Peeling Back the Mask

Peeling Back the Mask

A Quest for Justice in Kenya

Miguna Miguna

Peeling Back the Mask

Published by Gilgamesh Africa in 2012

ISBN 978-1-908531-21-6

CIP Data: A catalogue for this book is
available from the British Library

I'm for truth, no matter who tells it. I'm for justice, no matter who it is for or against. I'm a human being first and foremost, and as such I'm for whoever and whatever benefits humanity as a whole.

– Malcolm X

ALSO BY MIGUNA MIGUNA

Songs of Fire
Disgraceful Osgoode and Other Essays
Afrika's Volcanic Song
Toes Have Tales

For my late mother, Suré Miguna Nyar Njoga,
who sadly departed too soon

For my children Atieno, Biko, Suré, Anyango and Achieng',
for their love, support and trouble!

And

For the two departed beautiful Kenyans: Dr. Crispin Odhiambo Mbai
and Harrison Okong'o Arara, for their courage and patriotism!

TABLE OF CONTENTS

DECLARATION

I stood in front of the bathroom mirror and examined myself carefully. The man that stared back at me wasn't the same person who had arrived in Toronto as a frightened young political refugee from Africa almost 20 years earlier, on June 25, 1988. Of course, I remained the same ideologically. My core principles and mores remained intact. But I had grown older, worldlier and hopefully wiser. I had also become more socially and economically well-grounded. I was now a father and a husband, with all those roles' attendant social responsibilities and expectations. Most obviously of all, physically I wasn't the same penniless lanky fellow that I had been in 1988.

It was September 14, 2007, the same day we were set to leave our beautiful home in Bradford, Ontario, for good. For the past 11 years, this genteel suburban town is what I had called home. It hadn't just been a secure roof over our heads; it had been where I had finally made a proper home for myself after my first tumultuous decade in Canada. It was where I had raised a family. And it was where we had prospered together as a family.

As a member of the Greater Luo community, tradition did not allow me to call that house at 97 Dépeuter Crescent a home. Yes, Bradford is where I had lived and managed to transform myself from a recently called member of the bar to a well-established lawyer; from an ingénue father to a family man with five beautiful children. For Luos, however, a home isn't just where one lives or raises a family, no matter for how long you are there. To a Luo, a home is supposed to be where one's mother 'buried the placenta'; where the umbilical cord is cut. But that is just half of the story because even Luos born in modern health facilities in cities all over the world are still required to think of 'home' only as their 'ancestral' place – for Luos of Kenya this is the region on the shores of Lake Victoria (Nam Lolwe) that the community migrated to centuries ago from Southern Sudan.

A day before September 14, I had arrived back from Denver, Colorado, where I had been part of the inner cohort supporting Raila Amolo Odinga, then Kenya's leading presidential candidate and the head of the Orange Democratic Movement (ODM). Although the trip had been very successful, my mind had been distracted by my impending return to Kenya – my homecoming. Now – as I stood there looking at this 40-something man with a slightly greying, receding hairline – I could no longer suppress my emotions. Nineteen years previously, I had arrived in Canada with nothing but the clothes on my back and less than five Canadian dollars in my pockets. I had been 24 years old and had weighed not more than 68 kilograms. I hadn't been wearing glasses either. My damaged eyesight is a bitter souvenir of the inhuman and barbaric state-sponsored torture I endured in Nairobi's Nyayo House torture chambers – where the powerful light inside the 7x7 detention chamber never went off – after my unlawful incommunicado detention as a student leader.

After my release I had fled former President Daniel arap Moi's repressive regime on foot, at night, across the Kenya-Tanzania border. As we had walked for more than eight hours across the savannah bush, thickets, thorns and grass, all we had thought about was freedom. But more importantly, we had wanted to escape to a country – any country – where we could be alive and be free like human beings again: free to study, free to work, free to think and free to associate with whomsoever we chose.

The Kenya we had been brought up in was post-colonial: in fact, more accurately a neo-colonial banana republic. We had fled from it 24 years after its flag independence from British colonial rule. Yet, those dreams of independence had soured. We had lived under two successive autocratic one-man dictatorships. Kenya's first President, Jomo Kenyatta, had started off as a nationalist and benevolent dictator before mutating into a chauvinistic bone-breaking autocrat that rued any dissent. He, like his successor, the semi-literate Moi, had transformed Kenya into a country that the late Josiah Mwangi Kariuki would famously lament, before his assassination in 1975, was "A country of ten millionaires and ten million beggars." Under both Kenyatta and Moi, Kenyans had been turned against each other through artificial ethnic manipulation, competition and rivalries.

Now, in 2007, Kenya had become a country of 10,000 millionaires and more than 41 million beggars! Although multiparty democracy had been enshrined in the heavily mutilated 1963 Kenya Constitution, the country was only now emerging from a long period of being a *de facto* one-party state.

In 1983, Moi's then vice-president, Mwai Kibaki (now President) had moved the motion in Parliament that inserted that infamous section 2A that made Kenya an official totalitarian state. Kibaki was then one of KANU's chief puppeteers. By 1988, Kenya had been ruled by Moi as a *de jure* one-party state for five solid years. In those days, many perceived to be 'radical' – university lecturers, lawyers, writers, journalists, university students, workers and church ministers – found themselves either in detention without trial, in jail after trumped-up charges and kangaroo trials, dead, or in exile. Things became so bad that, between 1982 and 1988, all formal political opposition to the regime had been effectively stifled and only university students had still found the courage to openly stand up and challenge the regime.

In 1987, when I fled from Kenya, the City of Nairobi was not as expansive as it is today. Upper Hill, Kilimani and Hurlingham were then considered suburbs with a few neatly fenced residential quarters, mainly government houses occupied by middle-level and senior officers. Upper Hill was then almost entirely a Kenya Railways staff quarters; not the modern concrete jungle it has become. The reliable Kenya Bus Service – then a public transport system – was still plying all Nairobi routes and that of its environs. The Kenya Railways station in Nairobi was then a beehive of activity, with tens of thousands of commuters arriving from and departing to the countryside daily. Public telephone booths with functioning handsets and lines still dotted the city. Nairobi wasn't exactly 'safe', but muggers, car-jackers, robbers and pickpockets hadn't invaded it like locusts, the way they now have. But Moi's ubiquitous Special Branch Police were swarming everywhere, looking out for any sign of dissent.

It was in that smaller, yet febrile, city, that I had been involved – together with many other progressive university students – in the struggle for national liberation: liberation from totalitarianism, tribalism and institutionalised grand corruption. Our abductions, detentions without trial, and torture had interrupted that struggle, but never stopped it. While some of us were lucky enough to escape with our lives to foreign countries where we had continued the struggle, others continued with it from within Kenya, always being pursued by the Special Branch and Moi's political thugs.

From exile I had for two decades continued to campaign for democracy and academic freedom in Kenya through political activism: awareness-raising campaigns for, with and through human rights groups, my writings, and my organisation of political rallies and conventions abroad. Latterly, I had been a key player in exile of the nascent Orange Democratic Movement and a close personal ally of that movement's leader, Raila Amolo Odinga. Fortunately, through protracted struggles, we were able to have section 2A of the Constitution repealed and multiparty politics reintroduced.

But in recent years this involvement at a geographical distance, though valuable and valued, had begun to feel insufficient to me. I yearned to feel the rich soil of Kenya under my feet once more. Now it was apparently safe for me to return, I wanted to witness first-hand democracy taking root again and to help to nurture its growth. I had political ambitions of my own and felt that I could make more meaningful contributions to making Kenya a better society for all Kenyans from the 'ground', than I could from Canada.

I also felt that I had some unfinished business to pursue there relating to the assassination of my good friend, Dr. Crispin Odhiambo Mbai. This sage had been shot and killed at close range in cold blood one Sunday afternoon in September 2003. From Canada I had tried to do all I could to assist in the arrest of his killers who, to date, have not been prosecuted even though *The Standard* newspaper's investigative journalists traced some of them to a Tanzanian village. Senior Kenyan politicians who were alleged to have been involved in his death have never been investigated.

So, my return to Kenya in September 2007, would be to continue the struggle we had joined in the 1980s for true democracy in Kenya, to pursue my own political ambitions and to seek justice for my late friend.

"The truck is almost here," my wife Jane said, opening the bathroom door slightly, and returning me back to the present reality.

"Well, we are ready," I responded.

The children, especially Biko and Anyango, didn't look happy at all. Biko, my son, didn't want me to leave. He thought, wrongly, that I would never return to Canada. And because he was remaining behind with his sister Atieno, my eldest child, so that they could continue with their education (they were about to join high school), Biko cried uncontrollably, saying that I shouldn't abandon him; that I couldn't leave him behind. I could never imagine doing that, let alone plan it: I love my children so completely and unconditionally that nothing could make me abandon any of them.

This was the second time Biko had done this. The first time was when I had travelled to inspect the construction of the roof at our Runda house in Nairobi.

The boy had cried so much that I had had to buy an air ticket for him and we had spent one month together running around, supervising the construction. But the boy was visibly distressed. It took me time and effort to make him understand and accept that our relocation wasn't intended to hurt him or anybody else.

Suré and Atieno seemed nonchalant; they never expressed enthusiasm for leaving, nor any sense of loss. But fleetingly, Suré mentioned that she wanted to remain behind so that she could continue attending Fieldcrest Elementary School in Bradford and still be taught by Mrs. Lee. Our last born, Achieng', wanted us to "keep the house so that we could return to it". I explained to her that, unfortunately, we had already sold the house to someone else and that it was no longer ours. But being only four, Achieng' did not yet have a conception about ownership. Even the five-year-old Anyango didn't, as she insisted that we could leave her in the house so that "I can stay here and play in the park every day".

On September 19, our plane departed Pearson International Airport, Toronto, at 11pm. We hugged Biko, Atieno, their mother and my ex, Tracey, and Kathy France, my great friend and bookkeeper, before going through security. Although we suppressed our emotions, both Jane and I were crying within. (I could tell just by looking at her.) I was happy to be returning to Kenya and looking forward to the challenges and the opportunities that we were undoubtedly going to encounter. But I also recalled a question one of our friends had asked me: she sought to know if I would be able to work with Raila Odinga given his reputation of not brooking dissent or independent-minded people. I assured her that things would be all right, that I believed him, based on the short duration of time I had known him, to be open-minded, secure and progressive. Of course, this premature confidence would return to haunt me later.

During our eight-hour flight to Amsterdam, I didn't sleep much. My mind was clouded by thoughts, reflections and emotions. I thought about my struggles during the 19 years' sojourn in Canada. I felt sad that I had closed down my thriving legal practice, discarded and left behind a comfortable middle-class existence for the turbulence, the risks and the uncertainties of life in Kenya. I had laid down my roots in Canada, so to speak. In many ways, it was there that I had become a man as well as a respected member of the community.

Yes, I had been a student leader in Kenya and even made headline news when we were abducted, detained incommunicado and tortured for 14 days. During that dreadful fortnight – and after – we, the student leaders, became national figures and made history. It was in Canada, however, that I would complete my university studies and become gainfully employed. For more than 13 years, I had worked hard and built a law firm in a far away land from my country of birth; I had also built a family and had friends and colleagues with whom we had formed close and fulfilling relationships. There was social and financial stability in my life. In addition, the Canadian society (unlike in Kenya) provides social, health, educational, infrastructural and physical securities that make life liveable. We had begun to take for granted clean water, electricity, good roads, weekly garbage collection, pervasive security, and mundane things such as reliable and functioning landline telephones and home mail delivery – which aren't available in Kenya.

Leaving all that for an unknown, unpredictable and unstable life in Kenya with attendant political risks had been a difficult decision. My household had been sharply divided over my decision to relocate. My wife had preferred living in Canada. So had Biko, and one of our twin daughters, Anyango. Except for Achieng' who must have been genuinely confused, my other children had at first preferred to side with their Daddy, believing that I would know what I was doing. There was no doubt that my wife and the children had known I meant well and was trying to do the best to provide for them. I had quietly agonised over my decision.

I had political ambitions that, as a pragmatist, I knew I couldn't fulfil in Canada. There was an invisible ceiling that all African Canadians knew we couldn't penetrate or go beyond. Virtually every African Canadian I knew understood this unwritten law. As a lawyer, I could aspire to be, and perhaps even become, a superior court judge. But there was no evidence that Canadian society was ready to allow any one of us, no matter how qualified, talented, skilled, or experienced, to become a chief justice. In politics, it was possible to rise to the position of a councillor, mayor or parliamentarian. It was possible to become a cabinet minister – Lincoln Alexander and Zanana Akande had blazed a trail there. Yet why did they have to be thought of as trailblazers? I could not accept the fact that even my children (who were already exhibiting their father's strong-willed stamina and ambitious streak) would have to adjust their dreams to fit neatly into the colour-coded social stratifications of Canada.

Yes, I was musing over these things as Barack Obama had just started his audacious journey to the apex of American political power. But Canada wasn't the US and Obama, though born of a Luo father, had a Caucasian mother, and had been brought up in America as an American by his Caucasian grandmother. I couldn't claim to be a Canadian. Indeed I had never thought of myself as anything but Kenyan. I have always considered myself a proud, progressive pan-Africanist: one that believes in, and is fully committed to the unity and total liberation of the continent and all its peoples.

Admittedly, there were lots of challenges in Kenya as I prepared for my return home. There was ethnic exclusivism, xenophobia, discrimination and marginalisation of certain groups of people. There was flagrant nepotism and cronyism. Integrity, competence, education, training, experience and skills, which should be the basic criteria for employment and upward mobility, didn't matter as much as ethnic, racial and class affiliations. Caucasians, Asians, and the Kikuyu and Kalenjin elites – generally – were regarded to rank higher than other groups, in that order. The first and second categories derive their privileged status to colonial policies, while the elites of the third and fourth groups draw theirs from neo-colonial tribalism and abuse of power. In fact, growing up (and even up to this moment), I have never met an unemployed or homeless Kenyan Caucasian or Asian. Whether at Kenya's airports, hotels, restaurants or at social and political functions, those belonging to these two groups are always served first and more politely than their African counterparts. It's one despicable colonial and neo-colonial legacy I have never accepted, and which is what I felt the burning desire to help change.

And yes, there was runaway, systemic and institutional corruption. There were deep-rooted and serious iniquities and inequalities affecting more than 80 per cent of the population. The roads were far fewer, narrower and poorly constructed than in Canada. Clean running water was as rare as gold. Electricity was unreliable. There was no public health, education and transportation system to speak of. Political intolerance was a huge problem. The economy was stuttering along. Unemployment was uncontrollably beyond 75 per cent. Inflation had hit the roof.

Although I had constructed a beautiful house for my family in the gated Runda estate and felt positively about the elections scheduled for December 2007, when we landed at the Jomo Kenyatta International Airport that September 20, I was a maelstrom of emotions.

Nineteen years previously, on June 25, 1988, when my British Airways flight from Johannesburg to London had landed at Jomo Kenyatta International Airport, I had had to remain in my seat as we waited for the plane to deposit Nairobi-bound passengers and pick up London-bound ones. My fellow exile Erastus Omill Oloo and I hadn't been able to risk disembarking. The United Nations High Commissioner for Refugees (UNHCR) had forewarned us that we would be on our own if we made any rogue moves. We had been told that Moi's ubiquitous Special Branch police would be on high alert and would relish the prospect of nabbing those 'enemies of the state' and parading us to the media for propaganda purposes.

But here I was – back now for good. This time around, I didn't have to look over my shoulders; at least not in anticipation of a sudden and unjustified swoop by the Special Branch. When Kenyans had forced Moi to repeal section 2A, it had released the suppressed and frustrated energies of Kenyans, re-energised political activism and led to the formation of a torrent of political parties. Ordinary Kenyans had demanded and enforced their freedoms of expression and association. The hitherto muzzled and intimidated media had found its voice at last.

So, as we drove through Nairobi, I felt more liberated and excited than anxious about this new life. Yes, Jane, the children and I missed our spacious and clean Bradford house, but I was happy that I no longer had to worry too much about what I said and to whom. Even though Kenya remained in large measure an unmitigated totalitarian state where extra-judicial killings, police and military brutality of the ordinary citizen, looting of public resources and other abuse of power occur daily, I was happy that I could (working together with other progressive Kenyans, particularly in the ODM), confront these challenges without fear.

We were home. Not 'home' in the cultural sense because I wasn't going to settle down in Magina or Kisumu. But home because I was back in Kenya, my motherland. Emotionally, I was very happy. It had been many years. I had missed the food, the music, the landscape and the people, particularly the people. I had deeply missed being able to speak my mother tongue without feeling uncomfortable or looking over my shoulder. Politically, I felt ready to face the risks, challenges and opportunities that lay ahead.

I was determined to plunge headlong into the political process with the hope and commitment of trying to contribute towards making Kenya a model modern democratic state, governed by the rule of law, respectful and adhering to fundamental human rights, and guided by and practising constitutionalism. Whenever I thought of Canada with all those wide and well-built roads and its other infrastructures, I felt impatient. I knew that we were capable of catching up with the developed world if we fixed our politics, especially if we had visionary, committed and incorruptible leaders. If we were able to stamp out grand corruption from our politics and government system, I was sure we would be able to place our country on the path for national renewal and prosperity. I was certain that with good leadership, tribalism and nepotism were cancers that we could eradicate in less than five years.

As we settled into our new Runda home, I re-examined myself and smiled. The image I saw staring back at me was of a committed man, ready to give a humble contribution towards a more egalitarian, free, equitable, tolerant, just, united and developed country. The once all powerful Kanu party was limping into oblivion, having been mercilessly humbled during the 2002 elections. The massive coalition of opposition parties – Narc (National Alliance Rainbow Coalition) – that won those elections had also crumbled. President Kibaki had decamped from the once indomitable Narc and hitched a political ride with a new outfit called Party of National Unity (PNU), on whose ticket he was now fighting for re-election. Raila, too, had abandoned Narc to stand for the Orange Democratic Movement (ODM) less than three months before the 2007 elections. He would be gunning for the country's top leadership on an ODM ticket.

The political panorama was a quagmire. There were no clear ideological demarcations or distinctions between the political parties and individuals now competing for power. Although Raila's ODM had an impressive manifesto and a conglomeration of past liberation soldiers, it, too, had more than its fair share of former KANU plutocrats, looters and retrogressive characters.

This was a far cry from the political situation in the country in 1987 when I had fled into exile. At the time, there hadn't been any doubt who the 'enemies of the people' were. And it had been crystal clear who was genuinely fighting for the liberation of the country. In those days, one's liberation credentials were more valuable than the depths of one's pockets. Leadership had not yet been mortgaged and reserved for dubious political and business oligarchs. Parliament had not yet been auctioned off to people whose vast wealth had been acquired in murky circumstances.

Now, as I prepared to enter the political fray, I was deeply troubled by the fact that some of those 'enemies of the people' – plutocrats who had occupied exalted positions in Moi's government and assisted him in suppressing the popular will of the people – had not only escaped with impunity, but were perched high up in senior positions in both Kibaki's government and Raila's ODM. But I am an optimist by nature; perhaps I allowed my heart's hope that an ODM victory would usher in a better era for Kenya, to rule my head. I intellectualised that while the path to power might involve pragmatic alliances, once in power the ODM would be different from previous Kenyan governments. But I had perhaps philosophised on these issues too much.

My support for Raila Odinga was predicated on this vision of a cleaned-up Kenya; a Kenya where leadership would be acquired and retained through progressive ideological clarity, honesty, integrity and commitment to the public good, where impunity would be punished unremittingly. Up to the point at which

I returned to Kenya, Raila had shown (in my opinion) dynamism, vision and commitment. He spoke the language of a united, democratic, modern and developed Kenya. He espoused (if only rhetorically) pan-Africanism and social democratic credos. He asserted his belief and commitment in a country governed by the rule of law and constitutionalism; a country that respects basic human rights and is committed to social justice and cultural, social and economic equality and renewal.

Would we succeed?

As this book will, I hope, show, I came to believe that Raila wasn't honest or ready for the complete overhaul and transformation of the Kenyan society, starting with its leadership and politics. His rhetoric was intended to woo votes so as to ascend to power. Beyond that, he lacked genuine vision and commitment.

* * * * * * * * * * * * * *

On August 4, 2011, the Prime Minister of the Republic of Kenya, Raila Amolo Odinga, announced, through the Kenyan media, that he had suspended me indefinitely without pay as his senior adviser on coalition, legal and constitutional affairs. Until this sudden announcement, I had also been serving as the joint secretary to The Permanent Committee on the Management of the Grand Coalition Affairs.

Simultaneous with my suspension were the summary dismissals of all my staff. The locks to my office were changed; my personal effects continue to be detained illegally. The sealed suspension letter, marked 'top secret' was delivered to me 28 hours after the media started reporting its contents. Media reports – and the letter – alleged that I had been suspended for "misconduct". Yet I have never been given any particulars of this supposed "misconduct".

In other words, I had been accused, disgraced, judged and hanged without due process. And by Odinga, a man who had served eight years of detention without trial under Moi's repressive regime. Odinga has always billed himself as an 'agent of change' and as a 'progressive leader' who believes in the rule of law and constitutionalism. Yet here he was publicly humiliating his most senior personal adviser and friend. A friend who had supported his ambitions to become president of Kenya, stood by him loyally at his darkest hour in December 2007 after President Kibaki had stolen his presidential victory and had worked tirelessly for him ever since. Why had he treated me this way? What had I done? But even more importantly, had Odinga exposed himself as a man who couldn't be trusted with power? Was Odinga a true democrat and 'reformer' as he had for decades claimed?

In *Peeling Back The Mask*, I expose him as a selfish, confused, hypocritical and deceptive leader whose greed for power and money makes him unfit for the presidency of the republic of Kenya. The book contains details of Odinga's transgressions: from serial illicit sexual exploits with various married women to involvements in corruption; from his befuddled and inconsistent positions on the constitutional review and the International Criminal Court (ICC) process to his failure to negotiate effectively with President Kibaki, his partner in Kenya's grand coalition government; through to his disgraceful dozing through important meetings. The book depicts a cowardly and intellectually dishonest leader undeserving of all the praise and attention he has generated or received over the years.

The book also retraces my steps from early childhood in grinding poverty in Magina village; my arrest and torture as a student activist; my political exile in Canada; to the frustrations I faced while serving as Odinga's adviser.

The timing of the book is made even more pertinent by the fact that Kenya is set to hold general and presidential elections in less than one year from the date of its publication. In view of the post-election violence that engulfed the country (and nearly reduced it to rubble through ethnic-based conflagrations) in 2007, I am sure Kenyans and Kenyan observers will be interested in knowing the intrigues, discussions and power plays that have been occurring in Nairobi's 'corridors of power'.

Since my irregular suspension and later half-hearted reinstatement, I have become known as a thorn in the side of the grand coalition government and a critic of Odinga. Very few people dare to publicly challenge powerful political figures in Kenya. Rarer still is the decision of those affected –like me – to publish their experiences in book form. But at a tender age, I promised myself, my mother and my God that I would never compromise on matters of integrity, truth and social justice. I hope that after reading this book, many will confirm that I have kept that promise. As Ngugi wa Thiong'o says in his *Barrel of a Pen: Resistance to Repression in Neo-Colonial Kenya*: "silence before the crimes of the neo-colonial regime in Kenya is collusion with social evil".

I believe that the time has come for me to peel back the mask of injustice, betrayal and deception from Raila Odinga and other merchants of impunity and expose them for what they are: devious and conniving people who have abused the collective trust Kenyans placed on them to transform the country for national prosperity.

* * * * * * * * * * * * * * *

These are my memoirs.

Dates and incidents are not weaved together chronologically for the sole purpose of narrating a story. My life story is not told here to entertain anyone.

The book tackles (or so I hope) some of the key issues in my ongoing life, commencing with my early childhood experiences to the most contemporary highlights of my involvement in Kenyan politics.

It would be difficult (perhaps impossible) to appreciate what drives me if one does not understand my core values, ideals, vision, ideological beliefs, philosophical and political commitments and moral precepts. One cannot divorce me from the zeitgeist of my generation. Nor can one successfully separate me from the material and historical circumstances that have shaped my life. I belong to the generation of Kenyans born from the 1960s to the early 1970s who were too young to have experienced the nationalist aspirations and ferment that culminated in independence. But we were (soon) old enough to read the disappointments etched on the faces of those who had hoped for so much more from a Kenya where their own countrymen were now the masters. We were old enough to experience crushed dreams, grand corruption and barbaric abuses of power. We also witnessed the ravages wrought by the International Monetary Fund and the World Bank, through African puppets, mascots and cunningly creative structural adjustment programmes.

Our generation experienced the famines of the 1970s and the humiliation of having to line up for food aid. Many of us were already young adults in the sunset years of Kenyatta's despotism and the morning of Moi's tyranny. We knew who those independence figures, like Jaramogi Oginga Odinga, Pio Gama Pinto, Bildad Kaggia and Field Marshall Dedan Kimathi were; we were familiar with the thoughts of African freedom fighters from Amilcar Cabral to Marcelino dos Santos; we knew where to place the Mobutu Sese Sekos, Kamuzu Bandas and Daniel arap Mois; our teachers literally and ideologically had been the Ngugi wa Thiongos and Oki Ooko Ombakas; we had read all the great writings of the likes of Walter Rodney, Frantz Fanon, Paulo Freiré and Ruth First. Our heroes and heroines were Nelson Mandela, Graça Machel, Thomas Sankara, Steve Biko and Cynthia McKinney.

We sympathised with the politics of the Green and anti-globalisation movement, but above all I belong to a generation who unapologetically identified with and embraced Africa, the 'Third World' and all human progress; I am a man who is part of the generation that did not fear, despise or look down on our sisters – on the contrary we saw them as comrades, colleagues, friends – the half of humanity we have learned from and work closely with in all our aspirations. Not all of us were socialists, Marxist-Leninists or radicals, but we were united in our quest for another possible, alternative milieu. We pursued undiluted human dignity, equality, freedom and justice for all.

Even though I lived in North America for many years, my affinity for, identity with and passion for Kenya and Africa never subsided. I always wanted to be and still want to be part of the solutions. Without understanding some of these grounding principles it would be difficult to understand why I easily and consciously walked away from a comfortable Canadian lifestyle that I had struggled to attain, and plunged myself headlong into the uncertain vicissitudes of a cutthroat and turbulent Kenya.

As my narrative unfolds, it will become patently clear that my disappointment with some political personages I had earlier placed on a pedestal had a lot to do with my ideals and core values. Perhaps I was too idealistic; perhaps I expected too much from mere mortals with their inevitable foibles and frailties. Or perhaps, as I argue, one such disappointment – Odinga – was all along a 'political conman' who masked his true identity, nature and intentions and by doing so succeeded in fooling people, including myself, for a long time.

BOOK ONE

BEGINNINGS

CHAPTER ONE

MAGINA

I was born to a peasant mother in a village called Magina on the shores of the River Nyando in the Kano Plains in the former Nyanza Province of western Kenya. *Magina* is a name Luos (the community I belong to) use to describe something expansive or a weapon of mass destruction. It is, however, unclear how the village got its name.

My father had died when my mother was pregnant with me. I was her last child. I was born at home, so there are no records of my birth. My illiterate mother told me, however, that it was after the heavy rains of *Uhuru* or independence. Historians have confirmed that there were heavy rains during that period. It could have been in 1964 because I started elementary school in 1971.

Those days, you wouldn't be admitted to grade one if you couldn't touch the upper tip of your left ear with the right hand while standing straight with your neck upright. The first thing that teachers did was ask the newly arrived children to stand in a straight line and they would make each one try to touch the tip of their ear. Those who failed would be sent home. This process began in village nursery schools, which weren't real 'nurseries' because 'classes' were conducted under any large tree in the village. Children would mostly sing, narrate stories, and struggle with riddles and tongue-twisters. We were usually served rice and something that looked like rice but tasted differently called *mawele* (oatmeal).

The nursery 'teachers' were all local women from the village. I don't know whether they were officially employed or just volunteers. We didn't have exercise books, pencils, rubbers or text books. The 'teacher' would simply stand in front of us and begin singing or reciting a, e, i, o, u, ba, cha, da, and such like, and we would roar after her for a half day. The following day, we would do numbers, counting from 1 to 10, then from 1 to 20, and so forth. Once we mastered whatever we were being taught, we would proceed to the alphabet. Meanwhile, our parents or guardians or older siblings would have gone to the market, farms or schools. In a way, we were being baby-sat.

So, I never saw or had a father. My mother served both roles. I had one older brother and five sisters and four step sisters. My mother's seven other children had died as babies. Until my mother's death in 1987, our family home was a small one-roomed grass-thatched and mud-walled hut in Magina. Villagers used water from the river Nyando for everything: drinking, cooking, washing, bathing and disposing of all waste. Those days, there were hardly any pit latrines. The bush and maize fields were the ultimate destination for villagers, making the daily early morning exodus a sight to behold. Modern toilets are still unheard of in Magina to this day. It's amazing that epidemics didn't wipe out the village years ago.

Standing in Magina village facing north, Nyabondo Plateau would be to your back, to the south; Lake Victoria to the south-west; and Nandi Hills to the north-east and the blue skies connecting (literally) to the ground in the open spaces all around. From Magina, Kano Plains feels like a valley or a huge hole. Standing there as a child – and observing all around me – I sometimes felt physically trapped.

Two clans occupy Magina. They are the Kimira and Ka'Nyilum. My mother came from the Kimira clan, but not the one located in Magina. My mother told me that my father, Miguna *wuod* Jomune, was a tall brown handsome man. He must have been six foot four. That's an intelligent guess because both my brother and I are six foot four. Even some of my sisters are close to six feet tall. Both my parents had converted to Christianity. My father became "Joshua" Miguna Jomune and my mother 'Margaret' Suré Miguna. I was named after my father.

When I was about five years' old, I was taken to be baptised in our village church. I liked that particular church because they didn't beat drums and jump exuberantly as they prayed. I have never been a fan of loud and charismatic churches. When the village priest asked me to confirm if my name was 'Joshua Otieno Miguna,' I baulked. Apparently, my mother had asked the priest to name me Otieno because I had been born at night. Nobody had ever called me Otieno though. I told the priest, firmly, that I wouldn't accept the name. I explained to him that there were too many boys in the village with it and that I didn't like to be associated with a name that common. The priest was taken aback because no other child had ever refused a name proposed by the parents. But I stood my ground. My mother relented and asked me to choose what I wanted to be called. So, I chose Joshua Miguna Miguna. I explained that she had named me after my father who was Joshua Miguna *wuod* Jomune. However, since I was Joshua Miguna *wuod* Miguna, I needed to be called Joshua Miguna Miguna. That's how I ended up with my name. Over the years, I have tried to find the meaning of 'Miguna' with little success. Some people have told me that 'miguna' refers to something – anything – ancient, like a rock. Well, I really don't know. I'm OK with that. Later in 1997 – long after I had gone into exile in Canada –I officially excised 'Joshua' from my name and became simply 'Miguna Miguna'.

Folklore in the village spoke of my father as a hard working and frugal man who rarely parted with money. They sang songs about him in the village, calling him '*Oruko pesa mit makata minu kwayi*'. Loosely translated, it means 'Oruko the one who loves money so much that he can't part with it even when his mother begs him for some'. They didn't seem to narrate that as a way of rebuke. They seemed to marvel at my father's frugality. His name wasn't *Oruko*; so I'm unsure as to why they referred to him using that name. *Rukruok* in Luo means being in different places doing different things at the same time. In other words, he was agile; a multi-tasker. It could well be that that's what they meant. After all, he was a husband, father, farmer, trader and investment genius by the standards of the village. He used to be a trader in livestock, especially cattle, from as far as Aora Chuodho in Ndhiwa, South Nyanza. He would bring them to Sondu, Ahero and Kisumu, where he would sell them for tidy profits.

In the early1950s, my father had business partners from all over Nyanza. One particular business partner was called Migowe from Apondo village in Rachuonyo. They were so close that whenever Migowe accompanied my father to Ahero, Sondu or Kisumu, they would stay together in our homestead, and whenever my father was in South Nyanza, he would stay at Migowe's home. By the standards of that period, the two grew rich and influential. This was long before independence. And to show their wealth, they both became polygamists, with Migowe overreaching himself and marrying more than ten wives. My father had two. And to cement their friendship, my father married out my elder sister Jane Atieno to Migowe's eldest son called Dishon Osuma who was at that time a business apprentice of both my father and Migowe. Osuma went on to become, by then local standards, a real business magnate in Nyanza, acquiring fleets of buses called *Nyombulu*, as well as real estate along the Mikayi, Oyugis and Kisii road. But Osuma, like his father and my father, was illiterate. He, too, was a polygamist who married five women.

In contrast to my father's reputation of frugality, my mother was generous to a fault. She never had anything she didn't want to distribute and share with villagers and relatives. Her reputation in the village was of a fiercely honest person who was also too generous to be rich. In that time, peasants in Nyanza hardly understood money. Their economic worldview revolved around livestock and land. We are talking of a period when agriculture and fishing weren't developed and most Luos partook in them just to stay alive. There were no large scale farmers. Growing up, we rarely had anything in excess of our barest minimal requirements. Yet, whenever my mother had one kilogram of sugar in the morning, for instance, you could be sure that by evening it would have been shared out until she would end up with nothing.

As children, we used to be frustrated by our mother's generosity. Her situation following my father's untimely death had grown gradually worse. She told harrowing stories of how after my father's death, his brother Aoyi had taken away my father's cattle, ploughing equipment and other things considered "wealth" at that time. He had sold most of it before moving away to different places in South Nyanza. Eventually, Aoyi settled in Nyatoto village, in Lambwe Valley and became a rich landowner and farmer. Other male relatives of my father denied my mother access to most of the land. The situation was made worse by the fact that my mother refused to be "inherited" in accordance with the Luo customs. They left her without livestock and land, which were then the only investments and means of survival for peasants. She used her bare hands to toil on a tiny strip of land, growing vegetables, corn and millet.

The village was located between the River Nyando and its tributary Wailes. The river Nyando broke its banks in April, August and December every year. The floods would cover the entire village sending everyone in search of safety in higher grounds. The water was muddy, and it was everywhere, as far as the eye could see. During the rainy seasons, Magina village would be deserted. People would leave the village by swimming, using anything that floated: banana plants, reeds tied together, traditional boats, and on rare occasions on boats the villagers called *andururu* (motor boats with propellers that make 'ndruuu' noise).The first port of call would be the Chief's Camp in Ahero. However, since the entire locality would have been rendered homeless, the Chief's Camp would quickly fill up, leaving most people stranded. On those occasions, we would sometimes be supplied with blankets, tents, mosquito nets and food portions. Essentially, the villagers relied on relief assistance during the perennial floods.

As the floods subsided but before the place dried up, battalions of white men with long guns would descend on our village shooting at the swarms of geese and wild ducks. They would shoot sporadically as their black assistants ran off to catch any birds they shot down. The villagers didn't seem to know where the white people came from but they came every time during the floods. The geese and wild ducks were so numerous in those days that they would blanket large swathes of the water's surface.

When the village was flooded, all the schools closed. There wasn't any other activity except fishing. The men would go out, mostly at night, with flash lights, fish traps, nets and other contraptions. They would stay out all night. Sometimes they would return at dawn with lots of fish. Other times, they wouldn't be so lucky. Fishing at night had its dangers, such as the ferocious Nyando hippopotamuses. Because there was no man in our household – my father was deceased and my brother was working as a policeman away from the village when I was a young boy – my family rarely partook in the fishing exercises. That meant that as other families with adult men were feasting on fish, we at times did without. Fortunately, however, life in the village was such that neighbours always looked out for each other. And due to my mother's legendary generosity, it wasn't unusual for her to return home after a harrowing day in the fields and find that some anonymous person had left fish for her.

When I was in lower primary, I used to visit my maternal grandmother, Roda, in the Kimira clan, near Wang'anga, just a few kilometres from the Luo Kipsigis border. I remember vividly how the Kimira and Katolo clans used to organise wrestling contests of young men between the two clans. The matches were huge events that were held in a big field near my grandmother's home. In those days, wrestling was the biggest entertainment sport around Kano, not soccer.

In many ways, life in the village was idyllic. Between the ages of five and 15, boys in the village would gather in the evening, almost weekly (depending on when the cows gave birth), from one household to the other, drinking *adila* (which my wife tells me is called colostrum) with *ugali*, and on occasion, barbecuing the fatty portion from a ram's tail. There is nothing I loved more than those evenings.

This is what would happen: one week after a cow gives birth, it produces lots of brown milk – colostrum – which isn't really meant for human consumption. Ideally, the colostrum should be exclusively used by her offspring. But often, during the first week, the calf is still too young to feed on all the colostrum, which is extremely rich in nutrients (and I suspect antibodies). And as happened in those days, villagers were frugal and never allowed food to go to waste. It was this excess colostrum that our mothers would keep in large earthenware pots for weeks, allowing it to ferment until it was frothing with gases (and obviously friendly germs). On an appointed day, all the boys from the neighbourhood (except perhaps one or two greedy ones) would be invited for a 'feast' at the home where the cow had given birth. We would arrive dutifully and wait for the *ugali* and *adila*. That day, we wouldn't take dinner in our respective homes.

That wasn't the only food-related 'ceremony' the village reserved for boys. Magina village was famous for the abundance of 'food' – corn, millet, potatoes, vegetables, cattle, sheep and goats. There were more sheep than goats in the village. Nearly every household had some. So, before the young rams developed their huge, curled fatty tails (we called them *sembe*), boys in the village would wait until it had just enough girth before using a very sharp knife to cut off and remove a small portion from the tip. A red-hot machete would be used to burn the place from which we had chopped off our meal in order to help it heal.

For me, the only occasions that rivalled the *adila* and *sembe* feasts were the traditional weddings. On those occasions, there would be abundant food. We would eat bread with margarine spreads (a delicacy that was often reserved only for such special occasions) and feast on *sembe*.

If there are things I look back on with sentimentality, it is the *adila*, *sembe* and traditional wedding feasts. Those days, I wished for a wedding every week. This was because whenever my brother or another young man in the village was getting married, we would be sent to take the cattle for 'bride wealth' to the bride's home, especially if she hailed from any of the Kano clans. Taking the cattle to the bride's home was called 'sembo dhok'. There isn't anything close to it in English. But it essentially meant that we, the boys, would "walk" the cattle either from the market place or from the homestead of the groom. It was on such occasions that boys in the village bonded, shared stories and experiences.

Magina was – and remains – both an interesting and a depressing place. There were – and are – no real homes in the village; only clusters of huts. The huts were constructed very close to each other, each cluster forming large homesteads. The huts were thatched with a kind of grass called *seé* (*Cypress rotundus*) that only grows in swamps. Nothing was permanent in the village. At night – and except when the stars, the full moon or the fireflies were out in full force – the whole village was pitch-dark. Apart from local drunks, night runners and fishermen when there were floods, very few villagers ventured out after dusk.

Our lives were in constant flux, you could say we lived a life of nomadism. Nature dictated where and how we lived. For a while when I was still a teenager, Magina produced some of the best sweet potatoes, yams, arrowroots, pumpkins, cassava, peas (whose leaves are used as vegetables) and tomatoes I have seen in my life. Despite the grinding poverty, starvation hasn't been known to the people of my village. They have had very little throughout, yes, but the kind of famine we have seen on our television screens has been largely absent.

For as long as I lived there, I never heard of thefts. In many ways, life in Magina was and has remained very idyllic. There was no infrastructure to speak of, nor were there any social amenities. Sadly, this situation remains to this day. Magina is a village that has known no modern development. The floods continue to ravage the village many times each year. Successive governments have never bothered to solve, once and for all, the perennial floods problem.

Throughout my childhood, there was a man suffering from mental illness in Magina called Ogwang'. Many villagers called him *Ogwango*, which perhaps was a deliberate but insensitive mangling of his name intended to indicate his condition. Ogwang' had a family – a wife and three children. He wasn't around most of the time. He would be gone for extended periods during which time we heard rumours that he was either gainfully employed in Kericho tea farms or roaming in Nyanza and Western provinces, being chased from one market place to the other. But Ogwang' always returned to Magina, mostly when afflicted with severe bouts of schizophrenia. Invariably he would make loud noises, sing incoherently and run around for no apparent reason. Children and women were often scared of him though for the entire period he was alive, I never heard of any incident when Ogwang' actually hurt anyone. He was more of a danger to himself than to others. For instance, he frequently ran into trees, thickets and holes, causing serious injuries to his body. There were fears that he would jump into the Nyando or Wailes and drown. I never knew whether he could swim.

There were times when his relatives would tie him up with ropes and detain him in small shelters constructed specifically for holding him. It was a terrible, revolting sight as Ogwang' would start groaning and making animal sounds as he struggled to free himself. This would go on sometimes for whole days and nights. Eventually, he would manage to free himself and take off, running and singing. To restrain him completely, his relatives would then use chains, which Ogwang' would try to bite through.

As children, we used to sneak from our huts and take food to him. We would feed him, as his hands remained tied. He never threatened or harmed us. In fact whenever Ogwang' saw a child approaching he would give way for the child to pass. He was completely harmless. I have always wondered why Ogwang' was never taken for medical treatment. The sight of Ogwang' being held like an animal in small cages has never left my mind. It has traumatised me throughout my life. Barbarism, inhumanity and sadism weren't something I accepted even as a minor. I have strongly opposed them throughout my life.

I was breastfed until I was a big boy (or at least that's what I remember). It is amazing that even today when I close my eyes and try to remember that period, I can still see my mother kneeling as I suckled away, in full view of the villagers. The week my classmates were being herded to the first grade, I was busy playing *katolo*, *peke* or *kalongolongo* with other children who were not going to school. *Katolo* is what the English call hop-scotch. *Peke* is a throwing game. The girls' game was making *kalongolongo*. They would gather little twigs which they used as firewood. A small hole would be dug on the ground with three little stones like cooking stones. Small tins would be gathered and cleaned. These served as pots and pans. The girls would then prepare real vegetables or fake ones from weeds. From dust and soil, they would make mounds resembling *ugali*. After the 'meals' had been prepared, the girls, now pretending to be grown up mothers, would call smaller boys and girls, now acting as their children, 'to eat'. Older boys would sit separately from the children and would be served as the men of the households. 'Families' would huddle around their 'meals' and pretend to partake in imaginary feasts. After the 'meals', 'couples' and their 'children' would retire to different spots in the compound; some under trees, others under the stores called *dero* (granary made of reeds or twigs) where grains were kept; and others either behind or inside the huts. It was during these imaginary fiestas that naughty children tried to engage in sexual escapades. Probably that's why siblings rarely played the roles of 'mother' and 'father.' It was usually with the neighbours' children or preferably with children from other clans who had been brought to babysit for their aunts or other relatives.

In our village, my 'wife' was a young beautiful girl named Lalo. She was from Kobura near Kaluore market. She had come to help our neighbour, Mary Ochele, who was giving birth to baby boys every year in those days. We were about five or six years old. Mary had just given birth to a baby boy called Elisha. We kids knew whenever Mary was giving birth because it wasn't a quiet affair. As we watched her tummy extend and enlarge each year, we could predict with precision when the hilarious commotion would begin. The week Mary gave birth, she would be very restless; going in and out of her hut; sitting behind the hut and generally just walking around. Weekly before she delivered, she would visit my mother's traditional gynaecology and obstetrics clinic where my mother would use warm water and petroleum oil and herbs to massage her belly and check the condition of the unborn baby. As toddlers, we sometimes lay there pretending to be asleep but watching keenly what was going on.

Elisha was delivered in the morning, at about 10am. That day, we were playing around Mary's hut. Suddenly, we heard a loud piercing shriek. Mary opened her hut and ran behind it, squatting on the pumpkin plants, yelling "I want to *pee!* I want to *pee!* I want to *peeeeee!*" As Mary fumbled and cried, we took off to the fields, calling my mother at the top of our voices as we headed towards where she was weeding. "The baby is coming! The baby is coming!" We yelled as we ran towards my mother who responded "*Ang'o? Ang'o?*" She was asking what the matter was. As soon as we reached where she was, breathless, she had figured out the problem and taken off in the direction of Mary's hut. We remained in front of the hut as she retreated behind it. And hardly 30 minutes later, there was a whimper from a baby before my mother asked us for water in a basin. This was the baby Lalo had come to babysit. From then on, she became my partner; we became so attached to each other that even adults used to refer to her as my wife. However, shortly after I started elementary school and Elisha was ready for the village nursery school under the tree, Lalo returned to her home and I never saw her again.

For some reason, I liked baby boys so much in those days that whenever a local woman gave birth to one, I would spend hours carrying them and playing with them. I would rush there first thing in the morning and after chores or school. Perhaps it was a way of expressing my desire to have a brother. But as a fatherless last born, there wasn't any chance of that.

There came a time when my mother dressed me up and escorted me to school. For a week or so, I would pretend to be going but turn back when I knew she had gone off to the field or the market. Eventually (after two weeks), I had to be taken to school by force by a teacher and neighbour called Onditi Oriare, the son of the village priest. I remember that day as if it was just yesterday. I screamed and cried all the way there. I was missing my mother and playmates. At the end of school, I rushed home, where my mother knelt down to breastfeed me. But that was the only time I resisted going to school. Once I started properly, I became very keen on learning. My mother was very firm about the need for me to go. Despite her illiteracy, she knew that education would be my only salvation from poverty. I loved and valued my mother. To please her and prove to be a good child, I plunged into learning in a manner hitherto unknown to the village. I did my homework without prompting. I carried my school-work and books whenever I went to herd the few cattle we had. After spending hours in the fields digging with our hands, I would rush off to the river to swim before reading myself silly. Thankfully, that investment eventually paid off.

When I was a toddler, well before I joined elementary school, I spent time with my brother Eric Ondiek (*Owadgi Leah*) who was a policeman in various stations in the Western Province. My brother's first wife was called Deborah. She was a young beautiful Teso woman (at least to the eyes of a toddler). They had a lovely baby girl called Queen. I'm not sure which Queen she was named after. It's most likely Queen Elizabeth II of England. I say her because Queen was slightly younger than me, and I was born shortly after Kenya's independence.

During that period, my brother would most likely have been thinking of that English Queen. But it's also possible that he chose the name Queen to designate the special place his first daughter occupied in the young couple's lives.

My brother later separated from Deborah after he lost his job as a policeman and moved back to the village. Unfortunately, my brother never kept in touch with Deborah or his daughter. As a child, I blamed my brother for the break-up. I didn't have concrete reasons. It was just the thinking of a perceptive child who desperately wished that things could have turned out differently. What I know is that at some point after losing his job, my brother started drinking heavily and neglected his family. He would leave home in the morning with his drinking buddies and return at night, shouting and singing incoherently. There were days when he would just eat and go to bed without commotion. But on most occasions, he would engage his wife in unnecessary quarrels that inevitably led to a physical assault on her, often prompting my mother to intervene. It was extremely annoying to see him complain about the food he was served: either that it wasn't properly cooked or that it was vegetables and he expected meat, chicken or fish, even though he had rarely provided.

I used to sit there and wonder: why can't you, for once, stop drinking and go and look for fish, chicken and meat? Why are you blaming her? But I was too young to confront him. Other times he breached all boundaries of decency and good morals. He would hurl abuse at my mother, merely because she had tried to prevent him from assaulting his wife and told him to stop drinking. When he still lived in my mother's compound, she would even threaten to kick him out. Of course that was just an empty threat. Our homestead wasn't fenced. Nor did she have the capacity to implement the sanction. Ondiek was a big man at six foot, four inches.

The situation grew worse after Ondiek constructed his own homestead and now it was my mother's turn to go live there with us. He would go for his usual drinking sprees, return shouting and singing; only this time, my mother had little or no leverage. In his drunken stupor, the cultural and traditional restraints that compelled children not to answer back, quarrel with or fight their parents, especially their mothers, evaporated. He would threaten to kick my mother out from his homestead. Once, when I was only 15, I yelled back at him that he would have to fight both her and me. I swore I would never drink alcohol. That stopped my brother in his tracks. He looked at me bemused but actually stopped yelling, entered his house and went to sleep. I hated witnessing those scenes. I knew my mother was suffering innocently. I also knew that as my mother's second born child – especially after my elder sister's marriage – my brother should have tried to help out my mother. He didn't. Neither did he really help himself. From that day, I felt alienated from my brother and hated alcohol. And I have remained a bitter enemy of all alcoholic beverages to date.

The other reason why I have always hated alcohol revolves around an incident that happened when I stayed with my brother and his wife Deborah in Malakisi. I was only four yet it remains fresh in my mind as if it occurred just yesterday. One day, a fellow policeman came to my brother's house and asked to take me for a walk. My brother wasn't in the house, and on reflection, I believe that Deborah shouldn't have allowed that to happen. But I went with the policeman to a place where people were drinking a local alcoholic brew which Luos and Luhyas call *busaa*. He started drinking. And as he got drunk, he asked me to "taste" the drink, which I believe I did, but only once. Being a very young child, I didn't know it was alcohol. I didn't think. Moreover, it was given to me using a calabash, which I had hitherto only associated with porridge. In fact, *busaa* looked to me very much like porridge. So, I took one gulp and knew right away that it wasn't porridge. Once I felt the pungent taste, I refused to take another sip. When he returned me to my brother's house, I was singing and speaking in a language nobody could understand. My brother was so furious that he ended up beating Deborah and banned his fellow officer from his house.

At about five, I was returned to Magina from my brother's work station in Western Province to start school. It's possible that my stay with my brother only lasted a few months. To a child that young, however, it seemed like a lifetime. However, when I returned to the village, I realised, to my horror, that I had forgotten my mother tongue, Dholuo. In Malakisi and Bungoma, we had only communicated in Kiswahili. Deborah, my brother's wife, was a Teso. She didn't speak Dholuo. Hence, when I returned to the village, my first traumatic experience was how to relate to and speak with my mother, sisters and the children of the village. I couldn't even play with the other children because they didn't understand Kiswahili. In the village, life revolved around Luo; the culture and the language. It took me months of frustration and daily struggle before I learnt basic words and phrases. And as I learnt to roll my Rs, the village children made a spectacle of me, laughing and taunting. To them, not being able to speak my mother tongue was akin to being an alien or a village idiot. Within one year, however, I had learnt Dholuo and completely deleted Kiswahili from my system. Thereafter, my brain refused to absorb Kiswahili. It's as if the brain had concluded that Kiswahili wasn't good for its survival. It taught me an interesting lesson in human psychology: we are flexible, adaptable and reasonable. However, should our system detect danger, it will shut down.

I don't believe there is any place with a higher concentration of mosquitoes than Magina. At night, mosquitoes were all over, singing and biting. They were particularly mutinous against visitors, upon whom they unleashed their most vicious attacks, making them restless and ultimately bedridden with malaria. But not on the indigenous villager; strangely the mosquitoes knew us. They exercised great restraint: they feasted gently and harmlessly on us. It's impossible to know at what stage I developed immunity to malaria. But for as long as I was young and living in the village, I was never infected. Mosquitoes would feast on us daily but we never got ill. Much later after returning to Magina from Canada, I caught malaria. I had stayed abroad for six years and my body must have accordingly adjusted to the extended absence of risk.

Magina is a microcosm of Kenyan villages. Today, it remains painfully poor – almost desolate and abandoned by the state. There isn't any infrastructure to speak of except for Apondo Primary School, which, mainly through my efforts, has now got some poorly constructed permanent structures, modern wooden desks and chairs. The floor, which was supposed to be concrete, is still dusty and dirty. Money that was intended for it has lined the pockets of a few school administrators, school committee members and politicians. More than ever before, the villagers struggle on their narrow strips of dry land, trying to eke out a living. But the swamp is gone, together with the papyrus, mangrove, reeds and other foliage. With them went the fish and the birds, including the beguiling seagulls. The sweet potatoes, vegetables and sugar cane are no more. In other words, like most Kenyan villages, Magina has decayed and become poorer over the years. The culture of neglect has persisted. In many ways, Magina has never enjoyed the fruits of independence, politically and economically. This is both a tragedy and an unforgivable betrayal.

NYATOTO

Despite what my mother told me about what had happened after my father's death, she kept in fairly close contact with her brother-in-law Aoyi (my uncle) and his family. My mother used to visit them quite often in Nyatoto village, Lambwe Valley.

Aoyi's children never visited when they were young. I became curious about them, primarily because there were three male children close to my age. In Luo culture, they were my brothers. So one day, when Aoyi's first wife, Juliana, visited our village, I insisted on going back with her. That was in January 1974. I was supposed to join Standard Four and I arrived in Nyatoto in brown khaki shorts, one cotton shirt and a nylon shirt. I also had a school bag with a few pencils, an eraser, a razor blade for sharpening my pencils, and three exercise books.

Aoyi's compound looked prosperous. He had two large *kraals* full of cattle and hundreds of sheep, goats and chickens. The homestead had several houses, one for each of his three wives, and one belonging to his older son Jacobo Odhiambo. There were also numerous stores and a kitchen. In addition, Aoyi owned more than 50 acres of land, on which he grew corn, millet, groundnuts and sunflowers. Up to that time, I had never entered a homestead that big. Nor had I encountered such 'wealth'.

I was to attend Nyatoto Primary School with a younger son named Daniel and his two younger sisters, Rael and Rosa. On arrival at the school, I found children who believed Aoyi was so wealthy that he had earned the status of a demi-god. There were Aoyi songs, which I found embarrassing to sing, firstly because they weren't based on facts, and secondly, because they seemed to be talking about a mythical figure.

The first month went well; I found my bearings and settled down. But in the second month, things grew unbearable on the home front. I was supposed to wake up at 5am or earlier to go to the farm and plough with the oxen until 7.45am before cleaning up and rushing off to school for 8.30am. I hardly had time to do my homework, read or play. I was often so exhausted that learning became a challenge.

Although food was abundant at the home, I hardly ate. Aoyi wasn't a kind man at all. He would shout at me all day long. I couldn't focus. Over the weekend, I was on the farm for eight to twelve hours uprooting groundnuts, harvesting sunflowers, struggling to drive a huge plough and rambunctious oxen over rough terrain. While Aoyi's own children were in school I, an 11-year-old was toiling alongside the hired hands in the fields. When I was not ploughing or planting seedlings, I would be weeding or harvesting. After the harvest season, I was sent to roam the vast Lambwe Valley in search of grazing grass and water.

In those days, the Ruma National Park, which is within the Lambwe Valley, was not fenced. The whole area teamed with wild animals such as deer, elks, rabbits and zebras. The valley also suffered from a bi-monthly invasion of army worms, what the Luo call *kungu*. They would eat everything green in their path – grass, plants and leaves – and carpet the entire place. They were rapacious and destructive. They were also messy. People literally walked on top of those worms, crunching them as they went along, leaving trails of green goo. But even more, they left a trail of destruction in their wake. As I herded the animals and searched for grazing grass, the swarms of army worms would cover everywhere until there was nowhere to sit and nothing for the animals to eat. Each time I hurried and took the animals to a place the worms hadn't reached, it only took an hour before the worms swept in. Apart from the biblical stories about the invasion of locusts, it's impossible to imagine anything like the invasion of army worms. They made me hate Lambwe Valley even more.

At the end of the first term (or semester) at Nyatoto – and despite my intermittent attendance – I was still the second best pupil in my class. That was quite an achievement considering that I had often missed school in order to do manual chores. The one month recess that followed was hellish for me. My brown cotton shorts were now tearing off. My cotton shirt could no longer be worn. I now only had the nylon shirt that I had come with. I had no shoes. Occasionally, I would borrow the open shoes made of old vehicle tyres from Ojwang', the herdsman. Ojwang' was older than me, but he was my height and size. The problem with Ojwang' was that he was schizophrenic. He would be nice and generous one day or hour and be brutally callous the next. He was even violent. One evening as we lay on the mats in the kitchen where we slept (before Jacobo, the older son's, *simba* was constructed), Ojwang' suddenly plunged towards me with a pocket knife. It missed me narrowly.

In the absence of proper clothes, shoes, food and care, I became a victim of jiggers (parasites that burrow in to the skin) which were rampant in and around Nyatoto. After only three months, nearly all my toe nails had disappeared.

I was finding my life as an unpaid herder increasingly unbearable, I had also not seen my mother and siblings for more than three months. One day during the August 1974 holidays, I got into an argument with Aoyi's eldest son Jacobo. I cannot recall what the argument was all about, but I recall Jacobo asking me to leave his *simba* (a hut for boys). I was to go and sleep in the kitchen, which the girls were now using. To me that was ridiculous. I believe I must have refused to leave.

Before I knew it, both Jacobo and his brother Daudi were raining blows on me. I tried to defend myself with very little success. Both were much older than me and I was soon overpowered. I cried out as loudly as I could but no one came to my rescue. The physical assault lasted for about 30 minutes. I was writhing in pain. My mind was racing. I quickly gathered my books, the cooking stick I had prepared as part of arts and crafts for school, and took off into the darkness with dogs barking behind me. Jacobo and Daudi were in hot pursuit. I ran outside the gate and onto the path leading to the main Homa Bay-Sindo road. They didn't pursue me beyond the gate. I could hear them swearing as they returned to Jacobo's *simba*. My heart was pounding rapidly. I was mad, angry and sad. I was crying, but kept running. My clothes were in tatters. I was determined to get away for good. It was around midnight. I had no money. Nothing.

Luckily, after about one hour, I saw a large truck approaching at full speed with full headlights on. I began to wave furiously. The truck driver must have seen me because he suddenly slowed down and screeched to a stop, about 50 metres past where I was standing, my heart racing. I dashed towards the truck, shouting in Dholuo, "Please help me! Please help me!" He inquired what I was doing and where I wanted to go. I shouted back "Ahero! Please take me to Ahero!" He opened the back of the truck and I climbed in. As I got in, I told him that I was from Apondo in Kano Plains and that he could drop me off at Ayweyo Primary School before reaching Ahero. He nodded his head and closed the back of the truck. The man must have looked at my state and concluded that something terrible had happened to me. He never interrogated me.

It was dark and scary inside the truck. I couldn't see anything or where he was heading. But he kept driving. After about 30 minutes, he stopped and left the truck. I heard him talking with some people before the truck started moving again. And it moved and moved until I fell asleep. When I woke up, it was early morning. I could see the sky clearing. But I didn't know where I was. The truck kept moving. I knew that as long as the truck was moving, I was getting away and would be farther from danger. Aoyi didn't own a vehicle, so I knew there was no prospect of him catching up with me.

Then the truck suddenly stopped. The back door opened. The driver told me to climb out as we had reached my destination. My heart started racing again. I was excited. We were at Ayweyo. I climbed down, thanked him, blinked and took my bearings. It was now about 8 am. The journey had taken eight long hours. As I walked towards Magina, tears started flowing down my cheeks. I was sobbing uncontrollably. I couldn't walk. I sat down and held my head with both hands. I was ready to return to grinding poverty, but at least I was free from inhumane and barbaric treatment.

My mother was at home when I arrived. When she saw me approaching, she ran up to me and held me tightly against her bosom before breaking down, crying. She took another good look at me and told me to enter our hut. I was given cold water to drink and then porridge. My mother took water and washed my face. She then wiped my feet with a wet cloth. She did these things ritualistically. I was being cleansed.

As I sat there drinking the porridge, my sister-in-law Angeline arrived. She too looked at me with sadness on her face. I had no toe nails on my feet. My clothes were completely in tatters. My hair was shaggy. They knew what had happened. They could see that I had endured long and brutal abuse. Later, I recounted what had passed and how I had managed to escape. The story was so sad that my mother asked me not to repeat it. "We will survive", she said. "We shall not die of hunger my child."

Even at the tender age of 11, I knew what inhumanity was and how it felt. I also knew how and when to reject it. From that day onwards, I considered my uncle Aoyi dead. I never communicated with him again until much, much later and only then because I had no choice.

The first time was after I returned home on holidays from the University of Nairobi in 1987 and found one of my older sisters missing. Before my mother died, she had asked me to make sure that I took care of my older sister, Leah Achieng'. Leah had a learning disability. Apparently, she had gone to visit the Aoyi family, but she had not been heard from for about one year. Now, based on my experience, I didn't want to imagine what could have happened to her. So, I took off to Lambwe Valley, arriving late in the evening only to be told that nobody knew where Leah had gone. I was given the name of a lady who was said to have taken her to somebody else to marry. When I arrived at the lady's house that evening, she wasn't sure where Leah was, but she promised to take me to another place in Karungu where she believed Leah had been married. That evening, I saw Aoyi and we greeted each other though we never actually spoke.

The lady and I took off early the following day. We arrived at our destination in the late afternoon and began a search that took us to five homes. Eventually, we found Leah, thin and dazed. She was living with a man who didn't seem to know even how to greet a brother-in-law. When he saw me, he panicked. I told them that my mother had died in May that year. It seemed Leah hadn't been told. The man didn't seem concerned about all that; all he was thinking of was that I had come for his wife. I managed to take Leah home the next day.

The man actually held onto my sister's right hand as I pulled the left one. Leah was confused: she didn't know whether to follow her brother or to turn back with her "husband". The man hadn't even bothered to find out where Leah came from. He hadn't actually married her, traditionally or civilly. He had not visited Magina, nor had he brought any cattle to symbolise marriage in accordance with the Luo customary law. There was no marriage certificate.

On reflection, I actually think I placed myself in unnecessary danger. The man, his brothers, relatives or fellow villagers, could have murdered me thinking – of course mistakenly – that I was a stranger trying to take their wife away. I had good reasons for what I did. I had promised my mother that I would try my best to take care of Leah; protect her from this unfair society. I couldn't let my mother down. For that, I took a risk.

A week after bringing Leah to Magina, I went back to university. When I next returned home for the holidays, I found that Leah had returned to Karungu. She had stayed in the village for only one week. Years after I had fled to Canada, she left that man and returned home. But she later died of severe diarrhoea on her way to the funeral of one of my step-sisters. I actually believe Leah died of hunger. The tragedy is that I had sent her some money via my brother, who had either diverted it or kept it for too long.

The second time I communicated with Aoyi was after my relocation back to Kenya in 2007. Aoyi was by then an ailing old man. He had undergone prostate cancer treatment and was back at the Moi Referral and Teaching Hospital in Eldoret for further tests and treatment. While there, his son, Daudi, who was then teaching at a university in South Africa, called and asked if I could speak to his father. I did. That was the second and only time I had spoken to Aoyi since 1974.

To me, Aoyi was an embodiment of raw and unmitigated evil. By not trying to prevent an 11-year-old boy from disappearing into the night in a place where wild animals roamed, he had shown real barbarism. But worse still, he never bothered to find out where I had gone or whether I was still alive. He made no attempt to send anyone to Magina to find out if they had heard of or seen me. That was bestial.

Aoyi died in May 2011 and I attended the funeral. Death is the final equaliser. And since we were taught never to speak ill of the dead, I paid my last respects humbly, and forgave him, though I have certainly never forgotten his cruel treatment of me. Fortunately, years have healed some of the hurt and injuries I sustained in Nyatoto. My relationship with Daudi improved and we are now fairly close. I am also on speaking terms with Jacobo, his sisters and mother.

APONDO

That is how I rejoined Apondo Primary School, which by that time had been relocated to a place about 20 metres away from our homestead. But before I could join, there were minor issues that needed to be resolved. First, the school needed a record of my attendance at Nyatoto Primary School. Unfortunately, I had no records, having fled my uncle's home in such a rush. Then the Ministry of Education officials insisted that they needed evidence that I had paid the 12 shillings annual fee. I didn't have that evidence either. In fact, I knew that Aoyi hadn't paid anything for me. The Ministry of Education office at Ahero insisted that my mother had two options: either to get original receipts confirming payment or to proceed to Pap Onditi, where they could pay the balance before I could rejoin Apondo. My brother opted to go to Pap Onditi and returned with proof of payment of Sh12. And in September 1974, I rejoined Apondo Primary School, having nearly lost a year herding cattle, sheep and goats for Aoyi. For that, I have been forever grateful to my brother.

Throughout my youth up to and including the entire period I attended university, I was very thin, so thin in fact that I don't remember ever wearing any pair of shorts or trousers that fitted me. Belts were rare in those days, so I would make do with strings made from sisal fibre or discarded plastic. Whenever I didn't have these strings, I would walk around with one hand permanently lodged to my side that ensured that the shorts or trousers didn't fall right down and expose my skinny buttocks. But I wasn't always successful, especially when we had to engage in physical exercises or education in school. In elementary school, it made running or participating in sports extremely difficult.

When I was about eight years old I nearly died twice. One day, I went to herd our cattle between the river Nyando and its tributary Wailes with a boy from Magina called Ouma Nyakongo. He used to call himself *John Kirk*, a name he borrowed from a European explorer in the Kenyan history books. As we herded, Ouma decided that he wanted to make a club from a fig tree branch. He had carried a sharp machete with which to accomplish the intricate job. He climbed up the fig tree and asked me to hold the branch as he cut. Unfortunately, when he finally managed to cut the branch, the machete went through it and landed on my forehead. I lost consciousness immediately and came to as Ouma was frantically washing off the gushing blood from the wound in my head with the brown Nyando water. He had dragged me to the river's bank and laid me down, where the water lapped around us. I sat up for a while, and then stood up. Up to that point, I hadn't understood what had happened. Ouma didn't tell me until much later. And when he did, he pleaded with me to keep it a secret because he feared that he would be severely punished if he was found out.

Somehow, I found myself home as the sun was setting. I pretended that nothing had happened and for a few minutes even joined my sisters in playing hop-scotch. Suddenly, I heard a shriek from my sister Auma. She was pointing at me and screaming. She had seen the swelling on my forehead. *Obwongo! Obwongo!* She screamed. Apparently, she saw something white on my head and thought my brain was coming out. It was my skull. By then my head had swollen to such an extent that it was submerging my eyes. I felt dizzy and collapsed. When I woke up, I was in a hospital, but I didn't know where it was. I later learnt that it was called *Russia* (now New Nyanza General Hospital). The deep cut on my head had been washed and stitched. That explains the fairly large scar on my head just above the forehead. At Onjiko, some students used to make fun of it, claiming that it was a path for cockroaches.

The second time that year that I nearly died was when I attempted to cross the river Wailes. Children in Magina learnt how to swim fairly young. That day we had crossed the river using a log-bridge and spent considerable time playing and eating wild guavas. Later in the afternoon we came back to find the river rapidly swelling. And unfortunately we weren't at the same location where we had crossed earlier. We were at a place without a log-bridge. The other children knew how to swim, and they soon removed their clothes and swam across the river. I was left alone. I looked at the river and took a plunge only to find myself being swept away. I couldn't swim. I was drowning. But in a split second a creative thought came to me. I loosened my body and fell to the bottom of the river. My feet and hands could feel the sand on the river-bed. I held my breath and walked on the riverbed and across up to the river bank where I emerged to find my friends running along the bank wailing that I had drowned.

I emerged at the bank breathless, just at the point where my energy had begun to ebb away. My eyes were red. I was choking from coughing, having ingested too much water. I lay on the ground, not quite believing I was still alive. All I had was a strong faith and a determination not to die. After about one hour of deep reflection, I returned to the river and resolved that I must learn how to swim. I struggled for about three hours. I returned the next day and the day after that until I learnt how to swim. Since then I have held the belief that everything is possible with hope, faith and determination.

For a long time when I was growing up my brother owned both a shortwave transistor radio and a gramophone. He had lots of albums by Owino Misiani, Franco Lwambo Makiadi, Tabu Ley Rochereau, George Ramoji, Kolela Masee, Oguta Lie Bobo and others. Whenever my brother got some money, he would buy batteries and play the albums endlessly. I loved it. I also used to listen to the British Broadcasting Corporation news bulletins daily – in the evening and in the morning. The BBC used to bring more insightful news than the Voice of Kenya, which concentrated on narrating what the President and his retinue had done on a daily basis before announcing fundraising events, deaths and funerals. In those days, the singer Owino Misiani Ja Shirati was like a one-man army of resistance, satirically and lyrically pointing out the ills of society and the betrayals of the Kenyatta – and later the Daniel Moi and Mwai Kibaki – governments. I loved music and news bulletins so much that there were times between elementary school and university when I could only study with some music in the background. To date I have remained a strong lover of music (of all genres), news and current affairs. In fact I trace my political consciousness directly to the historical and critical lyrics of Owino Misiani.

In August 1978 Kenyatta died. I remember that day clearly because I was at home when the news broke. I believe it was a weekend because I remember rushing across the fence that separated my brother's home and the school and beating the old tractor plough that the school used as a 'bell'. It wasn't a school day. I beat that bell so hard and for so long until I felt pain on my right hand. Of course nobody joined me or came to the school. Many must have thought that I was either crazy or that somebody had died and I was announcing it. Regardless, as a 15-year-old I already had developed deep resentment for Kenyatta and his government. I was already aware of how he had betrayed the Mau Mau veterans, Jaramogi Oginga Odinga, Pio Gama Pinto, Bildad Kaggia, Achieng' Oneko, Kungu Karumba and Thomas Joseph Mboya.

At the time, I was preparing to sit for my Certificate of Primary Education examinations. I was top of the class in Civics in our school. I knew about the political repression and economic subjugation Kenyatta had subjected the Luos to, yet it was Jaramogi who campaigned for his release when Jaramogi had the option of taking power himself. Even at that tender age, I was babbling with rage at the palpable injustices and inequalities that many Kenyans, especially Luos, were experiencing under Kenyatta. The 24 years of Daniel arap Moi continued and intensified the political and economic strangulation of the Luos, in particular, and Kenyans in general. I had this consciousness even when I joined Form One at Onjiko Secondary School in January 1979.

ONJIKO

I got to Onjiko through a roundabout manner. At Apondo Primary School we didn't have a counselling department or teacher. This is hardly surprising, given the fact that only three out of the six teachers had actually been trained.

For as long as I was a pupil at Apondo Primary School, the headmaster there was Enock Obiero. Elkanah Otieno Ojuki taught me English. No one could forget Elkanah. He was erudite, loud, proud and brash, in his own unique way. He perpetually reminded us that he was the best English teacher south of the Sahara and north of the Limpopo river. James Okoko, a humble and dedicated teacher from Kagimba, taught us the Bible, or what was referred to, in secondary school, as 'Christian Religious Education'.

The current Secretary General of the Kenya Union of Teachers, David Okuta Osiany, taught me in my last years at Apondo when he was fresh from college, although many pupils claimed that he was an untrained teacher or "UT". This could have been due to his relative youth at the time. Looking back, you can't imagine that the Okuta who used to teach at Apondo is the same man we see on TV today. The Okuta of the late 1970s was young and trim. I guess Okuta has eaten well since the 1970s. That applies to me as well.

These were poorly paid, humble but extremely committed teachers. They lived in grass thatched and mud walled huts in and around Magina village. They either walked to school or arrived perched precariously on their rickety bicycles. But above all, they taught us with passion.

When we sat for the CPE exams, I was so confident that I would get 36 points – the maximum at that level – that I only chose the best schools I knew of: The Alliance Boys High School, The Starehe Boys' Centre and Maseno School. But when the results were released, I only managed 30 points, obtaining B+ in all three examinable subjects – Maths, English and General Subjects (History, Civics, Geography, Natural Science and Agriculture). Only three pupils at Apondo passed that year: Habil Ochieng' Odhiambo, Rose Akumu Ong'udi and I. Habil and I led with 30 points with Rose coming second with 28 points. Habil and Rose seemed to have been more modest in their expectations, choosing all local (Nyanza) schools. Habil ended up at Homa Bay High School while Rose joined Rang'ala Girls High School. In those days they were considered very good schools. They both received their admission letters within weeks of the results being announced. I waited for my admission letter to no avail. Then just one week before the secondary schools opened in January 1979, I received an admission letter from Onjiko Secondary School. I was stunned. It seemed that the Onjiko headmaster had noticed a candidate with fairly good points who was still floating, unattached and decided to pick him.

Onjiko was located near Ahero, which was about six kilometres from Magina. Onjiko had a chequered history. It fluctuated to the extent that one would have found it nearly impossible to predict how it would rank each year. Discipline was also a major problem at Onjiko. We heard of students drinking at Ahero, leaving school at night to go to discos and otherwise just being rowdy. However, by 1979 a new headmaster called Leonard Ochola had been at Onjiko for about three years. During those years, discipline improved considerably and with that academic performance.

Onjiko went up to Form Four, with each class having two streams of about 45 students. My letter indicated that I had been admitted to Form One Stream B as a Day Scholar, which meant that I would attend school only during the day. This was shocking. My big dreams of joining a national school had been shattered completely. Then, of course, came the real trouble: that of finding fees. Even though Onjiko was a public school, students were charged tuition (or fees) that catered for accommodation, food, water and other facilities.

This was long before private academies became chic. In those days, attending private secondary school implied that one was academically weak. Children who couldn't make the grade but were from rich homes were the ones who attended private academies. They weren't popular even with the rich. In fact, the rich spent time and money and tried to throw their weight around in order to curry favour for their children to be admitted to public schools. Even as modest as Onjiko was – infrastructurally and academically – I remember seeing the sons of ministers, members of parliament and judges being chauffeured in at the beginning of the semester and out when the semester ended.

Although I went about my daily routines in the village as if nothing was amiss, I was terribly worried that the prohibitive cost would put paid to my dreams of attending secondary school. I walked around like a zombie, worrying to death. I soon stopped talking to anybody. I watched for any sign, any inkling that the situation would improve but found none. I felt lonely though there were lots of people around. Despite all the hustle and bustle of village life, Magina became a very cold and lonely place for me. This was the second time I felt depressed; the first having been at Nyatoto. With only one week to the opening of schools, my mother also started worrying about my tuition and money for shoes, science equipment, required texts like an English dictionary, the Bible and the Koran.

Tuesdays were market days at Ahero. On the last Tuesday of December, my mother gave my brother Ondiek a fat cow to go and sell so that I could find the money to join secondary school. From the proceeds, they bought me the kit I needed and took the balance to Onjiko for tuition. I walked to school that day. I left home at 5.30am and arrived just before 8am when the students were assembling to be addressed by the headmaster and the rest of the teaching staff. We endured one hour of long and boring speeches about school rules, discipline and more rules. It was scary. The speeches were actually just threats. I began wondering if I was in a school or a prison. When we dispersed, I headed straight to the administration block and paid my tuition. I was given a receipt.

Before my admission to Onjiko, I had never even used a toothbrush and toothpaste. Soon, covering the 12 kilometres (both ways) daily to school was taking its toll. Firstly, there was no road between Magina and Onjiko. I walked through wet dew in the morning and sometimes through floods. It was often chilly. Soon I started feeling severe chest pains, which by the second semester, had brought me down with fever and flu. I eventually found myself admitted again to *Russia,* in Kisumu. I was diagnosed with pneumonia and stayed in hospital for two weeks.

After my discharge, my mother spoke to a distant relative who agreed to accommodate me in Ahero from where I would walk to school. That was a significant improvement. Rather than the 12 kilometres, I was now contending with two. But during the two weeks' absence, my classmates had marched on. I found them significantly ahead in Maths and Physics. Although I was able to catch up with them on all the other subjects, I constantly lagged behind in those two subjects. It explains why I later opted for arts subjects rather than science. My original desire was to pursue medicine at university. However, without Maths and Physics, I couldn't specialise in science.

Quite early, I knew that my career path had to be in the liberal arts. As we progressed to Form Two, I had emerged as the best student in English, Literature in English, History, Geography, Chemistry and Christian Religious Education. I was also among the top three students in Agriculture. I found Agriculture interesting because we learnt the botanical names of plants and weeds. My performance in Chemistry was surprising in view of how I struggled with Physics and Maths. But I found Chemistry easy to commit to memory, just like History.

In Form Two I became a boarder. The remaining three years at Onjiko passed quickly. As soon as I started residing at the school, my grades improved remarkably. By the second semester in Form Two I was ranking in the top five in our class. In fact, I could have ranked number one except for Maths, Physics and Kiswahili that were still proving difficult to master.

My best friend from Form One to Four was Henry Okulu Obadha. We used to call ourselves the *Mangi Brothers*. We bestowed upon ourselves that moniker, but the students, through some uncanny logic, reserved *Mangi* for Okulu and *Owadgi Onding'* for me. The nickname emerged out of the habit students had of going for additional food after the first round.

In 1980 when I started boarding, there was a shortage of white maize, or at least that is what we were told. The school begun to buy yellow maize, which many people suspected was diverted relief food that had been donated by the United States of America for famine relief – severe drought and famine had actually affected most parts of the country that year. We would eat yellow maize and beans for lunch daily. For dinner, we would be served yellow *ugali* with vegetables three times a week and yellow *ugali* and meat twice a week. In between we got rice.

Previously, the maize and beans had been full of weevils and the food truly repulsive. But the yellow maize looked clean and fresh and tasted good, at least to Okulu, myself and our other friends. Rumours quickly spread that the yellow maize the school was serving us wasn't meant for human consumption; that it was animal feed. The story was that the United States of America was dumping animal feed on Africans in order to control our population growth. I'm not sure where those rumours originated from, but most students believed them. I didn't. Yellow maize in Dholuo is called *bando mar onding'*. I tried to listen to the rumours but found all of it to have been without any foundation. After all, virtually everyone in Kenya was now eating yellow maize. I knew that. It was being served in all local schools; not just at Onjiko. Even in our homes, we were eating yellow *ugali.* I refused to join the bandwagon, but the rumours persisted and as the rumours and rumblings spread among the students, many began to boycott eating much of their lunch and dinner. This meant food became abundant for those prepared to disregard the rumours.

During that boycott – which eventually died off by itself – a few of us used to go back for more food. Sometimes we would go twice and on occasion even thrice. The reason was simple: the first portions were usually very tiny and we would hardly be satisfied by it. Unlike the well-to-do students who had adequate pocket money with which to purchase loaves of bread, coffee, tea, milk, butter, margarine and jam, we were given virtually no pocket money to buy extras. We were bought toothbrushes, toothpastes, body soap and washing soap and told to head to school. On very rare occasions, some of us got Sh20 extra with which we could buy sugar and tea. These would hardly last for three weeks. Once those provisions dried up, all we could do was try to go for additional food, whenever it was available.

Then, as now, I've never been particularly susceptible to peer pressure. I have never been conditioned to do things because my friends, relatives or classmates were doing them. Even in those days, before I did anything I had to analyse its utility, first and foremost for myself, before I went ahead with it. So, I never really cared that other students were boycotting the yellow maize. For the few weeks that the boycott lasted, I ate my fill without shame. That was the origin of my nickname *Owadgi Onding'*. And I wore it as a badge of honour throughout my stay at Onjiko.

Another nickname I wore with honour at Onjiko and much longer afterwards was *Gowok*, which I gave myself. This wasn't an original construct; it was a derivative from General Yakubu Gowon, the former head of the Federal Military Government of Nigeria from 1966 to 1975. It was Gen. Gowon's decisive leadership that prevented Biafran Secession during the 1966-1970 Biafran Civil War. (By no means am I disregarding the systemic and historical gross human rights abuses against the Ibo by both the Federal Government of Nigeria and northern ethnic groups like the Hausa). As our history teacher (the best teacher I have had), Enos Oyaya Rateng' would later explain, Gowon's name was a clever coinage: 'Go on with one Nigeria.' I decided that I would like a similar nickname: 'Go on with one Kenya' – *Gowok*. To date, there are former Onjiko students – close friends – who only call me, endearingly *Owadgi Onding'* or *Gowok*. Even at that time I had a belief in one united and indivisible Kenya. As a pan-Africanist, I have had an ideological commitment to a strong, united and developed Africa; an Africa that is modern and democratic. For us to get to that dream, pragmatic pan-Africanists believe that it's possible to liberate and establish small geographic and political units which should – and hopefully would one day – come together in the future as a united federation; democratic, industrialised and equitable.

Bullying was then rampant in virtually all public boarding secondary schools in the country. For a long time, Onjiko was well known as a bastion for student hooliganism. Until Ochola *Yamo* was posted as the new headmaster a few years before I joined the school, Onjiko and discipline couldn't be mentioned in the same sentence. However, following Ochola's arrival, things changed significantly. Ochola was nicknamed '*yamo*' (the wind) by the students because he moved without being seen. In other words, when the wind blows, all we see is the movement of leaves, branches or other things that sway in its direction. Wind moves invisibly. Ochola was the same. The students soon realised that whenever he drove into the school compound, he would place his vehicle in neutral and have it roll into the compound without any noise. Other times, he would park his vehicle more than 200 metres away from the main gate, wear a long grey coat and an Oginga Odinga flat hat before entering the school incognito. Using these methods, he would catch students who were arriving after the 6pm curfew on Sundays, those who were intoxicated, those smoking in the toilets, noisemakers and all manner of offenders. Ochola was unpredictable, apparently random in his choice of days and times. Whenever he came across offenders, he would quietly take them away to his office without attracting any attention. Those caught would face a variety of punishment. Some had to pull up tree trunks, cut grass, run around the field or clean the compound. Those who had committed more serious infractions, such as drunkenness, smoking or sneaking out of school, might receive severe corporal punishment or even a brief suspension.

Before long the students became paranoid. Anybody walking in the school compound after 6pm could be Ochola. He caused so much fear among students that before long, students began to obey the school rules. Both students and parents viewed him as a mysterious man; someone with extraordinary powers. But Ochola wasn't just a strict disciplinarian; he was also a good administrator. He bought adequate provisions for the school – the library and the kitchen, in particular, were well stocked. And as he continued to enforce the rules firmly, consistently and fairly, the students spent more time studying, the teachers spent more hours teaching and the academic performance drastically improved. In other words, Yamo brought the rule of law, order, discipline and stability to Onjiko. By the time I was joining Form One, Onjiko was already among the top ten schools in Nyanza.

My best friend Okulu hailed from Seme and had the characteristics that we associated with Seme in those days: fiercely and brutally honest, brave and quirky. He was one of the brightest students in Form One, and easily the best at Maths and Physics. He had a good memory, which meant he also did well at history. He was intellectually independent. He was also creative, original and had flair. But he was also charismatic: he entertained fellow students with weird jokes, farted in class liberally and was constantly restless. He hardly sat still in class for one hour. He would visit the toilet frequently. He got bored quickly. Unfortunately because of these eccentricities, he always attracted the wrath of the teachers who punished him regularly and mercilessly.

When we were in Form Three, I was appointed a deputy dining hall captain. Many students were astonished because until then nobody knew that the administration liked me. My appointment meant that the Mangi Brothers were now in charge of the kitchen and could eat their fill. I suspected that Oyaya had had a hand in my appointment. By that time I had consistently distinguished myself as the best Geography and History student in our class. Oyaya taught us both subjects. I have never encountered a teacher so disciplined, so knowledgeable and so committed to his students. The message the school was sending (I believe through Oyaya) was simple: 'We know that you are poor. We know that you don't have money for sugar, bread and butter. But we also know that you are a very good, resourceful and promising scholar. We are giving you access to enough food; now go out there and perform.' I never disappointed. I have been forever grateful for that helping hand – maybe I would not have come so far in life without it.

Another sterling Onjiko teacher was Joshua Owiti Osuri. He was the only agriculture teacher at Onjiko for the four years I was there. We nicknamed him *ja-gwen* (chicken owner) because he looked after the school's chickens with a single-minded focus and dedication. Teaching two streams of students from Form One to Form Four looked like an impossible task, but Osuri did it with joy. He was always in a hurry. He was a man of action more than words and was regarded with immense respect by the entire student body. When I joined Form One, Osuri had a student in Form Four called Joseph Ochieng' Owuor who seemed as dedicated as he was. Ochieng' was so keen a student that he would emerge top of his class in all subjects – science and arts alike. He emerged top in the national exams as well. But rather than proceed to advanced levels, Ochieng' chose to go for a diploma course at The Egerton College in Njoro (that was long before Egerton became a university) where Osuri had graduated from. Apparently Ochieng' was the first born in a family with very little. Doing A-levels wasn't an option for him as it would have denied his other siblings the opportunity to go to school as well. Recently I was happy to see Ochieng' being interviewed by Jeff Koinange on K24 television. When I saw Ochieng' on K24 I quickly called Osuri (who is now the principal of Agoro Oyombe Secondary School in Nyanza). We both marvelled at how hard and diligent Ochieng' had been throughout his life. During the interview, Ochieng' stated that he was a lecturer in Agricultural Economics at Egerton University. He also disclosed that he had become a dairy farmer in Njoro, one of the very few from the Luo community. This confirmed the adage that persistence pays – and that no matter how long it might take, hard work is always rewarded.

Some time in Form Three, an incident happened that would change Okulu's life trajectory forever. It was Sunday. Ochola *Yamo* had taken study leave and gone to the United Kingdom to study for his Master's Degree. The Ministry of Education replaced him with an erratic man called Opondo Nga. Opondo was so eccentric that he would address students in Dholuo yet he knew that Onjiko students hailed from nearly all the Kenyan ethnic communities. He would tell us irrelevant stories about his escapades abroad which always ended by proclaiming that he was "Opondo Nga, *pi chieth motamo joduar modho;*" (Opondo Nga, watery faeces that hunters cannot drink). He was an exhibitionist, boastful, unpredictable, flamboyant and not without charisma, especially when speaking Dholuo. At first the students liked the jokes and his contrast to the humourless disciplinarian Yamo. Soon, however, the students got bored of Opondo and quickly saw through the fact that though he tried to sound sophisticated and brilliant, he was a buffoon, fit only for the rowdy markets in Nyanza. They also discovered that he was pilfering school provisions, leaving the students hungry.

In those days, I used to walk more than ten kilometres (both ways) on Sundays to go and visit my elderly and only aunt, Beldina Owuor. Aside from my mother who visited me in school once a month, my aunt was the closest relative I had.

She never called me by my name, preferring to call me, endearingly, *'Nyar minwa.'* This literally meant: "my mother's daughter'. This is because I was named after her brother, my father. Instead of saying: '*wuod minwa*', or 'my mother's son' to refer to my father, she inverted it. Luo cultural linguists might be able to unravel that; but for me, it designated the deep bond and affection between us; and that is enough. Peasants like me didn't have or use telephones in those days. I usually just took my chances and visited, calculating that on Sundays my aunt would attend an early morning church service then retire. Sundays were generally considered resting days. And I always found her at home, sitting under a big fig tree in her homestead. We would sit there for hours, just talking in low tones about family and school. At about 3pm I would set off back to school.

Whenever I wasn't visiting my aunt I would visit another retiree called Stephen Ochieng' Okumu. For his entire working life Ochieng' was employed by the Ministry of Roads and Public Works. When he retired he purchased a piece of land, which was situated about 100 metres from Onjiko Secondary School. Ochieng' had become a cripple since his retirement, confined to a wheelchair. He was also an alcoholic. Whenever I visited him he would regale me with adventurous stories of his youth and places he had worked. Although he was always drunk, he spoke lucidly about the value of education. He encouraged me to study hard, pointing out that our village needed well-educated people who could try to change the miserable conditions under which the villagers lived. I listened keenly to Ochieng'. I found him wise and positive. He gave me lots of inspiration and a strong belief that I would succeed. In turn, I would prepare light meals for him and wheel him to the toilet.

One day I returned to school just before 6pm, after a visit to my aunt's, to find chaos. There was commotion and noise everywhere. A small group of about 30 students were running around the soccer field singing war songs. Another group had surrounded the kitchen taunting the cooks. Yet another one was in the field behind the school. I tried to find out what was happening but nobody was explaining anything. I made my way towards the kitchen and a few students started chanting '*Owadgi Onding'! Owadgi Onding'!*' I didn't know why they were shouting my name. I approached the entrance to the kitchen but found it locked. The cooks were too scared to open up. I knew that the situation was getting out of control. I also knew that sooner rather than later, there would be trouble.

I quickly went to my dormitory and packed a few clothes before proceeding to our classroom where I took some books. I found a large section of the students doing the same. We knew that soon the riot police would arrive with guns, truncheons and tear gas. They wouldn't distinguish between who had joined the protest against Opondo's profligate maladministration and cruelty and those who were just bystanders. As we made our way to the back gate, a small number of students had gone to Opondo's house and were frog-matching him towards the main gate. I later learnt that they intended to take him to Ahero Police Station. However, just as they were about to leave the main gate, the riot police arrived, shooting in the air and throwing tear gas. It was pandemonium. Students were beaten and injured. Opondo was rescued. The school was closed indefinitely.

When I arrived home at 8pm that day, my mother was outside, pacing up and down. The message of the "strike" had preceded me. She was happy that I was alive. But she was also upset with me. To her, all students were guilty for going on strike. I subsequently explained what had happened and my mother relaxed. Her worry all along was that I might get expelled. Anyway, after three weeks of suspense, I received a letter from Onjiko stating that I was to report to school the following Friday. When I arrived, I did not find Okulu there. Upon further inquiry, I was informed he had been suspended for one month, following which he would become a day scholar. For some reason, the school administration had concluded that Okulu was one of the ring leaders of the strike. There were about 15 students in a similar position.

On the day Okulu's father brought him to school, an unprecedented drama ensued. At about 8am Opondo quickly summoned the entire school, along with the parents who had brought in their suspended children, to an assembly. We dutifully gathered. The teachers lined up in front of us in a row with Opondo in the middle. Okulu, his father and the other children with their parents stood to the far left. After a long and hilarious speech by Opondo, he summoned each parent to say something before caning their sons.

The first three parents complied and Opondo moved on to Okulu's father, Obadha. Apparently both Obadha and Opondo were from Seme. The assembly was dead quiet. Okulu lay on his stomach like those before him. Obadha was handed a cane. However, rather than proceed towards his son, he turned the cane on Opondo, hitting him on his bald head thrice before throwing away the cane and wrestling Opondo to the ground. The students broke into a loud uproar, clapping. Some female teachers took to their heels and four male teachers tackled Obadha and rescued Opondo. It was a scene to behold.

For that, Okulu spent the rest of his remaining time at Onjiko as a day scholar. And with that his bright future went down the drain. He became a pariah. Fortunately our friendship wasn't affected. I used my privileges as the deputy dining hall captain to have Okulu served lunch, and, on a few occasions, dinner, as if he was a boarder. I know that was an abuse of my privileges, but I felt that

Okulu had been an innocent victim of circumstances. The students had legitimate grievances even if they had resorted to illegitimate means to resolve them. I'm not sure if Okulu was a ring-leader or not. He informed me then that he hadn't been. I believed him. By then, I had known Okulu close to three years. Yes, he was headstrong; but he wasn't dishonest.

He rented a room at Ahero market. I believe that the distractions of the market place played a significant role in undermining Okulu's concentration and ultimately his performance.

Eventually, Opondo was replaced by a tall fat man whom the students nicknamed *Kube*, because of the huge round shape of his belly that looked like the sort of tin the Luo use for measuring grains in local markets. *Kube* wasn't a good administrator. He was absent from school most of the time. The students threatened to go on strike if Kube wasn't removed. Soon, Kube was replaced by Ogoto Owuor who arrived at the school driving a *matatu* vehicle with *Odessa* written on it. There were rumours that Ogoto had studied in a place called Odessa. Some students claimed it was the one in Texas, in the US, while others swore on their grandmothers' graves that the Odessa on Ogoto's *matatu* was purportedly in the Union of Soviet Socialist Republics (the USSR). But regardless of the minor controversy over the origins of the name, it explained why Ogoto had chosen it.

It was during Ogoto's tenure that we sat for our Ordinary Level exams. In Form Three we had been allowed to choose eight subjects; Maths, English, two science subjects, and four other subjects of our choice. When that happened, I rose to the top of our class. Meanwhile, I was spending lots of my time writing and studying other things outside the academic programme in school. For instance, I regularly contributed to the 'letters to the editor' sections of both the *Daily Nation* and the *East African Standard*. The only other student who contributed articles to the national newspapers was Gordon Ondiek (who would later precede me as an elected official of the Students' Organization of Nairobi University and also worked as a journalist before his untimely death).

In those days, Form Four national exams were done for three weeks in November. During exams, candidates were exempted from doing some school chores. After sitting the last exam for the day, Form Four students used to congregate for two hours around the soccer and basketball fields. One day, after we had completed a paper, I accompanied some of my classmates to the basketball pitch. We were watching some students practice, when suddenly I felt something hit my left elbow. The impact was so hard that I moved forward and knelt down immediately. As I writhed in pain, I heard commotion behind me. Other students were chasing one of my classmates, Charles Okoth Nyawade (now deceased), who had taken off. He was, however, caught and brought back to where I was, my left elbow now bleeding and already swollen. A few of my friends roughed Nyawade up before the teachers intervened and took him to the staffroom. I was quickly put on a bicycle and taken to Ahero Dispensary where the wound was cleaned and dressed. When I returned to the school that evening, I was told that Nyawade had confessed that he had hit me with the stone so that I couldn't complete the exams. Apparently, that was his way of preventing me from performing better than him. This incident was one of the first times when I realised how toxic envy could be. Nyawade was actually a smart student, especially in Chemistry, Maths and Physics. Although he wasn't among the top five in our class, he was certainly in the top ten.

Fortunately the injury wasn't as serious as everyone had feared. Although my elbow was swollen and painful, it didn't prevent me from studying or writing the remaining exams, which we soon finished. In January 1983 the results were released. Unfortunately, my best friends Okulu and Obura Kola obtained weak third divisions and became primary school teachers. Nyawade passed with a strong second division and must have gone to do Advanced Levels because I eventually saw him at the University of Nairobi where he did Botany and Zoology. Charles Uhuru (who had been the best student in Form One but now deceased) and John Frederick Kennedy Olali (who reigned in Form Two, but is also now deceased) also scraped by with weak second divisions. I was the second best student in the exams, behind the top student, Willis Otieno Orondo from stream "A". Orondo got 21 points and joined Nakuru High School. I obtained 22 points and went to Njiiri's High School.

My school leaving certificate issued by the deputy headmaster at the time on February 4, 1983 noted the following about my ability, industry and conduct: "Resourceful, Hard-Working, Self-Confident". I am sure many people couldn't have been more accurate about me. Regrettably, Okulu received the worst leaving certificate, which compelled me to intercede on his behalf with the deputy headmaster, Mr. Odette, to no avail. Despite the fact that I still owed the school more than Sh1,500, I was allowed to sit for the Ordinary Level exams. This was because the school always made such allowances for its bright students.

NJIIRI'S

On February 7, 1983, I registered at Njiiri's High School (later renamed Njiiri School in the late 1980s). Njiiri's was in Murang'a District, but it operated its postal address from Thika town, which was in Kiambu District.

This time I was smarter in the way I had gone about applying to schools. One couldn't choose three of the top schools and expect to get a place if your first choice didn't pick you. At the time Njiiri's came in as either the third or fourth best school in the country. It had been awarded the trophy for best discipline in Kenya in 1982. It had retained the honour in 1983 and was still holding the title when I graduated in 1984. The previous year one of the best students at Onjiko had joined Njiiri's. So I chose Njiiri's first, then The Starehe Boys' Centre and Kanunga High School. This time I was admitted to my first choice and off I went to Murang'a.

The journey to Nairobi from Kisumu was traumatic. Even though I had spent four years at Onjiko, I hadn't been to Kisumu. During my four years at Onjiko, I had never gone on outings or educational tours because the school charged extra for them. My brother Ondiek travelled with me. We boarded the Kisumu-Nairobi commuter train one evening on February 6, 1983. The train was full. We were in the third class cabin. I later heard that the first and second class cabins were for rich people. That made my hatred for poverty even more intense. The third class cabin was filthy. It stank of urine and human faeces throughout the journey. Although the train seemed to have modern toilets they never had water in them. Passengers were sitting everywhere – even on the floor and inside the toilets. It was both disgusting and shocking to me. I clutched onto my things all the way. Unlike me, my brother wasn't bothered. He behaved as if he was used to the commotion, congestion and filth. Maybe he was. After all, he must have taken the trains many times before. I also found the train too slow. It was vibrating, jerking along frustratingly. It also stopped too frequently, though there were times when that was a relief as we had to dash outside during these brief stops to relieve ourselves in the bushes. Somewhere along the way, many hawkers entered the cabins, selling cooked food, mainly roasted corn, groundnuts and bacon. Ondiek bought some bacon and offered me a portion. I declined. Although I was hungry, I couldn't eat with the choking nauseating smell that enveloped the cabin. I eventually fell asleep and was only woken by the loud and continuous horn of the train as it approached its final destination. Soon, hundreds of people were rushing to alight. It was early morning. We had been travelling for close to 12 hours. Ondiek led the way towards the Machakos Bus Stop where we caught a commuter vehicle to Njiiri's.

Njiiri's was a large school, three times the size of Onjiko. But the buildings looked old, grey and dilapidated. There were students from virtually all the ethnic communities and regions in Kenya. I had been admitted to do History, Literature and Christian Religious Education. I was focused on becoming a lawyer.

During our final year at Onjiko, Anthony Ochieng' Owala, who had also graduated to Njiiri's, and I had become inseparable. We had spent lots of time together studying. Owala and I were so sure of ourselves that we called ourselves 'the gifted two'. After classes, we would sit under trees in the school compound with our notebooks and texts to revise. On many occasions (at Onjiko) I would lie on my back facing the sky with my eyes closed and ask Owala to open page one of the geography text, *East Africa* by White. I would start from the preface, go over the introduction, and move through the book up to the last page. As I recited the text, Owala would be quietly checking whether I had missed a comma, fullstop or an expression. He would then declare the result. Next, Owala would lie on his back facing the sky as he recited the same text before we moved over to the history text by Professor Were. We taxed and tested our memories on a daily basis on literature, history and geography texts. During school holidays, we visited each other's homes and did the same. We trained our minds so well that it wouldn't matter from which chapter or section of the books the questions came, we would be sure to excel in those exams. Through our relationship, our mothers became friends and used to joke that we might risk falling for the same woman when we grew up. We had many similarities: both of us were fatherless, both were last born, and both were fiercely competitive.

Njiiri's had many Ugandan expatriate teachers. Our two literature teachers, Ndyatuura and Mpalirwa, were Ugandan. Mpalirwa was a flashy young man who was rumoured to have been a lawyer in Uganda before getting into trouble with Idi Amin's brutal dictatorship. He taught us literary criticism and appreciation. Ndyatuura apparently used to be a literature lecturer at Makerere University. He always looked absent-minded but was as sharp as a razor. Ndyatuura taught us novels, plays and oral literature. It was Ndyatuura who introduced me to Bertolt Brecht's *The Caucasian Chalk Circle*, Bhabani Bhattacharya's *So Many Hungers*, George Lamming's *In the Castle of My Skin*, John Steinbeck's *Grapes of Wrath*, Sembene Ousmane's *Gods Bits of Wood*, John Ruganda's *The Floods* and Meja Mwangi's *Carcass for Hounds*. These are some of the best pieces of literature I have read; meticulously and vividly written accounts of adversities, wars, violence, cataclysmic social upheavals, turmoil, rapacious exploitation and triumph of good over evil. These books taught me that no matter how protracted the struggle for justice may be, ultimately, good always prevails over evil. That is why I will never give up struggling in the quest for justice. The struggle will take many forms and encounter many setbacks, but the result is guaranteed.

There were several maths teachers, but the most famous one was J.M. Humphreys, a relic of the British Empire who lived alone with a dog and called out students by their admission numbers. It was as if he thought African children were nothing but numbers. Humphreys was nonetheless a gifted maths teacher. Although he was also a strict disciplinarian, he was very popular with students and had genuine commitment to his profession. But he lived a socially detached and alienated life, which I felt was mainly self-imposed. The headmaster, Stephen Ndung'u, whom we nicknamed *Adhuk* because of the thick moustache he sported, ran the school like a boot-camp. He maintained very high discipline standards but he was inflexible and oppressive. Then there was the teacher everyone simply referred to as Mr. Kagwala; slow, heavy but quite good. Mr. Kagwala taught Ordinary-level English and had the singular distinction of producing the highest number of distinctions in English Language in the entire country. Folklore had it that for as long as Kagwala taught English at Njiiri's, no student got less than a "C" grade. Students looked at Mr. Kagwala in awe.

Until I arrived at Njiiri's I had never heard of a student caning a fellow student as punishment. In Njiiri's, a Form Five prefect could cane a Form Six student. Essentially, all the students were under the same rules and regiment. The school had been named after senior chief Njiiri, who was a Home Guard and a British collaborator. We were told that he had donated the land on which the school was constructed. It was a huge piece of land situated a few kilometres from the Aberdares. And of course, everybody knew how such tracts were acquired by colonial collaborators before and even after independence. In July, the weather around Njiiri's was so chilly that students from Nyanza, North Eastern, Northern parts of the Rift Valley and Coast believed that no other place could be colder.

After three weeks at Njiiri's, I met a young man who replaced Okulu as my best friend. His name was Duncan Osodo (now a high school principal).

Njiiri's students engaged in many extra-curricular and co-curricular activities. We had sports of every description, such as soccer, basketball, volleyball, field hockey, mountain-climbing, tennis and athletics. We also had clubs for debating, agriculture, first aid, history, current affairs, Christian Union and others. In May each year, we would wake up at 3am and go mountaineering. We would walk and run through the thick Gatare Forest, all the way to the Aberdare Range. There were lots of bamboo forests. As we made our way through footpaths, we saw elephant footprints and dung. At times, we passed places where elephants had just destroyed large sections of the forest. It was very scary. Eventually, we would climb up to where we saw Lake Naivasha below and Mount Kenya to the right. The panorama was breathtaking. But as it was always chilly at the top; we wouldn't stay there for long.

I quickly distinguished myself as a good debater and a current affairs expert, leading to my unanimous election by the students as the chairman of the Senior Debating Club as well as the treasurer of the Senior Historical Club in October 1983. Before we finished Form Five, I was appointed the first deputy school captain. There were two of us. The second deputy captain was studying Maths, Biology and Chemistry. Neither of us participated in sports. Many students were shocked because before then those positions had been reserved for good soccer and basketball players. Unlike the other prefects, I wasn't that interested in wielding power. I rarely bothered with smokers and noisemakers. What I was particularly keen on was the development of a democratic culture where students would be encouraged to present their arguments and positions without hindrance. Njiiri's prefects were encouraged to give lectures weekly on topics of their choices. As soon as I was appointed, I began to give lectures on a variety of issues. My favourite topics were popular democracy, pluralism, repression, detention without trial, the cold war and the arms race. As my lectures became increasingly popular with students, Ndung'u became restless. It was put to me that I should join the basketball team or be fired as a prefect. I chose to be fired and was only rescued when the students threatened to go on strike if he made good his threat. That was the first time I came face-to-face with deliberate attempts to stifle my rights. In a way Ndung'u, wanted to dictate what we as students thought and how we expressed our thoughts.

It was also at Njiiri's where I learnt how to sketch pictures. My roommate was a gentle but slow bespectacled young man from Western Province who was a real artist. He could draw everyone. We both resided in Kenyatta Dormitory. I used to sit there and marvel at his talent. Then one day, Ndung'u announced that President Daniel arap Moi, his then Vice-President and Minister of Finance Mwai Kibaki and the then Higher Education Minister Joseph Kamotho and other dignitaries would grace the school's 25th anniversary – the Silver Jubilee – celebrations on June 11, 1983. That was just three weeks away. We were asked to compete by drawing a portrait of the ex-senior chief Njiiri, whom the school was named after. Whoever drew the closest likeness to the ex-senior chief would receive a certificate and cash prize. I dutifully entered the contest.

For the next two weeks, my roommate and I struggled with many sketches. We used Njiiri's real pictures in the school library. The conventional wisdom was that my roommate would take the prize because he was by far the best artist in the school. The sketches would be judged by the visiting dignitaries.

On the appointed date, after much noise, songs, dances and speeches, Kamotho stood up to declare the winner. Everyone held their collective breath.

'Your Excellency, it is now my pleasure to announce that the winner of the drawing contest is Joshua Miguna Miguna'. The students erupted in loud applause. I was shocked and thought that the minister had made a mistake. Few people thought I would win. I had never drawn before. Nor had I taken courses in Fine Art. Yet there I was being photographed by an army of journalists as if I had won the 100 metres' dash at the Olympics.

I stood up and went up to the dais, shook the hands of President Moi, Vice-President Mwai Kibaki and Education Minister Kamotho and accepted the Sh50 prize. They also gave me a certificate, which I held aloft before returning to my seat. When Moi stood up, he congratulated me and the entire school. He then announced that since the school had retained the top position as the most disciplined school in Kenya, we would retain the trophy. (I have no idea how it was determined which school deserved the trophy). And to cap it off, he took out a bundle of notes in an envelope and called me back to accept our gift for being good students. It was Sh10,000. That was a huge amount at that time. Moi said that the money was for buying a bull for the students to feast on. Moi used to dish out such gifts to many schools over the country. It was a clever Machiavellian way of buying loyalty and support from students.

After the guests had left, I handed over the money to Ndung'u, who informed me I would accompany him to Thika the following week in order to select the bull for the students. We left early in the morning. I sat at the back of Ndung'u's Citroën car. For the next four hours, Ndungu' took me from place to place. Wherever we went, he would leave me in the car and come back only to drive off again without telling me anything. Eventually, we entered a place that looked like a farm. Again, he abandoned me in the vehicle and returned only to drive off after 45 minutes. In the evening, he dropped me back at the school and announced that "we" had purchased the bull. I believe it was a bare-faced lie. If he had bought a bull, I hadn't participated in its selection nor did I know how much it cost. But presumably to cover any fraud, Ndung'u had bothered to carry me along. I suppose he swindled some of the money Moi had given us. The long and short of it is that we ended up being served some portions of beef (presumably from the bull) with two slices of bread. That was our feast.

My last year at Njiiri's was extremely difficult. I was sent home on three separate occasions for tuition fees which I couldn't raise. Each time, I was called into Ndung'u's office with other poor students in the middle of class sessions and caned savagely before being sent away. I would use the fare meant for end of term transport to travel to Magina only to return empty-handed. Eventually, as the exams were getting closer, Ndung'u extended a reprieve and I was allowed to stay.

Unfortunately, I fell ill and spent a considerable amount of time visiting local health centres. I would get injections until there were no places on my buttocks to inject. Most of the time, I felt quite ill. Many parts of my body were quivering uncontrollably. I had pain in my stomach and groin. The situation got so bad that a teacher volunteered to take me to the Nyeri District Hospital where I was admitted for a week. They did a barrage of tests and placed me on a week's medication. I was discharged two weeks before the exams began. By then, I was beginning to resign myself to the idea that I might not be able to sit the exams. My classmates were extremely worried. When I sat the exams, I had not fully recovered. I was also feeling tired.

The results came out in early January 1985. I was able to find the fare to Njiiri's after one week. By then, most students had collected their results. I was restless. I eventually arrived at the school and found that I had passed with three principals. I had also passed the compulsory General Paper. I had 12 points. But I was worried. I had only selected two courses: Bachelor of Laws and Bachelor of Arts. I had only chosen the University of Nairobi. I'm not usually good at gambling. All my life I've been a focused and decisive person. It was a great relief to me when I was, in the end, admitted to the BA programme at the University of Nairobi. I missed the cut-off point for admission to Bachelor of Laws by one point.

CHAPTER TWO

GILGIL

In the 1980s, those admitted to public universities had an enforced year out before they could start. That was due to the frequent closures of the only public universities at the time – Kenyatta University and the University of Nairobi – due to student demonstrations against bad governance, rampant human rights abuses and frequent political assassinations. In those days, the University of Nairobi was closed three or four times in one year. One time it was closed for almost a year. Consequently, there was a one-year backlog. Meanwhile, Moi had also imposed a three-month mandatory National Youth Service (NYS) boot-camp for students admitted to public universities. Thus the next responsibility for me was to find gainful employment before I did my NYS, then proceeded to university. I got a teaching job at St Alloy's Gem Secondary School, a junior private day school in Gem Rae, founded and owned by the late Dr Pius Alois Okelo-Odiko, who had also set up the Makini School in Nairobi.

I started in February 1985. I was to live in, which was to present me with new challenges. As the younger brother of four unmarried sisters, I had never learnt to cook proper meals or look after myself domestically. My house was a four-roomed and mud-walled shelter with a corrugated iron roof. The floor was nothing but dust. There were large cracks on the walls through which you could see the outside. I often fretted about snakes crawling into my bed through those cracks. Sometimes I would lie on the bed, imagining the non-existent snakes.

I knew one family in the neighbourhood. I had attended Onjiko with a brilliant naughty young man called Jack Ojuok, who had excelled in his exams and joined Kakamega High School. Ojuok's younger brother Owen joined Onjiko in Form

One when I was doing my final year. I had taken care of Owen, ensuring that he wasn't bullied. For my acts of generosity, the Ojuok family welcomed me in Gem with open arms. In fact, for the first few weeks after I started teaching at St Alloy's, I either ate at Owen's home or one of his sisters prepared meals for me at the school. Owen's younger brothers Isaiah and Ochis brought me fresh milk in the morning. And in the evening, Owen's younger sister Rose brought me water for cooking, cleaning and bathing. This went on for about one month until my brother's daughter Caroline came over and taught me how to cook *ugali*, eggs, rice and vegetables. Later, I learnt how to cook *omena* by myself.

At St Alloy's Gem Secondary School, I taught English, Literature in English, History, Geography and Christian Religious Education. After four months, another untrained Form Six graduate called Elly Otieno Bodo (sadly recently deceased) was recruited. Elly had done his A-levels at Nakuru Boys' High school. He was also teaching as he waited to join the NYS before proceeding to the University of Nairobi for a general science degree. When Elly joined, he took over Maths, Physics and Chemistry. Elly moved in and shared the four-roomed ramshackle house with me. We developed a roster for cleaning and cooking. Because he was generally a better cook than I was, Elly prepared meat and *ugali* while I specialised in eggs, tea and rice. Over the weekend, we would go shopping in the local market.

Elly and I were sad to have to leave St Alloy's behind for the NYS boot-camp at Gilgil. It had been a happy and productive time. In contrast, the three-month boot-camp felt like a year-long endurance test.

We arrived at the NYS boot-camp to find the place dry, Spartan and hilly. There were many barracks, built like large school dormitories. They were long rectangular buildings with one entrance at the far end. There were two rows of single beds lined up on either side with an aisle down the middle. The floors were made of cement, the walls plastered and the roof covered with asbestos. We used to place our luggage, shoes and utensils under the bed. Everything was regimented and strictly controlled. We woke at 3.30am to carry out menial chores amidst a din of yelling and abuse from the *afandes* (the regular servicemen and servicewomen). The *afandes* were actually either elementary school graduates or at best Form Two dropouts that had been recruited to the regular NYS programmes to be taught commercial trades such as carpentry, masonry and tailoring. Some of these trainees chose to become 'trainers' of new recruits; mainly in physical education. These were people whose worldview didn't extend beyond Gilgil. They looked at us – the pre-university students – with envy. As a result, some of them vindictively mistreated us as if we had to pay for having excelled in the examinations that the *afandes* had either not done or failed in.

The morning after our arrival, we were taken for a medical examination. X-rays, blood and urine tests were done. Those who were found to be ill were told to return home. Many were rejected for chest complications, tetanus or malaria. The way those found to be ill were discharged made them feel as if they were failures. Some managed to convince those in charge that they would be able to endure the camp.

One of those was Nicholas Gumbo (now Member of Parliament for Rarieda constituency). Gumbo suffered from severe tetanus, which had affected his left foot, making it swell badly. For a period, his foot was so swollen that he couldn't actually walk. Neither could he participate in any strenuous physical activity. Eventually, it subsided, but even then, he could only limp. He couldn't wear closed shoes. I used to get food for him when he couldn't walk. I believe he spent the entire three months wearing rubber slippers. For the entire period we were at the NYS, Gumbo, whose bed was next to mine, never marched. He spent most of his time reading detective and mystery novels, especially Robert Ludlum's detective supermarket novels. Gumbo believed that returning home would lead to him being stigmatised as less of a man, some kind of weakling. I found that quite strange. But he showed great courage and fortitude. He completely refused to accept that he was suffering from severe tetanus. He refused to be an object of pity. I liked the fact that he endured his pain and suffering with dignified pride.

When we arrived at the NYS camp, we noticed neatly planted flowers around each barrack. The flowers were well watered. My barrack was *Ngamia*. At dawn the following day, we were woken up by shouts of what sounded like 'Fallen! Fallen! Fallen!' ("Fall in"). As they shouted this the *afandes* would be pulling off blankets and sheets from us and exposing our nakedness. Most of the students, including myself, didn't have pyjamas. A few didn't even have underwear. We quickly stood up, cowering and desperately trying to cover our bodies. We dressed in a hurry. Others were running to the bathroom to brush or take a shower. But our progress was thwarted by punches and kicks coming from a group of *afandes* who had invaded our barrack shouting at the top of their voices. We were forcibly herded together. One *afande* stepped forward, and using a bed next to him, demonstrated how we were supposed to prepare our beds. We were given three minutes to do that. And as we tried to do that, more blows fell on a number of us. The *afandes* were cursing us and saying we were lazy, stupid and useless.

Eventually, we were outside, in three lines, with the green-attired *afandes* in front of us. Soon we learnt that 'fall in' meant to stand outside in three straight lines. 'Fall out' meant to disperse. 'Up-iiz' meant 'at ease', which was another way of saying that our feet should be placed apart while we stood straight. 'Chain' meant to stand to attention. 'Kamneiiz' meant 'company', which referred to the entire barracks being assembled. Each one of us was given a spade, which we were taught to hold as if it was an AK-47. Spades soon took on a different meaning for us. We were made to line up with the tallest people being at the end of the line and the shortest ones in the middle.

The tallest people at both ends were referred to as 'right markers'. And since I was the tallest in *Ngamia*, I became a 'right marker'. These were the people that would lead the rest of the 'company' as we marched every day for the next three months. Right marking was such a burden. You stood out like a sore thumb. Any mistake and the entire team came crushing down, with the right marker's mistake being replicated through the chain. And the *afandes* watched right markers more closely than the rest of the team. A half of the company was called 'sikuodi'. That was their way of saying 'squad'.

We would march for one hour without a break. In-between marches, we would be forced to do multiple press-ups on the tarmacked field with our fists clenched. It was brutal. Immediately after that, we would be hustled around the barrack and made to uproot all the nice flowers – every single one of them. After that, we would dig up the ground where the flowers had been and water it thoroughly. As we did this, the *afandes* would be shouting expletives at us, pushing and shoving. No sooner had the ground been prepared and levelled, than we would be told to replant the flowers again and again.

Sometimes we planted and uprooted the flowers five times before we were shoved towards the kitchen to get our breakfast of one portion of porridge, which we took 'on the go'. By 9am each day, we were taken outside the camp for cross-country running. This lasted for two to three hours, after which we returned, showered and rested for 30 minutes before starting the marches again. During the day, the entire camp assembled on the field and practised, with *afandes* shouting discordantly. This was only interrupted by lunch at 1pm. Within an hour, we were back again, with '*lef, right, lef, right, lef, right...abautan...lef, lef, lef, lef...halt!'* This went on all day. The food was bad. Nights were chilly. The *afandes* exhibited perpetual hostility towards us.

This went on for about one month. Most students were becoming restless and despondent but nobody had enough courage to rebel. We were mostly new to one another. Mobilising the entire group would take considerable effort and time. In *Ngamia*, I had a few close friends. Benjamin F. Odhiambo Onienga, Ojwang' Hongo, Nicholas Gumbo, Chome and Abaja Yambo (now deceased). But of all of them, Abaja was by far my closest friend. In many ways, I considered Abaja more than a friend: he was a true confidant, a comrade. He was both outspoken and fearless in a funny way. He spoke his mind unreservedly. But he didn't do so by addressing large gatherings. He didn't have the gift of the gab. He was surreptitious, organising rebellion underground. He was the tiniest person in the entire barrack. That gave him lots of advantages that he utilised to the maximum. Because he was short and thin, it was always difficult to notice him as we marched, jogged or performed other chores. Aware of that, Abaja would always try to cause mischief. When the *afandes* were shouting at us, Abaja would hurl choice words back at them, hidden in the midst of the squad or company. He would do it in a manner that made it very difficult for the *afandes* to know who it was. For instance, whenever we were ordered to do press-ups, Abaja would blurt out: *"Afwaaaandeeee! Tim kendi"* (*Afande!* Do it yourself!) This would set the entire company roaring with laughter, which would in turn make the *afandes* run around with rage, but without knowing who to target. The whole company would be punished. And as we started doing more press-ups, Abaja would be saying, with each downward and upward movement: *"one, two, afwande, beast, one, two, afwande nugu, one, two, afwande, kondo…"* This would send us reeling with more laughter, and the *afandes*, unable to tell who was doing this, would stand there in an impotent rage. To their credit, no one in *Ngamia* snitched.

However, as the frustrations continued and the *afandes* persisted with their beastly ways, Abaja, Odhiambo B.F., Hongo, Chome Mwidau and I decided that we needed to teach them a lesson. We agreed that we would mobilise all residents of *Ngamia* and convince them to have a small strike. We didn't want it to involve all the other barracks – not only were the residents of the other barracks capable of taking care of themselves – but trying to organise the entire place was wrought with too many risks. All we wanted was one hour of civil disobedience. On the appointed day and hour, all *Ngamia* residents would lock the door from inside and refuse to wake up. We would remain inside until the *afandes* got the message. The subsequent investigations would disclose our grievances, which was the whole point. Everyone we spoke with agreed with the plan and a date was set. At exactly 3.30am, the *afandes* invaded *Ngamia* – as they always did – shouting 'Fallen! Fallen! Fallen!' For the first time since we reported to the NYS camp, *Ngamia* remained locked and nobody moved. The lights were switched off. It was dark. The *afandes* couldn't see anything from outside. They started banging the door viciously. Nothing moved. Eventually, after a 45-minute stand-off, a traitor opened the door and all hell broke loose.

Investigations were later conducted and some snitches revealed what had happened. They reported that Benjamin F. Odhiambo Onienga, Ojwang' Hongo,

Chome and I were the ringleaders. We were made to stand in the field for three continuous days from morning to evening, rain or shine. That time, Abaja escaped the dragnet. But it never broke our resolve. And we never betrayed Abaja. That act of defiance by an unarmed and a peaceful group of students in the face of grinding injustice signalled to the powers-that-be that we weren't taking things without resistance. It also showed that the students – mainly strangers to one another and as frightened as they seemed – could still come together in solidarity for a collective goal: that of removing oppressive shackles from their shoulders. It also disclosed that whatever we did, there would always be the risk of betrayal. And that if or when that occurred, only a few would be sacrificed. I was okay with that.

The students at the NYS camp were becoming radicalised as days drew into months. We continued to perform menial physical chores, marched and ran around Gilgil town. We were beginning to question the utility of the so-called pre-university training programme. On paper, we were supposed to undergo physical fitness, foot drill, first aid, camp craft, fire-fighting and attendance at a series of lectures on national development issues and strategies. In reality, however, we only received physical fitness and foot drill training, most of which were geared towards dehumanising us. The target was to break us down: physically, psychologically and mentally. At the end of each day, we were supposed to be so exhausted that serious thinking would be impossible. Denying us basic needs such as adequate and nutritious food, entertainment and recreation was supposed to turn us into beasts.

Hungry young men (and women, who were camped in Naivasha, more than 30 kilometres from Gilgil) wouldn't have time for serious discourses. Important national issues affecting the majority of Kenya such as detention without trial, extrajudicial killings, torture, political repression, runaway corruption, iniquities, rampant tribalism, excessively high unemployment and lack of multiparty democracy weren't things hungry and physically exhausted youths would bother with. Locking up young men aged between 17 and 20 for three months would inevitably cause them to crave for alcohol, tobacco and women. The primary idea was to make us feel like we were nothing. Those who conceived of the programme had the singular intention of 'proving' to us that we weren't as intelligent as we might have believed. Essentially the message was: you might be bright in the sense that you have passed a series of competitive national examinations, but without power and money, you are still nothing. Power and money were presented as the beginning and end of everything. This was supposed to cause insecurity in us thereby exposing us to political manipulation, misuse and abuse.

Each month, we used to attend 'political sermons' by Kanu and government big wigs from Nairobi. They would shout themselves hoarse about patriotism, *Nyayo* philosophy, development and the need for respect for elders. Afterwards, they would field questions from the students. Everything began and ended with *Nyayo Juu!* Indoctrination was up in their agenda. The only thing lacking was sophistication, tact and a well-thought-out strategy.

I had a dramatic encounter with the then Chief Secretary and Head of the Civil Service, Simeon Nyachae. Contrary to his concocted media-propelled reputation as an effective public administrator, Nyachae didn't sound intelligent, thoughtful or coherent. His presentation was scattered, erratic and retrogressive. He asserted that the Moi government was popular and ordained by God. He stated that those challenging Moi were drug addicts, deranged communists and dissidents. He warned us against falling into the traps of devious scholars whose primary intention was to propagate foreign ideologies and culture. Forget about academic freedom! Consistent with the scripts we had heard before his arrival, he concluded by invoking Moi's name and his glorious *Nyayo* philosophy of 'peace, love and unity'.

My hand was up before Nyachae resumed his seat. I had been burning with rage throughout his speech. It was the most insensitive and outrageous sermon since we had reported to the NYS. But I could see that G.W. Griffin, the director of National Youth Service and the one presiding over the session was avoiding my hand. I persisted. After the third person had asked his question, I posed mine: "Sir, thank you for that illuminating lecture. You have informed us of how democratic the Moi government is. You have also condemned those who are challenging the government, stating that they are drug addicts, deranged communists and dissidents. Could you explain to us, Sir, why this democratic government has refused to allow Jaramogi Oginga Odinga from forming his own political party? Secondly, even if you argue that he isn't allowed to form his party because the Constitution forbids the operation of any other party except Kanu; why then can't Jaramogi be allowed to exercise his rights, like everybody else, by being allowed to pursue his political ambitions? Why has the same democratic Kanu government banned Jaramogi from running for office on its ticket? Finally Sir, could you explain to us how detaining political opponents without trial is consistent with Kanu's proclamation of democracy and the Nyayo philosophy of 'love, peace and unity?'"

I stopped when I saw Nyachae charging towards the microphone in extreme fury. He was foaming and gesticulating. The students cheered and clapped loudly. Some were shouting '*Toboa! Toboa!*' (reveal! reveal!) before I finished. Griffin was unable to speak. Other dignitaries were fidgeting. We were supposed to have been 'worked on' for the last two months yet there I was still persisting with questions that only dissidents asked. NYS was intended to serve two primary purposes: to physically and psychologically break us through constant menial chores, humiliation, denigration and mistreatment, and to indoctrinate us into believing that Kenya had its owners; the rich, the powerful and the privileged. Something clearly wasn't right. That seemed to have shocked Nyachae.

First, Nyachae demanded to know my name. An NYS functionary sitting on the dais quickly went up to him and gave him a piece of paper. I assumed that my name was on it. I had been marked. He then raved and ranted about respecting His Excellency the President and the Commander-in-Chief of the armed forces who had brought peace and unity in the country. In the end, Nyachae forgot the questions I and other students had asked him and petulantly marched off the stage and headed to his vehicle, which drove off at high speed, with the other dignitaries in tow. The sermon was over. And I knew I had been marked.

Early in the morning the next day, I was summoned to the administration block and told that because I had been rude and disorderly the previous day, I would face disciplinary action. The first one was to run up to *Kioko* (a hill two kilometres away) with a white pillow carried over my head so that I could be seen going and returning. Once I reached *Kioko*, I was supposed to go round it ten times. After that, I was to uproot the biggest stump in the camp. I had to start on these tasks immediately. I was actually relieved. Although I had never gone to *Kioko*, many other students had. It was the most common punishment, with a slight caveat: going round it ten times wasn't humanly possible. It was also impossible to verify unless someone accompanied me. I knew that was out of the question because whoever was to accompany me would also be under punishment. So, I took off before they could change their minds and send me home. Within 45 minutes, I was approaching *Kioko*. It was then that an ingenious thought crossed my mind. Why couldn't I just go round the hill once then sit for the next two hours before returning? Nobody would stand at the camp peering at *Kioko* for that long, I concluded. And that's what I did, returning back after covering my face, legs and hands with dust. Subsequently, I spent five days removing the stump.

To the students – fortunately – this incident established my credibility and confirmed my liberation *bona fides*. Henceforth, they paid rapt attention to my ideas and contributions whenever there was a contentious issue. The three months soon ended. The young men who had arrived at Gilgil thin and weak were now muscular, fit and hardened. We hadn't learnt first aid, camp craft, fire-fighting or any national development issues or strategies; although our certificates dated August 22, 1986 listed all of those programmes. We had specialised in physical fitness, foot drill and press-ups. Yes, we might not have handled real guns, but we had learnt how to wield spades with lethal precision. We had conquered hills and mountains as well as learnt endurance. More importantly, living at close quarters for three months had allowed us to bond with each other – even created viable opportunities to understand each other. This was quite ironic. Those who had conceived of, devised and executed the plan to have us undergo a boot-camp hadn't intended it as a morale booster. On the contrary, our morale was supposed to have been in tatters within three months. The physical, psychological and mental abuses had been deliberate. Moi's unyielding desire had been to break us down and render us unable to organise and mobilise as students. His intention had been to create a society of robotic sycophants who would delusionally sing about his supposed wisdom, leadership acumen and God-given right to rule over us (not govern).

That entire grand plan had flopped.

NAIROBI

Arriving on our respective campuses that September, virtually all the students had identified those that they could trust as their future elected leaders.

I arrived in the capital by bus and walked to the University of Nairobi's main campus. Registration took hours. I was assigned to Hall 6 and given forms for the university students' assistance programme (popularly known as 'boom') and my student identification card. Raising funds for tuition and upkeep would have been impossible for a student from a poor background like me. Luckily, in those days, a student didn't have to come from an economically well-to-do-background to study at a public university. They just needed to qualify for admission and register for classes. Thereafter higher education loan forms and education grants would cover their basic costs. Thus there was a real incentive for poor children to study hard and pass the national exams.

I registered for Literature, Political Science and Philosophy. I loved research and reading. These courses provided me with more than enough reading material. I found philosophy very interesting. Logic, Metaphysics and Sage Philosophy were my favourite subjects. But I also enjoyed literature.

Before the end of the first semester, I met and befriended two female American exchange students from the University of California, Berkeley – Rachel and

Nancy – whom I took to Magina for one week during the holidays. They stayed in the village, accompanying me to the sugarcane farm I had – unhappily as it turned out – used my meagre university allowance, or boom, to cultivate, and bathing in the dirty river *Wailes*. Whenever we needed to cross the river with the two young American women, I would carry one across before returning for the other, to the amusement of the villagers. At night, the three of us would squeeze into my small bed; two sleeping facing one direction and the third facing the opposite direction. The villagers actually believed that the two young women were my wives.

At the university, I used to go out with both of them, dancing with each in turn. The three of us spent many hours discussing and arguing over oral literature and world politics. Students felt intrigued by the fact that the girls were always with me; it created a useful buzz for a budding student leader. Many found me intriguing. Here I was, a student from a dirt poor peasant background who seemed to have everything going for him: good grades, beautiful and sophisticated girls and student leadership.

At the end of the academic year, I emerged as the best philosophy student. But tragedy sneaked in suddenly without warning before I had completed my first year. On May 24, 1987, I was rushing off to the library at the main campus, when I saw my brother Ondiek crossing the State House Road towards Hall 6 where I stayed. He was in a hurry. It wasn't unusual to see him as he sometimes used to visit me at lunchtime – in those days, Ondiek worked at the Income Tax Department in the Community area. However, as soon as Ondiek reached where I was, I noticed that something was wrong: he was crying. Until then, I had never seen my brother cry. But before I could ask him what was the matter, he blurted it out. "Mother is dead. I just received the news this morning." By then it was about 11.30am. He was now sobbing uncontrollably. Almost immediately, I took off, shouting that I was going to get permission from the administration so that I could travel home that afternoon. A car missed me narrowly as I dashed across the road.

We arrived home the following morning to find our homestead overflowing with mourners, relatives and villagers. For the first time in my life, I broke down and wailed for more than four hours. At about 2pm on May 27, my mother was buried at my brother's homestead in Magina village. That very night, I travelled back to Nairobi to complete my examinations, which were actually in progress when my mother died. When my mother died, she had been the sole bread-winner for me, my sisters and a number of her grand-children. Suddenly, those responsibilities fell on my not-so-broad shoulders. I had to be creative and frugal if I was going to succeed in juggling the rigours of university studies with my new social obligations.

One day, as I lay on my bed revising for the special exams I had been entered for, because I had missed some papers to attend my mother's funeral, I heard some rustling movement near the door. When I looked carefully, I saw that someone had pushed through some literature. On careful examination, I noticed that it was a pamphlet on the financial scandal involving the then minister for sports Henry Kosgey (currently the 'reform' oriented Orange Democratic Movement chairman). The scandal revolved around the funding for the All-Africa Games that were due to be held in Nairobi in August of that year. However, because I was more concerned about passing my exams rather than playing politics, I put the pamphlet away and resumed my studies. On the day I completed my exams, I travelled home. Later, after I was abducted at night at gunpoint and detained incommunicado, this fleeting acquaintance with 'dissident literature' would return to haunt me.

Before the end of the first academic year, I was elected the vice-chairman of Kisumu District University Students Association. A fourth year medical student called Jobunga was chairman. This was a welfare organisation whose primary mandate was to create avenues through which the students could organise themselves and mobilise resources to assist their district in uplifting the educational standards of the area, advocate for quality and affordable health care and to accord the students with social and recreational outlets. The university district associations organised annual dances and offered students the opportunities to network and socialise. In addition, they were also leadership incubators that provided the necessary training and challenges in leadership. When I was elected, the association's patron was Dr Robert Ouko, then serving as the foreign affairs minister.

Dr Ouko was an articulate and urbane politician who served former President Moi loyally – and some have argued – blindly, until he was assassinated on 13 February 1990 by the same power barons he had served with such distinction. Ouko was down-to-earth. Whenever we had university or Kisumu District-related functions, he would attend and enjoy himself thoroughly, dancing, drinking and frolicking with the girls. The problem with Ouko was that he wasn't proactive and never followed up on anything that affected the students' welfare. He was very generous with drink and food. It was courtesy of Dr Ouko that I first dined in a fine Chinese restaurant. However, we soon replaced him with Joab Omino, who was then his political rival in Kisumu. Omino wasn't as affable as Ouko; but he was action-oriented. He never promised things he couldn't do; he kept his appointments and his word.

Following my mother's death, I resolved to be more politically active. Prior to her death, I had been reluctant to engage in active student politics. I feared that if anything untoward happened to me – and by then I knew names of so many victims of Moi's rapacious regime – my mother wouldn't have coped psychologically and I felt, even, physically. All I had dreamt of until then was a day I would be able to cater for all my mother's basic needs, starting with a proper permanent and decent shelter. My mother also liked taking tea. I had vowed that I would buy and put one sack of sugar in her house. While teaching at St Alloy's Gem, I had done that once already. However, now that my mother was no more, these hindrances receded to the back of my mind.

One of the most popular lecturers at the University of Nairobi during this time was Casper Odegi Awuondo, who taught sociology. When we joined the University, we found Odegi's radical credentials already established. One of the incidents that had solidified his reputation was a paper he delivered at an anti-apartheid symposium organised by SONU on Saturday, December 7, 1985. At the time, I was teaching at St Alloy's Gem Secondary School. Odegi's paper was titled "South Africa shall be free". His original draft, which I still have, courtesy of the SONU files, had "Azania" as the name for South Africa. In the file copy, Azania is crossed out and replaced with "South Africa."

Odegi exhorted students and the youth to lead the struggle, firstly, for the liberation of their countries and societies, and secondly, for the liberation of South Africa. "The Blacks in South Africa are not alone in the struggle against injustice," he declared. He heaped blame on all post-independent African governments, challenging them to put their houses in order first before pretending to condemn apartheid. He quoted the late literary scholar and university Professor Okot p'Bitek, who asserted that he didn't see much hope in independent Africa's ability to face apartheid as they themselves practised worse forms of discrimination in their own lands. Okot p'Bitek stated: "The most striking and frightening characteristic of all African governments is this, that without exception, all of them are dictatorships, and practice such ruthless discriminations which make the South African apartheid look tame…I leave it to political scientists to explore and analyse this strange situation, whereby independence means the replacement of foreign rule by native dictatorship."

After locating the 'roots' of apartheid in the United Kingdom, the US, Germany and other western powers with 'giant business interests in South Africa', Odegi added: "Me, I'm scared of Africa. I am astounded by an Africa that has no confidence in its peoples. For instance, we say we are too many yet we are completely incapable of raising just a token army of a few thousand, or 1 million, trained youth to liberate South Africa. And Africans are too many indeed! The Blacks (in South Africa) will liberate themselves; they will not wait for a pathetic Africa to liberate them."

Those were powerful, audacious and explosive words for those times. Odegi uttered them at the nadir of Moi's repressive regime and following the speech he was picked up and detained without trial (and possibly tortured). When I joined the University in September 1987, Odegi had only just been released. Although he had resumed teaching, Odegi was now constantly monitored. But he wasn't deterred. He kept mentoring new students like us and criticising the repressive regime.

Another catalyst to my becoming more politically engaged was the fact that as the year ended, Moi was becoming more repressive. He was continuing to crack down on his real or perceived political opponents, mainly university teachers, students, writers, journalists and critical politicians. By that time, Raila Odinga, Koigi Wamwere, George Anyona, Willy Mutunga, Edward Akong'o Oyugi, Oki Ooko Ombaka, Al-Amin Mazrui, Kamau Ngotho, Wachira Kamau and many others had been detained without trial or had spent time in jail following trumped-up charges and kangaroo trials. Many ex-servicemen of the defunct Kenya Air Force who hadn't been hanged were also serving indefinite terms under torture.

The Constitution had been amended in 1983 to make Kenya a *de jure* one-party state. There wasn't press freedom. Nor was there freedom of thought, conscience, expression, association and movement. Everything Moi said or commanded was the law. Moi transformed both the judiciary and parliament into instruments of oppression; they did whatever he liked. His ministers were now mere puppets, parroting whatever he wished. The few voices that tried to offer resistance – Jaramogi and Bishop Henry Okulu and valiant university students – faced severe sanctions. Jaramogi had become a virtual detainee; constantly under house arrest, followed, monitored and hounded. He had also been reduced to a pauper with no ability to earn a living.

Naturally, I felt an uncontrollable urge to resist and oppose those draconian conditions. At the time, the best avenue to do that was through an organised forum – some form of movement. A movement provided cover and some minimal insurance. Yet by then, all opposition and critical political formations had gone underground. Moi had managed to infiltrate, disorganise and scatter many of them through bribery, coercion and brutality. The only coherent political resistance in the country was through the student movement, which was becoming more visible and generating a lot of popular support from ordinary citizens. This had become the last bastion in the movement for the second liberation. Moi seemed acutely aware of this and was desperately trying to control and manipulate it to advance his selfish parochial political interests.

Over the years many student leaders had been used by Moi in his quest for permanent political dominance. Surreptitious nocturnal visits to State House by student leaders had become routine. But the overwhelming majority of students remained nationalistic, patriotic and progressive. Any time such nocturnal visits were discovered, the students would rise up and topple their leadership. The epicentre of that struggle was the main campus of the University of Nairobi. And being a conscious political operator, I used any free time I had to visit students' rooms, engage them in political discussion and try to understand their issues. I also used these opportunities to get ideas as to the popular solutions students would support.

Some of my friends used their free time to go to clubs, bars and discos; I spent mine preparing a political movement. I was pleasantly surprised that more than ninety per cent of the students understood the issues and were prepared to join in the struggle. The only other student who did this systematically was Kaberere Njenga, by then a fourth year medical student. I was accompanied during some of these exploratory initiatives by a former Onjiko student, Julius Nyadiango. Other times, Jacky Muca accompanied me. We did a thorough and comprehensive job of explaining the political options we had. As I would later learn, Jacky's interests were very different from mine. But she successfully concealed them.

By the end of the first academic year in June 1987, I had already established my networks throughout the university. I was increasingly becoming well known and well regarded at the University. By this time, many students were familiar with my radical poems and articles, which were either published in the *Campus Mirror* newspaper or being posted on the university notice boards. Another reason I was becoming popular was because I was among the very few students who were actively involved in our district organisation and yet was a teetotaller. My friendships straddled regional, ethnic and racial boundaries. I was also fairly popular with female students, especially from our year. My close friendship with the two American young women gave me additional (unusual) attention. On reflection, I now believe that Moi's special branch boys might have mistook that relationship to be that of a young impressionable student being infiltrated by the 'American CIA'. I can't be absolutely certain that my friends weren't CIA. But I can say that I never suspected it. They looked, sounded and behaved just as naïvely as any other of my colleagues.

The academic year of 1986-1987 turned out to be an eventful one. When we registered, Omondi Aloyo was the SONU chair. He was a short and thin philosophy major with a silver tongue. Aloyo was so good with his mouth that he could have sold anyone soil for the price of gold. That was the first practical example of the fallacy of Darwinian capitalistic theory of survival for the fittest. There we were with someone who, for all practical purposes, wasn't just physically weak; he was also tiny. But due to his rhetorical flair, Aloyo kept tens of thousands of students spellbound for hours. Ultimately, he rose to leadership, not because he was strong or rich; he was elected because he was the best orator. Which begs the question: why do human beings associate leadership with oratory? Is it because oratory has for a long time been associated with and treated like a duel? Or is it in recognition of the fact that to speak well, you must also think clearly?

Whatever the reason, Aloyo soon exhausted the credits students had extended him – courtesy of his tongue – and found himself in trouble. It was alleged – and most students believed – that Aloyo wasn't just a puppet of the university administration and the government, he was also misappropriating students' funds. A popular rebellion removed him. And as the students were chasing Aloyo up and down the campus, his deputy replaced him temporarily. There was a clamour for fresh elections. Unfortunately, the university administration managed to sneak in a fellow called Nduma Nderi. Now, Nduma deserves a chapter for himself. He was a third year law student. He was a disaster. He couldn't speak and had a very weak personality. Whenever he climbed the rostrum and attempted to address a student gathering, Nduma would start urinating in his pants. We would see his pants beginning to wet before drops of urine would literally start falling onto the ground below him. By then, students would be yelling and jeering at him so loudly that one could have mistaken it for a riot. He would be chased from the meeting. Nduma would engage students in a hide-and-seek comedy for weeks without end. Eventually, the students forced him out. His deputy, Odawa Francis Xavier replaced him temporarily before fresh elections were held.

Political activities had intensified on campus. The university administration, the national security agents on campus and the government were becoming nervous. They feared losing control over student politics. Their presence and activities were noticeable: agents removing critical literature from notice boards; both the university and administration openly sponsoring students to run as candidates for SONU positions.

And as these were happening, a small group of progressive student activists had come together to plot a SONU take over. Both Owen Mac'Onyango and Muca had declared that they would contest the SONU chairmanship. This was astonishing on at least three levels. First, both were now in second year with me. I considered both close friends of mine even though I was closer to Muca. They knew, like everyone else, that the SONU chairmanship was practically reserved for a third year student.

Strategically, I tried explaining to both of them that their candidatures would split the progressive vote and allow the university administration and the government to have a friendly SONU chairman. That would turn the clock back in terms of the students' interests and the overall progressive agenda for the country. Why don't you wait for just one more year, I asked them. Second, we knew that to win the chairmanship, one needed both well organised teams of mobilisers and considerable funds. Neither Muca nor Mac'Onyango were rich students. They knew that it was impossible to campaign on their student loans or boom. Unless they had a dubious source of funds – something most students would demand that they came clean about – they couldn't win.

On the other hand, I explained to them that we already had a team working for a radical change of direction in student leadership. They could join and become part of the winning team. In other words, divided they were sure to fail; but united we would all win. In my view, it was much better to be part of a progressive student government and work together for the necessary changes for the university and the country rather than to be a lone ranger. And third, it was becoming crystal clear that the main contenders for chairmanship would be Robert Wafula Buke (then a third year BA student) and Maina Kiranga.

Nduma Nderi – the pathetic government project – was graduating that year. So, the government replaced him with another stooge called Kiranga. Kiranga, like Nduma, was regarded as intellectually weak and morally and political compromised. Nduma had had lots of money, courtesy of the Special Branch agents on campus. They dutifully transferred the largesse to Kiranga, who traversed all the campuses with a well-oiled but tiny entourage. He also had glossy posters, which were strewn on every wall and lamp post.

Buke was no stooge. He had a reputation for fearlessness and was considered a natural rebel and a progressive. Older students told us that the university administration had frustrated him both academically and politically. We heard that he had transferred from Kenyatta University to the University of Nairobi. Physically, he looked lazy and unkempt. He also drank a bit too much. There were unconfirmed rumours that Buke used to visit the Libyan Embassy in Nairobi at night and would allegedly be given money, literature and copies of the *Green Book* for distribution among students. Rather than scare students away, these rumours endeared Buke to them. I don't recall Buke actually openly denying or admitting those rumours, although I never saw him with any significant money that would have confirmed the stories. But he did have a copy of the *Green Book*.

I remember borrowing it and making several copies of it, which I then distributed among students. For progressive students, therefore, Buke was the undisputed candidate. This was primarily in defiance of the administration and government. We wanted to demonstrate to them that we were masters of our own destiny. I explained to Muca and Mac'Onyango that it would be imprudent to go against the popular current. It was also the current that reflected the aspirations and dreams not just of the students; but also of the majority of Kenyans. By then, we were marketing ourselves as agents of change.

Our chief political ideologue was Kaberere Njenga. Munoru Nderi – a third year law student – was also in our camp. So was Oyuo Amuomo Ngala, Munameza Muleji, Peter Mutonyi Gakiri, Omill Oloo, Ogola J.T.O. and many others. Despite Buke's stated weaknesses, we felt that he was the right candidate. And to be fair, Buke was perhaps the most fearless third year student who had expressed interest in leadership. In addition, I believe that the circumstances had conspired in his favour. This is what superstitious people call 'fate.' The gods had beckoned to Buke and we, the progressive students, responded accordingly. Moreover, we needed somebody who was as fearless as Buke. We knew he wasn't a model student, nor was he a rousing orator. But we needed a fearless leader who wouldn't and couldn't be easily intimidated or used. We were sick and tired of student leaders who made secret nocturnal visits to State House. We had a solid team.

During those days, Kenyatta, then Moi had banned Col. Muammar Gaddafi's *Green Book*, Karl Marx's books including *Das Capital* and *The Communist Manifesto*, George Orwell's *Animal Farm* and *1984*, Ngugi wa Thiong'o's *Devil on the Cross*, *I Will Marry When I Want*, *Petals of Blood*, *Detained: A Writer's Prison Diary*, *Barrel of a Pen*, *Decolonising the Mind* and *Matigari* and many other books, especially those that were deemed Marxist, Socialist or revolutionary. The repressive authorities used the *Penal Code* and autocratic fiat to prescribe anything they deemed wasn't in the interest of "public order, public health, public morals or the security of Kenya". These were vague, general and over-broad catch-all phrases that were used with predictable regularity to suppress and control the country in order to perpetuate the illegitimate power wielders of the day.

Whatever the government restricted became popular with students. Rebellion was in vogue. I looked at the situation and saw the building up of a potential popular revolution. The national consciousness was rising against those in power. The students were becoming more assertive on national and political issues. We were consistently demanding democratic pluralism and the unconditional release of all political prisoners. Pamphleteering and publication of radical literature was becoming our weapon of choice. The public loved it though in a muted form. The media – except a Christian magazine called *Beyond* – was intimidated and muzzled. They regurgitated what leading politicians had said at funerals and harambees; but beyond that, there weren't any critical, analytical or investigatory reports. However, we students were energised. And those controlling the state were scared.

Earlier in that year in London – on February 18, the 30th anniversary of the execution by the British colonialists of the Mau Mau leader Dedan Kimathi – a new Kenyan opposition movement, *Umoja wa Kupigania Demokrasia Kenya* (Ukenya) had been founded. Addressing a press conference in London during the launch, its chairman Yusuf Hassan (now, ironically, a PNU Member of Parliament for Kamukunji constituency in Nairobi) stated: "We have reached the peak of many years of repression from the hands of the unjust KANU regimes of Kenyatta and Moi...Since February 1986, hundreds of Kenyans have been arrested; some have been sentenced to long terms of imprisonment or detained without trial and others have been intimidated, harassed and tortured. Others have been stripped of their citizenship and many more Kenyans have fled into exile. These patriots have been arrested because of calling for democracy. But it is not only they who are suffering, for throughout the country many more Kenyans have met with a similar fate because of struggling for democracy and human dignity.

"KANU has become an instrument of mass oppression...KANU's leaders have not done enough to consolidate Kenya's independence...The independence gained...did not bring any fundamental changes in the economic structure. For example, 80% of our industries are controlled by foreign companies...Corruption has become the guiding philosophy of the KANU regime...UKENYA is an anti-imperialist organization, committed to the struggle for democracy and the regaining of Kenya's sovereignty. UKENYA shall, therefore, strive for the unity of all patriotic Kenyans who are struggling against neo-colonialism and hence are fighting for a national economy; a national democratic society and a national independent culture which reflects the diversity of the nationalities of Kenya."

He stressed that Ukenya would not name all members of its executive publicly to protect them from harassment and victimisation by agents of the Moi regime.

As conscious, progressive and young political activists, we knew that the repressive regime was getting isolated. Patriotic Kenyans were becoming creative and resourceful in their resistance. In our small way, we resolved to engage the regime on all the issues Ukenya and other organisations were raising. After a rigorous nomination process where many candidates competed for almost all the constituencies, validly nominated candidates were listed. Only those listed as having been validly nominated had their names on the ballot papers and were allowed to compete for the elections. Out of more than twenty aspirants for the Faculty of Arts, ten were nominated, with me garnering the highest number of votes cast. The campaigns for various SONU seats were conducted between October 30 and November 3, 1987. After a spirited door-to-door campaign that must have taken me to 99% of all students' rooms, the elections were held.

For one month, I traversed the campus in a flowing Nigerian *agbada*, with a matching *kofia*. At the last *Kamukunji* (public gathering) at the sports field next to the main dining hall and kitchen, E.M. Nderitu, a law lecturer and SONU elections returning officer, attempted to grab the microphone from me on account of a statement I made castigating the university administration for kowtowing and ceding their statutory mandate to state functionaries. The students, in an instantaneous move, nearly lynched the man before he hastily dropped the microphone and I continued my address. Unlike previously, we had organised teams of mean-looking young men who stayed in the polling centres and left only after the final tally had been announced. They were all volunteers. And when the final results were announced, Buke beat Maina Kiranga, Muca and Mac'Onyango with a margin that hadn't been seen before. I emerged number one from the Faculty of Arts.

Immediately after the elections, Buke, as the newly-elected chairman, convened a meeting of the Students' Representative Council – the SRC – which comprised all SONU elected representatives. During that extraordinary meeting, Munoru Nderi was elected Vice-Chairman; Kaberere Njenga, Secretary General; Miguna Miguna, Finance Secretary; M.N. Kori, Assistant Finance Secretary; Omill Oloo, Communications; C. Michoma, Social Affairs; Morris P.O. Aluanga, Sports; Peter Mutonyi Gakiri, Catering; J.M. Owiny, Security; Oyuo Amuomo Ngala, Academic Affairs; Munameza Muleji, Foreign Affairs; Ombima H. Seruya, Health; Margaret Ben, Assistant Secretary General; J.T.O. Ogola, Assistant Catering Secretary; and Bimberia M'Mukami, Secretary Without Portfolio. Essentially that was the entire student government that year. In the history of the University, it was the most democratically elected student leadership. Despite attempts by both the university administration and influential politicians to interfere with and manipulate the elections, the overwhelming majority of students had sternly rebuked them.

On November 4, Buke chaired his first cabinet meeting where we discussed our priority issues, schedule and mechanisms of execution, as well as discussing the role and place of the students' newspaper, the *Campus Mirror* and how we would use it to articulate both burning student issues as well as national issues. We unanimously resolved to convene an extraordinary *Kamukunji* for the entire university at which all executive members of the student leadership would take oath of office, swear to serve the students without compromise and read out their individual pledges. Secondly, I was unanimously elected the Managing Editor of the *Campus Mirror* and mandated to institute a transparent process of recruiting editors and writers for the newspaper. Thereafter, I was to identify a new printer for the newspaper as the one that had been retained by the previous compromised leadership subjected publications to state censorship. Academic freedom was going to be one of our top priorities. I was also tasked to institute a process of auditing all SONU accounts, books and records. Thirdly, the S.R.C. was to begin a process of cleaning up the university from corruption, ineptitude and lethargy, starting with the kitchens and dining halls before moving to the library and other areas. And fourthly, we unanimously resolved to actively participate in national politics and development.

We were on a roll. There was a synergy amongst the student leaders. Everywhere the new student leadership went, there were fireworks. Things were moving forward. We performed our functions collectively and there was visible teamwork. There was also obvious ideological clarity and coherence as well as political unity which hadn't been experienced at the University for a very long time. We conducted daily inspections of all the dining halls and kitchens and ensured that they were clean, orderly and that high quality and adequate food, fruits and water were available for all the students. Pilferage of supplies significantly reduced. The Student Centre, which hadn't been well stocked for a long time, suddenly had enough supplies. It was also sparkling clean. The students walked with their heads raised high. Muggers who had become a major problem in the tunnels connecting the halls of residence and the main campus suddenly disappeared. Students were happy.

On November 5, the SONU vice-chairman Munoru and I held a meeting with Professor Festo A. Mutere, the Deputy Vice-Chancellor (Academic) to discuss an invitation we had received that same day from the International Union of Students Secretariat based in Prague, Czechoslovakia. We were invited to attend the World Student Conference as SONU delegates in Havana, Cuba, from November 6 to 25, 1987. Prof. Mutere wrote to the Principal Immigration Officer at Nyayo House, Nairobi, requesting that we be assisted quickly with Kenya passports so that we could travel without any delay. He explained that we hadn't applied earlier because we had just received the letter of invitation to the conference and the SONU elections had just been concluded. He mentioned that the University had approved our travel. We rushed with the letter to Nyayo House. We had earlier that morning applied for and obtained "clearance" from both the Ministries of Education and Foreign Affairs.

Upon reaching Nyayo House, we entered the elevator and pressed 24, which was then the floor where the principal immigration officer's office was located. Four other men squeezed their way in before the elevator doors closed. Munoru and I were now sandwiched in the middle. And as the doors closed and the elevator started moving up, one of the men pressed 22. Once the door opened on the 22nd floor, one of the men held my left hand and told me to follow him as another one softly pushed me from behind. As soon as we stepped out of the elevator, Munoru and the two other men disappeared. I could see that the elevator was heading up. I was quickly led to a medium-sized office where we found a man sitting behind a desk reading a newspaper. He continued reading as the two men accompanying me offered me a seat across the desk from the man reading the newspaper. After what seemed like 30 minutes the man carefully closed the paper and moved it to the right side of the table. He then slowly opened a drawer and pulled out a note pad, which he opened. He took out a pencil and wrote my name in block letters on the note pad before fixing me with a stern glare.

"You are Mr Miguna, are you?"

"Yes I am," I answered, unsure of what this was all about.

"Why do you want to go to Cuba? Are you a boxer?"

"I don't want to go to Cuba. And no I am not a boxer."

"Well, what is this thing about you going to Cuba then?" He closed the note pad at this point. I hesitated. I was confused. I didn't know what the man was driving at.

"Well, are you going to answer me? Cubans are only good in boxing."

"We received an invitation today from the International Union of Students. They would like us to attend their annual conference, which is being held in Cuba this year…" I started before the man cut me off.

"That's well and good. But why *you*? How did these people know *you*? Are *you* a boxer?"

"I don't know. Perhaps they just chose two SONU officials at random."

"We shall see about that. Anyway, go ahead and apply. Here, take the forms."

"But I thought we could get the passports today. The conference is starting tomorrow" I managed to say this as the man waved me away. The two other men took me to another room where I was made to complete many forms. After another 30 minutes, I was told I could go. When I inquired about the passport, they stated that they would be in touch.

It was only when I reached the ground floor that I remembered that Munoru had been with me. I stood there staring at each and every elevator that opened. I waited for 15 minutes then left. I proceeded directly to Buke's new residence on the State House Road and found Kaberere there. I told them what had just happened. Shortly afterwards Munoru also arrived. His experience was similar to mine. We knew then that the government wouldn't allow us to travel. But more chilling was our realisation that Special Branch officers were on our trail.

Clearly, the government was scared. It seemed like Moi had panicked when progressives had triumphed in the SONU elections. Buke, Munoru, Kaberere and I resolved to intensify our activities so that by the time the government got its act together, it would find that the entire university had changed so much that there would be nothing it could do. We knew the government believed Buke, Kaberere, Munoru and I were unrepentant Marxist radicals out to overthrow them. That fear had some basis only to the extent that Kaberere, Munoru and I were committed Marxists. Yes, we wouldn't have minded if the government fell; but we were also aware that at that time the people poised to take power from Moi were even more retrogressive: the Charles Njonjos and Simeon Nyachaes. These represented the darkest and most backward political formations in Kenya. We preferred a revolution led by the progressive forces, which we were keen to link up with except that almost all of them were in detention, jail or in exile.

Later that afternoon, I visited the Vice-Chancellor, Professor Phillip M. Mbithi's office in order to request the secondment of an auditor from the university. By then I had discovered major discrepancies in the SONU accounts. The new SONU leadership had resolved to investigate how the previous student leaders had mismanaged funds and students' resources. Prof. Mbithi ushered me into his office jovially. He inquired about how we were doing. I briefed him on the new developments and sought his assistance in obtaining passports. He promised to help. He then asked me about Kaberere. I told him he was well. Prof. Mbithi then leaned towards my chair and said in a low tone: "I've spoken with your lecturers and they tell me that you are a good boy – hard working, smart and well behaved. I've not heard any complaints from your teachers. But some Special Branch people came here and told me that you are very close to that boy Kaberere. I understand that in August this year, Kaberere induced you into engaging in dissident activities. The Special Branch believes that it was you and Kaberere that wrote and distributed dissident pamphlets about the All-African Games here on Campus. Now, I told them that I doubt your participation. But they insisted that it was you and Kaberere. They even told me that you had a meeting with other dissidents in August where Kaberere spoke very passionately against the President and in his over-excitement, he missed his seat and fell to the floor…What's your response?"

I explained to Prof. Mbithi what had happened: that I had returned to the University to write special exams because I had missed most of the exams when my mother died. I told him about the pamphlet being pushed under my door as I lay inside reading. I defended Kaberere of the accusations and categorically denied knowledge about the alleged meeting. Mbithi listened quietly before proceeding: "Anyway, I would like you to organise with your colleagues a trip to State House soon so that I can introduce the new SONU leaders to His Excellency the President. Secondly – and this concerns you directly – I would like you to call a press conference tomorrow and thank His Excellency the President for increasing your boom by Sh300. It's important that you express appreciation to the President."

This was exasperating. Mbithi expected too much out of our meeting. I explained to him that I had come for three things, namely: I needed him to recommend an auditor to help us put the SONU books in order; two, Munoru and I needed him to intervene so that we could get passports to travel to Cuba for the I.U.S. conference; and three, I had been asked by the S.R.C. to inform him that we were going to hold an extraordinary *Kamukunji* on November 13, 1987. I added that it's that meeting that could authorise me to thank Moi for the increment and also approve of the State House visit. We agreed that I would update him after the *Kamukunji.* Meanwhile, Mbithi called in one of his secretaries and dictated a letter to a Mr Shem Khasabuli of the Internal Audit Department at the University. I then returned to Buke's residence to update them of my meeting. Buke, Kaberere and Munoru agreed with the manner I had handled Mbithi. We unanimously agreed that we wouldn't thank Moi for his belated and inconsequential increment. Our position would be that it was too little too late; that we were entitled to at least a Sh1,500.00 increment. We would also take the position that we appreciated Mbithi's offer to secure a meeting with the President. However, the new student government wouldn't be a puppet of the government and that we would request a meeting whenever there was something important to discuss.

Not one to lose momentum, a follow-up executive meeting was scheduled for November 9 to discuss the drafting of the new policies, the issue of the students' allowances and for the receipt of implementation reports of the resolutions of our first meeting. On November 8, the agenda of the second meeting was circulated by the Assistant Secretary General, Margaret Ben, who, to our chagrin, later turned out to be a cleverly imbedded Special Branch officer. Meanwhile, I simultaneously summoned a meeting for the Kisumu District University Students' Association for November 10 in order to discuss a students' education trust fund we were establishing; a healthcare services scheme and the issue of meetings of the KIDUSA executive. I got the outgoing SONU Secretary General, Gordon Ondiek (now deceased), to write a letter to the bank manager of the National Bank of Kenya, Moi Avenue Branch, instructing them of the change of signatories to the SONU accounts from Nduma Nderi and Ndeda M.O. to Buke, Kaberere and myself. The handover was deliberately delayed by the University administration until we were abducted and detained.

On November 11, I received a handwritten note from Mr Khasabuli. He had received Mbithi's letter and an accompanying memorandum from me. He promised to return at 9am the following day. We met as scheduled and agreed on the course of action. I also provided him with all the files, records, books and bank statements. He undertook to complete the work by the end of the month. After he had left, I prepared a notice to all editorial board members of the Campus Mirror. The main agenda was to map out the paper's policy and assignment of duties. My final notice was to all students, inviting them to the *Kamukunji* on Friday November 13, 1987 at the Sports Field starting at 3.30pm. By then, Munoru and I had given up on our passports and the Cuban trip. The S.R.C. knew that Moi was jittery about us. The good news was that we were ready and prepared for war. The media was awash with stories of the "radicals that had taken over the student leadership and the looming confrontation". On our part, we focused on the students' agenda and avoided sideshows.

On November 13, about 10,000 students had converged on the main campus by noon. There was a carnival atmosphere. The media had also descended, taking pictures and interviewing students. Meanwhile, Buke, Kaberere and I were holed up in a meeting. We were preparing the "oath" to be taken by the student executive. We were also synchronising our speeches. There was intense anxiety. That day, we had eaten lunch at the chairman's residence. However, when I had returned to my room before the meeting started, I had noticed that the room across from mine was wide open and five men in leather jackets were seated facing the door. I greeted them and entered my room.

The meeting began on time. There was music and slogans. Then each SONU executive took a solemn oath to be faithful to the students and to serve them without fear. We then gave short speeches. When my turn came I reported to the students my conversation with Prof. Mbithi. I also explained how Munoru and I had been subjected to interrogation over an invitation to attend the I.U.S. conference in Havana, Cuba. I informed the students that despite the government's refusal to issue us with passports and allow us to travel, we would continue serving them with dedication. I then called:

"Comrades!" and raised a clenched fist aloft.

"Power!" The students roared back, with more than 10,000 fists in the air.

"Comrades, Power!"

"Power!"

"Comrades, would you like me to publicly thank President Moi for increasing the boom by Sh300?" I asked, facing them.

"Nooooo!" roared back their collective response.

"Comrades, do you want the SRC to pay a courtesy call on the President?" I posed again.

"Nooooo!"came the uniform answer.

Electrified and angered by the continued repression of Kenyans by the Moi-Kanu regime, and undaunted by the possible consequences of our activities, I delivered one of my best attacks against the regime. I aimed strong substantiated charges at almost all Kenyan departments, institutions and structures. Knowing that several secret security agents were in the crowd listening and taping our speeches, I patiently and painfully detailed graphic accounts of human rights abuses which had been catalogued by Amnesty International in their 1987 special report – "Kenya: Torture, Political Detention and Unfair Trials." Cases such as the long detention and torture of Raila Odinga, Koigi Wamwere and George Anyona; disappearances or deaths after barbaric tortures in custody of Peter Njenga Karanja and Gregory Byaruhanga; torture and ill-treatment of political prisoners like John Gupta Thiong'o, Karige Kihoro, Rateng' Oginga Ogego and Julius Mwandawiro Mghanga were recounted. I also offered specific cases of government infringement of our academic freedom, specifically the stationing of security agents in classrooms, halls of residence, and virtually everywhere where students and teachers happened to be. Finally, I publicly challenged the authorities to arrest me and bring charges against me if they viewed my utterances as constituting a criminal offence.

I was prepared for the consequences of both my actions and utterances. And the students were happy – at long last they saw and heard someone who could stand up to the state bullies. They thunderously shouted: 'Toboa! Toboa!' or ('Reveal! Reveal!') as I enumerated the machinations of the dreaded ubiquitous Special Branch police. Their faces beamed with satisfaction and I could almost feel their heart beats thumping in readiness for action – whatever the S.R.C. deemed appropriate. I was happy. For the first time in my life, I felt powerful. With more than 10,000 young and committed students roaring back at me, I felt unrestrainable. It was part defiance, part youthful exuberance and part revolutionary fervour. But it nonetheless felt good to openly defy the dictatorship as they stood there outnumbered and powerless. But, of course, their 'powerlessness' was brief.

I could feel the helplessness of those few Special Branch officers who had been given the task of monitoring our gathering. I knew that there was an urgent need for the removal of all vestiges of oppression and exploitation from the Kenyan society. And with almost the entire student body behind us, we were ready for that ultimate sacrifice. I felt like a bird, ready to fly high over the sacred skies of jail and detention; with the fear of being incarcerated disappearing from my mind.

I thanked them and concluded by stressing that the new student government was neither going to serve the administration nor the government; that we were willing, ready and prepared to work with them to serve the students; that we wouldn't betray the oath we had just taken. A few days before the *Kamukunji*, a few of us – Kaberere, Buke, Munoru and I – had discussed the possibility of forming a 'Kenya National Students' Movement.' I was tasked with preparing the draft constitution, including its vision, objects and aims. The aims and objectives of the national student movement were to promote the welfare of its members; to establish cooperation with other student bodies within and outside Kenya; the promotion of academic freedom; and to accentuate cooperation between Kenyan students and all other sectors of the society. In my outline, which I still have, I spelt out our opposition to corruption, especially grabbing of public land by powerful politicians; our political ideology as revolutionary Marxist-Leninists; foreign policy towards America and Western powers, the Eastern Block, South Africa's apartheid regime and the Frontline States. Finally, I had a paragraph on freedom and democracy. In other words, we were in the process of establishing a national movement geared towards promoting the students' involvement in national affairs, including politics. That must have scared the hell out of Moi and his autocrats.

The *Kamukunji* ended on a high note. Members of the S.R.C. gave each other high-fives and left. But I suddenly felt disturbed. It was as if I was conscious of being watched. This was more instinctive than anything. As I was leaving the sports field, I found myself in the midst of a thick crowd, debating, discussing and strategising ways of implementing what we had just proclaimed. In the midst of all this, I met Anthony, who had travelled from Kenyatta University to witness this historic occasion. He informed me that we had spoken very well. He was impressed with my speech but glibly expressed concern about my security. I didn't respond. At that point, we decided to have dinner first before proceeding to the

Women's Hall to see Anthony's girlfriend, who was actually my classmate. We proceeded there directly and spent the next two hours chatting and debating with a small group of students in her room. It was clear to me that we had fired up all the students – even the traditionally lethargic. At about 10.30pm, I walked back to my hostel. I took a shower and went to bed almost immediately.

I woke up with a start. There were timid knocks on my door. Could it be my cousin, Onyango Ong'or, just returning from Nyakach, his rural home; or was it Odhiambo B.F. Onienga, returning from his nocturnal escapades; or could it be that the S.R.C. had called an emergency meeting? One thing didn't cross my mind – the possibility that the ubiquitous agents of state were lurking, ready to swoop on me. I opened the door, still half asleep. It was about 3am on November 14.

"Shhh…shhh…!" Five pistols and equally murderous faces greeted me and silently motioned me to be quiet. Before I knew what was happening, they had forcefully pushed the door in, shoved me aside and closed it behind them. They were five fairly young males. They were wearing jeans and leather jackets. One could easily have confused them with fellow students. 'Your name?' one authoritative voice demanded.

'Miguna Miguna'. My answer was terse and confident.

'Ok. Dress up!' another voice ordered. Their voices quivered with anxiety. They frantically looked at the room's posters. One to the left was of Thomas Sankara. The one to the right was of Malcolm X. And another one near my bed was of Che Guevara. Many more were hanging precariously on the walls, defiantly staring at those state invaders.

"You a communist agitator? Eh?" one rough hollow voice shouted. Ngugi wa Thiong'o's arrest came to my mind. I started singing to myself one of Owino Misiani's latest hits – one about the cancerous corruption of those in power. I took my note book, student I.D. and keys. I noticed that I was still wearing only my underclothes. My uninvited guests seemed overwhelmed by all the posters, leaflets and books that were strewn on the floor. They all seemed to be reading the Che Guevara's poster which had a bold proclamation: "The duty of a revolutionary is to make a revolution!" For a moment, I actually pitied them. I pitied their ignorance, zeal and sense of duty to a corrupt regime.

"You a communist agitator? I don't know what's wrong with you Luos!" one of them remarked as they appeared ready, at last, to leave. I completely ignored this last outburst.

They then turned, looked at me from head to toe, and then shook their heads, as if in agreement about something, before one of them thundered: "You are under arrest!" "What have I done?" I managed to ask as they literally carried me three floors down. They buffeted me on both sides, bundled me up and violently threw me into the back of a vehicle that had been left revving on State House Road.

I couldn't sit up, with three men struggling to keep my head down while a fourth one tried to sit on me, as the vehicle zoomed wildly towards the Central Police Station, located less than 100 metres from the main campus. The car was followed by four others, obviously carrying more state agents. To the uninitiated eye, the entourage might have looked like a VIP escort, save for the supersonic speed of the cars, recklessly driven as if to cause fright or a politically orchestrated accident. It took just over two minutes to reach the police station; now I understand why that barrack of public coercion was strategically located near the University of Nairobi. It makes sense for a dictatorship, doesn't it?

At the police station, a strange name was entered in the occurrence book instead of mine; yet my protest and attempts at correcting this was brushed aside by a thunderous shout to the effect that as a 'prisoner', I had no rights. I had been declared a permanent resident of the state-run dungeons of death without due process; not even of a kangaroo court. My blood turned cold and I steeled myself for the worst. Yet, discovering more comrades through the iron bars of the police station calmed me. It was then that I realised that they hadn't just come for me: Buke, Kaberere, Margaret Ben and Ngala were already at the station. Munameza would be brought after me, bare-chested and barefoot, yelling and screaming.

My calm became defiance, and defiance grew into reticence. I waited for whatever awaited me. Shortly afterwards, I was hurriedly taken away, blindfolded, dumped inside a white van with heavily tinted windows and driven along what seemed like meandering roads until the vehicle suddenly stopped. The two heavily-built men who sat on me throughout got off. One took my right hand and led me into a building before ripping off the blindfold. As I was blinking, trying to get my bearings, I felt a hard thing against my cheeks. Then a man yelled: "Wewe nugu! What do you think you are? You Luos think you are very smart…?" The man was advancing menacingly towards me when another uniformed police officer restrained him and took me into a small room inside. The room was bare. There was no furniture of any kind. The walls looked like they used to be white; now, they had sprinkles of white, brown and many strange scrawls. There was no telephone or any gadget one could use for communication. I was beginning to feel hungry but I knew the dangers of eating at such places. There are endless lists of freedom fighters that have become statistics through poisoning, hanging or 'disappearances.' I was determined not to join their ranks.

Momentarily, my mind returned to the Central Police Station. Something didn't seem right. Why had they arrested Margaret Ben? Of all the SONU leaders that year, Margaret had seemed the most detached from our cause. Although she pretended to be with us, she never made any significant contributions. She would support the team and vote for each and every resolution, but she never generated any ideas. Curiously, she had accompanied President Moi to the Commonwealth conference in Vancouver, Canada, a few months before our abductions. Her invitation didn't come through SONU and Kaberere and I had wondered how she had got her name on the Moi list. Previously, Moi had used such invitations to infiltrate and control SONU. Margaret Ben wasn't really an influential SONU leader; she was also just an assistant Secretary General. She didn't have any significant following among students. Why would Moi invite her to accompany him to Vancouver?

Kaberere and I had asked these questions but never pursued them to their logical conclusion. That would prove to have been a fatal error on our part. When I had first been taken to the station, it had been Margaret Ben and Buke that I could see clearly from the entrance. I only saw Oyuo Ngala Amuomo's (Keg Lager's) famous jacket. Yet when I tried to look at her, her eyes would not meet mine. Could that have just been natural nervousness or was there more to Margaret Ben than we knew? What kind of a name was that anyway? I sat down on the cold cemented floor and dozed off.

About two hours after I had been dumped there, the door opened. A uniformed policeman was holding a bowl with two miserable-looking slices of bread and tea in a tin-cup, which he offered me then left the room. I looked at what must have been my breakfast and remembered all the victims of Kenyatta's and Moi's terror machines. I shuddered before pushing them into a corner. I couldn't take them. I also thought – naïvely I might add – that I would be released soon, after what I thought would happen: students rampaging over our illegal abductions and detentions, or upon the realisation by the authorities that we hadn't committed any crimes. I now realise that the main interest of the government was to quash any potential student rebellion by either removing or criminalising the student leadership.

The regime seemed to have realised that killing us wouldn't be in its best interest. Apart from the unprovoked attack on me by the enraged policeman, I was basically left undisturbed at the police station. However, about four or five hours after I had been brought there, a group of five walkie-talkie-carrying men in civilian clothing appeared at the door of the cell. They looked mean. I could tell from their expressions that hell was ready to swallow me whole. They swooped on me like anti-terrorist squads. The cold cell suddenly smelt of death. They blindfolded me again, scurried as they walkie-talkied, then pushed me down into the van and told to lie on my belly, which I did before they drove in circles, zigzagging, stopping and moving again, for what seemed like hours until I felt dizzy and nauseated.

Finally, I could feel the vehicle driving downwards then round as if towards a basement. Then the car stopped and two men held my hands from both sides and gingerly led me into a room. Once more, my blindfolds were ripped off and I found myself in a tiny brightly-lit bare room. It was about four metres by four metres. There were no windows. In the middle of the ceiling was a huge bulb that bathed me in blinding bright light. There was no switch in the room and my abductors refusal to switch it off even when I needed to sleep, I soon learnt, was another creative mechanism of torture. (Of course, the effects became obvious when, barely a year after this tragedy, my previously healthy eyes required prescription glasses to be able to function adequately!) The tiny room was also freezing.

I was abandoned and left to starve. And I starved for so long that I lost count of the days and nights. I would bang on the heavy-duty and reinforced metallic door whenever I wanted to visit the toilets, which were outside the room. A man would appear mysteriously and take me there, after ensuring that he had blindfolded me first. The blindfold would only be removed when I was in the toilet and tied again after I had finished. It would be removed once I was back in the hovel. The door locked automatically. I suspect it was remotely controlled. Then the torture began in earnest. I was blindfolded and transported through a special elevator to what sounded and felt like the highest point in the building. Here, I was made to sit, still blindfolded, for about one hour. Then someone abruptly tore away the cloth that covered my eyes and yelled at me to take off my clothes and sit on the cold floor. I refused.

What followed can only be characterised as frenzied violence. As if thirsty for my blood, seven torturers jumped on me, kicking, punching and hollering. Some reached for my testicles and tried to squeeze and pull them as hard as they could while I writhed in pain. They mocked me, saying that a true revolutionary did not have to cry. "Remember Che! Eh? Remember Che?" one kept yelling.

"Where is Ngugi to help you now? Where is Ngugi?"

"Where is Castro? Where is Marx? Eh? Where is Gaddafi?" They went on and on and on. They beat me and swore about my alleged foreign co-conspirators. They were panting and sweating. But however much they tried, I said nothing. I had long learnt that speaking to these idiots at such moment was both stupid and suicidal. They did not ask questions because they lacked or even wanted answers. They simply asked for the sake of asking. Again, it made them feel good about themselves; perhaps fooled them into thinking that they were actually working. Yes, building the lovely nation!

"I am not going to answer any questions until I am fed!" I managed to shout amidst insults and whips.

"Hahahahahaha…! Look what we have here! A chicken!" one huge beast snorted.

"Oh no! I thought you were a man…A REVOLUTIONARY!" another one sneered even louder.

"Yes, MISTER Marx, Engels, Castro and Che. Didn't you know that revolutionaries don't eat? They produce! Yes, communism is food. Isn't that what you learn at the University? Isn't it sweet my dear revolutionary? Isn't it?" the most vicious one thundered. He was excited, perhaps overestimating the effectiveness of their strategies. They continued to rain blows and kicks on me. They used rubber whips and wooden sticks. I writhed in agony, crying out for help. The beasts kept at it until I passed out.

When I regained consciousness, I found myself lying under the desk, naked. All except one had trooped out of the torture chamber. He seemed to have been given the task of watching over the state prisoner. When they returned, I was blindfolded again and returned to my cubicle. I could hardly walk. A few minutes later, some rotten vegetables and *ugali* arrived, via a tiny opening of the door. Within two minutes, I had finished eating, and my persecutors were already there, waiting. Back at the torture chamber, they forced me to sit on the floor before proceeding to fire a barrage of irrelevant, unconnected, questions at me. This time, however, they behaved in a civilised manner. Perhaps they had realised that brute force and intimidation did not or would not, work with me. So now they bombarded me with questions on Marx and Marxism, Libya/Gaddafi and the *Green Book*, the Ayatollah and Islamic Fundamentalism, Ngugi and Literary Criticism – everything. They seemed desperate, anxious and nervous. Perhaps they feared that they might have missed a golden opportunity to get a confession for the crimes they imagined. Perhaps they feared the wrath of their enraged bosses who might have given specific orders on what was to be extracted. What were they going to do now that they were unfortunate enough to meet an impervious activist, unwilling to budge? After all, their work demanded nothing but force and violence. They didn't care about the niceties of due process. As far as they were concerned, there was only one law and authority – and that was dictator Daniel arap Moi.

The state security boys desperately wanted to piece together rumours and lies and concoct a case against me to put before one of their corrupt grand juries and inept judges. Day after day they came and repeated their brutal rituals. Yet, day after day, they failed. Instead of a confession, I offered them free lectures on topics ranging from Marx to Ngugi. They gaped, their mouths hanging open. For hours – between whips, insults and threats – I patiently explained the plight of the poor. In addition, I explained the failures of capitalism and articulated our principled stand on revolutionary progressive change.

That did it. Again, they swooped on me like vultures. They swore as they tortured, frustrated with my apparent stubbornness. Then I was thrown back into the cell at the basement and kept in water for nearly 20 hours. Almost a day later, they pulled me from the water and locked me up in another cell, wet and shaking. They kept me there wet and ill for nearly a week, without food, medicine or a doctor. I nearly lost my voice, not to mention my life.

Afterwards, they came intermittently and at inconsistent intervals to bring me food, and to find out whether or not I was ready to, as they put it, 'cooperate'. However, each time they opened the door, I had only one answer – "NO". Meanwhile, I discovered inspirational words inscribed on the walls of the cell where I was kept. So, whenever I was left alone, I would preoccupy myself by reading these nearly illegible words, which had clearly been written by veterans of the struggle.

It was nearly impossible to tell day from night. The tiny cells didn't have windows. Whenever we were taken out of them, our eyes would be tightly blindfolded. But somehow, I detected a strange routine, which made me guess day from night. Throughout the period I was held incommunicado, and at intervals that suggested it might have been early in the morning, I would hear somebody walking on the floor immediately above like a female in stiletto shoes. The tap, tap, tap, tap noise was so predictable and refreshing that I actually looked forward to it. It was at times the only indication I had that I was still alive. There were days I needed to pinch myself and hear that tap, tap noise to know that I hadn't 'disappeared'. But sometimes the monotony made me doubt if indeed I was still alive. Strangely, those steps also rekindled my longing for female company. It might sound strange but it is true.

Later, I tried communicating with another comrade in the neighbouring cell-cum-hell by knocking on the thick wall that separated us. I occasionally heard this comrade's voice as he persistently called out for the guards to allow him to visit the toilet. He did it with such regularity that I thought either the man had bad stomach flu or he simply needed to hear his voice to know that he was still alive. However, all my attempts at communicating with 'the world out there', beyond the narrow confines of the hell that had now became my home, were impossible. But I was glad to learn, when we were released, that Ngala was aware of my attempts to contact him, except that he feared that if discovered, we might have suffered too much for it.

Having 'gotten used' to the routine of torture, or so I thought, I never reflected upon the possibility of our release. All attempts I had made through the merciless guards to contact a lawyer or any member of my family had been frustrated by the security men who believed that I actually had no rights. I was constantly reminded that the office of the President was directly responsible for whatever happened to us. The last revelation always made me smile; that a head of state would find our activities, as students, so personally threatening as to constitute treason, was certainly amusing. Of course, we were aware of the accusations regarding our alleged links with Libya and Uganda. Yet, I still did not understand why it was taking Moi's security agents so long to 'investigate' their trumped up charges against us. The delay was difficult to understand, particularly because we were being held incommunicado.

So, when they appeared with the blindfolds again, my heart leapt to my mouth. I wondered what sinister plans were afoot.

'Not another one of those state orchestrated suicides', I desperately hoped. 'Court. Maybe court', I repeated to myself silently as my heart thumped wildly. However, I knew that even in court, there was no salvation. What I already knew of the 'court of injustice' was that: contrary to section 77 of the Laws of Kenya (that was decades before the ratification of the Constitution of Kenya 2010), the whole exercise was normally cordoned off from members of the public. In addition, charges were often manufactured; the accused subjected to torture, cruel and unusual punishment and forced to swear falsely; evidence coaxed and witnesses bribed. In short, justice was, and still is, trampled underfoot. Yet I couldn't fathom the reasons for the delay in having us charged.

On November 27, 1987, I was blind-folded, lifted up and placed next to another body in what felt like a van. The body next to me later turned out to be Munameza Muleji. As with the day we were abducted, the vehicle made zigzag movements for what could have been 30 minutes. When the vehicle stopped and our eyes freed, we were ushered into a secluded building that looked like it had been abandoned a decade ago. We were later informed that it was the Criminal Investigations Department (CID) headquarters, and that we were meant to make statements before appearing in court. Munameza and I found Kaberere Njenga, Munoru Nderi and Oyuo Amuomo Ngala already seated and eagerly waiting for our promised arrival.

I lunged for a newspaper that was lying around. Then came a terse warning: no reading for prisoners! We were still guests of the state, and as such, still had no rights or privileges. At first we protested and demanded to see Buke, the SONU chairman before we could make any statements. However, we were told that asking any questions would be considered subversive. We were further assured not to worry about Buke because all of us would face the same fate –that we would all be 'reprimanded' before being allowed to continue with our studies. Of course, we didn't believe a single word these terrorists spoke, but there wasn't anything we could do given our limited options and the circumstances under which we had been kept. We decided to write the statements, as carefully as we possibly could so we weren't returned to the hell we had been in. As soon as we signed the statements, we were taken to court.

At approximately 6pm on November 27, 1987, we were taken to the Nairobi Law Courts where a kangaroo trial was conducted before Chief Magistrate Joseph Mango. The prosecution was led by none other than the dreaded and despised Bernard Chunga, who was then the Deputy Director of Public Prosecutions (in one of Moi's last acts of insanity and defiance, he was later appointed Chief Justice of Kenya; fortunately, Chunga was quickly hounded out of office after Kibaki took power in December 2002); the Director of Prosecutions then being the Attorney General. Chunga had a reputation as a meticulous, efficient devil. He did everything to ensure that anyone who thought about, imagined or dreamed of opposing Moi would be put away for a very long time. He considered the courts, judges, magistrates, law and procedure as inevitable irritants and inconveniences that one had to pretend to consider before ultimately convicting and incarcerating all dissidents to long and harsh sentences. When we saw Chunga pacing up and down with a thin manila file in his right hand, we imagined that all that was standing between us and the Kamiti Maximum Prison was the entry of the magistrate, which would be a formality in any event. Assisting Chunga was another prosecutor called Alex Etyang. It was the latter who completed our bond papers and witnessed our signatures. We weren't allowed to have legal counsel.

By the time the case was called, it was well past 7pm, but the robotic magistrate didn't care. Although we were neither required to plead to the alleged offences (I don't even recall hearing what they were) nor to have legal counsel, we were summarily handed suspended sentences and dumped back inside the van, this time without blindfolds. The "Bond to Keep the Peace", miscellaneous case number 13/87 at the Chief Magistrate's Court at Nairobi was interesting. It stated that we had been bonded to "keep the peace for the term of twelve months" and to refrain from "any act that may probably occasion a breach of the peace…" And that if I breached the peace, I would forfeit the sum of Sh5,000. That meant anything I did could be interpreted as a breach. We had essentially become prisoners even outside prison walls.

Thereafter, we were taken to separate police stations in Nairobi, to spend a last night in detention along with other Kenyans who had been welcomed as 'criminal visitors of the state.' I spent that cold night at the Lang'ata Police Station's holding cells. The night passed quickly because I spent it in discussion with some inmates who had been condemned to spend their entire lives in jails. No matter how depressing the conditions, I was excited to be among my fellow humans again.

Early the following day, I was taken to the University's administration block. There, I asked to speak to Prof. Mbithi, a request that I was surprised to be granted graciously. I climbed the stairs and before his secretary could manufacture a lie about Mbithi's absence, I had opened his door to find him on the telephone. He stared at the dishevelled figure before him in utter shock – my hair was long and shaggy; my beard was unkempt and my clothes were dirty and creased – and quickly replaced the receiver. "Why did you do this to me Professor? Why? Why did you make up stories about us when you know that we are innocent?" I cried out to him. But before Mbithi could answer, one of the Special Branch officers that had taken us there came into the office and politely asked me to leave. I did, glaring back at Mbithi with complete disgust. As I was stepping out of Mbithi's office, one of the orderlies handed me a letter addressed to me. I opened the envelope and saw a letter dated November 30, 1987 –three full days earlier.

It read:

> *Dear Mr Miguna,*
> *RE: YOUR EXPULSION FROM THE UNIVERSITY OF NAIROBI*
> This is a formal communication to let you know that the University of Nairobi Council, at its meeting of Friday, 27th November 1987 took the decision to terminate your status as a student.
>
> This decision has been necessitated by circumstances very well known to you including; firstly failure to comply with the terms of the letter of acceptance signed by you when you were admitted into the University [sic]; secondly failure to abide by the regulations governing the conduct and discipline of students at the University; and thirdly your involvement in a scheme of student politics designed to disrupt the regular operation of the University as an academic institution, which, in November, 1987 led to violent

> demonstrations and the subsequent closure of the University. [Sic] It follows that you cease forthwith to be a student, and you are not to make any unauthorised appearances at any of the University's campuses or any University property.
>
> Yours sincerely,
> Philip M. Mbithi
> Vice-Chancellor and Professor of Sociology.

It was shocking. A professor of sociology writing a letter that purports to expel a student without any particulars, supporting facts or evidence. Clearly, Professor Mbithi knew that he hadn't disclosed what I did, or how my purported conduct violated or breached the University regulations. He hadn't particularised how I had failed to comply with the terms of my letter of acceptance, when that failure had occurred, when and how I had been notified of the alleged failures.

Moreover, Professor Mbithi knew that as a student leader, I only acted in the best interests of the students. He failed to disclose what the "scheme of student politics" meant or how they had "disrupted regular operation of the University as an academic institution". If anything, for the few days we served as the student government, we enhanced not just academic freedom by ensuring that the intimidation of teachers and students was rebuffed; we also created a conducive environment for learning by making sure that there was adequate food and provisions for students; and that basic cleanliness and maintenance were no longer distracting concerns to students. On what basis, therefore, was Professor Mbithi (acting at the behest of Moi's repressive government), expelling me?

Lastly, Professor Mbithi betrayed his education, training and professional integrity by allowing himself to be a robotic tool for the oppressive regime. He knew that the so-called University of Nairobi Council's proceedings were meaningless without notice of the proceedings to me and without my participation. Natural justice demanded that I couldn't be condemned unheard. Asserting that the decision had been necessitated by circumstances very well known to me was balderdash. The onus was on Mbithi to detail those circumstances. And to ridiculously conclude, like he did, that I was responsible for the 'violent demonstrations and the subsequent closure of the University' when he knew that the students only rose in protest over our unlawful abductions and detentions was to demonstrate a callous disregard for the truth.

I was still shaking my head in disbelief when I entered the vehicle that took us to the Halls of Residence. They dropped each one of us next to our respective Halls then parked near the Student Centre. They gave us 30 minutes to collect our things. However, before I climbed the stairs up to my room, it was obvious that we didn't have anything to collect. The place was in a total mess. Windows and doors were broken. There was litter, torn clothes and broken furniture strewn everywhere. The hall was abandoned. There were no signs of life. It was like a deserted battlefield, minus corpses. You could almost smell death. You could sense that people had died, been injured and maimed there. I reached my room and found the door ajar. Apart from papers strewn about, there was absolutely nothing of value. My clothes, books, files, posters – everything was gone.

I walked down slowly and found my colleagues waiting, also empty-handed. We started asking nobody in particular about our things. It was now past 7pm and Special Branch Officers were becoming restless. They ordered us to get into the vehicle and leave. We obliged. "But where is Buke, the SONU chairman?" I kept asking. No one seemed ready or willing to answer that question.

The instruction was for each one of us to head home directly. They dropped us at the Akamba Bus Service and returned money they had taken from us on the day of our abduction. We first escorted Ngala to Kenyatta estate. Munoru and Anampiu headed to Meru. Kaberere took the Banana-bound *Matatu*. Later, I saw Munameza off at the Akamba Bus terminus before taking a Gold Line bus to Kisumu in the evening. We had been told that we weren't allowed to stay in or visit any urban centres without the express permission from "the authorities." They didn't explain who the "authorities" were. And upon return to our rural homes, we were required to stay away from all institutions of higher learning and public libraries. We were also banned from meeting with more than five people at a time. That included members of our families. And given the fact that Africans have extended families, we couldn't fathom what that command entailed. If we adhered to it, most of our family members would have to be permanently excluded from any gathering, get-together or meeting. Interestingly, because many African households comprise more than five people, what this meant was that we would be permanently in breach, thereby permitting the authorities to arrest us any time they felt like doing so. We were sitting ducks. What would five 'dissidents' be doing together if not plotting against the loving President? We could be gainfully employed as long as it wasn't 'formal employment'. In short, we were banned from doing anything. We basically remained prisoners. Yet we hadn't been charged, tried or convicted.

These outrageous conditions were intended to teach us a lesson and show the public the price one had to pay for dissidence. Look at them, they would jeer. 'Look at what disobedience brings!' Yes, the public was supposed to castigate us; we were to become objects of public ridicule. 'Look at what too much privilege does! We give them everything: food, clothing, free education…and what do they do? Insult us back? Spoilt brats! Who needs their strike? We are sick and tired of these university students!' Our friends and relatives were supposed to condemn us, and some did; publicly.

When I arrived at Kisumu on November 29, I bought a newspaper and saw that we had made the news: "Varsity Expels 45!" screamed the headline. We had been disposed of like garbage, without shame. The most annoying thing was that dictator Moi kept attacking us through the state-controlled media; accusing us of being unpatriotic and alleging, of course falsely, that he had unearthed a plot by us, working in league with the 'Boers' of South Africa and white supremacists from the United States of America, to overthrow his 'constitutionally legitimate government'. Nothing could be more preposterous!

On November 30, 1987, we learnt, through the newspapers, that Buke had been charged, tried, convicted and sentenced to five years in jail for allegedly "pinning seditious literature on university notice boards and spreading socialism on campus". The newspapers reported that Buke had "confessed" to these "crimes". That was astounding. The same newspapers also reported that Moi had kicked out Gaddafi's envoy to Kenya over allegations that he had been funding our activities. I knew the regime was shaken. And I swore never to give up the struggle. I swore to keep chanting, as my comrades in Mozambique had, "ALUTA CONTINUA!"

My letter of expulsion was identical to the ones issued to Munoru, Kaberere and Gakiri. I didn't see Ogola's and Anampiu's letters but I wouldn't be surprised if they were also carbon copies. However, there were other students who received conditional expulsions. Worse still, the university administration placed paid advertisements in the national print media claiming that the expelled "trouble makers have in the past been involved in activities of a similar nature in schools and at the National Youth Service." The ad referred to us as "a small vicious section of the student community lacking any sense of public responsibility." That we "attempted to burn university buildings and vehicles, stoned private motorists and public vehicles, manhandled lecturers, assaulted other university staff and engaged in numerous other acts and unsolicited behaviour" [sic].

This was vile and malicious propaganda designed to assassinate our characters and poison the minds of ordinary Kenyans. We were not involved in any acts of violence that occurred during the confrontation between the students and the police – we had already been illegally abducted and detained. And nowhere was it mentioned that it was those unlawful abductions and detentions that had spurred the students to riot. Prior to that act of state perpetrated terrorism, the university had been peaceful.

And how free would we now be? What sort of lives could we pursue in Kenya?

We had received two curious pieces of advice immediately before we had been forced to sign our statements. The first was from one of the goons responsible for ferrying us around. "This is friendly advice, an old man's words of wisdom to misguided kids," he had begun. "Take it or leave it." He was the oldest one amongst them. Until then, we hadn't really noticed him. The only time we became aware of his presence was when he had dropped us off at different police stations on the day of our court appearances. Then he was simply our chauffeur. Until he spoke, he had simply been our silent driver. He rarely said anything. He simply drove, as if to tell us that he was only doing it to make a living; that he had nothing to do with anything that had happened to us. His eyes kept pleading "I have a family to feed" each time we glanced at him, trying to appeal to his humanity.

But this time he spoke, his voice quivering with emotion, his eyes darting from one 'prisoner' to another. He looked like a disturbed father unable to control his children. "Yes, you are nothing but *boys*...boys. *Boys* need *girls*, not prison. So, go get yourselves young girls and get married. The world needs children. *Get married and have children*. Become Christians like myself, go to church regularly and forget about what your hot-headed friends say or do. Forget about this *stupidity* you call politics...student power or whatever they now call it. You hear me? Get married, have children, read your Bibles and become law-abiding, obedient servants of the Lord. That's all I have for you."

And that was all he had for us. He seemed visibly angry and distraught. He immediately withdrew and retreated into his usual absent presence again. To him we had choices; nothing was forcing us to confront authority. The best and most reasonable option, he thought, was to immerse ourselves in prayers and Bible-studies.

The second and last advice came from a very unusual quarter. Patrick Shaw was at the time a notorious figure in Nairobi, an ugly, flabby and ruthless British secret agent-cum-head-teacher of Starehe Boys' Centre. His involvement in our case made clear the extent to which we had rattled the government. In Kenya, Shaw's name was always associated with dangerous violent situations. The media always reported him as having captured this or that dangerous armed robber or heavily-armed "enemy of the state", none of whom ever escaped alive. And since dead people didn't tell their versions of those stories, only Shaw's versions were right. He was ubiquitous. He was lethal. He was feared. Shaw was always where the action was; he killed without feeling. He was brutal and cold. His sharp-shooting was legendary.

The newspapers praised Shaw. He was a one-man army. They portrayed him as the only crime-buster. Politicians and business magnates worshipped him. He was said to have single-handedly been responsible for curtailing violent crime in Nairobi. Like the Hollywood manufactured Rambo, Shaw was BAD! He took no prisoners. He was slippery. He was tough. He inspired fear in all political activists in Kenya. Thieves were scared away just by hearing his name mentioned. For it is said that once a thief stole something on Biashara Street in Nairobi and when someone shouted: "Shaw! Patrick Shaw is coming!" popular myth has it that the thief promptly dropped what he had stolen and took to his heels. He ran for his life. Everybody in the vicinity scurried for cover. However, seeing that everything was now safe, the alarmist burst out laughing. He had simply pulled a trick on the thief.

So, what was Shaw doing amongst us? We weren't violent. We weren't armed robbers. Why was Shaw here with us, poor students? After all, we were just university students.

Shaw certainly didn't look like Rambo. He was repulsive-looking; his entire body puffed up with slabs of fat, forming creases; and from this despicable-looking filth oozed a persistent, peculiar stench. He was a walking latrine. It had never occurred to me until then that one person could combine so many negative traits.

He bellowed at us: "Mine will be short, extremely short. You should cooperate with us, write your statements honestly; don't protect your friends. You are just individuals now. SONU is no more and will never be again. It's *dead!* You will be released. But from today henceforth, there shall be no more meetings, no more student power, no more politicking. I repeat: there shall be no more meetings and no politicking. You shall return to school and that will be that. No questions about anything or anybody. And there shall be no talk about the last few weeks. Remember that we shall be watching your every movement."

Shaw's admonition clarified some niggling queries of mine. Now I understood why they had been so keen on certain innocuous details about our lives. They had asked me about the type of clothes I liked to wear, what I liked to do during my free time, the type of women I find attractive, my favourite food and social places. Now I realised that these details were to allow the state to know how to place us under surveillance. It was then that we noticed Margaret Ben's absence; nobody mentioned her name – not the Special Branch and not Shaw. We realised that she had been an agent all along. Her arrest had been a subterfuge. She must also have been the one who advised the Special Branch of the top radicals and ideologues of the student movement.

So what was left for us? We couldn't work freely or study, and our presence at home would compromise the safety of our families and we would be subjected to continuous harassment from the authorities. A future that had once looked glittering now seemed grim. Yet the injustice of it all spurred me on. "Only death can stop me," I kept saying as I plotted my next move. Not even my mother would have tried to stop me at that point, for it was also her suffering and sense of justice that I now felt hammering in my chest.

BOOK TWO

EXILE

CHAPTER THREE

TANZANIA

The decision was made. Exile. That one word with an X slashing across its body. I was also going to have to slash my way out of the country.

But there were hurdles. One was my girlfriend at the time. How could I convince her that my decision didn't mean abandonment; for in a way, it did. The other was my relatives and close friends. Could I trust them to keep such information secret or even to understand why it had been made or had to be made? After all, they had never before known anyone who had been exiled.

Eventually, only the very closest of friends and relatives heard the bare bones of my plans. Absolutely no one was privy to the entire plan. One thing I had learnt living under a totalitarian regime was that you couldn't trust even the closest person in your life. So, one was told only about an intention, some desire. Another person heard about a 'journey' to an undisclosed neighbouring country – for how long and for precisely what reasons no one discussed or disclosed. It was just to ease off the pressure, I insisted. Some heard that the journey might be long while others were told that it might be short.

The good thing – and I must commend all the various people I spoke with – is that they never launched any serious opposition to these vague, unusual revelations. They offered only their love and unconditional support, with one exception: my girlfriend. The young woman was conflicted; on the one hand, she fully supported me and wanted me to be safe and prosper. On the other hand, however, she wanted me near her. She dreaded being left alone. To ensure that she either stopped me from leaving or delayed it significantly, she would try to be around me as much as she could; pleading with me to accept what had happened as God's plans; that I should find a teaching job and settle down with her. Unfortunately for her, I never gave those considerations any thought. I wasn't going to let Moi dictate what my life would be.

I knew that it wasn't fate or God's will; it was Moi's dictate. I argued that God could not have enabled me to pass all those exams only for Him to terminate my progress midstream without reason or justification. For me, God couldn't have been responsible for the suffering, the torture and the pain; only evil could have been responsible. Therefore, to settle down and forget about all those dreams I had would have been to allow evil to triumph. I refused to do that. She eventually relented even though it inevitably meant a permanent breakup.

Before I fled, I managed to trace my personal effects. A fellow student who had also been at Onjiko – Onyango Ogango – had had the presence of mind to pack up my things and take them with him to his rural home on Nyabondo Plateau in Nyakach. When I eventually made it to his home, I found him wearing one of my African shirts. Most of my other things were intact, including my books and the SONU typewriter, stationery and documents. For that, I am completely indebted to Ogango.

Soon after my release I typed up letters to the United Nations High Commissioner for Refugees in Dar-es-Salaam, Tanzania; Amnesty International, London, the United Kingdom; and the International Union of Students, Prague, Czechoslovakia. I notified them that I planned to flee into exile, through Tanzania. To prevent those letters from being intercepted, I gave them to my sister Juma who lived at Muhuru Bay to mail them in Tanzania. I then surreptitiously travelled back to Nairobi (incognito) and sought out the colleagues who had been detained or expelled with me.

The first person I approached – the Marxist-Leninist ideologue and former SONU secretary general Kaberere Njenga – turned me down flat. He wanted us to wait a little longer. He also thought the best escape route would be Uganda, not Tanzania. Kaberere was a fourth year medical student. He was exceptionally smart, but more than any other 1987 student leader I was aware of, Kaberere was also a fanatical ideologue. Once he had said "no", I knew there was no way of changing his mind.

I found one of Keberere's reasons to be naïve; he informed me that Kimani Wanyoike was going to help us not just to cross into Uganda, but would put us in contact with Yoweri Museveni's government and the National Resistance Movement so that we could undergo military training. But unlike Kaberere, I was less focused on military training than on completing my university education. My view was that we shouldn't allow Moi to ruin our future and determine our lives; that had Moi not arrested, detained and expelled us from the university, we would have graduated and moved on. Shouldn't we complete our studies first before thinking of military training? After all, even Fidel Castro, Vladimir Lenin, Karl Marx, Eduardo Mondlane and Nelson Mandela had first focused on their education before venturing into revolutionary politics.

But Kaberere also gave me a more practical and touching reason why he couldn't leave Kenya at that time. Kaberere feared that if he went into exile, his elderly mother would die. I could relate to that. I knew that if my mother was still alive, I would have found it extremely difficult to leave her behind. I understand that about one year after we had gone into exile, Kaberere crossed into Uganda and tried to pursue his military goal. Unfortunately, Ugandan security agents arrested and locked him up. After his release, he returned to Kenya crestfallen; military training having fallen off his priority list.

My next port of call was Peter Mutonyi Gakiri. Although I hadn't been very close to Gakiri – and he wasn't one of the arrested and detained student leaders – I found him focused and resolute. He had been one of the 45 students expelled. Gakiri had served the students diligently as the catering secretary. When I mentioned my escape plan to Gakiri, he said "yes" before I could complete the sentence. He only asked "when?" I gave Gakiri the date and place he must report to and went to meet Joseph Tony Ogola.

Ogola was popularly known as JTO. He had represented the faculty of science in SONU though he had held no executive position. Ogola also said "yes" and I moved onto Munoru Nderi. Munoru had been the SONU vice-chairman. Even before I had joined the university he had established his credentials as a fearless student activist. In 1984, he had served a six-month sentence for allegedly commandeering a university bus to drive to Kenyatta University to rally students against Moi. After a year in the wilderness he had been allowed to return to the university. When I approached Munoru, I found him ready, though he too initially favoured Uganda as our escape route.

I persuaded him that Tanzania was our better option. Moi had publicly claimed that the Ugandan leader, Museveni, was using us – the University of Nairobi students – to overthrow him from power. I argued that if we were unlucky and were caught crossing into Uganda, the repercussions would be more severe than if we were caught doing the same into Tanzania. I also reasoned that Museveni was more likely to arrest and deport us in order to prove to Moi that he wasn't involved in our political schemes. Furthermore, I pointed out that Tanzania was unlikely to deport us because the Tanzanian leader, Nyerere, was said to have never forgiven himself for having returned two Kenyan dissidents – the so-called leaders of the aborted 1982 coup against Moi, Hezekiah Ochuka

Rabala and Pancras Oteyo Okumu – on the understanding that they would not be killed only for Moi to breach his word and hang them within months of their return.

On the appointed day, my three fellow escapees arrived in Kisumu by bus from where we took another public service vehicle to Migori town. From there, we took yet another public service vehicle to Muhuru Bay, arriving late in the evening. I found my sisters, Juma and Herina waiting anxiously. We spent a few nail-biting hours in Herina's house before departing in the small hours for the Tanzanian border. It was pitch dark when we started out at 3am, but Juma, who was our guide, had travelled the route on foot numerous times and knew the way. We had one clear intention: to travel at least 50 kilometres before daybreak. That way, we would be deep inside the thick thickets that covered the no man's land between the two countries. The route we took was a footpath, so we knew that it would be near impossible for anybody to pursue us with any motorised vehicle.

We trudged along, sometimes in a single file, other times together. Many times we had to stop and wait for Gakiri, who was terribly out of shape. He panted that he was exhausted and in agony from the blisters between his thighs. But he couldn't actually go back. Firstly, he didn't know the way back and none of us was going to return with him. Secondly, he was as determined to get away as all of us. And thirdly, Gakiri knew that going back was more treacherous than reaching the border. So, we kept going and Gakiri kept faith and endured like the rest of us. And after eight long hours of trekking and constantly looking behind us, we crossed into Tanzania.

Crossing wasn't easy. The paths meandered. There were times our footpath came to an abrupt end and we had to decide whether to go back or keep going through the shrubs. We always kept going ahead. We knew that as long as we kept going, we would be getting further away from totalitarianism and closer to wherever fate would take us. We kept vigilant. If we noticed any movement behind us, we would stop until we knew what it was. We also monitored movements ahead. Nothing was left to chance. Tanzania was a friendly country, we kept repeating to ourselves. However, we hadn't forgotten how a few years before our flight, the Tanzanian government had collaborated with the Moi regime and 'swapped dissidents'. The two Kenyan returnees, Ochuka and Okumu had of course been hanged.

My sister knew where the Tarime, North Mara regional office was located. As soon as we had introduced ourselves, she said her final goodbye to us and headed back. It was getting late and she was alone.

We found the Tanzanian government agents knowledgeable and sympathetic. A few days after our abductions and detention from the University of Nairobi, Amnesty International had adopted us as prisoners of conscience. It had subsequently launched a global campaign for our release. Hence, by the time we were crossing the border into Tanzania, our plights were already well known in media, government and humanitarian circles. In addition, my letter to the UNHCR in Dar-es-Salaam had been received. The officials at Tarime recorded our statements with lightning speed and transported us to a government guest house in Sirati. We were booked in there two days before Christmas. The guards there informed us that it was where Nyerere would stay when touring the region – it was comfortable, but a far cry from the ostentatious living of the Kenyan ruling oligarchy.

Early, at about 5am on the morning of December 26, we were told to pack because we would be moving to a different and more secure location at Musoma, one of the 'major towns' on the shores of Lake Victoria. A day after our arrival in Musoma, we requested to be taken to the post office where we sent a telex to the UNHCR office in Dar. We got a prompt response that a protection officer would be dispatched to interview us within a week. Meanwhile, a Tanzanian newspaper had carried a story titled "No asylum to Kenyan students". The story was attributed to the Director for Africa and Middle East Affairs in the Tanzanian foreign affairs ministry, Ndugu Bernard Muganda. Ndugu Muganda was quoted as confirming our presence in the country and asserting that the Tanzanian government had no issue with our being there because we had entered legally. However, he added that: "The students have not asked for asylum in this country, and even if they did, the best we could do is register them with the United Nations High Commissioner for Refugees who would in turn allocate them another country of asylum". Ndugu Mugunda also confirmed that he had accompanied the foreign minister Ndugu Benjamin Mkapa (who would later become President of Tanzania) to Nairobi the previous week where they had discussed us with the Kenyan government. But the story had a more scary aspect; Ndugu Mugunda also stated that we had been given until January 20, 1988 to leave the country.

We were in a state of consternation. Luckily, a protection officer from the UNHCR arrived in Musoma the following day and took detailed information from us with a view to assessing our eligibility for recognition as conventional refugees. He was called Castro from Latin America. (That was a name I held in high esteem; Castro!) We were now six student refugees, not five. We had been joined by Erastus Omill Oloo, who had been SONU's representative in Kabete campus. Apparently, Oloo had taken off from Kenya the moment the media had reported that we had fled to Tanzania. He had managed to enter through the Sirare border crossing. Unlike Munoru and I, Omill had a Kenyan passport.

More anxious days passed then suddenly, at the end of January 1988 – and without prior notice – a Tanzanian government Landrover arrived at the guest house one breakfast time with four armed officers and a driver. At about 5pm that day, we arrived in Kigoma, a town on Lake Tanganyika. There, we were met by a rambunctious man who introduced himself as George Labor, a UNHCR protection officer based in Kigoma. He carried a small leather bag that looked packed with cash. George was a short fast-talking man who seemed to be always on the move. Right at the outset, he laid out the ground rules on meals, dos and don'ts. It was apparent that we were now under the control of the UNHCR. After completing a retinue of forms, our mug photos and fingerprints were taken. George also gave us two sets of relocation forms to complete: one for Australia and another set for Canada. However, after brief consultations amongst us, we decided to complete only the Canadian forms.

We were taken away from Kigoma at the end of February 1988. Just like with the 'evacuation' from Musoma – which we were later told was in response to a Kenya government attempt to kidnap us – one day, George just announced that we should pack our bags and board a vehicle, which was already waiting. We were then taken to an airstrip and told to board an old Soviet-era six-seater helicopter. It was tiny. Until then, none of us had boarded a helicopter or fixed-wing plane. We were excited not just because we were going to fly for the first time; we were happy because we knew we were getting away and hopefully getting resettled.

The flight was frightening. The helicopter was too small to fly too high. So, it kept just above the clouds. And each time it encountered strong head winds, air pockets or thick clouds, it would fall several metres down before climbing up again. Many times we thought we were crashing. We held tightly to our seats. Thrice, it fell so suddenly and dramatically that Gakiri, who was seated behind me, threw up. Finally, we landed safely at Dar international airport. We were met by the UNHCR country representative and taken directly to his head office. There, we filled more forms, took more mug shots and fingerprints. Within one hour, we were issued with special UN travel documents. Subsequently, we were driven to a small hotel from where, very early the following morning, we were driven to the airport again. We boarded a Swazi Airlines plane bound for Manzini, Swaziland. Until then, we hadn't been told where we were travelling to. But it was quite obvious that everybody was in a mad rush to get us out of Tanzania.

SWAZILAND

We landed at the Manzini airport late afternoon and were met by a UNHCR protection officer; a stunningly beautiful Tanzanian lady. It was the end of February and the weather was chilly. We were told that the South African winter was on. The lady quickly explained that we had been given temporary stay by the Swazi government as the UNHCR worked on our relocation papers. She was cagey. But she nonetheless mentioned that one of the countries considering our asylum applications was Canada. She put us in a large van blaring fantastic South African music. Thus gloom and doom were replaced with brightness and Afro fusion music. She offered us water and juice. Our faces brightened. I could see the sneaky glances of Munoru, Omill and Ogola towards the gregarious lady.

The ride between Manzini and Mbabane took about one and a half hours. The roads were smooth and large, but full of curves around the breathtaking undulating hills. The land was beautiful and green. And soon we were in Mbabane, the capital city of Swaziland. It was a tidy little city, with a population of about 40,000. By the standards of Swaziland, that was huge. Mbabane was the second largest city, after Manzini. In fact, the two were the only cities. One could even argue that they were the only urban centres. Although Manzini was bigger and hosted virtually all the industries and most of the King's palaces, Mbabane was the seat of government. It was also considered the financial hub. It was clean and neatly planned. As we drove into the city, we could see some people in traditional regalia: bare chests, what appeared like a leather loin cloth around the waist, a tiny knife stuck to the waistline, some trinkets around the ankles and feathers on the head. We were promptly informed that the three gentlemen that we passed dressed in that ceremonial regalia were possibly members of parliament, who were possibly also members of the royal family.

The vehicle entered the UNHCR compound and we alighted, finding a dedicated team of workers waiting for us, led by the country representative who looked like a Somali. We were warmly welcomed and taken in for a comprehensive debrief. The first thing we were told was that our admission and stay was granted by the government of the tiny landlocked kingdom for a very brief period of time. It was given on condition that while there, we would refrain from active political involvement. Emphasis was placed on our absolute discretion and commonsense. We would be free to move around Mbabane but we weren't to go anywhere else. We were also warned against speaking with the media. These conditions – it was explained to us – were in our best interests. The protection officer mentioned that we had been taken from Musoma because of specific threats of abduction. The Tanzanian intelligence service had information that a few members of the Kenya Special Branch had crossed into Tanzania and were tracing where we were. She told us that even Swaziland wasn't completely safe. South Africa routinely abducted members of the ANC and spirited them back to South Africa. Although they considered that a remote possibility with respect to Kenya, she nonetheless expressed concern that it could still happen. We were to be extremely careful with whom we spoke and associated with. The session ended with the filling of forms, fingerprints and mug shots being taken.

We were booked in a nice three star hotel in Mbabane, right in the middle of the commercial business district. The UNHCR arranged for our meals and accommodation. Gakiri and I quickly developed a routine: we would wake up by 8am, eat breakfast and head to the library. By 12.30pm, we would stroll back to the hotel and eat lunch. After lunch, Gakiri liked to nap as I went out walking. I would do this for about two hours before going back to the library for another hour or so. Occasionally, Gakiri would join me at the library in the afternoon. However, more often than not, I would be alone, returning at about 5pm, in time for dinner. Many times Gakiri and I only saw Munoru, Omill, Anampiu and Ogola at breakfast and dinner. They had a routine of their own, mostly roaming the outskirts of town in search of alcohol and women. They nicknamed themselves the *Inkosis* of Swaziland. An *Inkosi* is a Swazi traditional chief. We were okay with that for as long as we were all safe.

However, one early morning, two months after our arrival in Mbabane, our protection officer came to the hotel just as we were eating our breakfast. She looked unusually flustered. I noticed a few waiters and other customers looking at us curiously. That wasn't particularly unusual since most of them knew we were foreigners. The protection officer came over to our table and instructed us to finish quickly so that we could accompany her to the office. I knew that something was wrong but had no idea what it was. Strangely, Omill, Ogola, Anampiu and Munoru were visibly shaken. They had guilt written all over their faces. Then all hell broke loose the moment we arrived at the UNHCR office. We were taken to a boardroom where the country representative immediately launched into us. "What is this? What is this?" he shouted, as he held that day's *Swazi Times* newspaper. I hadn't read the newspapers that morning, so I had no idea what the commotion was about. Gakiri was sitting next to me. He whispered: "They addressed a press conference yesterday?" He was pointing at our *Inkosis* – who were now shifting in their seats. When I tried to make eye contact with them, they all looked down. I craned my neck to see what was on the newspaper and saw their photos on the front page. I knew instantly what had happened. The

Inkosis had defied the warnings we had been given and shot off their mouths about revolution and military training to a bunch of Swazi journalists delighted to get a 'scoop'.

"If this happens again…if you speak to the media one more time; you will be gone. We shall wash our hands of you!" The country representative warned sternly.

About one week after the *Swazi Times*' headline, the media carried reports about the recall of Swaziland's High Commissioner to Kenya, Mr Elliot Gamedze. He had been Swaziland's top envoy in Nairobi for three years. No explanation was given for the recall, which took effect immediately. Hardly two days later, there were screaming headlines again connected to Kenya: two Swazi air hostesses were arrested in Nairobi allegedly "in possession of drugs". They were quickly taken to a Nairobi magistrate's court and remanded in custody. Rumours started swirling in Mbabane that the Swazi government wanted the ladies repatriated in exchange for our return. The situation was becoming tense and volatile. That week, a strange fellow visited our hotel, claiming to be the first secretary from the Kenyan Embassy in Zambia. I wasn't there when he arrived, but I found him huddled with the 'chiefs' at a corner in the hotel; they were drinking. After the usual pleasantries, he introduced himself to me and invited all of us to a much fancier hotel in the evening. I gave it a wide berth though all my colleagues honoured the invitation. But Gakiri returned barely an hour and a half later saying he didn't trust the man. According to Gakiri, the man was a spy up to no good. He seemed to have a lot of money, with which he was inebriating the 'chiefs'. In the process, the 'chiefs' were busy "talking" unrestrainedly. Obviously the man was a Special Branch officer – whether based in Zambia or in Nairobi was completely immaterial to me. As far as I was concerned, our 'chiefs' were recklessly exposing us to danger. I wanted nothing to do with them. When the 'chiefs' returned to the hotel, Ogola was talking about "Moi's offer of forgiveness to us if we publicly apologise." Ogola seemed excited about that prospect.

"Apologise for what?" I challenged him.

"You, you just leave us alone to execute this. Moi has promised that we would be readmitted back to campus and we wouldn't be victimised," Ogola attempted an explanation.

I told them, firmly, that they should leave me out of their crazy plans; that I didn't need Moi to complete my education. Apparently, the "First Secretary" was waiting for a written declaration from the 'chiefs', which he undertook to deliver to Moi personally. I had no doubt that Moi desperately needed an apology from us. It would have been a huge PR coup. "Runaway student leaders ask Government for forgiveness!" That would be the headline.

But the UNHCR spoiled the drama, for very early the following day, we were told to pack our things and get into two separate vehicles. We were on the move again. Nobody told us where we were being taken until we arrived there. On the way, we saw Manzini and I wondered if we were getting repatriated to Kenya. Luckily, we passed Manzini and kept going. Eventually, the vehicles pulled out of what appeared like a secluded resort, tucked away on its own in a wooden area. The resort was located in a tiny town called Big Bend, which was less than two kilometres from the Mozambican border. By all accounts, we had been sent to Siberia due to the indiscipline of the 'chiefs'.

The Big Bend Resort was an interesting place. It was an old Victorian structure with less than 30 rooms. We shared rooms in the same pairings as we had in Mbabane. But here, we also shared the beds; two each to a double bed. There was one small dining room where we took our meals. Again we were given three square meals, though the level of service and hospitality was of a lower standard than it had been in Mbabane. There were two bars, which were about 30 metres away from each other. Adjacent to the bars were spaces for guests to dance. The bigger bar and dance space was commonly referred to as the "zoo". This is where Africans bought and took their cheap, local brews. It was always jam-packed with African farm hands, domestic workers and truck drivers between Friday and Sunday. The working and living conditions of most Africans in Big Bend – as in the entire country – actually resembled that of animals in a zoo. Swaziland was a sharply divided society. The royal family formed the political and economic crust of the society. Pockets of white South Africans shared that economic apex with the indigenous aristocrats. But there was no real middle class. At the bottom was everyone else, but of course, with different levels of access to social amenities.

There were large sugar cane, orange and mango plantations in the area around Big Bend. Virtually all the farms were owned and managed by white South Africans, who lived in tidy and well manicured compounds near the farms. Their workers, however, lived in ramshackle hovels made of pieces of zinc, tin, iron and plastic. Friday, Saturday and Sunday nights, these workers would fill up the "zoo"; dancing and drinking away their miseries as the white farmers, tourists and other visitors enjoyed their scotch whiskeys, beer and wine in the genteel, quiet bar, laughing loudly and telling each other stories, mainly about the stupidity of Africans. The lady who managed the resort was of mixed-race origin; what would be referred to in South Africa as a coloured. She had two daughters; young women who assisted her to run the place. They weren't actually running the place as they spent almost all their time 'entertaining' the white guests from South Africa. They occasionally paid us attention, probably because the UNHRC was paying our bills. A few expatriates teaching in the area also visited the place. Most of them preferred the zoo to the genteel exclusive white enclave. That is how I met Richard and Sheila Parthak, two Canadian expatriates, who became my friends, and with whom I would later meet up in Toronto, Canada, after they had returned from Swaziland. Needless to say, that was the first time in my life I saw and experienced a colour-bar.

Then on May 22, 1988, I received my letter of admission to Canada. It was dated May 13 and issued by the Canadian High Commission in Pretoria, South Africa. The Canadians had decided to split us into twos, with each pair destined for a different province and city. There was some internal logic to their pairing. Gakiri and I would go to Toronto. Gakiri and I were friends and had both indicated our interest to study law. The two leading law schools in Canada were in Toronto: Osgoode Hall Law School and the Faculty of Law at the University of Toronto.

Gakiri flew out first. Early one Saturday morning on June 25, 1988, Omill and I departed Manzini airport for Canada, via South Africa. We had brief stop-overs in both Nairobi and London. First, the Swazi Airline plane took us to Johannesburg. For the first time, we used escalators. Although we didn't leave Jan Smuts International Airport (now Oliver Tambo International Airport), Johannesburg was visibly advanced. From there we took a British Airline plane, landing in Nairobi about midnight the same day. We were scared to death of being arrested. Luckily, en route passengers were not supposed to disembark. The wait-time was also under one hour. I slept most of the way from Nairobi. We landed in London in the morning. This time, the wait was long. Also we were splitting in London; Omill was taking a direct flight to Edmonton and I another one to Toronto. One month earlier, Ogola JTO had made the same trip to Edmonton. Anampiu and Nderi would soon follow; to Vancouver, British Columbia.

We checked our departure times and gates before saying goodbye to each other, not knowing when next we would be in touch. There were no mobile telephones or emails in those days.

I recall arriving at Pearson International Airport in Toronto on the evening of June 25, 1988. It seemed like a miracle that we would land in Toronto on the same day we left Swaziland, and despite the stop-overs. I keenly followed the general direction of disembarking passengers. I knew someone would meet me but I neither knew the person's name nor how s/he looked. And since I hadn't been to any major international airport with multiple gates, exits and shopping centres, all I was interested in was finding customs and immigration officers so I could ask them where I would go. I held my UN-issued travel document, letter of admission and minister's permit tightly in my left hand. My duffle bag was in my right hand. When I reached the customs counter, I presented the documents and waited anxiously. The officer – a nice white lady – smiled and asked: "Where are you travelling from, Sir?"

"Swaziland" I answered confidently.

"And where are you going?" she asked.

"I actually don't know…"

That was the truth; I didn't know where I was going. I hadn't been given the name of any person; no address of a hotel or residence. And I had only $3.50 in my pocket, all that was left over from $50 I had earned as a letter writer for an old illiterate Malian businessman whom I had met in the hotel in Mbabane. Anyway, before I could finish answering the customs officer, I heard someone calling: "Maiguna! Maiguna!"

I looked up and saw another friendly female face beaming at me and approaching the counter. She introduced herself as the immigration officer who would take me where I was to stay. The customs officer had a brief chat with her before stamping my documents and saying: "Welcome to Canada!"

Within minutes, we had exited and found a limousine waiting. I marvelled at the large, smooth super highways. My mind fleetingly wondered whether I would ever manage to drive on what looked like a maze of highways. And I breathed a sigh of relief. A new chapter in my life had just begun.

CHAPTER FOUR

CANADA

I had landed in Toronto about 5.30pm. It was late June, but summer hadn't really begun yet. The weather was mild and dry. There wasn't humidity. The trees were green. Flowers of various colours, shades and variety were blossoming. As we drove from the expansive and ultra modern airport along wide and smooth multi-lane highways towards the city centre, we could see people eating and drinking in restaurants or on their apartment balconies. Through the car's windows we saw tall and spacious buildings. The general state and quality of infrastructure was so markedly different from what I had been used to in Africa. It dawned on me why the country was described as 'developed' while Kenya wasn't – isn't still – even developing. I am not saying that Canada isn't without many faults – including systemic racism – but first impressions count: starting from the airport all the way to the hotel, the customer service was superior to anything I had experienced previously.

We arrived at my new 'home' at about 8pm, yet the sun had not set and it was still bright outside. The streets were still milling with people. Within five minutes of my arrival, Gakiri walked into my room, which I was sharing with a fellow refugee from Ethiopia. Gakiri occupied another room next to ours, which he was sharing with a Southern Sudanese refugee. It quickly became apparent to me that the place was exclusively meant to accommodate newly-arrived, Canadian government-sponsored refugees. It was a five-storey building but the refugees occupied only two storeys. The upper storeys looked like offices. We would later learn that they were actually being used by officers from the Canadian Intelligence Service. They were meant to surreptitiously keep an eye on us. Strangely, the building was located on Jarvis Street which was well known as a red light district. I found it strange that in a large metropolitan city like Toronto, the Canadian authorities saw it fit to accommodate us newcomers on Jarvis Street.

Gakiri looked relaxed and contented. He always did. I've actually never met anybody in my life as patient and relaxed as Gakiri. He had an equable temperament; at least superficially. Even amid chaos, Gakiri would be as cool as a cucumber. He never spoke much either. Nothing excited Gakiri; the only exception – and these moments were extremely rare – was after taking a few beers. Then he would sometimes sing in Gikuyu. Although he had been in Toronto now for one month, he hadn't started looking for his own accommodation nor had he inquired about universities. I got those admissions out of him within 15 minutes of my arrival. Unlike him, I was restless. All I was thinking about was how and when I would resume my university studies. I was imagining, daily, that my classmates back at the University of Nairobi were now way ahead of me.

Our rooms had two double beds, a colour TV and a landline telephone. Local calls within Toronto were free though that didn't matter to me because I knew nobody except Gakiri there. By 10pm that day, I had eaten my dinner and slept. I was exhausted, but also fretting about the important errand I had to run on Monday – I was desperate to get to the admissions office of the University of Toronto, which Gakiri had told me was then the leading Canadian university in most fields.

I woke up at midday the following day, a Sunday. It was the longest I had slept in my life. It was also one of the few times I suffered from serious jetlag, which to me is just an accumulation of exhaustion and fatigue. After a late breakfast, I armed myself with the map of Toronto and the Toronto Transit Commission (TTC) map of street cars, the subway and city buses. I wanted to familiarise myself with all the places I would need to visit on Monday, which was the very next day: the Canada Immigration Centre at 443 University Avenue, the Toronto City Community Service Centre office at 1631 Queen Street East and the Registrar's office at St George campus of the University of Toronto (U of T). With Gakiri acting as a guide, we zipped through the city within one hour. We were back at our new abode by 2.20pm. That evening, we watched the 9 o'clock news together before getting an early night.

On Monday, June 27, I was awake by 6am. Soon Gakiri and I had made breakfast and headed out. Our first stop was the Canada Immigration Centre at 443 University Avenue. My admission letter had instructed me to report there first. For that day's appointments, I had been given enough Toronto Transit Commission (TTC) tokens. We were there by 8am, by which time I was third in line. By 9.30am, we were heading to the Community Service Centre (or Welfare) office at 1631 Queen Street East, where I would get advice on employment, education, accommodation and general upkeep.

When we reached the Community Service Centre we found the place was already full. There were men, women and children from all races and countries, though most of them were either African or Indian. For the first time since my arrival in Canada, I felt sad. Everyone in that room looked poor, disillusioned and depressed. The clerks weren't efficient. Nor were they polite. Racism was palpable. After two hours of waiting, a young Caucasian woman came to the reception area and called my name. She led me to a tiny room where she confirmed my particulars before explaining to me the basic regulations and policies. She informed me that I would be entitled to a basic upkeep allowance of $250 per month. That would cover all my basic expenses such as food and clothing. However, should I get an apartment, they would pay for it provided that there was a formal offer to rent, a lease and that the landlord was approved by them. The amount for rent couldn't be more than $300 per month. For transport, I would be given money for a monthly TTC pass, but I had to go to the Sherbourne TTC station and have my picture taken and the basic TTC identity card issued first. The minister's permit I received from the Canada Immigration Centre at 443 University Avenue identified my "occupation" as a "new worker". The social worker explained what that meant: I would be required to start job hunting right away.

My aspiration of getting a scholarship and being able to continue with my studies was beginning to look unattainable as the hard realities of life abroad began to sink in. Every week, she continued, I would be required to file with my respective welfare worker evidence of my job search. If or when I got a job offer, I would have to notify my "welfare worker" (that's what the lady sitting in front of me was called) immediately. Failure to inform the welfare worker of employment offers or actual employment would constitute fraud. The lady wasn't ready to discuss with me any issue about completion of my university education. Twice I tried to bring it up and twice she waved the discussion away. She wasn't actually rude, but she was distant and unconcerned. Her main focus was how I could settle down quickly and be independent. This wasn't necessarily bad, except that handling refugees, asylum seekers and immigrants, especially those with dramatically different cultural backgrounds, required much more sensitivity.

After what seemed like hours of dos and don'ts, she allowed me to leave the tiny room with my piles of paper, two weeks' worth of TTC tokens and $70. The money was for my meals for two weeks, after which I would have to make another trip to the office for more. Gakiri was still waiting when I came out. He was used to the routine. He had been in Toronto for one month after all. I asked him if he could accompany me to St George campus so that I could explore ways of joining the U of T. Gakiri wasn't keen and advised me to take it easy. He had met a few Kenyans in Toronto who had discouraged him from pursuing his university education. Their argument – which Gakiri, unfortunately, bought – was that due to systemic racism in Canada, a university education wouldn't improve our chances of securing white-collar jobs. They held the view – sometimes rightly – that the "best paying" jobs weren't necessarily white-collar. They told us that a plumber, electrician or taxi driver could end up earning more than a clerk. I was shocked that Gakiri was talking about settling down with a minimum wage income doing menial jobs. In my view, Gakiri had met the wrong people who were out to mislead him. I reminded him of the main reasons we had fled Kenya. First, we wanted to escape from any possibility of Moi arresting, detaining or torturing us again. But secondly – and equally importantly – we wanted to complete our university education. "We can't allow Moi to dictate our future by forcing us to settle on menial jobs", I told Gakiri. I argued very strongly that a university education wasn't just for employment. A good education is and by itself a value even if one remains unemployed. Knowledge is power. That's not just a cliché; it's the truth. Gakiri obviously knew this, yet he was allowing himself to be distracted by people who had given up. I was disappointed that Gakiri would travel that far only to settle down on things he could have done in Kenya. But I knew Gakiri; once he said no, it was no. So, I studied the TTC map thoroughly before we bade each other goodbye.

At about midday, I arrived at the U of T's Registrar's Office. The Registrar wasn't in but his deputy was. I convinced the secretary to allow me to see him for a few minutes. She did. I found a genial middle-aged man sitting behind an imposing rectangular shaped oak table. He offered me a chair and I introduced myself. He sought to know what he could do for me wherein I gave him an abridged version of the problems we had faced in Kenya as students and how I had ended up in Canada. I concluded by asking him how I could be admitted at the U of T so that I could complete my education. He fixed me with a worried frown. It was two minutes before he spoke. "Young man, you have a number of problems, which I am not sure I will be able to help you with," he said. He then passed me a piece of paper containing "application dates" and asked me to read it before we could continue. The document listed faculties and the deadlines when applications had to be received. I had already missed that year's deadline for all undergraduate course applications. Medicine and law weren't included on this piece of paper as their procedures were more elaborate. Both professions were considered post-graduate careers. One needed a first degree plus a sterling performance in their highly competitive entrance admission examinations. For law, one had to sit and pass the Law School Admission Test (LSAT). Both Canadians and Americans did the same exams three times a year. I was late for those by three weeks, in addition to not having the basic qualifications for admission to law school anyway.

"Sir, I can see the problem, but I still would like to try my luck just in case not everyone who applies meets the basic requirements or if some qualified applicants die, relocate or change their minds." I pleaded.

He inquired if I had my high school certificates and university transcripts. I had only the Ordinary and Advanced level and school leaving certificates. I didn't have any evidence that I had attended the University of Nairobi. He explained that for me to be admitted, I would have to submit an application to the Ontario University Admission Centre and have the University of Nairobi forward all my official transcripts directly to the Admission Centre and to the U of T. I explained that that wasn't going to be possible given the manner of my expulsion and flight. He reiterated that the deadline for applying had actually passed. He wasn't promising anything but he would try; I just had to do my part. If we weren't successful, he said, I could try in the next academic year. The man could tell from my facial expression that I was already distraught from the mere thought that I couldn't join the university that September. After 30 minutes of further discussions, the man – whom I later learnt was from Barbados – picked up the telephone and asked his secretary to bring admission application forms to the office. Thereafter, I completed one application form for the Ontario University Admission Centre and one for the U of T. Luckily I had brought what documents I already had with me. The man took these and assured me that I would be offered a conditional admission on the strength of my moving story, but that I still must submit all the required transcripts. He made copies, addressed the application and told me that he would discuss the matter with the Registrar and get back to me. Since I had just arrived in the country, I used the Community Service Centre address care of my Welfare Worker. Before I left that office, I held the man's hand tightly, looked him straight in the eye and told him matter-of-factly: "Thank you very much Sir. I shall not disappoint you!" He smiled and wished me good luck. I needed it. I then left.

My steps were light. My heart was beating fast. My face was glowing. For the first time since my abduction from the University of Nairobi halls of residence, I felt genuinely happy. On my second day in Toronto, I had made significant progress towards seeing a lifelong ambition – that of completing my university education – realised. I resolved not to fail myself, the deputy registrar and everyone who had faith in me. I would try to move out of the hotel as soon as possible and find a job. I knew that life would be difficult and full of challenges, but I also knew that no challenge was impossible to surmount. All I needed was an unflinching focus and a determination to not become despondent. I was sure that success or failure was in my hands. I had no desire to become a pessimist, cynic or a sentimentalist, forever harping on about what could have been.

On my way back to the hotel, I decided to pass by the *Nofrills* grocery store at the junction of Carlton and Parliament, just 500 metres from the hotel. I had calculated that $70 wasn't money one ate with in restaurants. Since our rooms had stoves in them, I felt that there wasn't a need to strain myself financially for nothing. As I was picking bananas, I heard someone say *"jambo"* behind me and I turned to see a broad smile from an African man in his late 50s. "*Jambo!* My name is John Masuka. I am from Tanzania," he said, as he extended his hand in greeting.

"*Jambo!* How did you know I spoke Kiswahili?" I responded as we shook hands.

"I don't know; I just knew. How long have you been here?" he said smiling.

"I just arrived on Saturday evening. This is my second full day here." I replied.

We chatted as we picked groceries with Masuka advising me on what was good and which foods to avoid, where to shop and which places not to go to. It was a quick orientation. After paying, we both walked to the hotel and found Gakiri watching TV. I introduced him to Masuka before we prepared dinner and ate together. Masuka lived with his family in Regent Park, which was a short walking distance away. So, at about 6.30pm, I walked with him to his family 'home'. We found his wife and six lovely children; two girls and four boys. They welcomed me to their home as a member of their family. And when I left to return to the hotel that evening Masuka promised me that he would find me an apartment that same week.

True to his word, he dropped by the following day – which was my third day in Toronto – and announced that I had an apartment at 247 Broadview Avenue. This was about ten minutes away by street car. I went with Masuka to see the place the same day, got a written offer to lease and a draft lease from the landlord, John Lambert. On the third full day, I took both documents to my Welfare Worker, who signed them after calling the landlord to confirm. She undertook to pay the rent so that I could move in as soon as I had purchased household goods.

I was given a list of places where I could collect a bed, a mattress, two bed sheets, one blanket, one bed cover, three cooking pots, two frying pans, utensils, a reading table, two chairs, an iron and an ironing table. Also, so that we would survive the treacherous Canadian winter, I was provided with a pair of winter boots, one winter jacket, some thermal underwear otherwise called "long johns", a thermal vest, a winter scarf, a sweater, a pair of winter gloves, four pairs of winter socks, a fan, an alarm clock and an electric kettle. Masuka who had become a very useful guide, a fatherly figure, told me where to shop for these items. And exactly five days from the date of my arrival, I moved out of the hotel. Because I had only found one room, I left Gakiri at the hotel but encouraged him to move out as soon as possible, which he did, after another month.

Now that I was on my own, the pressure from the welfare worker was for me to find a job, any job. But each time I showed up for a job interview, they would ask me for "Canadian experience," which I didn't have. It seemed like they needed Canadian experience even for cleaning toilets or cutting grass. Twice, my former roommate – the Ethiopian – took me to a side street at dawn where we were picked up by a truck and taken to a factory in Mississauga. That was quite an experience. We worked throughout the day carrying boxes, loading and unloading trucks until we couldn't remember our names. In-between, we had 22-minute breaks, once to rest and the other for lunch. After the second day, we were too exhausted to continue. In the end, we got paid $63, minus taxes.

Then one day in mid-July I received a telephone call from my welfare worker. She said she needed to see me urgently. I rushed there only to find her livid. She took out a letter from an envelope and said: "I received this yesterday. Who told you to apply for university?"

She handed me the letter. "I didn't know I needed permission to apply for university admission," I explained.

"Well, now you know. You cannot go to university at this time; you are supposed to work for one year before you can qualify for assistance. I want you to write to the university and decline the offer." It was more of a command than a suggestion. My mind was working overtime. I needed a solution – fast.

"Madam, I am sorry but before I came to Canada I explained to the people who interviewed me that I was desperate to complete my studies. If I knew that I was being brought here to work and not go to university, I wouldn't have come. So, I will accept the admission and go to university. That's my decision. Moreover, you had no right to open my letter. The letter was addressed to me and I didn't give you permission to open it." I said it with finality. The lady told me firmly that if I needed their support then I would have to do what she told me.

I was determined to join U of T that September come rain or shine. From 1631 Queen Street East, I went straight to my apartment and read the letter again, very carefully. I had a conditional admission to the Faculty of Arts at Scarborough College, one of the three constituent colleges of the U of T. When applying, I hadn't known where Scarborough was, I had just chosen it because I liked the pictures of the campus; it had lots of trees. I had been granted, preliminarily, four transfer credits towards my undergraduate degree programme but could get three more credits if I could deliver a detailed course outline to the admissions office promptly. That was accomplished with relish within three days. The four credits I was granted were in lieu of my first year of university in Kenya. However, the letter indicated that I had to pay a deposit towards my tuition by the end of August 1988. I was in a conundrum. I didn't have any money; not a dime. I didn't have a job. And I didn't have any source of income or support. Yet, I had also resolved not to return to the welfare office. Somehow, the good news was being transformed into something dreadful. I held my head in both my hands and sobbed uncontrollably. When I stopped, I pulled myself together, went to the bathroom and took a cold shower. As I was showering, a determination washed over me. "I must succeed. Failure is not an option," I uttered silently, shivering.

That night I went to bed very early, setting my alarm clock for 5am. I promised myself that I must find a job – any job -the following day. I didn't care what I had to do; I was going to look for a job and accept the first one I was offered. I was prepared to clean toilets if that's what was needed for me to raise the tuition fees. So, very early the following day, before it had even opened, I was at the Employment Centre at Pape and Danforth. From 9am, I spent the next three hours, writing down every job ad I felt I could do. I then retreated to a public telephone booth, where the unemployed were allowed to call prospective employers for free and started cranking the phone. An employer asked me to come immediately for an interview and off I went. After the interview, I was back at the Employment Centre again. This routine went on for two weeks until one day I just decided to walk into the Hotel Ramada at Carlton and Jarvis. When I spoke to a lady in the Human Resources department, she told me to report for work that same evening. I would work in the laundry cleaning and ironing linen at night. My hourly rate was $7. I was ecstatic. I rushed to my apartment, made dinner, ate quickly and took a shower before returning to take up my appointment. The same day, I telephoned my welfare worker and notified her of the job offer. She indicated that they would adjust my benefits depending on how much I was being paid.

My daily shift began at 5pm and ended at 6am. During the day, I was constantly sleepy or sleeping. It was now nearing the end of July. I needed more than $500 tuition deposit. I was also thinking of the children – young relatives – I had been paying school fees for in Kenya. One was supposed to sit for his advanced levels, yet I hadn't been able to send money to him for the past eight months. I realised that working night shifts would pose major problems for my studies. I quit working at Hotel Ramada at the end of July and instead started with a food company called Tosi, where my job was to make Caesar salads all day. For this I earned $6.50 per hour. That was a pay cut of fifty cents. But to my relief, the job was much lighter.

One day in the third week of August, I needed time off in the afternoon to go and pay my tuition deposit. I had saved $300. I approached my supervisor and explained to her my situation. She didn't look impressed. She told me, coldly, that I had two choices: either I kept the job, which meant no time off; or I could go to register for university and never return. I was astonished. That's how I quit preparing Caesar salad.

On the appointed date, I travelled to Scarborough College and paid my tuition deposit. I also completed and submitted my course registration forms. I had decided to pursue political science and philosophy; the same courses I was studying at the University of Nairobi. I picked seven full courses even though I knew that the maximum was five. I was in a hurry to complete my studies. I had resolved that if the classes didn't clash and I could squeeze in the tuition, I would do everything to finish at an unprecedented speed. The very following day, I went back to the Canada Employment Centre and got a shipper/receiver job at Danforth Lumber Company located at 25 Dawes Road in East York. I didn't know what 'shipping and receiving' was. I just saw the ad, applied, was interviewed and taken on.

Of all the jobs I have ever held, this was by far the worst. All the shippers and receivers were male and black. However, none except me was from Africa. When I had reported to work and saw that everyone looked liked me, I had assumed that we would get along easily, but the first problem I experienced was xenophobia. There was one particular man who I later learnt had emigrated from Jamaica who kept on yelling at me that Africans were cowards, because we had failed to *"Kill Bota"*. When he wasn't yelling at me about the Apartheid regime, he was accusing Africans of having sold his countrymen to the white slave traders. When he was tired of that line, he would ask: "How did you travel to Canada, eh? Did you swim?" He berated me constantly as we were loading and unloading the timber of all shapes, sizes and weights. Even though I felt like knocking his teeth out, I restrained myself. I couldn't allow my emotions to ruin my life; not then, and not ever. The whole place was full of dust. It was dirty inside the office and in the yard. Within three days of taking up the job, I had a terrible cold; my chest was burning and my back aching.

On August 23, 1988, I applied for a $462 loan from Employment and Immigration Canada. Having depleted my savings to pay for half my tuition deposit I still needed about $350. By the time I started my classes at Scarborough, I had quit Danforth Lumber and found a job with Taco Bell, a fast-food chain. It had dawned on me that the noise and conditions at the lumberyard weren't conducive to university studies. They were only paying me $8, but the better news was that my supervisor was pleasant, understanding and supportive. The work environment wasn't hostile, segregated or unbearable. Everyone was treated the same. I also finished work by 4.30pm. And the distance between my work station and the school was about 30 minutes by TTC buses. I used to study on the bus or subway train to and from work.

At the end of August 1988, I submitted an application for the Ontario Student Assistance Program (OSAP). The OSAP programme offered loans and grants to college and university students with residency status. Unfortunately, I hadn't by then received my permanent residence status. The social worker had also warned me that I couldn't qualify for OSAP until I had worked and lived in Ontario for one year. In Canada, everyone must have a social insurance number. Without a SIN, nobody can open a bank account, be employed or get admitted to college or university. Annoyingly, those without permanent residence were issued with social insurance numbers starting with the number "9". This was an indication that one didn't have landed status or citizenship. When an employer saw "9" at the beginning of the SIN, most would refuse to employ you. The good ones would demand to see one's "employment authorisation" and "visa." I had both. That's why I was able to get employment offers, but lack of permanent status excluded me from "better" jobs. Still more painfully as I would later learn, it also denied me access to OSAP. I was, however, determined to succeed. OSAP or no OSAP, I wasn't prepared to drop out from university.

My first class at Scarborough began on September 5 and it was taught by Professor Eboe Hutchful, a Ghanaian political scientist who specialised in political theory and militarism. Hutchful was well read, articulate, dynamic and challenging. His lectures were very contemporary. He never consulted his notes. He had done his PhD at the U of T. Speaking with 'older' students, one got the impression that Hutchful was both popular with students and well respected by his peers. That was rare in academia. He would turn out to be a teacher, a mentor and a good caring friend to me. In fact, it was Hutchful who made the suggestion that I should go to law school (that story will come later). In that first class, I met Joanne Bund, a young Canadian woman from Alberta, who had been in Kenya as an exchange student in November 1987, at the time we were abducted, detained and tortured. Joanne was sitting next to me. We hit it off immediately. She recognised my name as soon as I introduced myself.

Joanne was dashing, brilliant and politically progressive. She was the first Caucasian I met who fought really hard against racism. Later, she was to become my girlfriend and the first woman I cohabited with for one year. During my first week, I also met two professors who would play crucial roles in my life. One was Professor J. Esberey (now professor emeritus). Esberey was originally from Australia. She taught comparative politics. The other one was Professor Ronald Manzer (also now professor emeritus). Manzer taught me public policy, public policy analysis and the politics of bureaucracy. He was a quintessential scholar; precise and deep.

During the first month at Scarborough, Joanne introduced me to the "writing lab" where I could learn how to type and to use the computer. Virtually all my classmates were word-processing their assignments while I was submitting them in long-hand. After we had received back our first assignment, Joanne was astounded that I had gotten B+. She told me that it was because I hadn't typed my work. She was so concerned about it that she ended up typing all my work before I learnt how to type. My marks went up instantly. I quickly ranked among the top three in the class. Joanne also advised me to apply for bursaries, which I promptly did. By the third week of October, I had received a letter informing me that I had been awarded a Scarborough College, University of Toronto bursary of $350. The money was remitted directly into my tuition account. All I needed to do was to remain enrolled in my courses. I said Hallelujah!

In June 1990, I graduated from the University of Toronto with a first class degree in Politics and Philosophy. The bursaries I had been awarded as a student went a long way to help me achieving that goal. The faith that had been shown in me made me work extremely hard. I used to work like a robot, for 18 hours a day. There were days that when my alarm clock sounded at 5.30am I would wake to discover that I had fallen asleep on my bed, fully dressed and still in my work boots. I would remove the boots, put water in my kettle and rush to the washroom. Within ten minutes, I would dash out again.

Meanwhile, Kenyan exiles were arriving almost weekly. Politically and economically, things were getting worse at home. Unemployment, especially among the youth, had hit the roof. The Kanu-Moi regime had become fully totalitarian. That reality hit home even more profoundly as soon as one travelled outside Kenya and came across books and publications that had been proscribed there. For instance, in Toronto in 1989, I purchased Ngugi wa Thiongo's 1983 publication *Barrel of a Pen: Resistance to Repression in Neo-Colonial Kenya* and read it within two hours.

Independence had turned out to be a tragic farce, but there were incidents of heroic resistance. Through my small shortwave transistor radio, I followed the trial of Harrison Okong'o Arara, a former member of the now defunct Kenya Air Force, accused in August 1988 of being in possession of two 'seditious' publications, *Mpatanishi* and *Pambana*. The state alleged that both publications had been distributed by the Kenya Revolutionary Movement (KRM) and the Kenya Patriotic Front (KPF). After a *kangaroo* trial during which Arara denied the charges and asserted that he had been framed, a senior resident magistrate, Mary Ang'awa, sentenced him to five years in jail on each of the two counts. The sentences were to run concurrently. When asked if he had anything to say in mitigation, Arara laughed and stated:

> I don't ask for any leniency from this court for to do so is to recognise its right to judge me. I expect no mercy and ask for none, for if there is no mercy for millions of Kenyans, what will mercy to one individual serve? The documents I am accused of possessing are truthful and honest. It is unfortunate that truth and justice have been sacrificed for selfish interests. Those apostles who have attempted to rescue justice have found themselves in detention, prison or exile. I am proud and happy to join the company of such illustrious sons and daughters of the land…

At that point, the deputy public prosecutor, Bernard Chunga, who had earlier submitted that the accused was a first offender, objected to Arara's address questioning whether it was mitigation. Surprisingly, Ang'awa ruled that it was Arara's right to speak and that he should continue. Arara continued:

> …A society that regards the cry for freedom, the cry for liberation, indeed the cry for emancipation, as being seditious forfeits its place in the civilised community of nations. The people of this nation are simply demanding their fundamental rights and freedoms. They are simply demanding their rights to a decent living, right to education, right to proper medical care, in short, the right to be human beings.

> If that is sedition, so be it. To sum up: you are delivering your judgment but it is not judgment according to law, but according to the system…But to you as a judge, you have betrayed your knowledge which you acquired…Let us be detained, imprisoned, hanged, slaughtered like sheep, but as a sacrifice for greater hopes. The last thing I am leaving you with is that you are not contending against these simple bastards like Okong'o Arara, but you are contending against truth and truth you will not prevail over. *Ok unu nyal.*"

When asked by the magistrate to translate the final words that were in Dholuo, Arara said that the court could do the translation itself. The court clerk then translated the words to mean: "You will not succeed". Arara had earlier thanked the magistrate for allowing him to address the court, stating: "I have throughout my life cherished the ideals, truth and justice. These are the goals for which I've always fought and for which I am prepared to die."

Arara had achieved what many highly educated and prominent Kenyans hadn't: fearlessly telling off the system in open court in clear and detailed terms. Rateng' Oginga Ogego had tried to do that at his trial following the failed 1982 coup. But unlike Arara's, Rateng's address was brief.

For those familiar with liberation literature, it was clear that Arara was familiar with Nelson Mandela's famous "Rivonia Statement" from the dock on April 20, 1964. At the conclusion of Arara's trial, the magistrate said she had listened to Arara's mitigation and noted that he wasn't repentant. "In fact, you have said the two documents are truthful. It means you agree wholeheartedly with them," she continued. She asserted that one could obtain truth without the subversive documents as Kenya's laws provided for legal means of pointing out and correcting any defects of government. "You have failed to follow the right channels, the offence is serious and you are not repentant…The court totally rules out torture."

Unlike Mandela who was a highly sophisticated lawyer, Arara hadn't gone to university. His performance, when compared to the dismal role played by the university-educated magistrate, gave cause for hope. Although we were just a handful of Kenyan exiles in Toronto at the time – and despite our busy lives – we quickly assembled to discuss how we were going to organise ourselves in exile against the repressive Moi regime. We knew that most of the Kenyan students at U of T and York University wouldn't join us. Almost all of them were on government scholarships. Many were related to those in power. More still were conformist. But there were of course a few who were politically sympathetic and who had immigrated independently. These became our target, whenever we attended parties at the Graduate Residence at St George campus, we used that opportunity to gauge our fellow Kenyan students' politics.

In the autumn of 1988, a few politically progressive Kenyans – students, immigrants and exiles alike – had constituted an exploratory committee to come up with proposals of forming a "Kenyan Union in Toronto". By December that year, we had transformed the organisation into a "Committee for Democracy in Kenya". I was elected the coordinator of the group. Willy Mutunga (now Chief Justice of Kenya), who was then undertaking his doctoral studies at the Osgoode Hall Law School at York University and Omondi Obanda were elected committee members. In-between my studies and work, I was keeping a detailed diary, getting involved in Amnesty International campaigns, especially in Kenya and writing articles for publications like *Africa Events* on the human rights situation in Kenya.

Moi was increasingly becoming erratic; ordering the release of one group of political detainees as he put others in detention; cracking down on media and civil society as he pretended to seduce some of his former opponents. We knew that the regime was slowly weakening. By this time, most western governments viewed the Moi regime as a pariah. On February 8, 1989, President Moi released nine political detainees, including Raila Odinga. Most of them had been arrested and detained between March 1986 and August 1987 during the vicious crackdown on the underground opposition movement *Mwakenya*. The problem was that Moi had previously released political detainees, including Raila, only to lock them up again for no particular reason or justification. Indeed, Raila had been serving his third stint in detention. He was first detained after the government withdrew a charge of planning to overthrow Moi in the abortive coup of August 1, 1982. Raila's second detention was on August 30, 1988, after being mentioned as the leader of Kenya Freedom Movement during a sedition case. His third detention was when he, Kenneth Matiba and Charles Rubia were accused of plotting "to overthrow Moi". Of course, they had only been planning, with Jaramogi, Masinde Muliro and others, how to establish an opposition party, which later crystallised into the formidable Forum for the Restoration of Democracy (Ford).

In those days we used to go to the Toronto Reference Library located at Bloor and Yonge streets, to read Kenyan newspapers. Although they were delivered two weeks late, it was still a delight to read them. I got more immediate news from the BBC World Service, especially its Insight and Dateline Africa programmes. But the BBC only reported on major news; the newspapers filled us in on everything reported. So, I was surprised to read the headline story of the *Daily Nation* of April 28, 1989, attributed to Bishop Alexander Kipsang' Muge and Bishop David Gitari, claiming that they had met two men in Toronto in the late autumn of 1988, "who said they were *Mwakenya* operatives".

I wasn't surprised that Muge and Gitari might have met men who claimed, truthfully or falsely, that they belonged to *Mwakenya.* Indeed there were then Kenyans in Toronto who openly admitted to having belonged, worked with or to still be members of *Mwakenya.* What was shocking was the statement by Muge that he had "immediately contacted top government security officials and briefed them after the meeting," and that he had "handed over a scary subversive literature to a government emissary sent to collect them from him in London on his way back". That was most bizarre; that a church minister would "secretly" meet Kenyans claiming to belong to a movement that professed its aims and objectives to include the liberation of Kenya from dictatorship and then – five months after the alleged "secret" meeting – the minister would address a press conference to disclose that he had acted as a government agent during and after the said meeting, was astonishing. Firstly, why did it take Muge and Gitari five months to openly admit to their clandestine rendezvous? Secondly, were the two clergy confessing that they were now working as security agents for the Moi regime? And thirdly, Muge in particular, claimed that,

> … as a Christian, a pastor and an ex-police officer and as a bishop, for that matter, I took all the precautions before meeting the said men. I contacted the government officials back home and informed them of the people I was about to meet for discussions. I was given the green light. I met the two men in Toronto and indeed they turned out to be members of *Mwakenya* who found their way to Canada through Tanzania…The two men revealed that there were seven subversive groups, that *Mwakenya* was the umbrella organisation and that the seven have agents here in Kenya. They also pointed out that some of the neighbouring countries have promised a lot of support to overthrow the Government of Kenya by violent means and that there is a contingent of Kenyans being trained in Libya for this purpose. They also told me that the rampant killings of wild animals in Tsavo National Park at that time were part of their campaign and that the group behind the said killings was under the command of a Mr Hussein, who works for the British Broadcasting Corporation in London… The two

> gentlemen gave me a lot of subversive literature. Some were on programme on how and when to take certain actions against the legally elected Government of Kenya. [sic]

Muge alleged that it was apparent that *Mwakenya* had assumed that he was one of them as the group had "opened the whole file" to him. He said the subversive groups were spread out in the US, Canada and Western Europe. "They gave me very scaring things [sic]," Muge said. "I rang the government to tell them I would not bring these home. And they agreed to send a fore-runner to meet me in London to collect the documents."

Muge's behaviour struck me as deeply immoral. He hadn't had to meet the "*Mwakenya* men". He could simply have declined the men's request to meet him. But even having met them, there were no justifiable reasons why he played along only to report the *Mwakenya* men to the government. That was tantamount to entrapment. Moreover, by this reckless act, it was likely that Muge had endangered the lives of innocent family members, relatives, friends and colleagues of the two men. And why had Muge taken the so-called subversive literature only to turn it over to the government? Why would a bishop conscript himself as a government security agent? Moreover, why would the men have confided in Muge unless he had misled the men into believing that he was either sympathetic to them or that he was actually a member of *Mwakenya*?

Being a church minister is supposed to be a higher calling. Having been a policeman didn't mean that Muge had to continue serving the state (or its interests). He had many heroic examples of Latin American liberation theologists who openly and actively opposed repressive regimes and worked in solidarity with groups whose raison d'être were similar to *Mwakenya's*. Gitari's silence in the face of such treachery was equally instructive. Bishop Muge's heroic acts and summons came much later after, in my view, irreparable damage had been done. I concede that Muge's position and activities towards the end of his life were redemptive. However, for me, they never completely removed the moral stain he had gratuitously painted on himself.

The Muge/Gitari story caused consternation among the Kenyan exile community in Toronto. It took me a very long time before I could interact with fellow Kenyans without feeling suspicious. In a way, many of us became a bit paranoid; always looking over our shoulders.

Certainly this incident reflects the paranoid bunker mentality in Nairobi at the time. Moi was feeling the pressure from all fronts. He was receiving round condemnation from the international community for human rights violations.

Political activists based in Kenya and abroad were also getting increasingly emboldened, more creative and determined. The world media and human rights organisations were continually exposing Moi's excesses. Suddenly on June 1, 1989 Moi made an "amnesty offer" to all political exiles, beseeching them to return home. He added that they needed to apologise to him and he would grant them pardons. That did it for me; that the autocrat who had subjected Kenyans to untold suffering could have the temerity to demand apologies from his victims, before they could return to a country that was still under one-party dictatorship, was too much to bear. I instantly unleashed a long broadside on Moi, challenging his amnesty declaration and demanding to know what crimes we had committed.

I wrote that: "First, we would like to state categorically that we have committed no offence to warrant any kind of pardon, least of all from a dictator like Moi. Moi's hands are dripping with the blood of innocent Kenyan patriots who have perished in the notorious police dungeons like the 'slaughter houses' of Nyayo House, Nyati House and Kamiti Maximum Prison. We view Moi's political gimmick as yet another populist ploy from the increasingly isolated KANU minority regime to deflect attention from the grave socio-economic crisis within the country and to refurnish its battered image internationally..."

"There are sinister manoeuvres in these seemingly conciliatory gestures...It is our belief that this is part of a wider scheme of arm-twisting and pressurising countries that gave refuge to Kenyans to abandon their international human rights obligations under the pretext that the 'country conditions have changed'. Even as we write, there are over 60 political prisoners still languishing in Kenyan dungeons of death. At this very moment, there are thousands of innocent Kenyans being subjected to physical, mental and psychological torture among other cruel, degrading, inhumane and unusual treatment by the Moi regime. The 'swimming pools' at both Nyayo House and Nyati House where simulated drowning are inflicted on political detainees are in full operation. It is no longer a secret that all independent Kenyan publications are either banned or viciously censored to the point where nothing gets published unless the Office of the President approves..."

I pointed out that there was no evidence that Moi was becoming less dictatorial or less repressive. On the contrary, less than three weeks prior to the amnesty declaration, high ranking government officials were publicly calling for the arrest and detention of the regime's perceived Moi opponents who had just been released from detention. These demands were being made because some of the released political detainees had disclosed that they had been tortured while in detention. "It would therefore require an extraordinary degree of naïvety on our part for us to believe that Moi's amnesty offer is sincere. The onus is on Moi to prove to all Kenyans and the rest of the world that the 'amnesty offer' is both genuine and unconditional". And for us to determine that the offer was genuine, I listed ten conditions that Moi needed to satisfy. They were:

(a) That all political prisoners that were still being held be released immediately and unconditionally.

(b) That section 2A that made Kenya a de jure one party state be repealed immediately so that Kenyans could exercise their right to form and belong to political parties or associations of their choice.

(c) That Moi should admit that the 1988 "queue voting" exercise was a massively rigged travesty and was a system inimical to free, fair and transparent elections. In that regard, we demanded the nullification of the 1988 election results and fresh credible elections on the basis of a secret ballot of one-person-one vote be conducted.

(d) That an independent inquiry by reputable international human rights organisations and respected religious leaders be set up to investigate the human rights violations in the country. In particular, that the former student leader Titus Adungosi's death be investigated and all responsible for his death and all the other violations of human rights be severely punished.

(e) That the government must forthwith stop harassing, intimidating and mistreating former political prisoners.

(f) That the government should immediately cease the 'genocidal' policies being carried out in northern Kenya against the Pokot, Somali and other nationalities who inhabit the area. The massacres of innocent civilians by Kenya's security forces in those areas, where there had been a perpetual state of emergency, should stop.

(g) That the government ban on publications such as *Beyond* and *The Financial Times* should be lifted and that all forms of censorship should cease.

(h) That the government should halt the International Monetary Fund's austerity measures which has led to increasing privatisation of education and health services and resulted in thousands of Kenyans being rendered jobless and many indigenous firms collapsing.

(i) Those hostile policies of the Moi regime against neighbouring countries like Uganda, Sudan and Somalia must stop.

(j) Finally, we appealed to countries that were providing financial aid, grants or loans to the Moi regime to link any such 'assistance' to Kenya's human rights record.

Obviously, we knew that Moi wouldn't accept any of these demands. We weren't making them because we expected compliance. They were being made to expose the hollowness of Moi's amnesty offer. Our demands were made as a petition and delivered to all western governments, media, and human rights organisations and submitted to the Kenyan media as well. It worked. Almost without exception, no western country, media organisation or human rights group swallowed Moi's bait. The exile community treated the amnesty call with the contempt it deserved. In fact, some of the political prisoners he had released like Raila Odinga, Mukaru Ng'ang'a and Al-Amin Mazrui voted with their feet and fled into exile.

Politically, as well as co-founding and chairing the Committee for Democracy in Kenya, I had also joined the African Liberation Organisation in Toronto. Among the exile community, we were trying to establish a unified and pro-democracy organisation in order to push for the repeal of section 2A and the reintroduction of multi-party politics in Kenya. We had had a successful meeting of "patriotic and progressive Kenyans" in Toronto from June 30 to July 3, 1989. The idea was to reignite the "Kenya National Movement" dream we had had while still in Kenya. We actually launched the movement at the end of that conclave and sent out a three-page communiqué to the international and Kenyan press. Among some of the groups we worked closely with were the *All Africa Revolutionary Peoples Party* led by the late Kwameh Toure (formerly Stockley Carmichael, now deceased) and the Toronto-based *Black Action Defence Committee* (BADC) led by the dean of black activism in Toronto those days, Dudley Laws (also now deceased). Some of the prominent leaders of BADC were the veteran lawyer Charles Roach, teacher/poet Lennox Farrell and teacher/activist/politician Zanana Akande.

Charles Roach was an interesting person. Apart from being the leading African-Canadian lawyer (though born in Trinidad and Tobago before immigrating to Canada as a young man), Roach was also a poet, writer, painter, calypso artist and piano player of note. He was the only person I knew that steadfastly insisted that he wouldn't take up Canadian citizenship until Canada became a republic. His argument was that taking up Canadian citizenship meant that he had to swear an oath of allegiance to Her Majesty Queen Elizabeth II, a person who represented an empire that had enslaved his people and brought them to the Caribbean. He could become a citizen, he argued, if the oath was changed to remove all reference to "Her Majesty", or the "Crown", or the "Queen", or "Regina". Roach filed one constitutional challenge after another, losing a string of them but not giving up.

Roach had actually set precedents of sorts in the early 1960s. There was a condition then that one had to be a citizen to be admitted to the Bar of Ontario. Roach and others challenged that successfully and that restriction was removed. But then there was reference to the "Queen" and "Crown" in the oath of admission. Roach successfully challenged that as well and he took a special oath that omitted all reference to "Her Majesty". It was that struggle that Roach was continuing to wage by the time I arrived in Canada. He was constantly on the news; picketing, demonstrating, filing challenges and arguing before all levels of tribunals and judicial system. Meanwhile, his practice was thriving. African-Canadians and other "people of colour" thronged his law firm with cases. He was rightly considered a 'defender' of the rights of all non-Caucasian people, especially that of African-Canadians. Interestingly, Roach himself could pass as a Caucasian; he was a product of an interracial relationship. But he deliberately chose to identify with and fight the cause of Africa. In fact, Roach was the first pan-African non-continental African I had met. He soon became my mentor.

I had also maintained contact with a number of fellow university students back in Kenya. In late November 1989, I received a letter from my former classmate at the University of Nairobi, Samuel Abonyo. Abonyo's letter was written and mailed in Dar-es-Salaam, Tanzania where he was seeking asylum with another former student, Dennis Oduor. Oduor had been studying law. Abonyo and Oduor had been readmitted following our expulsion. However, on February 5, 1988, they were suddenly summoned to a Special Senate Disciplinary Committee and handed expulsion letters. They were accused of having attempted to "conceive, design and effect a scheme or strategy whose object or logical consequence is to disrupt the due operation of academic programmes" at the University. They were specifically accused of having participated in an alleged gathering at the University sports grounds between 11.30pm and 12.20am between February 3 and 4, 1988; and that between January 23 and 25 they had "participated in two illegal meetings as a result of which two anonymous circulars were prepared and published with the intention of discrediting the University administration and cause disenchantment and disaffection between the students and their chancellor". The "chancellor" was Moi.

Abonyo and Oduor had fled to Tanzania before they could be arrested. Unfortunately, the Tanzanian government had declined to help them. They had subsequently applied for asylum to Canada through the UNHCR, but the Canadians had rejected them under the pretext that they will "find it hard to fit into the Canadian society". I guess they had filled their annual quota of Africans! Apparently, they had foiled an attempted abduction in Dar by some Kenyan security agents and sought refuge at the Swiss and Japanese embassies respectively. Abonyo had sent me an eight-page handwritten letter on legal sized paper and attached copies of their expulsion letters from the University of Nairobi. Immediately I received Abonyo's distressing letter, I typed a two-page "Urgent Action" appeal to Amnesty International in the UK. At that time, my contact at the Amnesty International was a Mr Hill, Northeast Africa Research Section. Luckily, Mr Hill acted fast and both Abonyo and Oduor were given asylum in Norway where they eventually settled.

Hardly a week had passed when I received another call of distress from a former Onjiko schoolmate who had joined the University of Nairobi a year after me, Onyango Ogango – the young man who had retrieved my personal effects after our abductions and detentions. He, too, had been summarily expelled. Unlike Abonyo and Oduor, he had fled to Uganda. He was also desperate for asylum. Once more, I cranked up my typewriter and appealed for help, even managing to insert $10 inside an aerogramme letter to him in Kampala. And like Abonyo and Oduor, Ogango got asylum in Norway where he settled. During that period, I also sent Canadian tourists to Kaberere. Thereafter the two of us renewed our friendship. It was then that I learnt from Kaberere that he had also tried fleeing through Uganda but the Ugandan authorities had ended up placing him in custody for months before releasing him. Buke, too, had faced the same fate when he crossed into Uganda. They had both returned to Kenya crestfallen. Fortunately for Kaberere, he later successfully petitioned the University of Nairobi for readmission and completed his medical studies – more than ten years after our inhumane expulsions.

By year-end, my grades were top-notch. I had nearly completed the requirements for the award of a bachelor's degree. And I was gearing up to go for further studies. So, I quietly submitted applications for admission to Master of Philosophy programs at Oxford, Cambridge and Sussex, with a provision of a progression to their PhD programs. I approached my teachers for letters of recommendation that were to be sent directly to the respective graduate school's admission departments. Professors Esberey and Manzer sent off their recommendations within days. But Prof. Hutchful seemed reluctant. I found that surprising. After one week of waiting, I went over to his office to remind him that I was still waiting for confirmation that he had forwarded the letter. Instead of confirming, Hutchtful invited me to his home the following Sunday. He insisted he just wanted me to spend that day with him so that we could chat.

On the appointed day, I arrived at Prof. Hutchful's home at about 11am. I found him reading the day's newspapers on his porch. He invited me inside the house where I met his wife and children. And after the usual pleasantries, he asked me into his study. It was wall-to-wall with books, magazines and journals. I had hardly sat, when he began:

"Miguna, look at me. I want you to have a good look at me. What do you think of me? Do you think I am a successful happy professor, hmm?"

"B…but…but Professor, you are; aren't you?" I asked.

"No!" He boomed.

"What do you want to do after your studies?" he asked.

"Well, I am planning to go to Oxford or Cambridge or Sussex to do my graduate studies in politics after which I would like to teach at the university level." I replied.

"Teach what?" he boomed again. But before I could respond, he continued.

"That's why I invited you here. I have seen your application. You want to go to England to do your graduate studies. You want to teach…to end up like me! Well, I have a suggestion for you; just a suggestion. You are a very good student. You have a good analytical mind; just the way I was at your age. So far, you are way ahead of everyone in your class. I have spoken with your other teachers and they say the same thing. You are good with words also. I think you can make a good lawyer. I am not telling you not to go and do your graduate studies in England or anywhere else for that matter. I am not asking you not to teach at the University if that's what you want. All I am saying is that you should reconsider the sequence of how you want to do all those things. I want you to consider applying for law school. You will make it. Yes, people fail in LSAT but I'm sure you will pass. After law school, you may decide to practise law for a few years before going for your PhD in politics. That way you will have more choices than I have had. If things were reversed and I was in your position right now, that's what I would do. OK? Think about it. Meanwhile, I will send your letter to those English schools tomorrow. You may think that I am comfortable because I have this small house and teach at U of T, but you are mistaken. Look at all my white colleagues there – even those who have no PhDs and haven't published as much as I have; they are either tenured or they have better packages than I do. Imagine, I've been teaching here for the past ten years with more than five acclaimed books, one even recommended by this very university for their PhD students, yet I have no tenure. I don't want you to go through what I'm going through. I care about you. I want you to have options I don't have because I didn't have someone like me – like you do now – to advise me."

We later ate lunch and discussed politics, racism and discrimination before I went back.

That's how I ended up at Osgoode Hall Law School. Since arriving in Canada, the idea of becoming a lawyer hadn't entered my mind. I received admission at all three English universities, but only Cambridge and Sussex gave me some small financial assistance. I tried applying for the Commonwealth Scholarships but I wasn't successful. I subsequently shared with Joanne what Prof. Hutchful had told me. She seemed to agree with Hutchful. Even though I hadn't studied for the LSAT, we decided that I should give it a try. I picked up the application forms and Joanne paid the fee with her credit card.

* * * * * * * * * * * * * *

The summer of 1990 was historic in my life. I had a first class degree in my pocket and an admission letter to the most prestigious law school in Canada. I had also received my permanent residence status, without which admission to law school would have been out of the question. I had now lived in Canada for two years. I was fairly well known at the U of T, in the media as a regular commentator on social issues, and within the African-Canadian community as an outspoken critic of racism. As such, I had been on the periphery of an ongoing demonstration against an exhibition of African artefacts at the Royal Ontario Museum (ROM), which had been marketed as "Into the Heart of Africa".

On the face of it, there wasn't really anything wrong with the exhibit: they were actual historical artefacts, mostly pillaged from Africa during the missionary and colonial incursions. The main problem with them was that they depicted (out of context) a period in Africa's history far removed from 1990. There were pickets outside, which led to the arrests of 11 protesters, charged with assaulting police officers. ROM also sought and obtained an injunction restraining all demonstrations against the exhibition. The court appearances and ensuing trials for the group labelled the ROM 11 ignited further confrontations. While some of the protestors went for plea bargains, others argued that it was they who had been assaulted, not just by the "racist" Toronto police officers, but also by the "racist" society who had the audacity to portray Africans as primitive.

Suddenly, one could clearly see the divisions among the communities in Toronto. The façade of a multicultural society was rupturing. Matters were made worse by an article published in the *Globe & Mail* newspaper supporting the ROM by Philip Rushton, a University of Western Ontario professor, whose research and writings have led to frequent accusations of unrepentant racism.

That did it. More protests were organised. At this point, I attended a few of the pickets, but to me they seemed ineffective. I also had problems with the fact that although we had made a lot of noise about the "racist" exhibition and museum, none of us seemed to have seen it, so we couldn't be coherent or authoritative in our criticisms. Speaking from a position of ignorance wasn't something I was good at. So, I suggested two things, both of which were adopted by the protest's organisers. Firstly I suggested that we needed a counterweight to Prof. Rushton – another scholar who could provide a coherent position on why the exhibit was anachronistic. I suggested Professor Molefi Kete Assante, the author of the popular book, *Afrocentricity,* then based at Temple University in the US.

Next, I suggested that we shouldn't treat the confrontation as a "one off", that we needed a systematic and well planned intellectual engagement with racists. Consequently, I suggested that we invite Ngugi wa Thiong'o, then teaching and living in Boston, to visit and give a lecture in Toronto. That's how I met Prof. Assante that summer. It was also how I ended up convening, and playing the role of master of ceremonies for the *African Liberation Day* event in Toronto that August. It was to be the first time I had met Ngugi.

Because the African Liberation Day was being organised by a loose and informal group of individuals and organisations, the Convener and his residence became the "organising" body. We rented the hall from the City of Toronto. To get funds for Ngugi's air fare, honorarium and to be able to provide refreshments and entertainment during the event, we sold entry tickets, solicited donations and sold soft drinks during the Caribana festival. Unfortunately, only Gerald Pokhobye, one of the ROM 11, helped me hawk the soft drinks; literally on our shoulders.

Ngugi lived up to his billing; he thrilled the audience with his concise, clear and candid exposé of the diabolical western systems – class stratified, racist, exclusionist, alienating, exploitative and inhumane. His lecture placed the African worldview and perspective at the centre of modern intellectual thought. In person, Ngugi presented as a modest, humble, simple and down-to-earth man. He was soft spoken, listened keenly and responded precisely. He was inquisitive and observant, making comments whenever necessary. He also had a good memory – not surprising from such a behemoth of a writer. He had travelled the world – literally. Asked how he managed to travel around the world without a Kenyan passport in view of the fact that, until then, he hadn't been known to have acquired any other country's nationality, Ngugi answered me matter-of-factly: "I've always used a Ghanaian passport." Clearly, there was no need for the artificial colonial boundaries, was there?

But on the day Ngugi was leaving, the people who were taking collections at the entrance disappeared with the money. Even others who were selling refreshments couldn't be traced. The sales Gerald and I made at *Caribana* amounted to less than $100. Yet we had promised Ngugi $2,500 honorarium. Luckily, the return air ticket had been paid for. I explained the situation to Ngugi and we agreed that I would try to trace our people and hopefully send him the funds within days of his return. Ngugi expressed his understanding and flew back. A few days later when his publicist contacted me to ask for the money, I hadn't received a dime from the people who were supposed to give me the gate collections. I telephoned Ngugi and disclosed my predicament. Regrettably, Ngugi wanted his money; he didn't care that I was a refugee struggling to pay my own way through law school. Eventually, I depleted my meagre savings and sent Ngugi his honorarium. That was another valuable lesson learnt: people espousing revolutionary rhetoric won't necessarily practice what they preach.

The admission letter from Osgoode Hall had indicated that all first year law students were expected for orientation during the last week of August. Classes would start in the first week of September. But I had a few personal issues to sort out. The first one was Joanne. What was I going to do? Would I commute to and from Osgoode Hall or was I going to live on or near campus? What about our relationship; was it heading somewhere or we had reached a cul-de-sac? Since it became apparent that I was determined to move out so as to be near the law school, we had started arguing. Joanne rightly felt that now that I was going to law school – thanks in large measure to her generosity – I wanted to "abandon" her. That was most unfortunate because I truly loved and cared about Joanne. The only problem was that I had to make a decision that was good for both of us. I wasn't going to change my mind about joining law school that September. Postponement – which is what Joanne initially suggested – was out of the question. I was aware that once I "settled down" and became comfortable, it would be near impossible to continue with my university studies. Once you are encumbered by mortgages, loans and children, those ivory towers seem less alluring.

I was also conflicted. For the two years we had been together, Joanne had been extremely supportive, loving and caring. In fact, truth be told, it is difficult to imagine how I would have managed to complete my studies in such record time and with such good grades without her support. But I also faced many challenges. A lot of African and Caribbean students 'violently' disapproved of our relationship. Most of it was out of sheer ignorance, 'reverse' racism or green envy. But there were a few who had genuine 'reasons' and 'legitimate' concerns. Racism was still rife in Canada. Was I ready to bring children into this world who would be subjected to gratuitous taunts, bullying, insults and all kinds of unfair treatment because they happened to be products of a mixed-race relationship? How about my decision that I would 'soon' return and settle in Kenya? More profoundly, how about my decision – strange as it might sound for many people – that I wanted to retire, die and be buried in Kenya?

We broke up, first slowly, then gradually, then permanently. Joanne did her LSAT, passed and was admitted to study law at the University of Calgary, her home city. In the autumn of 1990, she moved there – permanently. We would talk on the phone, and for a few months she visited during her school holidays, but that was it. We both knew that the long-distance relationship couldn't work. The relationship had died.

* * * * * * * * * * * * * *

I moved to the graduate residence at Osgoode Hall Law School in October that year, where I would live until I graduated with an LLB degree in June 1993. My CDK colleague, Willy Mutunga, was also there. He lived at 8 Assiniboine, which was next to my apartment at 6 Assiniboine.

To survive and pay my tuition at Osgoode Hall Law School, I took up three jobs. First, Professor Toni Williams, the one black teacher in the Osgoode Faculty, was kind enough to appoint me her research assistant. Toni taught Law and Economics and Urban/Municipal Planning law. I would crawl through the Osgoode and main York libraries in search of old municipal maps, planning manuals and archaic monographs. There were times I would read about banking, finance and stock market. These weren't my areas of intellectual interest. But I needed the job, the experience and ultimately, I needed to pay my tuition. I am forever grateful to Prof. Williams for having given me a chance. I hope that she found my contributions to her research projects invaluable.

The second job was as a researcher at the Race and Ethnic Relations office at York University. I reviewed cases of discrimination against students either by teachers or the university administration. I made inquiries. I researched the applicable policies, regulations and legislation. I consulted the Canadian Charter of Rights and Freedoms. I then analysed the evidence and the facts before making recommendations for possible resolutions. In addition, I also made recommendations on how the race and ethnic relations policies could be reformed or changed. The director of the Centre was called Chet Singh. He was a great guy. He was supportive; always encouraging me and offering solace.

My third job wasn't formal, though it was the one I really felt passionate about. I've always engaged in writing, primarily as a means of changing the environment and society in which I live. Since secondary school, I've written thousands of letters to editors, articles, poems, essays and more recently, I've written books. Writing is in my DNA. I like ideas. I also love intellectual debates. There is nothing I enjoy more than reading and writing. Through writing, I provoke discussion over important issues of the day. I am a typical iconoclast. I hate totems and myths, especially those intended to protect unfair, unjust and unequal status quo. Throughout my life, I have arrogated myself the role of a myth buster. Perhaps the only other things I relish in equal measure are music and political campaigning for truth and justice. Everywhere I have studied, worked or lived, I have always associated, affiliated and worked with progressive elements and forces to bring about a just society. I'm extremely passionate: once I focus on something, I rarely let go. So, while at Osgoode, I quickly decided to use my writing to earn a modest sum. Apart from the few dollars writing placed in my pocket, it was also intellectually and socially stimulating. People took my work, which appeared regularly in *The Toronto Review of Contemporary Writing Abroad* very seriously, which was a needed morale booster.

From October 1990, for the three years I studied for my LLB degree, I had a popular weekly column in the Osgoode Hall Law School student newspaper, the *Obiter Dicta.* In order to highlight what I perceived as racist tendencies at Osgoode, I provocatively called my column "Disgraceful Osgoode". Subsequent instalments would bear numerical monikers – "Disgraceful Osgoode II", "Disgraceful Osgoode III", et cetera. The column made me very popular with a section of the York University population; but it also equally made a few others loathe me with a passion. A group of extreme right wing students even formed a new association called the "Objectivists" to counter my views.

The other non-curricular activity which gained me some notoriety during my time as a student at Osgoode, even beyond its hallowed walls, was my role in a protest against the Metro Toronto Chief of Police, William McCormack, addressing Osgoode students about "ethnic relations" in the city. I had co-founded an organisation called the Pan African Law Society (PALS) to oppose racist and discriminatory practices at the school. These were in admissions, hiring, retention and promotion of employees including teachers. At a minimum, we were demanding that Prof. Toni Williams be given tenure and two more professors "of colour" be hired. We wanted the number of African Canadian students to be increased to reflect their demographic representation in the Canadian society, which was about five per cent Canadian.

We knew that many African Canadian students were applying but were being excluded due to stringent GPA and LSAT score requirements. PALS made recommendations for an evaluation based on everything including background, life experiences, work experience, progressive record of overcoming adversities and academic potential. Our aim was to create an awareness of all forms of systemic and institutional racism. Specifically, we exposed "hidden" institutional forms of racism in the syllabi, the examinations, the teaching methods and in the way scholarships and other awards were given at the school.

PALS petitioned both the Osgoode administration and the York University senate. We lobbied for a course at Osgoode specifically dealing with the experiences of Africans starting from slavery, emancipation, the civil rights movement, up to and including the way the western legal regimes treated them in their so-called "modern democratic states". This would cover the civil rights movement and its impacts on the western society in general and on the institutions of power, including the judiciary, in particular. In addition, such a course would have sections dealing with how racist laws had been used to isolate, alienate, degrade and inflict abuse.

We were in the midst of those intricate and delicate negotiations with both York and Osgoode when the Osgoode Hall Italian Cultural Society invited McCormack. Our feeling was that the invitation was a provocative act intended to scuttle the ongoing negotiations. A year before McCormack's visit, an African Canadian man suffering from disability called Donaldson had been shot and killed by Metro Toronto police officers. Following an outcry by the African Canadian community over this death, McCormack and other senior police officers had been reported to have reassured the "black community" that there had been no foul play in the shooting. However, investigations soon revealed that one police officer had used excessive force. He was charged and prosecuted. Yet when the officer was acquitted – as they always were – the media reported that McCormack was among those who had celebrated his acquittal.

In 1989, Metro Police officers shot and killed an African Canadian teenager called Wade Lawson. The Chief of Police and many of his officers had implied that the murdered teenager had got what he deserved for dangerous driving of a stolen vehicle.

Before the end of 1989, Sofia Cook had been shot and left permanently paralysed by Metro Toronto police officers. She had been a passenger in a stolen vehicle. The Toronto Police Services Board had suspended the officers who had shot her on full pay and benefits.

Another African Canadian casualty was 16-year-old Marlon Neal, shot in the back while allegedly speeding. And what did McCormack do? At first he tried to "quell" the anger of the African Canadian community in Toronto by accusing it of lacking "proper leadership". Later, he promised "thorough investigations". When investigations concluded, the responsible police officer was only charged with "misuse" of a firearm. This was a misdemeanour. The charge of "attempted murder" was only instituted following three months of relentless demonstrations and pressure from the African Canadian community for the officer to be charged with an appropriate offence. And as if to prove to us that the Canadian legal system wasn't for Africans, this officer was later acquitted. McCormack and a few of his officers later blamed the community of being "responsible for a disproportionate number of crimes and victims of drug addiction".

From June 25, 1988 when I arrived in Toronto to the date of McCormack's visit to Osgoode, more than 20 African Canadian youth had been felled by the Toronto police in questionable circumstances. Yet, in each case, the culprits hadn't been punished. So, on March 13, 1991 when McCormack came to Osgoode, there was palpable tension. As McCormack was preparing to mount the rostrum to begin his address, the Moot courtroom thundered with music. It was reggae! Bob Marley was thundering: "Stand up, stand up! Stand up for your rights!"

McCormack stood like a statue; speechless. No one except PALS members made any movement. In a split second, we had taken over the room: raising placards, waving pamphlets and shouting: "The racist metro police force… murderers!! Murderers! Murderers! Where is Sofia Cook? Where is Marlon Neal? Where is Donaldson? Where is Wade Lawson?"

Our *Operation McCormack Out* made headlines around the country. *The Globe & Mail,* the *Toronto Star* and the *Toronto Sun* – the largest circulation newspapers in Canada – published screaming headlines about 'McCormack's humiliation at Osgoode'. That was good for our cause. If it was just the *Sun* reporting, many would have dismissed it as 'tabloid sensationalism'; but not when it was the prudish, starchy, self-important and venerable old lady of Canadian journalism – *The Globe & Mail.*

Soon, I started receiving interview requests from the national Canadian press. I was also interviewed by Naomi Klein who was then the editor of *The Varsity* – a U of T student newspaper. Naomi did an exclusive feature interview, which headlined in *The Varsity*. Canada's largest national newspaper, *The Toronto Star*, also did an interesting piece on the "next 40 most promising young leaders in Canada". They had young people – mainly university students from across Canada. I was the only one featured from York University; that gave me a bit of a spring in my steps and for a while kept the racist hounds at Osgoode at bay.

And Osgoode did respond to some of our demands. Soon after Prof. Williams was given full tenure. Two new courses dealing with race and racism were introduced. They covered the civil rights movement well. The following year, Osgoode hired an African professor, one Indian, and one Japanese. Over time, most Osgoode students began to understand that we weren't against white people; far from it. Our problem, as they came to appreciate, was racism – mainly the historical, systemic and institutional type.

Unfortunately, over the years, many African Canadian students have been chewed and spat out by racist teachers and administrators at all levels of the Canadian learning process. Many have dropped out in high school, their future destroyed. Others have managed to join the many colleges and universities only for their confidence and futures to be ruined by callous, uncaring and malicious teachers.

Michael – the only African Canadian student in my section at Osgoode – fell by the wayside in the second year. He had joined Osgoode with a high GPA and a decent LSAT score. Yet, barely two years in, he was deemed to be insufficiently intellectual. This would prove tragic for Michael. He didn't take it very well and drifted, losing his mental and psychological bearing in the process. Rather than use his excellent Bachelor of Arts degree to earn a living or pursue graduate studies, Michael went into a deep depression from which he never recovered (at least not that I was aware of). He lost his skills and became unemployable, drifting and wandering from one homeless shelter to the other, while trying to hide from people he knew who could have offered him solace, encouragement and assistance.

My friends Joma and Gerald would later go through the same debilitating experiences when they couldn't pass the Ontario Bar. They had both graduated from Osgoode. But strangely the Bar Admission Course suddenly became an obstacle to their otherwise bright futures. By the time I relocated to Kenya in 2007, Joma and Michael were still wandering Sufis in the Toronto shelters. After failing the Bar for the maximum number of times allowed, Gerald eventually returned to South Africa where I heard he later died. If for nothing else, I'm writing this book in their memory and in celebration of their lives and heroic struggles.

* * * * * * * * * * * * * *

In 1991, the Kenyan pro-democracy organisation that I coordinated in exile – CDK – organised three important events. First, we held a series of meetings with

Kenyans in Ontario that culminated in a communiqué issued on October 27, 1991. We made important demands, which the Kenyan media picked up and reported on. The second one was the visit by various pro-democracy opposition leaders like Gitobu Imanyara, Paul Muite, Raila Odinga, James Orengo and Prof. Peter Anyang' Nyong'o. In those days, Orengo, Nyong'o, Muite and Gitobu had more political and international gravitas than Raila. My friend Dotse Tsikatsa from Ghana helped me organise these events.

Gitobu was the first to visit, alone. This was after the fallout in Ford-Kenya. Gitobu, Muite and Leakey had formed Mwangaza Trust, then Safina. When I had a private chat with Gitobu, he told me something I still remember. He said that Raila was a dishonest and self-consumed hypocrite that he could never work with again. I was shocked. Those days, the Kenyan exile community – including myself – was desperately praying for the "opposition" to unite so that we could remove Moi faster. The more we heard or saw anything that exhibited or confirmed disunity, we coiled up in pain. So, I sought to know if there was absolutely nothing he or we could do to repair the damage. Gitobu fixed me with a piercing gaze and answered: "No. Nothing can be done to repair the relationship between me and Raila. He is a megalomaniac." That was Gitobu in the early 1990s. At the time, he was still publishing the *Nairobi Law Monthly*.

When Anyang' visited, it was Dotse Tsikatsa and I who accompanied him to Ottawa and introduced him to the then top leadership of the Liberal Party of Canada, including Jean Chrétien who would later become Prime Minister of Canada for three terms. Anyang', then, as now, struck me as intellectually sharp but without charisma, dynamism and strong commitments. He wasn't charming either. His lectures lacked wit. He had a silver tongue all right; but it emitted dry and withering words. He was knowledgeable of what other people had written centuries ago, but barely applied that learning to his immediate environment. I found him lethargic. At the end of his visit, Anyang' called me to find for him a lady who could take him "shopping". I dutifully introduced him to a nice Kenyan lady. And that was the last time I heard from him or saw him in Canada. The next time I met him would be in 2007 at Orange House. It gave me a glimpse of Anyang's priorities in life.

I never really engaged Raila. He was dozing off – or pretending to doze off – most of the time he visited. For instance, we had a lengthy meeting with the visiting Kenyan delegation of opposition leaders in my friend Obanda's apartment at York, yet Raila slept throughout the meeting. He never made a contribution. In the end, only Muite, Gitobu and Orengo made any sense.

Soon, my Osgoode sojourn came to an end but not without a final drama. I had managed to pass all the exams and met the academic requirements for graduation in June 1993 with my class. The only problem was that I hadn't cleared my tuition and therefore couldn't graduate. I owed the school $800. By then, I had completely exhausted all my savings. I couldn't borrow from a bank because I had no job or collateral. Nor did I have somebody to guarantee such a debt. There was no benefactor I could rely on. Prior to the completion of our final semester, I had applied and been offered a job as an articling student at the firm of *Roach, Schwartz and Associates* where Charles Roach was the management partner. But our articles could only start after we had graduated and completed the first six months of the Bar Admission course at the Law Society of Upper Canada.

To imagine that I had gone that far only to falter due to financial handicap sent me into temporary depression. I retreated into my apartment and refused to venture out much. I felt that I couldn't disclose this information to many except two of my closest friends, both female and both Osgoode students. One of them – Sheri – approached my favourite professor, Hutchinson, and told him what was happening. He in turn telephoned me. He first apologised for breaching Sheri's confidence and for butting in. He explained that he had already disclosed the nature of my problem to the then Dean Marilyn Pilkington, who had requested if I could meet her that afternoon.

Dean Pilkington had taught me evidence and criminal procedure. She was a fine and meticulous lawyer and scholar. She had a clinical approach to teaching; everything was lean, precise and to the point. She was also very dignified. But above all, she was a human being. Until then, she hadn't struck me as generous. That afternoon, Dean Pilkington explained to me some of the experiences in her life, her teenage close friendship with a Ugandan student and assured me that there was nothing to be ashamed of in my situation. She promised to keep whatever she was about to do strictly confidential due to the sensitive nature of people's financial circumstances. At the end of the meeting, she wrote me a personal cheque of $800 and had me sign a promissory note. She kept one original copy and I kept one. I undertook to pay her in the first month of my articles.

That's how I managed to graduate from Osgoode. And after my full month at *Roach, Schwartz and Associates* – and true to my word and honour – I sent Dean Pilkington a personal cheque of $800. However, being the epitome of human generosity, Dean Pilkington never cashed my cheque. That promissory note was both a humble cover and a way of ensuring that I treated her intervention seriously. I have forever been grateful to and respectful of Professor Marilyn Pilkington. I have also never forgotten Sheri's and Prof. Hutchinson's timely and sensitive interventions.

* * * * * * * * * * * * * *

From September, I began my articles of clerkship with *Roach, Schwartz &Associates*, in Toronto. I strategically found an apartment about 500 metres away which meant I could walk to and from work, saving me about $30 monthly.

My articling principal was Charles Roach. He was a very good lawyer. He was keen and passionate about his work. The firm was small compared to the large "factories of law" on Bay Street. There were four senior lawyers: Roach himself, Peter Rosenthal, James Willoughby and a semi-retired partner Schwartz. Despite his age (he must have either been in his late sixties or early seventies then), Roach reviewed each and every letter, pleading and submission we prepared, making corrections on grammar, spellings, case citations and arguments. Initially, there were times he would cross through large chunks of my work, sending me back to investigate the case, re-examine the cases and refine the pleadings. The daily taking of facts from different clients before dashing off to the court libraries or the U of T faculty of law library was tiresome in the beginning. However, as I got my hands dirty, so to speak, and got used to the grind, I enjoyed the work so much that some days I would stay at the firm until late at night. On many occasions, I would go to the office over the weekend and work for hours without end.

Peter Rosenthal was a full-time mathematics professor at the U of T. His practice as a Barrister and Solicitor with *Roach, Schwartz & Associates* was restricted to issues of social justice. He specialised and did only human rights and civil litigation cases. He did inquests of those killed by government authorities, especially by the Toronto police. He sued government authorities over human rights violations and abuses. He did judicial reviews of refugees and immigrants. He conducted numerous detention reviews. He represented civil society groups in challenging government decisions, legislation and orders. Rosenthal was passionate, brilliant and fearless. He must have been around Roach's age. I learnt a lot from him.

By then, I had become a well-known writer, cultural critic and prominent political activist in Toronto. And because Roach was the reigning dean of African/black activism in Ontario as well as a published poet and a well-known musician, there were days – mostly over the weekend – when the two of us spent hours discussing politics, poetry and music. Roach was into calypso and reggae while my musical taste was eclectic; I loved and enjoyed virtually all genre of music. We shared a libertarian streak as well. From the beginning, Roach didn't treat me as a typical student-at-law; he viewed me more as a colleague. In fact, he hadn't subjected me to the kind of interviews prospective students went through. When I appeared for the interview, Roach told me he had gone through my resume and decided to offer me the position. He didn't go round in circles like most employers. He didn't play games. He was straight forward and to the point. The year I spent at *Roach, Schwartz & Associates* was intellectually, artistically, politically and professionally stimulating and productive. This was the first and only employment environment where both my boss and I were soul mates.

When I wasn't busy researching and drafting pleadings and submissions, I was penning newspaper and journal articles and poems. I was also preparing notes for three books – one book of essays and two books of poetry. I had become a member of the Canadian Writers' Union, the League of Canadian Poets, PEN International and a group called "Writers Thru Race". The latter were "writers of colour" who belonged to the *Writers' Union of Canada*, but who felt that there were issues that affected them but which the bigger union had ignored.

I attended various writers' conferences, workshops and symposiums and engaged in lively debates on the role of the writers of colour in Canadian society, including within the *Writers' Union*. I also read my poetry and essays at a number of these colloquiums. Sometime in 1994, I started and coordinated a poetry reading group of African writers. This group eventually started an African journal called *African Voices*. Members included my good friends Beth Gebroyohannes and Yvonne Vera. This was before Yvonne became a world-renowned writer. The idea was to create a forum or institution that would mentor and encourage young African writers in Toronto.

By this time – thanks to Charles Roach – I had also become heavily involved in the Pan-African movement. So, in April 1994, Kiké Roach (Charles's lawyer daughter) and I travelled to Kampala, Uganda and attended the 7th Pan African Congress. At Pearson International Airport in Toronto, the US Customs and Immigration quizzed me for two hours over my alleged connections to the Palestinian Liberation Organization (PLO). I found that odd and told them so, asking why they would be concerned about my alleged membership of a group the western nations, including the US, had embraced. That was after the PLO's Yasser Arafat had been awarded the Nobel Peace Prize. They seemed fixated on a stopover I had made in Cairo, Egypt a few years before. They also wanted to know why we were flying through Chicago, then London, before heading to

Kampala. That was quite bizarre as our stopover in Chicago was for only five hours. The London stopover was longer – a full eight hours. But that wasn't my fault. The organizers of the conference had booked both Kiké's and my flights. We didn't choose which routes to take or which countries we would stop over. Moreover, they didn't interrogate Kiké; they were only focused on me. I knew then that I had been noticed. I was happy that my relentless pursuit of justice had been noted by the number one self-appointed world prefect.

Dr Tajudeen Abdul Raheem – the organizer of the 7th Pan African Congress in Kampala – had personally invited me. This was a historic gathering. It was being organised more than 30 years after the 6th Pan African Congress in Manchester, England. The 6th Congress had been organised by George Padmore and Kwameh Nkrumah. Other big names who had attended that Congress were Jomo Kenyatta and Sir Williams of Trinidad and Tobago. The theme of the 7th conference was: *Pan Africanism: Facing the Future in Unity, Social Progress and Democracy*. The motto of the conference was: *Africa Yetu! Organize, Don't Agonize!* These were apt reminders to the African youth, intellectuals and activists to stop their perennial lamentations, recriminations and sentimentalisms and to begin organising and mobilising themselves for change. The unity, liberation, democratisation and social progress of Africa weren't going to be brought through emotional outbursts. It needed hard-nosed strategies, tactics and unrelenting focus.

It was regrettable that it had taken more than 30 years for a follow-up congress and that the Kampala one was the first to be held in Africa. More than anything else, that was proof that lots of work needed to be done. It was also proof of how resilient imperialism and its forces of repression and exploitation were. Undoubtedly, the progressive arm of Pan Africanism of Kwame Nkrumah and George Padmore had lost out to the opportunists like Kenyatta and Kamuzu Banda. Now was the time to reconsolidate, expand and make gains. Just looking around the conference and having discussions with various delegates, I was aware that the task was daunting. I was startled by the open animosity and disdain Kwame Toure exhibited towards Dr Abdul Alkalimat. Both were delegates from the US. Both were African American. But they couldn't agree on anything, even on who was to speak on behalf of their delegation. The disagreement turned nasty and created chaos, which, as tiny as I was at the congress, I tried to mediate. I found Kwame Toure to be impulsive and unreasonable.

Then, of course, was the hodgepodge 'delegation from Kenya', with some from the US, Canada, Kenya, South Africa, et cetera. Intriguingly, I found Maina wa Kinyatti incoherent, illogical and quite frankly a pale shadow of what I expected him to be. He was incapable of communicating even in the most basic, simple English. He resorted to speaking with Ngugi in Gikuyu in the presence of other non-Gikuyu delegates. That was both shocking and extremely disappointing. I had held Kinyatti in very high esteem, until then. From then on, I began to view all his writing as artificial parody and pastiche in the greatest tradition of modern European mimicry, not worth spending anyone's time on. Unfortunately, I also found him to be paranoid, reclusive and ethnocentric. He kept glancing over his shoulders in Kampala in April 1994 – two whole years after the repeal of section 2A and the reintroduction of pluralism in Kenya. Kinyatti appeared perpetually in fear of some ubiquitous special branch officer who could pounce on him from nowhere any time. Unlike Ngugi and Micere Mugo, Kinyatti didn't give me the confidence I expected of a man of his stature and notoriety.

Tajudeen was a fiery, dynamic, razor-sharp and an original Pan African intellectual to the core. He walked proudly in his flowing Nigerian *agbada*, which he kept gathering with his left hand at intermittent moments, as if in some solemn ritual. He had a massive bushy beard and constantly had a pipe hanging from his lips. It gave him the old aura of an eminent African intellectual, which he was. Tajudeen also spoke fast and very loudly, punctuating his speeches with funny short laughter.

Tajudeen had invited all the major Pan African intellectuals and political heavyweights of the day. Graca Machel, Ambassador Thomson from Jamaica, Ngugi wa Thiong'o, Dr John Garang', Kwame Toure, Dr Abdul Alkalimat from the US, Mohammed Farah Aideed (then President of Somalia), Mohammed Abdulrahman Babu (the celebrated Tanzanian writer and thinker), Karim Essack from Tanzania, Maina wa Kinyatti (Kenyan exile in the US), Patrice Lumumba Jr. (then based in Germany). Delegates had travelled from all over the world: Cuba, Mexico, South Africa, Nigeria and Ghana. Unfortunately, leading Kenyan politicians did not attend. Neither did the opposition. It was the clearest indicator that no leading political actor in Kenya was a serious pan-Africanist.

That's when I met Atsango Chesoni, Tirop arap Kitur and Irungu Haughton. We were then in our twenties; idealistic and impatient. Ugandan President, Yoweri Museveni played host. The discussions were quite refreshing. But more importantly were the contacts we made. Before the end of the conference, I was given a chance to address the plenary on the role the young could play in shepherding the African revolution. After my 15 minute speech, I was invited to address a group of Ugandan youth at Kampala City Hall. On arriving there, I found both Atsango and Irungu had also been invited. Atsango and I gave short speeches and read our poetry to universal acclaim from the youth gathered there.

On April 6, 1994 – a day before the week-long conference ended, both the Rwandese President Juvenal Habyrimana and the Burundian President Cyprien Ntaryamira were killed in a plane crash near Kigali, precipitating the Rwandese genocide. Credible reports blame the Rwanda Patriotic Front militants, then headed by Paul Kagame, for the assassinations of the two presidents. And in my view, the situation wasn't helped by the casual manner in which Museveni announced the sad news to the conference. This, coupled with the fact that Museveni was not just a confidante of Kagame – the latter worked as his regime's head of military intelligence for years before leading the audacious incursion into Rwanda – left reasonable doubts in my mind as to his (Museveni's) innocence. Moreover, both Habyrimana and Ntaryamira were returning from a visit to Kampala. For me, the twin tragedy wasn't something I could put past Museveni. As subsequent events would attest Museveni's unbridled ambition to be the first president of a federated East Africa and his expansionist tendencies would be cited in both Dr John Garang's tragic helicopter crash as well as Laurent Kabila's assassination in Kinshasa.

Before Kiké and I headed back to Toronto, we did a rendezvous in Nairobi where I met my sisters and other relatives at my Cousin Awino Ong'or's Kenya Railway residence in Upper Hill. We arrived at night and departed at night, cautious that Moi's Special Branch could have struck again.

At the beginning of 1994, I published my first collection of poems, *Songs of Fire*. The book contains poems I had written from the time I attended the University of Nairobi up to 1994. By the end of that year, I had published my second book, *Disgraceful Osgoode and Other Essays*. Later that year, writers of colour belonging to the Writers' Union of Canada organised a conference called *Writing Thru 'Race'* in Montreal, Quebec. We had spent one whole year lobbying, pushing and cajoling the Writers' Union to recognise and fund our group. Eventually, it agreed, but with a caveat; that our meeting couldn't be exclusively for writers of colour. If we insisted – like we were doing – that Caucasian writers couldn't attend, then we had to forfeit the funding. We agreed, strategically, to accept the funding but intended to try to lock out writers with European backgrounds once the conference began. We thought it inconceivable that Caucasian writers would want to gatecrash our meeting. But when the conference began, the 'writers of colour' found ourselves outnumbered one-to-ten by white writers in the hall. We were astounded. Silvera Makeda who founded and headed Sister Vision Press in Toronto stood up and protested at "this insidious invasion of our space". She stated that she hated a situation where she had to justify to a bunch of white people why, as people of colour, we needed to meet alone and discuss amongst ourselves.

But Pierre Berton, a white veteran historian, would have none of it. With a loud quivering voice, agitated face and flailing hands, he lambasted us for "squandering" his money – contributions to the Writers' Union – organising racist, exclusive conferences to talk about nothing. He said we were all writers; it didn't matter what the colour of our skins were.

A few other whites spoke, more or less, in support of Berton's line of argument. There were counter arguments from writers of colour. A few liberal whites supported the conference as a breath of fresh air. When my turn came on the podium, I blasted Berton for his insensitivity. I pointed out that Europeans like him should feel ashamed for complaining about peanuts that had been "donated" to our conference from our taxes when for more than 500 years, they had used our labour to build their empires. I told the gathering that we weren't going to *beg* them to "*bring* the money and clout" to our cause as some had suggested we should do; we were going to "*take* the money and clout". There was a lot of commotion and jabbering. In the end, the *Writing Thru 'Race'* conference achieved nothing. The white writers refused to leave the hall. And in their presence, we couldn't discuss freely. They had managed to set the agenda and tone of the conference for us.

* * * * * * * * * * * * * *

When I finally cleared my Bar Admission Course and was placed on the roll of those to be admitted on February 16, 1995, I exhaled. I exhaled not just because I was exhausted and needed rest, which I wasn't going to have, because starting a new practice as an African immigrant who had gone straight to university without first settling down or integrating wasn't tantamount to 'taking a holiday'; I exhaled because I had used the previous six years of my student life thoroughly immersed in the political mire of Toronto. I had made a name for myself. Many openly acknowledged that I had, within a very short time, distinguished myself as fearless, analytical, progressive and an indefatigable activist. Not only had I participated in almost all political activities involving Africans/black people in Toronto – from political to artistic engagements – I had also published popular articles and books. In fact, many were surprised to learn that I had been studying law. They assumed I was a writer and an activist; not a lawyer.

I took my chances with a new practice even though Roach had been kind enough to offer me a job as an associate immediately I was called to the Bar. I needed to test my mettle. But another reason was money. I knew that if I opened my firm, the sky would be the limit. If I worked very hard, and got enough clients – even if they were only people of modest means on legal aid – I could easily earn more than $100,000 per year. Knowing my zeal and determination, I chose to go solo, and I never regretted the decision.

By then, I had met and started a relationship with a young beautiful woman called Tracey Wynter who would soon give me sparkling new children, Atieno and Biko. The journey had been long and turbulent. There had been treacherous terrain throughout, but I had triumphed.

In the course of 1995, I published two books: a book of poetry called *Afrika's Volcanic Song* and a novel called *Toes Have Tales*. Since graduating from Osgoode, I had managed to publish four books and hundreds of articles in reputable publications. Now, I could concentrate on my practice, try to make a small difference in the lives of the vulnerable and also make some money in the process. Despite everything else, I promised myself that I would become a successful lawyer.

Within three months, I had managed to purchase a vehicle, a two-year-old Buick Lessabré. And in October 1996 – less than two years after starting my practice – I purchased land and constructed a spiffy one-storey four-bedroom, three-toilet house in Bradford, Ontario. It was a lifetime achievement. I put a down cash payment of $30,000 and took out a mortgage of $209,000 from the Bank of Montreal. As a first-time home buyer, I didn't need collateral.

The decision to purchase my own house within such a short time of practice would turn out to be one of the best decisions I have ever made in my life. Every week on Fridays, I would drive to Bradford and inspect the progress of the construction. Within one month – on October 30, 1996 – the house was ready. I promptly took possession and Tracey, my first born Atieno and I moved in. Biko would come on December 4, the same year. Many people have never understood how I ended up living in an exclusive white suburb of 10,000, 65 kilometres from Toronto. Many detractors even started a rumour that I was trying to move away from the Kenyan community in Toronto. Well, let me explain the background to that move here.

When my daughter Atieno was born in July 1995, Tracey and I were renting a one-bedroom apartment at 199 Chatham Avenue in Toronto. I had just been admitted to the Bar. The apartment was small. My practice was growing fast. I was beginning to make good money. At the end of August, an estate agent showed me a beautiful three-bedroom house in Richmond Hill, which Tracey and I loved. We promptly put in an offer, which was just $3,000 shy of the asking price. We knew nobody else would make such an offer. It was the rule of thumb those days to deduct 10 per cent from any first offers in order to leave room for negotiation. But because resale houses were going like hot cakes in Richmond Hill that year, we didn't want to risk being gazumped. The vendor was supposed to respond to our offer within 72 hours or the offer would automatically lapse.

My real estate agent waited for a week without hearing back from the vendor's agent. That was very strange. Although houses in Richmond Hill were extremely popular with buyers; the Ontario real estate market wasn't overheated. Out of curiosity, he checked the listing to see if the house had been bought by someone else. He found it was still listed. Why hadn't they responded to our offer? He then placed a call to the vendor's real estate agent who told him that his client had decided to remove the listing. She no longer wanted to sell.

Stranger still. My agent had the feeling that the vendor had removed the house from the market so as not to have to sell it to a black man. The house was in a Jewish neighbourhood. Most people knew that in order to keep such neighbourhoods "pure", property owners deliberately refused to sell to "people of colour" especially Africans. They believed, wrongly, of course, that black people wouldn't maintain the standards of the neighbourhood and that that would result in their property values going down. Others also feared that once Africans or black people started buying property in the neighbourhood, white people would start fleeing, resulting in a sharp plummet in property value.

I was extremely angry and distressed but there wasn't anything I could do to redress the wrong. But the injustice made me have an unrestrained sense of urgency to purchase a house if only to prove to racists that they couldn't keep us down forever. So, on that Sunday, I drove from one new development to another, while keeping a northerly trajectory. I drove until I lost any sense of distance. When we reached Bradford at about 12.30pm and saw a nice announcement for a new development, I parked the vehicle and we went in. I signed the agreement of purchase and sale that day for a prime corner lot at 97 Dépeuter Crescent that would become my home until I relocated from Canada in September 2007.

Dépeuter Crescent would prove to be a quiet, genteel and interesting place to live on and raise a family. We were the only non-whites on the street. On the day we took possession the man opposite welcomed me with a crate of cold beer and a trolley of barbecued hamburgers. He was genuinely disappointed when I politely declined the drink. A few houses from ours, there lived a retired lady called Ann who made life on the crescent fun. She was very friendly to everyone. One interesting story she told and which stood the test of time was that women on the left side of the street gave birth only to girls while those on the right side gave birth only to boys. When my wife did a physical headcount she discovered that she was right. Her word would be confirmed again and again as women became pregnant and gave birth precisely in the order she had sketched, starting with my wife, whom she approached each time her tummy became visible with "another beautiful girl; I tell you that's another girl". I guess my son escaped her accurate predictions because he was conceived in Toronto before we moved. But I will never forget the lady.

Opening my law firm would provide an avenue for advocacy that had hitherto been restricted to two firms in Toronto. As soon as I placed my advertisement in the newspapers and the Law Society's and Legal Aid Ontario's "lawyer referral services", an avalanche of refugee, immigration, civil and criminal matters started pouring in. Many Africans/blacks who felt that their rights had been violated by government authorities be it the police, customs, immigration or city authorities, trooped to my office. I also did professional malpractice cases, especially against physicians and both against and for lawyers. Within two years, I had solidly established myself as a leading lawyer on actions against public authorities. My enviable record on refugee and immigration law was nearly one hundred per cent success rate.

That's not to say I didn't experience racism from judges, court administrators, court clerks or even fellow lawyers. I couldn't pretend that everything was rosy. Once, shortly after my call, I arrived at the Brampton courthouse and encountered an elderly white judge who was as obnoxious as he was ethnocentric:

Mr *Maunda*, something fell on your head!

Pardon me Your Honour?

Yes, there is something on your head!

Oh, Your Honour, it's religious.

Is it a *recognised* religion?

Your Honour, what do you mean by *recognised*?

Well, like Christianity or Jewish religion?

Your Honour, it is *Islam*. Isn't that *recognised*, too?

There was complete silence. You could hear a pin drop. After my last answer, the judge never uttered another word. Immediately my matter was disposed of, I was on Highway 401 heading back to the office, singing and whistling. No matter what racists tried, I refused to give up. Eventually, I decided to use my pen to fight back. I penned several probing and searing articles and poems in publications including the *Law Times*, *Lawyers Weekly*, *Share*, *Pride*, *The Globe & Mail* and the *Toronto Star*, as well as in the *Toronto Review of Contemporary Writing Abroad* in which I raised issues of systemic and institutional discrimination and good governance in the legal profession, in the justice system and in the Canadian society as a whole.

I subsequently published an article in the *Toronto Review of Contemporary Writing Abroad* and in *Elements of Essays: Patterns, Purpose, and Perspectives* (Toronto: Thomson Nelson, 2002), highlighting some anecdotes of egregious racism in the judicial system, including that incident at the Brampton Court. The article is now taught to Canadian high school English students.

> *Anecdotes of Racism: A View Across the Aisle*
> *Part I: Racist Thorns at the Gates of Injustice: A Biased Reflection*
> I slowly climb the stairs leading into the August House, the House so revered by most Canadians that one often will witness fright, genuine fright, and wobbly legs in many a soul so unfortunate as to be brought to it by members of the all powerful Metropolitan Toronto Police force and duly christened "an accused." As I reach the top of the first set of stairs, I turn right and take the elevators. The climbing feels good for my legs. But this is enough exercise for today. As the elevator chimes and comes to a brief halt, the doors open wide and I emerge, with a briefcase in hand and a stern face, I enter the tenth-floor Registry of the Superior Court of Justice (formerly the Ontario Court, General Division). I can hear my heart pounding, my chest moving up and down and small strings of sweat crawling lazily down my cheeks. I momentarily observe my protruding paunch and swear at myself for allowing my weight to become this bothersome. "It's either because I am overeating or it is due to lack of exercise," I say silently to myself. I try to rationalise by adding that the private practice of law requires too much reading and sitting down and I actually do not have time to exercise.
>
> Still smiling at my thoughts, I approach the Court Clerk, seated on a high stool looking important. I quickly retrieve the nicely bound Motion Record. I then immediately produce a cheque for $75.00 that I had written to the order of the Minister of Finance, Mr Paul Martin, as required, and wait for service. The Clerk looks briefly at me over her thickly rimmed glasses and sighs deeply. "She must be tired already," I think to myself, but say nothing. She suddenly turns and begins what appears to be an endless tap on her computer keyboard. "Hi." With my voice slightly quivering, I manage an embarrassing greeting. She ignores it and continues her laborious tapping. I continue to wait.

Occasionally, the Clerk answers the incessantly ringing telephone and engages in small talk. However, as soon as her conversations end, she continues her endless tapping on the keyboard without any discernible sign that she is aware of my presence right here in front of her. Finally, after thirty minutes (time that seems to me like a decade), I hear a growl:

"Yes! What can I help you with?"

Having resigned myself to what appeared as a long wait, I quickly stand at attention and stammer out my words…

"Ooh…I…I…I…I would like to file an ex parte motion, returnable on…"

"Wait, wait a minute!"

She cuts me in mid sentence, strongly waving me to stop what I am trying to say. Then she props her chin on her clenched fists, her knuckles reddish, and strained. She inquires:

"Do you have a LAWYER SIR?"

"I AM THE LAWYER," I answer back, firmly and deliberately.

Repressed anger begins to show on my face. I am slowly gaining my composure, my confidence. I am beginning to show my displeasure at this unnecessary discourtesy.

She quickly grabs the package I had placed on the counter before her and scans through it.

"Hmm…Hmmmm…Hmm…Yah…ya…" She hams her way through the document.

I can swear that she is planning to pull some trick, blame me for a missing comma, maybe a full stop. But I am sure there are no mistakes. Not even minor typographical ones. I had taken the trouble to spell-check and I literally read through every single word, line, sentence, and paragraph three times. I stand proudly and wait.

"Where is your affidavit of service sir?" she asks firmly but does not bother to wait for my answer before she continues.

"If you are really a lawyer then you must know that we can't accept any motion materials without proof of service…"

"But it is an ex parte motion madam. We are not required to serve ex parte motions," I manage a response and hope that my explanation will put this fishing expedition to an end. I am sure she has read the Rules of Civil Procedure and is aware that ex parte motions are a unique breed, allowing parties to bring an urgent motion on short notice without necessity of notifying the responding parties since the granting of such motions would not result in any injustice or serious prejudice to the other side. "She has to know that," I say silently, in a rage.

"Says who?" she shoots back, unabated.

"Well, if you must know, says the Rules of Civil Procedure," I reply.

We are clearly at a standstill. We have reached a point of no return.

"She does not want to accept my argument, not because it is illogical or baseless; she simply does not want to lose face," I think to myself once more.

"Show me which Rule says that SIR?" she is determined to push me to the wire.

"Subrule 37.01 of the Ontario *Rules of Civil Procedure* states that 'A motion shall be made by a notice of motion (Form 37A) unless the nature of the motion or the circumstances make a notice of motion unnecessary," I read aloud, exasperated.

"Clearly this Rule was intended for precisely the same set of circumstances as this one. The nature of this motion and the circumstances make service entirely unnecessary. Please take your time and read under our 'Grounds for the Motion' and you will see that we have been unable to contact the respondent. All our registered letters to him, sent pursuant to Subrule 16.06(1), have been returned by Canada Post unclaimed. Please read the affidavit in support of our motion and see the attached exhibits. In any event, we are also seeking relief under Rule 16.04(1), for an order dispensing with service. This is plain and clear. I honestly don't see what you find so difficult to understand…"

I am beginning to get agitated.

She sternly fixes me with her gaze and calls out "Next?" without pomp or ceremony. She then motions to the person behind me to move forward to be served and pushes my documents to the side of the counter. The white process server behind me eagerly rushes to take my spot. I have been dismissed.

"You can stand aside as you look for a better Rule to persuade me that what you are attempting to do is valid. Meanwhile, I have to serve the next person on line. We have a lot of people waiting." As she says this, she reaches out and takes the process server's motion materials and proceeds to file them without even a brief examination as to whether or not the documents were in good order.

I momentarily reach for my briefcase and retrieve my 1998 Ontario Civil Practice text. I want to make sure that my rendition of the Rules has been accurate, that I have not made any mistakes. I quickly confirm that all my citations were accurate. By this time, some people seem to have noticed our protracted "discussion" and are watching it with obvious delight.

"Well Mr Lawyer, I set the RULES here! At this counter! If I say that you need an affidavit of service, then that's what you must produce before I can file any of your documents. Case closed." Whatever reservations I might have had about her, this last statement completely changed my mind. I immediately concluded that it would be a waste of time to continue talking to her and I ask to speak to her supervisor.

"Be my guest," she says, walking slowly away from the counter after serving the process server.

Thirty minutes later, a young man emerges and inquires about my problem. I briefly explain it to him, and without apologising for the discourtesy and unprofessional behaviour of the Clerk, this man, expressionless, simply takes my motion record, quickly taps on the computer, takes my cheque and issues a receipt.

"Done," he announces.

I hurriedly pick up my bags and leave, exhausted and wishing that I had never become a lawyer. However, as soon as I reach the subway stop, my mind rapidly moves to my next case and the incident at the court registry recedes to the back of my mind, only to be retrieved later as part of my literary effort to chase after John Grisham. I intend to make it a heated pursuit.

TINDA! May I grow as tall as my uncle's pine tree!

(...)

This would prove to be but one in a series of poignant episodes during my more than 13 years as a Barrister and Solicitor in Canada. I would encounter and overcome numerous attempts to humiliate and frustrate my efforts in the search for justice for all manner of clients.

But, to be brutally honest, as the old judges retire or die, new, more modern and enlightened ones are taking their places. Most of this new breed have fully embraced not just the multicultural society that Canada – especially Toronto – is, but also the principles entrenched, protected and guaranteed in the *Charter of Rights and Freedoms* and a myriad other human rights legislation.

In April, 1998, I visited Kenya. The intention was to purchase for one of my sisters a flour (posho) mill and for myself a piece of land in the Awendo/Migori area. I had earlier renewed contact with my old friend Anthony Ochieng' Owala, who was then the head of security at South Nyanza Sugar Company at Awendo. I travelled to Awendo, via Eldoret, with my first cousin, Ochieng' Aoyi, arriving minutes before midnight. The following day, before we departed to inspect the pieces of land that were available for sale, Anthony introduced me to a lady who would later become my wife. The relationship between Tracey and I had broken up around January that year. We had amicably agreed to have joint custody of the children and were raising them together. I continued to live at my Bradford house while Tracey lived in Toronto. The introduction to Jane was very brief; we just greeted each other and exchanged personal contacts. That day, after purchasing a two-acre plot in Uriri, I departed for Muhuru Bay to see my sister, who lived there with her family. I completed by business and returned to Toronto. Jane and I maintained contact through emails and long-distance calls.

During my visit, I managed to reconnect with my old comrade Wafula Buke and new ones Waikwa had introduced me to like Kabando wa Kabando, Njagi Jemedar and Kamau Ngugi. Many people had reported to me that Buke was seething with unexplained anger over those who had fled and sought exile abroad, but I didn't detect this in Buke when we met. However, much later, after I had relocated to Kenya, he exhibited this negative attitude towards me in particular. He felt, quite unreasonably, that those who had fled into exile didn't deserve any consideration, especially for public jobs.

In April 1999, I visited Kenya again and was reacquainted with Jane. I also visited her home and got introduced to her parents and siblings; thus began a courtship process that culminated in a traditional customary marriage rites being performed on 6 August 2000, in Kenya. On October 29, 2000, Jane landed at the Pearson International Airport and joined me in Canada, as a permanent resident, her sponsorship having been processed in a record six months.

Thus started our lifelong journey, through which, we have been blessed with three daughters – fraternal twins, Suré and Anyango, born on September 1, 2001 (just ten days before 9/11), and another daughter, Achieng', born on April 11, 2003, during the severe acute respiratory syndrome (SARS) outbreak. I never witnessed Achieng's birth, as I had done of each and every other child, because the Canadian health authorities had sealed off all health facilities, disallowing 'expectant' fathers, to all except for the most essential staff, expectant mothers and emergency treatment.

The birth of my five children isn't something I had intended to write about. But the more I reflect on those experiences, the more I cannot bury those beautiful memories. My daughter Atieno came on July 14, 1995, at The Wesley Hospital in Toronto. Atieno took time to come. As we waited patiently in the labour ward for eight hours, she went on strike. Our obstetrician and gynaecologist was a fellow African friend originally from Nigeria called Dr Titus Owolabi. After nine hours of waiting, with Tracey in agony, the physicians suggested an epidural. I wasn't completely convinced, but Tracey was the one in pain. She basically said, "Look, let's get it over with." She also decided on a c-section. Soon, around dawn, a healthy baby girl was removed from the mother's tummy, crying softly. I wanted to name her Akinyi (the Luo name for a girl born at dawn), but Tracey, being an African-Canadian originally from Jamaica, found Atieno – a name given by the Luo to a girl born at night – easier to pronounce, hence 'Atieno' she became. I added Suré, which was my mother's name.

On the third day, we took Atieno by taxi to our one-bedroom apartment at 199 Chatham Avenue. And for the next three months we could hardly sleep; Atieno had severe colic, and cried daily most of the nights. We were green in child rearing and didn't know what to do. Before I bought my first vehicle, we used to push Atieno everywhere: to grocery stores, to the park, to the malls, to Afrofest to listen to African music and cultural performances, to the Harbourfront to listen to jazz, to the Caribana… The tiny Atieno was a fixture on my shoulders, enjoying the view from above; so much so that after the first Afrofest I took her to, TV cameras showed us on the prime-time news. Despite the challenges and difficulties, we managed.

Biko was born at the same hospital on December 4, 1996. But unlike his sister, he came out on time and on schedule, through the birth canal.

Five years later, their twin-sisters – Suré and Anyango – arrived. Although we had then moved to Bradford, which was 65 kilometres from Toronto, and should have had them delivered at the South Lake Hospital in Newmarket, once it was detected that Jane was carrying twins, we were advised to attend a multiple-birth clinic, located at the Sunnybrook Women's Hospital in downtown Toronto. As with Atieno's delayed birth, Suré and Anyango refused to come when expected. We had arrived at the hospital in the morning of August 31, 2001, before Jane was actually in labour. Labour pains had started at 1pm. By 4am on September 1, Jane had had enough and, despite misapprehensions about the procedure, had an epidural. The first baby charged outside about 45 minutes later.

"Congratulations! Baby Number 1 is out; she is a girl," the obstetrician shouted with unrestrained joy. She looked healthy and strong. I immediately called her Suré; again, after my mother. I pride myself as perhaps the only person who has named his children for his mother twice. And within four minutes: "Baby Number 2 is out; she is a girl! Congratulations!" I didn't name her immediately. My mind was elsewhere. Something was amiss. Baby Number 2 appeared breathless. I thought she was dead. For about three minutes she didn't have any visible signs that she was alive. The doctors and nurses fawned around her until she cried. Apparently, she had had an umbilical cord around her neck. The doctors also speculated that Suré must have been kicking her in the tummy. Anyway, by the time Anyango came out, Jane was too exhausted to watch.

Unfortunately, the nurses and doctors left the delivery room too soon after both babies came out. In their absence, Jane started shaking violently. I pressed the button to motion the nurses and doctors back. Nobody came. I pressed again. Nothing. Then I pressed again, and again. Still nothing. Jane began to cry as she shook even more violently, saying she was dying. "I am dying. I'm dying and leaving my twins." Looking at me and grabbing my hands, she said "Please take good care of the girls."

I panicked and started yelling "Doctor! Doctor! Nurse! Nurse!" until they came, rushing in. They got busy and managed to stabilise Jane's condition. But by then, someone had already called 911. Later, I was told that there were several police officers swarming outside the delivery room. Fortunately, they never entered nor tried to speak with me. It's during those times, when a man is watching his loved ones facing imminent danger that he can easily send someone to the cemetery. For the next six months – from September 2 to February, 2002 – Jane experienced severe headaches that required regular medical intervention and strong painkillers. September and October were the worst. We vowed never to request or allow the epidural procedure performed again.

Achieng' came on April 11, 2003, without an epidural. As I couldn't witness her birth due to the SARS epidemic, I stayed home and took care of Atieno, Biko, Suré and Anyango. This time, Jane was a pro. She waited until the last minute before calling a taxi after the labour pains had started. When I called the hospital after three hours, they transferred me to her room and she answered: "Achieng' was a walk-over!" She had delivered uneventfully and named the girl after my sister, Leah Achieng'. That's how I got my five little Angels!

* * * * * * * * * * * * * *

In 1999, I travelled to Kenya and applied for admission to the Kenyan Bar. The application would be kept in abeyance for no apparent reason for ten years. The first roadblock thrown on my path was over the determination of exemptions. I had sought complete exemption from pupilage and all examinable subjects except ethics. This was in line with the reciprocal treatment Canadian Barristers and Solicitors received from the UK. Being a commonwealth jurisdiction, Canadian lawyers were routinely exempted from both academic and practical requirements of all commonwealth bars. That explained why many British lawyers had, over the years, either served in high profile positions in the Kenyan judiciary or been permitted to practice in the country without being subjected to licensing examinations. Usually, the only other condition imposed would be the writing of an ethics exam.

Anyway, after much toing and froing, the then Principal to the KSL wrote to confirm that I had been exempted from all academic exams and pupilage except two exams: land law and succession law. I was subsequently invited to travel to Nairobi in August 1998 to dispense with the two exams. Ironically, when I travelled as required, I ended up spending three weeks waiting for notification of when to sit the exams to no avail. One day, after having waited in vain, I went to the Principal's office and discovered to my horror that both the land law and succession exams had already been written. Nobody had bothered to notify me. And, of course, nobody offered any apologies for the inconvenience caused.

The next ten years would be replete with false promises, misleading information, written notices faxed to me in Toronto a day or two after the examinations had been conducted, a lecturer extorting money from me so as to "facilitate" my passage of the bar and many dramatic twists and turns, only ending, eventually, in 2007 after I had relocated to Kenya and managed to sit and pass the three exams that had now been imposed on me. The time and money wasted in the process was compounded by the many inconveniences caused to me, my family and my clients during the ten years it took for such a simple administrative affair.

Meanwhile, my practice in Canada was expanding exponentially. I was handling very interesting cases. Helping people find legal recourse, protecting them from the harsh environment and otherwise ensuring that their rights were guaranteed gave me great pleasure and satisfaction.

* * * * * * * * * * * * * *

At dawn on Millennium Night of January 1, 2000, something happened that would propel my modest practice to the stratosphere of notoriety and set me on a collision course with the Metropolitan Toronto Police Service, and the notorious Toronto Police Association. A 26-year-old African-Canadian man, whom I knew very well, had been shot dead by the city's Emergency Task Force at the St Michael's Hospital in downtown Toronto where he had taken his three month old son, who was having trouble breathing. He had rushed the baby there for emergency treatment. Apparently, the young man had called 411 and been promised prompt attention at home. Just before midnight on December 31, he had, after waiting in vain, taken the child in a taxi to the hospital's emergency department, panting and panicking as he went.

The police later put out an elaborate story, quoting 'sources in the hospital' – though it was never proven – that the man had been armed with a pellet gun, which was later variously referred to as a 'toy pistol' or a 'stun gun' (whether or not that was true or it was conveniently planted on him there, was never, ever established), attacked emergency room doctors, holding one hostage for hours as he 'violently' demanded treatment for his seriously ill baby. So, they claimed, he was shot in order to save lives, protect and rescue the doctor held hostage. This begged the question: how would the man – who had no known history of erratic behaviour or insanity – have expected a dead doctor to have treated his son? One plausible, logical explanation is that the man had waited for a doctor to attend to his baby in vain, forcing him to demand, perhaps aggressively, for immediate attention. The all white doctors and one Chinese quickly dialled 411, unleashing an unfortunate course of events.

The young man was Henry Hidaya Masuka, the son of John Hidaya Masuka, the first African man I had met in Toronto on June 27, 1988. As expected, John was on the phone to me within hours, and I was immediately coordinating media and legal issues surrounding this tragic and untimely death. John appointed me the Masuka family spokesman. This was going to be my first high profile case and one that promised to involve a titanic battle against the largest, strongest and meanest police service in Canada as well as one of the largest, most established, prestigious and richest hospitals in Canada. I quickly consulted my mentor Charles Roach, who advised that I should bring Prof. Peter Rosenthal on board as co-counsel, which I did, instantly.

Press conferences, media briefs, press releases, TV and radio appearances, pleadings, contestations, discoveries and inquests followed. Peter and I were engaged on this case almost daily for the next two years, fighting for the family to find justice and compensation. Unfortunately, the police and hospital had deeper pockets.

Whereas Rosenthal and I were handling the case pro bono, the two well-healed institutions hired the best, most expensive and ferocious lawyers and law firms in the country. They tried every strategy and tactic available to them. The Toronto Police Association – a union of uniformed police officers – even filed a complaint against me with the Law Society complaining that I had acted unprofessionally during one media brief. To their credit, the Law Society gave the complaint short shrift, without formal investigations. The Police Association filed another complaint. That, too, was summarily dismissed. But I was now constantly monitored and intimidated. Again, and again, they tried to derail me without success.

An inquest was conducted, with Peter leading the show. Unfortunately, both the inquest and lawsuit didn't return positive verdicts for Henry, his son's 19-year-old widow, John and the rest of the family. The family was satisfied with our efforts. The African-Canadian community appreciated our courage, commitment and service. We were humbled, but very proud. We might have made no money, but we cemented our integrities, reputations, credibilities and bona fides. From there on, we earned our bragging rights as being the most courageous lawyers in Toronto. I honestly think it was well deserved. We lost a battle, but not the war.

For the more than a decade I practised law in Ontario, I met tens of thousands of people and acted for tens of thousands of clients. Many of these people were referred to me by word of mouth, by people who had confidence in my abilities, skills, commitment and courage; people I might have touched through my professional legal work, political activism, social and cultural criticism, or through myriad other ways in which I participated in the welfare of the community in which I either lived or belonged to; as my reputation grew with the exponential expansion of my practice.

Most of my clients were Canadians. However, of the Kenyan clients I had, more than 70 per cent were Gikuyu, followed by Kisiis and then Luos. I had Luhyas and people from other communities sprinkled here and there, but among Kenyan communities, my core practice was GEMA (Gikuyu, Embu, Meru Association), perhaps because I was called to the Bar earlier than all the other Kenyan lawyers and the only one who had a well established firm, and a near perfect success rate in the courts and refugee/immigration tribunals. This was also partly because, by then, more than 60 per cent of Kenyans who were settling abroad as economic immigrants were Gikuyu and Kisii. The rest were Luo, Luhya, Kalenjin and the rest, in that order. Incidentally, up to that point, only Gikuyus and Kisiis had served as ministers of finance, and given the draconian restrictions on foreign exchange by the Moi regime, it's conceivable that those ministers were only assisting members of their ethnic communities to get scholarships or obtain the necessary foreign exchange to travel abroad. Another reason is the relative prosperity of both communities compared to say the Luo or Luhya. Yet another reason could well be that most people from the Mount Kenya region assumed, wrongly, that I was either a Meru or a Gikuyu, based purely on the phonetic sound and spelling of my name.

My own feeling is that I got the majority of my clients – from all racial, ethnic, cultural and linguistic backgrounds – due to my proven near-perfect record. I was – and most people knew it – completely blind to ethnic and linguistic differences, didn't consider it in any form, shape or manner, to be a determining factor in who, what or how my services were to be rendered, so much so that I was once accused by a Meru client, who was entangled in a silly, petty dispute with a Gikuyu roommate – who was also my client – of being 'biased' in favour of the Gikuyu because I was allegedly a Gikuyu. They sought my services as a mediator. After the conclusion of the mediation exercise, the Meru suddenly blurted:

"You are biased! You are only supporting her because you are a Gikuyu!" She yelled.

"Who told you I am a Gikuyu?" I inquired, politely.

"You are! Everybody knows you are a Gikuyu! Look at your name. If you are not, why are your secretaries and the other man Gikuyus?"

"Actually I am not; not that it matters or should bother you. I am a Luo from Kisumu. I have never pretended to be anything else, except that we are all Kenyans, and what I have done today is in everyone's best interests. I am not against you. I advise you strongly to change your attitude about life. Don't view people from other communities as enemies."

The two women reconciled and I never heard any complaints from them again. Clearly, the suspicions, mistrusts, apprehensions, hatred and open hostilities we have against each other by virtue of our differences – perceived or real – are largely baseless, misplaced and unjustified. At its core, we are all human beings; endowed with basic human instincts, wants, needs, desires, aspirations, expectations, rights and dreams. None of us was born bearing any peculiar cultural, traditional, customary, linguistic or intellectual traits. We acquire all these as we grow, from our immediate environments. And those environments can change, be moulded, improved or worsened. There shouldn't be any entitlements based on one's pedigree. My intention is to work both individually and collectively with others with similar beliefs and orientations, for a socially, culturally, economically and politically humane, fair, equitable and just environment for all, regardless of race, ethnicity or other grounds.

BOOK THREE

RETURN

CHAPTER FIVE

PRELUDE AND AFTER

To some of my comrades, exile ended when they first returned home, however fleetingly, whether it was a midnight foray to their rural homesteads or a weekend stint in Nairobi to attend a conference. Those were people who considered exile a matter of geography.

For me, however, exile was something more fundamental; an entire way of being. For so long as my primary home was abroad, I would be in exile, emotionally and spiritually, too. Yes, I had made trips to Kenya from the early 1990s. My first foray had been a surreptitious one, when I had slipped into what the Afro-Caribbean literary icon Aimé Césairé referred to as my "pays natal" (native land), while attending the 7th Pan African Congress in Kampala, Uganda in April 1994. After that initial discreet visit my trips had become more frequent. I had come back from Canada to bury three of my sisters and other close family members. When I chose to get married I had gone into the Kenyan countryside to complete all the customary formalities. I had also returned for work-related reasons. And prior to my proper return, I had travelled back and forth between Canada and Kenya as I oversaw the design, construction and completion of our new family home in the Runda suburb of Nairobi.

But in my mind these were only frequent visits to Kenya; just trips if you will. For me, exile is a complex socio-economic, political, ideological and psychological reality, which in my case, had been forced upon me by harrowing circumstances. It was only after I took the bigger mental step of deciding to permanently relocate my family to my homeland that I began to feel my two decades of exile were coming to an end. So, my return from exile wasn't merely a physical act; it went further and deeper than that.

The idea of 'return' had been gnawing on my mind since about 1997, but it became a more persistent trope in my thoughts from the time I graduated with an LLM degree from Osgoode Hall Law School in 2001. I had a huge emotional longing for home, but initially, in 1997, I repressed that feeling because of the tender ages of my children.

Biko was then just one and Atieno had just turned two, so this was a genuine reason, not an excuse. If I had moved back to Kenya, the bond between the children and I would have been permanently severed. The effect on their future could have been profound, permanently unbalancing their confidence and emotional well-being. Then, of course, there were off-putting logistical considerations. Matters like employment, income, accommodation and other things stubbornly imposed a reality check on me. As well, I still had a mortgage to pay off on my home in Canada, but at least I had a home and a secure livelihood there. In Kenya, I would, to a great extent, have to start over.

I investigated whether I might be able to return to East Africa with my work. But when I looked into jobs with the United Nations, which has a huge presence in Nairobi and East Africa, I was stunned to discover that I would need a Master's degree to even apply. But still I yearned for 'home'. Two years later, I was admitted for a Master of Laws programme at Osgoode. I undertook the course part-time from September 1999, attending classes in the evening and on Saturdays, doing my research and writing the assignments, papers and thesis. Despite juggling these studies with a heavy legal practice, I still managed to graduate, with distinction, in June 2001.

But even having completed these studies, I still felt that I needed to get admitted to the Kenyan Bar. Kenya's institutional lethargy and corruption conspired to delay this process for more than five years. My stern refusal to pay bribes to teachers and administrators at the Kenya School of Law meant that my file either 'disappeared' or became 'low priority'. A three-month LLM practicum I had organised through a Canadian non-governmental organisation, "Project Ploughshares" turned out to be a complete waste of time, because of the willful belligerence of their Kenyan contact who refused to assign me any work.

At least, however, by then I had saved enough to purchase or build a decent house in one of Nairobi's most desired neighbourhoods. I resolved to build in Runda, a tranquil suburb which felt a little like a Nairobi equivalent to Bradford, near enough yet not too near to the hustle and bustle of the city centre. I had fallen in love with Runda at first sight. By the time I had inspected the available plots being sold, I'd made a decision to buy. I signed the agreement of purchase and sale on the spot and undertook to submit the instalment payments starting one week from that day, with a further undertaking to complete paying the Sh2.5m for the half acre plot within six months. Again, that was one of the best decisions I have ever made. I have never regretted it.

Within six months of signing the agreement of purchase and sale for the Runda property, I had completed making my payments and was now only waiting for the delivery of my title deed. By early July, 2003, I had, working alongside an architect and engineer, devised a plan. And then for the next four years, I would travel three or four times a year in order to inspect the construction. I was in Kenya for the groundbreaking ceremony, the foundation being laid, the walls going up and the roof going on. In time I felt that the tens of thousands of dollars I had spent travelling back and forth were an investment as they would otherwise have been lost through theft, fraud and mismanagement.

And so despite a lawyer absconding with funds early on; some theft, pilferage and misappropriation during the construction; and the distance between Kenya and Canada, the shell of the house, including the roof, was completed by September 2004. By the time my family and I had returned to Kenya in September 2007, the house was almost ready for occupation. By then of course, as I was running around trying to finish the house, I was also helping Raila with his presidential campaign and trying my hand in Nyando constituency politics. The house project would turn out to be a sparkling triumph, but the two political projects weren't as successful. One would be the major motivating factor for this book.

* * * * * * * * * * * * * *

I returned to a Kenya that had gone through a bewildering number of political mutations and alliances over the past decade. It was only five years earlier, in 2002, that Moi had finally given in to pressure at home and abroad and announced his retirement as Kenya's President after 24 years of totalitarian rule. He had 'won' his last term in December 1997, beating his former finance minister and Vice-President Mwai Kibaki, Michael Wamalwa Kijana and Raila Amolo Odinga, respectively. Many believed that apart from rampant rigging, Moi's 'victory' then had been mainly due to the failure of the Kenyan opposition to unite. At the time Kibaki headed the Democratic Party (DP); Wamalwa had been the leader of the Forum for the Restoration of Democracy – Kenya (Ford-Kenya); while Raila had stood for the New Development Party (NDP) following his abandonment of Ford-Kenya.

Soon after the 1997 elections, Raila's NDP had started a loose alliance with Moi's Kanu (Kenyan African National Union) party, that culminated in a merger between the two parties on March 18, 2002. The Moi-Raila marriage was a remarkable political union, not least because Raila had for years been one of the repressive Moi's most high-profile victims. Shortly after the August 1, 1982 attempted coup d'état against Moi's government, Raila had been arrested and detained without trial over his alleged involvement in the coup, having earlier been charged with treason. However, before his trial commenced, the charges were suddenly withdrawn and the prosecution terminated. He was released on February 5, 1988, but Raila had by then already served more than five years of unlawful detention and incarceration. His freedom was to be short-lived. On August 14, 1988 as he tried to rebuild his life, Raila was arrested again. He served his second stint of detention without trial until June 12, 1989.

On July 5, 1990, Raila was arrested and detained for the third time – again without trial. Shortly after his release on June 21, 1991, Raila fled into exile in Norway. He returned after the repeal of section 2A and the reintroduction of multiparty politics and joined the newly registered and popular opposition party the Forum for the Restoration of Democracy (FORD) then led by his father and Kenya's first Vice-President, Jaramogi Oginga Odinga.

It is these liberation credentials that first attracted me, and many others, to Raila. True, when Raila, as leader of the NDP, joined Kanu and Moi's government, he had come full circle, but this seemed an expedient and strategic move to place himself as a future leader of the country. Certainly, his 'journey' was quite different from that of Kibaki, George Saitoti, Kalonzo Musyoka, Moody Awori or even Michael Wamalwa Kijana, with whom he would later work against Moi.

Moi appointed Raila minister for energy and the then ruling party Kanu's secretary general. Raila might have intended to use his newly acquired power to position himself to succeed Moi in 2002, but unknown to him, Moi had already decided to support former President Jomo Kenyatta's son, Uhuru Kenyatta. In the process – and quite inexplicably – Moi caused a major political realignment in Kenya. As far back as 1988, Kibaki had fallen out with Moi and had taken over the DP. Now, Professor George Saitoti who had served as Moi's Vice-President for ten years was facing the worst political fight in his life. Prior to openly endorsing Uhuru, Moi had fired Saitoti from the Vice-Presidency and publicly ridiculed him as being unfit for the presidency. Moi's other close political associates, Kalonzo Musyoka, Musalia Mudavadi and John Joseph Kamotho, had also been sidelined. They would all soon rally around Raila in rebellion against

Uhuru's endorsement. Eventually, it was these internal Kanu wrangles and power struggles that led to the formation of the 'Rainbow Alliance'.

By October 2002, the Rainbow Alliance had become extremely popular. Most of its leaders held important national positions within the ruling party Kanu and in government. Raila was then both the Minister for Energy and Kanu's Secretary General. Kalonzo Musyoka had been Kanu's organising secretary before being chosen as one of Kanu's vice-chairmen and a senior cabinet minister. George Saitoti had been Moi's Vice-President for ten years, but when the Rainbow wave swept the country, he was serving as Minister for Finance and one of Kanu's vice-chairmen. Musalia Mudavadi was both a senior minister and one of the four national vice-chairmen of Kanu. Although Moody Awori wasn't a full cabinet minister, he had been an assistant minister for more than a decade, hailed from a well-known political and business family, and was considered not just fabulously wealthy, but also a decent, respected statesman. In other words, the Rainbow team was both popular and well-heeled. Its open defiance of Moi within the Kanu establishment in many ways triggered the kind of euphoric excitement that had not been experienced in the country since the struggle for liberation that culminated in Kanu forming the first legitimate and popular independence government in 1963. Ordinary folks identified with it because it was perceived to be courageous and openly defied the independence monolithic and despotic party, Kanu, and the decaying Big Man, Moi. (Admittedly, some of the anti Moi/Kanu popular revolt might have been motivated by self-interest and the burning desire of its leaders to succeed Moi, but by now Kanuism and Moism had become so unpopular that anyone who courageously stood up against them won instant support.)

In order to formalise themselves into a coherent political formation, Rainbow 'bought' a briefcase political party known as the Liberal Democratic Party (LDP). Meanwhile, however, two other politicians – Charity Ngilu of the Social Democratic Party and Michael Wamalwa Kijana of Ford-Kenya – had formed a loose association with Kibaki. These three started having what amounted to 'public breakfast' at the Norfolk hotel in Nairobi. These choreographed breakfast sessions created a further buzz. Their association would later coalesce into the National Alliance Party of Kenya (NAPK).

Simeon Nyachae, who had served the colonial government as a junior administrator, Jomo Kenyatta as a senior civil servant and Moi as both the head of the public service, chief secretary and cabinet minister before falling out with Moi to form his own political party, the Forum for the Restoration of Democracy – People (Ford-People), had his own ideas, which he confided to Raila. Nyachae wanted to contest the presidency. He had a colourful reputation as an effective administrator. Nyachae and Raila were both from Nyanza Province; the first being an ethnic Gusii, while the latter is a Luo. Initially, Raila pretended to be supportive of Simeon Nyachae's plans, promising to endorse him for the presidency.

One day, Raila arranged to meet Nyachae at the Serena Hotel to sign a Memorandum of Understanding supporting Nyachae's presidential candidacy. An alliance was to then be announced at the Serena Hotel between Raila's newly acquired shell, the Liberal Democratic Party (LDP), and Nyachae's Ford People. Coincidentally, the same day, Ngilu, Wamalwa and Kibaki, calling themselves the National Alliance Party of Kenya (NAPK), had decided to hold a massive political rally at Uhuru Park. As Raila was leaving the Serena Hotel, having signed the MoU, he came across the NAPK leadership and throngs of supporters walking towards Uhuru Park. Raila saw the park overflowing with people and his heart missed a beat. He greeted the walking band and decided to join it. He wasn't going to pass up an opportunity like this. "This is the winning team," he must have said to himself.

Back at the Serena, Nyachae could not have had any idea that things had changed so dramatically in the space of a few minutes. He had made a fatal mistake that others, including this author, would make, again and again, to our individual and collective peril: of trusting Raila Amolo Odinga. Within one hour of signing Nyachae's MoU Raila, the quintessential opportunist, stood before the crowd and declared "Kibaki Tosha!" (Kibaki is fit for leadership!)

This incident has been debated with intensity for many years. I regret to say that the media, Nyachae and others who know what Raila did have done this country a great disservice by not calling Raila out on his duplicitous behaviour. Raila must have calculated that if Nyachae became President (through some miracle), it would have complicated his (Raila's) presidential ambitions since both of them hailed from Nyanza. He might also have realised that the Norfolk Hotel Breakfast Confederacy had gained considerable steam and might have become unstoppable. Being an opportunist, he ran after the train and boarded it, just as it was leaving the station, taking a seat next to the driver.

In short order, the LDP and the NAPK merged and formed the National Alliance Rainbow Coalition (Narc). Narc – the popular new political outfit – was headed by a 'Summit' composed of Moody Awori as chair, Kibaki, Raila, Saitoti, Ngilu, Kalonzo and Wamalwa as members. Even though Moody was the titular head of the Summit, everyone recognised Kibaki as the first among equals (due to his advanced age and experience), followed by Wamalwa, Raila, Saitoti,

Kalonzo and Ngilu in that order. But it is unlikely that Raila ever really accepted that arrangement; he considered himself equal to Kibaki and certainly ahead of Wamalwa.

Fate and circumstances then conspired to thrust Raila further into the limelight. Weeks before the 2002 parliamentary, presidential and council elections Kibaki was severely injured in a motor accident. With its primary candidate indisposed, Raila, an indefatigable campaigner, assumed leadership of the Narc juggernaut. At the time, Kibaki, a cunning tactician, let Raila assume he was the second-in-command. Once Kibaki had been elected President, however, he cut Raila down to size. Immediately after the elections, Raila suddenly found himself locked outside the inner sanctum; he neither had direct access to State House nor Kibaki's Muthaiga residence where the real decisions were being made. And when Kibaki named his first cabinet, Raila was relegated to the lacklustre ministry of roads, public works and housing. Kibaki preferred Wamalwa as his deputy and second-in-command, although Wamalwa was by then seriously ailing and would die within two years of the Narc ascendancy.

Raila was, with some justification, extremely offended. He had played a pivotal role in campaigning for Narc and Kibaki, especially following Kibaki's accident. He had traversed the country, rallying diverse sections to Kibaki's support. Indeed many credited Raila, more than any other member of the Narc Summit with the 2002 victory. It was in that context that many of us had poured overwhelming praise on Raila's head, probably turning the already megalomaniac into an autocrat.

Raila had also brought Kibaki the support of the so-called Luo Nation. The Luo had put all its hopes in Raila; their 'only stick with which they could hit the snake' as the saying goes. If he faltered, the community believed it would falter, too. If his star looked bright, the community believed that its star would be bright too. That is how the Luo Nation found itself supporting Kibaki more vigorously than the level of support Kibaki got from his own Gikuyu community; it was because they felt that through Raila's pivotal role in Narc, the Luo would reach Canaan. It was a similar mirage of power to the ones they thought they had glimpsed during the short-lived Jaramogi-Kenyatta marriage from 1963 to 1966 and the Raila-Moi cooperation between 1998 and 2002. And, ironically, the Kibaki betrayal of Raila would closely parallel that of Kinyatta to Raila's father, Jaramogi, more than 25 years previously.

Raila, feeling he had been betrayed, resolved to start an insurrection within Narc, as he had before from within Kanu. The rest, as they say, is history. But this specific narrative says more about how morally fickle Raila is than about anybody else's trustworthiness. In a word: Raila betrayed Nyachae within minutes of signing the MoU with him. Given what I now know, I'm not surprised that Kibaki and his henchmen felt they couldn't trust Raila.

At the time though I did trust Raila and put my faith in him. Fleeting misgivings I had had about his ideological and philosophical coherence had been quelled by his stellar performance in the run-up to the November 2005 referendum on the constitution. A new constitution had been one of Narc's pre-election commitments. But in office, instead of allowing the draft constitution to be prepared through a credible, transparent and accountable process, Kibaki had authorised former Attorney General Amos Wako and former cabinet minister Charles Nyachae to go on secretive retreats and prepare a retrogressive draft constitution whose sole intention was to consolidate power in the hands of the sitting President. It was this draft constitution that was later derisively referred to as the Wako Mongrel. Raila had led the campaign against the Wako Mongrel, urging the people to vote No in the November referendum by ticking the no box that had an orange as its marker. His was a brave stance that saw his LDP kicked out of the coalition government. From then on, I had a soft spot for Raila and the party that he then co-founded, the Orange Democratic Movement (ODM) – so-called because of the orange that had been on the referendum ballot paper. I started openly supporting Raila, publishing numerous articles in national newspapers in Kenya supporting his candidacy for President. His liberation credentials were of course a key factor in my support too. Raila had been detained without trial for slightly more than eight years in the aftermath of the 1982 coup attempt. Raila has never publicly disclosed his involvement, if any. He has never renounced the coup. If anything, he has maintained (correctly in my assessment) that the coup was inevitable due to the unacceptable totalitarian policies and practices of Moi and his Kanu henchmen. He has consistently stated that the people who should have faced treason charges were Moi and his cronies. This reticence to exploit the past, his sporadic radicalism and the fact that he is the son of the doyen of Kenya's liberation politics, Jaramogi Oginga Odinga, plus, of course, his defiance against Moi and Kibaki when they transgressed, instilled his image in the psyche of the ordinary Kenyan as brave, progressive and selfless. Many Kenyans thought and believed that Raila had a vision for the liberation of all Kenyans irrespective of ethnicity, race, class, gender or other primordial classifications.

When I first endorsed him publicly, these were the reasons. I wasn't supporting him because he was a Luo or because he was from Nyanza Province. These primitive considerations have never inspired me. I fervently supported Narc in

2002 for the same reasons. I thought and believed (I now know that I was mistaken) that together, despite the inherent contradictions, they had the country's interests at heart and that they would deliver. I knew that they couldn't deliver 100 per cent. But I believed, hoped and expected that they could achieve 50 per cent. I had hoped, for example, that they would work tirelessly, as one team, to expedite the realisation of a new people-focused constitution, something they had undertaken to do, during the 2002 campaigns, in 100 days after assuming power. The second major public policy issue I had hoped they would address themselves to immediately was the fight against grand corruption. They had promised to deal with the Goldenberg scam among other major public rip-offs. And the third issue I had expected them to tackle was the problem of tribalism. This was a cancer that threatened to divide and destroy the country. It was a disease that I thought and believed (wrongly, of course) that the Narc team would deal with because their Summit comprised Kibaki (a Gikuyu), Raila (a Luo), Kalonzo (a Kamba), Awori (a Luhya), Saitoti (a Gikuyu), Ngilu (a Kamba) and Wamalwa (a Luhya). It wasn't a perfect face of Kenya all right; but it was a diverse group representing five regions of the Republic! Of course, they never delivered on any of their promises and undertakings after taking power. In fact, they never even tried to. Instead, they started looting public assets and fighting each other over real and imagined 'differences'. They mutated into the worst and most corrupt and tribalistic beasts imaginable.

But immediately before the 2002 elections, I was as euphoric as most other Kenyans. I believed that we were going to be able to turn the tide against the culture of impunity that had taken our country hostage. I longed to be in Kenya to make my contribution. I was determined not to watch others slay the dragons of totalitarianism, grand corruption and tribalism as I watched from the sidelines.

* * * * * * * * * * * * * *

Those who have recently hurled abuse at me because I have openly criticised Raila conveniently forget that for more than six years, I fought for Raila perhaps more than all of his turncoat kitchen cabinet. I worked tirelessly, researched on, wrote about and published widely on public policy issues that helped Raila define, refine and explain what he made me believe was his political philosophy and platform. I also responded to, fought off and scattered many of his political enemies. I peppered over and excused Raila's indiscretions because I thought they were normal human contradictions. I did all these things for more than six years because I believed in him and what I thought was our common vision for the country.

It was a newspaper column that I wrote about Kalonzo Musyoka in early August 2006 that first brought me to Raila's attention. By this time, Raila was a member of parliament for Lang'ata constituency in Nairobi. He had stood for the constituency as a LDP candidate within the Narc coalition, but had since been fired from the Cabinet by Kibaki and so was now with the LDP, before they later transformed themselves into the Orange Democratic Movement-Kenya. At the time I was still based in Canada, but I had become a popular commentator on political and social issues in my homeland, contributing regularly to the *East African Standard*, the *Daily Nation* and the *Kenya Times*. The article headlined *Opinion polls are not the best bellwether of voters' choice* urged Musyoka, then Raila's main opponent for the leadership of the ODM-K – which the ODM had at that point had to rename itself because of a problem with registering their original moniker – against growing complacent after polls had portrayed him as the most popular presidential candidate. I noted that the relationship between Kalonzo and Raila had reached a point of no return; that by Kalonzo insisting on being the most suitable candidate in the LDP, and appearing to be desperately trying to avoid internal party competition, he had actually crossed the Rubicon.

The piece led to my introduction to Raila Odinga, via email. After initial introductory correspondence and discussions between us, I would occasionally forward briefs, comments and observations on various national issues, especially on the constitutional review process, the emerging political issues and strategies of dislodging Kibaki from power.

By this time, Narc had descended into disarray, with Raila trying to cause insurrection from within. Although LDP was still, technically, part of the Narc government, it was practically operating alone, away from Narc. Both Kalonzo and Raila had emerged as the leading figures within LDP. Both wanted to run for President. But neither was prepared to concede defeat in any party nominations, no matter how democratic, transparent or fair. Given their respective public credentials, I took Raila's side. Unlike Kalonzo, Raila had been detained without trial for a long time under Moi. Another reason I was keen to ally myself with Raila was that I saw him – wrongly – as someone who would intervene to have the murder of my late friend, Dr Crispin Odhiambo Mbai, properly investigated. Mbai, who had chaired the devolution committee of the Bomas constitutional process, had worked closely with Raila. Mbai had been senselessly assassinated one bright Sunday morning on September 14, 2003. The government's lack of effort to apprehend his killers, has since led me to wonder if it, or sections of it, might have been complicit.

For years my haranguing of the government to step up their investigation had been met with silence. I felt that if I joined a leading political party, I could influence some action that might culminate in a judicial inquiry, which would at least bring some much needed answers to light, perhaps reveal the identity of the killers leading to accountability, even justice for Mbai. The best person to do this, I thought, was Raila. He had known Mbai. They had worked together very closely. They were friends and colleagues. I'm not afraid to admit that I was extremely naïve. I had seen Raila cry at the Nairobi Hospital where Mbai had been rushed following his fatal shooting. Today I believe those were crocodile tears.

I decided to cultivate a relationship with Raila, firstly, in order to try and find justice for my good friend who had been assassinated for standing up for the country, and secondly, so that I could help in the process of transforming our country. I also wanted to contribute towards the democratic removal of Kibaki from power. I believed that Kibaki was a tribalist; a nepotist; and a man who abetted corruption, if not willingly partook in it, all together. These were my thoughts and beliefs. In addition, I wanted to play a significant role in the constitutional review process, a project that finally came to fruition with the popular enactment of the Constitution of Kenya 2010 on August 4, 2010.

* * * * * * * * * * * * * *

Following numerous email exchanges, and a few telephone discussions, between Raila and myself for about two months in the summer of 2006, I floated the idea of a Canadian visit during which time he could – and would – explain to Kenyans living in and around Ontario, what his political agenda, platform and 2007 election manifesto was. It was July 2006. I suggested September 2006, but Raila thought October would give us more time to arrange the logistics; so October 26 it was.

Although internal Orange Democratic Movement – Kenya (ODM-K) nominations hadn't yet been held, and there wasn't a clear indication whether or not Raila would emerge victorious in such a nomination contest, we agreed that, from a purely strategic standpoint we had to operate as if he had already won. Image and perception are important in politics. It was imperative that Raila spoke and acted as if he was *the* ODM-K candidate.

Kalonzo might have still been being artificially projected as being ahead in the polls, but the chattering classes and the ordinary people considered Raila *the* de facto leader of ODM-K. He had received extensive media coverage. Hardly a day went by without a newspaper, television outlet or radio station featuring Raila, positively or negatively. The conventional wisdom is that 'any coverage is good coverage for a politician.' We understood that most people wouldn't remember the story lines; they would only remember the name of the person at the centre of the story. The mere fact Raila's name was on everyone's lips, from the market place to the private members' clubs, was good for his candidacy. We intensified the positive buzz about Raila by feeding the media all kinds of information on Raila; his childhood, his detention without trial, his brief Kenya Bureau of Standards stint, his exile, and his escapades in opposition politics. The media was saturated with information about Raila and as I had predicted, his popularity ratings started to grow steadily. As soon as he began conducting himself as the *de facto* ODM-K candidate, he was seen as the *de facto* ODM-K candidate.

Raila visited Toronto for four days in late October 2006 with a delegation that included three other politicians, Kasipul Kabondo MP, Paddy Ahenda, Amagoro MP, Sospeter Oteke Ojaamong' and the Hamisi MP, George Munyasa Khaniri. I paid for Raila's business class ticket, their full board accommodation at the Sheraton Hotel in Richmond Hill and covered the costs of their local transport, food, drinks and other refreshments almost entirely from my pocket. My compatriots in exile, Waikwa Wanyoike, Ben Otieno and Leonard Wandili helped me ensure that the visit was a big success. They quickly formed a core group that organised a small fundraiser that generated about $2,500. The total cost of the visit was $50,300, out of which I happily doled out $47,800 from my savings. It was a sacrifice I was willing to make because of my commitment to defeating Kibaki's Party of National Unity (PNU) agenda, which I was convinced wasn't good for the country.

During Raila's visit to Toronto, I arranged an exclusive dinner for him with Professor Richard Sandbrook and a few fellow Africanists at the University of Toronto Club on St George campus, where we discussed the liberation struggle from 1950s to 2006. Prof. Sandbrook was an Africanist of note, having written many books and peer-reviewed journal articles on Kenya, specifically, and Africa, in general. He had taught me political economy and international development economy at the University of Toronto. As we enjoyed our meal, the affable well respected don held us in thrall with stories of TJ Mboya the legendary charismatic nationalist Kenyan politician, whom Prof. Sandbrook had known and worked with closely as a young academic. Sandbrook had been in complete awe of TJ and told us how ill he had felt when Mboya had been assassinated. He did not conceal his utter disappointment that successive regimes in Kenya hadn't resolved the mystery surrounding Mboya's cold-blooded murder. He then mentioned, quickly and in passing, that I had been one of his brightest students, having graduated with distinction in politics and philosophy from the U of T. Raila would later repeat this to a mutual friend-cum-journalist, who relayed it back to me.

I had prepared Raila for this encounter. Because I knew and understood Sandbrook very well, I had given Raila a quick rundown on his academic areas of interest, summarised some of his books and explained Sandbrook's interest in international development and political economy. As we enjoyed our sumptuous lunch and discussed "Africa's future", I could see the veteran Africanists' minds weighing and balancing up their main guest. They would casually inquire what "an Odinga Administration" might look like and showed keen interest in Raila's responses, which were disappointingly vague, general and lacked deep understanding of the political economy of Africa. For instance, Sandbrook asked Raila what mechanisms he would put in place to address the issue of corruption in government, historical human rights abuses and the "regional" imbalance in development that could prove to be a powder-keg in the future. Raila repeated his usual mantra about the 'founding fathers' dreams; the words of the national anthem and their purported inner import; with the inevitable comparison and contrast between Kenya and Singapore, Hong Kong and Malaysia before and after decolonisation. He failed to articulate core ideological beliefs, nor did he explain the basic policy platform on which his administration's actions would be based. Raila's exposition on Kenyan and African political-economic affairs left me underwhelmed and engulfed with embarrassment; I surmised that he had not made an indelible impression on the eminent scholars at the dinner table. But I also knew that political leadership required progressive vision (which I then believed he had) and not first-class academic or philosophical acumen (which I now knew he lacked).

After lunch, we headed straight to the CBC studios on Front Street in downtown Toronto, where Raila fielded questions on politics, the divided opposition, Kibaki's legacy and ethnic divisions in Kenya. As we say in Dholuo, *opuk ogoe pige* (the turtle is happy inside its familiar waters). Raila proved himself an agile swimmer in front of the cameras. He waxed lyrical about "ongoing negotiations" between and among different opposition leaders and political formations. That interview was a glowing success.

On Saturday, October 28, we held a successful political meeting with Kenyans, again at the University of Toronto. Raila, to his credit, rose to the occasion with a rousing inspirational speech, peppered with appropriate historical anecdotes and jokes. I thought it was an outstanding performance. It was a bit of an anticlimax though, during the question and answer session, when he fumbled and meandered, sounding slightly defensive, when Adongo Ogony, a long time Kenyan political exile and resident of Toronto directly challenged him on the actual track record of the so-called 'Young Turks' in the Narc government, in which Raila had served as a senior minister. Rather than admit the dismal performance of the Young Turks in government, Raila tried to heap all the blame on Kibaki.

Afterwards, Raila sought to know what I thought about Adongo. I told him that he remained sharp, probing and progressive; that he shouldn't mistake the question Adongo had asked him as a sign of hostility. Inexplicably, he sought to know my views about Onyango Oloo (David), who incidentally, wasn't present during that visit because he had relocated to Kenya. Just like with Adongo, I told Raila that Oloo was an honest, hard-working guy, who was also very prolific; that he was writing and publishing many good essays on Kenyan politics in the blogosphere.

Raila then asked about Okoth Otura, an eccentric self-styled 'preacher' who had sought asylum in Canada claiming that Raila and other members of the opposition wanted to kill him. I told him that I didn't know Okoth very well, but that from the little I knew, he didn't seem credible. "Okoth is a conman; he made me attend an inauguration of a fake church in Kano before he ran away to Canada. Avoid people like Okoth," Raila told me. That choice of words would haunt Raila five years later when I had had more of a chance to judge Raila's own dealings with those he had worked with closely.

It was also during this visit that I asked Raila why he had fallen out with his longstanding strategists and personal assistants, Rateng' Oginga Ogego and Herbert Ojwang'. I knew Rateng' well. He was a close friend of mine. Rateng' was then Kenya's High Commissioner to Canada. Based on my discussions with him, I knew that he no longer had any respect for Raila. Although Herbert hadn't then disclosed anything regarding his fallout with Raila to me (because I hadn't met him), it was common knowledge in Kenya that Raila had fired him unceremoniously. Even though I hadn't then met Herbert, I felt that it was important for me to understand why there was a very high turn-over in Raila's core political staff. We were on the road; just me and him, zooming in my newly acquired Mercedes Benz ML 320.

Raila told me that nothing had actually happened between him and Ogego; that contrary to popular myth, it was he, Raila Amolo Odinga who had presented

Ogego's name for appointment as Ambassador to Canada after Narc took power in December 2002; that it was Kibaki who had delayed in making the appointment, thereby providing Raphael Tuju (then Minister for Tourism, Information Communications) with the opportunity to claim undeserved credit for it.

So, quite clearly, Raila tried to claim credit for something he hadn't done. He didn't know that I had discussed the matter with Rateng', who had told me that Raila hadn't helped him at all; that his name had been presented for appointment by Tuju to Kalonzo Musyoka, who was then Foreign Minister and had been with them in LDP, before Narc was even formed. Rateng' also informed me that Moody Awori (then Kenya's Vice-President) was also willing to push for his appointment had Kalonzo failed. Again, Moody had also been in LDP before joining Narc prior to the 2002 general elections. And as happens with such matters, I didn't know what or who to believe. My head was telling me that Rateng''s version was more credible; but my political 'heart' and instinct were warning me that there might have been other forces involved. On reflection, I wish I had trusted my head. Since then, I've learnt to respect and pay close attention to both my head and my instincts equally.

On Herbert Ojwang', Raila claimed to me that he had sent Ojwang' to South Korea to go and collect some campaign finance; that Ojwang' had been given Sh200m to deliver to Raila, but that Ojwang' had returned to Raila with less than Sh50m. Raila alleged that this is what had destroyed their friendship. Essentially, Raila claimed that he had fired Ojwang' for stealing about Sh150m of his campaign funds.(Presumably, hundreds of millions of shillings were funnelled to Raila's non-existing campaign kitty. The truth is that Raila didn't contest the 2002 presidential elections; he chose instead to support Kibaki. So, where did all those hundreds of millions disappear to?)

Of course, four years following my relocation to Kenya, I heard and learnt of more salacious stuff surrounding the fallout between Ojwang' and Raila; stories that have refused to go away despite many years of suppression and denial from Raila's quarter. They can be found in Chapter 13 – Betrayals.

The point I'm trying to make is two-fold: first, at the time I was working with Raila with my eyes wide open. That's a fact. However, although I had heard many rumours, there was nothing concrete.

More importantly, in 2006, I might have been a bit politically naïve and believed, like many Luo intellectuals, that the broader goals, aspirations and dreams that we were fighting for were higher, much higher than individual interests; that Ogego might have had genuine cause to be aggrieved, but that if we could still pursue and achieve "our goal" (of making one of us President of

Kenya) which, unfortunately, meant allowing Raila to continue abusing, degrading and discarding individual members of the Luo Nation, then it would be worth it for the higher national good. I, like many others, still believed, of course mistakenly, that Raila was now our only chance to the "Promised Land"; that anything that threatened to trip him had to be blocked, diverted, and even destroyed. I was only interested in the "bigger picture"; the "national good of the Luo". To us, Raila embodied our collective struggles, aspirations and dreams. So much so that even when we caught Raila contradicting his well-orchestrated public image and persona, we turned a blind eye. It was as if Raila had convinced an entire community that he was both invincible and indispensable. I would have to confess today, publicly, that, like the overwhelming majority of Luos, I was naïve; I might also have been wrong.

The day before Raila and his entourage flew back to Kenya from Toronto in October 2006, I had arranged a generous reception for him and his delegation at my friend Joseal Igbinosun's home. Kathleen France, Millicent Agola, Veroline Otto and my wife Jane prepared delicious dishes of *kuon, dek, mito, akeyo, osuga, obambla, aliya, and rice* – which we feasted on. Veroline came with traditional Acholi vegetables and foods, which everyone loved; licking their fingers. As the party progressed, I noticed an uninvited visitor; a female who looked Rwandese. When the party ended, at about 2am, I made sure that our visitors were taken to their hotel. However, after I had dropped them at the hotel, Ben called to ask if the Rwandese should be given a ride to the hotel as she was claiming to be '*Jakom's* guest'. I told Ben to leave the lady behind as *Jakom* hadn't told us about her. Ben did that, but on his way to the hotel, he received a call from Raila, confirming that indeed, the lady was his 'guest'. Ben headed back but found that the lady had already taken a taxi. Next morning at 8.30am, I met the lady leaving Raila's room.

That, plus another incident that happened many years later, when Dr Odeya Ayaga sought to inform Raila, through me, that a lady he often "saw" in New York wasn't reliable and "safe", troubled me. When I discreetly passed Odeyo Ayaga's message to Raila at a lunch date we had at the Nairobi Club a few months later, Raila reacted with so much fury that I was completely taken aback. Odeyo was simply trying to help Raila by cautioning against someone he knew. Well, Raila turned against Odeyo, refusing to answer his calls.

Even before Raila returned to Kenya from the Toronto trip, the Kenyan print media was heaping praise on the speech he had made. The Toronto visit became a major cog in Raila's 2007 presidential campaign. But something else happened that, on reflection, should have forewarned me not to trust Raila.

When we dropped them at the airport, I noticed that Raila had failed to say one magic word – Thank You – to those hardworking, selfless and generous people who had made his visit a success: Waikwa, Ben and Wandili, who had volunteered their time and resources to assist; Joseal Igbinosun and his family who had opened up their magnificent home, spent their time and immense resources to make Raila feel welcome; my friend and bookkeeper, Kathy France, who had spent her money, time and other resources to make *mandasis* (Kenyan donuts) and other assorted foods for our guests before playing chief host; and my wife and children who had worked tirelessly in order for Raila and his delegation to feel comfortable, remaining loyal despite my many absences and the huge amount of resources I had dedicated to Raila's visit, most of it removed from their nest eggs. Raila didn't even thank the photographer, the filmmaker and the drivers I had hired to look after each guest throughout their visit. That serious lapse ought to have sent alarm bells ringing in my head, especially in view of the fact that Raila would go on to behave with the same outrageous sense of expectation, again and again, but each time I found some reason to excuse or to overlook it. I was being blind, silly and naïve. For that, I've not forgiven myself.

* * * * * * * * * * * * * *

One late evening in mid-February 2007, as I sat in my office preparing pleadings for a new client, my office phone rang. It was Agwenge Mbeche. Agwenge was one of Raila's staunchest supporters (or was it 'acolyte?') in Texas. He told me that Raila had called him from Dubai, asking him to request me to accompany him [Raila] to Minneapolis, Minnesota, the following day. That sent me into temporary confusion.

If I said no, I thought, Raila would be devastated. Yet, I had to finish the pleadings and make arrangements for its filing on Monday before I could say yes. I quickly asked Mbeche to call me later in the evening, probably by 9pm, by which point I would be in a better position to give him an answer. I also asked him to tell Raila to call me directly. Mbeche said Raila had told him that he had been trying unsuccessfully to reach me. He actually called me that evening before I left the office.

Apparently, Raila had been invited to the "31st Pan African Student Leadership Conference" at the Minnesota State University at Mankato from February 22-24, 2007. Raila was the main guest speaker. Unfortunately, Raila told me, he had no written speech. He wasn't just asking me to drop everything I was doing and use my own funds to get to Minnesota within a matter of hours, he was also asking if I could prepare his speech for the event. "Good Gracious Lord! Doesn't this guy have a secretariat and staff?" I wondered to myself, astonished at the level of confusion, casualness and obvious incompetence of the 'leading presidential candidate'.

Presidential and general elections were scheduled for December 27 of the same year, yet here was the candidate, who by all accounts many believed stood the best chance of succeeding Kibaki, calling me in a panic because he had no written speech for a major international conference in the US with which to woo the Kenyan Diaspora, the international community, and indirectly, the US administration. However, because I believed in Raila and felt that he was our only hope to steer the country from a course of inevitable self-destruction to democratic progress and prosperity, I did what I would otherwise not have done: I told Raila that it would be difficult but that I would try. Before I left the office, I checked the online flight availability, booked on my credit card and sped home on Highway 400, whistling one of Owino Misiani's hits as I went. Raila didn't even know what topic he had been assigned to speak on. But because the conference was on "pan-Africanism," I knew that writing his speech would be a piece of cake for me.

When I told my wife about the call, she exclaimed: "Are you guys crazy? How does anyone expect you to just fly out to Minnesota without notice or an air ticket?"

"Well, it's a bit late for that now. I've already promised him that I would go. Sometimes we have to sacrifice for the higher cause!" I tried saying as an explanation, which sounded flat, even to me.

"Higher cause? What higher cause? It's all about Raila! Why isn't Raila Odinga's family being inconvenienced for the higher cause? Why must it be us? Why couldn't he just let you know in advance, since he must have known, probably months ago, that he would be speaking at the conference? Raila is much richer than you; so, why isn't he paying for the trip?" She was fuming. And I frankly had no good argument to prop up Raila's sudden act of madness, but I truly believe in honour; my wife knew (and still knows) that. She knew that once I had given my word that I would be there, then I would be there. My word is my bond. I have always told my wife that of all things in the world, I hate lying more than anything else. No matter how aggrieved my wife was, I wouldn't renege on my word to Raila.

Almost immediately after I had checked into my hotel near the University of Minnesota at Mankato, Raila revealed that Sarah Elderkin, the veteran Kenyan journalist who was now working in his campaign as his principal speechwriter, had discovered that the speech which had been prepared for him for the occasion by Dr Adams Oloo had been plagiarised, almost word-for-word, from one of Thabo Mbeki's speeches on pan-Africanism. Having ordered room service and asked the hotel's reception to make sure no one disturbed me, from 7.30pm until 3.30am, I worked furiously. By 7am, on February 22, 2007, I had the draft of a 22-page speech to show to Raila. After going through it thrice, he said he was very satisfied with it, but he needed it pared down to between 15 and 19 pages. By 10am, one hour before he was scheduled to deliver the keynote speech, Raila got his 18-page document, which he read at the conference, to much acclaim.

Immediately following the first day's session, we went into two private meetings with leaders of the university administration, led by its Provost, Scott Olson and Dr Fagin. At the centre of the discussions were the potential future institutional collaboration between Maseno University and the Minnesota State University at Mankato. Raila's instructions were that I should lead the negotiations. I advised Raila to request two broad areas of collaboration: firstly, that since the MNSU was home to one of the best physical science centres in the US, it could assist Maseno University with technical and material assistance to establish a fully-fledged faculty of engineering; and secondly, that the two institutions of higher learning could develop an academic exchange programme. I even mentioned that we could explore ways of seeking some technical assistance from the famous Mayo Clinic, which is located a few kilometers from the MNSU.

The MNSU administration was quite enthusiastic and promptly began exploring viable mechanisms of having the two proposals realised. But when they sought to know the name of the contact person at Maseno they would be dealing with, I was both surprised and disappointed when Raila whispered to me to propose his wife Ida. How could Raila expect anybody to respect him if he wanted to push his wife like this? I had expected him to connect me with the chairman of the Maseno University board or the vice-chancellor; but his wife? Until then, I had no idea that Ida was a member of the Maseno University board. In any event, despite both MNSU's and my best efforts, Ida never followed up on our correspondence, and nothing productive ever came out of those discussions and the many hours I subsequently spent on telephone and formal communication with the MNSU. I had high hopes for that project, unfortunately Raila never acted on any of my recommendations, advice or promptings. After months of wasted time, both MNSU and I gave up, most regrettably.

On February 26, I had flown back to Toronto, exhausted, $6,000 the poorer, but exhilarated.

* * * * * * * * * * * * * *

We had still been at Mankato, when Raila and I had discussed – just the two of us – the setting up of the '2007 Raila for President Campaign Team'. We had spent a considerable amount of time discussing the role of the campaign manager; the basic qualifications, background, training, experience and exposure. Raila intimated that he was thinking of hiring a foreigner – Atul Vadher – as his campaign manager. According to him, Atul had helped many leaders around the world win presidential elections. He gave me the example of Bakili Muluzi (1994-2004) of Malawi and others that I no longer remember.

Now, Atul was supposed to be a political expert, who had been, for a long time, an advisor to the eminent British Liberal politician, Lord David Steel; Atul would be 'donated' and paid for by Steel. I remember telling Raila, firmly, that it sounded like a disaster in waiting. How, I asked, could a foreigner without hands-on political experience, cultural, social and historical knowledge of Kenya manage such a potentially risky campaign? After a bit of back-and-forth, Raila asked me to prepare a short outline on how I thought his campaign team should be structured, including the roles of various central players.

By April 2007, I had delivered the draft to Raila (during a trip to Kenya), whereupon he introduced me to Caroli Omondi, so that – in his words – "the two of you can fine-tune the document together". I ended up doing the document without Caroli's input, not because I didn't seek it, simply because he never responded to emails and didn't seem particularly bothered. Within two days, the document had been finalised. The ideal campaign manager I suggested would be dynamic, efficient, knowledgeable, quick on his feet, frugal, competent, loyal, progressive, well organised and incorruptible. Two other attributes that I thought key were: ruthlessness and strong leadership skills. He/she must be capable of saying no, even to their candidate. Above all, s/he must be a leader who can correct, stop or prevent mistakes from happening, regardless of who the perpetrator might be.

I was meeting Caroli for the very first time and had no idea that he had once served in YK'92, the notorious lobby group set up in the early 1990s by William Ruto, Cyrus Jirongo and other 20-something right wing hawks in the ruling Kanu party to campaign for the re-election of the incumbent despot Daniel arap Moi, or that he had been associated with some of Kenya's worst economic racketeers. (More recently, Raila appointed the former chairman of Youth for Kanu '92, Micah Kigen, to head his 2012 presidential 'Friends for Raila' lobby group. In my mind, it proved the adage: 'the more things change, the more they remain the same.')

Raila also introduced me to Dick Ogolla, Caesar Asiyo, Tony Chege and Mike Njeru as members of his strategy team. After just one hour of meeting that team, I had a severe migraine. Apart from Dick, they just seemed a group of bumbling bumpkins: intellectually lazy, morally decayed and without an ounce of progressive blood in their veins. Why in the world would Raila do that to his campaign? That's a question I've never been able to answer.

* * * * * * * * * * * * * *

I regret now that I didn't raise more objections when I found out that Raila had appointed Mohammed Isahakia as his campaign manager. Purportedly a veterinarian, with absolutely no political training, experience or background, he struck me as a lethargic, lazy character. He had also been implicated in a list of alleged corruptions as long as the River Nile. There are a few court judgments on these. I was befuddled.

My brief inquiries revealed that Isahakia had served as the managing director of the National Museums of Kenya before leaving under a dark cloud of corruption which saw him arraigned in numerous criminal courts for theft, fraud and misappropriation of millions of shillings of tax payers' money. He had then apparently been dismissed twice as a permanent secretary for incompetence under Moi's government. There were also all manner of allegations regarding financial impropriety and illegal land transactions, culminating in the recent return of many public houses he had allegedly fraudulently seized more than 20 years ago in the Woodley estate. He possessed none of the qualifications I had put down as the bare minimum. He wasn't robust, nor dynamic and he lacked rigour. Isahakia was by all accounts idle, an intellectual underachiever and incredibly corrupt. Why had Raila hired such a dubious character?

When I later confronted him with that question, he first explained that Isahakia had been proposed by the leading and highly respected National Muslim Leadership Forum (NAMLEF). On another occasion, however, he claimed that he had met Isahakia when Raila worked as Moi's Minister of Energy; that it was there that he had discovered that Mohamed Isahakia was "among the best permanent secretaries". However, my friend Athman Said who served as the secretary general of NAMLEF subsequently advised me that NAMLEF, which he belonged to, had never proposed Isahakia's name, and were, in fact, he claimed, opposed to him; they knew Isahakia's chequered history and wanted nothing to do with him.

Was this the *best* person Raila could get? Did he even understand ODM's message, platform and programmes? Was he capable of managing volunteer resources, campaign information, communication and financial resources? With no progressive credentials or agenda, was Isahakia going to appreciate the trajectories of the struggles we had been involved in since 1966? If pilfering public resources was an Olympic sport Isahakia would have been a medallist, but was he capable of fundraising?

It was much later – perhaps in mid-December 2007 – that us sceptics in the strategy team began to understand why Raila preferred what I would perceive as a rotten apple like Isahakia to any clean, progressive person. This must be understood within the context of there not being a campaign finance law in Kenya, enabling presidential and parliamentary candidates, specifically, to seek funding from corrupt businessmen, drug dealers, tax evaders and gun runners. Usually, the funding wouldn't come in the form of a cheque, money order or a banker's draft; it would come in neatly packed cartons, huge sacks and dark plastic bags. One Saturday, I met Caroli at the OiLibya Petrol Station in the Westlands suburb near The Mall shopping complex ferrying piles of cash in his vehicle, stashed in plastic bags. He told me that it was Sh54m he had just collected from Moi's former personal assistant Joshua Kulei. Apparently, Raila had sought help from Kulei in order to pay ODM presidential agents, a job which he had then tasked Caroli with. I shook my head and walked away.

Raila probably knew that someone like veteran journalist and former UN functionary Salim Lone (who served as his spokesman both during the 2007 campaigns and for one year after he became Prime Minister), former political prisoner Professor Edward Oyugi, Sarah Elderkin or myself couldn't and wouldn't carry Sh54m in plastic bags, leave alone collect it from Kulei and run around town with it in broad daylight. He might have figured that he needed people without scruples to do that. Such people would be easy to deal with in case there were scandals; Raila could simply cut them loose and hardly anything would stick to him. Everyone, he must have figured, would say 'aha, we knew they were dirty'. This is the deeply-entrenched working political culture of Kenya. Raila, like Moi before him, was just perpetuating it. I have never subscribed to that culture. I've never been a follower. Iconoclast? Maybe.

On reflection, I should have left the Raila campaign that afternoon. Had I done that, I would have saved myself some of the moral dilemmas and angst I later faced working for Raila as Prime Minister. But hindsight is of course a wonderful thing and if wishes were horses, beggars would be riding them. I was beginning to understand the role of dirty money in Kenya's politics. But at the time, I excused it by arguing that if Kibaki could raid the treasury to fund his re-election campaign, why shouldn't Raila fight fire with fire? Well, as I should have known and appreciated, once you start sliding down that moral and legal slippery slope, you can't apply any brakes until you reach the bottom.

* * * * * * * * * * * * * *

Looking around at the Raila Odinga Centre (ROC) in Upper Hill, which for a while served as the nerve centre of Raila's presidential campaign, there wasn't any organisation. In the campaign manual I had prepared, there was a position for a polls research director, which naturally should have been filled by Dick Ogolla. Dick had gained extensive experience as a researcher working at the Nation Media Group. He knew polling inside out. He could analyse well. Unfortunately by 2007, Dick was facing many health challenges, and was in and out of hospital often. Without competent research and analysis, the campaign would be flying blind. Yet that position remained vacant until I assumed it, informally, but *de facto*, between November and December 2007. It wasn't just Dick's health that relegated him to the periphery of Raila's presidential campaign. I never knew why or when that had happened, but much later Dick whispered to me that Caroli had fed Raila with unfounded rumours about him so that Caroli could take charge of the campaign, which would put him in charge of the money.

During the ROC so-called strategy meetings, nobody took notes. There was only one laptop which Dick carried and used. Raila distrusted note-taking. He has, on occasions, lashed out at me with fury, out of the blue, for my note-taking. Perhaps this was partly a throwback to his "underground" past, when everything was committed to memory for fear that Moi's Special Branch boys would use any written record to obtain quick and easy convictions from trumped-up sedition and treason charges. But this was a new era. (Much later, I came to wonder if Raila might have been consciously trying to discourage record-keeping as a way of concealing his various business deals. He didn't want someone recording what might turn up later as 'evidence' against him.)

At one point, I asked if they had discussed and agreed on the campaign policy platform. Dick shot in, backed by Caroli and Raila's fundraising manager Tony Chege that Raila's campaign was going to be "against the Gikuyu hegemony". "We are going to win this campaign on the policy of 1 against 41. All we need to do is to make Kenyans hate the Gikuyus. We need to ask Kenyans whether they are prepared to elect another Gikuyu when we have had Kenyatta and Kibaki already…Propaganda, not public policy will win this campaign…" Dick explained, as the others nodded excitedly in agreement.

I was aghast. I looked around the room again and saw nodding heads. Here was what I thought was a high-powered strategy meeting of the leading presidential candidate, yet what I was hearing wasn't just irresponsible rhetoric and propaganda couched as public policy, but what one might even venture to say, was outright ethnic hatred.

I was glad, about five months later, when I attended a strategy session without any of those jokers. Happily, Prof. Oyugi was now chairing a proper strategy team, operating from the Rainbow House in Lavington, composed of a diverse group of people with an array of backgrounds, experience and competencies. Prof. Oyugi and his group laboured mightily, against all odds, to produce some of the best campaign manuals, regional manifestos and briefs I have ever seen. Dave Anyona, Ken Ombongi, Athman Said, Jacqueline Oduol, Oduor Ong'wen, Paddy Onyango Sumba, Kibisu Kabatesi and many other patriotic Kenyans worked as a team and managed to salvage a campaign that had been stuck for months. It was this team that I later joined.

* * * * * * * * * * * * * *

On May 6, 2007, Raila Odinga launched his presidential bid at a colourful, glitzy event at the KICC, where, standing amid the hundreds of people who attended, he read his "application for the job of servant of the people", from a laptop. This was not out of design, but because, only that morning, Sarah Elderkin, operating from Nairobi, and I, doing the heavy lifting from Toronto (with Adongo Ogony providing some much needed munitions on the side), had made the final touches on the "application" and Raila's Nairobi team hadn't found time to print it by the time Raila was addressing the crowd that had gathered inside that KICC amphitheatre. The speech was a tour de force: skillfully crafted in simple, plain English; ideologically and politically balanced, and yet containing all the ingredients of a practical, solid platform. There weren't any grandiose promises: we only included what we believed Raila should be capable of fulfilling. Quoting Mahatma Gandhi, Raila stated that we must guard against "politics without principle; pleasure without conscience; wealth without work; knowledge without character; business without morality; science without humanity; and worship without sacrifice."

Some of the highlights in Raila's speech might return to haunt him given his, in my opinion, pathetic record as a co-principal of the grand coalition government and the Prime Minister of the republic of Kenya. For instance, he asserted that: "I am deeply committed to a new Constitution and a parliamentary system of government, as contained in the Bomas Draft. The USA is the only country among the major western powers with a presidential system. All the rest are parliamentary democracies, and this is what we must aim for in Kenya."

This was to prove to be mere rhetoric post in the wake of the 2007 post-election violence when, during the final Harambee House negotiations over the system of government in the draft constitution, co-chaired by President Kibaki and Raila, it was the latter who proposed the adoption of the presidential system, to the consternation of everyone around that table, including Kibaki, who smiled but said nothing. Clearly, by then, Raila was prepared to jettison what had only months earlier been one of the building blocks of his campaign. He no longer desired a parliamentary system because it tended to scatter executive power. Raila wanted all executive power concentrated in his hands, if he were to become President.

At the KICC that May 6, Raila undertook to "remove power from the power-brokers and give it back to the people of this country, so that the people have a real say in their destiny, and are not just dispensable pawns in a complicated game being played by our leaders to rules that only they know." He stated that "presidential systems are associated with lower public spending and few benefits for the people, and this eventually results in the kind of inequality that characterises our system. That is what I will change. Power-sharing in a people-driven and consultative process is the way forward, along with devolution of power, as provided for in the Bomas Draft. This is something I am 100 per cent committed to...And to move the economy forward, we must immediately invest heavily in three things: number one, infrastructure; number two, infrastructure; number three, infrastructure!"

He then stated how social security was "a fundamental human right, and it is the responsibility of the government to provide it, in order to protect the people from destitution and other vagaries of life," and how his government would establish an "effective social protection policy framework under (a) a universal social welfare insurance scheme; (b) employer-driven contributory pension schemes; and (c) private savings, insurance policies and co-operatives."

The KICC launch looked more like a coronation than a presidential campaign launch. It had a carnival atmosphere and the colour, pomp and ceremony more associated with installations of foreign monarchs than a prelude to a serious political electoral contest. There was music, jubilation, dance and a firework display. Many of Raila's staunch supporters and strategists at the time recoiled in embarrassment at the extravagance, the presumptions and the elitist nature of the whole exercise. "If Raila was truly a 'people's president' as we had chosen to market him, why was he holding his launch in an exclusive amphitheatre rather than at Uhuru Park, or any such historic place?

But there was still the issue of which political vehicle Raila would ride on. There were subterranean power-struggles within ODM-K. Uhuru had peeled off already and declared support for Kibaki's re-election. Kalonzo was pulling in a different direction from Raila. And meanwhile both Ruto and Mudavad were growing restless. In July 2007, Kalonzo took off from Raila – taking the ODM-K name with him – leaving Raila partyless. It was the lawyers Paul Muite and Mugambi Imanyara who then saved Raila's skin, by allowing him to use the original ODM name that Mugambi had surreptitiously registered in 2005 at the time of the ODM's formation.

Now that Raila had a party of his own, he was determined to lead it to State House. On September 1, 2007, he 'won' the ODM nominations, 'defeating' Musalia Mudavadi and William Ruto. In the run-up to these party elections, Najib Balala and Joseph Nyagah who were supposed to run, had strategically thrown in the towel, in order to give Raila momentum. That was choreographed and stage-managed beforehand. What many Kenyans didn't know – what has never been publicly spoken of – is that Raila didn't actually win the ODM nominations at Kasarani fair and square; he rigged the nomination ahead of time. This is a fact that Janet Ong'era and Caroli Omondi have confirmed to me repeatedly: that they doctored the delegates' lists, interfered with accreditations, blocked legitimate delegates at the Moi International Sports Centre, Kasarani, and admitted mostly Raila people to ensure a smooth ride. This is not to suggest that Raila might not have emerged victorious in a fair, open, transparent and democratic process where the principle of one person one vote would have been practised. All I am saying is that Raila didn't win *fairly* at Kasarani on September 1, 2007. And anyone who could cheat so brazenly at Kasarani in 2007 could cheat any other time.

Let me make one confession: although I wasn't involved in this high-stakes electoral fraud (I wasn't even in Kenya then), I have always known about it – and I never reported it to the 'authorities.' From an ODM perspective, the 'authorities' were historically perpetrators of fraud. And the 'authorities' were our opponents. I was between a rock and a hard place, but I could still have blown the whistle, by publishing an op-ed or delivering a surreptitious letter to Raila's opponents.

For that, I apologise profusely to ODM members, specifically, and to Kenyans in general. I'm a human being with human frailties like any other person. I mistakenly believed that Raila acquiring power so that he could transform Kenya was more important than the electoral infractions he had committed to get the ODM nominations.

* * * * * * * * * * * * * *

More than five years on from Raila's job application speech, many Kenyans, including important figures within Raila's strategy team for the 2007 elections, are wondering what has happened to the promises he made at the KICC that evening. Raila has been the Prime Minister of Kenya since April 2008. He is a co-principal with President Kibaki. He sits atop the office of the Prime Minister, a humongous and elevated institution in Kenya, with a budget that runs into billions of shillings, a large staff and extensive reach and influence. What is preventing him from using his office to pursue some of his pre-election commitments? Five years after taking up office he is still behaving like an opposition activist, complaining about the 'government', despite being one of the leaders of that same government.

Another fundamental pledge he made in that KICC speech was to be accountable over corruption, nepotism and tribalism in government. He declared that staffing at his office "will reflect our national diversity". He then challenged anyone to hold him accountable. He correctly decried the existence of "informal government structures that allow family members, personal friends and moneybags more access and control of State House than elected officials – more even than cabinet ministers. These will go…the informal structures that currently exist are rooted in tribal alliances and cronyism, and our history tells us that these have been the real engines running our past and current government."

Yet, from the off, the office of the Prime Minister has seemed to me to be a den of corruption and nepotism. While I was his senior advisor and joint secretary to the permanent committee on the management on grand coalition affairs, I tried to remind Raila, repeatedly, of those solemn undertakings to the people of Kenya. I openly challenged the decision to appoint his older brother Oburu Oginga as an assistant minister for finance; his cousin Jakoyo Midiwo as both the ODM and joint coalition government chief whip (which is essentially a full cabinet position); sisters Akinyi Wenwa to a diplomatic post in Los Angeles, California and Beryl Achieng' to chair the Railway Workers' Pension Board; as well as the appointments of his cousin Carey Orege as PS in ministry of regional development; Elkanah Odembo (Jakoyo Midiwo's brother-in-law) as Kenya's Ambassador to the US; his cousin Paul Gondi as the executive chairman of the Geothermal Development Company; another distant cousin from Sakwa in South Nyanza, Ochillo Ayacko, as the executive chairman of the Kenya Nuclear Electricity Project and another cousin from Sakwa, Bondo, Joe Ager, as a senior officer of the Kenya Power Lighting Company. There were even credible stories that the newly appointed Controller of Budget, Agnes Odhiambo, was Ida's first cousin. Even the (then) National Social Security Fund's Managing Trustee, Alex Kazongo, and the Auditor General, Edward R.O. Ouko, were said to be related to Raila. In fact, immediately Raila was set to become Prime Minister, even before he was sworn in, he hand-picked another relative of his, James Ogundo, to be a member of the lucrative Constituency Development Fund (CDF) board. That was perhaps Raila's first appointment as Prime Minister.

But we should have detected Raila's nepotistic tendencies earlier. Or more accurately, I should have. Twice, when I accompanied Raila to Minnesota and Colorado, I noticed that funds donated by diaspora Kenyans were handled by either his step-sister, Akinyi Walkowa, or his daughter, Rosemary Akeyo. Other times, he would summon another relative (whom everyone at Raila's offices refer to as "Kulei"), George Opondo, to handle cash. These weren't personal funds. Kenyans were donating in order to support the ODM and Raila's presidential campaign.

The personalisation of power is largely responsible for the Big Man syndrome and the vicious abuse of power, the tyranny and pillage of public resources that have occurred all over Africa for the last 50 years. Raila's hiring of his family members, relatives and village-mates would be one of the worst kinds of nepotism I would ever encounter in my life, and in many ways, a harbinger for worse things to come. Raila, whom I had called an agent of change – a bridge between the old rotten system and the new progressive era – a person I had termed an enigmatic political genius of all times would turn out to be worse than Moi in my considered opinion and much, much, worse than Kibaki on every score.

Unlike Kibaki, Raila had no honour and loyalty to his friends. His word meant nothing. He betrayed his close friends more than he did his enemies. He couldn't be trusted not just with petty promises, but also with the power and leadership of Kenya. In a word: I would painfully discover that Raila was a dangerous man.

More than once (after Raila became Prime Minister), I sat in meetings where investors would propose to fund the development of various initiatives, including such things as garbage incineration. The French government made proposals of improving the infrastructure of Kisumu. But each time, Raila would crassly steer the discussions to Siaya County, specifically Bondo Town where he hailed from. The only place where a university college has been commissioned, built and opened since Raila became Prime Minister is Bondo.

Is this what we worked so tirelessly for? The nepotism, cronyism and plain irresponsibility defies reason, logic or commonsense.

CHAPTER SIX

NYANDO

By August, 2007, I had, with some regret, sold our Bradford house and closed my law office in Toronto in readiness for our relocation to Kenya. I was planning to contest the Nyando parliamentary seat, though first I would have to be nominated as the ODM candidate. I also wanted to make direct and significant contributions to Raila's and ODM's campaigns in the general elections scheduled for December 27.

Nyando was my home constituency. Magina village, where I was born and had grown up, was administratively in the South East Kano location of Nyando division. Between 1963 and 2007, Nyando had had nine members of parliament, only two of whom had ever been re-elected. Since independence, Nyando has been split and reconfigured three times, exemplifying how political gerrymandering has played a pivotal role in its leadership. The major economic activity in Nyando is subsistence farming, but the area is perennially ravaged by floods, which means the grinding poverty of my childhood is still the norm. As of 2007, some of my siblings, relatives, former schoolmates and friends still lived in Nyando. Although I had fled it to go into exile, I knew and loved Nyando more than any other place. I still do. But more importantly, I understood its problems, challenges, strengths and the opportunities it offers for positive change. Canada, where I had lived for 19 years, has super-modern infrastructure, social amenities and all the basic necessities of life in sufficient quantity and quality. But Nyando doesn't have even the most rudimentary of these.

So, when I decided to venture into politics in 2007, Nyando was the logical place to start. It cried out for change in every sphere – political, social, economic and cultural. I had a vision for Nyando, which I developed into a 12-point manifesto which focused on strong advocacy, legislation, public policy and development for the constituency. But the centre-piece of my campaign for Nyando was a plan for flood control.

As I've mentioned before, politics is in my DNA; it forms part of my essential daily diet. Without politics, music, writing, and agitation for social justice, I'm not sure what my life would look like. What I know is that I wouldn't have been, or be, the same person I am now. Although I had been away from Kenya for close to 20 years, I could still roll my Rs like the natural-born Luo that I was. It surprised many people, including myself, that I could actually still address rural constituents in flawless Dholuo, punctuated with poetry, riddles and metaphor. Adjusting my daily routine from the manicured lawns, hallowed courtrooms, well-paved roads and highways and comfortable lifestyle that I was used to in Canada to the muddy and dusty neighbourhoods of Nyando came naturally to me. After all, my passion was with the long suffering people of Kenya, but especially those of Nyando. This was home!

That's how I ended up running around the villages and market places of Nyando with hordes of youth in tow and dancing with local women and children. And I discovered, as I traversed the entire constituency, that in more than 50 years, the place had not qualitatively changed. If anything, it seemed like it had actually deteriorated. There were less mud-walled and grass-thatched buildings inside the school compounds, but many people were still dying from preventable and treatable diseases like malaria, bilharzia, meningitis and dysentery. Unacceptably large numbers of expectant mothers were also dying during child birth. HIV/Aids continued to ravage Nyando, as it has now done for decades in many African countries. Positively, in many of the local schools, children had wooden desks; not stones like we had had during my time. However, the conditions of local secondary schools had significantly worsened. The buildings were rickety. Most of them hadn't seen paint for decades. But even more worrisome, the academic performance for both primary and secondary schools had plummeted so badly that hardly any village children were proceeding to provincial or national secondary schools. Sadly, it seemed like no public health facilities had been constructed since I had left Nyando.

It was depressing. And yet I felt inspired to do everything I could to improve conditions here. I felt strongly that I could be effective as the people's representative in parliament; that I could place my legal training, experience and the exposure I had had abroad to the service of my people.

* * * * * * * * * * * * * *

But we had to get to Kenya first. We planned to ship out our household goods to Nairobi at the beginning of September and to move out of the Bradford house by September 15. Indeed, we had packed and were just waiting for the arrival of the movers early on the morning of September 9, when my home telephone rang. It was Raila.

"*Ja-Nyando*, how are you?"

"I'm well Jakom; congratulations! That was a remarkable victory for the ODM ticket [he had just won the party's presidential nomination]. At least now we can breathe easy that the progressive forces have a party of their own, with a leader who can deliver… How is Nairobi?"

"Thank you! Oh Nairobi was OK earlier today when I left. I'm in Dubai, catching a flight to Denver Colorado. Look, I'd like you to accompany me to Denver. I'm scheduled to attend a Pan-African conference at a place called Mankato tomorrow. Please if you can…"

"That was marvellous. You swept Kasarani clean. I just read it on the net." I was still stuck on the results of Raila's nomination as the ODM presidential candidate which had been reported by the electronic media a few hours before. It hadn't dawned on me that the man expected me to drop everything I was doing to rush to Denver right there and then. But that's what he expected. How could I maneouvre myself out of it?

"Thanks *Ja-Nyando*. I think they knew I would win – Musalia and Ruto; they are the ones who put up stiff competitions. Balala and Nyagah were, of course, on our side all along. Anyway, will you go with me?" he chimed in.

"Hmmm, *Jakom,* it's tricky because I'm planning to travel to Kenya…me and the entire family in a few days. You know that we are relocating…"

"Oh, time runs fast. Of course, I know. When are you coming?"

"We are scheduled to depart here on September 19, arriving in Nairobi on the 20th."

"I hope you can make it to Denver; please try. I know it will leave you no time to pack, but I really need you there."

"I'll try *Jakom*. What's the trip about?"

"Oh, I've been invited to give a talk at the University of Denver. You know, I once attended that university, many years ago. I'm going with Kipkalya Kones, my daughter Rosemary and Jacqueline Oduol."

"Ok, *Jakom*…"

"Who was that?" My wife asked as soon as I replaced the handset.

"Raila; who else?" I answered, feeling confused and a bit frustrated. Why was Raila trying to take advantage of me?

"I knew it! Why is he always calling you to go with him to places yet he doesn't want to spend his own money on those trips?"

"It's OK; it's for the struggle!" I responded limply.

"The struggle? What struggle? It's for Raila Odinga, full stop. Are you going?" She asked.

"I don't know. I guess I will. I'll disappoint him if I don't," I struggled with my words.

"Well, when is it? I hope it is not tomorrow."

"Actually, it is. We'll manage; don't worry."

"Hmm! Just remember that we are moving out on September 15th!" She sighed and we called it a night.

"I know, I know," I said, sighing heavily as I packed my carry-on luggage and said goodbye to the kids and my wife who was getting increasingly rattled by Raila's demands. She wasn't like her normal self – repeating things over and over again. As I drove out of the driveway, I called my travel agent, Freweini, and placed my booking for early the next morning, which she confirmed before I arrived at the airport. My head was whirring. I booked into the Toronto Sheraton at Pearson International Airport. My flight to Denver would be very early the next day. And since Bradford was 65 kilometres away from Toronto, I feared that I might not wake up early enough to catch the 7am flight. The flight was on time on September 10. We had one stop-over and a connecting flight and we landed at the Denver International Airport by 2pm that day. I found Raila's former personal assistant Ochido at the airport. We waited for Raila, Kones and Rosemary who arrived at about 3pm. Jacqueline Oduol arrived later in the evening.

Once we were at the hotel, Raila told me that he had no speech. That was becoming predictable. My friend Banda Nyaware travelled from New York to join us late that evening. That night, as with the Minnesota visit, I didn't sleep. Not only was I preparing Raila's speech, I also needed to prepare one for myself in view of my last-minute inclusion in the programme. On top of all that, I had already spent about another $6,000 of my personal savings in the cause of the Majestic People of Kenya on this Denver trip.

On September 11, 2007, after Raila and Kones had spoken, I delivered a long tribute to "The Majestic People of Kenya", and concluded with an exuberant prediction:

> I am extremely honoured today to be speaking in the presence of Honourable Raila Odinga, Kenya's foremost agent of change and the next President of the Republic of Kenya.
>
> As one that we have humbly named *The Majestic People's President,* let me signal to Honourable Raila Odinga that Kenyans from all walks of life fully expect that when he finally takes over the reigns of government in January 2008, the country will turn its back, for good, on the politics of blood, rapacious looting, tribalism, exploitation and oppression.
>
> With the pre-eminent agent of change presiding over a progressive administration in Kenya, we have confidence and hope that, finally, Kenyans will say, in memory of all our people who have perished, been maimed, detained, imprisoned, exiled or impoverished, fighting for the total liberation of our country: Free at last! Thank God Almighty we are free at last!

It was exuberant, defiant and uplifting, at least for me, and clearly for many people in the audience who applauded after I had finished. We needed to explain the arduous journey of our struggle to the audience, the overwhelming majority of who were foreigners with little, if any, knowledge of Kenya.

At that point, I was absolutely confident of the outcome of the scheduled general election. Though I wonder now if someone had been able to forewarn me of the impending chaos that electoral malpractices would bring about if I might have planned my own life differently. This is not to say that I was completely blind to the potential danger of rigging or of someone refusing to relinquish power after a convincing defeat at the polls. I recall raising this matter with Raila, privately, during the Minnesota and the Denver visits. However, in his characteristic style, Raila had brusquely brushed my concerns aside, telling me that rigging had become practically impossible since the 2005 referendum when the Orange brigade, led by him, had humbled Kibaki's Banana republicans. He was cocky and told me that I should remember how he had forced Moi to concede power to Kibaki in December 2002 by threatening to lead "a one million-man march" to State House; that just as Moi had eaten humble pie then, and as he had forced Kibaki to do in November 2005; so would Kibaki be forced to in December 2007.

I also tried to raise the issue of the politically lop-sided composition of the electoral commission, the security and intelligence agencies, including the provincial administration, but Raila would have none of it. He was adamant that Kibaki would not be able to rig the 2007 elections just as he had been unable to rig the constitutional referendum of November 21, 2005. I mentioned that Kibaki had had far less to lose in 2005 than now, in a presidential election. "*Jakom*, do you really think Kibaki is behaving like someone who is ready to vacate power?"

"*Ja-Nyando*, Kibaki has no option but to leave," Raila answered.

"But where is the evidence that he is going to leave? Forgive me for asking again *Jakom*, but look at the way he has trashed the Inter Party Parliamentary Group (IPPG) agreement that all parties entered into in 1997 by unilaterally naming members of the Electoral Commission of Kenya without regard to other parties' involvement; why didn't he consult you and other members of the opposition if he doesn't plan to rig? Look at the way his inner circle are speaking: Njenga Karume [then Minister of Defence], and John Michuki [his internal security and provincial administration counterpart], specifically. Why do they look like they are digging in for a long fight when they should be preparing for any possibility; a win or a defeat and a peaceful handover of power?"

"*Ja-Nyando*, on this one we disagree," responded Raila. "Kibaki will leave power after we defeat him in December 2007."

That ended our debate on the potential rigging by Kibaki. We moved onto the tricks and tactics Kalonzo had tried to use to win the ODM-K presidential nominations (before he eventually ran away with the party). Raila had told me a memorable thing, which I should share. He said, "*Ja-Nyando*, in wrestling; when two people wrestle, they do everything to win. One may try to grab his opponent's crotch; the other may try to trip the opponent; but in the end, the one who wins is either the one who remains standing or on top of the other. Politics is not any different. Everyone must do whatever he can to win. So, let Kalonzo do everything he can to win..."

It is a very close paraphrase; but it nonetheless captures the gist of what Raila said. "But *Jakom*," I began, trying to be as polite as I could, while conscious that I needed to tell him that there are rules in both politics and wrestling, "you are speaking as if the games of wrestling and politics have no rules...I understand what you are saying, but I'm not sure that a wrestler is allowed to grab his opponent's crotch and win; nor do I really think or believe that electoral laws allow politicians to break the law in pursuit of votes. If I understand you correctly *Jakom*, you are saying the end justifies the means? And that victory is all we should worry about; that it doesn't matter the infractions and violations one commits in the pursuit of victory?"

"Yes *Ja-Nyando*, in this game, the end justifies the means," he said this with unusual energy, as he kept smiling, slyly.

This left me scratching my head. I was beginning to form misgivings about Raila. I was slowly seeing a politician solely motivated by a burning desire to win at any price, who might be prepared to do anything – legal, extra-legal or outrightly unlawful to win. That was very clear from his last assertion, which he spat out with vigour, as if to tell me he wasn't prepared to continue the discussion.

Later, after Raila became Prime Minister and we were sitting in his presidential suite in a hotel in Geneva in 2009 – with Salim Lone next to me – I asked if he could ever work with Kalonzo again, especially now that they were both holding important positions in the grand coalition government. Raila looked at us and answered, deadpan: "Kalonzo is so shallow and self-absorbed; I can never work with him again. He believes that he was ordained President because his mother, who was a 'seer,' predicted it." Salim and I looked at each other and we moved on to another topic.

* * * * * * * * * * * * * *

On September 20, 2007, we landed at Nairobi's Jomo Kenyatta International Airport; my wife, Jane, the twins, Suré and Anyango, and our last born, Achieng'. My two older children, Atieno and Biko, remained in school in Toronto. The children, not being used to long-haul flights, were exhausted.

Five days later my campaign to be nominated as the ODM candidate for Nyando began in earnest with my purchase of a Toyota Land Cruiser, pickup truck and Corolla. I also purchased campaign equipment; an *auja* system (public address system equipment) and loud speakers. Posters, calendars, hats and t-shirts were also ordered. Then I hit the road, covering practically all the Nyando villages; meeting women, youth and men of all ages. We traversed the constituency with a team of dedicated campaigners and supporters: attending five to seven meetings each day; discussing issues with the constituents; singing with women and the youth; dancing and fundraising throughout Nyando. All the time, we were also recruiting members for ODM, urging voters to turn out in large numbers – not just during the ODM nominations scheduled for 16 November 2007 (my first hurdle) – but more particularly for the general election on December 27.

On October 8, I submitted my nomination forms to Orange House. The following day, various aspirants met with the then ODM election board chairman, Justice (Rtd) Richard Otieno Kwach, a haughty figure who treated us to a bizarre, disjointed and confused presentation where all questions were summarily dismissed. There were no discussions, deliberations or debates; only Kwach's autocratic fiats. I sought reassurance that all nomination materials would be produced in time and securely delivered to all constituencies at least a day before November 16. And that the ballots and boxes would be tamperproof. Kwach's irritated response was to tell the gathering that we should know that anything he presided over would be perfect; that perfection was his first and last name. He would repeat this once more at a meeting he had with aspirants from Nyanza at the Tom Mboya Labour College in Kisumu.

My worries were not allayed. I could see danger lurking ahead. Beneath the thin veneer of confidence that Kwach exuded, I perceived a man whose head was being turned by the tens of millions of shillings that were pouring into Orange House each week. Parliamentary aspirants were falling over each other to curry favours with Raila, Nyong'o, Musalia Mudavadi, Henry Kosgey, Omingo Magara, William Ruto, Najib Balala, Joseph Nyagah, and Kwach – even Raila's wife Ida. These people – most of them former Kanu leaders (those we call "Kanu Orphans") – would arrive carrying briefcases and brown envelopes filled with cash, in the hope of buying favour and influence. At the end, it was this cash that guaranteed a nomination certificate to an aspirant; not votes.

But why were we really surprised considering that Kwach's tenure at the Kenya Court of Appeal had suddenly ended following serious allegations of corruption? In fact, stories had been doing the rounds in Nairobi that a well-known Nairobi lawyer, Ahmednasir Abdulahi, had videotaped Kwach in the basement of the Nairobi Hilton Hotel as he handed parcels stuffed with marked notes over to the judge in a sting operation. Even though Kwach was never prosecuted over this, credible allegations had been made against him at a tribunal President Kibaki had established shortly after taking power in December 2002 to deal with corruption in the judiciary. Conveniently, however, Kwach had retired instead of facing the tribunal and exonerating himself of the allegations.

Although I visited every village, market place and primary school in Nyando, and spent Sh5m in less than two months, I soon realised that I hadn't given myself enough time to campaign. Clearly 46 days was insufficient to cover as large a constituency as Nyando. Many Nyando residents were supportive, understanding and appreciative of the efforts I was making; they attended my meetings in large numbers and hailed my speeches; but they were also almost uniform in their verdict: I needed more time to traverse the constituency, familiarise myself with the people and connect with them. This is important not just in politics, but in every human endeavour. However, it was particularly significant in a political environment that had been infested, infected and 'corrupted' with money. I now regard this experience as a learning process.

Whenever all the Nyando candidates met, I was picked to chair or draft any joint communiqués. That was because there was no history of bad blood between me and any of them. I had approached the contest positively, consistently arguing that it was an in-house competition that had to be conducted peacefully, fairly, transparently and democratically. I reasoned that Kenyans would be judging Raila Odinga's and ODM's abilities to govern the country on the basis of how they conducted the party nominations; if the nominations were fraudulent, most Kenyans would inevitably conclude that Raila and the party would perpetrate electoral and other frauds on the Kenyan public. However, if the nomination exercise was conducted faultlessly, then Kenyans would pass judgment positively. I also stressed that even though we were competing against each other, we would remain Luos, residents of Nyando and Nyanza, members of ODM and Raila Odinga's supporters. I argued that if we fought viciously then the end result would be deep, irreconcilable divisions within the party. These arguments helped calm nerves, though whenever my fellow contestants met alone – in the field or in public places like bars and restaurants – they not only publicly exchanged bitter words, but almost always engaged in physical brawls. Whenever I met them alone or in ODM meetings, they expressed their appreciation about the level of maturity and tolerance I had brought to the campaign; they claimed it was because of my time in Canada.

I recall meeting Otiende Amollo at the Nyanza Club one day during the ODM nominations campaigns. He was then a candidate for Rarieda constituency where he was going head-to-head with my old friend and former classmate Nicholas Gumbo. I asked him why there was so much animus, even physical violence, between him and Gumbo and their supporters in Rarieda, when they had so much in common. They were both young, urbane and highly learned professionals. Amollo told me, in exasperation: "I don't know what the problem with your friend is. It looks like violence is in his DNA. I think that's the way he was created."

I didn't believe Amollo about Gumbo, nor did I credit his theories about genetic inheritance. However, Amollo's comments worried me, because they expressed such resignation about an alarmingly widespread culture of intolerance towards people with divergent political opinions. The quick resort to physical violence demonstrated our society's failure to manage conflicts peaceably.

In Nyando, there were deep schisms between Eric Opon Nyamunga and Frederick Outa; Nyamunga and Paul Gogo; Nyamunga and Apollo Owuor; Outa and Paul Omanga; Outa and Charles Aguko; and Outa and Laban Oyuke. So fierce, corrosive, virulent and personal were the rivalries that Outa and Nyamunga's supporters had fought numerous times, guns had been drawn and two innocent youths had lost their lives. These two could never meet peacefully unless I was around. In fact, I was the only candidate who campaigned in Nyando without armed goons. I was also the only one who didn't bear a firearm. Twice, Gogo and Outa had separately and individually held joint rallies with me. My youths and security freely mingled with those of my opponents'. So, it was natural that they would appoint me their spokesperson.

But there were two other reasons. Firstly, it was an open secret that I was a member of the Raila Odinga 2007 strategic team. Many knew that I had not only hosted Raila in Canada in 2006, but that I often accompanied him on his many foreign trips. They believed that among them, I was the 'closest person' to Raila. And secondly, I was the only candidate in Nyando who carried a laptop and had proven writing skills.

* * * * * * * * * * * * * *

On November 16, all the candidates for Nyando, save Eric Nyamunga, gathered at the Ahero Multipurpose Centre, which was to serve as the Nyando constituency nomination centre. We were all apprehensive, not just about the election result, but because by 1pm our returning officer was still to report to duty. Even worse, the actual election paraphernalia – the ballot boxes, ballot papers and other nomination materials – had not yet arrived. My telephone calls and text messages to Orange House weren't being responded to.

We were getting increasingly anxious, restless and annoyed. An Orange House insider gave me the registration number of the vehicle – a matatu – that was supposed to be ferrying the materials to Muhoroni, Nyando and Nyakach. Rumours were spreading that the outgoing MPs for those three constituencies had intercepted the vehicle and were busy marking ballot papers in some secret location(s). I promptly marshalled 20 youths to stand on the road and intercept the vehicle if they saw it on the road, which they did, within 45 minutes. And to our astonishment, the vehicle was indeed carrying about 17,000 marked ballot papers for the outgoing Nyando MP, Eric Nyamunga, and more than 15,000 for the outgoing Nyakach MP, Peter Odoyo. Apparently, the MP for Muhoroni constituency, Ayiecho Olweny, had already received his "deliveries". Strangely, at around the same time as we apprehended the vehicle and discovered the marked ballot papers, Nyamunga arrived at the Centre, expressing as much shock as we did.

After careful examination of the vehicle, we found voting materials for many other constituencies, most of it already opened and tampered with. They were for Rarieda, Alego Usonga, Ugenya, Uriri, Karachuonyo and many constituencies in Western Province. The situation was a complete farce: those who were supposed to escort the materials and ensure their security and safety looked dazed and were unable to explain what was going on. It was obvious to us that we had interrupted a major electoral fraud being executed.

After quick consultations with the other candidates and the returning officer, I drafted a protest note, which was then faxed to Justice Richard Otieno Kwach. It informed him of our discovery and advised him of our collective hope that the nominations process could be extended to the following day, November 17. The letter was couched carefully to cover all legal loopholes and signed by all the candidates.

> Dear Sir:
> Re: Resolution by Nyando ODM Candidates
> Please be advised that Nyando ODM Parliamentary and Civic Candidates have unanimously resolved that the ODM nominations that were scheduled for November 16, 2007 shall take place today, November 16th, 2007 and to continue and conclude on November 17, 2007, between 6am and 3pm.
>
> This resolution has been made because the ODM Elections Board failed to deliver ballot papers and boxes in a timely fashion. The ballot boxes and electors' cards were only received at 2pm on November 16, 2007. Some of the ballot boxes and papers were torn and shredded. The individuals that were sent to deliver the materials could not explain why they were late or why the voting materials were tampered with. In addition, the ODM Elections Board failed to provide presiding officers, polling clerks and transport for the nominations. Consequently, we were compelled to provide logistics, security, transport, additional ballot boxes and papers so that the nominations could be conducted fairly, transparently and securely.
>
> We could not expose the Returning Officer, candidates, polling officials and voters to insecurity by extending voting at night as ordered by you, sir. We recognized that the Elections Board never made provisions for lighting and security.

> Our attempts to communicate the foregoing anomalies to the Board were unsuccessful because the Returning Officer's calls were not answered by either you or any of your officers.
>
> We have carefully considered the implications of conducting elections at night in a rural constituency where security, transport and logistical issues were not taken care of and unanimously resolved that this problem can only be resolved by us holding the nominations today up to 6pm and resuming tomorrow at 6am until everyone would have voted.
>
> It is further unanimously resolved that the Nyando ODM nominations shall not be conducted through dictatorial, arbitrary, irresponsible and capricious orders from either the ODM Elections Board or from the Board's Chair.
>
> Yours very truly,
>
> Miguna Miguna, Eric Opon Nyamunga, Frederick Outa, Apollo Owuor, Laban Oyuke, Paul Omanga, Charles Aguko and Paul Gogo.

That is how we rescued what little still remained of the ODM's electoral democracy. That exercise opened my eyes to some of the most fundamental problems in our governance system. For instance, Nyamunga and Outa openly bribed voters (in broad daylight as we watched) as they lined up to vote at various polling stations. The two and their agents moved from one polling station to another, paying voters Sh200 each to cast their ballots for them.

On the day of the delayed Nyando nomination – November 17 – there was palpable tension in and around Ahero. There were rumours of mysterious ballot boxes appearing or disappearing on the way to Ahero Multipurpose Centre. Most of these rumours seemed to suggest that Outa and Nyamunga were largely responsible for the electoral thuggery in Nyando. There were similar reports of electoral misdeeds all over the country. ODM members were up in arms, demonstrating against the disorganisation, incompetence and corruption of the ODM Elections Board. I voted at Apondo Primary School in Magina village at about 8am. Immediately after I had cast my ballot, my Blackberry vibrated; it was Raila calling.

"Good morning *Ja-Nyando*?"

"Good morning *Jakom*"

"How are things? How are you doing?"

"Well, I've just cast my ballot at my local primary school and will tour the constituency to see the progress. I'll let you know how things are in the evening."

"Ok *Ja-Nyando*. Good luck."

That was very thoughtful of Raila. He had actually surprised me. He rarely called unless he wanted something done urgently. That was a very rare and special occasion. I appreciated the gesture.

At around 7.30pm on November 17, I went to Karanda Primary School with Outa to follow up sensational claims that Nyamunga's youth had taken over the polling centre. Now, Karanda wasn't just any ordinary station, it had the largest number of registered voters in Nyando – more than 12,000 of them. Lela Primary School was the second richest vote centre, with about 11,000 strong. Outa considered the latter his strong-hold by virtue of clan affiliation. Therefore, securing both Karanda and Lela votes was crucial in ensuring that whoever emerged the overall winner would have a legitimate mandate of the voters. Similarly, whoever "stole" votes from either or both centres would most likely emerge the overall winner. That was well known.

Upon our arrival at the main hall there, we saw that there was still a long line of anxious voters, presumably worrying that the polls would close before they had been able to cast their vote. Outa almost immediately started a commotion; pushing, shoving and threatening everyone on sight. He drew a long, sharp and shining sword, which he had concealed in a leather sheath that looked like a walking stick. As he advanced towards the man in charge of the station, many people began to surround him, daring him to strike. I intervened and calmed the crowd before they began tearing Outa to pieces. I could see that nothing untoward was happening there; voters were just anxious that the station might be closed before they voted.

As we drove away from Karanda, I was still worrying that Nyamunga might have conspired with the polling officers to harvest all the votes there. But those suspicions soon dissipated as results began to trickle in. Outa took an early lead and maintained the momentum throughout. By midnight, I knew that Outa was most likely going to win, followed by Nyamunga. By the time I left the tallying hall for my hotel in Kisumu at around 11.30am on November 18, I had 2,545 votes while Outa had passed the 10,000 mark. I believed the game was up. I said goodbye to my colleagues, agents and supporters and drove to Kisumu.

But what Outa had done kept gnawing on my mind. As he had drawn out his sheathed weapon and charged at ordinary voters and polling officers, I had wondered what might be going on in his head. He had been talking gibberish about Nyamunga having bribed everybody, yet he hadn't even investigated those reports. And besides, as I have indicated before, Outa himself wasn't entirely innocent of such accusations: I had watched as both he and Nyamunga had bribed voters in at least three polling stations.

But notwithstanding any suspicions we might have had – legitimate or illegitimate – how could Outa justify threatening voters, assaulting or battering them and still expect to win their support, respect and confidence? How was he going to salvage the situation by being a combatant? For the first time, I realised how shallow and irrational Outa could be. He had behaved like a common thug. Later, in parliament, he would seem incoherent, silly, incapable of thinking beyond the most rudimentary and therefore apparently ill-equipped to be a legislator.

Looking back, I can say confidently that had I not intervened and had that vehicle carrying nomination materials intercepted on the Nairobi-Kisumu road, Nyamunga and Peter Odoyo would have rigged themselves back to parliament. That is not to say that I found Outa or Ochieng' Daima good or better parliamentarians than Nyamunga and Odoyo; on the contrary, they were dour, lacklustre and clueless; their contributions in parliament couldn't fill a two-lined paragraph. It is also why, as we go forward as a country, our focus as a nation mustn't just be on legal and institutional reforms per se; it must equally be on fundamental changes in our culture and attitudes, individually and collectively. This is because no matter how progressive a constitution might be, it must be implemented by people. The values and broad principles in the Constitution of Kenya 2010, are quite far reaching; but unless there are men and women of integrity ready to enforce them, they will remain just words on paper.

At about midnight, as I sat in my room at the Nyanza Club, Raila called me to find out how things were.

"*Ja-Nyando*, how were the nominations?"

"There were ok. Nyamunga and Outa bribed voters but I guess that's the way things are done in this country..."

"Well, who won?"

"I think Outa has won, despite the serious malpractices. When I left the tallying hall, he had an unassailable lead over Nyamunga."

"It's ok. Take it easy. When are you returning to Nairobi?"

"I'll be there tomorrow *Jakom*. I'll henceforth concentrate my efforts in the Presidential Strategy Team."

"Ok. Good night *Ja-Nyando*."

"Good night *Jakom*."

* * * * * * * * * * * * * *

On November 18, we woke up to an outcry. Amid the hullabaloo, there was universal condemnation of the ODM Elections Board, the ODM Secretariat, Kwach and Anyang' Nyong'o, specifically. Reading the newspapers that morning, one couldn't help but notice the hypocrisy of the party. Although selections had been organised for Kisumu Rural and Mugirango South, where Anyang' Nyongo' and Omingo Magara, as secretary general and national treasurer, respectively, were facing stiff competition, just days before the nominations Orange House had announced that both candidates had been issued "direct nominations".

Everyone was aghast. Ochoro Ayoki, who was supposed to have been opposing Anyang' in Kisumu Rural, was furious. I used to see him whenever we went for meetings with the provincial administration and ODM Elections Board as Nyanza candidates. He struck me as a gentleman. But whenever the issue of Kisumu Rural came up, Ochoro was always insistent that Anyang' knew that he [Ochoro] was going to win; that that was why he [Anyang'] was trying to either rig or get himself a 'direct certificate.' At the time, I thought Ochoro was exaggerating things. However, when Orange House announced that it had issued direct nominations to the two national officials from Nyanza, I was angry and extremely disappointed.

Weeks before that, Orange House had issued all members of the Pentagon – Raila, Musalia, Ruto, Nyagah and Balala – with direct nominations. They had also given Henry Kosgey, as chairman, the same. Now, this dubious practice was being cascaded downwards. Orange House justified these moves by insisting that 'the party wanted to free up officials to concentrate on the presidential campaign'. Although the argument defied every ODM platform, almost all staunch supporters backed it (in my case, grudgingly). The idea of direct nominations defeated the very principle of free, fair and transparent elections. It was 'high table' rigging.

At about 8.30am on November 18, I took my return flight to Nairobi. Before boarding, I telephoned Caroli to find out how he had fared. He told me that he had won but that the returning officer had changed the results and inserted John Mbadi's name. He wanted to petition Orange House to revoke the results and declare him a winner. I advised him not to pursue the matter as we were better off trying to help Raila win the presidential election. Fighting among ourselves, I argued, wasn't in the best interests of the party.

Before the plane departed at 8.45am, I called Jacqueline Oduol, who was devastated, also complaining about massive electoral fraud perpetrated on the people of Alego/Usonga. "Jacky, let's now dedicate our efforts towards a Raila victory. Join the strategic team. I think that's where your skills are in dire need."

"Ok, Miguna let me mull over it and I'll get back to you once I'm back to Nairobi later this week," she said. That is how Jacky joined the Raila Odinga 2007 presidential secretariat full time in November 2007. She and I plunged headlong into the campaign, working tirelessly, with many others, without compensation, day in, day out, until the elections were held on December 27.

At Jomo Kenyatta Airport, you could tell from people's expressions that they were disappointed with ODM. Everyone I spoke with at the airport was breathing fire: "We are going to teach Kwach and his group a lesson," many threatened. The party was turning inwards. Before I reached home that day, there were riots, demonstrations and violence. ODM members threatened to burn down Orange and Rainbow Houses. An irate group from Kasarani charged on Orange House with stones and other crude missiles, raining them on the national party officials until the riot police arrived with tear-gas, batons and guns. The Kasarani youth were repulsed by the police, but they didn't disband; they headed straight to Rainbow House where they unleashed terror, keeping members of the strategy team hostage for hours until police arrived. Similar events were happening all over the country; ODM officials were being chased around villages, towns and cities like wild dogs. The situation wasn't looking pretty, yet Raila, his Pentagon and ODM national leaders were nowhere to be found or seen. It was pure chaos.

It was Sunday still, but you wouldn't have known that from the number of people swirling around Orange House when I arrived there. It was pandemonium. It looked like a military garrison that had been run over by an invading army. There was litter and debris everywhere. Windows and doors were shattered; broken shards of glass and broken furniture strewn everywhere. You could still see smouldering embers, where flames had just been doused. People were shouting incoherently at the top of their voices. Many were gesturing wildly, pointing at each other, shoving and pushing.

The Orange party was now a mess; at the secretariat and throughout the country. I saw small pockets of people huddled together, whispering in low tones. I looked around for anyone I could recognise to ask where people were 'meeting', but I couldn't see anyone familiar. After 30 minutes of walking around, I saw Janet Ong'era and approached her, but she waved me away before I could say anything. Eventually, I saw Anyang' with a small group of people. I recognised Ken Ombongi, Amukowa Anangwe, Peter Wanyande, Mary Nyamongo and Janet Ong'era, though, at that time, we didn't know each other well. I approached tentatively and pulled up a chair, unsure whether to relax or to flee. Everyone glowered at me. Caroli arrived and pulled a chair up next to me. He whispered to me that he had already secured a nomination certificate for Gwasi

Constituency. I inquired how he had managed to do so and he told me there were "ways". I told him, still whispering, that I didn't think that was right; that he shouldn't get himself entangled with the ensuing confusion. He didn't look convinced either. The meeting was in a small tent in the compound. We discussed damage control; how to prevent a complete fallout of the party. In the end, nothing much came out of the meeting. There weren't resolutions; only an agreement to meet the following day to continue with the discussions.

On Monday November 19, I presented a document to the strategic team on the "way out" of the nominations' mess. I had received an avalanche of emails from ODM enthusiasts all over the world. There were obviously real concerns the party might go up in smoke. Many people believed that Raila urgently needed to call a meeting of all ODM candidates – those with certificates and those without (we had to avoid referring to those without as "losers" because, in truth, it was impossible to say who had lost or won). The party had to reassure all those who had stood that this was a marathon relay race, not a sprint, that each person had a contribution to make; and each person stood to gain something in the end – after our victory. A suggestion was flagged, which I thought offered the best reassurance to those who hadn't secured certificates, that once Raila had won the presidential election, those who had run as candidates would be considered for positions in government, as a matter of priority.

That November 2007, with only about six weeks to go until the presidential election, I found the members of the election strategy team, despondent. I heard lamentations of how its briefs, advice and recommendations were being ignored; how it had failed to secure meetings with Raila and other members of the Pentagon. The team complained that Ong'era, Kosgey, Magara and Anyang' ran the secretariat as a personal fiefdom; that everyone at Orange House was allegedly corrupt, starting with Nyong'o going down; and that Kwach was a disaster. Examples of alleged corruption and other malfeasance were legion. For instance, I was told of how Nyong'o, his wife and other relatives had opened up merchandising shops at Orange House and in other locations where they were selling ODM t-shirts, hats, jerseys and other things for profit. Apparently, Nyong'o had allegedly diverted all ODM printing work – of manifestos, constitution and basically all election-related materials – to a family company run by his wife from their Runda home.

There were credible stories of aspirants bribing national, secretariat and elections board officials. As well, many, including members of the strategy team, were raising questions about where the more than Sh2.5 billion that the party had collected during the membership recruitment drive and the rush for ODM nominations had disappeared to. This was in view of the fact that every time money was needed – even as little as Sh50, 000 – to buy lunch for strategy team members – they were being asked to go on 'begging' missions to Indian businessmen based in Migori and Nairobi. It was embarrassing to see private individuals – some with unknown political affiliations – carrying bottled water and food to Orange House, Rainbow House and Pentagon House. Everyone in ODM, including the senior most leaders, could have been poisoned and wiped out within minutes.

One assurance I gave to my colleagues after formally joining the strategy team in November 2007 was that I would ensure that all our resolutions reached Raila, directly. I was perplexed that neither Prof. Oyugi nor Prof. Wanyande could reach Raila on the telephone. Although Ager would boast of his frequent meetings with Raila, I discovered that the team was unanimous in its mistrust of Ager. Neither did they trust Caroli, another person who only made technical appearances at the meetings. I heard, over and over again, that both Caroli and Ager distorted, misrepresented and withheld vital information whenever they were sent to Raila. Prof. Oyugi and Ong'wen kept telling me not to trust Caroli; they stated that he was not just on the take from State House and PNU mandarins; he and Ager had allegedly told Raila that the strategy team was a "talk shop" that should be ignored; that it was because of Caroli and Ager that Raila and his Pentagon group showed disrespect to the team and rarely met it. I was even more surprised that up to the time I joined, Raila hadn't really held one formal meeting with the team. This was horrifying in view of the fact that it was now less than one and a half months to the general election. Prof. Oyugi was at his wit's end about his failure to get to Raila.

Once I joined the strategy team, my colleagues quickly gave me the responsibilities of leading research, drafting and propaganda initiatives. The core strategy team operated from the Rainbow House in Lavington, which used to be the headquarters of the LDP. Others who played central roles in strategy but were located at the communications centre at a place we called "49 Communications" – also in Lavington – were, Rose Lukalo (head), Salim Lone (spokesman), and Sarah Elderkin who was in charge of "special projects," doing everything from writing speeches to production of special advertisements and brochures. She operated from her home office in the Hurlingham area.

There was another shadowy group headed by Mohamed Isahakia based at his private offices located in a building called the "Titan" – which I understood was being paid for by the national security intelligence service throughout – made up of Isahakia's sidekicks Nehemiah Ng'eno, Caesar Asiyo, Iddris (a man who claimed to have been a Major in the Kenya Air Force, but who was dishonourably discharged allegedly due to a corruption-related incident), Tom Ogutu, Tony Chege and Mike Njeru. This group, though in charge of hundreds of millions of shillings, apparently did absolutely nothing. In fact, they undermined, subverted and sabotaged the campaign by constantly leaking information to the media, to the PNU and the security agencies. It was widely believed within the campaign that the Titan group's main motivation was how much money they could make out of the campaign. They didn't care who won. According to reliable sources within the campaign, this selfish and destructive group believed that they would gain either way. Each one of them had deep and strong connections with former President Moi's government, with the NSIS and, unfortunately, also with Raila. It was tricky working around this group. Many a time, the strategy and communications team would go quiet whenever any member of the Titan group chanced in on their meetings.

On the evening of November 19, as I sat watching the 9 o'clock news, Raila called. After the usual pleasantries, I got to the point, "*Jakom*, there is a big problem that needs to be addressed. You know that I'm now with the strategy team and I can confirm that there is a lot of discontent there. As well, there is a general feeling that you should call an extraordinary meeting with all ODM aspirants – with or without a certificate – so that you can assuage their fears, apologise to them for the way the nominations were mangled, in order to free your hands for the looming battle…I have prepared a detailed brief, with practical strategic options for you to consider…"

"OK *Ja-Nyando*, when do you want to bring it over?"

"I can do so tomorrow before I fly out to Toronto to see my children for a week before I return…"

"OK; come to the ROC at 10am. When are you leaving tomorrow?"

"I'm leaving at 10.45pm in the evening *Jakom*. I'll be there."

That is how ODM summoned all the candidates from all over the country to the Bomas of Kenya in early December for a heart-to-heart family discussion that re-energised the Orange team and put in motion a force that would threaten to run Kibaki out of State House within weeks. Thereafter, I was the main link between the strategy team and Raila. Ultimately, however, Raila and the entire ODM leadership exposed a serious weakness: they preferred operating through personal, informal channels rather than formal and institutional ones. This wasn't how modern governments were run.

BOOK FOUR

IN THE TRENCHES

CHAPTER SEVEN

KNOCKING ON HELL'S GATE

At around 2.30pm on Friday December 28, 2007, I drove my vehicle into the Kenyatta International Conference Centre (KICC), which was serving as the national tallying centre for the Electoral Commission of Kenya (ECK) and parked at a spot reserved for local observers. Seated beside me was Caroli Omondi. He had hitched a ride from Pentagon house, where we had left chaos. The security officers at the KICC gate recognised me and waved us in without checking our credentials.

As we climbed down the stairs into a large hall which had been converted into a media centre, I saw hundreds of anxious, angry and frustrated people, all trying to speak at once. Polling had closed in the parliamentary and presidential elections more than 24 hours earlier and now the results were overdue. At the far end of the hall, perched high on an elevated portion, were the Electoral Commission of Kenya commissioners, but their chairman, Samuel Kivuiti, was missing. There were a dozen other people seated beside and behind the commissioners. It wasn't clear who they were, where they had come from, or what they were doing sitting with the ECK commissioners. But they too looked anxious. Nobody on that dais was speaking. Their eyes were fixed on the space in front of them. There was media everywhere; print, electronic and TV. Journalists had come from all over the world: Africa, Europe, Asia, North America, India – you name it. They all looked wired, as they tried to record all the comings and goings.

Caroli and I spoke briefly with some ODM observers that were seated at the back of the hall. They told us that Kivuitu was supposed to address the gathering at any moment. We snaked our way towards the front. I could see the ODM

Chairman, Henry Kosgey, ODM Secretary General, Prof. Anyang' Nyong'o, ODM Pentagon member, Charity Ngilu, Justice (rtd) and ODM Elections Board Chairman, Richard Otieno Kwach, Bob Arunga, Dr Joseph Misoi, ODM Executive Director, Janet Ong'era and other ODM luminaries seated right in the middle of the front row, chatting animatedly. We were about two feet away from them when Caroli turned to me and said, matter-of-factly:

"Miguna, these people are not giving us *this thing*."

"What do you mean *they are not giving us this thing*?" I shot back.

"Kibaki will not hand over power," Caroli replied.

Still struggling with the enormity of what Caroli had just said, I proceeded to where our luminaries were seated and squeezed myself right behind them, next to Kwach.

"What's going on?" I whispered to Ngilu.

"Well, we are just waiting for Kivuitu to come down and start announcing the results…it's getting late already," she replied, sounding worried.

"But where is the National Tallying Centre? This is a media centre. Where *are* the tallying clerks, the 16A and 17A forms? Why are we all here?" I said rather loudly, turning to where Anyang' and Kosgey were seated. They both shrugged their shoulders.

I had opposed the idea of appointing ODM politicians and officials from Orange House as national presidential and party tallying agents. Raila, members of the Pentagon and all MP-elects had unfettered access to the KICC, but I hadn't seen the point in appointing them agents. I thought the role would have been better suited to young, brave, committed ODM members, who were good at crunching numbers and who would have been prepared to push and shove as necessary.

After hours of increasing restlessness, Kivuitu appeared, looking chirpy and carrying a brown file. "Ladies and gentlemen, I know you have been very patient," he began. "Unfortunately, I have no news for you. We are still trying to find our returning officers, some of them have switched their phones off and we don't know where they are. But we'll find them. When we do, I'll come down and start announcing the results, as they come in…"

"Nooo! Noooo!" the crowd roared back.

I decided to go in search of the National Tallying Centre, which was on the second floor. It was guarded by two solid reinforced wooden doors, which were in turn manned by several heavily-armed administration police and the General Service Unit (GSU) officers, none of whom looked like they were in the mood for any conversation.

As I stood outside, I saw people arriving in pairs, carrying briefcases, plastic bags and large brown envelopes. As soon as they reached the door, the security opened the door for them. Some would disappear inside, while others would emerge after a few minutes, either empty-handed or carrying something. I saw several Party of National Unity (PNU) big shots – among them Uhuru Kenyatta, Martha Karua, Amos Kimunya, Njeru Githae, Mutula Kilonzo, Beth Mugo and George Thuo of City Hoppa – entering and leaving in this way. But no Orange Democratic Movement mandarins were coming upstairs alongside them.

After spending close to 45 minutes monitoring PNU bigwigs coming in and out of the place where, I presumed, the election results were being 'cooked', I gathered my courage and approached one of the heavily armed security men stationed at the door. "Soldier; *habari*! What's going on here?"

"I don't know," he replied sullenly.

"I see. Isn't this the National Tallying Centre?" I continued, using the leading-question approach that lawyers find handy in such situations.

"Maybe; what do you want?" he responded. Two more officers had joined him by now and a small crowd was forming around me.

"Well, if it is the National Tallying Centre," I said removing my observer badge from my shirt pocket, "then I would like to go in and see what's happening inside."

"No you can't!" a newly arrived officer said, blocking my path.

"Why is that?" I asked, inching forward and stretched my hands as if trying to open the door.

"Because you can't!" another one answered, blocking my way. There were now about ten heavily-built, muscle men, carrying AK-47s, glaring at me.

"But I have seen PNU politicians like Karua, Uhuru and the rest going in and out of this place...Why are they allowed to do that when I can't?" They didn't respond. They just stood there glaring at me. The crowd behind me was becoming louder.

"How can you stop me, an observer, from witnessing how results are coming in and tallies are prepared?"

"You must leave now!" Two of them yelled in unison. I stood my ground. It was tense. I knew I couldn't go inside by force. But I also knew that with the crowd growing every minute, there was not much they could do to me.

At that moment, Anyang', the ODM Secretary General, and Kosgey, the ODM Chairman, arrived where I was. They looked worried. "What's going on Miguna?" Anyang' asked.

"This is the National Tallying Centre, not that noisy media centre down there," I blurted out, exasperated. "It is here that PNU are doctoring the results. We need to be inside here, observing, rather than down there, watching TV!"

"Miguna, you must leave here at once or I'll remove you myself!" said Kosgey, menacingly.

"Why when Uhuru, Karua, Githae, Mutula and all those PNU people have been going in and out of this place. Chairman, they are cooking the results here!" I replied, refusing to move.

"I said *leave now*, Miguna, or I'll order them to eject you!" Kosgey yelled, as Anyang' stood there, helplessly.

I left, reluctantly, because I didn't want to create a scene with the ODM chairman and secretary general. But I was furious. How clueless could a group of people be? I shook my head as I went back downstairs to the media centre. There, things had deteriorated to a point where sections of the media (both local and foreign), observers (both local and international), politicians from all sides, and ODM and PNU youth were baying at each other; ready for a grand finale. "Kibaki and his PNU thieves will not intimidate us with his heavily armed security forces!" I shouted, as I approached the front of the hall.

"Mr Miguna, you will not intimidate me. I know you…I know you are huge, but I'm not scared of you!" responded the ECK Chairman, Kivuitu, completely gratuitously, since I was not trying to intimidate anybody; all I was trying to do was demand, very strongly, for the results to start being announced. I wasn't deterred: again and again I charged forward, loudly demanding the results; telling Kivuitu off; squaring up to PNU power 'men' like Martha Karua, Uhuru Kenyatta and Amos Kimunya; arguing, haranguing, and shouting. Standing beside me, urging me on, yelling, pointing and demanding results were the ODM youths George Ayugi (popularly known as Mbuta) and Kadundo. Meanwhile, our luminaries stuck to their seats, looking pensive and petulant. Occasionally, Ruto and Ngilu provided necessary fire power.

Every so often, Kivuitu or another ECK commissioner, Kihara Mutu, would brave the cacophonous fray to announce constituency results, which nobody was interested in, primarily because they had already been announced at the constituency level more than 24 hours before. Just before midnight, they had released a provisional national presidential tally that gave Raila about one million votes ahead of Kibaki. But we were neither happy nor satisfied because, curiously, Kivuitu was withholding nearly all the results from Central Province, the large and populous constituencies in Eastern and the constituencies in Central Rift Valley, which is home to the Gikuyu Diaspora (Gikuyus who reside outside their ancestral home of Central Province). We suspected that the ECK must have been waiting to see Raila's votes before deciding how many votes they needed to add onto Kibaki's so as to legitimise his "victory." I texted my wife a simple message: "They are stealing this thing from us."

None of my strategy team comrades were around. Neither was Caroli. As soon as he had noticed the palpable tension in the hall, he had melted away. It was now nearly 15 hours since I had last eaten. But I wasn't feeling hungry or exhausted; I was too incensed to think about food. The only thing on my mind was how we could effectively repulse the forces of darkness intent upon destroying progress in Kenya. My focus was now big, much bigger than anything else I had previously encountered; it was about our destiny as a country; whether the country was ready to embrace democracy – in both theory and practice – or remain stuck in the past. There were no grey areas for me on that issue. One either belonged to the group of the majority of Kenyans demanding change; or one was with the merchants of impunity.

The media centre was closed at 1am. I rushed home, ate, showered and napped for two hours before heading out again. This was war and I wasn't going to watch it on television. I arrived back at the KICC at 4.30am to find it completely surrounded by security forces in strange military jungle fatigues. Their faces were hidden behind heavily reinforced red and black metallic helmets. Outside the media centre, I met Ugenya MP-elect James Orengo. He had just arrived from Ugenya. I briefed him on the previous day's events and we agreed that we would do whatever it took to force Kivuitu to announce the results. Scanning the troops, I felt it was better to die on my feet fighting for democracy, than to be killed fleeing.

December 29 was essentially the same as the previous day, except that Kivuitu and his team of despicable electoral thieves came down more frequently to announce constituency results, which were, by then, already known. They were releasing results of parliamentary candidates more or less accurately. However, they were withholding the presidential tallies, despite the fact that at the constituency level these had already been released by the returning officers. The media had also been reporting these figures now for close to two days. That was a pointer to trouble ahead. Orengo, Ngilu, ODM Pentagon member William Ruto and I now formed a four-person ODM platoon barraging the ECK officials for more results. Some of our PNU counterparts, meanwhile – I remember Josephine Ojiambo, Beth Mugo, Amos Kimunya and George Nyamweya – seemed determined to distract us with cat calls and heckling. From their conduct, it's difficult to imagine that they didn't know what was going on. They kept smiling scornfully at us. Except for Karua who was extremely agitated, most of the PNU people seemed relaxed, as if they knew that a "decision had already been made".

Just before 3pm, Kivuitu released a bizarre tally that put Kibaki, for the first time, far ahead of Raila. As if they had been waiting for that cue, results from Central Province and some other PNU enclaves in Eastern and Rift Valley now began dripping in. As each new constituency result was unveiled, Kibaki's lead seemed to be becoming unassailable. Eventually, Kivuitu would declare that Kibaki was now ahead of Raila by more than 350,000 votes. The gap was mysteriously widening. Based on previously released results, we couldn't see where those Kibaki votes had come from. We believed that someone was playing games with the tallies.

That is when Orengo, Ngilu, Ruto and I panicked. We were now in no doubt that PNU had massively rigged the vote. We went straight for Kivuitu. Orengo mounted the rostrum and snatched Kivuitu's microphone. I came behind him, shouting. Ngilu, too, climbed the steps and snatched another microphone from one of the ECK commissioners. There was pandemonium. More than 100 General Service Unit (GSU) and Administration Police (AP) officers invaded the hall. They pointed guns at us and wielded truncheons to shove the protestors back. Yelling loudly, they struck many people, repeatedly. Kivuitu and his disgraceful team were shepherded upstairs, out of sight.

That night, the ODM, through Orengo, Ruto and Ngilu, vociferously demanded for an audit of the tallies. After more than three hours of deafening commotion, the ECK officials acceded to those demands. Raila called members of the Pentagon at the KICC and nominated Orengo to lead the exercise on his behalf. But Orengo had no experience in forensic examination of documents. They picked Dick Ogolla as backup for Orengo specifically to look at the figures. There was no handwriting expert to help with the complicated matter of how, when and by whom the forms 16As and 17As had been filled. I immediately sniffed danger and cautioned Raila (by telephone) and Orengo. PNU picked Martha Karua as their lead "auditor." Ironically, none of the so-called auditors had any forensic training or experience.

As soon as the ECK opened up the National Tallying Centre for the 'auditors', I knew there was a trap. There were documents everywhere: piles and piles of them; some on tables, others lying on the floor, and all kinds of people running in and out. The place hadn't been secured. Orengo hadn't demanded that non-auditors were to stay out of the hall until the review exercise was completed. People operating computers were still proceeding with whatever it was that they had been doing and nobody sought to know what that was. Curiously, I noticed some people shredding documents in a corner, with nobody bothering to stop them. I pointed all these things out to Orengo and warned him that the exercise was bound to end in futility unless he investigated all those anomalies. When I approached the people who were literally tearing documents into pieces inside the hall, some hawkish ECK official – I believe it was Chege – insisted that I had to leave. Orengo didn't raise a finger in protest.

More egregiously, Orengo hadn't taken charge of the 'review process' at all; whatever they 'examined' were selected and brought to them by individuals Orengo had no knowledge of. (I suspected that most of them were either PNU or PNU-allied ECK officials. Some might even have been members of the National Security Intelligence Service.) He never asked the logic behind the choice of the documents brought. All Orengo had was a list of 34 constituencies whose presidential results ODM disputed. They were mainly Kieni, Molo, Nithi, Juja, Limuru, Mwea, Lari, Kirinyaga Central, Kandara, Gatundu South, North Imenti, Igembe South, Igembe North, Tigania West, Malava, Kimilili, Ol Kalau, Naivasha, Mandera West, Kajiado North, Tetu and Laikipia West. Although we had issues with Dagoreti, this wasn't on Orengo's list. Matuga was also a problem but no one seemed bothered about it. The ODM top honchos were convinced that Raila had won. They were contentedly waiting for the final victory whistle.

Disappointingly, Orengo never requested copies of the documents his team 'examined'. At the conclusion of the process, he left the hall with his hand-written notes and a tepid request jointly signed (with Martha Karua) to Kivuitu to "note" some "anomalies". Later, a section of the media reported that Orengo and Martha had "agreed that there were no major anomalies and that, barring minor errors, the tallying had complied with the relevant law". In other words, the dubious audit had approved the electoral fraud. I nearly collapsed. Initially, I blamed the press for misreporting. I even challenged Jeff Koinange of K24 to interview Orengo live, so that his clarification could be placed on the record. This was because when I challenged Orengo to explain why he had issued the joint statement with Karua, giving a green light to the doctored results, he had strongly denied having done so. He claimed that the media had misrepresented his views. But Jeff had actually interviewed Orengo live, and he (Orengo) hadn't corrected or clarified anything. It would turn out that the person whom Raila had sent to the tallies to audit the results was a perennial fumbler.

There were very serious anomalies that we expected Orengo – as ODM's chief auditor/verifier/examiner – to have clarified or sorted out before the ECK announced the final results. The total votes cast for all presidential candidates and those cast for all parliamentary candidates in the same polling station/stream were expected to be equal except for the spoiled votes, which would be duly marked "rejected" by the presiding officer. While we recognised the fact that there was no law requiring a voter to mark his or her ballot in any particular manner – and that it was both possible and probable for a voter to cast a ballot for a presidential candidate and not for a parliamentary candidate or councillor, or vice versa – the fact was that it was highly unlikely that a person would go to a polling station and refuse to mark the ballot for all three candidates – for President, MP and Councillor. Thus there shouldn't have been any significant difference between the total votes cast for presidential candidates and all parliamentary candidates in a polling centre, but if there was a *significant* difference, this would be an indication of rigging. When such anomalies ran into tens or hundreds of thousands of votes, one couldn't simply pepper over them. But Orengo did.

Moreover, under the relevant elections law, the results of the presidential election in a constituency shown in form 16A was supposed to be subject to confirmation by the ECK after a tally of all the votes cast in the election. On receipt of the returns from the parliamentary constituencies, the ECK Chairman was required – as the national returning officer for the presidential elections – to publicly receive and transparently tally the results in the presence of the candidates or their agents. Concomitantly, the candidates or their agents had a right to peruse, review, confirm or dispute the authenticity of each return submitted by the returning officers. The law recognised form 16A as the only source of an election result. Any 'results' that failed to conform to these requirements were deemed invalid.

Prior to being permitted to conduct the limited audit, Orengo knew, or ought to have known, that the ODM presidential candidate or his agents hadn't been allowed to peruse, review, verify and authenticate the form 16As that Kivuitu had used and was continuing to use to announce results of the presidential election. He also knew, or ought to have known, that no duly filled and signed form 16As were displayed to candidates or their agents in the media centre, before, during or after the announcement of the results. He (Orengo) had only been allowed into the tallying centre following two days of intense struggles and demands by the ODM contingency at the KICC. And his role there was restricted to 'auditing' forms from constituencies that we had raised red flags on; forms whose sources or authenticity he had no way of verifying.

It is imperative to underline that the procedure of reporting presidential election results wasn't followed in more ways than one. First, returning officers in some constituencies didn't deliver form 16As to the ECK because the forms were allegedly 'unavailable'. Second, there were credible reports and some evidence that the ODM presidential agents were forcefully evicted from or denied entry into some constituency tallying centres, thereby preventing them from verifying the tallying of votes, authenticating the votes cast in favour of the presidential candidates and challenging any irregularities. Third, the ECK deliberately failed to establish a national tallying mechanism for the presidential election. Fourth, the ECK Chairman, in many instances, announced presidential election results that were different from the results issued and confirmed at the constituency level by the returning officers and validated by duly completed and signed forms 16A and 17A. Fifth, Kivuitu read out presidential election results from computer printouts with figures that were materially different from those contained in forms 16As and 17As, contrary to Regulation 40(3) of the National Assembly and Presidential Election Act (as it was then). Sixth, the ECK didn't adhere to Regulation 40(6) of the National Assembly and Presidential Election Act (as it then was). Numerous times, Kivuitu comically announced that he couldn't reach some ECK commissioners because "they had switched their mobile phones off". In my view, these were the issues that Orengo was supposed to raise and insist on, instead of engaging in pedantic and menial addition and subtraction of numbers provided by both the architects and implementers of the massive electoral fraud.

Despite all these infractions and ODM's public, written and prompt dispute of the results – within the stipulated 24-hour period – the ECK refused to order, nor did it supervise the recount or re-tally of all or some of the votes, as required and expected. Instead, Kivuitu proceeded to issue Kibaki with form 18, and declared him "duly elected President of Kenya". Kivuitu, as he would later admit, only had the capacity or mandate of announcing the results; not determining who was or was not 'duly elected president'.

Meanwhile, outside the KICC, and far beyond it, tension was rife. Reports were beginning to flood in of sporadic and rapidly spreading violence around the country. As constituency results had been announced, youths had gathered in villages, market places, towns and cities, lighting fires and barricading roads, as they waited for the presidential results. Motorists were being attacked. Government vehicles, buildings and facilities were being vandalised, burnt or threatened. "No Raila, No Peace!" was being chanted in many parts of Kenya.

Before voting day, thousands of security forces had been deployed in many parts of Nyanza, especially Kisumu, Migori, Homa Bay and Ahero. There had also been a large deployment of troops to Nakuru, Eldoret, Kericho, Nairobi's Kibera and Mathare Valley slums, Kakamega in Western province and Mombasa

– all ODM strongholds. At first, most demonstrations were peaceful, with youths carrying twigs, hand-written placards and Raila's election portraits. However, as soon as the security personnel started recklessly shooting at peaceful civilians, the people countered with resistance militias. The situation soon got out of hand, with more than 1,500 civilians murdered, tens of thousands maimed, injured and raped, more than 600,000 displaced and billions of shillings' worth of property destroyed or burnt. An abyss beckoned for serene, beautiful Kenya. The world held its breath.

* * * * * * * * * * * * * *

The indicators that the election would be stolen had been there all along. Kibaki wasn't prepared to relinquish power; not in 2007, and not to Raila Odinga anyway. It was odd that almost everyone else had accepted that as a foregone conclusion except Raila. I had warned him more than once. Former cabinet ministers Njenga Karume and John Michuki (both now deceased) had alluded to PNU's intentions, repeatedly, in the months and weeks prior to the elections, yet Raila had remained convinced that he would be President after the 2007 elections. He had refused to put measures in place – as we had strongly recommended – to prevent or counter the civilian coup that Kibaki eventually carried out. On December 27, and subsequently, Raila spent entire days and nights drinking and partying at the Palacina, the Hotel Intercontinental, Serena Hotel, Osteria Restaurant, and at the Karen, Nairobi and Parklands members' clubs, as well as in other nondescript hotels and bars around Nairobi.

At around 8.30am on December 30, Uhuru Kenyatta, Kalonzo Musyoka, Amos Kimunya, Kivutha Kibwana, Raphael Tuju, Beth Mugo, Njeru Githae, John Michuki, George Thuo, Martha Karua, Mutula Kilonzo, and many other PNU Alliance leaders arrived at the media centre at the KICC and seated themselves in the front row. This was unusual. From the afternoon of December 27, when many of us had started attending the farcical ECK media presentations, most of the PNU top leadership had only made technical appearances. I couldn't recollect having seen any of them there for more than three hours on any particular day, and none had previously arrived that early in the morning. So, we (ODM agents) knew something was afoot.

Sitting beside them in the front row were the usual ODM members. I sat next to Kimunya; and the two of us engaged in small talk. At some point, as we sat waiting for Kivuitu and the ECK commissioners to come down and announce the final tallies, I mentioned to Kimunya – as Tuju who was sitting next to him was within earshot – that I hoped that they were prepared to hand over power that very day because it was Kibaki's last day in office.

"Are you sure of that?" Kimunya asked, turning quickly towards me.

"Of course I'm sure; Kibaki was sworn in on December 30, 2002; today is exactly five years from then. So, we shall not allow any illegitimate extensions; not even for one second," I explained to him. He whipped out a mobile phone, stood up and went outside. After 15 minutes, he returned and sat down, fidgeting. The ODM contingent started making noise, demanding the results. The room was now lined with security forces. Everywhere you looked, there was a protruding muzzle of a gun, pointing in our direction.

At about 9.30am, Kivuiti entered, accompanied by his fellow commissioners. Silence immediately engulfed the room. The media focused their cameras and microphones on Kivuitu. The scene was being beamed live to the world. Kivuitu had a thin brown Manila folder before him. He hesitated. Orengo stood up and loudly demanded the results.

Someone shouted: "Don't waste time; give us the results, or don't you know the country is burning?"

"I'm prepared to burn with the country if that's what it will take…I will announce the results even if I have to do so from a military submarine…", the old man responded, as cranky as ever. But these careless, provocative and irresponsible remarks caused more tension and anger.

"Do you want us to read the results ourselves?" It was Orengo, his voice quivering with anxiety. I yelled something too. It was now just Kivuitu, his commissioners and multitudes of police officers on one side and ODM leaders and supporters on the other. By this time, the PNU leaders had left the hall, one after another. They were in a hurry.

"Read out the results! Read out the results! Read out the results!" a chant broke out from behind me. When I looked up to check, I saw that the media, agents, even some local election observers had joined in the shouting match. Kivuitu stood up and made his way towards the door. The police and commission members followed. He had just cancelled whatever announcement he had wanted to make.

Within minutes of Kivuitu's departure, Raila arrived with a phalanx of ODM leaders, MPs-elect, youths, busy bodies and groupies. This was his first and only entry to the KICC during the entire episode. As he entered the hall, we could see security reinforcements arriving. They now completely outnumbered the civilians in the hall. They looked vicious. We stood firm around Raila, as he approached the dais. Raila mounted the platform and sat in Kivuitu's chair. Members of the Pentagon sat on chairs previously occupied by the ECK commissioners. The country held its collective breath. Then Raila condemned the "ongoing electoral fraud" and warned Kivuitu against succumbing to Kibaki's and the PNU leadership's attempt to undermine the will of the Kenyan people. He then stopped and introduced a man who was standing in front of me; Kipkemoi arap Kirui. Kirui took the microphone and recounted numerous electoral malpractices he had witnessed at the so-called National Tallying Centre, which he had been seconded to by the Parliamentary Service Commission. He concluded that his conscience couldn't allow him to keep quiet in the face of such massive electoral fraud. Raila then ended his speech by urging Kenyans to exercise restraint, but promised that he would be addressing them again if Kivuitu hadn't announced the results by that afternoon.

As Raila and the Pentagon members squeezed themselves between the thick cordon of police and GSU officers, some people started pushing and shoving. It felt choreographed, as if an intended security breach. Raila's security detail was overpowered and outnumbered. Before we could reach the door, an enraged GSU officer aimed his baton at Balala's head but missed narrowly. It grazed his temple before landing heavily on his left shoulder. Balala, startled, moved quickly to his right, causing pandemonium. In the confusion, I saw a man edging closer to Raila. I quickly tackled him to the ground, and was still holding him by the scruff of his neck, when I heard Omingo Magara shouting, "Hey Miguna, that's one of our MPs!" I let go of the man quickly, apologised, climbed the steps and exited the KICC through the main entrance. The man I had nearly squashed was Chepalungu MP-elect, Isaack Rutto.

Outside the KICC, I saw the US Ambassador, Michael Ranneberger, addressing the press. I overheard him saying that Kibaki had won the election. He was urging the "opposition to remain peaceful and accept the results". It was unbelievable. How could he say that in the face of such extraordinary electoral theft, I wondered, as I followed the throng of ODM supporters now trying to leave the KICC. I got into my vehicle and headed straight to Pentagon House.

The country was now on fire.

THE BIG SCRAMBLE

It was now December 30. Raila and the ODM inner circle were in the doldrums. Our first instinct was defiance. We couldn't allow Kibaki to run roughshod over the Kenyan people. From the results Kivuitu had announced so far, it seemed logically impossible that Kibaki had won. How could he have done, with only Central Kenya votes? Based solely on the provisional results, Raila had defeated Kibaki in Nyanza, Western, Rift Valley, Coast, North Eastern and possibly even Nairobi provinces. That was more than three quarters of the total population of Kenya. Kalonzo (possibly) led in Eastern. That left Kibaki with Central province. How many voters were in Central province and how many of them had voted for Kibaki? That was the question that perplexed observers.

At ODM's first meeting at the Pentagon House after the KICC fiasco, it was unanimously resolved that we would resort to peaceful mass action until Kibaki accepted defeat and relinquished power. But it was also agreed that the newly constituted Technical Team (which was made up mainly of former strategy team members) would meet later and map out a comprehensive SWOT (Strengths, Weaknesses/Limitations, Opportunities and Threats) analysis on mass action and report, within a day, to the ODM Pentagon.

The meeting agreed that by blatantly rigging the presidential election, Kibaki had declared war, and executed a civilian coup d'état against the popular will of the Kenyan people. In response, many felt that we needed to take the war to Kibaki's doorstep. We knew that Kibaki and his PNU Alliance controlled the coercive arms of government – the police, the intelligence and the military. But force alone wasn't enough. History is replete with lessons of mighty military forces being humbled by ragtag formations. As a student of history and politics, I believed that the Kibaki regime could be forced to relinquish power.

We resolved that Raila should declare himself President and prepare to be sworn in at Uhuru Park within hours. This suggestion elicited heated debate, with those opposed, warning about treason charges. Treason, those of us who supported the idea insisted, couldn't be preferred against the people; it was the people who had, and who would inaugurate Raila as their President. The majority in the room felt that most Kenyans were prepared to rise up against Kibaki's civilian coup.

Salim Lone, Kibisu Kabatesi and I prepared a statement declaring Raila President. It was now around 3.30pm. We had summoned the media to the Pentagon House. The consensus was that the Narok North MP-elect and octogenerian, William Ole Ntimama, not Raila, was best suited to read the statement. Firstly, he supported this option more than any other senior member of ODM. Secondly, he was elderly and the feeling was that Kibaki would be reluctant to haul such an elderly man to jail. My view, however, was that as the person whose victory was being snatched, Raila should have been courageous enough to lay claim to the victory. I also felt Raila's voice would have galvanised the country against the injustice being perpetrated against them by Kibaki. This was no time for half-hearted shadow-boxing.

At 3.45pm, just as Ntimama began to read the prepared statement, the lights went off. As the media scrambled to switch on their backup generators, an announcement was beamed through all TV and radio stations: Michuki, the then Minister for Internal Security, had imposed a total ban on live broadcasts. On hearing this (even before determining whether or not the order was legally binding), the local media started packing up. It was about 4.50pm, when there was a second announcement on the TV screens: Kibaki was due to be sworn in at State House that same day, at 6pm. We were crestfallen. We had been outmanoeuvred again.

At about 5.30pm, the ECK Chairman Kivuitu and his fellow commissioners came on the Kenya Broadcasting Corporation (KBC) TV channel and formally declared that Kibaki had won the presidential election by 4,578,034 (46.4%) to Raila's 4,352,993 (44.1%). Earlier a statement released by the Presidential Press Service – even before the ECK had announced the results – had claimed that Kibaki had won with 4,584,721 (47%), while Raila had allegedly received 4,352,860 (44%). Amazingly, the KBC TV and Citizen TV figures were carbon copy of the PPS results, putting into question the independence of the media houses, especially the latter, which is supposed to be a commercial concern. The Kenya Television Network (KTN) had been more fair, accurate and balanced; its figures matched closely those of reports we were receiving from ODM's agents (whenever they could be traced). The Nation Television (NTV) numbers were distorted but they were still much closer to reality than Citizen TV's. Notwithstanding all these, the three media houses (NTV, KTN and Citizen) would later refuse to share their polling figures with the public, or the independent commission of inquiry into the elections of 2007 (the Kriegler Commission). Within minutes of the bizarre announcement, we watched Kivuitu handing over the "victory certificate" to Kibaki on the State House lawn in front of an assembled but jumbled group of PNU boys and girls. Minutes later Kibaki was sworn in by the then Chief Justice Evan Gicheru and the High Court Registrar, a Ms Christine Meoli.

Kibaki's low-key State House swearing-in ceremony was conducted at dusk. We could see people arriving, rushing into the tent, (on live television) as the ceremony was going on. There were no foreign diplomats; nor were there foreign correspondents. Clearly, whoever had put that show together was in a great rush and hadn't had time to plan properly. Nor had they had time to invite guests, which made me wonder how those in attendance (most of whom were dressed up in suits and ties) had known Kibaki would win and that a swearing in ceremony had been arranged for that evening. They had done well to leave whatever they were doing, dress up, beat the horrendous Nairobi traffic and clear the impenetrable security at State House, all before Kivuitu had declared the results. However, the attendance of those empty suits, Evan Gicheru, then Chief Justice (gowned up and grinning), the High Court Registrar (also excited) and the local media, all made me certain that the rigging had been premeditated and planned.

Except for President Yoweri Kaguta Museveni of Uganda no head of state attended. Only he, President Robert Mugabe of Zimbabwe and the US State Department issued congratulatory messages to Kibaki (but the latter was quickly to retract that rash and irresponsible endorsement). Kibaki faced a major diplomatic isolation from most governments. He was now marooned at State House, unable even to venture out to attend a church service, because of the chaos that reigned outside. The Kenya-Uganda Railway had been uprooted in Kibera; no goods were travelling to Uganda by train or road. Tourists had fled. Businesses, factories and offices were closed. The national economy had ground to a halt. Yet, Kibaki did not address the Kenyan people to convince them he was their legitimate leader.

On January 3, 2007, Kenya resembled a burnt-out tomb. There was death and misery everywhere. Thousands lay dead or injured, most of them either shot at by the security forces or hacked or shot at by marauding gangs wielding machetes, bows and arrows. More than 600,000 civilians had been forcefully displaced. Tens of thousands had even fled into Uganda to seek refuge. In Eldoret more than two dozen young children and women would be burnt alive in a church where they had sought refuge. A man would lose his family of nine in a murderous inferno in Naivasha, as he hid watching. Hundreds would be butchered, maimed, mutilated and gang raped in Nakuru and Naivasha. Peaceful demonstrators chanting "No Raila, No Peace!" were being hunted down and shot at like wild animals. There was blood everywhere.

I published an article titled *"The civilian coup was premeditated"* in which we expounded on our theory that Kibaki had stolen the presidential elections. Consistently during the presidential campaign, Lucy Kibaki had warned Ida Odinga that she would not enter State House. We reminded the country that two weeks before Kenyans had gone to the polls, high ranking PNU leaders like Njenga Karume, John Michuki and the Police Commissioner Hussein Ali had made alarming statements outlining the level to which they would respond to any post-election unrest. Maj-Gen. Ali had also revealed that the swearing in ceremony for the "winning" presidential candidate would be a state function, instead of the public event Kenyans had, in recent years, become used to. The question that begged an answer was: If Ali had no intelligence or information about electoral malpractice, how did he know that there would be civil unrest?

While stating that Mwai Kibaki "cannot lose this election," Njenga Karume (now deceased), had, without any prompting, warned Kenyans to remember that he was the Minister for Defence. Both before and after these eerie statements had been made, the above named individuals had engaged in scaremongering, warning innocent civilians that they would be arrested if they participated in "any political event" after the announcement of the results of presidential elections. In response to Karume, ODM's Deputy Captain, Musalia Mudavadi, had declared: "Kenyans can only interpret Karume's boisterous statement as a threat to Kenyans. Essentially, Karume was saying that whatever the outcome of the elections, KIBAKI MUST be declared the winner."

It was unclear why Karume had believed that violence would erupt after the elections. Admittedly, in the run-up, there had been sporadic violence around the country: in Kuresoi, Eldoret, Molo, Kisumu, Mount Elgon, Mombasa, Nairobi, Vihiga, Taita, Kakamega, Wundanyi and Tana River areas. But these eruptions had appeared spontaneous reactions to reports of planned rigging and other perceived injustices. Further – and sadly – inter-ethnic conflicts had been instigated, encouraged or deliberately allowed to continue by the government for parochial and selfish interests. Most of the areas where violence had erupted were considered ODM strongholds. As such, the government's unstated wisdom had been to let the conflicts spiral out of order, dislocate thousands of voters sympathetic to ODM and ensure that they did not vote on December 27. That way, PNU would be chipping away at ODM's acknowledged lead.

We noted that during polling day on December 27, 2007, Kenyans had conducted themselves peacefully. The turnout had been huge in most parts of the country. Tallying and reports of election results in most constituencies throughout the country had been conducted without much incident save for in PNU strongholds where they had refused ODM agents and independent observers to be present in the voting and tallying halls. Contrary to the legal requirement that Forms 16, 16A and 17 must be completed and signed by the returning officer and all candidates' agents, these mandatory forms were never used in Central and most parts of Eastern Provinces.

Whereas virtually the entire country tallied their results and submitted them to the ECK at the KICC using Form 16A, results from the two PNU strongholds were purportedly submitted by telephone. In many cases, there was no credible evidence that those reports were even submitted by ECK officials and even as recently as January 3, 2008 the Chairman of the ECK had admitted that there was ongoing "tampering with previously submitted Form 16As and 17As" at the KICC.

Most of the figures Kivuitu was reading between December 27 and 30 were never authenticated by the legally required Form 16As, duly signed. Even when these anomalies were raised by ODM and repeated requests made for early intervention to prevent the impending electoral fraud, the ECK boss persisted in reading the disputed results. Months following the electoral fiasco (about February 2008), Kivuitu confessed publicly on national television that between Raila and Kibaki, he didn't even know who won the presidential election. More than five ECK commissioners, of a total of 21, had broken rank with their fellow commissioners and confirmed that PNU had massively rigged the presidential elections.

Subsequently, an ODM in-house 'audit' of the results determined that despite massive rigging through falsified and inflated figures in favour of Kibaki, Raila Odinga still won convincingly by more than 400,000 votes.

The ODM report was like a breath of fresh air in an otherwise polluted environment. We were shocked that the local media had refused to expose the massive rigging. Subsequently, I did interviews with the CBC, the BBC, Voice of America, Radio French International, Al-Jazeera and many other international media outlets, trying to explain the root cause of the crisis and what I thought were the viable options out of it. Throughout, I insisted that the world needed to put pressure on Kibaki to accept the popular will of the Kenyan people. Strategically, I felt that the world hadn't expressed sufficient outrage against Kibaki's defilement of democracy. Salim did the same; addressing press conferences and fielding numerous telephone interviews, even for the few months he fled to the US because of threats on his life. We slowly rallied world public opinion to our side and managed to completely isolate Kibaki.

By January 3, 2008, more than 600,000 had been forcibly displaced in Kenya. Thousands had fled and sought refuge in Uganda. There was a shoot-to-kill order. The security forces were shooting at peaceful demonstrators like wild animals. There were smouldering infernos everywhere. Yet, the response of Samuel Kivuitu, the disgraced ECK Chairman, was to publish a preposterous letter dated January 6, 2008 on the letterhead of "Kivuitu & Company Advocates," addressed to "My Beloved Fellow Worshippers," in which, he stated, among other things, that it was "Satan" who had appeared and taken control of the tallying process.

Kibaki had imposed what amounted to a state of emergency. No meetings and demonstrations were permitted, however peaceful. Civil liberties were arbitrarily suspended. Meanwhile, ODM agents from all parts of the country were descending on the Pentagon with 16A and 17A forms. Two people were tasked with collecting these documents: Caroli Omondi and Ceasar Asiyo, with Caroli in charge. (So, we were shocked that during the Kriegler inquiry – slightly more than six months after the fiasco – when ODM needed these forms to be able to demonstrate the "massive electoral fraud" it alleged Kibaki and PNU had committed, Caroli couldn't provide any of those documents. It remains a mystery where he took them to or why he refused to produce them when we needed them. It's mainly due to Caroli's failure or refusal to disclose those documents that Johan Kriegler, the chairman of the Independent Review Commission (IREC), declared that based on the information that was available to his commission, "there was no evidence of rigging at the KICC". Yet, this is the man Raila subsequently chose as his private secretary after becoming Prime Minister!)

In early January 2008, there were intense efforts to find both temporary and long-term solutions to the post-election crisis. Raila was daily receiving dozens of telephone calls from world leaders, former presidents and prime ministers, statesmen and diplomats. Members of the strategy team who had been retained by the Pentagon to advise them during this crisis renamed themselves the "Pentagon Technical Team". After long, extensive and intensive deliberations, this group came up with a three-pronged approach. First, it recommended that ODM should try to use mass action to peacefully remove Mwai Kibaki from power. The second option (if we tried but failed on the first), was to galvanise the country and the international community into demanding a rerun or fresh presidential polls. We knew that with the widespread electoral malpractices and chaos Kenyans had witnessed during the 2007 presidential election, they would "punish" Kibaki and the PNU in any subsequent poll. (Moreover, as a lawyer, I was also aware that if a rerun was allowed, Kibaki couldn't run because, technically, he would have served "two terms", which were the maximum number the constitution permitted.)

And the third option was for an audit or retallying of the presidential results. Although some members of the technical team argued for this, I strongly opposed it. This was due to the fact that all electoral infrastructure and voting materials like ballot papers and boxes were in the sole custody and control of the Kibaki government. Technically, the ECK was supposed to be the body in custody of those items. However, the ECK didn't have its own police force, storage or capacity to ensure the integrity of the materials. Moreover, as I have explained before, the ECK wasn't independent; all the commissioners and secretariat staff had been chosen unilaterally by Kibaki.

Unfortunately, Caroli, Isahakia, Ng'eno and a few other busybodies had convinced Raila that undertaking an audit and retallying was the best option. He almost fell for it. Decision making is not one of Raila's greatest strengths. He takes too long to decide; dithering and taking too many calls; consulting his wife, children, sisters, brothers, cousins, village elders – even magicians and witch doctors. Wide consultations, especially on such important issues are good and desirable; however, if it results in inaction, then it doesn't serve any useful purpose at all. In fact, it might demonstrate intellectual vacuity. This was the case with Raila. During that period, Raila was constantly on his insecure mobile telephone. (I am sure Kibaki's state security agents loved that!)And because he had increasingly surrounded himself with empty sycophants who told him what he wanted to hear, any decision he made based on their advice was bound to be deeply flawed. I remember incessant arguments with Salim, Prof. Oyugi and Prof. Hino after Raila became Prime Minister. These three believed that it was useless telling Raila what he wouldn't accept; that as advisors, we should recommend things we knew and expected Raila to accept, preferably without any argument. My unyielding view was – and has always been – that an advisor fails in his or her role if s/he doesn't tell whoever they are advising the truth. My view is that advisors owe it to themselves, their training, professional ethics and ultimately to their principals to disclose all facts and surrounding circumstances; that it is better to be candid than to mislead. I preferred to be unpopular but right. Salim and Oyugi largely agreed with me on this, but they held the view that telling Raila what we suspected he wouldn't accept was a waste of time. Hino was of the old totalitarian school: he believed that an advisor couldn't and should never argue a case before his principal if s/he thought that the principal wouldn't be positively predisposed to the view being advanced. Unfortunately, I have to admit that I was mistaken: Raila loves sycophancy.

Meanwhile Kibaki, supported by a restless cast of puppeteers like then Justice Minister Martha Karua, Internal Security Minister John Michuki, Finance Minister Amos Kimunya, Uhuru Kenyatta, then Foreign Affairs Minister Moses Wetangula and then Attorney General Amos Wako, parroted a cynical clarion call of "Go to Court!" They dared ODM to put up or shut up. They knew that the unreformed Kenyan judiciary was a den of corruption; that the judiciary had earned a distinct reputation for being incompetent and prone to manipulation from politicians, business people and even crooks, in its dispensation of 'justice'.

The Economist reported in early January 2008:

> A small cabal of politicians almost certainly stole the result by fraud. In the parliamentary vote, President Mwai Kibaki's ruling party was

> routed. Yet in the presidential vote, Mr. Kibaki emerged victorious at the last moment and had himself sworn in only a few minutes later, forestalling pleas from all sides – even from the head of the election commission he himself had appointed – for a pause to investigate mounting claims of malpractice. (...) Initially, America, which sees Kenya as a front-line ally in a war against Islamist militias in neighbouring Somalia, made the mistake of endorsing the President's re-election. Now Britain, America and the African Union are urging Mr. Odinga and Mr. Kibaki to talk in an effort to stop the bloodletting. That lets Mr. Kibaki off the hook far too easily. All the violence should certainly be condemned, but most of the diplomatic pressure should be exerted on Mr. Kibaki's supposed new government to annul the results and organise a recount – or a new vote.

I held the same view as *The Economist.* As time went by, the whole world came round to this view and began to call Kibaki to account. Jeffrey D. Sachs and John McArthur, two eminent global personalities, sent Raila "Notes on a Strategy for a Peaceful Democratic Resolution to Kenya's Current Political Impasse" dated January 7, 2008.

Sachs and McArthur's overall assessment of the crisis was correct:

> The international community needs to understand that peace and stability in Kenya can be achieved only through political legitimacy, and legitimacy can be achieved only if election results are treated with respect.
>
> It makes no sense for international observers or foreign governments to push for a "compromise" or "national unity" if basic democratic processes are disrespected.
>
> We believe that the leaders of Kenya's democratic opposition, including the ODM and the wider democratic movement of Kenya's civil society, should join forces to help the world to understand how Kenya's democracy is under fundamental and urgent threat as the result of major election fraud followed by a brutal crackdown on the rights to free speech and free assembly... The over-riding need is therefore to re-assess the election results (or to hold a new election if a retallying proves to be impossible). (...) We suggest five points in such a strategy of international public education.

1. Focus sharply and repeatedly on the 27 December vote results.
   - The most important public strategy should be to demand the accurate re-tallying and investigation of the...vote.
   - If a re-tally later proves to be impossible, a "forensic audit" of the vote counting should still be conducted in order to explain the nature of the vote fraud.
   - The democratic opposition should also forward its own credible numerical estimate of the true results, based on its observations of local tallies on Election Day.
2. Emphasise the need for peace, freedom of peaceful assembly, and freedom of the media.
3. Explain that the political fight is one of "the old guard versus the rest of the country" rather than one of ethnic divisions. The Kenyan public is demanding democracy, human rights, and the sharing of the gains of economic development among all Kenyans, while the old guard is defending the prerogatives of the few.
4. Call for electoral and constitutional reform to consolidate Kenya's future democracy. The December 27th election results reflect the need for stronger accountability systems to ensure votes are counted accurately, including the true independence of the Electoral Commission. The constitution should also be reformed to devolve more democratic power to local communities and regions.
5. Emphasize that global security in East Africa can be ensured only through democratic legitimacy in Kenya. (...)

We recommend the following key mechanisms for explaining these points to the global public:

1. Kenya's democratic opposition, including the ODM and wider civil society, should establish regular daily press briefings to convey and emphasize these 5 points...
2. The websites of the ODM and other democratic opposition groups should be updated regularly with progress reports on these five points. International observers will turn to these websites to get the latest news, yet the websites have not been updated.
3. The democratic opposition should draw daily attention to the growing support that Kenya is getting domestically and from abroad for the re-tallying of the elections, and for protecting Kenya's democratic institutions as well.(...)

This was much needed intellectual, political, strategic and tactical firepower, but other than the regular briefs ODM leaders held and the detailed communiqués we sent out, most of Sachs' and McArthur's recommendations went unheeded. ODM's website remained a dud. The so-called "democratic opposition" didn't unite. In fact, it wasn't clear what that beast looked like. First, there was ODM – united and massive at the time all right – but it was just one political party. The rest of the opposition wasn't united. Second, the opposition wasn't democratic. In ODM, all major decisions were made in Nairobi between one to four people. Then of course – opposition to what? Up to that point, it was obvious ODM wanted power. It also opposed Kibaki and PNU. But beyond that, what did ODM represent?

Clearly, Raila and the rest of the Pentagon saw themselves as an alternative power fulcrum to Kibaki and his cronies. But were they necessarily qualitatively better than Kibaki and his PNU thugs, philosophically, ideologically, intellectually or morally? What was the content of their so-called progressive credentials? Many of the leading lights in both political formations had had their names mentioned in mega corruption scandals and impunity cases. Almost all had worked hand-in-glove with Kenyatta and Moi; two leaders whose distinctive characteristics were megalomania, excessive repression, tribalism and looting. Both political formations had their fair share of suspected drug dealers, money launderers and people who had allegedly committed or been complicit in serious human rights abuses. Even Kenya's civil society and press weren't united in opposing the worst electoral fraud in Kenya's history; their loyalties were divided on the basis of their ethnic affiliations.

But like Sachs and McArthur, I still had a lot of hope invested in ODM. Compared to PNU, it had less skunks. That's partly why I stuck around to give this battle my all. These issues did, however, trouble my conscience. And I would, of course, later establish that I might have been right in my assessment of the two political formations but wrong in my conclusions regarding the depth and extent of the rot in both. I later learnt that what might have looked like superficial mould in ODM had actually penetrated to the core of the organisation and rendered the entity incapable of effecting any far-reaching or fundamental positive changes.

The forensic audit option was never pursued, partly because Caroli couldn't produce ODM's "evidence". The audit report, though well-intentioned, didn't prove much. It was also somehow amateurish. It was primarily prepared by Dalmas Otieno, Mohamed Isahakia, Jeremiah Ng'eno and James Ogundo. Dalmas had joined the technical team after one of the Orange House meetings. He had claimed to have "expert" knowledge as a "forensic" auditor and analyst and promptly relocated to the Pentagon. Before this, Dalmas had been on the outside of the periphery of the ODM power hierarchy. The inner sanctum had wanted nothing to do with him. In fact, he was considered "lucky" to have made it to parliament. Raila and most ODM politburo supported the former Rongo legislator, Ochilo Oyacko. During the ensuing meetings, Dalmas would prove to be as clueless about forensic audit as he was of ODM's political platform. To many of us, Dalmas was just cunningly positioning himself in the event of a power-sharing deal. He would eventually make significant gains, ending up being appointed cabinet minister even though the core strategy team opposed his inclusion. He had used his one-month presence at the Pentagon House to worm himself closer to Raila. And Raila, being easily influenced, failed to see through Dalmas' strategy. Ridiculously, Dalmas and his audit committee buddies concluded that Kibaki had stolen the election but they presented a margin tighter than Kivuitu's. They also concluded (although this wasn't included in the report that we later made available to the country), that Raila would lose in a rerun.

The technical team dismissed the report before reading it, in the belief that its authors' primary motivation was to force Raila to join a unity government, so that they themselves could reboard the gravy train. They had done this for so long under the Kanu regime that, for them, joining or staying in government – any government – was their preferred course. Caroli and Isahakia had certainly found common ground in pushing Raila to initiate talks with Kibaki over the formation of a "unity government".

Caroli even confided in me that he was desperate to have Raila become Prime Minister so that he could salvage two of his properties whose mortgages hadn't been serviced for months. One was a Sh45m mortgage at the ROC in Upper Hill. The other was a Sh25m mortgage on the property in which Orange House stood, in Hurlingham. He claimed to own both properties, which he was renting out to Raila. Apparently, he had received notices that if he couldn't discharge both mortgages by the end of April 2008, they would be repossessed and sold on a "power of sale" or auction. The World Bank office in Nairobi had terminated Caroli's account under mysterious circumstances. There were credible rumours swirling around that the World Bank had requested his arrest over some financial improprieties. Whether these allegations were true or false isn't significant, except to say that the man looked extremely worried and like he would do anything to save his skin, through Raila.

* * * * * * * * * * * * * *

Raila, meanwhile, was confused and fatigued. He was always dozing off. His eyes were constantly streaming. He kept wiping at them with a white handkerchief he would pull out from his trouser pocket. He continued talking too much on his mobile telephone; refusing to have his calls screened, which I thought was irresponsible. He was getting too much conflicting advice. He didn't pay attention to detail; never read his letters, briefs, newspapers and questions forwarded by media houses (often telling Onyango Keta or his then secretary, Susan Utugi, to "give those to Miguna to respond to"; or simply calling me in and saying, "*Ja-Nyando*, you know all the answers to those ones…" before dozing off again.)

However, on most days (between January and February 28, 2008), he would arrive at Pentagon house by 7.30am and leave at around 7pm; almost daily. So, it's arguable that he was too tired to think straight, but Raila didn't have a choice: there were too many things requiring his attention; too many people expecting him to be in too many places at the same time. In my view, it would have been better if the Pentagon had structured its operations better, with specific people analysing information, before presenting summaries to Raila, with precise recommendations on what to do. Raila, too, needed to cut down on his public and private engagements. He seemed to be trying to escape from the swirling crisis by drowning himself in alcohol (virtually every night) and surrounding himself with people of dubious backgrounds. To me, that was tragic.

Sarah Elderkin kept vigil at the Pentagon House, constantly recording proceedings at most meetings; trying to capture everything. But Raila was difficult to track in the evening: he was constantly on the move; still keeping up daily appearances in local bars, restaurants, members' clubs and hotels; still going to bed late and waking up too early; not having enough sleep. Fatigue was written all over his features. Prof. Oyugi, Salim and I tried several times to urge him to go slow, but he never took heed.

Atul Vadher, Raila's 'consultant' from the United Kingdom, was still around, walking like a duck. Ceasar Asiyo, Dave Arunga and Tony Chege had disappeared from view. Apparently, Raila had instructed the guards at the Pentagon gate to block Dave from entering the place. It was unclear why. Ceasar had been blocked because of allegations of financial misappropriation during the 2007 campaign. The same situation applied to Chege. But I didn't understand why Caroli and Isahakia hadn't been barred even though they were alleged to be the worst offenders.

Many strategy team members peeled off gradually. I could see why. By January 2008, I had been working for Raila full time for four months pro bono. My savings were rapidly dwindling. But I was focused and positive. Though the children asked when we were "going back to Canada," I distracted them with diversionary stories.

ODM supporters countrywide were getting restless and disillusioned. Nyong'o, Ruto and Mudavadi would call press conferences at the Pentagon or Orange House and announce a grand march to Uhuru Park or declare that "Monday would be mass action," and then call another impromptu press conference to cancel. Once, members of the Pentagon, secretariat and Pentagon technical team went to the city centre in order to precipitate nationwide vigils, protests and demonstrations, but the second they saw a handful of police officers approach, they ran away like idiots.

The stalemate was frustrating the world. Information leaked out that the World Bank country director, Dr Colin Bruce, had met with Patrick Otieno Lumumba and other Kibaki affiliated professionals to draw up a strategy document for the endorsement of Kibaki's controversial "re-election" by world leaders. ODM swung into action and Bruce was quickly recalled. Meanwhile, the US Deputy Secretary for Africa, Dr Jendayi Fraser, had visited Kenya and recommended that the US give qualified recognition for Kibaki. Again, ODM, through Dr Sally Kosgei, piled pressure on Dr Condoleezza Rice, seeking a retraction. We got that, plus more: Rice hastily arranged a tour of Kenya (detouring from a whirlwind trip she had made with President George W. Bush to a few African countries, including Tanzania), where she tried to knock some sense into the PNU. Former Presidents Kenneth Kaunda of Zambia, Joaquim Chissano of Mozambique, Quett Ketumile Joni Masire of Botswana, John Kufuor of Ghana and South African retired prelate and Nobel Laureate Desmond Tutu, also made the pilgrimage to Nairobi.

It was those international interventions that resulted in a mediation process being proposed. After telephone conversations with world leaders – and following unrelenting pressure from Caroli, Isahakia and Dalmas (for their own reasons) – Raila became more and more interested in the idea of "sharing power" with Kibaki, though the logistics of it all remained hazy. Who would mediate these discussions and whether they could even be called mediation became an issue in itself.

CHAPTER EIGHT

THE GRAND RESCUE

On January 7, 2008, the ODM went on a retreat to Maasai Lodge to debate its parliamentary agenda. Among the main topics for discussion were: the strategies we were going to adopt in order to ensure that ODM parliamentarians were elected speaker and deputy speaker, respectively; how we were going to use the swearing in ceremony for maximum political, media and theatrical effect; and, since parliament would be adjourned until March, 2008, shortly after the swearing in ceremony, whether or not we would challenge Kibaki mounting the presidential rostrum in view of his contested legitimacy and the fact that he would be attending the session as the MP for Othaya and not as head of state or government. We maintained that Kibaki had not been elected and therefore had no mandate to govern.

During the session, the ODM Secretary General, Prof. Nyong'o raised two critical issues, which were at the heart of the ongoing crisis. Firstly, since ODM maintained that Kibaki didn't win the 2007 presidential elections and therefore had no mandate to govern, what authority did he have to summon the opening of parliament? And secondly, that ODM's call for and participation in a mediation exercise should only be done so as to prepare the country for a rerun between Raila and Kibaki. He added: "our supporters have been calling and instructing us not to go to parliament".

The ODM Chairman, Henry Kosgey, meanwhile felt that ODM should view the temporary calm that had followed the party's suspension of mass action as a "ceasefire". He acknowledged that reports in the newspapers of thousands of unarmed innocent civilians having been killed by the security forces were deeply harrowing, but he still felt that while we could talk about mediation as an issue, ODM should prepare to return to mass action. He also felt that we as a party had to take advantage of the forthcoming scheduled visit of President John Agyekum Kufuor, President of Ghana and the then serving Chairman of the African Union. PNU officials had been insisting that Kufor was only coming to "take tea with President Kibaki at State House". Kosgey was adamant that when Kufuor arrived (which was in a day or so), "we should immediately go into mediation; he needs to see our point of view and background information". That point was quickly picked up by then ODM Pentagon member Najib Balala, who suggested restructuring the meeting's agenda, asserting: "We have come here to discuss mediation. (...) What is our stand? Are we prepared? What's our view of Kibaki's statement today? How do we participate in parliament?"

Nyong'o reminded Balala that this was a discussion that would have to wait until all the Pentagon members had arrived – it was noted that Raila, Musalia and Ruto though due soon, were not in the room. Meanwhile, Otieno Kajwang' aka the Mapambano man (so-called because he sings 'the struggle' songs at ODM rallies and functions) stood up and spoke eloquently, his voice booming: "Kibaki is in office illegally," he said, gesticulating animatedly. "The Law Society of Kenya has articulated that position. The people of Kenya have identified with the position of the LSK. (...) In parliament, MPs must stand up when the President enters the chamber...Being there, aren't you recognising him? How do you walk away from that reality? If we attend and stand up as he comes in, how would we fail to recognise him afterwards? We also need to consider what the consequences are of not being there. Whether we are there or not, they will elect a speaker. The speaker will adjourn parliament; he will swear in MPs. He will declare seats of the absent MPs vacant. And we will disintegrate as a party; won't we? What do we do? What will Raila do? He was elected President; do we want him to attend? How will Raila take his oath? How does he accept Kibaki as President? If you don't swear at all, you are not an MP; they can declare the seat vacant..."And so, Otieno Kajwang' the choirmaster started well but ended up muddling himself up. Essentially, Kajwang' didn't want ODM to jeopardise his position as an MP.

Ugenya MP-elect, James Orengo stood up and spoke. This was long before he graduated into being a 'lyrical sycophant in the king's court'. This was Jim the intellectual activist. He was concise, clear and on target. He pointed out that when parliament opened, there would only be three items on the table: election of speaker and deputy speaker and the swearing in of members before parliament adjourned. There would be no other business. He went on: "The office of the speaker can never be vacant. Parliament must always elect a speaker...The first day, Kibaki comes as a voter. Standing orders don't allow him in the chair of state…After finishing the business of voting in the speaker and deputy speaker, we can refuse to swear in…If the MPs aren't sworn in, then nobody can take their seats in parliament. MPs-elect can then state that the issue of the presidency is not resolved. It is completely watertight if you have your speaker and deputy speaker. Whoever we elect speaker must be both friendly and loyal. The question is: how do we ensure that Kibaki does not use parliament to transact business? By electing our own speaker and deputy speaker and ensuring that no business is transacted…"

The MP-elect for Emuhaya, Kenneth Marende, who would later be handpicked by Raila to become speaker, listened intently and raised no objections. He neither supported nor opposed any of the arguments raised. This, on reflection, should perhaps have raised our suspicions. And sure enough once parliament convened, Marende never raised a finger (not that he could have as speaker). He went ahead to allow parliament to engage in other business, contrary to what ODM had pre-agreed. (Kibaki would stroll in when parliament convened and climb onto the seat of state reserved for the President with no objections raised by Orengo – who had eloquently argued that Kibaki would only attend parliament as the MP-elect for Othaya constituency. The pugnacious MP-elect for Budalang'i, Pius Tawfiq Ababu Namwamba, would be the lone voice, challenging Kibaki's authority, which Marende would over-rule, again and again.)

To boost ODM's numbers, it was suggested that our MP-elects strategically reach out to members of the other parties and convince them to support our speaker and deputy speaker candidates. We were prepared to use ethnicity and regionalism to get the requisite numbers. Non-ODM members from Western, we reckoned, might find it attractive to support Marende. Likewise, non-ODM members from North Eastern might support Farah Maalim on the basis of shared ethnicity, language, culture, religion and region. But looking around the hall, we could see just a handful of skilful parliamentarians to execute this grand strategy.

One of the unanimous resolutions adopted at the meeting was one proposed by Farah and strongly supported by Omingo Magara, that "ODM MPs should swear in their own President, so that we go to parliament with our Speaker, Deputy Speaker and President and if there is chaos, that might be the beginning of a solution," was abandoned before the meeting concluded.

When supporting Farah, Omingo was fiery: "Kibaki has broken all the laws in this land. I cannot swear allegiance to Kibaki. I support Farah – we swear in our own President. If we are charged with treason, so be it…Let's create a crisis; some of us are prepared to go to jail," Omingo concluded, jabbing his finger in the air.

"Are we going to parliament or not? That's the question. The issue of a vote of no-confidence will not work." Belgut MP, Charles Keter shouted from the back and sat down.

"Attend parliament; go there very early; occupy the government side; Captain (that was Raila's nickname as presidential candidate) and Deputy Captain (Musalia Mudavadi's nickname, as ODM's deputy leader and Raila's running mate) enter, and they are acknowledged as President and Vice-President, respectively…Parliament does not have to sit in Nairobi; it can sit elsewhere…" That was Orengo again.

The room was growing excited. Before Orengo had spoken for the last time, most MP-elects had been leaning towards attending parliament. Their concern was that having been elected as constituency MPs it would be a dereliction of duty to refuse to attend. Meanwhile, Raila and other Pentagon members had arrived at 10.30am and were sitting quietly, listening to the contributions.

At 11.45am, after Orengo's comments, Raila stood up, cleared his voice and spoke without the usual preliminary verbiage. He sounded upbeat. "We are at a very critical point," he began. "You are part of a movement of the people of Kenya for fundamental change. The people of Kenya want to see change in the country. You saw the wave for change during the recently concluded elections. Ignore the tendency of believing that the people of your constituency chose you and therefore you must be sworn in and sit in parliament…People gave you a mandate. If you betray them, a popular national democratic revolution will topple you.(…) It cannot be stopped. If you try to betray them, you will be swept by the wayside.(…) Yes, Kibaki and his PNU control the judiciary and the military; but parliament is supreme. The law says to elect a speaker there must be a two-thirds majority of all elected members of parliament. Business cannot start without two-thirds of the MPs…We have 106 members; they have 101, unless others are bought. If you vote together as one bloc, you will have the speaker and the deputy speaker. We need to agree on the name of a speaker and a deputy speaker today. Once you have the speaker, then nothing else will happen unless the speaker agrees… Then as the proceedings near an end, one of you can stand up and state that 'Parliament is not properly constituted because we don't have a President. *We have two Presidents in the House.* We don't know which President should be sworn in…' Then nature will take its course.

"All is not lost. Don't be enticed. *We don't want to share cabinet positions with Kibaki.* This government will not last. *The UK Prime Minister Gordon Brown told me not to accept every half-baked position; to accept a long-lasting solution. A rerun is what we need.* So, let's say, we will retally, then we have a rerun… Remain united. Begin to bond... The future of this country depends entirely on you. The whole world is going to use Kenya as an example. We refuse to be judged by African standards. Let's be judged by international standards.

"Even as we go for mediation, Pentagon should not forget that Kenyans voted overwhelmingly for change. *Anything short of a rerun will be a fraud.* Kibaki's invitation to the Pentagon to State House was a PR exercise. Kibaki admitted to some church leaders that he had lost the election. *Kibaki is in State House illegally.* What we recognise is the mediation exercise headed by Kufuor..."

He was crisp, coherent, logical and focused. It had been a very long time since I had heard Raila speak that way. He didn't equivocate. He didn't pull punches. He didn't sound cowardly. He was in his element. If only he could have remained that way throughout the negotiation process and the life of the grand coalition government.

When a leader conducts negotiations with that kind of clear-headedness and courage, he makes significant progress. How I wish that Raila had taken Gordon Brown's brilliant advice not to be tempted by half-baked positions in government and the trappings of power! How I wish that Raila's sentiments had been adhered to by everyone in theory and practice. I wish that Raila hadn't betrayed his own words and ended up doing exactly what he had warned others about that day at Maasai Lodge! Regrettably, he went on to do precisely what he had condemned that day.

After Raila sat down, a tea break was called, which lasted until 1.15pm. During that break, Raila moved from one cluster of MP-elects to the other. He was cajoling and confiding as he talked to them about his nominee for speaker. And when the meeting resumed, Nyanza, Western, Nairobi and Eastern provinces returned only one name: Kenneth Otiato Marende. Nairobi went ahead and nominated Maalim Farah as deputy speaker. That wasn't Raila's choice. Coast returned with Willy Mutunga's name as speaker and Farah as his deputy. Very quickly, the meeting voted, choosing Marende as speaker designate and Farah as his deputy. Other names that had been thrown around the hall were: Martin Shikuku and Peter Castro Oloo Aringo. My observation was that Shikuku would have taken the speaker's position had Raila not interfered.

The rest of the day's discussion concerned the humanitarian crisis that had engulfed Kenya in the wake of the elections.

The next party meeting was scheduled for a few days later at the Kenya Commercial Bank training school in Karen. Then we would have to finalise the strategy of how ODM was going to conduct itself in parliament. We also had to agree on the final list of nominated MP slots. The latter had turned to be divisive and full of intrigues, most of which were perpetrated by Raila himself. Reports reaching the technical team were that Raila had promised too many women nominated slots. By this time, Janet Ong'era wasn't attending any ODM meetings. Neither was Dave Arunga. Both were sulking because Raila had already discarded Arunga; and Ong'era was claiming that Raila was planning to short-change her by nominating Rachel Shebbesh. Milton Mugambi Imanyara, Jacqueline Oduol, Rosa Buyu, Millie Odhiambo, Esther Passaris – had all been promised nomination.

So the atmosphere was tense at the KCB, Karen. The technical team, of which I was a member, had prepared detailed briefs for all members of the Pentagon and MPs-elect, based on the earlier agreement that the MPs-elect would elect a speaker and deputy speaker before scuttling the swearing in ceremonies. However, in the intervening days several members had got cold feet about refusing to take their oath. Their worry was that would result in their seats being declared vacant and they feared that they might then lose a by-election. The 1969 KPU conundrum (when MPs who had resigned from Kanu to join KPU in solidarity with Jaramogi Oginga Odinga were forced to resign their parliamentary seats and contest them afresh, resulting in their massive 'defeats') hung over the MPs-elect like a Sword of Damocles. This issue became a huge bone of contention. After a lot of unnecessary arguments, the top honchos conceded to the recalcitrant group that they would take their oaths. However, it was agreed that they would precipitate a crisis before, during and immediately after being sworn in, culminating in a deadlock over the legitimacy of Kibaki's election.

But there was a parallel simmering problem. Media reports that morning had claimed that ODM had already submitted the names of its nominated MPs to the ECK. (In Kenya, there are two categories of MPs – elected and nominated ones. After election results have been declared, the ECK would provide political parties with slots for nominated MP positions to parliament and municipal councils, based on their respective performance in the general elections. It's a formula based on the total number of votes cast for each party. In other words, the ECK would add all votes cast for each party's parliamentary and presidential candidates and use that, on a sliding scale, to determine the number of nominated MPs each party would be entitled to.) Janet Ong'era was the one accused of having submitted the names and she had reportedly done so without consent from Raila, the Pentagon or the party hierarchy. This led to a serious full-scale dispute pitting Raila against Ong'era. Rumours were also swirling around the meeting that Ong'era and Dave Arunga (who was her common law spouse), had been taken to see Kibaki at State House, Nairobi, by Martha Karua, and that her attempt to unilaterally nominate MPs for ODM was part of a large-scale PNU strategy. These could just be rumours. However, they disclosed a recessive schism and angst deeply rooted at the heart of the Orange party; and which was threatening to burst into the open and scatter all the gains so far made by the party.

Raila ended up nominating Mrs Rachel Shebbesh, Mrs Millie Odhiambo, Mrs Sofia Abdi and Sheikh Mohammed Dor from Mombasa. More than a dozen women whom he had promised those slots and Mugambi Imanyara, who had given him ODM at his greatest hour of need, were left in the lurch. Even Roza Buyu who had obtained about 17,000 votes in the 2007 general elections was overlooked (she had contested on Charity Ngilu's Narc party ticket after the disputed ODM nominations in her Kisumu Town West constituency). From a party viewpoint, it was inexplicable that Raila had chosen Shebbesh who had garnered less than 1,000 votes during the ODM nominations in Kasarani constituency, or Millie Odhiambo who hadn't contested and who hailed from the same constituency as Otieno Kajwang', whom he would later pick for his cabinet. Many people believed – justifiably – that there was no logic or reason except the personal relationship Raila had with the two ladies. That was extremely disappointing for a man many Kenyans had fondly referred to as "The People's President."

President Kufuor of Ghana visited Kenya as scheduled and held brief meetings with both Kibaki and his PNU team on the one hand, and Raila and the Pentagon, on the other. Unfortunately, Kibaki stuck to his guns and refused to accept Kufuor's offer to mediate the conflict. Kufuor returned home. That same day – January 10, 2008 – Raila issued an "Address to the Nation" on the state of the mediation process. He criticised Kibaki for blocking mediation and appealed to Kenyans to remain vigilant and "to take all appropriate steps to protect our hard-won democratic rights and gains, which face imminent death through Kibaki's autocratic and brutal action…" He encouraged Kenyans to "be brave and gallant in reclaiming our electoral victory that was unlawfully stolen from us by Kibaki…" and "to come out in large numbers and demonstrate to Mwai Kibaki and the illegitimate usurpers of power that Kenya belongs to all of us". He indicated that despite the best efforts by Kufuor, the ODM and himself to seek a mediated settlement to the political turmoil afflicting the country due to "the open theft of the presidential election by Mwai Kibaki, the latter refused to even acknowledge that Kenya is on fire because of his actions". He went on further to declare that Kibaki had "dishonoured the mediation process that everyone knew he was supposed to be a party to" and that "by that act of betrayal, Kibaki has once more failed to place the interest of the country ahead of his personal interests". Audaciously, Raila signed the statement as President-Elect of The Republic of Kenya.

On January 11, 2008, President Kufuor sent Raila a letter, confirming the discussions they had had during his visit to Nairobi. But unlike Raila's stinging "Statement to the Nation," Kufuor's letter was positive. He noted, significantly, that "as we agreed together, I have constituted the team of Eminent Persons who would use their good offices to facilitate the process of finding a durable solution to the problem. I wish to inform you that H.E. Mr Kofi Annan has accepted to lead the team. Other members are President Benjamin Mkapa of Tanzania and Madam Graca Machel of Mozambique.(...) I shall keep a personal interest in the work of the team of Eminent Persons, with your side and President Kibaki's side".

When Annan landed in Nairobi, I had given Raila, the Pentagon and technical team the following draft document, which, in my considered view, had it been signed, even in an amended form, would have saved time, energy and lots of unnecessary ruckus that afflicted the coalition.

> *Mediation Memorandum*
> Between Raila Amolo Odinga/Orange Democratic Movement (ODM) and Mwai Kibaki/Party of National Unity (PNU)
> This is a Mediation Memorandum between His Excellency Raila Amolo Odinga (hereinafter referred to as "H.E. Raila Odinga") and the Orange Democratic Movement (ODM), on the one hand, and His Excellency Mwai Kibaki (hereinafter referred to as "H.E. Mwai Kibaki") and the Party of National Unity (PNU), on the other (herein referred to as "the parties").
>
> The parties agree that apart from the signatories to the Mediation Memorandum and the Parties' Mediation Teams, no other political party or individual will be permitted to take part in the Mediation Process.
>
> The Mediation Memorandum sets out the terms of the mediation and the understanding of both parties regarding the mediation process.
>
> The parties expressly agree to have their differences and all issues of contention regarding the 2007 presidential election results mediated and amicably resolved in the interest of justice, fairness, truth and democracy.
>
> The parties hereby appoint the Panel of Eminent African Personalities, namely, His Excellency Kofi A. Annan, as Lead Mediator and Her Excellency Graca Machel and His Excellency Benjamin Mkapa. The Panel was constituted pursuant to an

agreement between the parties and His Excellency President John Kufuor, President of the Republic of Ghana and Chairman of the African Union, as contained in President Kufuor's letter to the parties dated 11 January 2008. President Kufuor's mandate to find a durable solution to the political and humanitarian crisis in Kenya was given to him in his capacity as the Chairman of the African Union.

Subject to the parties' agreement, mediation shall be conducted by any one, two or three named Mediators. Further details of the mediation process are to be agreed upon by the parties with the assistance of the Mediators.

It is understood and agreed that the Mediators are neutrals with no direct or indirect connection to any of the parties and no personal interest(s) in any mediation outcome.

The parties commit themselves to respecting the mediation process and to be bound individually and collectively to both the mediation process and any agreement reached at the end of the mediation.

The parties agree that they will conduct mediation at a neutral physical location and in good faith. They will also refrain from uttering any statement or taking any action that might undermine the process of mediation.

H.E. Mwai Kibaki agrees to forthwith order members of the regular police force, the Administration, General Service Unit and any other security personnel to refrain from shooting at and beating unarmed civilians.

H.E. Mwai Kibaki agrees to forthwith order all members of the disciplinary forces and his supporters not to interfere with the rights of association, assembly and expression of all Kenyans.

H.E. Mwai Kibaki agrees to order that press freedom, including live coverage of events, be reinstated and respected forthwith.

H.E. Raila Odinga agrees to appeal to all his supporters to exercise restraint and remain peaceful.

The parties expressly agree that H.E. Raila Odinga will participate in the mediation process both personally and through representatives. H.E. Raila Odinga shall be the ultimate decision maker on behalf of ODM. Decisions made by H.E. Raila Odinga during the mediation process shall bind ODM. No decision shall be binding on either H.E. Raila Odinga or ODM if not agreed on or consented to in writing by H.E. Raila Odinga.

The parties expressly agree that H.E. Mwai Kibaki will participate in the mediation process both personally and through representatives. H.E. Mwai Kibaki shall be the ultimate decision maker on behalf of PNU. Decisions made by H.E. Mwai Kibaki during the mediation process shall bind PNU. No decision shall be binding on either H.E. Mwai Kibaki or PNU if not agreed on or consented to in writing by H.E. Mwai Kibaki.

Both H.E. Raila Odinga and H.E. Mwai Kibaki hereby confirm and undertake to be accessible during mediation when not physically present at a mediation session.

H.E. Raila Odinga and H.E. Mwai Kibaki formally consent to have six witnesses to the final Mediated Agreement, namely one representative of the African Union; one representative of the European Union; one representative of the United Kingdom; one representative of the United States of America; one representative of Japan; and one representative of the United Nations.

In addition, the Mediators shall also append their signatures to this Mediation Memorandum and any final Agreement thereto.

The Parties agree that the mediation process shall be concluded within one month from the date the Mediation Memorandum is executed and duly witnessed.

The Parties agree to make the contents of this Mediation Memorandum and any Agreement thereto publicly available to the Kenyan people.

The Parties, Mediators and Witnesses to the Mediation Memorandum hereby confirm that they have sought and obtained independent legal advice and append their respective signatures hereunder voluntarily.

Any amendments, changes or alterations to the Mediation Memorandum are hereby declared null and void.

Dated at the City of Nairobi, Kenya on this..............day of January 2008

H.E. Raila Odinga/ODM H.E. Mwai Kibaki/PNU

Signing as Mediators

H.E. Graca Machel H.E. Kofi Annan H.E. Benjamin Mkapa

Signing as Witnesses

Representative of the AU Representative of the UK

Representative of the US Representative of the EU

There were several mischiefs that this document aimed to cure. Firstly, both Kibaki and Raila needed to be recognised simply as two principals representing parties to a dispute – equal before the mediators in all respects. Before the process, Raila and Kibaki were merely two presidential candidates; competitors in an electoral race. Neither took precedence over the other. Titles, powers and positions irregularly acquired, or bestowed, or arising out of the conflict, should never have been used. The mediators ought to have recognised the status quo before Kivuitu declared Kibaki President; he was an outgoing President, whose term had effectively ended on December 30, 2007.

The draft documents neatly locked out Kalonzo and his ODM-K formation from the mediation table. If he or his ODM-K party were to be present, they had to get to the table (indirectly) as Kibaki's nominees; not on their own standing or merit. Conventional wisdom held that it was Kalonzo that made Kibaki's electoral fraud easy to execute. The document also sought to bind both Kibaki and Raila to the process and the final resolution reached. As well, it opened up the mediation exercise to all issues, including the legitimacy of Kibaki's presidency and that of the half-cabinet he had named (barely a day before Kufuor's first visit). It equalised the parties and had them formally appoint and instruct the mediators. In addition, it sought to have the security forces stop shooting and infringing on the rights of unarmed civilians. It then tied the cessation of mass action to Kibaki's lifting of draconian actions he had taken. Media freedom and other civic rights were to be restored. Finally, a tight deadline of one month was imposed. This was important because open-ended processes would advantage the incumbent.

Thus began the process of mediation, which, on February 28, 2008, would culminate in the signing of the National Accord and Reconciliation Agreement.

But Kibaki and the PNU formation refused to accept the term "mediation". Raila and his team didn't have the stamina and fortitude to stand their ground, conceding quickly, as would subsequently become their *modus operandi*. They didn't insist on the agenda items we had recommended and that had been unanimously endorsed by the ODM party: that we should demand a rerun as the first and best viable option; joining a "unity," "inclusive" or "coalition government" wasn't even a second or third option. Unfortunately, it is this option that, secretly, Raila, Orengo and other Kanu orphans who had now surrounded Raila – preferring even a whiff of power to being left out in the cold – supported.

Taking a long-view picture of the situation, Kofi Annan agreed to call the process a "National Dialogue on the Resolution of the Political Crisis in Kenya". Later, this concession would prove to be fatal. These aren't mere academic quibbles with the manner Annan conducted the process. They are practical, structural and philosophical issues. Firstly, Annan hadn't really been "appointed" by the parties to the dispute. His name was first suggested by the US and UK administrations; and had been backed by Kufuor, partly because they were both Ghanaians. Essentially, Kibaki and his PNU cohorts had been bludgeoned into accepting him, grudgingly.

In my view, the process of choosing a mediator or negotiator was too important to have been treated in this manner. Both parties' confidence and trust in the mediator and the process as a whole are two significant ingredients in the process. Once both ingredients are missing, it's always a sign that the process is fundamentally flawed and might not succeed. Most alternative dispute resolution professionals and experts consider the so-called world powers' imposition of Annan on the parties as an error. There was a high risk that either or both parties could (and indeed PNU eventually did for some time) disown the process, the results or the implementation of the process. Moreover, without full confidence and trust of the parties, a mediator's mandate and authority is greatly undermined. And we saw how frequently Annan pussy-footed around all kinds of problems and Kibaki's numerous blatant abrogations of the national accord afterwards. Annan's mantra of "Let the parties resolve those issues on their own" was neither responsible nor convincing. What then was the role of the mediator? If his role hadn't ended (and he and his Kofi Annan Foundation continued getting paid huge amounts by the 'guarantors' of the process), like he kept reminding Kenyans, why couldn't he deal with open violations of the accord? Issuing regular one-page letters and general "assessments" couldn't have been the main function or mandate of a mediator.

I wasn't that naïve nor inexperienced enough to imagine that Annan or his fellow eminent African personalities would babysit the coalition. Nobody expected or wanted that. However, it was important that they took practical steps to prevent or manage egregious violations of the accord. (I would later come to see the arrangement as a ceasefire primarily intended to end the post-election violence and that it was never meant as a genuine real 'power sharing' arrangement.)

Later, Raila would be convinced by the then US Ambassador to Kenya Michael Ranneberger to accept mere departments as the 'first steps to real power sharing;' and to 'give Kibaki time to agree to the sharing of other positions in government.' "Ranneberger gave me his personal guarantee," Raila would tell me naïvely when I politely requested him to explain to the Pentagon technical team 'the insurance policy' ODM had that Kibaki would agree to 'share civil service, diplomatic, security, intelligence and other government positions,' which, in my view, was what would constitute 'real power sharing'.

Notwithstanding the problem with how Annan had been chosen mediator, he should have prepared and had Raila and Kibaki sign a detailed "Memorandum of Principles and Agenda" in which both parties would have committed themselves – as equal parties – to both the process and the outcome of the process. Annan never did this, hence he opened up the process for disownment later, which Kibaki did frequently. Instead, the "Annotated Agenda and Timetable" dated February 1, 2008 was signed by Martha Karua, "for the Government/PNU Delegation," Musalia Mudavadi "for the ODM Delegation," and H.E. Kofi A. Annan "Chairman, Panel of Eminent African Personalities." This was the first document that initiated the process. Why couldn't he have both Raila and Kibaki to sign, as the chief protagonists? Why didn't he involve his co-mediators? In my considered view, proceeding without written and unequivocal commitment and undertakings from both principals was another fatal error.

On February 12, Annan suddenly "disappeared" with the Serena Teams to a secret location, which we later learnt was the Kilaguni Lodge at the Tsavo National Park. The idea was to hold talks away from the media glare and the incessant interference from political saboteurs. But this came too late in the process, after the parties had become increasingly intransigent. So, after three days, Annan and the negotiating teams returned to Nairobi crestfallen. The secret talks had failed to yield any dividends.

When Raila and Kibaki signed the "Agenda Item Three: How to Resolve the Political Crisis" on February 14, 2008, Raila signed as "Hon. Raila Odinga, Orange Democratic Movement," while Kibaki signed as "H.E. President Mwai Kibaki, Government/Party of National Unity." I thought it was a huge mistake to allow Kibaki to be referred to as "President" in all the mediation documents. The presidency was at the centre of the dispute. Both Kibaki and Raila had laid claim to the presidency. Both were claiming to have been "duly elected". Therefore, to refer to Kibaki as "President" in all the documents, including the accord, erroneously ring-fenced the presidency for Kibaki and elevated him above Raila. The result of the process was thus illegitimately predetermined: it felt like it had been rigged for Kibaki. How could Raila later demand and Kibaki accept that the presidency was in contention when all the documents underlined that it was "occupied" and wasn't subject to discussion?

Once I saw the initial documents that Orengo et al had signed on behalf of Raila, I knew the game was up. I explained my misgivings to Raila, the Pentagon and the technical team. Unfortunately, only Ntimama, Dr Kosgei, Charity Ngilu and the technical team saw and appreciated my points. Raila was now clearly focused on joining the Kibaki government merely as a "minister". And a junior partner. Many could only speculate as to the real motives behind that move.

I recall one of the villagers in Magina – Mary Ochele Oyando – confronting me after the accord had been signed, and asking: "Miguna *Oruko wuod Jomune, pesa mit makata minu kwayi*; we voted for Raila as President; not as Prime Minister. Why can't Kibaki take the Prime Minister's position and leave the presidency for Raila? We can't accept this Prime Minister thing," she addressed me using my father's nicknames. She was expressing a popular view among the vast majority of Kenyans. They had voted for Raila as President. For them Kibaki had lost the election; his continued stay at State House wasn't just due to a fraud; it was an imposition. The presidency wasn't reserved for anyone; Kibaki included. There was no reason why Kibaki had to stay on as President and Raila given the hollow post of Prime Minister. I had made the same argument and had advised Raila accordingly, I told Mary. But it was Raila who had chosen to be Prime Minister. "Why?" Mary kept asking me; "does he fear Kibaki?"

"Maybe he does; I don't know." I answered Mary and politely excused myself and returned to Nairobi. That was in early March 2008.

I would meet the same sceptical questions from ordinary parishioners at a public event organised by the Catholic Church at St Mary's Yala School in Siaya County at the end of 2008. My good friend Reverend Joakim Omolo had invited me to address some questions the congregation had on the national accord, the coalition government and the constitutional review process. Unsurprisingly, virtually everyone was convinced that Raila wasn't showing grit in his ongoing dealings with Kibaki and the PNU side. I was also pleasantly surprised when one elderly lady said 'From the way you have spoken, I believe that Raila should have you as one of his advisors…'

To my mind, Annan also made an unforgivable error in not instituting a process on how information about the discussions would reach the media and ultimately the public. Ordinary Kenyans weren't just the biggest stakeholders of the process; they were its owners. The country was theirs. Both Raila and Kibaki were mere political players; trustees if you will. In any credible and professionally managed mediation process, information is relayed through the mediator via joint communiqués, signed by both parties. It was crucial for Annan to have compelled the parties to sign a written undertaking not to unilaterally release information or comment on the process, including its outcome or implementation, except through joint communiqués. However, because Annan had failed to secure such an important undertaking, both PNU and ODM consistently issued contradictory, divisive and conflicting information about what had been discussed or agreed on, thereby creating unnecessary tension in the country and placing artificial impediments that would later imperil the smooth running of the grand coalition government.

The duration of the mediation wasn't established either. No timelines or deadlines were set. There was no equality in the negotiations, as Annan kept driving into State House for meetings with Kibaki and joint meetings between the principal protagonists were usually held at Kibaki's Harambee House offices, with Kibaki chairing all sessions, and Annan tagging along as a note-taker, and Raila as just another "visitor" to the office. Although Kibaki had named his "half" cabinet days before Kufuor's arrival in Nairobi, Annan made no demands that, technically speaking, that cabinet wouldn't be considered for purposes of the mediation. In other words, Annan failed to take charge of mediation; failed to establish clearly understood ground rules; and failed to compel Kibaki to submit to the process, in the same manner that Raila had done; thereby failing to ensure that there was equality of and between parties; which is both essential and necessary for the success of mediation.

Unfortunately, probably before the negotiations had begun, Raila had abandoned all the core ODM demands. He had decided – without explanation or reason – to go for a coalition government, which was what Annan had announced as the "best way forward" upon his arrival in Nairobi, before he had even held meetings with the parties. This "grand coalition" idea didn't emanate from the parties or from the process; it was probably manufactured in Washington and London and delivered by Annan to Kenya; another dubious foreign experiment on Africa! Unfortunately, Raila and the ODM team then treated Annan like a judge of the 'supreme global court,' not as a mediator, thus Annan's role became prescriptive rather than explorative.

The Pentagon technical team had unanimously picked me as the secretary to the ODM mediation team. Initially, there was no problem. I actually attended the first two sessions, and accompanied Raila when he signed the 'Annotated Agenda' to the mediation process. Later, Caroli insisted that he should join me as a joint secretary, but the technical team balked at that suggestion – they didn't trust Caroli.

Initially, the ODM mediation team had no lawyers. Both the PNU and ODM teams comprised of politicians – elected members of parliament. Orengo was brought in much later, through the intervention of Dr Kosgei, who candidly admitted that "our side is disadvantaged; PNU has three good lawyers: Karua, Mutula and Wetangula, and we have none." Unfortunately, the sly Caroli went behind the technical team's recommendations and had himself "chosen" as the ODM liaison officer. His counterpart, Gichiira Kebaara (a civil servant who was then secretary to the Ministry of Justice and now acting permanent secretary in the same ministry) represented the PNU side. (Another good example of the civil service being PNU dominated.) Within no time, Caroli brought me "a message from Jakom" that I wouldn't be attending the mediation sessions.

The technical team did its best to try and steer the process. We tried to meet with the ODM mediation team before and immediately after each session. But ODM would rue the day Orengo and Caroli joined the mediation team as the only lawyers. They were terrible negotiators. They consistently and unstrategically withheld crucial information they were supposed to table (and then presented information they ought to have withheld); they presented partial information when they were supposed to present full information; they offered all ODM options and fallback positions to the opposite team without the technical team's approval and in direct contravention of our strategic recommendations; and they deliberately undermined our strategic positions.

In the end, a National Accord was signed that many believe to have been poorly crafted and uneven. Then a coalition cabinet was named that saw all the significant positions go to Kibaki's PNU. Raila and ODM had been again short-changed by Kibaki and PNU, but I believe that they only had themselves – with the principal culprits being Raila, Orengo and Caroli – to blame.

On February 14, 2008, when Raila and Kibaki signed the "Agenda Item Three: How to Resolve the Political Crisis", virtually all Kenyans breathed a sigh of relief. As if on cue, most combatants on both sides pulled back. In most areas, there was a de facto ceasefire. Sporadic incidents of violence persisted here and there, especially at the epicentre of the conflict in Rift Valley province. Of course, the hundreds of thousands of internally displaced remained homeless, cold and hungry. Those who had been raped, maimed, injured and dispossessed had still not been recompensed; even today accountability still remains a chimera. But on that St Valentine's Day, Kenyans and the rest of the world had hope. We had (been) pulled back from the precipice, but we were not yet completely safe.

On February 26, Annan suspended the talks (because they were heading nowhere) but kept insisting that they hadn't broken down. The following day, Tanzanian President, Jakaya Kikwete travelled to Nairobi and joined Annan and his team. He had just assumed the chairmanship of the AU. On February 28, Kibaki, Raila, Annan, Kikwete, Graca Machel and Benjamin Nkapa spent virtually the entire day behind closed doors at Harambee House in intense negotiations. As the talks proceeded, the country held its collective breath. TV cameras were fixed on the steps of Harambee House for any signs of progress or deterioration. Speculation was rife that if there was no deal, the country would relapse into civil strife, destruction and death.

Raila and the ODM were expected not just to seek justice for the thousands of innocent civilians who had been killed, maimed, tortured, brutalised, gang raped (and many infected by HIV/AIDS), injured and forcefully displaced; but also for those who had been arrested and detained. However, when the Accord was signed late that evening, Raila, Orengo and a faction of ODM still loyal to him had squandered all the opportunities they had had to seek justice for the victims of Post Election Violence (PEV). Instead, they played opportunistic politics with the destiny of the country and signed an Accord that was long on hope but short on detail. The document didn't specify how power was to be shared, how the coalition government would be established and the core policy areas the two parties were going to fulfill. There was nothing about how the coalition government would deal with the security forces who had mowed down thousands of unarmed and innocent Kenyan civilians; and nothing about the tens of thousands of youth who had been arrested and whose whereabouts were unknown to their loved ones. ODM leaders refused and failed to remain firm in demanding accountability for those who had perpetrated the heinous crimes committed in Kenya between December 27, 2007 and March 2008. And for that, history shall judge them harshly.

It was the first significant indication that those (like me) who had put their hopes in Raila as an agent of change, were going to be disappointed.

CHAPTER NINE

'PLEASE SAVE ME FROM KIBAKI'

"Eeeeh…eehhhh…eiiii…please save me from Kibaki! Eeeeeh…eiiiii… Please don't let me go back to that man…I don't want to go back to Kibaki! Eeeeh…eiii…Please save me from Kibaki!" Raila broke down and cried, torrents of tears flowing freely down his cheeks. He was shaking uncontrollably.

It was about 3.30pm on April 6, 2008. Everyone in the room was stunned. They had never seen Raila cry before. We looked at each other, unable to move. No one was prepared for this heart-wrenching scene. I guess we had assumed that Raila was 'superhuman'. He had a larger-than-life image in the consciousness of Kenyans. He had been given many nicknames, all describing his courage, mystery and enigmatic qualities. In fact, there wasn't any Kenyan – living or dead, with the possible exception of the ancient legendary Gor Mahia (from whom the famous Kenyan soccer team derives its name) – that I knew of who had so many nicknames. He was (endearingly called) 'Tinga' (the tractor), 'Agwambo' (mysterious one), 'Owad ga Akinyi' (Akinyi's brother), 'Wuod Nyar Alego' (Son of a Daughter from Alego, an area reputed to excel in magic and witchcraft. Most Kenyan men grew up being told and constantly reminded that "A real man doesn't cry".

But there he was, someone we all held in awe, wailing uncontrollably in front of everyone.

We were about 25 people in the room; members of the ODM Pentagon, a few ODM national leaders and the Pentagon technical team. Raila had just returned from a face-to-face meeting with Kibaki over the formation of the grand coalition government following the signing of the national accord and reconciliation agreement on February 28, 2008. By then he had attended numerous meetings and most had ended in stalemate or Raila's capitulation. Raila's debriefs and reports of those long meetings had become a routine in itself, with him repeating "Kibaki can't accept this" or "Kibaki is insisting on that".

Crying as such wasn't really the issue. I have cried many times before. But this was distinctly different. Context is important: Raila wasn't just another Kenyan; he was the leader of ODM – our general and commander-in-chief – and the person we all believed the majority of Kenyans had elected as President on December 27, 2007. If Kibaki hadn't executed his civilian coup, Raila would have been not just the head of government and state; he would have been the commander-in-chief of the armed forces of Kenya. He would have had the heavy responsibility of making decisions that could take our country to war and with it our men and women in uniform to unimaginable risks, including their deaths. Those are responsibilities that require courage, wisdom and steel.

During this period, members and supporters of ODM considered ourselves to be 'at war' with PNU. We needed a leader who could go into battle gallantly and return victorious. A man who couldn't face Kibaki eyeball-to-eyeball, unflinchingly, at a time when the country relied on him to be steadfast, in my mind couldn't effectively handle the onerous state responsibilities required as a President, let alone lead ODM. As Sun Tzu says, "it is the unemotional, reserved, calm, detached warrior who wins…"

Perhaps Raila was too fragile, having not fully recovered from eight years of detention and torture. It's even possible that in Kibaki he saw his former tormentors – his jailors; which in a way, as someone who was Moi's Vice-President when Raila was detained, Kibaki was. Yes, it's possible that Raila might have been having flashbacks. Or perhaps he had suffered irreparable damage following those long years of detention and needed counselling …I don't know. I sympathised with him. However, what I know is that at the historical juncture at which we were – and still are – we deserved a man of grit; not a fragile man.

Raila was not only crying; he was also sweating profusely. As he raised his right hand to wipe his brow and eyes, he exposed a drenched armpit. The then ODM's national treasurer and South Mugirango MP Omingo Magara moved gingerly towards Raila and placed his right hand on our Captain's shoulder, speaking soothingly to him, telling him it was all right. Then Pentagon member and Kitui Central MP Charity Ngilu and nominated MP, Joseph Nyagah, did the same before Raila sat down and asked for something to drink. Someone (it could have been Sarah Elderkin) dutifully offered him water, which he took in one gulp.

Salim and I looked at each other and said (quietly to each other where we stood), almost in unison, "Holy Moly! What the hell was that?"

We moved outside discreetly. "Can you believe that Miguna? He cried. Raila cried," said Salim, clearly agitated.

"Yes my friend, we all saw that," I answered softly. We said nothing more, before returning to the room.

* * * * * * * * * * * * * *

February 28, 2008 is a date etched into the psyche of contemporary Kenyans and the annals of history. On that Thursday, Kenya was at a standstill. For most of that day, all the television and radio stations, internet chat rooms and blogs were glued to President Kibaki's Harambee House offices, where Raila, Kibaki, Annan, Machel, Mkapa, President Jakaya Kikwete of Tanzania and both ODM and PNU Serena Teams were holed up in meetings, or simply pacing the corridors. The world media's analysis was that a peaceful future for Kenya hung by a thread; one wrong move and the whole country could slide into an even more cataclysmic chaos than the nightmarish days and nights that had ushered in 2008. There were even grim comparisons with Somalia and the Democratic Republic of Congo. We were peering into the abyss.

In the run up to that day, Annan, Machel and Mkapa had tried to cajole the two warring parties towards an accord. The fear was that if stalemate continued, then the angry violence that had raged in the wake of the contested presidential election results might reignite. In frustration, Annan had even suspended the Serena talks and 'secretly' taken the mediation teams to the Kilaguni Lodge in Tsavo National Park. But even that initiative had come a cropper, because the parties could not agree on the critical issue of whether they should have a grand coalition government or a rerun of the election. Nor, when a coalition was discussed, could they agree how executive power was to be shared out between Raila and Kibaki.

I didn't attend the February 2008 Kilaguni talks. But I understand from reports relayed to me by Athman Said, a member of the technical team, and ODM mediation team members Orengo and Sally that temperatures boiled to fever pitch; that at one time, Mutula and Ruto came up with a bizarre "compromise" proposal (that had its origins with Caroli, but which, thankfully, was summarily dismissed by the ODM team) where the Prime Minister was to be appointed by the President under the old Constitution, minus any other statutory or constitutional guarantees. Finally, however, a compromise agreement that would appear to move things forward, was reached, days after the team had returned to Nairobi. The country exhaled late in the afternoon of February 28, when the two principals appeared together, grinning, on the steps of Harambee House, along with the international mediators and their negotiation teams, plus a galaxy of both local and international media.

"Ladies and gentlemen, we have a deal!" Kofi Annan announced jubilantly. He then unveiled a two-page document, The Agreement on the Principles of Partnership of the Coalition Government, popularly referred to as 'the National Accord'. Kibaki and Raila, seated beside each other on the steps of Harambee House, and surrounded by Kikwete, Annan, Mkapa, Machel and the PNU and ODM negotiators, signed, as cameras flashed. It was this historic document that would form the basis of the National Accord and Reconciliation Act 2008. In fact, it was attached as an addendum to the Act. It would also form the basis for the Constitution of Kenya (Amendment) Act 2008.

The world hailed the signing of the Accord as a milestone – a historic event. Almost every Kenyan smiled, hugged or celebrated. The media was ecstatic. They hadn't at that stage analysed the fine print; for them just the act of signing was enough. Of course, once people read the accord and started the painful process of analysis, they saw gaping loopholes, vagueness, ambiguities and plain ineptness that forewarned them of real dangers that lay ahead.

I had seen all this coming and felt that, as usual, Orengo and Caroli had messed up. In the run-up to the accord meetings, the technical team had debated all the points for discussion and agreed that ODM shouldn't be party to any deal that wasn't detailed on all aspects of power sharing. We had emphasised that since the accord would be ratified publicly, all provisions in the old Constitution that contradicted it would first have to be amended to conform to the new governance structure.

I had been proactive and taken the time to prepare a five-page draft agreement (national accord) that outlined in great detail, all areas of the political settlement. I painstakingly reviewed the old Constitution and highlighted all provisions that had to be amended. The latter document was six pages. Subsequently, I convinced the technical team to adopt both documents before we presented them to Raila and the Pentagon. Both Raila and the Pentagon adopted them without any changes. Raila then instructed me to present them to Orengo so that he could in turn submit them for discussions and adoption at Serena.

One whole week before February 28 – Orengo and I had had breakfast at 7.30am at the Java Coffee House in Gigiri, close by our respective Runda homes.

It was there that I had briefed him on the technical team's discussions with Raila and communicated the latter's instructions with respect to the National Accord. I then presented Orengo with both drafts and urged him to ensure that the ODM team made a strong pitch for either their complete adoption, or the inclusion of their most salient features. Orengo gave me his word that he would do all that was necessary; after all, in his own words, "PNU had presented a shoddy two and a half-page document that Annan had dismissed as insufficient". I wonder to this day what then happened to my proposals.

* * * * * * * * * * * * * *

In the immediate aftermath of the signing of the Accord, I wrote an editorial for *The Kenyan Tribune,* a journal that Prof. Oyugi, Oduor Ong'wen and I had just started using our meagre savings. The editorial, "Raila-Kibaki Deal: the Landmines Ahead", appeared in the March 21-27 issue of the newspaper. Looking back, I'm surprised at how prescient that piece was. It highlighted many of the issues I had pressed the ODM team to take into account when they were negotiating the Accord.

We argued that although the Accord had been hailed as a major milestone in the history of Kenya, and in many significant respects it was, there were important deficiencies that might imperil its implementation if not immediately addressed.

Firstly, we asked the Accord provided that "There will be a Prime Minister of the Government of Kenya, with authority to coordinate and supervise the execution of the functions and affairs of the Government of Kenya." However, no date was stipulated when the Prime Minister's position would be created. Nor was there a precise legal mechanism enshrined on its creation. In addition, and contrary to standard drafting principles, there was no clause which defined important words, phrases and concepts such as "real power sharing", "power", "government", "coordination","supervision" and "execution of government functions".

Secondly, the Accord stated that "The Prime Minister will be an elected member of the National Assembly and the parliamentary leader of the largest party in the National Assembly, or of a coalition, if the largest party does not command a majority. This particular provision raised a few fundamental questions. To begin with, the term "coalition" wasn't defined. It was similarly not defined or provided for in the repealed Constitution of Kenya. As such, it was conceivable that anyone could craft a coalition as contemplated in the Accord from the existing parties and members of the National Assembly and create a majority of members outside the Parties to the Accord, namely, the ODM and the PNU.

What would happen to the National Accord in that situation, we asked. But even more importantly, how secure were Raila Odinga and ODM from political mischief by Kibaki, PNU and affiliated parties? Why was Kibaki's position secure and protected and not Raila's? On what basis was the Prime Minister's position a power-sharing arrangement between ODM and PNU if the latter could easily use state resources and instruments to woo members of the National Assembly (including ODM members) in order to undermine the spirit of the Accord?

Was the Accord simply based on trust? Although trust is important in such undertakings, it must be premised on concrete things. In this case, what was the basis of the trust in view of Kibaki's trashing of the Memorandum of Understanding of 2002 (between Raila's Liberal Democratic Party and Kibaki's National Alliance Party of Kenya) and the alleged massive and blatant rigging of the 2007 presidential election? Was history repeating itself?

Thirdly, the Accord stated that "The Prime Minister and the two Deputy Prime Ministers (one from ODM and the other from the PNU Alliance) can only be removed if the National Assembly passes a motion of no confidence with a majority vote." This was tricky. At that moment in time, ODM had a majority, albeit a slim one (with about six MPs), in the National Assembly when compared with any other existing parliamentary political party or coalition of parties. In fact, compared to the PNU (not the PNU Alliance which consisted of PNU, ODM-K, Kanu, Narc-K, New Ford-K, Sisi Kwa Sisi and many other tiny parties), ODM had a commanding majority. However, when one factored in a coalition comprising PNU, Kanu, ODM-K, Safina and other smaller parties, ODM's majority evaporated like the morning dew.

There was also the role of corruption in parliamentary affairs in Kenya. Coupled with the fact that Kenyans would be faced with six by-elections in the next coming month or so (due to four deaths of ODM MPs – two in a helicopter accident and two in murders, and judicial nullifications of others following successful petitions), the power equation might shift drastically in favour of either ODM or PNU and its affiliates.

Moreover, there was no provision in the Accord that required the reconstitution of the Electoral Commission of Kenya (ECK) or at a minimum, the replacement of the commissioners and the senior staff that were involved in electoral malpractices, including fraud. It was common knowledge that it was the ECK officials who were directly responsible for the fraudulent presidential elections and the attendant consequences, and yet they were likely to preside over the forthcoming by-elections. Under those circumstances, ODM had to be very careful not to fall into the traps laid by its so-called coalition partners. The Accord went further to provide that whereas the President would retain the power to appoint cabinet, ODM would only "nominate" persons for consideration to cabinet positions. In fact, there was no provision that guaranteed that ODM's nominees would be appointed by Kibaki (who remained the sole 'appointing authority'), in what numerical strength, or in what portfolios. In our view, this was a recipe for disaster. Why couldn't the drafters explicitly provide the two-thirds majority vote that was required for the removal of the President to also apply to the Prime Minister?

Fourthly, the provision that called for "portfolio balance" in the formation of the coalition government based on the relative "parliamentary strength" of parties was so vague and convoluted that it rendered itself to potential misinterpretations. Ordinarily, any reasonable person would have thought that the party with a majority in parliament would be entitled to more positions than a minority party. In other words, ODM should have had the lion's share in government. At the very least, it shouldn't have been relegated to a bystander's role in the management of government affairs. (Interestingly, however, it was Raila, members of the Pentagon and other national ODM leaders who began talking about a "50-50" power-sharing arrangement. The ink with which the Accord had been drafted had hardly dried before ODM started short-changing itself. When I requested Raila to challenge Kibaki on these issues, he retorted "that's not the way to speak to a President Miguna".)

Clearly these vague, inexact and general provisions were capable of abuse, especially by an untrustworthy and unwilling coalition partner. For instance, we asked, what would happen when the two coalition partners disagreed on the meaning of "portfolio balance" or "real power sharing?" Would Kibaki and his tiny PNU party simply proceed to run the affairs of state without any reference to ODM? In view of PNU's previous recalcitrance over all the major issues in contention, where was the guarantee that PNU would cede ground to ODM in reorganising cabinet portfolios?

It would have been prudent for the negotiators to outline what portfolios PNU and ODM would be assigned or allocated beforehand. Any competent and experienced mediator(s) couldn't conceivably have left these gaping loopholes in such an important document, more particularly in view of the crisis and violence that had engulfed the country for two months just prior to the signing of the Accord.

Obviously, many well meaning observers and 'Accord apologists' kept insisting that "it was understood" or "it was common ground" that ODM and PNU would share power equally. Nonetheless, it was one thing to say that one would share power "equally" and quite another to actually share power EQUALLY. The meaning of "equally" in the context of power sharing had also not been defined. Did it equate each cabinet position with the other without regard to factors like budgetary allocation, reach, influence and number of employees? Additionally, even if "it was understood" (as Orengo and Caroli kept singing to me) that the 50-50 sharing of power meant that ODM and PNU would share the entire "government" including but not limited to cabinet positions, senior civil positions, diplomatic and parastatal positions; where was the mechanism of doing so in the Accord?

Fifthly, the Accord stipulated that, "The coalition will be dissolved if the Tenth Parliament is dissolved; or if the parties agree in writing; or if one coalition partner withdraws from the coalition." Well and good. But what would happen if either party deliberately broke the Accord, or one or more of its fundamental provision(s)? Did it mean that the new-found peace could be unilaterally ruptured by any party for any reason under the sun? What would prevent either party from destroying the Accord merely because it had changed its mind or its fortunes had changed? What happened if one party whimsically withdrew from the coalition?

Prior to the signing of the Accord, various media houses carried stories about there being fresh elections if the Accord broke down. Where did that go? In our view, this was a good deterrence; a mechanism for preventing a selfish party from wrecking the Accord (and the country); especially a party not sure of emerging victorious in any subsequent electoral contests. Yet still, where were the inbuilt insurances from such mischief? What would prevent Kibaki or his PNU party from continuing to govern in complete disregard of the Accord after precipitating such fallout?

I had earlier proposed to my party that there should be a provision for automatic fresh elections if either party or both parties withdrew from the coalition, or in the event of a fundamental breach of the Accord. That would have provided accountability in the sense that the public would have been placed in a position of control over their leaders through fresh polls. With that condition now removed, where was the guarantee that Kenyans wouldn't revert to the much hated status quo?

And finally, although there was a provision that the Accord should be entrenched in the Constitution; once more, there was no time-frame for such entrenchment and no inbuilt mechanism for achieving that purpose. Nor was there an express commitment from both parties that they would ensure that it was done.

Even more significantly, ODM had failed to insist on a basic joint national policy framework, which the two coalition partners could sign and commit themselves to for the life of the coalition. This is standard fare throughout the world. Routinely, before coalitions are formed, partners engage in long and protracted negotiations over economic and foreign policy and plans for legal and constitutional reform. These are the pillars on which coalitions in Italy, Israel, Greece – and more recently in Great Britain – stand or fall. It is through these delicately negotiated policies that national interests (not petty and parochial interests) are adhered to. Forming a coalition government without first agreeing on policies affecting taxation, public investment, employment, education, health care (including universal health insurance policy) poverty eradication and spending, indicated that the power deal between ODM and PNU had been done more for the benefit of the parties concerned than for the public. At least, that was my deep held fear that unfortunately has been vindicated. Even though I had mentioned earlier on that we needed both a coalition agreement and an institutional mechanism for managing the coalition government, Raila, the Pentagon and the ODM mediation team never took steps to ensure that these key instruments were put in place before rushing into a one-sided political marriage that would forever haunt them.

I believe that my warnings about the Accord both during its negotiations and immediately after its signing were timely interventions, shots across the bow as it were, that deserved to be heeded by Raila, the Pentagon, the party leadership and members.

* * * * * * * * * * * * * *

Within weeks of having written this article, I was to witness my party leader reduced to tears of frustration by Kibaki's refusal to cede power. After February 28, Kofi Annan had rushed off to Geneva leaving many loose threads in the patchwork coalition. By early April, nearly two months since Raila and Kibaki had agreed to share 'real power' so as to end the ongoing political and humanitarian crisis, they seemed no nearer to forming a working coalition. Raila and ODM had approached all negotiations in good faith (one might add a bit naïvely), in a spirit of give and take, and had naïvely believed Kibaki would do the same. However, all Kibaki seemed to be doing was taking.

Raila's shocking breakdown must have happened on April 6, 2008, because the following day we prepared a letter for him, which was sent to Kibaki, that registered Raila's strong objections to the manner in which Kibaki was conducting negotiations over the formation of the coalition government. It addressed our party's concerns about Kibaki trying to weasel out of 50-50 power sharing; our sensible worries about the size of cabinet he was proposing and our anxieties over what real powers the Prime Minister's office would have.

To be honest, we sent a letter because we were trying to create a mechanism that could avoid Raila meeting with Kibaki face-to-face. Whenever that happened, Raila returned to us empty-handed. We had seen it during the negotiations for the Accord. We saw it again and again when we sent him to extract some concessions from Kibaki over the proposed structure of the coalition government, and over real power sharing. We would see it repeatedly over the constitutional review process; over the negotiations regarding the International Criminal Court's potential investigations and prosecutions into post-election violence; and we would continue to see it over the implementation of the Constitution of Kenya 2010.

It didn't help matters that Raila was a disastrous negotiator, disorganised, often confused and unstructured. He was also apparently completely cowed by Kibaki. Raila was a different man when he was with us from the pitiful wretch he became around Kibaki. With us, he would wail about his stolen election and Kibaki's obtuse arrogance and insolence during their meetings. He had a sharp memory. His vast knowledge of Kenya's history was remarkable. But once in Kibaki's orbit, his confidence would evaporate. Raila became like a schoolboy before a cruel headmaster, checking himself incessantly, straightening his tie, looking at his suit, fidgeting and talking incoherently. He couldn't even look Kibaki in the face, and would embarrassingly refer to him as "Your Excellency" and bow repeatedly before Kibaki at every national occasion.

Kibaki knew that Raila suffered from a twisted inferiority complex and exploited that to the maximum: he always kept Raila waiting; sometimes for as much as an hour; he never added any honorific to Raila's name (choosing to simply call him "Raila"); and he made sure that more often than not, his own seat was different in size and form from that of Raila's.

Kibaki intended to diminish Raila to a level – psychologically, visually and politically – that it would be very difficult for Raila to rise from. And he has continued to do so to this day. Kibaki has many state ceremonial chairs, the presidential lectern bearing the national emblem, a large national flag, presidential flags designating him as both head of state and government and a neatly dressed brass band that accompanies him everywhere he goes. But at no time has he allowed Raila, as Prime Minister, his co-principal and coalition partner, to use or share in the use of any of these ceremonial items. Kibaki's handlers and State House orderlies have made sure that Raila's name is consistently placed on the official 'presidential' programmes after Kibaki and Kalonzo; and that he never uses the 'presidential lectern' with three microphones. And on the few occasions when Kibaki has chosen to address parliament, the presidential security have blocked Raila from using 'State entrances to Parliament'. On two separate occasions, the media have beamed live pictures of the presidential security personnel shoving and pushing away Raila's security detail as they have tried to accompany Raila to Parliament and Madaraka Day celebrations at the Nyayo National Stadium. During one such incident, two of Raila's bodyguards were injured and disarmed by Kibaki's security personnel.

One of our greatest frustrations at the time of the Grand Coalition negotiations was that there was absolutely no need for Raila to flail, fumble and behave desperately. The country was mostly with him following the mismanagement of the elections. Even some of the people who hadn't voted for him on December 27, 2007 now sympathised with him. But he failed to cash in those credits. He was always well prepared before he went to meetings with Kibaki. Moreover, we constantly reminded him that we were ready to tag along and sit in adjacent rooms, in case he needed technical backup, even if he didn't want any of us to be present in the room. He never took us up on those offers, yet on the PNU side Uhuru, Saitoti, Wetangula, Mutula, Karua, Muthaura, Wanjohi, Kimemia, Thuita Mwangi, and many other PNU strong men – and, in Karua's case, of course, a woman – were always with Kibaki during those meetings.

It wasn't easy to comprehend why Raila was disadvantaging himself by attending the meetings alone. There were a few occasions when he took in Isahakia or Caroli, though more often they kept vigil in adjacent rooms, waiting for hours without being consulted or involved. But anyway they weren't the best people on our team to offer advice. Isahakia wasn't useful, since he knew nothing. Caroli, meanwhile, had too much baggage; he was desperate to look good to too many people to whom he owed favours. I was also disappointed in Orengo. Most Kenyans have an image of Orengo as a brave and candid advocate and politician (images he legitimately earned through decades of heroic struggles both at the University of Nairobi and as a young radical parliamentarian), but in these negotiations he suddenly became reticent and withdrawn, and almost always said "yes" to anything Raila suggested. I found that unnerving and a bit distasteful.

Time and again Kibaki had Raila on the ropes. One of the reasons for Raila's breakdown that day was Kibaki's intransigence over the formation of the grand coalition cabinet. In early April 2008, ODM had proposed the disbandment of the pre-existing cabinet and the establishment of a fresh one composed of a maximum of 24 ministries. Kibaki had rejected that out of hand, and Raila had returned to the Pentagon squirming, having conceded to PNU's insane proposal of an excessively large cabinet of 40. When I heard that, I laughed, thinking that it was some kind of April fool's day joke. That would be one of the largest cabinets in history.

"How would we afford it?" I asked, still thinking that it was a cruel joke. Many of my colleagues thought so, too. For instance, we couldn't understand how any sensible person could come up with a "Ministry of Nairobi Metropolitan," let alone think that Raila would accept such silliness. (This was to render, and it did render, the Ministry of Local Government, which Kibaki had ceded to ODM, into a hollow ministry.) They did the same with the Ministry of Health, which was divided into medical services (given to ODM) and health and sanitation (for PNU). Education was divided into (basic) education (for PNU), and higher education (for ODM). Home Affairs was split into home affairs (for ODM-K, a member of the PNU Alliance) and immigration and registration of persons (ODM); et cetera. At each ministry that had an ODM minister, there were PNU affiliated permanent secretaries, secretaries and directors, but the converse wasn't true for ministries where there was a PNU minister.

Without pre-agreeing it with the party, Raila had also already given Kibaki both finance and security portfolios, yet Kibaki hadn't reciprocated. We had sternly advised him that neither party could take both finance and security. It defied logic and commonsense that not only would Kibaki remain as head of state and government, but that Raila, Orengo, the ODM mediation team and the Pentagon had also agreed that he would continue as commander-in-chief and to chair all cabinet meetings. When I confronted Raila, Caroli and Orengo over this lunacy, they boasted of how Raila would be "chairing five cabinet subcommittees". "That's where most decisions will be made," stated Raila confidently.

"But *Jakom*, decisions of the cabinet subcommittees don't bind cabinet, do they? And moreover, unless you are in control of the main ministries, how will you control what those ministries originate? Whoever conceives an idea dictates its implementation."

"*Ja-Nyando*, I will be *supervising* and *coordinating* the government, including all the *ministries!*" He stressed the words "supervising", "coordinating" and "ministries" as if these words were self-enforcing. I could see adolescent excitement in his eyes, as if that was all we as Kenyans had been fighting for. He made it sound like he had suddenly forgotten about the massive electoral fraud and was now more than satisfied to be given the prime ministerial job.

Undeterred, I pressed on, suggesting that for his job to have meaning, significance or content, he should lay stake on either internal security or finance to be placed within the office of the Prime Minister and for him to be directly in charge of either of them; at which point Caroli jumped in. "No, that would dilute the Prime Minister's role and reduce him to the level of a mere minister," Caroli said, sounding knowledgeable.

Exasperated, I continued: "Right now, it is the President who is the substantive minister for defence, internal security and provincial administration; that hasn't diluted or weakened his position as President. On the contrary, it strengthens his hand; he is not just the head of state and government, and commander-in-chief of the armed forces; he is also directly, as minister, responsible for intelligence, police, and military – name it. In addition, he is directly in charge of foreign affairs. He gets to control money, weapons, all instruments of coercion and foreign relations. These to me are the meat of government."

Raila then concluded the discussion by reminding me that as Prime Minister, he would be coordinating and supervising even the ministries of defence, finance, foreign affairs and internal security and provincial administration. I sensed that he took the vague wordings of the National Accord quite literally.

Looking back to those events after four years, it is clear that I have been vindicated; Raila has never been consulted, nor has he had any significant input on any matters dealing with foreign affairs, finance, security and defence. He has been openly defied, belittled and ignored on matters dealing with the illegal occupation of Migingo Island by the Ugandan security forces; the attempts by Kibaki's faction within government to stall or scuttle the International Criminal Court investigations and prosecutions against prominent Kenyans alleged to be responsible for crimes against humanity committed in Kenya between 2005 to 2009 and the pending trials against the four whose charges were confirmed by the pre-trial chamber of the ICC ; human rights and economic policy.

A further impediment to ODM's negotiations was, to my mind, the part played by Ambassador Francis Muthaura. As the country's most senior civil servant and permanent secretary to the cabinet, his role should have been to impartially shepherd the two parties towards a coalition. Instead, he worked for Kibaki. In fact, at no time did Kibaki personally and directly respond, by letter, to Raila; he chose to communicate to Raila through his permanent secretary; thus clearly indicating the level at which, at least in his mind, Raila belonged.

The Pentagon technical team had told Raila that the entire government – not just the cabinet – had to be named. We had insisted that ODM had to lay stake to half the number of ambassadors and high commissioners, half the permanent secretaries, half the heads of state corporations and half the number of heads of other state institutions.

On March 10, 2008, Muthaura issued a provocative "press statement" on behalf of Kibaki, seeking to clarify the "structure of government":

> There have been various media reports that have created concern as to the roles of the position of the Prime Minister, Government appointments and structure of the Government following the national Accord. In that regard the Government wishes to clarify the following:
>
> - The President remains the Head of State and the Head of Government.
> - The Vice-President is the Principal Assistant of the President and the Leader of Government Business in Parliament.
> - The Prime Minister will coordinate and supervise the Government functions under the authority of the President.
> - The Prime Minister and the Deputy Prime Ministers will also have ministerial portfolios.
> - The President will appoint the Vice-President, Prime Minister, Deputy Prime Ministers and all Ministers subject to the terms of the Accord. The Vice-President, Prime Minister, Deputy Prime Ministers and all Ministers are directly responsible to the President. The President will continue to Chair the Cabinet.
> - The Accord does not include sharing of jobs in the Public Service. Therefore, it should be clear that appointments in the Public Service are governed by the Constitution or Acts of Parliament.
>
> To this end:
>
> - Holders of Constitutional offices, Permanent Secretaries, Ambassadors, Judges of the High Court, Chairpersons of Boards and a few Chief Executives of Parastatals are appointed by the President.
> - All other civil servants in Central Government and Local Authorities are appointed by the Public Service Commission or through its delegated authority.

> - Judicial Officers including Magistrates, etc are appointed by the Judicial Service Commission.
> - Teachers are appointed by the Teachers Service Commission.
> - Almost all Members of the Boards of Parastatals, except the Chairmen, are appointed by their respective Ministers.
> - Chief Executives of Parastatals are appointed by the Ministers on recommendation of the respective Boards.
> - All other staff of Parastatals are appointed by their respective Boards.
>
> I wish to assure public servants that there is nothing to worry about the safety of their jobs or the politicisation of the Public Service. I urge public servants to embrace the implementation of the Accord. It is extremely important that professionalism in the Public Service is maintained and free from partisan politics.

If there were any lingering doubts as to whether or not Muthaura was partisan, this press statement proved it beyond any reasonable doubt. The so-called government wasn't a party to the mediation process. There were only two parties: ODM and PNU. The fact that Muthaura essentially signed on behalf of PNU under the pretext of doing so "under the direction of Kibaki" as President, exposed the link between Muthaura and PNU.

Secondly, Muthaura's statement was another clear indication that Kibaki and his PNU group didn't recognise the Accord and the power sharing deal. Even though the Vice-President's position hadn't been a bone of contention during the mediation, Muthaura was intent on imposing that office (that was now occupied by Musyoka) as taking precedence over the Prime Minister. In other words, Muthaura's statement had unlawfully and irregularly established a pecking order in government that was contrary to the provisions of the Accord. If Raila was Kibaki's coalition partner and a co-principal, how could Muthaura, reasonably, relegate Raila?

Thirdly, Muthaura set out to reduce Raila's power, influence and authority; not just in the coalition arrangement, but also in government. By stating that the Prime Minister will operate "under the authority of the President," and that "The Vice-President, Prime Minister, Deputy Prime Ministers and all Ministers are directly responsible to the President", Muthaura was signalling to the government bureaucrats and functionaries that the buck still stopped with Kibaki, and that the Accord hadn't changed anything.

When that statement was issued, Raila summoned me to his office at the Pentagon and sought my opinion and advice. A few Pentagon members like

Balala, Ngilu, Mudavadi, Nyagah and Ruto and other ODM members like Ntimama and Magara were there.

I explained to Raila what I had told him before, that Muthaura's mischief was enabled by the flawed drafting of the Accord; the gaping loopholes that had been left there by the drafters, whoever they were. However, when one closely examined the language and political context of the deal, then one could argue that Muthaura was playing fast and loose with "power sharing" principles. How would one share 'real' power if that same person was "subject to the authority and direction" of his coalition partner? Legal interpretation cannot be done in a vacuum. Consequently, I suggested that ODM, through Raila, should respond to Muthaura's statement. I suggested Raila because the matter needed to be hammered by the biggest muscle we had.

Although Raila agreed with me that the statement had to be responded to, he took umbrage that I revisited the weaknesses of the Accord. He felt – like Orengo – that the Accord was ironclad and its provisions were as "clear as daylight". He insisted that I should have been "talking like our lawyer". That meant blindly supporting their position no matter how untenable or illogical it might be.

Raila didn't seem to appreciate that this was no time for sycophancy. In the end – and paradoxically – only Ntimama (that old Kanu fox) openly lauded my input. Raila directed me to draft a statement to be read by Dr Amukowa Anangwe that same day. I tried to bring out the real issues underlying the rift.

> Our attention has been drawn to a statement attributed to Amb. Francis K. Muthaura, Permanent Secretary/Secretary to the Cabinet and Head of the Public Service on March 10, 2008. This statement has caused shock and alarm amongst ODM supporters.
>
> The Grand Coalition Government is to be established between PNU and ODM as a result of a mediation exercise facilitated by a Panel of Eminent Personalities namely H.E. Kofi Annan, President Mkapa and H.E. Graca Machel, and with the goodwill and support of the international community, Kenyans managed to transform an otherwise dangerous conflict into an opportunity for national healing, peace and reconciliation.
>
> The National Accord reflects the good will and positive attitude of not only both our parties' leadership but also the genuine desire of all Kenyans.
>
> Both ODM and PNU are in the process of ratifying the National Accord through Parliament. They are doing so as equal partners.

> Kenyans from all walks of life have expressed their unqualified support for real power sharing as provided for in the National Accord.
>
> Appropriate bills have been published and will be tabled in Parliament for debate this week. Their passage will entrench the National Accord into our laws.
>
> For avoidance of doubt, the National Accord provides as follows: "The Prime Minister shall have the authority to co-ordinate and supervise the execution of the functions and affairs of the Government, including those of ministries."
>
> It further provides that "the composition of the coalition Government shall at all times reflect the relative Parliamentary strength of the respective parties and shall at all times take into account the principle of portfolio balance."
>
> It also expressly provides for a 50-50 power sharing formula. The power sharing is at two levels; Cabinet and Government, and that includes the Civil Service and Parastatals.
>
> Any statement clarifying, interpreting or explaining the content of the National Accord must be jointly released by the two principals, namely President Mwai Kibaki and Honourable Raila Odinga.
>
> The structure of the new Grand Coalition Government is being worked on before it is announced to the public by the two principals.
>
> Kenyans have begun the slow process of healing, reconciliation and rebuilding their shattered lives. They will not accept to be dragged back to the period of mayhem, violence and disruption by retrogressive forces bent on resisting change.
>
> Any other interpretation of the National Accord undermining, circumventing or delaying its ratification, in both spirit and letter, is mischievous, unacceptable and must be rejected by all Kenyans.

But this ended up being nothing but bluster. Raila had no interest, capacity or fortitude to fight for the full implementation of the Accord; nor was he going to protect the interests of ODM, its supporters, or those of the rest of Kenyans. Undeniably, the vast majority of Kenyans were sympathetic to Raila and wanted to see genuine power sharing and the formation of a legitimate coalition government.

One day in the middle of early April, 2008, there were media reports that Raila and Kibaki had "disappeared to a secret location to finalise the deal". Members of the Pentagon technical team quickly congregated at the Pentagon House and turned on the TV. From one channel to the other, the screens were blank; only scrolling messages that "the President and Prime Minister were holed up somewhere in a secret location, drawing up the cabinet list." The media were already speculating that both principals had decided to sideline their "hard-line advisors in their respective teams who had interests in the outcome of the negotiations". At the political level in ODM, those had now become code words for William Ruto and Prof. Nyong'o, while at the technical level, they meant me. There were even more 'hard-liners' on the PNU side; people like John Michuki, Martha Karua, Uhuru Kenyatta, Nick Wanjohi and Francis Muthaura.

For more than eight hours after Kibaki and Raila had disappeared from the radar, Raila's mobile telephone was switched off. So was Isahakia's. Everyone else seemed to be in total darkness. Then as suddenly as they had disappeared, media footages (without any sound) were released showing Raila arriving at the Sagana State Lodge in Nyeri with Isahakia.

When the subsequent 40-member Grand Coalition Cabinet was unveiled, it was nothing but a face-saving exercise. It was also a subterfuge to mislead the ODM supporters all over the world that the party had secured some gains; that it was in government. The truth, however, was different; Raila had become Prime Minister all right; he had nominated 20 MPs for cabinet positions, and another 20 as assistant ministers. A few permanent secretaries, diplomatic positions and state corporation places would be thrown his way (and he would throw these mainly to members of his family and the greater Jaramogi Clan); but ODM would lose its former lustre, forever. And when Raila exposed himself as a deceptive, opportunistic, weak, cowardly, disorganised and nepotistic leader, he sparked off internal dissent. This quickly developed into a full-blown rebellion by a section of Rift Valley MPs as the disaffection became widespread and uncontainable, ultimately threatening to cripple the party from any future prospects of electoral victory.

Four years later, the seeds of betrayal had grown and spread far and wide. As I complete writing this book the ODM Pentagon is no more. Former ODM luminaries that campaigned, fundraised and mobilised the support for the party in 2007 like Musalia Mudavadi, William Ruto and Najib Balala have peeled off and abandoned Raila, citing personal betrayal, dictatorship, lack of vision and conmanship as the primary reasons for their actions. They were accompanied by Omingo Magara, Aden Duale, Chacha Ganyu, George Khaniri, Chris Okemo,

Isaac Rutto, Charles Keter, Joshua Kutuny and many others. Reports indicate that even Charity Ngilu is preparing to decamp 'at the right moment'.

When the coalition government was sworn in on April 12, 2008, few of ODM's demands had been met. We had tried to save Raila from Kibaki, but he had constantly fallen back into the lion's jaws. Nothing could restrain, discipline or teach Raila a lesson. Contrary to popular myth, Kibaki was the more focused one. He never slept during meetings. He remained alert even if the meetings took more than three hours. He never wavered; never veered off his script. Kibaki was tough as a nut. When he said no, he meant it. He rarely said yes during negotiations. He took and took. He rarely gave.

It was apparent that Kibaki had studied and mastered Raila. He knew Raila's legendary weaknesses. The little trappings of power Kibaki had extended to Raila had turned his head. Unfortunately, Raila forgot too quickly where he had come from and who had got him there. He began to self-destruct. He quickly discarded his most loyal, most courageous and most brilliant generals. Yet, the war was not yet over. He hadn't won. Neither had Kenyans achieved what they deserved, wanted and needed. Although members of the technical team had advised him to restructure the party secretariat and revamp his office to make them effective, efficient and reform-oriented, he was either stuck in the ways of the past, or was now more interested in making billions using the 20 ministries that Kibaki had thrown his way.

For the most ardent patriots, the only relief was that Kenya had been saved from the cauldron through patriotic resistance of ordinary Kenyans who courageously refused to accept the wilful disrespect of the expression of their popular will through a free, fair and democratic election and the blatant perpetration of a civilian coup and international intervention. It's difficult to know what would have happened had Kibaki not interfered with the electoral process and denied Raila the coveted crown. I'm not a seer. I don't have a crystal ball. I don't know what could or could not have happened.

But I now know Raila very well. I know that he is a very weak leader. I also know that he doesn't believe in, is not committed to, and doesn't represent the new dispensation. In fact, he never did. For one, he has no commitment to the fight against impunity. He isn't dedicated to the fight against corruption either. He has no loyalty but to himself and his immediate circle. He has – as I will explain in more detail later – forgotten friends and former allies and betrayed numerous people and groups that helped him to achieve office.

Through the numerous preferential treatments of his family and relatives, it's obvious that Raila is a nepotist. He might not be a classical tribalist, but he represents what can be described as "reverse tribalism"; a tribalism against his own people, the Luo. But even more worrisome has been Raila's tolerance and proclivity towards financial graft. In my considered view, Raila has also shown that he can be greedy; greedy for power; greedy for money and public assets; and greedy for land. These aren't qualities Kenyans need of a national leader; not at this moment in time when we need leaders committed to constitutional implementation, good governance, democracy, rule of law, transparency, accountability and public participation in the management of public affairs.

BOOK FIVE

STANDING TALL IN THE CORRIDORS OF POWER

CHAPTER TEN

KILAGUNI

On April 17, 2008, Raila Amolo Odinga was sworn in as Prime Minister of the Republic of Kenya at State House, Nairobi. It was a low-key event that most members of the Pentagon technical team, including myself, watched on TV from Pentagon House. We hadn't received invitation cards, but many of us wouldn't have gone anyway. We were dejected and disillusioned, not just because of events since the post-election crisis; we were also very unhappy with the way Raila and the rest of the top ODM leadership had conducted the power sharing negotiations. We were livid at the surreptitious manner Raila had 'disappeared' from everyone only to be seen in media photos at the Sagana Lodge in Nyeri, having made some secret deal with Kibaki. We felt that Raila and ODM had made too many unnecessary compromises and ended up as a junior partner in the coalition government. We were also unhappy that Raila had agreed to have an exclusive and inaccessible swearing in at State House rather than a public event at Uhuru Park that ODM had wanted. There was now little difference between Kibaki's earlier swearing in and Raila's. The overwhelming majority of Kenyans – most of whom who had supported and still had faith in Raila – were locked out; they could only watch the event on television – assuming they had one.

ODM (with three affiliated parties) was by far the single largest parliamentary party with 106 members compared to Kibaki's PNU, which didn't even have 50. The so-called PNU Alliance was an informal mishmash umbrella organ with no united or coherent leadership. ODM-K presidential candidate, Kalonzo Musyoka and the then Kanu chairman Uhuru Kenyatta, had conveniently ganged up with Kibaki – together with many tiny parties, some of which just had one MP – in order to deny Raila the chance of forming a government following the hotly-contested elections. But even with their cynical 'unity', the PNU Alliance still only had a total of 97 MPs.

With a parliamentary representation of 207 members, ODM had a right to insist on having the lion's share of the cabinet and senior political appointments in the bureaucracy and diplomacy. But without a significant presence in government, it would be difficult – if not completely impossible – for ODM to implement any of its pre-election promises. But we could still try. During the 2007 campaigns, Raila had projected himself as "the bridge between the old and the new Kenya"; the leader who would ensure that the old order was buried and a new one emerged. ODM had promised Kenyans "Maisha Bora" (good life). We had undertaken to bring about a complete overhaul of the institutional, legal and constitutional structures in the country. We were committed to the realisation of equity and equality among Kenyans; a Kenya where ethnic, racial, religious and gender discrimination would have no place and where historical disparities and injustices would be addressed. Yes, a Kenya where justice would be our "shield and defender" as the National Anthem proclaims.

Raila Odinga had danced on podiums and loudly proclaimed that under his leadership tribalism, nepotism, cronyism and corruption would be things of the past. He had correctly ridiculed and chastised the tendency of previous Kenyan Presidents to make public policy decisions by the roadside. He had promised that ODM would introduce, practise and entrench mature politics, democratic governance and a strict adherence to the rule of law. ODM hadn't just promised these things in its manifesto; it had detailed them in the regional manifestos we distributed to all the eight provinces – Nairobi, Rift Valley, Central, Western, Nyanza, Coast, Eastern and North Eastern.

Following the signing of the National Accord and the formation of the grand coalition government, the Pentagon technical team conducted a comprehensive SWOT (strength, weaknesses/limitations, opportunities and threats) analysis on where we were. The conclusions were worrying. We established that whereas ODM's strength at the time was its widespread popular support among ordinary Kenyans, this was likely to dwindle, especially when people began to realise that its position in government was more of form rather than substance and that it couldn't deliver on most of its pre-election commitments. We foresaw a situation where the PNU Alliance, due to its enhanced position in government, would sabotage ODM's agenda. We predicted that just as Kenyatta (1966-1969), Moi (post 1982) and Kibaki (post the referendum results of November 2005) had used their state power and instruments to bribe, intimidate and coerce members

At the library in Onjiko Secondary School, swotting for the Kenyan Secondary Education ("O" Level) exams, November 1982. From left to right: the author, Andere, Ochieng' "Alick", Anthony Ochieng' Owala and, standing, Gumba.

The author at Njiiri's High School where he did his A-levels.

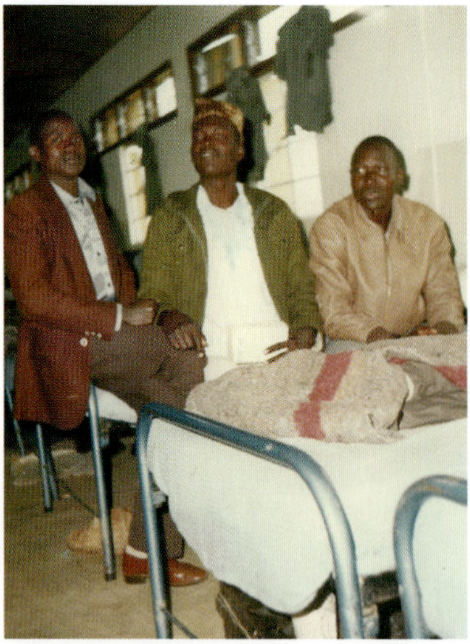

With friends at the National Youth Service in Gilgil, from left to right: the inimitable Abaya Yambo (deceased), the author, Osewe Mula.

At the National Youth Service, Gilgil, 1986, being punished for leading a 'riot' in Ngamia Barracks. From left to right: Chome Mwidau, the author, Ojwang' Hongo and B. F. Odhiambo Onienga.

The author addressing a Kamukunji at the University of Nairobi, November 13, 1987.

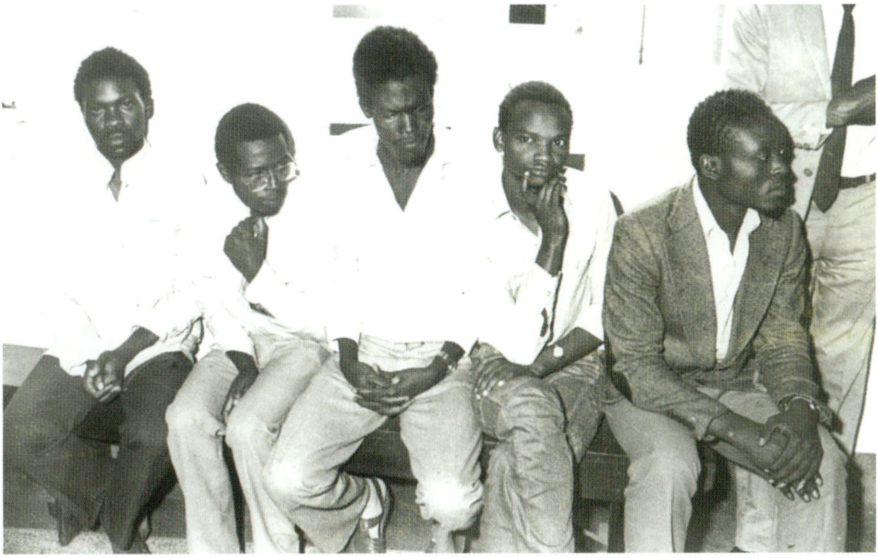

Nairobi Law Courts, 27th November 1987, the day we were released from incommunicado detention. From left to right: Munameza Mulegi (Foreign Secretary), Kaberere Njenga (Secretary General), the author (Finance Secretary), Munoru Nderi (Vice Chairman), and Oyuo Amuomo Ngala (Academic Secretary).

In Musoma, Tanzania, on 17th January, 1988, plotting our way out of Tanzania. From left to right: the author, Peter Mutonyi Gakiri, Munoru Nderi and Erastus Omill Oloo.

Joanne Bund, Toronto 1988 – my girlfriend through Toronto University and the one who paid for my Law School Entrance Exam, December 1988.

On the day of my call to Ontario Bar, 16th February 1995.

Graduating with an LLB degree from the Osgorde Hall Law School, York University, June 1993, with best friend, comrade and PALS co-founder member, Livingstone Wedderburn.

Kathy France on the occasion of her 60th birthday, July 2000 – my treasured bookkeeper, best friend and "mother".

My wife and I on our wedding day at the City Hall, Nathan Philip Square, Toronto, on 18 December 2000.

The author's house in Runda estate, under construction in 2004.

The author welcomes Raila Odinga on his arrival at Toronto International Airport, in October 2006.

With my family. Clockwise from top left: Atieno ('Atis'), my wife Jane, Biko ("Abuki'), Anyango ('Nyangi nyar Apondo mariek"'), Suré ('Asuro'), Achieng' ('Chichi').

Securing democracy in the shambollic ODM Parliamentary nominations in Nyando constituency, November 15th 2007 at the Ahero Multipurpose Centre. In the picture, the author has intercepted 17,000 marked ballot papers that were to be used in the aborted rigging exercise. Next to the author, from left to right, Aguko Charles, an aspirant in the election; the Returning Officer, Kopere; Apollo Owuor, another aspirant, now deceased; and an unidentified man, dressed in black, who was ferrying the marked ballots in the "Matatu" vehicle shown on the right.

At the Pentagon House in Nariobi with a member of the ODM Pentagon Think Tank, Sylvester Kasuku (wearing a suit), "Ja-Suba achiel mariek", February 2008.

Prime Minister Raila Odinga and the author at the Runda residence of the late Hon. Joshua Orwa Ojode (Sirkal), the former MP for Ndhiwa and Assistant Minister for Internal Secueity and Provincial Administration, on Sunday afternoon, 10th June, 2012, where they had both gone to console the bereaved family of Hon. Ojode, who died tragically in a freak helicopter crash earlier that morning.

of the opposition into supporting or joining the government, Kibaki would try to do the same in the aftermath of the formation of the coalition government. In addition, we warned that unless ODM restructured and strengthened itself, disgruntled members, who had hoped to be appointed to cabinet but now had to contend with less seniority, might decide to join the PNU Alliance with the hope of achieving more. We clearly foresaw the PNU Alliance erecting roadblocks and creating impediments on the path to constitutional, legal and institutional reforms. Finally, we advised Raila and the ODM to do everything possible to keep the party united and to honour as many of its pre-election promises as possible; because without the continued support of the Kenyan people, we argued, both Raila and ODM's future prospects would be doomed.

As usual Raila listened keenly and assured us of his total commitment. He stated that he wanted to have the party restructured, but that this had to wait until we had funding, possibly following the passage of the Political Parties' Act which would guarantee each parliamentary party state funding. (We would wait forever.)

The day after he had been sworn in as Prime Minister, Raila left Pentagon House in the company of Caroli Omondi, Mohammed Isahakia, Tony Gachoka and Abdilrahman Iddris (the so-called retired or disgraced major from the Kenyan military who had become a bodyguard, busybody or hanger-on depending on who you asked) to inspect the new offices allocated to the Prime Minister at the Treasury Building on Harambee Avenue. Raila left in a huge motorcade of five vehicles and two motorcycle outriders, with screaming sirens. Caroli, Isahakia, Tony and Iddris drove their vehicles at high speed, chasing after the motorcade.

In the 15 minutes Raila had stopped over at Pentagon House that day, something had jarred. He had looked and sounded different. Even his gait had changed. He had walked, gestured and spoken with a new 'authority'. We had all been astounded: the trsansformation seemed too fast to be believable.

But there were other more serious concerns we had. He hadn't chosen the security detail that had been dispatched to him. Some of us raised eyebrows about him being guarded by mostly total strangers who hadn't had any kind of vetting by Raila's or ODM's security team (or whatever was left of it after former Police Commissioner Edwin Nyaseda who had been in charge of Raila's security during elections had suddenly been discarded. He passed away on December 30, 2008). We felt that Raila was recklessly exposing himself to danger. We also took issue with the ostentatious security detail; arguing that as the 'People's President', it wasn't right for Raila to behave as if he needed to be 'protected from the same people'. "The people are your security," one of us blurted out. Another chimed in: "You are not Kibaki. You must not drive around with such heavy security..." But Raila dismissed us as either being "paranoid" and "refusing to accept the changed reality". He assured us that he was now "getting along well with Kibaki". Apparently, the animosity between the two gentlemen that had almost plunged the country into civil war and resulted in untold suffering, the deaths of more than 1,200 and injuries, rapes, displacements and a devastating destruction of property had all been "forgotten and forgiven" by the two leading protagonists. It was as if all Raila had ever wanted was the trappings of power, which Kibaki had now given him.

But there was no opportunity to discuss these concerns with Raila. He didn't return to Pentagon House that day, or the one after that. After two weeks, he suddenly reappeared one morning on his way to Kisumu. He was dressed casually. The technical team was now in disarray, with only a handful of us still meeting. That day, Raila announced his appointment of James Ogundo – his relative – as a board member to the Constituency Development Fund. We also learnt that Isahakia, Caroli, Tony and Iddris had been allocated offices at the new Prime Minister's Office, although they had not been appointed formally.

By May 2008, the Pentagon technical team had disbanded. By then, the grand coalition cabinet had been named. A few ODM nominees – mainly Raila's relatives and a few cronies – had been appointed to senior positions in the civil service. Even though Pentagon House remained open with one kitchen and one general domestic worker;. these two were also growing increasingly restless and despondent because they hadn't received their salaries for two months. In fact, apart from that one impromptu appearance by Raila on his way to Kisumu, no ODM leader had visited Pentagon House since April 17, 2008 (when Raila had been sworn in). It appeared as if the entire ODM political leadership had abandoned the party and all its operations as soon as the grand coalition government had been named. All party activities had shifted to the Office of the Prime Minister. Occasionally, the ODM parliamentary group met; but such occasions were extremely rare, and most of them were held at Raila's 14th floor offices at the Treasury Building along Harambee Avenue. Orange House had become a ghost building; haunted by bad memories.

I continued to provide pro bono advice and services to Raila and his office. He would call or summon me whenever he needed a speech, talking points or brief on an issue that his office wasn't in a position to provide. Other times, I dropped in to see him or Salim who was then working as his communications director. If I went for three weeks without calling him or dropping by his office, Raila would call, complaining that I had 'disappeared'. Between January and April

2008, when Salim had fled into temporary exile in the US over legitimate fears about his safety, I became the primary speechwriter for Raila. I don't quite remember where Sarah Elderkin had gone to. Whenever Sarah and Salim were around, the three of us would collaborate on the work. But since neither Sarah nor Salim had legal backgrounds, most of the legal, constitutional review and parliamentary work ultimately became my responsibility. Soon, Salim would formally take up the role of Raila's communications director. Although he had a nice corner office allocated to him on the 14th floor at the Treasury Building, he hardly had any other resources with which to perform his role. A secretary and an "assistant" had been seconded to him from the Office of the President – as with all the other senior staff at the Prime Minister's Office. But Salim didn't trust them. Not only did they look and sound clueless; we suspected that they might be national security intelligence agents posted there to collect and relay information to the PNU side of government. Salim's office also lacked such basic stuff as a functioning fax and photocopier machine. Perplexingly, for a communications director-cum-spokesman of a Prime Minister, Salim didn't have a television set or even a radio in the office. All the other staff – even those with no known responsibilities like Iddriss – had TVs, fax machines and photocopiers. Salim submitted numerous requests to the PM's Permanent Secretary, Mohammed Isahakia, without success. Unlike other senior staff, Salim hadn't been allocated a government vehicle or driver or bodyguard. Not that he was particularly keen on such trappings; but Salim was a very senior member of the PM's staff and it should have been routine to be assigned these. After the tenth request for some of these vital amenities, Salim gave up on Isahakia and tried to discuss the issue with Raila, who made him one promise after another, until Salim started getting disillusioned. He would openly discuss his frustrations with me.

The Prime Minister's current spokesman and communications director, Dennis Onyango, hadn't been hired yet. He would replace Salim after the latter left in a huff, due to frustrations with Isahakia and other senior staff. Twice, I felt so bad for Salim that I interceded for him with Raila. Salim had told me that he was planning to quit. He had had enough. But Raila laughed it off, telling me "Miguna, Salim has been talking about leaving forever…he will not leave…" This was now around July 2008.

Meanwhile, Kibaki had started reneging on every single item Raila claimed they had agreed on; even the bare minimum powers the old man had grudgingly conceded to him. For instance, he had apparently declined to appoint the few people Raila had allegedly put forward to be permanent secretaries and other senior government officers following the naming of the bloated (40-member) grand coalition cabinet. We were told by Raila that Kibaki had deleted the names of Peter Wanyande, Jacqueline Oduol, Kenneth Ombongi, Athman Said, Andrew Mondoh and I from the list of proposed permanent secretaries. Instead, Athman and Jacqueline got appointed secretaries for the departments of culture and children's affairs.

It was now nearly one year since I had returned to Kenya. For that entire time, I had used my savings to take care of my family and to participate in the democratisation of Kenya. It was now more than 12 months since I had last earned anything. My savings were quickly dwindling. Unlike other members of the Pentagon technical team who were either retired (and therefore in receipt of a pension or serving on state boards) or gainfully employed elsewhere, I had no income. The situation was compounded by the fact that my family hadn't really settled before the eruption of the post-election violence. Now, I was feeling the squeeze and beginning to think that perhaps I should return to Canada to reopen my legal practice. On many occasions, I mentioned my plan to Raila; trying to assess whether or not his informal (unrealised) offers were serious. He always assured me that he did indeed have a plan for me. However, he consistently complained that Kibaki was the one stalling on all the options he had. "*De mana nyuok Ja-Nyando, gik moko biro losore*" he would tell me. He was asking me to persevere as things would soon change.

But his 'plans' (if he indeed did have them) for me to be the Solicitor General fell through. Moreover, it was obvious that Caroli and Isahakia didn't want me and other members of the Pentagon technical team to work near or around the Prime Minister. Caroli seemed jealous and insecure of any competent lawyer with integrity being close to Raila. It wasn't just me. He behaved the same way towards Mutakha Kangu and Otiende Amolo. Even the Kenya High Court Judge Nicholas Ombijah would later call me to furiously complain that Caroli had allegedly conspired to have his name omitted from a shortlist of qualified candidates for the position of Director of Public Prosecutions that had been created under the new Constitution. As a judge with extensive experience in criminal law, Ombijah correctly felt that he couldn't have fairly been excluded from the shortlist. "If they can't shortlist a judge who has been primarily in charge of criminal trials for years, what justifiably could have been the criteria of selection?" Justice Ombijah posed before our telephone conversation ended.

Caroli seemed more insecure around young Luo professionals than with non Luos. He felt threatened by their access to Raila. He wanted to be the only one that fitted that bill. As for Isahakia, his attitude was a bit more complicated. He was always suspicious of Luos generally, especially those who had a history of political struggle or some perceived ideological connection with Raila. Because he had never participated in any political struggles and wasn't progressive, he always tended to disparage or undermine anyone who was. He might genuinely feel intimidated, insecure or conflicted around the Prime Minister because he considers himself 'an outsider' – culturally speaking. Yet, as far as the Kenyan status quo goes (which is what seems to be important to Raila anyway), Isahakia is actually more 'valuable' to Raila than most progressive Kenyans, hence his permanent presence and tenure at the 'King's Court'. "Isahakia might be lethargic, incompetent and corrupt; but Raila finds him more useful than a whole bunch of you," I was once told by one of Raila's longstanding confidantes. "Now that Raila is in power, he doesn't need competent and morally upright Kenyans; he needs those with deep knowledge of the intricacies of the inner workings of the murky corridors of power," my friend added.

In any event, I continued to persevere until suddenly I received a telephone call from Raila to see him very early in the morning one Monday in January 2009. After the usual preliminaries, he got down to business and offered me a job as his director of political affairs. It was now nearly one year since the formation of the coalition government. I had told Raila that I wanted to leave in two weeks' time. It looked as if he was offering the job to prevent me from returning to Canada. Essentially he wanted me to be his principal political strategist, advisor and coordinator. The position was unique in the sense that he wanted me to be hired through the Public Service Commission. My concern was that if I was hired by the PSC, my remuneration wouldn't be enough to enable me to maintain the standard of living my family was used to. Raila said that his office could secure funds to top up any deficiencies. That day, I completed a PSC form and left behind my updated resume.

Then a waiting game began. After another month, Raila summoned me again. I hadn't received any feedback from the PSC. Usually, the PSC's role was perfunctory once the Prime Minister or the President had submitted a name for a position. Yet, my name seemed stuck somewhere in the bureaucratic system. On Friday, March 6, 2009, Raila indicated that a contract was now ready for me to come in and sign. However, as I sat in the VIP waiting room outside his office, I read in a newspaper report that the previous day Caroli had announced the appointment of Dr Adhu Awiti as Raila's political affairs director. I was stunned. That was the same job I thought I had been offered.

That day's meeting was tense. As soon as I sat down, Raila tried to assuage my feelings by telling me that he had found a job "more suitable to your skills and qualifications. I would like you to be my advisor on constitutional, legal and political affairs and on matters pertaining to the constitutional review. I would also like you to be a joint secretary with Professor Kivutha Kibwana to the newly constituted Permanent Committee on the Management of Grand Coalition Affairs…"

"Jakom," I interrupted, breathing with suppressed fury, "I'm tired of being led a merry dance. You don't have to place me anywhere if you are finding it difficult. I would like to return to Canada and practise law. What you have said is quite attractive, actually more attractive than the job that you offered earlier. But why did you ask me to come and sign a contract if you had already given the job to Adhu?" I was glaring. Raila was now shifting in his seat, unable to speak. After ten more tense minutes, the meeting was over. As I was on my way home, Isahakia called. "The Prime Minister would like you to go and meet Ambassador Muthaura today before 6pm…"

I found Francis Karimi Muthaura, the Permanent Secretary to the President, secretary to the cabinet and head of the civil service, Prof. Kivutha Kibwana, the President's advisor on constitutional matters, and Sam Mwale, Principal Secretary at the Cabinet Office, seated around a large oak conference room. After brief introductions, Muthaura formally offered me the job Raila had spoken about that morning. He informed me that I had two options. I could be either a senior advisor to the Prime Minister on constitutional affairs or a senior advisor to the Prime Minister on coalition affairs. I would also be joint secretary – with Kibwana – for the Permanent Committee on the Management of the Grand Coalition Affairs. He was effusive about my qualifications, especially my master of law degree in alternative dispute resolution. He asked Kibwana to take out his pay slip and show it to me. He then asked me to write down all the items on Kibwana's pay slip as we would be paid the same amount, including all the benefits and privileges. He indicated that he would issue the letter of appointment that same day and that my official government vehicle, security and driver would report for duty on Monday, March 9.

Despite niggling concerns, I plunged into my new engagement as Raila's advisor with gusto. It was now more than a year since the National Accord had been signed and it was obvious to observers that President Kibaki and his PNU cohorts had no intention of adhering to the power sharing agreement. Kibaki had placed one roadblock after another in Raila's path. The President continued to make all the important decisions without any regard to the provisions of the National Accord that compelled him to consult the Prime Minister. Of course, things weren't helped by the fact that the Accord was full of loopholes. With neither a coalition agreement nor good faith from Kibaki, Raila was finding it impossible to exercise any of the supervisory or coordinating responsibilities that the Accord granted him. PNU ministers and senior civil servants affiliated to the party openly disregarded and defied the Prime Minister.

Although Raila kept himself busy chairing five cabinet subcommittees, rarely were any of the resolutions reached at these, ratified at the cabinet meetings chaired by Kibaki. If anything, the cabinet either completely ignored them, or routinely reversed them. The police commissioner, the head of the intelligence service and the military didn't recognise Raila's authority. Whenever Raila issued directives to these and other government officials, you could be sure they would never be complied with.

Things weren't any better in parliament. There, a new 'coalition against Raila' had emerged that was becoming increasingly virulent and well-organised. Raila's deputy party leader, ODM Pentagon member and minister for agriculture, William Ruto had openly broken ranks with Raila and the orange party. Meanwhile, a few vocal MPs calling themselves the "Grand Coalition Opposition", under the leadership of Raila's erstwhile and articulate ODM MP for Budalang'i, Pius Tawfiq Ababu Namwamba, were breathing fire down Raila's neck. Then there were the ODM MPs who, dissatisfied with having not been appointed into cabinet, were threatening to rebel against both the ODM and its leader.

Although I strongly advised and urged Raila to put his foot down and demand the respect and full implementation of the Accord, I was conscious of the anxieties among Kenyans over the potential return to violence. Both the media and the international community were extremely nervous of any sign of instability in the government. Any slight disagreement between the President and the Prime Minister was likely to be (mis)interpreted as an indication of the imminent collapse of the coalition. The risks were real. The world had witnessed the horrid images of tens of thousands of innocent civilians being hacked or shot to death; hundreds of thousands being rendered refugees in their own motherland; and billions worth of property being destroyed.

In view of this, I advised restraint. But it was restraint with a caveat. We needed to engage Kibaki in structured discussions over the outstanding issues. Whereas Raila publicly downplayed the tensions within the coalition as "teething problems", in private, he was reeling with rage. He had nothing positive to say or report about his coalition partner. He blamed Kibaki for everything. He told us how arrogant, obtuse and selfish Kibaki was. Raila hated meeting Kibaki. He felt – with lots of justification – that almost all meetings they held, just the two of them, never bore any fruit. Raila preferred meeting Kibaki with others from our side. Ironically, however, whenever such meetings were held, Raila not only failed to press Kibaki for concessions, he didn't encourage any of our members to confront Kibaki. This was quite frustrating for me.

Even before the Kilaguni debacle of April 2009, I found myself protecting Raila from Kibaki, quite literally. The first and one of the most memorable moments occured in late March 2009, at the very first meeting of the Permanent Committee on the Management of the Grand Coalition Affairs. I had proposed and Raila had agreed that to be effective and efficient, the Permanent Committee needed specific instruments that would guide its operations. We needed to agree on and ratify 'Terms of Reference'. I also thought that since the coalition was running on a PNU autopilot (with ODM as pliant passengers), it was imperative that we quickly developed a coalition agreement and a document on the 'mechanisms of consultation'. My view was that once these important documents were in place, Raila's ongoing wrangles with Kibaki, on the one hand, and Vice-President Kalonzo Musyoka, on the other, would die a natural death.

I drove in Raila's official limousine to the President's office at Harambee House that morning. The meeting was on the third floor of the same building. When we arrived, we could see the presidential motorcade and a beehive of security swarming around. The President was clearly in. As soon as we approached the President's boardroom adjacent to his office, Muthaura emerged and requested that the Prime Minister should go into the President's office. Caroli, Isahakia, Orengo and I entered the conference room and waited. Within minutes other members of the Permanent Committee also arrived and joined us.

There were only two things on the agenda: introductions and agreeing on the terms of reference and modes of working. When Raila, his nominees to the committee and I arrived, we found that Muthaura and his group had arranged the President's conference room, with Kibaki's chair sitting right at the head of the table with all the other seats lined on both sides. As soon as the ODM team entered, they sat on the seats presignated by Muthaura. I was aghast.

First, I placed my documents on the spot I had been reserved. Then I moved back to where the Prime Minister and the President were seated, positioning myself between them. I cleared my voice and announced that the joint secretaries needed time to "arrange the room". Muthaura said everything was in order. Orengo glanced at me and smiled slyly. That day Isahakia and Caroli had accompanied us even though they weren't members of the Permanent Committee.

"Excuse me sir, I hate to do this but the table hasn't been properly arranged. We would require just five minutes to put everything in order before the meeting commences," I addressed the President, while fixing Raila with my gaze, trying to tell him not to say anything.

The President stood, followed by Raila, then everybody else. As soon as the President's chair was vacant, I got hold of it and carried it to the middle of the table on the side that the PNU were seated. I moved the other chairs sideways and created space for the President's chair as Raila, Uhuru, Saitoti and Wetangula followed Kibaki into his office. I then created space for Raila's chair across from where Kibaki's chair was as I moved the other chairs around in the same manner I had done on the opposite side.

The other members of the committee were speechless. Isahakia and Caroli slithered away quietly. They knew that I was ready for war – both intellectually and otherwise. Nobody dared mess with me on such occasions. Muthaura, who had run off after the President, returned and started protesting that I had no authority to rearrange the seats.

"With all due respect Ambassador, *I am a joint secretary* to this committee; *you are not even a member;* so, you *shouldn't even be in this room*, let alone dictating to me how seats should be arranged. Secondly, Sir, this is *the Permanent Committee on the Management of the Grand Coalition Affairs*. Both President Kibaki and Prime Minister Raila Odinga are *co-chairs* of this committee; they are also *the two Principals in this Governmnent.* Unless you want to suggest, Sir, that you don't recognise the Accord and the Constitution which put this government together..." That shut him up. I continued to shuffle chairs around as I spoke. After three minutes, I was done and said to Muthaura: "Please you may invite them back in." I had set the tone for the meeting.

Consequently, the ensuing discussions were civil and productive, resulting in the ratification of the "Terms of reference and working modalities of the Permanent Committee on the Management of the Grand Coalition Affairs." It gave the Permanent Committee responsibility for resolving disputes within the coalition and any other matter referred to it by the two principals. The Committee confirmed that all its meetings would be co-chaired by the President and the Prime Minister and that its membership would be limited and restricted to "nominees from each grand coalition partner appointed by the two principals".

In addition, it was agreed that the Committee's Agenda and related documents would be prepared and circulated by the joint secretaries at least two days before the meeting. The grand coalition partners were to propose the Agenda through their delegated member of the Permanent Committee. In other words, neither party could impose its will on the other. Equality in form and substance was reaffirmed. All proposed Agenda items would automatically be included in the

Agenda. As well, the parties agreed that the Committee would hold monthly meetings. The joint secretaries were each to keep a set of the Committee's documents, a separate set of which was to be kept by the cabinet secretariat.

It was further agreed that the coalition partners were to appoint and establish a joint secretariat led by two joint secretaries to facilitate the work of the Permanent Committee. As well, the Committee was authorised to appoint task forces from among its members to deal with any specific grand coalition issue. Such task forces would be serviced by the joint secretariat. Decisions of the Permanent Committee would be by consensus.

Finally, the joint secretariat was empowered to monitor the implementation of the Permanent Committee's decisions and report progress to the Permanent Committee. Non-members of the Permanent Committee could only attend the meetings of the Permanent Committee upon formal invitation by both the President and the Prime Minister or through a delegated authority. And the budget of the Permanent Committee was to be sourced from the Exchequer.

These resolutions, which were unanimously adopted and signed by all present, should have been a good start. Significantly, the meeting purported to give the joint secretaries considerable power and responsibilities, not just over the day-to-day management of the Permanent Committee Secretariat (which was never established), but also a coordinating and supervisory role over all the institutional, legal and constitutional reforms that were ongoing. But this important instrument needed implementation by the two principals first. For instance, to establish the joint secretariat, the joint secretaries required an office, staff and equipment. To do that, we needed funds. Even though the document stated that funds were to be "sourced" from the Exchequer, the mechanism of doing that wasn't spelled out. Neither Professor Kibwana nor myself had authority to incur expenditure and the instrument granted none. This meant that to perform any of the duties itemised above, the joint secretaries had to rely on the head of the civil service and President Kibaki's permanent secretary, Francis Muthaura. More than anything else, this onerous task given to us – and not to the cabinet office where Muthaura held sway – would soon put us on a collision course with the senior bureaucrat.

My experience of working in the inner sanctums of power was that once Raila and Kibaki made a joint decision and followed it through in writing, the decision would cascade downwards and permeate through government. But if their decision required further action by Muthaura or others to be effective, it would invariably not be done. There were too many conflicting forces at play. My thinking is that had Raila insisted that day on providing autonomy (and resources) to the joint secretaries to coordinate the affairs of the Committee, things might have turned out differently. The persistent wrangles, the parochial disputes, the constant sabotage of rival parties and the confusion and lethargy that engulfed the government could and would have been avoided. Ultimately, with Raila's position strengthened, there would have been an effective check and balance at the executive level.

Clearly, the "terms of reference and working modalities" needed to be implemented for Raila and ODM to share in major decisions within government. I knew there would be resistance, especially from people like Muthaura and Gichangi who felt that they would be ceding power to "new interlopers". It wasn't in Kibaki's and PNU's interests to implement these "terms and working modalities"; it was in Raila's and ODM's. However, although I wrote numerous letters to Muthaura and sought Raila's intervention on many days without end, the latter never did anything substantive to move things along.

Had I not moved Kibaki's chair that day, Raila would have continued to sit on the sidelines, just like any other minister, as he continued to do at cabinet meetings where Kibaki took centre stage, with Muthaura on one side and Kalonzo on the other. In cabinet meetings, Raila was nothing but an inconvenient appendange.

From that day henceforth, seating arrangements at the committee were in the order I had set. Agendas were jointly drawn between Kivutha and I. Except for that first meeting, non members like Muthaura, the National Security Intelligence Service Director, Michael Gichangi, the President's Private Secretary, Prof. Nick Wanjohi and so-called Government Spokesman, Alfred Mutua, were kept away. But my suspicion is that when Kibaki's "power men" saw how I had brought down the President to the Prime Minister's level, they tried everything to prevent frequent committee meetings. They knew that with substantive equality around the table, they had absolutely no chance of manipulating or taking advantage of the process. With a fair, transparent and democratic process, they knew also that the outcome wouldn't and couldn't be one-sided. That scared the hell out of them. They had been used to processes they could dominate. Until then, they had armtwisted everybody: Annan, Raila and the cabinet. Every meeting Raila went into with Kibaki, he returned empty-handed. Now, they could see that might not be happening again.

On careful reflection, I can now vividly see why the scheme to besmirch and undermine me within the grand coalition might have been conceived after that meeting. I had ruffled the egos of some powerful people. Subseqently, working hand-in-glove with Isahakia and Caroli, those powerful forces seconded me staff they had primed to spy on me, with the aim of being able to build a fraudulent case against me when the time was right. From that moment on, I had to watch my back, which was going to be a monumental task given the fact that Raila would later join the schemers and the conspirators. But I was undeterred. I knew that we were up against a deadline. The National Accord had set a tight schedule of one to three years for the legal, constitutional and institutional reforms needed to stabilise the country and ensure that the next elections would not result in another orgy of violence and mayhem.

Under the mediation agreements, Agenda One addressed how to "stop violence and restore fundamental rights and liberties." By early 2009, stability, security and civil liberties had been restored to most of the country, only Mount Elgon was still smouldering. People were going about their business without much hindrance. Freedom of expression and press freedom were fairly back on course, although the right to peaceful assembly hadn't been restored; the police were still violently breaking up peaceful protests, and some human rights defenders had been executed under circumstances that disclosed systematic and deliberate state complicity. Although it was generally felt that the security forces remained trigger-happy and continued to commit many extra-judicial killings, overall the country was relatively peaceful and stable.

The Agenda Two reforms comprised the "immediate measures to address the humanitarian crisis, promotion of reconciliation, healing and restoration". Careful analysis and evaluation revealed that government initiatives to this end were patchy at best. Although relief food and token assistance were being given to tens of thousands of internally displaced persons, there were inherent weaknesses in the delivery system. The Ministry of Special Programmes targeted displaced persons from one ethnic group and completely neglected many other groups, which inevitably undermined reconciliation efforts. The same applied to attempts at resettlement. Land was identified and allocated to people in internally displaced people camps, most of whom were from the same ethnic group. But many critics asked why the displaced couldn't simply return to their original homes and farms if the security situation in the country had greatly stabilised, as claimed. Why was the government buying land for people instead of ensuring that they returned to wherever they had been displaced from? In the meantime though there were also accusations that the government was putting too little money into the resettlement efforts.

But even more disturbing was the fact that the government, as it was presently constructed, was perceived to be incapable of ensuring an impartial, effective and speedy investigation of the human rights violations that had occurred during the post-election violence. Members of the government and the disciplinary forces were so heavily implicated in the atrocities that occurred that no one expected them to deliver justice to victims or the accused. Moreover, the judiciary itself had been under popular indictment for decades; it needed a complete overhaul, not just patchwork reforms. Without a completely revamped police and judiciary, no justice could be obtained.

Agenda Three dealt with overcoming the political crisis that arose out of the 2007 presidential election. Fortunately, the main protagonists – PNU and ODM – had signed the *National Accord* and the grand coalition had been formed. So the political environment was tense, but stable enough for the search for the elusive new constitution.

Finally, Agenda Four sought to address "poverty, the inequitable distribution of resources and perceptions of historical injustices and exclusion on the part of segments of the Kenyan society" which were deemed to constitute the underlying causes of the "prevailing social tensions, instability and cycle of violence". Specifically, this agenda item required that the country undertake constitutional, legal and institutional reform; tackling poverty and inequity, as well as combating regional development imbalances, tackling unemployment, particularly among the youth, consolidating national cohesion and unity, undertaking land reform, and addressing transparency, accountability and impunity issues.

Then Kilaguni suddenly exploded and scattered the carefully crafted myth of Raila's 'close working relationship with Kibaki'. The myth was actually a Raila creation. It was his convenient cover. It hid his cowardice and presented him as a co-president, which was a far cry from what was actually happening on a daily basis in government. The reality was that Kibaki never consulted Raila on any major decision.

In late March, I had accompanied Orengo, Justice Minister Mutula Kilonzo, the Attorney General Amos Wako and Justice Permanent Secretary Amina Mohamed, to Geneva to meet Kofi Annan before travelling to The Hague to meet the ICC Prosecutor Luis Moreno-Ocampo, in order to discuss the ongoing ICC investigations and Kenya's cooperation with that process. We were able to secure a 90-day extension from the ICC, which allowed Kenya to try to institute criminal proceedings against those most responsible for the crimes against humanity that were committed during the 2007 post-election violence in Kenya. The delegation signed an undertaking, on behalf of the government of Kenya, that Kenya would voluntarily refer the situation to the ICC as required by the Rome Statute, should the Kenyan authorities fail to satisfy the ICC with their undertakings within 90 days.

Prior to travelling to Geneva and The Hague, both coalition partners had agreed that the Permanent Committee on the Management of Grand Coalition Affairs would go on a retreat at the Kilaguni Serena Lodge for five days from April 3 in order to address some simmering differences and put in place concrete mechanisms for the future management of the coalition government. Prof. Kivutha Kibwana and I had prepared a draft agenda. It had been shared with teams on both sides, including with the principals, who had agreed to it. I had also prepared two draft documents – "mechanisms of consultation" and a "coalition agreement" – pursuant to the resolutions of the committee. ODM committee members had extensively discussed and approved both drafts. Even the PM had approved them. I subsequently gave them to Prof. Kibwana to review and share with members of his side. My attempts to have a meeting with him to discuss the drafts with a view to preventing or ironing out any potential disagreements were unsuccessful. Prof. Kibwana kept promising to call me in order for us to agree on the date, time and venue of the meetings, but each time he never came back to me.

A week before the Kilaguni retreat, Kibwana informed me that he had shared the drafts with members of his team, though he refused to confirm whether they had raised any issues. On the agenda, however, Kibwana stated that there were no problems. Both sides had agreed to discuss and possibly approve the "mechanisms of consultation", "the coalition agreement", the issue of appointments of senior officers in government – permanent secretaries, state corporation executives, boards, commissions, diplomatic service, et cetera – and how these positions could be shared fairly equitably between the two coalition partners. We had agreed to relook at the issue of portfolio balance and the concept of "real power sharing" as contained in the National Accord. Finally, both sides agreed that the issue of "protocol" in government, especially pertaining to the position and place of the President, the Prime Minister and the Vice-President would be discussed. And of course, there was a provision for "any matters arising".

In a way, the agenda was a straightforward affair. The items sounded controversial, but both sides agreed that they needed to be discussed. The coalition could not be expected to run smoothly if the controversies – or teething problems, as the politicians referred to them – weren't resolved, hopefully amicably.

So, I wasn't particularly surprised when I landed at the Jomo Kenyatta International Airport, activated my local mobile telephone and found Kibwana's short text: "Hi ndugu! Have you returned? Please call me upon your return." I called him before I left the airport. He advised me that there might be a few changes on the agenda for Kilaguni and that I should meet him as soon as I arrived in town. I became curious and shared Kibwana's message with Orengo who advised that I should call the PM and let him know. I did that within 30 minutes of my discussions with Kibwana.

The PM told me not to worry about Kibwana as he was always full of drama. That I should meet with him the following day so that we could go over the agenda. I subsequently met both Kibwana and the PM. Kibwana informed me that some PNU members didn't want to discuss the protocol, power sharing and appointment issues. They were arguing, belatedly, that they didn't want to renegotiate the National Accord. I told him that I would come back to him after speaking with the PM.

For his part, the PM stated that neither side could dictate to the other what it could or couldn't bring to the table for discussions. He instructed me to tell Kibwana that they could include any agenda item for discussion and we would do the same. And after another round of discussions with Kibwana, we agreed that the original agenda would be tabled, but that if the PNU side needed any other item discussed, they were free to table it at the meeting. I explained to Kibwana that one key term of reference for the committee was to focus on matters that promote or hinder the smooth running of the coalition government and that this could not be achieved unless and until we courageously dealt with all such issues.

Since the formation of the coalition government, protocol issues had occupied a lot of our time. Similarly, issues of power sharing and appointments to key government positions had brought grief and despondency to the new government. Not a week passed without senior officials affiliated with both sides going at each other's throats. It was therefore impossible to have the retreat without discussing these issues. I pointed out that the country expected that we would return from Kilaguni having addressed all controversial issues.

As we approached Kilaguni, my focus was on how to manage the coalition in a way that could give Raila and ODM more real power. But Raila would be anxious about doing anything that challenged Kibaki. Indeed, he seemed to have accepted his small role in government and to resent my suggestion that he use sharp elbows to better his position. As some members of his think tank quipped, "Raila only wanted a motorcade, the title of Prime Minister, a huge office and salary. Why are you bothering him with useless details?"

The following was the instrument that detailed our mandate. It was ratified and signed by both principals before Kilaguni.

"Terms of reference and modalities of the Permanent Committee on the Management of Grand Coalition Affairs

Terms of reference

1. Focus on matters of concern which promote or hinder the smooth running of the Grand Coalition Government within the framework of the National Accord dated 28 February 2008, and the implementing legal instruments, as long as it does not perform the functions of the Grand Coalition Cabinet.
2. Managing the affairs of the Grand Coalition, including but not limited to dispute resolution mechanism of the Grand Coalition.
3. Undertake any other responsibility referred to it by both the President and the Prime Minister, or by Cabinet.

Working modalities of the Permanent Committee

1. The Permanent Committee will be co-chaired by the President and the Prime Minister.
2. The Permanent Committee shall be composed of nominees from each Grand Coalition Partner appointed by the two Principals.
3. The Agenda and related documents will be prepared and circulated by the Joint Secretaries at least two days before the meeting.
4. The Grand Coalition Partners will propose the Agenda through their delegated member of the Permanent Committee.
5. All proposed Agenda items will automatically be included in the Agenda.
6. The Permanent Committee will hold monthly meetings to take place from 10am on the First Friday of each month or at such other time or times as the President and Prime Minister deem fit.
7. All documents of the Permanent Committee will be Secret. The Joint Secretaries will each keep a set of the documents. The Cabinet Secretariat will also keep a set of the Committee documents.
8. The Coalition Partners will appoint and establish a Joint Secretariat led by two Joint Secretaries to facilitate the work of the Permanent Committee.
9. The Committee may appoint Task Forces from among its members to deal with any specific Grand Coalition issue. Such Task Forces will be serviced by the Joint Secretariat.
10. Decisions of the Permanent Committee will be by consensus.
11. The Joint Secretariat will monitor the implementation of the Permanent Committee's decisions and report progress to the Permanent Committee.
12. Non-members of the Permanent Committee can only attend the

meetings of the Permanent Committee upon formal invitation by both the President and the Prime Minister or through a delegated authority.

13. The budget of the Permanent Committee will be sourced from the Exchequer."

Many months following the adoption of this document, Muthaura had still not signed off on it going fully operational. Kibwana and I continued to work from our respective offices at the office of the President and the Prime Minister's office, without a budget and necessary staff. There was no joint secretariat, no resources, no support and no meetings. I was becoming very disillusioned. Raila didn't seem to care. I had a well paid job, he seemed to think; so what was my problem? In order to facilitate productive discussions, I returned to the "Mechanisms of Consultation" and the "Coalition Agreement" documents, which I had drafted previously and which the ODM side, including William Ruto, had unanimously approved. I distributed copies of both of these to my committee colleagues, but the PNU members refused to even discuss them. They were never signed, adopted or used. That's extremely sad and unfortunate. In any functioning modern democracy, the documents wouldn't be considered controversial and they wouldn't lead to an eruption of conflict between two coalition partners, not least of all just a mere presentation of them for discussions. Nobody was carrying a gun over another person's head with a dictum: "accept or I blow your head off". But issues had come to the fore and were threatening the stability not just of the government, but also of the country.

There wasn't any rational basis for Kibaki and his PNU team to refuse to discuss these agenda items. There wasn't any justification for either side to claim that the documents or the issues listed for discussion constituted an attempt to renegotiate the National Accord. A coalition is a relationship, albeit of a political nature. Relationships must be built on mutual understanding, respect and trust for each other and the ability to appreciate differences. There certainly were areas such as protocol issues, which could be disposed of quickly in view of the clear provisions of the National Accord, especially the fact that only Kibaki and Raila signed the accord on behalf of themselves and the political formations they led. The Vice-President and leader of the Orange Democratic Movement – Kenya wasn't a signatory to the accord. Consequently, he ought not to have featured in the pecking order.

Only Kibaki and Raila were the two principals. The debate could have ended there and we would have moved on to more important matters such as the meaning and content of real power sharing; the formation of the grand coalition government (not only of the grand coalition cabinet); and mechanisms of consultations so as to avoid unnecessary disputes. The only basis for the refusal, therefore, was because the Kibaki faction failed to engage their coalition partners in good faith negotiations.

Yet PNU refused to treat ODM as a partner. Kibaki, too, refused to accord Raila the respect he deserved as a partner. Kibaki and his PNU Alliance intended to take unfair advantage of the incompetence of Raila and the ODM negotiators during the writing of the National Accord in order to perpetuate their dominance in government. They saw any attempt at leveling the field as an aggressive act.

We boarded a rickety old military helicopter at the Wilson Airstrip in Nairobi at about 8.30am on April 3, 2009. I didn't know where Kilaguni was. I just knew that it was somewhere in or around the Tsavo National Park. The flight was horrible. The helicopter seemed unable to fly in a straight path. It kept jerking up and down whenever it encountered air pockets or thick clouds. Once or twice, it dropped about ten metres. I looked at William Ruto and Mohamed Elmi who were sitting next to me and they could only shake their heads. There we were, almost the entire ODM team, in one rickety helicopter. With us from the PNU side were mainly civil servants. PNU's head honchos were going to travel with the President in a relatively new state-of-the-art jet. It was clear where the power lay.

We all breathed a sigh of relief when we touched down at 11am. At reception, I immediately noticed something amiss: all the ODM members, including the Prime Minister and his Deputy Party Leader and Deputy Prime Minister, were booked in smaller and less elegant rooms than their PNU counterparts. As the person responsible for coalition management on the ODM side, I was very sensitive to these matters. They might look small or petty for those unfamiliar with how power is played, especially in coalition arrangements. However, for me, the fact that Kibaki, Uhuru and Saitoti had bigger rooms than Raila presented an immediate problem that cried out for a solution. I immediately sought out the hotel manager who referred me to the "government receptionist", a Ms Lydia. When I explained my problem to her, she was defensive, arguing that everybody had been assigned a room by the hotel and that all rooms were the same. I didn't budge. I insisted that she had to reallocate the Prime Minister and Mudavadi new rooms and that all ministers (regardless of their party affiliations) should be assigned the same type of room. When she saw that I wasn't going to relent, she acquiesced. I had long learnt from the American anti-slavery crusader, Frederick Douglass, that power concedes nothing without a fight.

Nothing describes what happened in Kilaguni more than the word "debacle". Things started going wrong shortly after Kibaki's arrival at the resort. The ODM contingent had arrived more than three hours earlier. We had showered, refreshed and held preliminary consultations amongst ourselves. We were unanimous that the meeting should commence that evening on the basis of the agreed draft agenda. If the Kibaki group insisted on tabling another agenda – we resolved – then either both documents could be used separately or merged. It sounded simple, but it proved to be anything but, as the subsequent hours would show.

That first night Raila went to see Kibaki in his room and subsequently made us fall about with laughter at his bizarre description of what had passed there. According to Raila – and we believed him –Kibaki spoke with him from behind the curtains, which were fully drawn. They didn't see each other. There was no face-to-face meeting as such. At first, Raila thought the old man was dressing up or using the washroom and that he would join him in the spacious living room. However, after 30 minutes of odd 'communication', Raila politely excused himself and left.

But the gist of what Raila stated Kibaki had told him was this: that both teams should just relax and take it easy for the four days; treat it as a well deserved holiday before addressing a joint press conference to lie to Kenyans that the "discussions had been productive" without actually disclosing the details of what had been discussed or resolved. To Kibaki and his team, Kilaguni should have been a huge PR exercise for the coalition partners. Kibaki wanted Raila to help him deceive Kenyans. We couldn't believe our ears. But there we were.

So, that evening, we ate a sumptuous dinner, under the watchful eye of state security agents. Raila sat with Kibaki and Kalonzo on a separate table while the rest of the two teams mingled freely. Later that evening, I prepared enough copies of the two agenda items and drafts of the three instruments including the "Terms of Reference and Working Modalities" that had been ratified by the permanent committee some time back. I also attached correspondence between the joint secretaries and Muthaura in which we sought his assistance, as directed by the committee, in securing a joint secretariat to be headed by us jointly; formal direction to permanent secretaries and senior government officials to cooperate with us whenever we would seek their assistance; and authority to incur expenditure so as to fulfill our mandate. Muthaura never acknowledged receipt of the letters and never acceded to our requests. (Subsequently – and sensing the reluctance of Muthaura and co to relinquish some control – even Kibwana declined to sign follow-up letters. I ended up sending letters to Muthaura without receiving any replies.) Even though the "Terms of Reference and Working

Modalities" document specified that the committee was to meet monthly from 10am on the first Friday, or at such other time or times as the President and Prime Minister determined, it never did. Yet the Prime Minister refused to summon any meetings himself. Nor was he willing to push the President for meetings. The problem was that Raila didn't realise that lack of meetings was in Kibaki's, and by extension PNU's, favour. ODM as a party, on its part, was asleep. It made no demands on Raila and had no structured mechanisms of engagement with PNU.

I worked in the calm before the storm erupted. After breakfast, the first session was scheduled to begin at 9am. Raila and his contingent were inside the hall by 8.45am. The meeting room had a long rectangular oak table around which I had arranged seats on both sides; each side for each coalition partner. At the head of the table were two similar chairs for both principals. I had placed the agenda item we had agreed on and the other one PNU had insisted on. The draft documents for the mechanisms of consultation and the guiding principles and institutional framework for managing the affairs of the grand coalition affairs were also in each member's folder. Present were, for ODM: Raila, Charity Ngilu, William Ruto, James Orengo, Amason Kingi and Mohamed Elmi. For PNU were: Uhuru Kenyatta, George Saitoti, Chirau Mwakwere and Kalonzo Musyoka. Kibaki was still in his room. Also Mutula Kilonzo and Noah Wekesa, who were not members, were in the room. Absent members were Musalia Mudavadi (ODM) and Martha Karua (PNU). Musalia was absent with apologies while Karua had decided not to be part of the process since her resignation from the cabinet. Later, Kibaki would appoint Beth Mugo to replace her. My counterpart, Kivutha Kibwana sat at the far end on the PNU side as I did the same on the ODM side.

Tension was palpable in the room. The ODM side, including Raila, didn't know what was going on; why the President hadn't joined the gathering. We had suspicion that Kibaki and his PNU battalion didn't want to proceed. It was April 4, 2009. The meeting was supposed to have started the previous evening, but it hadn't due to wrangles over the agenda. Raila called the meeting to order. He asked for prayers. I am not sure who prayed, but I think it was Wetangula. Before Raila could clear his throat, Mutula's hand shot up. "The Right Honourable Prime Minister, I would like us to be sensitive to the importance of this gathering. We shouldn't start the meeting without His Excellency the President…" Mutula began.

"Order, Waziri! First of all, are you a member of this committee? Joint secretaries, can you read out the names of committee members?" Raila ordered.

"Sir, on the PNU side, the members are: His Excellency the President Mwai Kibaki (co-chair), Hon. Uhuru Kenyatta, Hon. Prof. George Saitoti, Hon. Moses Wetangula, Hon. Kalonzo Musyoka, Hon. Martha Karua and Hon. Chirau Ali

Mwakwere. And on the ODM side: The Rt. Hon. Raila Amolo Odinga (co-chair), Hon. Musalia Mudavadi, Hon. Charity Ngilu, Hon. William Ruto, Hon. Amason Kingi, Hon. James Orengo and Hon. Mohamed Elmi. Sir, Hons. Karua and Mudavadi are absent today. Thank you!"

Raila: "Can your counterpart, Prof. Kibwana confirm that information?"

Prof. Kibwana: "Yes the Right Honourable, I confirm that the information my colleague, Mr Miguna has read out is correct."

Raila: "Well then, we must purge the room of non-members. First, Ambassador Muthaura, Mr Gichangi, Mr Wanjohi, Dr Alfred Mutua and Mr Isaiah Kabira, you are not supposed to be here. Could you please leave the room?"

As they were leaving, Raila continued: "And Honourable Mutula and Noah Wekesa, you know that you are not members. It follows that you, too, must leave before we can proceed."

There was no movement. Then Raila proceeded. "Let us talk frankly and openly so that we can resolve these problems. I would like to know from the PNU representatives present what they consider harmful about the bullets on the ODM's Draft Agenda.

Kalonzo: We are not ready for this retreat. We should prepare for a proper and well-coordinated retreat. We should hear the President's and PM's remarks and discuss them and then close the meeting so that we can arrange for another retreat.

Kingi: Let's give hope to Kenyans based on the truth. If you are not ready to discuss these issues, or we don't have a meeting at all; then there is no need to pretend that we met. We can't use tax-payers' money for a PR exercise.

Uhuru: I can see a consensus, except that we issue a statement for PR purposes. If we start a meeting on the basis of "you" versus "me"...if we can't create an environment of genuine discussion, then we can't have a fruitful discussion... Why does it have to be you versus us? Kenyans are looking at us to give them hope. We needed time to develop this Agenda.

Ruto: What are we doing now?

Orengo: Members of this Committee. Let's start by what we have agreed on. We should go to the first meeting. We agreed on a Coalition Agreement...in the Minutes. The two Joint Secretaries agreed on "Terms of Reference and Modalities" and a Draft Agenda, which was circulated to us. To sit here and talk generally will not help matters. These meetings are to be monthly and we are not meeting monthly.

Raila: Mutula and Wekesa are not members and therefore shouldn't be here.

Mutula: I would like to speak as a lawyer...

Raila: You are not a member. Even Miguna and Kivutha there are lawyers. This is not a public *baraza*!

Kalonzo: Mr PM, you are not even chairing this meeting.

Elmi: Let's start on the how; Terms of Reference and Modalities…

Raila: Let the President come and we agree on the Agenda or agree to disagree.

Saitoti: There is confusion. There were two sets of Agenda. We have to agree on the *modus operandi*. What was conveyed to the President was not correct. I have a proposal: (i) The two principals to consult on these matters by themselves. At this particular stage, the two principals should consult. (ii) We shouldn't come out that we are incapable of dealing with our issues.

Ruto: The committee was set up in recognition that some issues that were to be resolved by the principals were not being resolved. So, we cannot go back.

Uhuru: We aren't on the same page.

Ruto: We are running away from the problems that brought us here…brought in a way by the principals that have failed to address the issues affecting the management of this coalition…

Ngilu: We are meeting here on very serious issues. We cannot agree on the Agenda. If we don't want to discuss these issues, then why are we here? You are trying to keep the President away when issues are affecting the country.

Mutula: I want to speak. It is my democratic right. You are denying me the right to speak…

Raila: This is not a public *baraza*! I am ordering you and Hon. Wekesa to leave the room.

At this point, Mutula and Wekesa leave. The meeting continued.

Kalonzo: Ordinarily, the principals should be the last resort…

Raila: There are two sets of Agenda. We can add and subtract. We can agree on both…what goes where. We can also marry the two so that we can have one Agenda. We can add "Image Building" and "Waki Report" on our Draft.

Ruto: Let's have a meeting first…

Wetangula: We are looking very bad. Kenyans are waiting for us so that we can address their problems. We made a mistake by coming here without an agreed Agenda. I would encourage you to discuss with the President and resolve the issues and give us a "Way Forward". We are talking among ourselves. You need to make a decision on the "Way Forward." We made a mistake of dragging the press here. These meetings are normally held under very tight security.

Saitoti: We should agree on what should be discussed. If we are unable to agree…

(Saitoti looked relieved to have been cut short.)

Raila: Gentlemen and a lady, we are going to look very bad that we cannot agree to discuss issues affecting Kenyans. In coalitions the world over, each partner must bring its own agenda. Don't refuse to have a partner's agenda on the table. Disagree with the agenda; but we must allow each other to speak. I can disagree with you but I shall defend unto death your right to speak. The right to be heard is an important right. We are trying to cheat each other. Say whatever you want to say, disagree, but you can't say that if we disagree, we can't meet. We agreed with the President that we must openly and honestly identify and discuss the issues…

Orengo: The country is hurting because we are dysfunctional. If the government can't function harmoniously, then we can't deliver. We had an agreed agenda, which was circulated.

Mwakwere: We are the problem. Maybe the committee should be dissolved. The principals have agreed that we develop an agenda.

Ruto: I agree with Mwakwere on a different context: If we are not going to deal with the issues, we should be disbanded.

Ngilu: We are not barred from discussing any issues…

Uhuru: There was no agreed Agenda. Our position was clear that if we can't agree on this (PNU) Agenda, then there is no need for a meeting.

Raila: I would like the joint secretaries here to explain to the meeting how the Agenda was developed. Miguna, can you explain to us what happened?

I explained that Prof. Kibwana and I had met about four times to discuss and agree on the agenda based on instructions from our respective sides, including inputs from the two principals. I pointed out that the agenda that I had placed before all members of the committee had been agreed on before Honourables Orengo, Mutula, Amos Wako, Ms Amina Mohamed and I had visited Geneva and The Hague for meetings about the International Criminal Court process. I mentioned that it was upon our return from Geneva (two days before Kilaguni) that Kibwana had informed me of what he termed "suggestions" from the President's side to have the agenda changed. We discussed the so-called changes and realised that they were so fundamental that the two of us couldn't make a decision on them. I then took the proposal to the Prime Minister who advised me to tell Kibwana that PNU was free to propose those changes at the meeting, but that the agreed agenda had to be tabled at the meeting also. I never heard back from Kibwana. I had assumed that his silence meant that he and the side he represented agreed with the Prime Minister's position on the matter. I also added that the previous night I had held discussions with Kibwana and we had both agreed that we could solve the problem by having two agenda items by both parties. In fact, those two proposals were also in the members' folders. I therefore appealed that the meeting should proceed on the basis of both agenda items. It might mean extending the sessions or days of the meetings; but I didn't see any insurmountable problems.

Raila: Is that an accurate and correct reflection of what happened, Prof. Kibwana?

Kibwana: Mr Chairman, I don't want to indulge in that kind of discussion. Yes, Mr Miguna and I had several discussions and we came up with an agenda. However, that's now academic in view of the PNU position.

Raila: Prof. Kibwana, can you deny or acknowledge what Miguna has just said?

Kibwana: Well, I can't deny what he has said…

Raila: In that case, let's break briefly for consultations…

We broke for lunch between 1 and 2pm. During lunch, Kibaki came out and had lunch with both Raila and Kalonzo. Watching them from our table, they looked relaxed and cracked jokes. After lunch, both teams went for brief consultations.

As the ODM team went to the break-away room reserved for the ODM for private consultations, Raila grabbed my right hand and we walked 50 metres, talking in low tones as the media scrambled to take our pictures. Raila told me that he knew Kibaki didn't want the discussions to proceed because he realised that the proceedings might resolve all outstanding issues, thereby "watering down" their illegitimate stranglehold on power. He confided in me that if Kibaki refused to come out to the meeting hall, we would address a press conference and then depart for Nairobi. He wanted me to surreptitiously start working on that communiqué. I was to assume that the meeting had collapsed.

In the break-away room, Ruto confirmed what Raila had told me. But he insisted that three of us – Orengo, himself and I – should go and meet three PNU representatives – Uhuru, Wetangula and Kibwana – to see if there was a way out of what now looked like a quagmire. The media was already depicting Kilaguni as a mess. We went and consulted with the PNU team. They were adamant that Raila must go and meet the President alone and separately before the meeting resumed. They wanted the two principals to break the impasse over the agenda. I knew then what the plot was: Kibaki and his PNU team were aware that when left alone with Raila, Kibaki always prevailed. That's how ODM had been stitched up at the secretive Sagana Lodge meeting before the unwieldy large cabinet of 40 had been unveiled.

Uhuru and Wetangula believed that once the President went into a secret meeting with Raila, the President would stick to the script given to him by his hawks, while Raila would start panicking and worrying unreasonably over non-existent things. Raila would be sweating about the small stuff – the media, the civil society and the international community blaming him for being intransigent. Under pressure, Raila would crumble even before a stalemate developed. I never tired of advising him that stalemates and stonewalls are good for negotiations. So, when we returned to our break-away room, Ngilu, Kingi and I took a hard stance: Raila would only meet Kibaki in the conference room in the presence of the committee. We took the position that the government and the country were larger than the two principals; that they couldn't hold everyone to ransom.

After much back and forth, the ODM team unanimously agreed that Raila would not meet Kibaki separately before the meeting resumed. It was agreed that Ngilu, Kingi and I would escort Raila into the conference room and that he would go straight to his chair. As we expected, both Uhuru and Wetangula rushed to the Prime Minister as we approached the conference room. Muthaura, Wanjohi, Gichangi and Mutua were with them. Wanjohi and Gichangi were Kibaki's submarines: they operated beneath the surface. Those two were lethal, but operated largely out of sight.

Wetangula spoke first, pleading with Raila to go upstairs to where Kibaki was waiting for him. Uhuru chimed in, too. Apparently, as we huddled in our consulting room, Kibaki had left his room and headed to the conference room. However, instead of taking his seat at the head of the table, he climbed the stairs to a holding room, which was situated directly over the conference room. This is where he was now insisting that Raila should go and consult with him. We didn't understand why Kibaki was refusing to participate in the committee proceedings.

The meeting resumed at 2.15pm. Raila and all members of the committee sat there and waited for the President to come down, as Muthaura and other State House power barons shuttled up and down. Honourables Uhuru, Saitoti and Wetangula said the President would like to see the Prime Minister upstairs. The Prime Minister insisted that the President should come down to the meeting room. Everyone on the PNU side scurried upstairs. After a few minutes, they came down, minus the President. After two tense hours when nothing got done, Kibaki came downstairs and walked slowly down the length of the room without making eye contact with anyone or uttering a word. He skulked out, as the TV cameras trailed him back to his room. The meeting collapsed at this point. If one single individual was responsible for the debacle, it was President Mwai Kibaki.

When Kilaguni collapsed, so too did any hopes that the coalition would be managed smoothly. The tension across the country was reminiscent of the period before February 28, 2008, when the National Accord had been signed. Ordinary

Kenyans feared that fighting might break out again. The talking heads speculated that the coalition had collapsed. Some predicted that we were going to have fresh elections. Others stated that PNU would kick out ODM from government and proceed as if there was no coalition.

As the media scrambled for pictures and scraps of information, the ODM team gathered its things and headed back to Nairobi. There would be no press conference at Kilaguni. This, from my perspective was no bad thing, because I'd had no chance to complete a press statement. But as we ODM delegates were boarding our plane back to Nairobi, Kibaki was "speaking to the nation from Kilaguni".

He tried to put a spin on things. His message was that the committee had had very fruitful discussions over important national issues, but that unfortunately the ODM team had felt that they needed a break and consultations to proceed further. Kibaki said that he and the rest of the PNU had granted ODM the break they needed and "talks would resume soon". Those were blatant lies and the country knew it.

On arrival at Nairobi's Wilson airstrip, Raila and the ODM team headed to the Serena Hotel where a press conference had been called. By this time, it was impossible to keep up with events. It was also difficult to know who Raila was speaking to or whose advice he was listening to. He was constantly on the phone. This was something I had complained about for years. A leader needed quiet time, especially during a crisis, to think and reflect. Many a time, I advised Raila to take time and listen carefully to presentations from different people – analysts – before making a decision. It was also my considered view that during a crisis, the Prime Minister's telephone needed to be carefully screened. Not every Tom, Dick and Harry that called should be listened to. There are many busybodies who comment on things they have no inkling about. Moreover, discipline dictates that a good leader must control even the sources of advice he consults. If he fails to do that, he will be inundated with irrelevant, poorly researched and badly thought-out positions, which is risky.

But Raila just went on talking to all and sundry. Then he gave a speech which mentioned all manner of things I was sure he would never do. That was another grave error: a leader should never threaten or promise things he knows he cannot deliver on. He undertook to ensure that from then on all meetings between him and Kibaki were structured, minuted and that resolutions were followed to the letter. He promised the country at large that ODM would pursue the implementation of all the Agenda Four reforms. He specifically mentioned the constitutional review process, and the electoral, civil service and police reforms.

Interestingly, Musalia Mudavadi never showed up at both Kilaguni and at the Serena Hotel. Mudavadi had been expected at Kilaguni and had confirmed his attendance. As stated before, I had even struggled with the State House and hotel management to reserve for him a room of equal size and value as that of Uhuru Kenyatta's. But Mudavadi neither showed up, nor telephoned to explain why he hadn't shown up, despite members of our team – Raila, Orengo and I – trying to reach him to no avail. My suspicion is that Mudavadi, being a natural survivor, knew that there would be fireworks at Kilaguni. He is known to have no stomach for controversy or a fight, partly I think because he likes to be loved by all sides, but also because, not falling out with people, has allowed him to emerge as a compromise candidate. Mudavadi never learnt an important lesson during his time at university: nobody succeeds without taking calculated risks. He can't be President if he isn't ready to sacrifice something. It's as simple as that: overcaution is cowardice and Kenyans have repeatedly shown their disdain for political cowards.

A flurry of activities followed Kilaguni. Important telephone calls were made and received. Raila spoke to all the world leaders including President Obama, the then British premier, Gordon Brown, former UK premier, Tony Blair, French President Sarkozy and a plethora of diplomats, mostly from Europe and North America. (That's another Raila trait: in the topology of races, Raila seems to place premium value on Caucasians, followed by Asians. Among African Kenyan communities, he seems to value Gikuyus, Luos and the rest in that order. My suspicion is that it has something to do with his upbringing. Having gone for his studies in Eastern Germany as a young child – and at the height of the Cold War – Raila must have gone through a severe culture shock. This could have transformed him either into a rebellious pan-Africanist or a shambolic figure. Unfortunately, we got a strange mixture of both. The ultimate product defies description. One day Raila could be sounding very revolutionary and defiant; the following day he would turn out to be the most colourless and cowardly individual imaginable. Before Caucasians, he always played what African Americans term "a quintessential Uncle Tom". It's strange and embarrassing. But that's whom we've got: a thoroughly conflicted individual.)

The week following Kilaguni, the ODM team held numerous meetings. Curiously, however, I started noticing William Ruto – who had been so robust on the retreat – and Mohamed Elmi, drifting away towards PNU. Whenever we held meetings, Ruto would either be late or not attend at all. When he attended, he tended to keep quiet, which was quite unusual. As for Elmi, he kept reporting to us "what the other side is thinking". He continued to do that until one day I confronted him and asked him, "Waziri, I didn't know that you have replaced

Kofi Annan." He insisted that we needed to build confidence with "the other side" and that "not everybody there is bad". He seemed to have developed a very close working relationship with Uhuru. He actually believed that Uhuru not just respected him but trusted him as well.

My feeling, however, is that Uhuru and the PNU side only used Elmi. Any perceptive person who has worked closely with Elmi knows that he is generally clueless. He tends to ramble over everything. He is incoherent, confused and shallow. Above all, he is desperate to be liked and appreciated. Elmi didn't care about PNU's repeated infractions. In fact, he believed that PNU had legitimate reasons to complain that ODM had taken better ministries than them. (I first heard this argument from Raila shortly after the grand coalition cabinet had been named. The majority of the technical team – his think tank – had complained that he had chosen useless ministries and left all the good ones to PNU. To our utter shock, Raila defended the 20 departments he had taken. He argued that those "ministries are closer to the people". He had said, "You see, these ministries look useless when you look at them with your naked eyes; but when you put on the magnified glass or a microscope, you will see that they are better than the ones PNU got. Look at water, roads, agriculture, public works, land, health and immigration; you see they render real services to the man and woman on the ground…" I have to admit that Raila was persuasive. True, those departments actually offered services to Kenyans "on the ground". But can we argue that finance, defence, police, intelligence, transport, energy, communication, public health, education, provincial administration, livestock and environment didn't offer services to the people on the ground?

I argued instead that the importance of ministries was defined first and foremost on the basis of budgetary allocation, reach/presence and what people perceived. All over the world, finance, foreign affairs, defence, intelligence, energy, education, communication, transport and environment are considered the most significant ministries. These are the muscles of any government, without which nothing could be done. In fact, no coalition in the world would allocate finance and foreign affairs to the same party. Kenya and Zimbabwe were the only exceptions to the rule! If one were to judge the value and importance of ministries based on budgetary allocation alone, the PNU controlled more than 85 per cent of government. They had the money, the intelligence, the weapons and the information. Kibaki even took the office of the government spokesman and placed it under him. With the Presidential press service continuing to churn out partisan PNU propaganda, having the office of the government spokesman under his firm control essentially meant that Kibaki was going to be able to say pretty much what he liked.)

Absent trust and good faith in coalition management, these were structural problems that could have been effectively addressed through competently crafted legal instruments. It had been primarily the responsibility of Caroli and Orengo, as the only lawyers in the ODM Serena mediation team, to ensure that all the legal instruments met the highest international standards, were balanced and fair to the Orange party and its leader. As they say in ordinary parlance: they should have made sure all the Ts were crossed and the Is dotted. Well, they didn't.

And even after I had convinced Raila to instruct them – before the Accord was signed (which he did) – they again failed to present what I had prepared for discussion. Why were they doing that? Is it possible that these two weren't acting alone all along? Is it entirely surprising that within two years of Caroli's appointment into the OPM formally as an administrative secretary (but informally as Raila's chief of staff and private secretary), he had managed to accumulate within the shortest period imaginable an asset portfolio that is as baffling as it is scandalous?

Many people have argued that Caroli might have been on the payroll of PNU and Kanu Orphans all along – that the apparent errors and omissions made during the drafting of the Accord, during the Serena mediation and throughout the life of the grand coalition government weren't errors at all; they were deliberate and strategic sabotage.

Clearly, Kofi Annan and the Panel of Eminent African Personalities continued to play a significant role in seeing through the implementation not just of the Agenda Four reforms; their role was crucial in ensuring that the coalition held together. My view is that had Annan and his team (if they had acted as professional mediators) facilitated the crafting of dispute resolution mechanisms, instruments and organs for the coalition, his continued role would have been significantly diminished as the coalition government would have been – institutionally speaking – capacitated to resolve all disputes by itself. But since the Panel had left before having these instruments and institutions developed, it was now imperative for Annan and his team, as part of their ongoing mandate, to implement the short-term and long-term reforms that were necessary to prevent a recurrence of the same conflict Kenya had experienced in 2007/2008. Without the coalition holding together, the stability, peace and development of Kenya couldn't be guaranteed. After all, what was the Panel of Eminent African Personalities still doing if it couldn't help the parties to resolve outstanding issues?

Telling them to go sort out their problems, as Annan often did whenever ODM sought his intervention, wasn't, in my considered view, the best way to deal with the problems. But it is what Hans Corell – Annan's legal advisor – was recommending. I had privately consulted Corell and other senior UN officers to assist us prepare airtight documents that met the highest international standards possible. I also sought their assistance in reigning in Kibaki and his PNU hardliners on the implementation of the National Accord.

I had believed that Corell, having served as an advisor to the Secretary General of the UN, would automatically adhere, subscribe and uphold the highest international standards in the conceptualisation and drafting of such instruments. Granted, Corell didn't have any problem with the contents; his objection was more philosophical: that there wasn't a need for such instruments, as coalitions were built on and supposed to operate on the basis of mutual trust. That was quite a noble theoretical position. That's what should happen, ideally. But the reality is that we don't live in an ideal world. We live in a world occupied by selfish human beings.

The Permanent Committee had another meeting on April 6, 2009, at the President's office at Harambee House. In attendance were: the President, the Prime Minister, Kalonzo Musyoka, Musalia Mudavadi, Uhuru Kenyatta, Charity Ngilu, William Ruto, George Saitoti, James Orengo, Chirau Mwakwere, Mohamed Elmi and the two joint secretaries, Kibwana and I. Those absent with apologies were Amason Kingi and Moses Wetangula. As usual, Martha Karua kept away without apologies. The meeting commenced at 11.26am and concluded at 2.25pm It was a marathon, perhaps because we needed to show the country that we were still able to work together. The only problem is that nothing was achieved apart from in PR terms. We were twirling in the wind, as it were.

The meeting started with prayers. Before adopting the agenda, both the President and the Prime Minister, as co-chairs, made opening remarks. The President stated that the Grand Coalition Government is one government and it would continue to be so. He urged the members of the committee to continuously deliberate so as to agree on what it meant to serve in one government. He emphasised that the government should be free from acrimony. He further urged the committee to observe the rule of confidentiality.

The Prime Minister expressed appreciation that the meeting was taking place after the unsuccessful Kilaguni retreat. He indicated that members of the Grand Coalition Government had been talking at each other (not with each other) thus creating a negative picture to the public. He stated that the government could correct that situation. He emphasised that the government must work as one. He called for frank and open discussions that would lead to the resolution of the issues affecting the grand coalition. He urged all-round respect and understanding among members of the committee and the government.

It was all hosannas from both Raila and Kibaki. The two old political goats knew how to bleat for the gallery. They knew there was a throng of both local and international media outside and the entire country waiting for a signal that the coalition would hold. Businesspersons, investors, entrepreneurs, tourists, diplomats, neighbouring countries – the world – watched keenly to see if Kenya was going to slide back into the anarchy they had seen following the mismanaged presidential elections of 2007.

From Kibaki's body language, I knew nothing had changed. Raila looked anxious and slippery, as he always did under pressure. His eyes kept producing deltas of tears – his eyes seemed to get worse by the day. He had had several surgeries to those eyes but nothing seemed to have improved. He kept taking out a white handkerchief from his jacket and wiping away his tears.

Tension in the room was so thick you could have cut it with a knife. To ease things, the committee quickly discussed and unanimously adopted the agenda. Nobody wanted this PR exercise to derail on the agenda. The minutes for the meetings of that day, April 6 and February 11, 2009, were exactly the same. It was amazing that the committee didn't notice the irony of approving February minutes in April. If this was a corporate board of a going concern, it would have been disbanded. Yet there we were, sitting at the apex of a country, squandering time over nothing.

The issue of whether or not members of the Serena mediation team should join the Permanent Committee was extensively discussed but no decision was made on it. The joint secretaries presented the Draft Terms of Reference and Working Modalities of the Permanent Committee on the Management of Grand Coalition Affairs. The document was discussed and adopted.

The meeting resolved that information about its meetings, deliberations and resolutions would be communicated to the public through joint communiqués by the joint secretaries. The joint secretariat was formally constituted and mandated to establish an institutional framework that could effectively facilitate the work of the Permanent Committee and to monitor the implementation of the National Reform Agenda.

After some discussion, the joint secretaries were mandated to prepare a Draft Document on the "Guiding Principles and Institutional Framework for Managing the Affairs of the Grand Coalition Government" for discussion at the next meeting. I tried to point out that those documents had been prepared and were ready for discussion and possible adoption, but Raila waved the matter down because "they hadn't been prepared jointly with Kibwana". Before Kilaguni, I had informed Raila of Kibwana's refusal to sit down with me so that we could jointly draft, that he had cancelled six meetings we had scheduled for that purpose and then been unable to reschedule. Eventually, I completed drafting the documents and forwarded them to him for comments and observations. Yet after more than three months, Kibwana hadn't responded. I knew that Kibwana wasn't acting alone; he was under instructions from higher ups in both the Kibaki faction of government and the PNU leadership. That's why I was frustrated with Raila when he swiftly announced that the joint secretaries should meet and come up with drafts by the following Wednesday.

The joint secretaries then presented the "Matrix of Implementation of Agenda 4" of July 30, 2008, prepared by the Serena mediation team. The Permanent Committee noted its contents and discussed the status of the implementation of the National Reform Agenda. There was consensus that the fast-tracking of the National Reform Agenda under the National Accord must get priority treatment by both the Permanent Committee and the government. Again – lip service.

The Permanent Committee observed that line ministries were implementing certain aspects of the reforms and resolved that the joint secretariat should determine from each ministry and department the status of the implementation of these reforms and to report to the Permanent Committee on or before its next meeting. This was getting comical. The committee was busy making academic resolutions. I had earlier tabled three letters the joint secretaries had sent to Muthaura, seeking his assistance to carry out our mandate effectively. Without Muthaura's instructions to permanent secretaries, heads of departments, heads of state corporations and other government departments, agencies and functionaries, they wouldn't cooperate with us.

So, we had requested Muthaura to issue a letter to all government departments, directing them to cooperate with the joint secretaries. We had also asked Muthaura to secure an office for the joint secretariat. In addition, we sought to be issued with the authority to incur expenditure so that we could make the joint secretariat operational. Muthaura had simply ignored us. And here we were being given instructions again, over matters both Kibaki and Raila knew they had no commitment to undertake. Why were we deceiving the country? I tried several times to have the meeting call Muthaura (who was attending the meeting this time even though he wasn't a member) to account, but nobody was interested.

I had earlier primed Orengo, Ngilu and Kingi to back me up. But when I glanced over to them as I made my argument, they all stared blankly into space, pretending that they could not hear me. When we reached the thorny issue of executive or political appointments, I could see the ODM members squirming in their seats. Uhuru, Wetangula and Beth Mugo (who had replaced Karua) put in a spirited effort to have the matter deferred indefinitely. Eventually, with ODM in retreat (again), the committee directed that the joint secretaries should at the next meeting present a paper on the "Mechanisms of Consultations required for Executive Appointments to be made bearing in mind the Existing Law". That was another cowardly about-turn. Everybody knew that the document was ready for discussion. What did they fear? They also knew that there was no way Kibwana would agree to participate in drafting such a document.

PNU had made up its mind that it would never voluntarily accede to ODM's demands that Raila be consulted and his concurrence obtained before any major decision or appointment was made. Given Raila's poor record during previous consultation sessions with Kibaki, PNU didn't really have any justification for refusing to allow that document to be prepared and adopted. It was finally resolved that the Permanent Committee would resume its meeting on Friday, April 24, 2009.

That meeting never occurred. None of the resolutions passed were ever implemented. I tried more than 50 times to have the committee meet but nobody seemed interested; not even Raila. He would pretend to be angry, direct epithets at Kibaki and the PNU, but yet he did absolutely nothing to force his point. I kept explaining to him that he didn't need Kibaki's permission or endorsement to call a meeting. The Terms and Modalities we had adopted didn't prevent either principal from convening a meeting. After singing to the wind for months, I gave up. The committee then died a natural death. It never met again.

Under the circumstances, it was difficult to see how the implementation of Agenda Four reforms could be coordinated, monitored and evaluated. The committee was the best institutional framework wherein that work could be done. And the joint secretaries should have been the people best positioned to get the committee's work done. Unfortunately, petty and parochial political interests took over. The national interests were relegated to the backburner. Any time partisan and selfish politics gains, the ordinary people lose. That's what happened in this case. There are those who will disregard the facts and the evidence and blame me for all these failures. All I can say is that I did what was humanly possible to move the national agenda forward. If I failed, it wasn't because of lack of foresight, courage, discipline or persistence.

CHAPTER ELEVEN

WARNING SIGNS

By March 2010 I had become too many things to too many people. Beyond my committee work, I still had a role for Raila as his strongest general, defender, thinker, writer and fire-fighter. Whether it was in meetings or negotiations with his PNU counterparts, I was always the first and last port of call – particularly now that Salim had left and Sarah, for personal or family reasons as well as a growing disillusionment, had taken a very low profile. I prepared virtually all press statements, responded to a number of important correspondences and sat through many meetings.

On top of this – and despite propaganda to the contrary – I would actually later intercede for Raila whenever Caroli, Isahakia or Raila himself had caused a ruckus with one of his ministers, or when one of them had simply failed to cover Raila's too often exposed flank.

Kenyans deserve to know that in late 2008, before the fallout between Raila and William Ruto became public and toxic, James Orengo, Prof. Edward Oyugi, Oduor Ong'wen and I met Raila for dinner at the Serena Hotel in Nairobi and discussed the genesis of the problem. Prof. Oyugi and I strenuously advised Raila to try and build fences with his erstwhile friend. Regrettably, Raila insisted that he didn't want to mend their cracking relationship; that "Ruto was insolent and disrespectful; that reaching out to Ruto amounted to coddling a wayward child". Those were his exact words.

From late 2008, William Ruto, the then ODM Pentagon member and Minister for Agriculture, had grown increasingly restless. During the campaigns for the 2007 elections, there had been credible rumours that Raila would appoint

Ruto Prime Minister, should he become President. His deputy within ODM and running mate, Musalia Mudavadi, would have become Vice-President. Of course, after the power sharing deal, it was Raila who became Prime Minister and Mudavadi his deputy. Ruto in turn was appointed Minister for Agriculture, a portfolio Raila claimed Ruto himself had chosen. With about 50 parastatals and a budget more than ten times that of the office of the Prime Minister, the ministry of agriculture had heft. And Ruto, who had a reputation as a man with a sharp nose for making money, must have known that the Ministry of Agriculture was where 'excess fat' was; to put it in Kenyan business parlance.

But Ruto felt short-changed nonetheless and started making rumblings that would culminate in the near total collapse of the Orange party. Initially, Ruto alleged that he had 'brought more votes to Raila than Mudavadi'. Incredibly, Ruto credited himself with the approximately 1.5m votes that Raila had received from a conglomeration of diverse ethnic groups that had become known as the Kalenjin; comprising mainly the Kipsigis, the Nandi, the Keiyo, the Marakwet, and the Tugen. (Of course, this was a bit of an exaggeration. It was true that Ruto had worked extremely hard and did indeed 'bring' lots of votes to ODM and Raila. But he hadn't worked alone. People like Kipkalya Kones and Sally Kosgei had been equally instrumental. Many analysts felt that in 2007, Raila could have been more popular in the Rift Valley than Ruto.) Ruto's argument went that Raila had only got about 800,000 votes from the Luhya to whom Mudavadi belonged and should have been responsible for, hence, Mudavadi wasn't entitled to be appointed Deputy Prime Minister and deputy party leader of ODM.

Initially, Ruto couldn't come out openly and challenge the appointment of Mudavadi. To begin with, Mudavadi's appointment as deputy party leader was by virtue of the fact that he had obtained the second highest number of votes to Raila's during the ODM presidential nominations. Ruto had come third. Even though it's an open secret that the 2007 ODM presidential nominations weren't free and fair, and in fact are said to have been massively rigged in Raila's favour, those who participated in them like Ruto and Mudavadi, didn't openly voice their opposition to them. (I'm not suggesting that silence meant agreement or consent.) Neither did Ruto challenge Raila's appointment of Mudavadi as his deputy. Many people, therefore, had mistakenly assumed that both Ruto and Mudavadi had genuinely accepted those nomination results and were content. (Of course, we would learn much later that they hadn't accepted them.)

Ruto is charismatic, articulate, hardworking, rumbustious and ambitious. He is also extremely restless. Unlike both Raila and Mudavadi, he is also a teetotaller, and thus less distracted from political campaigning. But even more importantly,

Ruto is also fabulously wealthy. And notwithstanding the mystery surrounding the sources of his wealth, unlike Mudavadi and Raila, he can be very generous, especially when he has a political agenda to execute. He also has charisma. Mudavadi is the exact opposite: dour, technocratic, patient and soft spoken, he exhibits the characteristics of a traditional English gentleman. Mudavadi rarely shows emotion no matter how angry or aggrieved. He projects the image of a slow, methodical and calculating person; difficult to agitate. I would observe that he never openly opposed the party leader. He rarely spoke during meetings, but took care to always present cogent and logical arguments. The Kenyan media complain that he is boring and doesn't have the knack to give them soundbites. I have never heard him shout. His ambitions, although barely concealed, would never be displayed up to the very end when he would eventually openly rebel against Raila. But that would not happen until May 2012!

From mid-2008 until the end of 2009, when a decision was made to accommodate him, Ruto engaged in a political carpet bombing of Raila. I remember holding numerous separate private sessions with both Ruto and Raila over their unending running battles. James Orengo, Salim Lone, Edward Oyugi, Oduor Ong'wen and I held numerous discussions with Raila at his Karen home in July 2008, during which time we tried to persuade him to make amends and accommodate Ruto, whom we believed had legitimate grievances. We reminded Raila that of all the communities that had supported him in 2007, none had acted more gallantly than the Kalenjin, especially their brave youth. Many believe, with merit, that had the Kalenjin youth not fought in defence of Raila's 'stolen vote', Kibaki wouldn't have agreed to share power with him. And it was universally acknowledged that if there was one person who deserved praise for mobilising the Kalenjin youth during that period, it wasn't the ODM chairman Henry Kosgey, it was William Ruto. To a lesser extent, credit also went to the late Kipkalya Kones. Thus, we argued, we, as a party, owed Ruto some gratitude.

I subsequently held three meetings with Ruto at his Kilimo House offices, in which I tried to persuade him to show respect to our party leader and to remain in ODM. "I know you have political ambitions. But you are still relatively young. I believe that whatever ambitions you have – even for the presidency of this country – you would achieve more easily within ODM than outside it…" He listened intently and denied that he planned to abandon ODM.

Eventually, after months of attrition, Raila agreed to lobby the ODM executive committee members and the parliamentary group to create a second position of deputy leader responsible for strategy for Ruto. This extraordinary meeting took place at the Simba Lodge, Naivasha. Even though there were protracted debates, in the end, the proposal was carried. The ODM constitution was amended to formalise the change. But by this act, Musalia Mudavadi's position as deputy leader was diluted. And I suspect Mudavadi must have felt that his position was no longer guaranteed.

But still Ruto wasn't satisfied. After a lull of a few months, he erupted once more with more demands and spouting incendiary rhetoric not just against Raila, but also against ODM. His scattergun allegations were general, ambiguous and unsubstantiated. Out of the blue, he started attacking ODM and the "party leadership," which he was a part of, "for failing to defend the rights of the Kalenjin youths" whom he claimed "had disappeared" during the post-election violence. Admittedly, hundreds of Kalenjin youths – like other Kenyan youths – had been arrested and brutalised. Many might have been killed and buried in mass graves by state security agents. The sight of a lone policeman shooting to death two unarmed youths in Kisumu in broad daylight had been captured on live TV and broadcast around the world. Similar scenes had been replayed around the country. It had been barbaric and inhumane. Ruto knew that neither Raila nor ODM had been responsible for those ghastly acts of barbarism. Moreover, Ruto – like Raila – sat in the cabinet. He was a senior member of the executive and could have raised similar concerns at the cabinet meetings he attended. He could also have raised them directly or privately with the President. In addition, nothing prevented him from doing the same in parliament. Despite all these options, Ruto persistently attacked Raila over the "disappeared Kalenjin youth".

And as soon as Raila introduced a cabinet-approved national initiative to rehabilitate and restore the Mau Forest Water Tower Ecosystem, Ruto erupted with yet another lambasting of Raila. The Mau Forests Complex (MFC) is considered the most important of the five main watershed areas in Kenya because of its economic, social and environmental contribution to the country. These watershed areas are commonly referred to as "Water Towers". The Mau forests ecosystem has a high and rapidly growing population. Yet the forest is under increasing threat from irregular and ill planned settlements, encroachments and illegal forest exploitation, particularly logging (mainly by politically-connected businessmen and firms) and looting of public land. Over the last decades, approximately 25 per cent of the Mau forest has been lost to politically-directed encroachments. Currently, most of the forest areas are under the management of the Kenya Forest Service. The exception is the Maasai Mau forest which is a Trust Land Forest under the management of Narok County.

After decades of irresponsible dithering, the government had recognised that the "continued destruction of the forests is leading to a water crisis: perennial rivers are becoming seasonal, storm flow and downstream flooding are increasing, in some places the aquifer has dropped by 100 metres while wells and springs are drying up. In addition there are global concerns resulting from loss of biodiversity, and increased carbon dioxide emissions as a result of forest cover loss. Poor conservation of the deforested land is causing soil erosion and decreasing crop yields in an area of high agricultural potential; on the commercial tea estates, yields are being affected by micro climatic changes."

Consequently, the government took significant steps towards addressing the threat of rapid ecological degradation of its forest resources, particularly that of the Mau Water Tower Complex. A new forest policy and law, that placed significant emphasis on co-management of forest resources with local communities and the private sector and laid the foundation for the strict control of logging and human settlements, was adopted in 2005.

In view of the foregoing, the government established a 30 member task force (reporting to the Prime Minister) whose responsibility was to study and make recommendations on the immediate, short and long term options for restoring the entire Mau Forests Complex. The task force completed its work and submitted recommendations to the government in March 2009. Consequently, Raila led the government's initiative to restore and conserve the Mau.

Unfortunately, the government, including Raila, failed to take appropriate steps to ensure peasants and other ordinary citizens who had encroached on the forest were removed and resettled humanely. Instead, orders were issued that saw hundreds of ordinary civilians rendered homeless and exposed to numerous risks and dangers from wild animals, rain and the elements. But in the meantime, the Mau Forest Task Force Report dated March 2009 disclosed that wealthy and well-connected individuals who had looted, destroyed, desecrated and converted into personal use tens of thousands of hectares of forest land – like former President Daniel arap Moi at his Kiptagich Tea Farm – had not been ordered to hand over the public assets they have been occupying and profiting from for decades.

Ruto went on the offensive, attacking Raila as callous and anti-Kalenjin. He turned the worthwhile Mau restoration initiative into ammunition with which to hit Raila. Raila, many members of ODM and I considered Ruto's attacks concerning the Mau issue to be mainly gratuitous. Whereas he had a basis for breaking ranks with Raila over the manner in which 'the forest evictees' were treated, I believe that Ruto had no reason to attack the restoration exercise as a whole. The alternative was to allow the wanton and complete destruction of the water tower, which would lead to flash floods, famine and ultimately, the death of millions of innocent people not just in Kenya, but in the East African region.

Even more mischievous, was Ruto's target of Raila yet not Kibaki, when it was the latter who chaired the cabinet meeting that not only resolved to restore the Mau Water Tower, but also decided to evict all forest encroachers, including the Kalenjin peasants. It was for that reason I wrote – on instructions from Raila – articles critical of Ruto.

As Ruto was busy crucifying Raila, Franklin Bett – an ODM MP and the Roads Minister – joined in. Shortly after his appointment (which I had played a significant part in lobbying for, as many people around Raila were insisting on Langat Magerer or Musa Sirma), there was a brief period when Bett was publicly outspoken in his criticism of Raila's stand on the Mau Water Tower restoration exercise and for ODM's stance on the International Criminal Court process. During that period, Bett always seemed to be on the TV, the radio, or in the newspapers, hurling abuse at Raila, threatening that he would leave ODM and join Ruto, who had effectively decamped from the Orange party by then.

For two months, Bett and Raila never spoke directly. During that period, I acted as a go-between, relaying Bett's concerns to Raila and passing back Raila's response to Bett, almost on a daily basis. I recall one day things became so heated that when I telephoned Raila to communicate Bett's sentiments, he started yelling at me: "*Ja-Nyando*, leave that inciter alone! I don't want to speak with him or see him again! OK? Bett is an inciter!"

"*Jakom*, he is still one of your ministers. Even if you aren't happy with him, you need to tell him your concerns. It's better to discuss these things than to spar with each other through the media. I think the two of you should meet soon. I have spoken with Bett and he is OK with a meeting."

"No! No! No! I've told you stop speaking with Bett; he is an inciter! He is inciting people in South Rift to oppose the Mau exercise. I'll not meet him!" he continued to shout. Then he hung up.

But I didn't give up. I continued to hold meetings with Bett, trying to explain Raila's point of view; that he was genuinely interested in the Mau restoration as an environmental issue, not because of politics, and that Raila felt hurt that he [Bett] was addressing Raila through the press and making provocative statements that could incite disaffection in the South Rift. After numerous meetings, and back and forth messages between the two politicians, things soon thawed between them.

There were also three disputes with Dr Sally Kosgei that could have destroyed her and Raila's working relationship, had I not salvaged that situation. The first one occurred during the constitutional review process. Sally was then the Minister for Higher Education. One day, Sally accompanied Raila to a public function at

Taifa Hall at the University of Nairobi. Raila's wife Ida was also present. As the minister responsible, Sally had the task of inviting Raila to speak, which she did, professionally. In turn, protocol demanded that before proceeding to read his speech, Raila was to formally acknowledge the presence of his entourage (at least that's what Sally expected), including that of his wife and Minister for Higher Education. But Raila being Raila, assumed that he was only required to acknowledge the presence of those who hadn't accompanied him, people he was seeing for the first time on the podium. He did so and went straight into his speech.

As Sally later reported to me, this elicited curious glances from Kenyans who were used to the "usual thing". Whispers started that Sally had fallen out with Raila. Sally was furious. She felt belittled and spurned. After the function, they parted ways, with Sally swearing not to talk to Raila again. That afternoon, I was with Mutakha and the ODM team at the Kenya Institute of Administration at Kabete, trying to hammer out a deal on the draft Constitution, which had been mangled by the Parliamentary Service Commission (PSC) on the Constitution at Naivasha. During a tea break, my mobile phone rang. It was Sally. She recounted to me what had happened and why she hadn't attended the consultative meeting at Kabete; she was still very mad with Raila. After my conversation with Sally, I called Raila and politely asked him to try and speak with Sally, explaining that I believed Sally was right to be annoyed at the apparent slight.

"Forget about Sally, Miguna! She's childish. I didn't even introduce Ida at the function. Why should I have introduced them when they accompanied me there? Sally is like a member of my family; I don't have to introduce her…Everybody saw her arriving with me…" insisted Raila, clearly forgetting the fact that Sally was a cabinet minister, not a member of his family, and that the function they had both attended was an official state/government function, not a family affair. I found it strange that Raila often didn't know the boundary between the party ODM and the larger Jaramogi family, and between state or government and the Odinga clan. Leaders need to internalise such distinctions because if they don't, they may start to treat state or public assets or resources as family assets. It has happened many times in Africa (even from those previously hailed as 'Africa's great hope' – Ghana's Jerry Rawlings, Uganda's Yoweri Museveni, Zimbabwe's Robert Mugabe and Ethiopia's Meles Zenawi), and I was already harbouring grave concerns that Raila was either prone to such temptations or had already fallen victim to them. Such lapses in judgement didn't sit comfortably with his carefully honed image of being a champion of modern democratic practice.

Raila was as livid as Sally. I was stuck in the middle. Sally had become a valued friend to me; a source of intellectual strength, someone I could discuss complicated matters of governance with for hours every week, and a person I had brought into my confidence. And Raila was my boss. I didn't want to be placed in a situation where I had to make a choice between them.

The Bett situation had been easier because between him and Raila, I would have opted to be with Raila, any day, any time. I didn't trust Bett. He was full of drama and intrigues. Based on my conversations with people who had worked closely with Moi, but who had never been sucked too deeply into the *Nyayo* ways, Bett was considered a loose cannon; someone you couldn't rely on. But Sally was different. She was learned, urbane and sophisticated. She was remarkably bright. Among the ODM cabinet ministers, Sally and Orengo were closest to me. We spent hours upon hours arguing, debating, reasoning, intellectualising, philosophising. Sally had an interesting background and history. As a brilliant young university student at the University of Dar-es-Salaam, she had studied under the inimitable Dr Walter Rodney of Guyana, the author of the irreplaceable *How Europe Underdeveloped Africa* – required reading in my student days along with Franz Fanon's *The Wretched of the Earth* and Paulo Frèire's *Pedagogy of the Oppressed.* At Dar, Sally had been a fiery radical, associating more with Marxist-Leninists than with the dour reactionary types like Mutula Kilonzo, who was a good crammer, but a lousy intellectual, even in those early days.

I respected both Sally and Orengo tremendously. I deeply valued their friendship, although the two had what could only be described as an "interesting love-hate" relationship. One day they would be very chummy with one another – kissing and hugging – then the next they would be frosty and refuse to take the other's calls. Orengo and I frequently visited each other at our respective homes and offices. We often went for breakfast and lunch together. On numerous occasions, Orengo would visit me at home without notice; just driving in late at night. We would sometimes stay up as late as 3am, especially when there were important strategies, tactics or documents I was working on that Raila also wanted Orengo to look at, or Orengo and I had decided we needed to work on together. Occasionally, Anyang' Nyong'o and Prof. Oyugi would join us. But mostly, it was just Jim and I, alone, burning the midnight oil. We met almost daily during the constitutional review process. Similarly, we met frequently when the ICC got involved in the Kenyan situation. My house was the hub for activities related to these two important processes. I also used to visit Sally at home and at her offices frequently.

Many times, Mutakha, Kirui arap Kemboi, Nabii Nabwera and Salim would visit too to clarify a few things. They provided fruitful interactions and relationships. These were the thoughts and memories that crowded my mind as

I spoke with Raila about Sally that day. I was not just speaking about "another ODM minister". This was Sally, my friend. And I value, honour and cherish friendship more than most things in life.

"*Jakom*, Sally is extremely hurt. She was expecting you to recognise her at the function; just like you did to the other ministry and university officials and other people who were seated at the high table. She complains that you recognised people on her left and right and missed her out; she says you made her feel awkward and silly. She is genuinely hurt. In addition *Jakom*, it was a formal event and Sally was *the minister* responsible; she wasn't attending as a member of your family, sir. Kindly call the lady and just assure her that it wasn't deliberate."

Raila insisted that he had done nothing wrong and would not call Sally to apologise. We then spent 40 minutes discussing the progress of the constitutional negotiations. As soon as we were through, I called Sally back before returning to the session. I assured her that Raila seemed to have genuinely misapprehended the situation and had honestly mistaken her for being a member of his family, hence the lapse. Eventually, after many days, her anger subsided. But Raila never apologised.

There was another nasty spat between Sally and Raila that was caused – more or less – by Caroli and Isahakia. Perhaps unknown to Raila (although Sally told me she thought those were Raila's Machiavellian machinations), Caroli and Isahakia were "backing" different sugar companies in Western Province; Butali and West Kenya. Butali had applied for a licence to operate its factory less than 40 kilometres from West Kenya. Apparently, Butali had earlier been given a green light by the Kenya Sugar Board to construct a factory in Housing Minister Soita Shitanda's Malava constituency and it had spent a fortune doing so. However, as soon as Butali applied for a licence from the regulator, Kenya Sugar Board, West Kenya submitted a challenge at both the Board and at the High Court.

When the dispute started, Sally wasn't the Minister for Agriculture; Ruto was. Unfortunately, it was claimed that Isahakia was supporting West Kenya, while Caroli was rooting for Butali. I'm not aware why they were getting involved in what looked like a commercial dispute between two going concerns in Western Province. By the time Sally was appointed the Minister for Agriculture, the matter had already reached the courts and Sally, being a cautious and experienced professional, would not be dragged into a conflict whose source she didn't know.

The matter became worse when Sally was invited to a meeting at Raila's office. She arrived quite early – I believe she was there 45 minutes before the scheduled meeting. Soon Housing Minister Soita Shitanda, Deputy Prime Minister and Minister for Local Government Musalia Mudavadi, and Planning Minister

Wycliffe Oparanya arrived, in the company of Regional Development Minister Fred Gumo and Forestry Minister Noah Wekesa. The matter had become a Western Province/Luhya issue; not a straightforward matter of licensing. Sally hadn't been told the agenda of the meeting or who else was expected to attend. As a courtesy and good management and leadership practice, Raila should have briefed the minister responsible for agriculture prior to calling her into the meeting with the other ministers. Instead, she was kept waiting for close to one and a half hours as Raila met privately with the ministers from Western Province in the presence of Caroli and Isahakia.

Caroli should also have never been allowed to interfere in the running of the Ministry of Agriculture. His animus towards Sally was a matter of public record. He made no secret of the fact that he hated her. Ambushing one of Raila's most experienced and important ministers wasn't wise. This was one of Raila's worst mistakes. And it was an early warning of poor judgment and leadership acumen. In addition, Caroli ushered in the three late-arrivals who proceeded to have a private meeting with Raila for one and a half hours before Sally was called in. That slight was uncalled for. And as soon as she sat down, it was Caroli who began talking about "a legal opinion" on the case, concluding that there wasn't anything preventing Butali from getting the green light to have the new sugar factory inaugurated.

Caroli wasn't Raila's advisor on legal and constitutional affairs. He wasn't responsible for parliamentary or political affairs either. Strategically, Raila should have sought various opinions: from the Attorney General as well as his advisors on political, parliamentary, legal, constitutional and coalition affairs. Since the matter had grave political and legal implications for both Raila and the Orange party, I felt that even the think tank and the Orange party leadership should have been briefed.

Sally reported to me later that before she could even get a word in, Oparanya and Shitanda told her, intimidatingly, that she had no option but to go along with their decision. She said that Musalia wasn't nice to her either. Meanwhile, Raila just sat there and watched, pretending to be 'neutral'. Everything looked choreographed to her.

People who have worked closely with Raila know his style, and that incident bore his DNA. Of course, Sally as Minister for Agriculture was privy to information that not even Raila had heard or knew about. She had discussed the matter with a number of stakeholders, held extensive meetings and consulted with senior ministry officials and lawyers in order to form her opinion. But, of course, the mob was on the prowl. Raila continued pretending to be listening on the sidelines, but when the meeting ended, Raila announced that he would be granting Butali the licence at a public function in three days' time. Sally's consent wasn't sought. Nobody even bothered to find out whether she was free to attend on that day. That is why when, on January 14, 2011, Raila went to open the new Butali sugar factory, neither Sally nor her permanent secretary, and any other senior Ministry of Agriculture officials were present. They hadn't even been invited.

Meanwhile, Caroli was boasting to me and other people of how he had "fixed Sally". "Sally will not mistreat me under the government of Raila son of Odinga… She did that to me during Moi's reign when I was working at the Energy Regulatory Board; but not any more. You guys know what Sally did… It's all there in Raila's *Enigma* book. She would call and abuse Raila when she was Head of the Civil Service. So, she can go to hell!" It was amazing. Caroli didn't care that he was shouting about this in the presence of junior employees in the office, thus undermining Sally even in the eyes of quite lowly subordinates. I guess power had gone to his head. Following my irregular suspension, Caroli went on national television to cast aspersions against me, claiming that I was "responsible for the conflict within the coalition government". It was bullcrap!

The last incident concerning Sally occurred in late 2011. Sally was among ODM cabinet ministers and MPs who were travelling to Rusinga Island for the burial of Millie Odhiambo's mother. She had arrived at the ferry pier at Luanda Kotieno in the morning and boarded with others. By mid-morning, the ferry was in the middle of Lake Victoria heading towards Rusinga when the captain received an emergency call from Luanda Kotieno that he had to return to the pier. At first he resisted, arguing – correctly – that returning would expose the ferry, himself and his passengers to unnecessary danger; that he preferred to reach his destination first before turning back. As the captain was still arguing with his manager, the District Commissioner of Luanda grabbed the communication device from the manager and commanded the captain to "return at once".

On arrival at the pier, the captain found a furious Ida Odinga, who ordered him to remove three vehicles from the ferry in order to create space for her vehicles. Ida pointed at the three vehicles she insisted had to go. Unfortunately, one of them was Sally's, with her cabinet flag flapping. Sally and everyone else was stunned. Ida wasn't in any mood for an argument; she demanded that she had to travel with her bodyguards, personal assistants and other hangers-on in the same ferry. Realising that she would have to wait another hour for the ferry to return from Rusinga, and angry at having been humiliated by Raila's wife, Sally left in a huff for her home in Aldai.

Later that evening she called me and relayed what had happened. "Miguna, if she could do this to a cabinet minister now, what would she do if Raila became President? Raila called me a few minutes ago and suggested that Ida hadn't known that it was me; that she thought it was Minister for Public Health, Beth Mugo's vehicle. Does it matter?" That was Sally's only question. I could feel the anguish, frustration and disappointment in both her voice and questions.

Unknown to many Kenyans, Raila's relationship with ODM chairman Henry Kosgey wasn't (and hasn't always been) rosy either. Right from the beginning of the coalition, Raila constantly complained to me and Prof. Oyugi, Salim and Ong'wen that Kosgey was persistently disregarding his directives over the management of the Ministry of Industrialisation. One sticky issue was over Kosgey's unilateral decision to fire the Kenya Industrial Research and Development Institute's (KIRDI's) Managing Director Dr Tom Ogada and a board member, Dr Robert Arunga (Raila's longstanding friend). Raila recounted how Kosgey once saw Arunga alight from Raila's vehicle and became so envious that he resolved to get rid of him; something he managed to do within months of that incident. And despite Raila's interventions (even written directives), Kosgey went ahead and irregularly removed both individuals from KIRDI. Raila's view was that Kosgey was a 'closet tribalist' who hated Luos. Raila carped about Kosgey and others in their absence but never did anything to stem their infractions, even though he told Orengo, Salim, Oyugi, Ong'wen and I at his Karen residence that Kosgey had repeatedly ignored his written directives on this and other matters.

Some time in 2009, Raila travelled to France and Scandinavia. Henry Kosgey accompanied him on that trip. One of those that helped Raila while he was overseas was a former schoolmate of mine at both Onjiko and the University of Nairobi – Onyango Ogango – who currently resides in Norway but works as a consultant in Oman. Ogango informed me that while in France, he introduced an important investor to Raila, someone who was interested in setting up a major industrial production plant in Kenya. All the man was looking for was land and an assurance from the Ministry of Industrialisation that his investments wouldn't be interfered with by the state. Raila introduced Kosgey to the man and they all agreed that the investor (who Ogango advised me had flown to France in his own plane) would travel to Kenya shortly to formally meet with Kosgey and other ministry officials. The trip eventually happened in November 2009. Ogango called Raila and Kosgey in advance to agree on dates, time and locations of the meetings. Both Kosgey and Raila assured Ogango of their utmost cooperation and confirmed the meetings. Ogango also telephoned me that he was on his way to Nairobi.

Upon arrival in Nairobi, Ogango, the investor and his team booked into the Serena Hotel. The following morning – and as previously arranged – they turned up at Kosgey's Teleposta offices. Kosgey's secretary informed them that the minister was in the office but would be with them shortly. They made themselves comfortable, read the newspapers in the reception area and took tea. After waiting for one hour, Ogango placed a call to me asking if I could contact Kosgey and find out whether he knew they were waiting for him in his reception area.

I promptly called Kosgey, who confirmed that he was aware of the guests' presence. He undertook to invite them into the office shortly. I explained to Ogango that I was on my way to the KICC to attend a joint ODM/PNU Parliamentary Group meeting to be co-chaired by Raila and Kibaki. The meeting was scheduled for 10am. As soon as I sat down at the meeting, I saw Kosgey making his entrance. He made his way to the front. I immediately texted Ogango and advised him that Kosgey had just arrived at the KICC. Ogango was surprised. I requested him to rush to where we were so that I could reintroduce him to Kosgey at the end of the meeting. That's what Ogango did, arriving 20 minutes later, breathless.

Ogango told me that Kosgey must have left his office through a side door leading directly to the VIP lift, without even bothering to greet them. After the joint PG meeting ended, I quickly went over to Kosgey, with Ogango in tow, warmly greeted him and reminded him of the delegation from France and the meeting they had scheduled with him that morning.

"Oh, I'm off to the Intercon. Can you come there with the delegation?" Kosgey told Ogango, without any apology. As he entered his official limousine, three bodyguards tried to push away Ogango. Ogango and I stood there, embarrassed, but resolved to follow Kosgey to the Intercon. They had already wasted half a day. Ogango took off immediately so that he could collect his guests before proceeding to the Intercon. But within 30 minutes, I received another distressed call from Ogango. "Kosgey is not at the Intercon," he said. "Miguna, the man just lied to us."

I placed a telephone call to Raila and complained about Kosgey's irrational behaviour. "*Ja-Nyando*, I don't know what's wrong with Henry. I'll talk to him," Raila assured me.

On Friday of that week, I accompanied Raila to Eldoret for a few political functions. I intended to raise the issue with Raila during the trip. Ogango had been livid all week. He and the investor had already stayed three nights at the Serena. Their plan was to wait around for two more days before returning to Europe. The investor was flustered and confused. He couldn't believe this uncouth behaviour from *a government minister*. I told them to be patient and that I would try to intervene. Once in Eldoret, I briefed Raila on what had happened. "Henry will be here in a short while; I'll raise the issue with him," he said. That was the last I heard of this matter. As a consequence, Kenyans were denied a much-needed investment in the country that could have led to jobs being created. But as worrying, was the conclusion drawn that Kosgey must be a conman. Ogango and I suspected that Kosgey had been waiting for the investor to bribe him before he could facilitate the business transaction. Kosgey would later be charged with fraud over the irregular importation of used vehicles. The case is still in court in Kenya.

Another similar case involved James Orengo, ODM MP and Lands Minister, Soita Shitanda, PNU MP and Housing Minister, and I. While on a trip to Mombasa and Malindi with Raila in early 2010, I was introduced to a businessman called Hezron Awiti Bolo, the owner of the Habo Group of Companies. He was a highly motivated, hard working and successful entrepreneur. He was also a major Raila supporter and fundraiser. Awiti eventually introduced me to a Turkish businessman called Osman Erding Elsek, the director of Elsek & Elsek Group of Companies and Elsek & Elsek (K) Limited. The company had innovated the use of fibre, cement and steel in constructing affordable housing. This is a global company with considerable investment in many countries.

Elsek had set up a pilot project in Mombasa where he had put up model homes, which he took me to inspect. He was interested in putting up affordable housing for government key workers like policemen and teachers. Talking with Hezron and Elsek, we formed the idea that these houses could significantly alleviate the housing problems of urban centres like Nairobi, Mombasa, Kisumu, Nakuru and Eldoret. Elsek explained that his company's priority was to construct "low-cost houses which would suit middle and lower income earners, including slum dwellers". In a subsequent letter to the Ministry of Housing, he stated that: "Our project has already been test-proven, not only in our country of origin, but in Europe, USA, Canada and other Asian countries. Our specifications and quality have been Kenya Bureau of Standards-approved... Our future plan is to transfer the manufacturing plant and machinery to Kenya to facilitate easy production and make further cost reduction in terms of overall production which would give a further added advantage to the country in employment. Our current plea to the government is to support this project by looking at the best way to handle... duty and other taxes that would otherwise exaggerate the cost of this project. We also [wish] to express our interest to put up some housing units for your ministry at any appointed or designated site of which our company would take up the initiative to commence and complete the project...[sic]"

Elsek explained to us that a self-contained, ultra modern, one storey four-bed-roomed house would cost consumers about Sh1.5m. The difference in production cost was incredible. Kenyans would get very high quality housing at less than a fraction of the normal construction cost. If executed properly, such a scheme could help solve the slum problem once and for all. From a political strategist standpoint, I saw a golden opportunity for Raila and ODM to introduce something so revolutionary that it could do for us what Mau's forest conservation had promised but failed to do for an earlier generation.

Blown away by Elsek's demonstration and the quality of model houses, I promptly took Elsek to Orengo, who was equally impressed. Both Orengo and I took the man to Raila and we instantly triggered a process that was intended to facilitate Elsek & Elsek to start full production in Nairobi as soon as possible. Upon our return to Nairobi, I obtained an appointment with Housing Minister, Soita Shitanda, who promptly allocated time for Elsek to travel to Nairobi and make a presentation, which he did within days.

Within two weeks, Elsek & Elsek had submitted an application to Shitanda for a team of experts within the Ministry of Housing to travel to Mombasa and conduct a thorough evaluation of the company's capabilities. The report came back positive. Appropriate land on which to begin the construction began to be sought in the Mlolongo area.

Shitanda and Orengo showed genuine interest and cooperated fully, until something curious happened. Just before Shitanda was due to sign off on everything, Orengo asked me to invite Elsek to Nairobi so that we could have a three way meeting with Shitanda. All this time, I was only involved in order to help Elsek through the maze of government bureaucracy. Both Orengo's and Shitanda's offices are located at Ardhi House just across the street from the National Hospital Insurance Fund building where my office was. As soon as Elsek and I arrived that morning, we were immediately ushered into Orengo's office. That was normal. Orengo rarely kept me waiting. But this day was different. Usually, Orengo would be standing next to the door, relaxed, wearing a broad grin and with his hands outstretched. On this day, however, we found him rummaging through his desk, "trying to find the title deeds for the allocated land", which he was supposed to have handed over to Shitanda with a report, but which he was now claiming to have "misplaced". Elsek and I watched in astonishment as Orengo went through all the drawers, piles of documents and even telephoned someone to ask where the documents were. Sweat started forming on his face. The man was panicking. I thought he might have genuinely misplaced the items and suggested that maybe we should just proceed upstairs to Shitanda's office, have the discussion, and other "procedures" could happen later, a suggestion Orengo seemed relieved to hear.

Shitanda was cordial and receptive, but he firmly stated that nothing could happen until Orengo delivered the papers to him. There was an awkward scene as Elsek temporarily lost his cool and demanded to know what was going on. "Why did you make me travel all this way?" he fumed.

As we left Shitanda's office, Elsek told me straight to my face: "Miguna, he is lying. He didn't lose nothing [sic]. I think these people are corrupt." I looked at him, expressionless. Elsek drove off and I never saw him again. It was clear to both of us that Orengo hadn't lost or misplaced the title deeds; he had just refused to hand them over. Could he have been expecting something from Elsek? Well, I cannot be sure. But Orengo's behaviour left serious doubts in our minds about his intentions.

* * * * * * * * * * * * * *

Meanwhile, the Ruto problem wasn't going away. From the end of 2008, Ruto had become increasingly and openly critical of Raila and his style of leadership. He wasted no time in reminding the country that in his view, Raila was not just "a dictator; he was also an ungrateful betrayer". Eventually, Ruto wasn't just encouraging disaffection against Raila within the Orange party, he was now consorting with a hitherto ODM-allied party called the United Democratic Movement (UDM). Within months, Ruto and other MPs supportive of him were busy traversing the country promoting the UDM.

In early 2009, Mugambi Imanyara, a Nairobi lawyer and member of ODM's legal committee, General John Koech, the chairman of UDM and a staunch supporter of Raila, and I, had devised a number of strategies to neuter Ruto within both ODM and UDM. As Ruto announced that he would run for the presidency on a UDM ticket, we resolved to lock him out from both parties. Our first strategy was to ensure that Gen. Koech clung onto the UDM chairmanship in order to prevent Ruto from taking over the party. This he did through filing a petition with the Political Parties' Tribunal challenging Ruto's irregular "takeover of UDM". This forced Ruto to hire lawyers in order to fight the move to kick him out. And after petitions and counter petitions between Ruto and General Koech at both the Political Parties' Tribunal and the High Court, Ruto – in frustration – abandoned the UDM and formed his own party, the United Republican Party (URP) on which he now intends to run for the presidency. I subsequently persuaded Raila to fund Koech's litigation at the tribunal, which he did, through Orange House.

The second move was my idea. In view of the fact that Ruto had gone to the High Court to challenge the jurisdiction of the Tribunal, I knew that the tribunal might take a very long time before dispensing with the petition. In the meantime, I thought that ordinary members of UDM could file an urgent case before the High Court against the ODM rebels, Ruto, Isaac Ruto, Aden Duale and Joshua Kutuny, arguing that under the *Political Parties' Act*, these men could not belong to two competing parties, nor be promoting UDM's interests against those of the ODM when they had been elected and remained ODM MPs.

The legal action's aim was two-fold. I hoped it might force the MPs to resign from ODM, thus triggering by-elections in their constituencies – by-elections that they were unlikely to win, and that would be an expensive and time consuming distraction from their destabilisation of ODM. Or, the court could find that they had breached the *Political Parties' Act* and order the Speaker of the National Assembly to order their seats vacant. In either case, they would cease being a nuisance to ODM. When I explained my plan to the ODM strategic meeting called by the ODM deputy party leader and then Minister for Local Government, Musalia Mudavadi, the ODM Secretary General and Minister for Health Services Prof. Anyang' Nyong'o and Lands Minister James Orengo, they were very enthusiastic about it.

On or about March 2, 2011, ODM had finally resolved, through a joint national executive council and parliamentary group meeting at Orange House, to begin a process of expelling its members of parliament affiliated with the Eldoret North MP, William Ruto, who had had running battles with both its party leader, Raila Odinga, and the party itself. Although there were fifteen to twenty rebel MPs, ODM strategically resolved to target Ruto's underbelly first; it chose to go for what it considered 'soft targets' – MPs it perceived as weak in their constituencies and therefore weren't likely to win by-elections that were likely to be called after their expulsion. The *Political Parties Act* stipulated that MPs who had formed or joined another political party, or who were publicly supporting or advocating for the formation of another political party other than the one that sponsored them to parliament, were deemed to have resigned from their parties, and would be presumed to have forfeited the right to continue sitting in parliament under the sponsoring party. Fearing a potential backlash and euphoric sympathy for William Ruto and his acolytes if it targeted a large group of the rebel MPs, especially because the overwhelming majority of them represented constituencies in the vast Rift

Valley Province, ODM tactically picked Dujis MP Aden Duale and Chepalungu MP, Isaac Rutto.

But the Orange party hastily issued expulsion letters to Duale and Rutto without following the due process of law. In fact, it violated provisions of its own constitution, which required notices to be issued, disciplinary proceedings to be conducted and the affected MPs provided with fair and adequate opportunity to defend themselves before their expulsions. As well, the ODM overlooked or disregarded the requirement that only a national governing council's meeting had the mandate to expel. Consequently, the attempt to crack the whip turned into a legal quagmire, with threats and counter-threats, and the registrar of political parties disregarding ODM's expulsion letters. When I learnt of the decision, I advised against it, pointing out the constitutional imperatives. But I also questioned why the party had shied away from taking action against the chief mutineer – William Ruto. Why couldn't the party be courageous enough to take action against all mutineers, starting with their commander-in-chief?

After months of frustrating unending debates, dithering and recriminations, that decision was eventually reached on Tuesday, June 28, 2011. Almost one year before, the think tank had debated the pros and cons and unanimously agreed that action must be taken against the rebels. The problem had been the division within the political leadership of the party. Raila blew hot and cold. Anyang' and Orengo expressed their support for action but dithered; unsure of whether agitating for immediate action would be construed as contradicting Raila. But at two meetings at the United Kenya Club in Nairobi on June 28 and July 1, 2011, chaired by the deputy party leader, Musalia Mudavadi, and attended by about six ministers including Mudavadi, Nyong'o, Orengo and Dalmas and eight members of parliament including Ababu Namwamba and Alfred Sambu, I managed to rekindle the issue. It was unanimously agreed that subject to the Prime Minister's concurrence, we should initiate a legal process of getting rid of *all* the rebel MPs. Orengo was detailed to consult with Raila, who was vacationing abroad, and deliver his instructions.

Within two days, I got Raila's instructions through Orengo, to find a lawyer who could go after William Kipchirchir Samoei Ruto, Aden Bare Duale, Cherangany MP, Joshua Serem Kutuny, Belgut MP, Charles Cheruiyot Keter and Isaac Kiprono Rutto. There was consensus that Ruto, as the king-pin, had to be included this time. Duale, Kutuny, Keter and Rutto were the best foot-soldiers Ruto had; articulate and indefatigable. Except for Keter, they were also deemed to be 'weak on the ground,' hence the excitement to 'take them out,' politically. If ODM won the resultant by-elections, that would be a major boost to its dwindling fortunes, especially in the Rift Valley. However, we reasoned that if ODM lost some or even all of the seats – which was highly unlikely then – it wouldn't make any significant difference because 'they were gone anyway.' The by-elections would compel the party to reactivate its networks in the region. The ensuing recruitments, mobilizations, campaigns and jostling might just be what the party needed to rejuvenate. The contests would be morale boosters for the Orange troops. In other words, we believed that it was a win-win situation for ODM.

I acted with alacrity and tracked down Senior Counsel Paul Muite, whom Orengo and I believed would have been the best lawyer for such a high profile and potentially politically volcanic case. Muite advised me that he couldn't handle it because he had declared his candidature for the presidency in the forthcoming elections. But he arranged to meet me on Sunday, the following day at the Muthaiga Country Club. I relayed this development to Orengo and Nyong'o, who urged me to proceed. All I needed was Paul's guidance on the best lawyers around. And as expected, he immediately recommended Cecil Miller. I called Miller instantly and he gave me an appointment for the next day, Monday July 4 at 8.30am. I arrived thirty minutes before our scheduled meeting and waited. At Miller's office, I used my mobile telephone to connect him with Nyong'o, James Orengo and Janet Ong'era so that they could be in the loop. Moreover, since the party – as the client – was paying, it was only wise to make sure that Miller got instructions directly from the party. Miller promptly agreed to act for the party even though he mentioned, as an aside, that he had represented one of the affected MPs in a matrimonial case many years previously. I advised Miller to draw a retainer document setting out our understanding and his fees, which he did the same day. After a brief back and forth over the initial retainer deposit which Anyang' thought was too high, I was mandated to persuade Miller to discount a significant chunk, which he promptly did. Anyang' and Janet issued him with an ODM retainer cheque by Tuesday, July 5. And I breathed a sigh of relief.

Miller requested copies of the MPs' membership and party nomination documents, which Anyang' and Janet quickly placed at my disposal. I had these delivered to Miller's office on July 5, as well.

Although I had a complicated relationship with both Anyang' and Orengo (one characterised by my deep suspicions that while Orengo is more genuine than Anyang', they both tend to be intellectually dishonest and duplicitous on most political and ethical issues); they were still – by far – the most intellectually and ideologically progressive leaders within ODM. They also had solid liberation credentials. Whenever I wanted something radical initiated by the party, I always consulted them first. In fact, I consulted Orengo more often than any other ODM leader. Contradictions aside, to a large extent, I considered him both a role model, a comrade and intellectual soul mate. There were many issues that I trusted Orengo on not only because I thought he showed genuine interest and concern; but because he had, on a few occasions, stood firm when they came to the fore. Anyang', on the other hand, was very eloquent and persuasive when discussing issues with you one-on-one, but as soon as the matter was to be presented publicly or before Raila, he would invariably curl up and not defend the positions he would have taken just minutes before such meetings. Eventually, I didn't respect or trust him at all. Yet, as the ODM Secretary General, we couldn't do certain things without his buy-in, approval or involvement. It's akin to being between a rock and a crocodile.

As I was enjoying my summer holidays with my children before bringing them back to Kenya, Miller, Nyong'o, Orengo, On'gera and I corresponded and agreed on the contents of the application, which I also shared with Senior Counsel Paul Muite. By the time I returned to Kenya in mid-July 2011, the application had been polished and finalised. Nyong'o and Ong'era had also paid Miller his initial retainer. They had also signed his retainer letter. However, Nyong'o had substituted the three UDM members Gen. Koech had given us with ODM members known to him. I wasn't privy to the discussions that necessitated the change (as those discussions occurred in my absence), but I wasn't violently opposed to it. My only concern, which I shared with Orengo, Nyong'o and Ong'era, was the direct link that was now between the ODM and the application. I knew the media and public would see Raila and the Orange party hiding behind the litigants, which is actually what happened.

"Raila takes decisive action against Ruto and ODM rebels," screamed the media headlines the day following the filing of the applications. I gave an interview to the Nation Television (NTV) and published an article in *the Star* in which I explained that the five ODM rebels were between a rock and a hard place; that they couldn't file responding documents stating that they hadn't left ODM, for that would show cowardice and a clear indication that they weren't ready to take over UDM. If they did this, they would lose face and political credibility with their supporters. And if they filed anything admitting having decamped from ODM, then they had to resign and precipitate by-elections. Victory wasn't guaranteed in either Kutuny's or Isaac Ruto's or Aden Duale's constituencies. My calculation was that even if Rutto only lost in one or two (most probable ones were Kutuny's and Duale's constituencies), the only thing the media would scream about would be: "Ruto loses to Raila".

In my analysis, no matter how anyone sliced the issue, ODM would emerge on top. It would also show the country that Raila could be decisive and that he wasn't afraid of Ruto, two things that most Kenyans were no longer sure of. But, as ordinary members of ODM savoured the positive twist of events, I began to hear grumblings from quarters close to Raila. Ong'era called to inform me that the Gem MP and ODM Chief Whip, Jakoyo Midiwo (who also happens to be Raila's first cousin) had called her fuming; threatening whoever was behind the court case. She told me that Raila had also called shouting. According to Ong'era, Raila kept yelling, "Who the hell is Miguna Miguna? Who the hell is Miguna Miguna? I've not seen him in six months!"

As Raila was yelling about me, Ong'era could hear people speaking in the background, making her believe that Raila might have been acting for the gallery. Ong'era, Orengo and Nyong'o were worried and scared. They had not seen or heard Raila that angry in a very long time. All three called me, trying to find out why Raila was 'mad with us' while the ODM rank and file was excited about the move.

I spoke with my friend and ODM National Executive Committee member, Rosa Buyu and she confirmed what Ong'era had told me. Rosa had been contacted by nominated ODM MP Rachel Shebbesh, who had relayed Raila's feelings about me to Rosa.

That evening Orengo, Prof. Oyugi and I met up at Java Gigiri, and later at my Runda home. The idea was to develop a strategy to counter that of Jakoyo et al, who weren't privy to the strategy on the legal action. It was now Saturday. Raila had called an emergency National Executive Committee and Parliamentary Group meeting at Orange House the following day – Sunday. Raila, Jakoyo, Oburu, Kisumu Town West Member of Parliament Olago Aluoch and a few opportunistic Luo MPs were all frothing at the mouth about me. Suddenly, fault had been squarely placed on my shoulders. Ong'era had told me that Raila had also threatened to have her fired that Sunday over the issue. Raila and co were desperate for a fall guy. And the most visible sacrificial lamb was me. Conveniently for them, I hadn't been invited to the NEC/PG meeting. But that was OK. I wouldn't have wanted the meeting to be turned into a contest between Raila/Jakoyo on the one hand and I on the other.

As Orengo, Oyugi and I spoke, a brilliant idea struck me. I said "What if you Jim go to the meeting tomorrow and pose a few questions, viz: (a) Two ordinary members of the ODM party – citizens of the Republic of Kenya – who have a constitutional right to go to court and seek any remedy allowed by law, are reported to have filed a case in court challenging Ruto and other ODM rebel

MPs to state which party they belong to, and if they state it is UDM, to resign from ODM so that they can face by-elections; why is ODM overly concerned about that? The two individuals have stated in both their pleadings and to the press that they took the action to protect ODM – their party – from being destroyed from within by Ruto and his fellow rebels; why would ODM leadership complain of that? Does ODM or its leaders have power over individual members of the party to the extent that they can dictate to them who they could or could not sue? By calling a meeting at Orange House to discuss a case taken against the five ODM rebels by ordinary members of the party, is the ODM leadership admitting that it was behind the court case? If not, on what basis would it have the power to order the litigants to withdraw the matter? Isn't ODM admitting that it actually initiated the action? Does ODM want Ruto and his rebel MPs to continue undermining the party from within? What does the party fear? Finally, what would be the political or legal consequences of a resolution by ODM that the court case would be withdrawn; how would such a resolution compel the two litigants to withdraw the case?"

The intention was to expose the backpedalling by Raila, Jakoyo and Oburu as being completely bereft of logic, intellectual foundation and political content. My view was that all the activity seemed more motivated to "cut Miguna down to size" rather than for the well-being of the party. The court case was a major proactive decision that had met with overwhelming support from the rank and file membership of the party. Nearly everyone I had discussed this matter with felt that ODM had dithered over the issue for too long. And lo and behold, when the meeting ended on Sunday, it voted – with a 70 per cent majority – that the court case was a brilliant political move that the party must support rather than condemn. When Kipkelion MP Magerer Lang'at, Orengo and Ong'era called me to relay the information, we couldn't suppress our jubilation.

But I also knew that Raila, Jakoyo and Raila's elder brother, Oburu (who is also Bondo MP and an assistant minister for finance) wouldn't take the humiliation lying down. They must have been incensed that the meeting backed what they had openly credited me with, yet I hadn't even attended the meeting. In hindsight, this could be one of the real 'reasons' (or more appropriately an excuse) why Raila acted in such a barbaric manner when he purported to suspend me less than one month later.

On another occasion, Orengo, Nyong'o, Ong'wen, think tank members Nabii Nabwera, Martin Oloo, Salim Lone and I met at the Tribe Hotel in the Village Market to discuss the Ikolomani by-election. We were concerned about the confusion emanating from stories circulating that Raila, Fred Gumo, Wycliffe

Oparanya, Oburu Oginga, Jakoyo Midiwo and other 'prominent' ODM politicians were secretly supporting Bony Khalwale, the New Ford Kenya candidate, and had promised him that ODM wouldn't field a candidate against him. Apparently, these promises and money were being given to Khalwale without having been discussed within the party. The story was that these promises were being made out of fear that ODM would lose the by-elections, and that if the party supported Khalwale, his victory wouldn't be deemed a loss for the Orange party. But others saw more sinister motives.

The deputy ODM leader and the Deputy Prime Minister, Musalia Mudavadi, hadn't been consulted. Mudavadi's confidantes viewed the promises that were being made as direct attacks on him. A further problem was that the view that Khalwale was unbeatable wasn't scientific. Nobody had conducted an independent poll in Ikolomani. Moreover, parties don't participate in by-elections or elections purely on the basis that they have to win. Consequently, I argued that ODM shouldn't back Khalwale and that if it had to do that, care should be taken to seriously consider Mudavadi's views and interests. My view was that if the party proceeded without consulting Mudavadi, that would send a negative signal that Raila and the Orange party were undermining the deputy party leader. Weakening Mudavadi in Western Province would ultimately weaken ODM and its chances in the 2012 elections.

Luckily, the meeting agreed, and minutes after it ended I received a telephone call from Mudavadi's private secretary, Kibisu Kabatesi, thanking me for 'standing up for the DPM'. That proved to me not just that my arguments were correct, but also that our team was an open sieve. Martin Oloo was the sieve.

Raila called an extraordinary meeting of the strategy team, the ODM Parliamentary Group from Western Province. The meeting backed the same decision we had made. ODM subsequently fielded a candidate, albeit belatedly. But credible rumours continued swirling that Raila and others continued to send money to Dr Boni Khalwale.

I also found myself in opposition to Raila over his passionate campaign to have judges placed under 'performance contracts' just like civil servants. In one brief after another, I strongly argued against this, pointing out the significant differences between judges and other public servants. Firstly, I pointed out that the judiciary is supposed to be independent – both theoretically and practically – from other arms of government. Independence entails that the judiciary must have budgetary, administrative and institutional independence. The only acceptable exception to that independence is the involvement of the judicial service commission (JSC), which has a mandate to hire, promote, remunerate and discipline members of the judiciary. (But of course the judiciary is represented in the JSC.)

Secondly, I argued that the attempt to bring the judges under executive control through performance contracts would dilute, interfere with and compromise judicial independence. Essentially, it would place the executive on top of the judiciary. Yet, it is the judiciary and parliament that are institutionally authorised to supervise the executive.

And thirdly, I argued that determining the effectiveness and efficiency of the judiciary cannot be based on the quantity of cases processed or heard; nor even on the number of negative or positive judgments. In any case, in an adversarial system like Kenya where a legal dispute routinely involves more than one party, there would always be a winner and a loser. Justice isn't determined by the length, quality or quantity of a few judgments; justice is determined by neutrality, objectivity, competence and fairness of the judicial officer both during the process and final judgment, and the fairness of the ultimate outcome. It's only after a long period of time that objective assessment can determine whether or not justice would have been dispensed and seen to have been dispensed by the judiciary; not through an analysis of one case. Even more fundamentally, I advised Raila that as a person who had himself suffered under a politically and financially compromised judiciary – and as someone who was projecting himself as an 'agent of change' – it was imperative that he defended the independence of the judiciary as a way of promoting the rule of law and the culture of constitutionalism. Unfortunately, Raila refused to listen to reason or logic and kept persistently demanding that judges must sign performance contracting documents.

These and other incidents demonstrated that Raila wasn't decisive and reliable, but wobbly, cowardly, confused, opportunistic and deceitful. Above all, he wasn't loyal to his friends and comrades. He was also duplicitous. For three years, Raila couldn't decide whether to take Ruto on, push him out or accommodate him within the Orange party. That's a dangerous way for a leader to behave. As Tony Blair states in his autobiography, *A Journey*, "It's good to think before you act, but the thinking has to be of finite duration and the action must follow...when leading a country...failure to act is an action with consequence. Inaction is a decision to maintain the status quo. Maintenance of the status quo has its own result, and usually its own dynamic."

Whether it was Raila's flip-flops during the most immediate period after the 2007 presidential election crisis when he called and then cancelled more than a dozen mass action events thereby demoralising his supporters; or it was his yoyo (yes-no-yes-no) decisions during the Accord and formation of the Grand

Coalition Government negotiations; or it was with respect to the ICC process; or the House Business Committee and Leader of Government Business stand-off; or regarding Kibaki's unilateral and irregular extensions of tenure for Maj-Gen Gichangi as head of the National Security Intelligence Service or Prof Njuguna Ndung'u as Central Bank Governor; or the appointment of Githu Muigai as Attorney General; the appointment of Keriako Tobiko as DPP; or his embarrassing utterances over the continued illegal occupation of Migingo Island by the Ugandan Defence Forces; or of many, many other important decisions affecting the country, the point I wish to underline here is that Raila has demonstrated, time and time again, that *he is an ardent and staunch defender of the status quo*.

I tell these stories to explain the circumstances that led me to lose trust and hope in Raila's leadership abilities. I also tell them to disclose the warning signs that stared me in the face all those years but which, because of loyalty and commitment, I decided to ignore, at my peril. These and other incidents, show a pattern of behaviour that, viewed together and over a period of time, depict a person who not only lacks administrative, managerial and leadership skills capable of steering the country to national cohesion, progress and prosperity; he also lacks ideological clarity, intellectual rigour and commitment to a progressive agenda for Kenya. In other words, Raila might have excelled as a rabble rouser and opposition leader; however, once he was placed in a position of responsibility where performance was easier to audit, his record triggered warning signs that could not be ignored.

CHAPTER TWELVE

SKIRMISHES

After the signing of the Accord on February 28, 2008, I had strategically decided to stop publishing articles in my name criticising Kibaki, PNU or our political opponents. I had also stopped giving comments to TV, radio and electronic media. I was conscious that making critical or even constructive remarks about our coalition partners might be misinterpreted and could damage the goodwill that we needed to cultivate between the former warring parties. There was a general feeling that the grand coalition experiment deserved our support and we were determined to make best efforts to see it succeed. It was a painful and difficult decision to make. Many of my colleagues and friends had reasoned that I would be more useful and effective "working the system from within". For that one year of calculated silence, I conducted research, wrote briefs and prepared speeches and statements for Raila quietly.

However, that modus operandi soon changed. We realised that the more Raila and ODM tried to be civil, the more Kibaki and PNU became aggressive and disrespectful of him. Whereas ODM had completely discarded its claim to electoral victory and approached coalition management in good faith, in the spirit of give and take; PNU became increasingly insolent and repeatedly and consistently disregarded the power sharing arrangement. They largely acted unilaterally. Kibaki made decisions as if he had a popular mandate from the people and therefore could govern alone. Despite the provisions of the National Accord that required that he consult the Prime Minister prior to making appointments in government, Kibaki continued to ignore his coalition partner. Day after day, ODM was bombarded with negative attacks by PNU politicians, self-styled strategists and media commentators either sympathetic to it or on its payroll.

With Raila's encouragement, I went on the offensive, spending virtually every single day of my waking life fighting off attempts by Kibaki and the PNU high command to reduce the Prime Minister from being an equal partner to a flower girl. I was also fighting for the full and prompt implementation of the Accord and its four agenda items. The struggle was multi-pronged: at the ODM party level; at the Grand Coalition level; and publicly – through the media.

For instance, on April 26, 2009, I published an article in both the *Daily Nation* and *the Star* titled "The truth about power sharing and the place of the National Accord in the Constitution". It was a rebuttal to an article that had been published by Prof. Kivutha Kibwana, my committee counterpart as President Kibaki's advisor on constitutional affairs. In his article, Prof. Kibwana had asserted, as fact, that I was "the architect of the jurisprudence seeking a redefinition of the constitution" that was causing conflict within the Grand Coalition. He argued that the National Accord hadn't changed or diluted the imperial powers of the President and that Kibaki, as President, had the ultimate authority to make all decisions and senior appointments in government; that the Prime Minister's role was limited to 'coordinating ministers under the authority of the President'. In response, I exposed Kivutha's article as merely "a clever attempt to draw me into a political debate I would rather not be party to and deflect attention from the real issues". I pointed out that "no one is calling for the 'redefinition of the Constitution'. We are, however, insisting on a correct, reasonable and fair interpretation of both the Constitution of Kenya, as amended, and as it is since the entrenchment into it of the National Accord, as well as the latter's full implementation".

It had been the best part of a year since I had published a commentary in the newspapers or made my views known about the National Accord or the way the grand coalition was being managed. In my view, Prof. Kibwana was being mischievous by publicly blaming me for the wrangles within the coalition. He knew or ought to have known that the origins of virtually all the disputes in government were emanating from his side of the coalition. Having been both a university professor and cabinet minister – and now as a presidential advisor – Prof. Kibwana must also have known of the limited influence a person like me would have had on a political party and group of very senior politicians. Yes, I did hold sway then, especially with Raila and the think tank; but I wasn't really "the architect" of the political differences between the two coalition partners.

I reminded Kibwana that ODM's insistence that the National Accord be entrenched in the Constitution "was informed by President Kibaki's trashing of the Memorandum of Understanding (MoU) he signed with Raila Odinga and the Liberal Democratic Party (LDP) in 2002"; and that "only a fool would fail to be informed by past betrayals". I pointed out further that ODM was neither redefining nor attempting to renegotiate the National Accord. "In the preamble of the National Accord", I argued, "both Kibaki and Raila openly acknowledged that given the current situation, neither side can realistically govern the country without the other; and that there must be real power sharing to move the country forward and begin the healing and reconciliation process".

I underlined the commitments both principals made in the Accord that "The composition of the coalition government will at all times take into account the principle of portfolio balance and will reflect their relative parliamentary strength. The entrenchment of the National Accord into the Constitution gave it constitutional authority and mandate with respect to the management of the Grand Coalition Government".

Because Kivutha had posited that Kibaki retained the sole prerogative to make all executive appointments in government, I referred him to the wording of the Accord, which captured both principals' undertaking: "As partners in a coalition government, we commit ourselves to work together in good faith as true partners, through constant consultations and willingness to compromise." The two principals recognised that "constant consultations and willingness to compromise" are not just necessary but essential for a coalition government to function smoothly. I also reminded Kivutha that the term "government" was defined in the Constitution. The definition cohered with both common sense and the dictionary meaning. Government, I argued, meant the act or manner of governing; and the system by which a state or community is governed. In Kenya, that system is enshrined in the National Accord.

I stated that "It is crystal clear that he [Kibaki] intends to dominate the legislature as well. In fact, Kibaki deems himself to be the 'government'. But such a parochial and sectarian view of government cannot be sustained in law, logic or common sense. Neither ODM nor Raila Odinga is obligated to accept such self-serving interpretations. I am astounded to read that both PNU and President Kibaki have resolved to act as if Raila and ODM are not their coalition partners and that they will run the Grand Coalition Government whimsically without constant consultations or willingness to compromise. The Grand Coalition Government is not about the 1963 Constitution!"

I asked: "But more pertinently, why is the President refusing to consult the Prime Minister on all matters relating to the running of the Grand Coalition Government, when he committed himself to do so in the National Accord? Why did he write to the Speaker of the National Assembly, Kenneth Marende, stating that he is not willing to consult the Prime Minister on the issue of Leader of Government

Business, Chair of the House Business Committee (HBC) and the HBC's composition? Is it because he still operates under the 1963 Constitution rather than the current Constitution, which has the National Accord as an integral part of it?"

Kivutha and other Accord deniers knew that the Prime Minister's position was a creature of the National Accord and the Constitution. They also knew that the PM was not a presidential appointee, as they had mischievously claimed. The Prime Minister assumed his role and constitutional mandate from the fact that he was leader of the largest party in parliament. The formality of appointment, I argued, was superfluous. That was why the President couldn't fire him. Only the people of Kenya through parliament may remove either the President or the Prime Minister. More importantly, I reminded Kivutha that neither President Kibaki nor Prime Minister Odinga has the mandate of the people of Kenya to govern the country alone!

In conclusion, I urged senior advisors to the President to give him cogent advice. "The best route for streamlining the operations of the Grand Coalition Government and for resolving issues between the grand coalition partners is still negotiations, constant consultations and compromise through the Permanent Committee on the Management of the Grand Coalition Government. Without an amicable resolution to the issues afflicting the Grand Coalition Government, no reforms can be implemented. Both grand coalition partners must fully implement, adhere to and respect the National Accord. It is futile for some senior presidential advisors to deny the obvious: the National Accord exists, and it is part and parcel of our laws and constitutional dispensation. Anybody who says or does otherwise is only interested in chaos".

That response sent Kibwana into a brief hibernation. However, it didn't stop all the mischief. Almost immediately, the brouhaha over "the pecking order in government" erupted, with senior members of the PNU arguing that "the vice-President, as the President's principal assistant, ranked higher than the Prime Minister". They were demanding that not only should the Vice-President be paid more than the PM, he should also have precedence and be accorded 'higher' protocol treatment at state and government functions than the Prime Minister. Op-eds were published in various newspapers making this argument. A few times, there were even physical altercations between the presidential security and those of the Prime Minister over protocol matters.

On May 29, 2009, I published an article in *the Star*, correcting the impression that the Vice-President was senior to the PM. I argued that the issue of Vice-President Kalonzo's place in the coalition hiearchy was immaterial as he wasn't a coalition partner. Kalonzo's party, ODM-K, had joined the PNU Alliance prior to the signing of the Accord. Although one of its members, Mitula Kilonzo, participated in the Serena negotiations as a member of Kibaki's PNU Alliance, he wasn't representing Kalonzo or ODM-K. In addition, Kalonzo's name isn't on the Accord. He was appointed by President Kibaki, who could fire him at will. Moreover, he wasn't a co-principal; only Kibaki and Raila were. Accordingly, I concluded, Kibaki and Raila were first on the pecking order; followed by Kalonzo.

It was imperative that I reminded the country, firmly, that Kibaki and Raila were equal, pursuant to the Accord, which had been entrenched in the Constitution. I wasn't doing so because I loved Raila. Without a doubt, I did then love him, too. But I was doing so because I loved and cared for my country, its laws and the Constitution more than anything else.

As of this time, I hadn't yet started a regular column in any newspaper. All the articles I published in 2009 – except for an article on Moi's controversial ownership of the Kiptagich tea factory and two where I explained pertinent issues on the constitutional review process – were rebuttals to commentaries by either Kibaki's senior staff and PNU operatives; or the ones against ODM rebels like William Ruto, which Raila had specifically authorised. Raila was happy and satisfied with my pieces. Soon, he would request me to take out a column following a savage attack on him by a seasoned political commentator, Mutahi Ngunyi, in a column in the *Sunday Nation* of December 6, 2009. Raila, Prof. Nyong'o and Ida Odinga called me, pleading with me to respond to him, which I did, submitting a reply the same day.

Raila wanted me to have a national newspaper column so that I could not just react to other (perceived) offensive publications, but also use the forum to explain his (Raila's) and ODM's stand on national and international issues. In fact, he would instruct me to write articles explaining various issues or defending him, such as one I wrote about the role of a parliamentary whip; one in defence of Musalia Mudavadi with respect to the cemetery scandal and one in which I compared William Ruto to Joseph Goebbels. He also encouraged me to write two rights of reply when the *Daily Nation* had published critical op-eds on him.

In the case of the article I published in *the Star* on March 30, 2010 – *Is Bill Ruto the Kenyan Joseph Goebbels?* – on the Eldoret North MP, William Ruto, it was Raila who suggested that the best comparison was with Goebbels; I had wanted to say Machiavelli but Raila stated that comparing Ruto to Machiavelli would have been a compliment. (The nonsensical complaints later, by envious buffoons who claimed that I shouldn't have been writing, don't deserve any response.) In fact, on the same day the full page article was published in *the Star* Gitobu Imanyara, the veteran human rights lawyer and MP for Imenti Central, who was my co-author, called me and jubilantly advised that he was being treated like a rock star in a drinking joint he had gone to; that people (his friends and even strangers) were buying alcohol for him by the truckload. He was ecstatic. "Thanks to you Miguna, I'm being treated like a star," he had told me before hanging up. I therefore knew that I was making a positive contribution that many Kenyans of goodwill appreciated. Although Raila rarely called to say anything; he never complained. I knew Raila. I knew that it wasn't in his character to congratulate anyone, no matter how well one might have done. Over the years, I had come to accept that as just being him.

In fact, around August 2009, the former US Ambassador to Kenya, Michael Ranneberger met me at the Prime Minister's office, tightly grabbed my hand and said: "Here is the man who has been flying under the radar!" Ranneberger and many other foreign ambassadors would subsequently invite me for breakfasts, lunches, dinners or visit me in my office to discuss politics and other national initiatives. The Agenda Four reforms were the hottest thing then. Kofi Annan, foreign ambassadors, the press, the civil society and a few progressive politicians were piling pressure on the government to accelerate the unveiling of the reforms. The disgraced electoral commission, the judiciary, the national police and security agencies needed to be reformed. The civil service still operated in an opaque and insular manner. Major financial scandals such as the irregular and purported sale of the Grand Regency hotel to a shadowy group claiming to be an investment arm of the Libyan government under Gadaffi had emerged. The public had reportedly lost billions of shillings in that scam. The Triton, Maize and other scandals had hit the headlines.

Foreign ambassadors, a section of the civil society and the press frequently sought my opinion or input on these issues and sought to know which government ministries, institutions, projects or players they should support as a way of helping the reform process. They feared that some of the much talked about government initiatives could just be clever conduits for looting public funds. There was mutual respect between them and I. In other words, even though I hadn't taken out a newspaper column at the time, my quiet interventions were getting noticed.

However, almost weekly, during the regular meetings between the think tank and Raila, the latter consistently complained that I should have been publishing critical articles on Kibaki and the PNU Alliance. He openly encouraged me to start writing again. He wondered, wryly, why I was prolific in Canada but not in Kenya. "Have you suddenly encountered a writer's block?" he asked, sternly, with my colleagues looking on sympathetically. Eventually, I decided to resume writing, following a full and frank discussion with Raila over the utility of my articles. Raila made it clear that he not only loved my style; he also agreed wholeheartedly with virtually all my thoughts and opinions. After all, he often assigned me the role of responding to media questions and written interviews for him and would authorise me to forward the same for publication without correcting my answers. I thought everything was kosher; that Raila and the ODM team had confidence in my abilities and were in sync with my thoughts. I had no reason to think otherwise.

Throughout 2009, Raila was embroiled in controversy concerning his pivotal role in the reclamation and restoration of the Mau Forest Water Tower. Although this was one of the very few positive bipartisan government initiatives, Kibaki and his PNU contingent had taken a strategic low profile. Even though two crucial implementing line ministries – environment and forestry – were headed by PNU cabinet ministers, it was Raila, now acting as the coordinator and supervisor of the ministers, who was visibly in charge. Peasant encroachers into the forest had been evicted and were now stranded along local highways and roads. Almost daily, we were seeing pictures on television of women, children, the infirm, the sick and the elderly cowering under trees or temporary shelter, sometimes being rained on. Yet, the wealthy oligarchs like former President Moi who had 'encroached' tens of thousands of hectares of forest land continued to farm and extract profits from areas that everyone recognised as part of the water tower that needed to be restored. After trying to influence action against these rich and influential environment degraders to no avail, I published a stinging article in *the Star* on December 29, 2009 titled "The Genius and Madness of President Moi". I wanted the country to be repulsed by the hypocrisies, the ironies and the double standards of the power barons.

"For a former bare-feet goat herder and son of poor peasants to have risen from rags to become the President of Kenya in a short period of 15 years, Daniel Teroitich arap Moi was either a genius or a beneficiary of the most intricate historical conspiracy of all times," I started. (In order to give him a knock-off punch, I needed to build him up first.) Further in, I got to my main subject: " Moi and his coterie focused on public land as a theatre for control and a source of personal wealth. Loyal politicians, senior army officers, civil servants, diplomats and political fixers were rewarded with public land. In the process, forests, public toilets, roads – name it – were invaded, occupied and converted into personal property by the politically well-connected.

"That is the origin of the Kiptagich tea estate. Kiptagich is a massive tea estate with a modern factory located within the Mau forest water tower. It covers more than 5,000 acres. Although Moi has recently claimed that the land on which Kiptagich stands is 'trust land' that was 'given' to him by the 'Maasai community', the truth is that the tea estate is located on public land. Trust land is public land. Even though Moi has alleged that the land was transferred to him 'legally' he has failed to disclose by which legal entity, for how much and for what purpose. 'Maasai community' is not an entity known to law. As such, it could neither own nor transfer the land in question.

"According to Moi, because '75% of the tea processed at Kiptagich belongs to the public and only 25%' to him; Kiptagich 'belongs to the public'. Why then is Moi protesting when the public wants to repossess its land? Ironically, Moi claims that the 'title deed' for Kiptagich estate belongs to him; title he believes cannot be challenged, however fraudulent its acquisition. Public records, however, disclose that Moi never paid a dime for the land; never invested a penny to clear it; never spent anything to buy seedlings; and never purchased the factory equipment. Records also show that Kiptagich is not a state corporation. It is not listed in the Nairobi Stock Exchange. In other words, although the land, tea plantation and infrastructural developments belong to the public, Moi has been the primary beneficiary of the estate.

"It means that Moi has been extracting hundreds of millions of profits annually from a public asset without guilt. It is said that Kiptagich owes Kenyans billions of shillings in unpaid taxes, workers paid from public coffers and Ministry of Works tractors working in the farm without payment to the government.

"On the environmental front, Moi had this to say: 'I did not destroy trees to pave way for tea growing. It was originally a bamboo forest.' To Moi, the wanton destruction of a bamboo forest in order to plant tea on a water tower is justified!

"Understandably, Kiptagich is very close to Moi's heart. He loves the farm and factory. They are his cash cow, so to speak. Any inkling that Kiptagich might be repossessed by the people of Kenya makes Moi not just nervous but violently confrontational. Yet no one – not even Moi – has claimed that he purchased the land or that it isn't in the Mau forest complex. Moi and his supporters have not indicated that the proceeds from the tea estate are being donated to charity or used in the public interest. If Moi bought the land, he has not stated from whom and for how much. However, if he simply took the forest land when he was President, he must still explain to us why he did so. Kenyans are also interested to know why he deserves compensation of Sh760m for public land he has been unlawfully profiting from.

"After Moi has produced credible answers on the Kiptagich tea estate, we should also ask him a follow-up question on how he acquired Kabarak University. Later, we will seek explanations from the intractable genius about the construction and use of Nyayo House torture chambers."

The publication of this article was followed by an eerie lull, then a huge storm broke. After one week of silence, the Kanu orphans found their voices and responded with fury. And they did so in torrents. There were letters to the editor, commentaries and even threats – most posted on blogs, but there was one, under a fake name, in an article in *The Standard*, Moi's own newspaper. It was around then that a chorus started up, calling for my deportation under the pretext that I was a Canadian and therefore couldn't hold a senior government position. These timings were odd. Nobody had raised these objections when I had been offered the job. Many of them had been equally quiet before I began the struggle to defend the Accord and the Constitution. Suspiciously, the attacks reached a crescendo at a crucial stage during the constitutional review process when I, more or less, singlehandedly repulsed PNU repeated attempts to scuttle the process. My detractors knew that these allegations about me not being Kenyan were false, but they persisted, encouraged by ODM renegades, including, I now suspect, the duplicitous Raila Odinga.

Looking back, and following meticulous analysis of those events, I have concluded that along the way, Raila must have joined the PNU conspiracy against me. I should have seen it coming. But why do I say Raila was involved? The day the news broke (with every TV station, radio and blogosphere heating up with "Miguna is a Canadian; deport him" chant), I called Raila and sought his input as to what my response should be. He told me to leave things alone as "we would deal with it politically"; he didn't say when or how they were going to "deal with it politically". I expected that it would be soon since the media onslaught was getting worrisome. My pictures were plastered everywhere. Full page and coloured advertisements were published in all the national dailies – the *Daily Nation, The Standard, the Star*, and *the People* – by the self-styled PNU spokesman, Moses Kuria, whom many believed was working at the behest of both Uhuru Kenyatta and State House – demanding that I should be deported from Kenya. They also argued that as a Canadian, I shouldn't hold senior public office. I gave a crisp, standard answer to all the media outlets: "I am a Kenyan by birth. I have never renounced my citizenship. Citizenship isn't determined on the basis of passports. Many people, including Nelson Mandela, Jaramogi Oginga Odinga, Mwai Kibaki, Raila Odinga, Robert Mugabe, Koigi Wamwere and Ngugi wa Thiong'o have travelled on other countries' passports; that didn't change their citizenship. My case isn't different." Then I left it there, anxious about Raila's "political response".

I was driving back to Nairobi from Migori with Professor Edward Akong'o Oyugi and his lovely wife, Scola, when I had spoken to Raila. As we drove, with all radio and TV stations screaming "foreigner" at my name, both Oyugi and I found it odd that Raila had reacted with unusual coldness at the scandalous propaganda. I arrived home and was greeted by my worried children, who thought that we would be departing for Canada that very minute. That night, I couldn't watch both the seven and nine o'clock news. I went to bed at 9pm, earlier than usual. I was still expecting Raila's call. I needed him to assure me that he and the rest of ODM weren't going to just sit there, twiddling their fingers; that they were going 'to do something' about this offensive, outrageous and most vile invasion of and savage attack on my integrity.

I waited and waited but nothing came from the ODM. Then, after two weeks, Otieno Kajwang', the ODM Minister for Immigration and Registration of Persons, released a tepid statement, asserting that I was indeed a Kenyan citizen. It came too late. The lynch mob had already feasted on my corpse. Peter Kagwanja, who repeatedly claimed to be the 'Chief Strategist' for both PNU and office of the President, would later tell me that, "PNU was only acting at the behest of ODM; how else do you think we knew you had a Canadian passport?" he would ask, fixing his gaze on Caroli. So, when an opportunity presented itself in the case of the *Republic* v *Mahamud Muhumed Sirat*, I pressed the pedal so hard, it hit the bottom, with an article titled "A Kenyan born citizen does not lose citizenship by acquiring a foreign passport".

Desperation knows no length. And the brouhaha dissipated as soon as it had arisen. But the long knives weren't sheathed; they were just concealed under the clothes of the malicious renegades. It had given me an opportunity to see who my true enemies were. And they weren't PNU; they were right with me in ODM.

Barely three days after Otieno Kajwang's tepid statement on January 13, 2010, 12 ODM MPs from Nyanza called a press conference – not to respond to the odious PNU attacks on me – to condemn me for "criticising Moi," whom they praised for "leaving a legacy all Kenyans should respect". Their press conference was coming about one month after my article on Moi's murky acquisition of the Kiptagich tea farm and factory, which had actually appeared in *the Star* in December of the previous year. It was a pathetic display of intellectual bankruptcy from an area previously known for producing some of the best brains and the most fearless fighters for the liberation of the country; people like Jaramogi Oginga Odinga and Tom Mboya. Dalmas Otieno, Otieno Kajwang' and Nicholus Gumbo were among the 12 who issued this despicable handwritten statement. They had had more than adequate time and opportunity to rebut, but hadn't, no doubt because it is difficult to refute something that is blatantly true: truth vaccinates impunity.

Unlike these buffoons, I had stood against Moi's despotic and repressive regime throughout, had never joined Kanu and never sang, "*nyayo*". Indeed I have never idolised a fellow mortal. Yes, I supported and defended Raila valliantly, but it was because I genuinely believed he was an agent of change, a progressive political catalyst. I was wrong. Admitting it requires humility and strength; not arrogance, which my detractors love to accuse me of having whenever they run out of ideas. I have no apologies to make for my consistency, honesty, fearlessness and vision.

I was told by credible sources that Caroli Omondi and Dennis Onyango from the OPM coordinated the logistics of the press conference. I was also advised that Orengo, Nyong'o and Oburu deliberately witheld their signatures for strategic and tactical reasons, so that I could continue to believe that they were my friends. Clearly Raila had authorised the statement – 12 Luo Nyanza MPs, including two senior cabinet ministers wouldn't have issued the statement (no matter how poorly written) against the advisor of the party leader and the Prime Minister of the Republic of Kenya if they hadn't been briefed. I know that having worked with and around Raila for more than four years.

Shortly after the cowardly statement had been published and widely broadcasted, Karachuonyo MP, James Rege, Nyatike MP, Edick Anyanga (Omuk Lela), Nyando MP, Frederick Outa, Mbita MP and Minister for Immigration, Otieno Kajwang', and Alego-Usonga MP, Edwin Yinda called me and pretended to apologise. I refused to speak to Outa and Omuk Lela, because the press had quoted them being quite malicious. Based on my discussions with the others, I found Kajwang', Rege and Yinda somehow genuine and contrite. In fact, Yinda denied signing the statement and insisted that someone had placed his name there without his permission. Rege blamed Gumbo for misleading him. I'm not sure what Gumbo might have done to force him to sign. Gumbo himself stated that he was "proud to have initiated and drafted the statement". I found that unfortunate and told him so.

Indeed I felt betrayed by Gumbo. We had come a long way together. I had taken care of him at the NYS, after he had suffered a severe tetanus attack. We had remained friends over the years, but more recently I had felt that something was amiss in his dealings with me. Shortly after the formation of the Grand Coalition Government, he had sent me a harsh text message, accusing me of having refused to "recommend" him for a cabinet post. I had explained to him then that I hadn't been involved in making appointments at all; but that I had heard Raila say he was in a tight spot with Jakoyo and Oburu breathing down his neck, and that after naming Jakoyo Chief Whip, Oburu an Assistant Minister for Finance and Orengo minister, Raila (correctly) thought that Siaya District had had its fill. My view was that Raila shouldn't have given Oburu and Jakoyo anything, particularly because they were his relatives. However, I thought, once he had done so, it would have been an act of recklessness to proceeed and appoint

Gumbo either as an assistant minister or minister. Other areas and regions also deserved slots. I was being candid with my friend. Unfortunately, he blamed me for his "misfortune". I guess there is little one can do in such situations. I moved on and never troubled Gumbo.

By orchestrating this statement Raila exposed himself as a closeted Moi/Kanu orphan, desperately seeking to please his former boss. On reflection, I shouldn't have been surprised at all. After all, three long years after Raila initiated the Mau forest restoration exercise, oligarchs with large swathes of farms on the water tower, including Moi, were still sitting pretty. There were even rumours that Raila had appointed Moi's son Gideon, the chairman of a team tasked with resettling the evicted peasants from the Mau Forest. Audaciously, Moi would later issue a press statement "defending the right of Gideon, as a Kenyan, to be appointed to any position he is qualified for."

In other words, Raila excitedly and quickly evicted peasants and homeless encroachers of the forest, yet he became completely useless when he reached the stage of removing the real land grabbers, the main destroyers of massive portions of the water tower. On careful thought, Raila seemed to have resolved to use the Mau evictions for petty political gain. He was desperate to win back a portion of the Kalenjin after William Ruto had decamped from ODM with a huge chunk of their support. And since I had published an article questioning how Moi had acquired Kiptagich, I had to be humilated so as to show Moi that Raila hadn't condoned or been party to my article. It was Machiavelli 101! But I wasn't deterred. There was important work to be done for Kenyans on the constitutional review, and I wasn't going to roll over.

The onslaught was in full swing from all sides. The Committee of Experts had started serious work on the constitutional review. It had produced a summary of the process, identified contentious issues and given the country a "way forward" or roadmap in terms of process and timelines. I was the person representing the Prime Minister and ODM during the process, including at the consultation workshops organised by the CoE – and they were numerous. I had already attended a number of sessions when I received an urgent telephone call from Ekuru Aukot, the secretary and chief executive officer of the CoE. Ekuru said he had some urgent business to discuss with me and could I please rush over and meet him. I was there within one hour. We met at a restaurant in the Hurlingam area at about 11am.

He handed over a copy of a letter from my counterpart, President Kibaki's advisor on constitutional review, Prof. Kibwana to the CoE, in which he was accusing them of not conducting their consultations with the public as required. Prof. Kibwana was essentially laying the groundwork for a PNU challenge to the

CoE's work. Our suspicion was that the letter was a precursor to some sinister move to sabotage and scatter the constitutional review process in the same manner that Kibaki's inner circle had done to the defunct Constitution of Kenya Review Process in 2005. After reviewing Kibwana's letter, which was eight pages long, quickly I got the impression of what Ekuru was asking me to do.

"My brother, we need a strong response to this. A few of us have discussed this as a committee and we all agree that you are the one to do this." Ekuru explained.

"Of course my brother. I'll do my best. This is mischievous," I assured him. And before the end of that day, the reply to Kibwana had been delivered to him and to the media.

The struggle for a popular, people-driven Constitution had to proceed. The gist of my comprehensive 17-point-by-point rejoinder to Professor Kivutha Kibwana (contained at the end of the book as an annexure) was that there was a need for caution and restraint in matters dealing with the new constitutional dispensation and that the Committee of Experts required encouragement and support; not vilification, lectures and threats. Kenyans had waited patiently for far too long for a people-focused Constitution to permit any diversionary tactics aimed at undermining the quick completion of the process that would allow ratification of the same Constitution by August 2010. I also challenged Kibwana's assertion that the CoE hadn't fully consulted with all stakeholders. In addition, I accused Kibwana of attempting to create more bottlenecks to the process by inventing more contentious issues than Kenyans had stated and the CoE had published.

The letter was copied to the Prime Minister and all the stakeholders and it finally succeeded in sealing Kibwana's mouth, permanently. Occasionally, he would raise his head and I would knock it down gently, or firmly, depending on when, how or on what issue the head had popped up. One good lesson during that period was that one could never rely on Kibwana's word, no matter how well-intentioned or in what tone such word seemed to have been given.

It wasn't just Kivutha Kibwana and others who were trying to muddy the coalition waters. The "embodiment of the culture of impunity in Kenya", that ever-smiling snake, Amos Wako, the then Attorney General, was adding his own legal clay and intellectual alluvial soil, and I quickly sent out a right jab to Wako in February 2010 that lit up the blogosphere and re-energised ODM. Essentially, Wako continued to argue that the National Accord hadn't changed the executive power arrangement at the top of Kenya's political system. As far as Wako was concerned, "The President is the absolute and sole appointing authority". To Wako, Raila was nothing but a joy-rider in government. After this article went live, hundreds of readers sent me congratulatory emails from all over the world.

I knew that the country was keenly listening. That gave me the motivation to continue.

Once I had effectively blocked the mischief makers from defiling the sacrosant Accord (for me it was sancrosant in spirit more than in letter) and intellectually strengthened the Prime Minister's place within the coalition, my enemies started scheming about creating conditions that could destroy the coalition and precipitate either an early election or the removal of Raila from the Prime Minister's position.

Many of my comrades in the struggle will agree that the retrograde are tenacious in the most perplexing ways, that their strength is often in the patience they exhibit. They know that no matter how intense, controversial or heated something is, when given time, it cools down. Time, our reactionary friends know, tames everything. The most spiritual amongst them would say that "time heals everything". They fight, then hunker down and wait, until they have worn you out.

So, when the PNU 'strategists' started the false debate on a presidential versus parliamentary system, as they tried to project Kenya's old constitution as 'presidential', I knew that the country was in need of some free tutorial lessons. More than thrice in March 2010, I challenged utterances by politicians indicating that the system of government under the repealed constitution was a 'presidential system'. There had been false claims on what the majority of Kenyans purportedly wanted. Contrary to a myth being propagated by those who had exploited the existing schizophrenic system, I pointed out that it was *not* a presidential system. Although it had parliamentary roots, due to numerous mutilations under both Jomo Kenyatta and Daniel Moi, the repealed constitution had mutated into a fully-blown mongrel with no singular genetic trait. Because it was neither parliamentary nor presidential, the essential ingredients that distinguished one system from the other were missing; even the benefits of either system could not accrue to the people of Kenya.

Many people believed, wrongly, that a system was presidential when the head of state and government bore the title 'President'. This wasn't an argument one would want to have with people who had more than basic education. Unfortunately, it was a debate that had been forced on us and which we could only ignore at great risk to the future of this country. I gave the example of South Africa where the head of state and government is called a President even though the system – from top to bottom – is a federal parliamentary system. South African Presidents assume office when their political parties win majority seats in parliament. In South Africa, no one votes *directly* for the President and members of parliament. Parliamentary seats are allocated to parties premised on a formula based on the overall performance of each party in the general elections. Yet, we have never heard complaints that the mandate the South African Presidents derive from winning majority seats in the elections is somehow inferior to the so-called "directly" elected persons.

In Kenya, I argued, the basic system of government was actually parliamentary. Members of parliament, including presidential candidates, were required by law, to contest parliamentary seats in demarcated constituencies. At independence, the head of state was the Crown/Queen whose representative, the Governor General, acted in her absence. The head of government was a Prime Minister who assumed that position by virtue of being the leader of a political party with majority seats in parliament. Both the heads of state and government derived their mandates and legitimacy differently. The method of assuming office didn't and couldn't determine the functions, responsibilities and privileges of each office.

When Kenyatta repeatedly mutilated the independence constitution in order to merge the functions of "state" and those of "government" in one office, which he chose to call the "presidency" – I argued – he created a mongrel. The mongrel he created was at the executive level with no corresponding and/or accompanying structures, institutions and laws that would ensure accountability, transparency and checks throughout the system. Sadly, Kenyatta did not stop the demolition of the structural foundations of a parliamentary system at the executive level; he went out of his way to weaken and eventually emasculate both the legislature and the judiciary. As a result, the checks and balances that were necessary in both a presidential and parliamentary system were destroyed. Needless to say, I also reminded the country that Kenyatta never won an election throughout his life. Kanu won the independence elections when Kenyatta was in jail. He became Prime Minister straight from jail because Jaramogi Oginga Odinga turned down the offer to form a government after Kanu had won the elections.

Without an independent and effective legislature and judiciary, and with the Senate discarded, Kenyatta became an emperor, king, president and prime minister all rolled up in one. Conveniently, impeachment laws were never considered. The constitution was amended making the President beyond criminal and civil liability. Although a tiny window was left for parliamentary censure, the threshold of 65 per cent in a *de facto* one party system was impossible to garner. Thus, the emperor became a tin god. He could not be questioned, challenged, censured or removed. Anybody who dared criticise the "god" invariably got himself or herself arrested, detained, tortured, exiled or killed. Opposition parties were destroyed through being banned or through force, coercion, threats and intimidation.

With opposition weakened, compromised or destroyed, the African Big Men, the tyrants, reigned supreme. Whether it was Mubutu Sese Seko's Zaire, Kamuzu Banda's Malawi, Sani Abacha's Nigeria or Idi Amin's Uganda, the verdict was the same: there was an all powerful Imperial President at the top. Accountability to the people was zero. Transparency was a forgotten word. But even with perpetual barbarism and repression, the Big Men of Africa and the world could never forestall the movement for change, democracy and freedom. Forced compliance could not protect the Big Men from the popular movements that eventually removed them. The barrel of the gun could not protect them forever.

As I continued to articulate these issues in my weekly *Star* column, Kenyans from all walks of life responded positively. ODM supporters, in particular, loved my column and many used to call, text or simply walk over to my office to say "thank you". I am aware that many also communicated their gratitude directly to the Prime Minister. Thrice, Caroli told me that a newspaper vendor in his Karen neighbourhood used to stop him almost daily and demand to be brought to me. According to Caroli, the man, who was from Central Province, would always say: "Please take me to Miguna Miguna. I want to hold his hands…that's a real man I can go to war with!"

But I suspect that the more my column and articles became popular, the more Raila and a few of his relatives like his cousin and ODM Chief Whip, Jakoyo Midiwo, his elder brother, Bondo MP and Assistant Minister for Finance, Oburu Oginga, and his wife Ida, became jealous and resentful. To them, I was becoming too influential. In the process, they believed that the public was and would continue to give me credit for any or all the successes Raila or ODM made. That, they might have believed, placed me too close to the succession equation within Luo Nyanza. Raila was now approaching 70. These members of the kitchen cabinet must have panicked that should something happen to Raila, I would present as a serious contender for the Torch. Of course, I didn't know all these speculations and schemes and conspiracies were going on. I just charged full steam ahead with the national agenda. But as I would soon learn, Raila, his family and the kitchen cabinet had confused their parochial agendas with the national agenda. Put another way, they were using the rhetoric of "national agenda" as a ruse to hide their selfish motives.

For more than three decades now, I've tried to use words carefully and deliberately – and intend to continue using them – in the liberating tradition of Frantz Fanon, Frederick Douglass, Malcolm X, Václav Havel, Steve Biko, Vladimir Lenin and Karl Marx. As Václav Havel stated in his acceptance speech of the Peace Prize of the German Booksellers Association on July 25, 1989, "…words are a mysterious, ambiguous, ambivalent, and perfidious phenomenon. They can be rays of light in a realm of darkness…They can equally be lethal arrows. Worst of all, at times they can be one or the other. They can even be both at once!"

BOOK SIX

CIRCLING WOLVES

CHAPTER THIRTEEN

BETRAYALS

When it came to forming the grand coalition government, the most progressive, competent, experienced, morally-upright and hardworking members of the ODM strategy team – in particular – were left out completely. Yet if one took a close look at most of the individuals that were initially appointed into cabinet and senior civil service positions by Raila, one found names that deserved to reverberate with infamy, because of their close associations with corruption, human rights abuses and organised crime. Here were people that one wouldn't have expected to hold any public office, let alone in a political formation led by former liberation soldiers that had campaigned under the banner of 'Progressive Change'.

Right at the outset, Raila named Musalia Mudavadi (Deputy Party Leader, Deputy Prime Minister and Minister for Local Government; now only Deputy Prime Minister after resigning as both ODM Deputy Leader and Minister for Local Government); Henry Kosgey (ODM Chairman and Minister for industrialisation; now suspended over corruption allegations); William Ruto (Deputy Party Leader and Minister for Agriculture, then Higher Education; now fired over disagreements with Raila and facing prosecution by the International Criminal Court); Dalmas Otieno (Minister for Public Service); William ole Ntimama (minister for National Heritage and Culture); Fred Gumo (Minister for Regional Development); Dr Sally Koskei (Minister for Higher Education; now Minister for Agriculture); Joseph Nyagah (Minister for Co-operative Development); and Kipkalya Kones (Minister for Roads; now deceased). Caroli, Isahakia, Orege, Ng'eno would also be appointed to prominent civil service positions. All of these were veterans of the one-party dictatorships of Kenyatta and/or Moi. Although a few of them (mainly Sally and Nyagah) had tried to shed off the Kanu colours; the overwhelming majority of them were still loyal and tied to the old Kanu ways. They were deliberately chosen over vibrant, young and progressive members of the Orange party; people with certified qualifications, proven track records and liberation and integrity credentials.

It was as if Raila, his family and his 'inner circle' were made insecure by the presence of these progressives, perhaps worried that they might challenge the status quo, especially when these former liberation soldiers started consorting with known looters and organised criminals. Others speculated that 'Raila has been captured by the Old Corruption Networks'. I really don't know what happened or why he behaved the way he did. What I know, however, is that Prof. Edward Oyugi, Oduor Ong'wen, Mutakha Kangu, John Otieno, Salim Lone, Hussein Mohammed and Sarah Elderkin were the most obvious omissions. Yes, Salim "worked" at the Prime Minister's office for about one year after Raila had been sworn in as Prime Minister; but what many people don't know is that Salim basically worked pro bono; he told me himself that he never got a contract, and he never got paid for all the heavy lifting he did. And of course, Sarah continued to work as a consultant for Raila, primarily ghost-writing his yet-to-be-published memoirs, on the sidelines.

For a very brief period of time – about three months – Mutakha was given a contract to shepherd the devolution taskforce. All the work Mutakha and I did during the constitutional review process was done pro bono.

Raila repeatedly lied to many staunch ODM members about employment. When one looks across the aisle to the PNU side, Kibaki has given jobs to virtually everyone who campaigned for him. He at least understands that loyalty buys loyalty.

There are personal, as well as ideological reasons, that people will devote their energies to helping others get to power. At its most rudimentary, they expect a "thank you", and if possible, an opportunity to be considered for employment. I toiled in the trenches for Raila from 2006 to March 2009 absolutely pro bono. There are those who are aware that I spent tens of millions of my own money in order to fight for change; firstly for Kenyans including myself, but secondly for Raila. These are undeniable facts.

Shortly after the national accord was enacted into law and Raila became the Prime Minister designate, the strategy team disbanded, with misty eyes. We left Pentagon House without ceremony. Despite several reminders and urging from Prof. Oyugi, Raila refused to send personalised "thank you" cards or letters to the team.

None of the Pentagon, secretariat or new honchos at Raila's swanky office bothered even to invite the team members for tea, lunch or dinner as a way of expressing their appreciation for the team's efforts, time and energy. After about six months of waiting, one of the members, Hanningtone Gaya, organised a nice dinner for everyone at the Holiday Inn in Westlands. Raila didn't show up. He didn't even acknowledge his invitation to the event.

Many members became discontented, disgruntled and hostile towards Raila to the extent that, soon thereafter, following Raila's public falling-out with William Ruto, Dr Tom Namwamba, who had been brought to the strategy team by Raila himself, left and joined Ruto. He would later be appointed the executive director of the "Red Card Centre", which was set up by Ruto and allies, who were opposed to, and campaigned against, the 2010 draft constitution, before its enactment by popular will on August 4.

Only one member of the Raila's 2007 presidential strategy team is now with him. This is due to the fact that Raila abandoned his former inner circle as soon as he tasted power. He would do the same to former Butere MP, Martin Joseph Shikuku, whom he had promised appointment as the first chairman of the Truth, Justice and Reconciliation Commission.

Once Raila had no use for someone, he discarded and forgot about them.

On January 29, 2008 Mugabe Were, an ODM MP for Embakasi, was brutally murdered in front of his Nairobi home. Mugabe had been a very brave young man. At the very beginning of mass action, it had been Mugabe, Nyagah and I who had led a handful of youths past the Department of Defence headquarters just as the party big wigs chickened out, turned back and called off the march to Uhuru Park. Even before Mugabe's body had been laid to rest, ODM lost another MP, David Kimutai, who represented Ainamoi. Kimutai was shot to death by a policeman named Andrew Moache on January 31. To date, their killers haven't been punished. In Mugabe's case, the trial hasn't even started – almost five years later. These were huge loses for ODM. They also significantly reduced ODM's majority in Parliament. Raila quickly forgot about both MPs. He never pressed hard for the police to investigate, apprehend and prosecute the killers. That was the least he could have done. These fallen soldiers were useful to him during his quest for the presidency. But once dead, he had no use for them.

In Mugabe's case, there was a woman at the centre of the assassination; to date, nobody knows what happened to her. In the second brutal daylight murder, there were more than a dozen witnesses who saw the culprit pull the trigger that killed both Kimutai and his companion who was cut down struggling to get away from the scene of grisly carnage. Raila's behaviour regarding these murders was consistent with the way he had forgotten his alleged comrades in the 1982 attempted coup; the youth that fought running battles for him when trying to remove Michael Wamalwa Kijana from the leadership of Ford Kenya; and the thousands of youth who mysteriously disappeared, or were maimed, or jailed, or summarily executed during the "No Raila, No Peace" mass action following the mismanaged elections on 2007. Raila has made a tradition of climbing over others bodies in his scramble to the top.

There were betrayals closer to home too. Before his father Jaramogi died, he had a dedicated personal assistant called Dimba Jakobuya who nursed, cleaned, fed and washed Jaramogi until his demise. Raila then inherited Dimba, only to conveniently discard him like a piece of used toilet paper once he had joined government as a minister. He has done this to many people across Kenya: The Paul Muites, Gitobu Imanyaras, Martin Shikukus, Mwandawiro Mghanghas, Tony Gachokas, Rateng' Oginga Ogegos, Dick Ogolas, Herbert Ojwangs, Mugambi Imanyaras, Reuben Ndolos, Crispin Odhiambo Mbais and Mutakha Kangus.

And he has betrayed the whole country. Five years since Raila became Prime Minister, he hasn't done anything – not even make meek demands – to have many of the culprits of post-election violence face justice; or to have the hundreds of thousands of victims of the post-election violence (and police brutality) compensated, or resettled. On the contrary, he has hired some of the people implicated in the commission of crimes against humanity to his office. Hassan Noor – Provincial Commissioner of the Rift Valley, where thousands of Luos, Luhyas and Kalenjins were brutalised, killed, maimed and displaced in Nakuru, Naivasha, Eldoret and Kericho – became the coordinator of the Mau Water Tower restoration. Abdul Mwasera – Provincial Commissioner for Western Province when Luhyas and Luos were humiliated and mown down primarily in Kakamega – became Raila's Director of Administration.

Shamefully, when Raila turned against me, he dredged out so-called complaints from Administration Commandant Mbugua purportedly claiming that one of my Administration Police bodyguards had asked to be reassigned. Of course there is no doubt in my mind that Mbugua only did that (if at all) because I had consistently published articles demanding for him to be called to account for his transgressions during the post-election violence. Mbugua's forces are credited with the unrivalled distinction of committing the most and worst atrocities during PEV – that's according to the CIPEV findings! It's shameful! Needless to say, the so-called allegations were never disclosed to me before the suspension. Nor have I been presented with any particulars.

* * * * * * * * * * * * * *

Raila's treatment of fellow Luos within ODM has also been disgraceful. John Otieno, a brilliant young journalist, busted his behind during the 2007 presidential elections, and for close to one year, worked at the OPM; again largely pro bono. When he sought a contract or placement on the government payroll, Raila told him – to his face – that he couldn't be hired because he was a Luo. Being a Luo suddenly seemed to have become a crime for Raila. It had not been a crime when battalions of young, talented and hardworking Luos had been campaigning and raising funds for his election; nor when thousands of young Luos (and many from other communities) had bared their chests for police, GSU and AP bullets; nor when unarmed and innocent Luo civilians were shouting "No Raila, No Peace," and facing the security forces for months on-end, forcing Kibaki to the negotiating table and making Raila Prime Minister; nor when tens of thousands of Luos had been maimed, raped, gravely injured and displaced. But once Raila was in office, being a Luo, unless you were a relative of Raila's, did seem to be a hurdle to advancement.

Ironically, when it came to his siblings, family or relatives, Raila conveniently forgot that they were Luos; hence the formal employment of Oburu (assistant minister, elder brother), Akinyi Wenwa (diplomatic post, sister), Beryl Achieng' (board chair, sister), Ruth Adhiambo (personal assistant/MD Spectre, sister), Rosemary Akeyo (personal assistant, daughter), Fidel (personal assistant, son) and Raila Junior (personal assistant, son), Jakoyo Midiwo (chief whip, cousin), Elkanah Odembo (ambassador to the US, Jakoyo's brother in law), Carey Orege (permanent secretary, cousin), Joe Ager (Kenya Power, cousin), Paul Gondi (chairman, geothermal authority, cousin), James Ogundo (CDF board, cousin) and many, many others. These people are earning lucratively, courtesy of Raila's current position. Yet he has had the audacity to tell Luos not to seek or even think of government employment.

Why the double standards? Don't Luos – like other Kenyan communities – have the right to seek and be considered for public and state jobs? What is the most basic need of a human being; isn't it oxygen, food, water, clothing and shelter? How do Luos access these things if they are automatically excluded or disadvantaged on the basis of their ethnicity and affiliation to Raila? Of what good is Raila to Luos anyway?

The list of those Raila has betrayed is long. But the stories of Raila's treatment to Herbert Ojwang' and Hussein Mohammed deserve to be told here. When

Raila had visited me in Toronto in 2006, I had asked him about his relations with Ojwang', who had for many years been one of Raila's closest associates, but who had by then been exiled from Raila's inner court. Raila, you may recall, had told me a story concerning some campaign funds that Ojwang' had failed to deliver from a South Korean businessman.

Five years after Raila had made this serious claim against Herbert in Toronto, I had the opportunity to diligently inquire further into the matter. I obtained credible and reliable information from a number of independent sources, including from Ojwang' himself, that sharply contradicted Raila's version of events. Firstly, I learnt that the individual Raila had sent to a Mr Lee Jang-Soon, the then owner of *Unichem Mnt Company limited* of Seoul, South Korea for campaign contribution, was one Amondi Okul (the nephew of Ed Okul). Mr Lee was purportedly a shrewd international businessman who had earlier sought Raila's assistance with respect to securing lucrative contracts for water treatment and provision of water meters for the Kisumu Municipal Council. Raila had then apparently introduced Lee to the then Mayor of Kisumu, Shabir Shakeel. My information is that Herbert Ojwang's only involvement with Lee was that as Raila's then personal assistant, he was the one who scheduled and facilitated the appointments between the two men, on the one hand, and between Lee and Shakeel in 2001, on the other. In other words, Raila was less than candid with me on the issue of his fallout with Herbert Ojwang'.

Apparently, Lee had invested heavily in Raila, with the genuine but mistaken belief that Raila would win the 2002 presidential elections. My sources informed me that it was Okul – and not Herbert Ojwang' – who could have withheld Lee's funds, precipitating the eventual 'fallout' between Ojwang' and Raila. Lee himself later declared bankruptcy due to the colossal sums he had used to bankroll Raila, but which he couldn't recoup due to the fact that Raila never became President after the 2002 presidential elections.

Raila had originally hired Ojwang' – a long-time KANU operative – in 2000, for the purpose of soliciting funds (both irregularly and regularly) from Asian, Arab and foreign businessmen. (Indeed, for a considerable amount of time, even former President Daniel arap Moi used Ojwang' to funnel illicit funds to members of the Kenya opposition, including Raila and his other colleagues in Ford-Kenya.) In fact, with the benefit of hindsight, it is now crystal clear to me that Caroli Omondi, who tripled up as Raila's private secretary, 'chief of staff' and dealmaker, simply replaced Herbert. It is my contention that unknown to many Raila supporters, friends and compatriots, Raila had long discarded his fake 'revolutionary' attire and adorned Moi's kleptomaniac ones.

It was actually Herbert who used one of his business contacts in Tanganyika, Mr Ali Ahmed Said – the chairman of *Tanganyika Investment and Oil Transport Company Limited* and a wealthy oil magnate – to link up Raila with a South African business tycoon, Antònio (Tony) Teixeira. Teixeria was the chairman of *Petroplus Africa*, a multimillion dollar company with interests in Africa, Europe and North America. He also owned *Energem*, an oil, diamond and gold trading company. In 2006, Teixeira acquired the controlling interests in *A1 Grand Prix Series*. Unfortunately for him – I later learnt – Teixeira's heavy financial investment in Raila (he also gambled on him becoming either the President of Kenya in December 2002 or a major player in the subsequent government) largely contributed to the premature liquidation of the *A1 Grand Prix Series* in 2009.

It was Texeira who gave Raila his distinctive black helicopter, its pilot and a team of mechanics for the entire 2002 general election period. Teixeira was obviously buying influence through which he expected to gain financially. For his part, Raila was deeply involved in a serious conflict of interest. As Minister for Energy, he shouldn't have been a business partner of someone trying to invest not just in the country, but also with the Ministry of Energy. Unfortunately for Mr Teixeira, this dubious arrangement only benefited Raila and his family. It ultimately precipitated Raila's buyout of all Teixeira's 90% interest in the Odinga family business flagship, *Spectre International.*

As soon as Raila became Moi's Minister for Energy, Ojwang' quickly fixed a meeting between him, Teixeira, Bruce Holmes, one of *Petroplus Africa's* directors and Mr Vaughan McTaggart, the then manager of international trade and finance at the ABSA Bank in Nairobi. The initial meeting took place at Raila's ministry of energy offices at Nyayo House. During that meeting, Teixeira indicated that he was interested in buying Kenya's oil refinery in Mombasa. Raila instructed Herbert to travel with Teixeira and his team to Mombasa within a few days so that they could discuss their proposals with the managing director of the refinery. Eventually, that deal fell apart, partly because Moi's relationship with Raila had deteriorated and the latter decamped from Kanu before it could be concluded.

But Raila was particularly keen on having Teixeira inject the much needed capital into his purchase of the Kisumu Molasses Plant (later renamed *Spectre International*). To pursue that interest, the meeting proceeded the following day, at one of Raila's favourite restaurants, the Tamarind, next to the Central Bank of Kenya. By then, Raila had summoned his brother Oburu Oginga, his wife Ida, and Israel Agina who was, until recently, the family's longstanding business manager. It was during that lunch where the idea of purchasing the then stalled Kisumu Molasses Plant was made concrete. My sources tell me that it was actually

Ojwang who came up with the name "Spectre International". And since this was supposed to be a joint-venture between Teixeira, Raila and Ojwang, the latter's son then residing in London, UK, was proposed as both Raila's and Ojwang's nominee or proxy in the deal. Neither Raila's nor Ojwang's name could appear on any legal documents since both were then government employees – one being a cabinet minister and the other his assistant.

Teixeira agreed to contribute 90% of the total purchase price of the Molasses Plant. Raila and his family were supposed to come up with the remaining 30%. But there was a problem. Raila and his family stated that they couldn't come up with the money – roughly about SH90m. Thereafter, Raila came up with the innovative idea of having the "local population of Kisumo where the Plant was located buy shares of the Plant".

Raila appointed the late Joab Omino and Odeny Ngure, former Rarieda Member of Parliament, as the principal person in charge of collecting "contributions" from the local people. Conservative estimates indicate that Omino and Ngure "collected" Sh72m from ordinary Luos in Nyanza. This money was apparently deposited into the Kenya Commercial Bank branch in Kisumu. Raila and his family are said to have contributed not more than Sh20m towards the acquisition. In other words, Raila and his family should have held less than one third of the total value of the plant. However, as soon as the transaction was concluded, Raila, being a senior minister and Secretary General of the ruling party Kanu, unilaterally converted the public asset into an Odinga private enterprise and renamed the plant Spectre International. Ojwang was never compensated for his role. As usual, Raila's expression of gratitude was a kick in the ribs. But even more egregiously, members of the public who had depleted their savings (with some taking bank loans) to "purchase shares" in the Plant to the tune of Sh72m have not received their share certificates, dividends or refunds for their "contributions". In-between, Teixeira also sent Raila and Ojwang on an all-expenses-paid-tour of Houston, Texas, in order to familiarise themselves with the oil business. Raila was also given $40,000 pocket money.

Soon thereafter, Raila also expressed an interest in meeting high-ranking officials of the African National Congress (ANC). A meeting was soon organised for Raila and the ANC bigwigs by Teixeira in Johannesburg. Teixeira paid for first-class air tickets for Raila, Ojwang and Rateng' Ogego. Another Kenyan then working in the technology company in South Africa, James Rege, also accompanied them to this meeting though he paid for his ticket. Raila and his team stayed at the Hilton Hotel in Santon, Johannesburg – courtesy of Teixeira. Both the political and business meetings were very successful, and Raila returned to Kenya a happy man. As a souvenir, Teixeira had purchased 12 top-notch suits, shirts and matching ties for Raila. I understand that Raila didn't buy even pick up a pair of socks for Rateng' and Ojwang. Upon return to Kenya from Johannesburg, Raila decided that Ojwang's son couldn't act as a nominee or proxy in Spectre International. Instead, he brought back his younger sister, Ruth Adhiambo, from London and made her his nominee. When Ojwang' asserted his right to participate in the deal, he was summarily fired and replaced by Dave Arunga.

In 2009, Teixeira and many of his companies were facing problems in the global financial meltdown. His A1 Grand Prix investment in Italy went burst and was liquidated. His investment in Kenya had produced little in returns. Raila hadn't become President in either 2002 or 2007. The influence Teixeira had intended to buy with the vast investment in the Spectre International had proved a miscalculation. Raila saw an opportunity not to be missed: he bought out all of Teixeira's shares (through *Petroplus Africa Group*) in Spectre International, transforming the company into an Odinga Crown Jewel! I understand the relationship between Raila and Teixeira was extinguished by that sweet deal. So not only had Raila's relationship with Lee ended badly; the one between Raila and Teixeira ended the same way.

"Raila said he couldn't work and do business with Herbert," my source lamented, shaking his head in sadness. "That's the way Raila is; use and dump. He is very ungrateful!" Herbert did, however, continue to introduce Raila to other business magnates from China and other places. For instance, I was with Raila and Musalia Mudavadi in Beijing, China, in October 2010 when Ojwang' took executives of the China WuYi Company to see Raila at his hotel, where the construction of highways and roads in Kenya was discussed. Truth be told, a considerable amount of Raila's initial wealth is directly traceable to "business contacts" Ojwang' brought to Raila.

It's my observation that Raila loves money and power more than he loves anything else. In my assessment, he has never been interested in democratic governance for this country. He might have been (fleetingly) sometime back. But that was then. He has used his positions of influence and power to get rich. Regrettably, many of his followers and supporters have never clearly understood that.

Needless to say, I have heard that Ojwang' remains relatively 'close' to the Raila family. He continued to attend social events and consort with them in various businesses. Perhaps it's because he is fairly wealthy and continues to have vast business interests, many of which were solidified during his tenure in Raila's office. In Kenya, the process of wealth accumulation and retention is shrouded in muck. As a long-time Kanu operative, Ojwang' understands that 'if you acquired wealth mysteriously, you can also lose all of it mysteriously,' hence his unfathomable one-way 'relationship' with Raila.

But had Ojwang' openly disclosed the 'reasons' behind the cessation of his working relationship with Raila; it might have helped Kenyans in their quest for truth, justice, transparency and accountability; it could have enhanced good governance. The citizens of Kenya deserve to know the moral turpitude of their leaders or those aspiring for public office.

This brings me to the frustratingly sad story of Hussein Mohammed. Hussein is a dashing young Kenyan; articulate, brilliant, charismatic, hardworking and successful. Born in the slums of Nairobi's tough eastlands, Hussein has never let being raised in a tough environment hold him back. In his early 20s he founded his own marketing, telecommunications and information technology business.

But Hussein is also a progressive young Kenyan. So in 2007, his presidential candidate of choice was Raila Amolo Odinga; a man many believed embodied progressive politics in Kenya. Unlike most Kenyans, Hussein is tribeless. He could be Arab or of mixed race. He looks and speaks like Barack Obama. Perhaps his only affiliation on which he could legitimately claim a political platform is being a muslim. But that's tenuous since almost all Kenyans are religious.

In Kenya, that has its drawbacks. It means Hussein does not have immediate access to a racial conglomeration with whom he shares genetic traits, language, traditions and customs. His mother-tongue is Kiswahili. His second language is English.

In 2007, Hussein – alone – raised more than two million US dollars for the Raila Odinga presidential campaign kitty. That's approximately Sh164m. In addition, he raised and spent about one million US dollars trying to secure an ODM nomination certificate for the Kasarani constituency in Nairobi. Those are tidy sums by any reckoning. It is not easy to raise that kind of money in Kenya. But even more significantly, Hussein was not raising this money for himself, or for a relative.

In late April 2012 – weeks before this book was published – Hussein told me that he had put everything he had into the Raila campaign because of his strong commitment to progressive changes in Kenya. He yearned for a new people-focused constitution; a constitution that would bring accountability, transparency and wider democracy. Yes, a constitution that would empower the people in all respects, especially in governance, resource allocation and use, and in entrenching the rule of law and the culture of constitutionalism.Although Hussein didn't expect anything in return; he wouldn't have minded a word of appreciation from Odinga. But what was Hussein's recompense after all the hours he had put in and all those millions he had raised?

Well, just before the ODM parliamentary nominations in November 2007, Raila 'prevailed' upon him to make way for Rachel Shebbesh.This was not because Shebbesh was more popular than Hussein in Kasarani. Far from it. It seems more likely that this was because Shebbesh was Raila's 'squeeze.' Raila promised Hussein a nominated MP slot which he never got.

But there was one minor detail Raila hadn't ironed out in Karasani. Raila's wife, Ida, considered Shebbesh her arch-enemy and miraculously managed to 'prevail' upon the ODM secretariat to hand over the Karasani nomination certificate to Shebbesh's rival, Elizabeth Ongoro (now MP and assistant minister for the Ministry of Nairobi Metrpolitan).

Shebbesh ended up with less than 1,000 votes in the shambolic ODM nominations in Kasarani, but in spite of that Raila still nominated her to parliament. Unlike Hussein, Shebbesh hadn't raised any funds for Raila's or ODM's campaigns in 2007. She is not more educated, articulate, committed or loyal than Hussein. She is a woman, but more deserving women such as Rosa Buyu (who obtained more than 17,000 votes in her constituency), were not nominated.

After the post-election violence and the formation of the grand coalition government that made Raila Prime Minister, Hussein continued to volunteer for Raila and the ODM. Away from politics, he also raised funds for the cash-strapped national soccer team, the Harambee Stars and Raila's favourite football team, Gor Mahia.

On March 31, 2010 Hussein, who also runs a sports promotion outfit in Nairobi, Extreme Sports, hosted the "Extreme Sports Super 8 Soccer Ceremony, 7th Edition." This is an awards ceremony for a soccer tournament between teams from Nairobi's eight constituencies that Hussein has been organising for the past seven years of so. In 2010, he invited Raila as the guest of honour to the glitzy event held at the the Kenyatta International Conference, attended by more than 3,000. At the event, he found Raila unsettled and distracted. Rather than congratulate Hussein for work well done, Raila kept wondering how he had managed to organise such a hugely successful event. Hussein says Raila wasn't happy, and after that event, he noticed that he couldn't access Raila easily anymore.

In early 2011, Hussein approached Raila with a suggestion. He wanted to stand as a candidate in the upcoming Kenya Football Federation elections and asked Raila for his support. This is because soccer is predominantly played by Luos and Luhyas in Kenya. Raila is a former national soccer player. But more importantly, as the *de facto* leader of the Luo, he has significant influence over Kenya Federal of Football members who vote in new officials. Raila's quiet endorsement would therefore provide Hussein with the much needed boost. "That's a good idea. I can ask the former Safaricom C.E.O, Michael Joseph to run for chairman, and you can become the secretary of KFF," Raila told him before he had disclosed his specific interest.

"Captain", Hussein corrected him. "I'm actually interested in the chairman's position."

"But you know that Michael Joseph, being white, can help us raise more funds, which we can divert to our 2012 election kitty…" Raila said, trying to justify his decision. (Essentially, Raila was suggesting that if he was able to place Michael Joseph as chairman of KFF, they would have been able to raise hundreds of millions of shillings; and that in return for having been assisted to become KFF chairman, Michael Joseph could be 'prevailed upon' to divert some of these funds to Raila's political cause. That's what Hussein told me Raila had suggested to him.)

After that meeting, Hussein informed me that he had telephoned Michael Joseph to find out if he would be interested in being the chairman of K.F.F. "I know nothing about soccer or soccer management Hussein. I couldn't do that."

Armed with that answer, Hussein returned to Raila, hoping that this time, their encounter would end positively. Raila listened to him but made no commitments; only mumbling "hmmm…hmmm…hmmm," as he often does whenever he wants to deceive or conceal his intentions.

Hussein ran a disciplined campaign for the chairman's position. For a while, the KFF management tried to lock him out, arguing that he was too young. They even published some fake rules stating that anyone below 35 couldn't contest for the chairmanship of the KFF Raila never raised a finger to help Hussein even though such a policy was clearly discriminatory and unconstitutional. Hussein continued undeterred; he challenged these new rules both in court and in the court of public opinion. Eventually, the rules were quashed and Hussein was able to run.

On October 29, 2011 after months of campaigns, Hussein was defeated narrowly by Sam Nyamweya, a man from Raila's home province of Nyanza. Hussein believes that he lost because Raila refused to support him. He also believes that another candidate, Ambrose Rachier, who is a long-standing confidante of Raila – and a Luo like Raila – split the Nyanza votes, which if

Hussein had received as a block, would have carried him over the hump. Hussein told me that he suspects that Raila used his Chief of Staff, Caroli Omondi, to influence the outcome in Nyamweya's favour (by asking Rachier to contest at the last minute). According to Hussein, Nyamweya, being a Kisii, is considered more 'valuable' than Hussein, who as a tribeless Kenyan, brings no solid tribal vote block.

That is sad. Hussein would have represented change while Nyamweya represents the status quo. Nyamweya has been involved in soccer management in Kenya for the past 20 years and is considered part of the mess that needs cleaning up.

But then are Raila's choices necessarily guided by moral or ideological reasons, or is power all he cares about? Is he also fearful of strong, intelligent and charismatic people who might threaten his power and succession?

About six years after joining the Raila bandwagon, Hussein is dejected, disillusioned and embittered. He feels betrayed and has come to the conclusion that Odinga is not a genuine and true reformer. "Empty rhetoric; that's all," he said. And when the conversation turned to the fight against corruption, Hussein turned cynical, asking: "Who was allegedly involved in Triton, Maize and Kazi Kwa Vijana Scams in Kenya?"

Hussein won't be supporting Raila Odinga for President in 2012, or whenever the next elections are held."I will support someone who is genuinely committed to the full implementation of the Constitution; someone who can fight impunity. And I'm now sure that person is not Raila," Hussein told me. He believes that there are two sets of leaders clamouring for the presidency in the next elections. One group represents the status quo (Uhuru Kenyatta, George Saitoti, Musalia Mudavadi, Kalonzo Musyoka, William Ruto and Cyrus Jirongo). He calls these the "Kanu Orphans" – people who grew up, worked for and supported the most oppressive, corrupt and retrogressive regimes in Kenya's history – and he says firmly that he can't support any of them because they can't implement the new constitution. He calls the second group "reformists". These are Martha Karua, Raila Odinga, Mutava Musyimi. From this group, he believes only Martha Karua sounds genuine.

And he calls the third group "new blood". These are: Raphael Tuju, Eugene Wamalwa, Peter Kenneth and Prof. James Ole Kiyapi. Because Kiyapi openly opposed and campaigned against the enactment of the Constitution, Hussein believes that he cannot be trusted with its implementation. "Parliament has recently raised serious issues about Kenneth's integrity. They have raised concerns about how he acquired certain public assets in the past. Kenyans don't know how he managed to recently acquire two helicopters. If he is a billionaire we should know how he acquired his wealth. I don't think we need anybody with questionable backgrounds in State House," Hussein said this with pain in his eyes. Regarding Wamalwa and Musyimi, Hussein stated that these two aren't ready in any form or shape. "They can't even effectively run their own households," he said.

"So, that leaves Tuju and Karua?" I asked.

"Yes, I guess that's what we have to work with," he said as we hugged each other goodbye and parted for the day. I felt sad to see him go. Apart from the millions he sourced for Raila's 2007 presidential bid, he was also instrumental in attracting muslims to support Raila.

"I will soon speak out, too," he told me, referring to this book, "because self censorship means you lose your individuality. It's worse than state censorship." True, self-censorship is a complete corrosion of one's moral compass.

* * * * * * * * * * * * * *

Mohammed is just one Muslim. Raila has actually betrayed the whole community. In August 2007, leaders of the National Muslim Leaders Forum (NAMLEF) held a meeting with Raila where they discussed how they could receive an unequivocal commitment on various issues close to the hearts of Kenyan Muslims. The first one was on the issue of the renditions of Kenyan Muslims to Ethiopia and the US that has been going on since the 9/11 attacks. The Muslim leaders explained that they were going to peg their support for a presidential candidate on how he addressed this matter. They made it crystal clear that they would oppose President Kibaki for having allowed the renditions to happen. In the words of Said Athman who attended the meeting: "we wanted to teach Kibaki a lesson and we didn't care who the presidential candidate was as long as we were sure he would keep his word with or to us; we wanted somebody we could trust; a honourable leader."

Secondly, dovetailing neatly with the issue of renditions was their interest in the fortification of the bill of rights. Prominent Muslim leaders and human rights defenders like Athman and Zein Abu-Bakr were unwavering in their support and commitment for the resuscitation of the constitutional review process. They had both played significant roles during the constitutional review process at Bomas. They were very disappointed when President Kibaki and his henchmen stalled and then completely sabotaged the Bomas Draft. They were, therefore, interested in mobilising the Muslim community in supporting a candidate who wouldn't renege – like Kibaki had – on his promise for a new people-focused constitution that would contain a robust bill of rights and devolution of power.

"By this time, Moi had publicly endorsed Kibaki. We needed to back a candidate who could help Kenya bury, for good, the old order and bring to life the new dispensation," Athman told me.

In July 2007, NAMLEF had met with Raila and agreed on broad issues. The August meeting was in many ways a clincher. It was at that meeting that the now (in)famous Memorandum of Understanding (MoU) between Raila and the Muslims was signed. Athman confirmed to me that he is the one who drafted the MoU. He explained to me that before Raila signed the MoU, he did something unusual: he stretched his right pinkie finger, placed it in his mouth, bit it slightly and said: "In the Luo culture and traditions, an old man with white hair doesn't lie and whenever an old man makes an oath or makes a solemn undertaking, breach of which would result in one's death or a tragedy striking the offender; he must bite the pinkie finger and say 'I swear in the name of my grandmother that if I violate this oath, I shall perish.'"

At a subsequent convention that August, Kenyan Muslims openly endorsed Raila's candidature and went out full throttle to campaign for him. They also persuaded Najib Balala, who had been competing with Raila for ODM's presidential nomination ticket to shelve his bid. In fact, Athman told me that when NAMLEF had put pressure on Balala to relinquish his presidential ambitions – a few weeks before the ODM nominations in September 2007 – Balala had broken down and cried, shedding copious tears.

Later, during the ODM Convention at Kasarani, Balala stood up and openly endorsed Raila before the ODM delegates cast their ballots, as a way of sealing a deal that had been struck weeks previously. Ironically, Athman explained, it was Raila who "imposed Balala on the NAMLEF by suggesting that he [Balala] should serve as Raila's political contact person for the Muslim community." He did this and was a witness when the MoU was being signed.

On 24 December 2007 – when it looked almost certain that Raila would win the presidential election – NAMLEF met with him again and reviewed their agreement. During that meeting, Raila undertook to allow structured engagement and access between him and NAMLEF after assuming the presidency. It was also agreed that Athman would be employed in Raila's new office as a way of guaranteeing such access.

At that point in time, the Muslim community was assured of Raila's commitments and undertakings. They had no reason to doubt him.

As I have described above, President Kibaki and PNU didn't allow Raila to assume the presidency. They didn't allow him to go past The Serena Hotel towards State House. The crisis that engulfed the country shortly thereafter led to an international intervention that culminated in Raila 'sharing power' with Kibaki and becoming Prime Minister. During that period, Athman was toiling away with us at the Pentagon Technical team.

Yet, after Raila became Prime Minister, it took NAMLEF more than six months to secure a meeting with him. And when they eventually did, Raila shocked them. By then Raila had appointed Athman secretary to the Ministry of Culture and National Heritage, not to the Prime Minister's Office. Earlier, Raila had orchestrated rumours that Athman, Wanyande, Jacqueline Oduol, Kenneth Ombongi and I were destined to some elevated permanent secretary positions. These, of course, never panned out.

"I'm not a beautiful woman that you should want to see all the time," Raila told the NAMLEF leaders at his Treasury Building offices. He didn't apologise for not having met them earlier. Nor did he explain why Athman hadn't been placed as agreed. Instead, Raila pointed at Isahakia who was seated next to him and said: "You see, I have hired him to protect the Muslim interests." That meeting was a disaster.

According to Athman, this wasn't the first significant breach. During the ODM convention at Kasarani, Raila stood up – and to everyone's consternation – held aloft the MoU that had been agreed with the Muslims and selectively disclosed its contents to the country. He wasn't supposed to have done that. The MoU was supposed to be a confidential deal between him and the Muslim community. Consequently, he was subsequently summoned to the Jumia Mosque in Nairobi and sternly reprimanded by the Imams in the mosque.

The failure to hire Athman was the second major breach. NAMLEF hadn't proposed Isahakia's name. Isahakia wasn't their member. As far as Athman is concerned, Isahakia wasn't a practising or devout Muslim. "He never attended Friday prayers," Athman informed me. "We also didn't like the reputation he left behind during his long tenure under Moi," Athman explained further.

So, within months of the formation of the grand coalition government, NAMLEF wasn't just shut out in the cold, unable to get the "structured engagement and access" Raila had promised them at the risk of a major personal catastrophe; they couldn't get Raila to fulfill even one of the undertakings he made in the MoU. For more than four years now, Raila hasn't taken a clear and firm position on the inhumane renditions. In fact, he hasn't spoken about them at all. The issues about the realisation of the new dispensation were also in abeyance.

Regarding Athman, the betrayal was tripled: not only had he been appointed to some backwater department instead of in the Prime Minister's office; also he faced serious challenges of insubordination, frustrations and ethnic bigotry at the Ministry of Culture and National Heritage. When I approached Raila with Athman's grievances, which he had put in writing three times, Raila waved me away. Athman eventually got transferred to the Ministry of Housing through the intervention of the principal secretary at the Cabinet Office, Sam Mwale.

At the end of the day, Raila had effectively betrayed everyone and every significant constituency that had backed him in 2007. Looking back five years later (and with the benefit of reflection and time), I can say that the boil of deception, mistrust and opportunism had ripened and grown – it needed lancing.

Who would do it?

Ruto ended up intervening on behalf of some Muslim human rights defenders like Al-Amin Kimathi who had been renditioned to Uganda. Apparently, Ruto travelled to Uganda and convinced Museveni to release them after Raila and the entire government had failed to protect their own citizens. In fact, it was the Kenyan authorities who arrested and handed over their own citizens in complete abrogation of our own laws and the constitution. Those human rights defenders were never charged and taken to court in Kenya. Their rights to arbitrary arrests and detentions; habeas corpus; the right not to be detained for more than 24 hours without being produced before a court of competent jurisdiction, were flagrantly violated. And Raila never raised a finger!

Raila repeated this (pledge to Kenyan Muslims) and other pledges, many times, during his 2007 presidential campaign. Yet, four long years after becoming Prime Minister, we have not heard even a squeal from him on this monumental matter.

The same applies to ODM – the so-called "party of change". Why hasn't Raila said anything about Anglo Leasing or the Goldenberg or Triton or K-Rep or Grand Regency or the Embassy alleged scams through which the Kenyan taxpayers lost hundreds of billions of shillings?

Prior to the 2007 elections, Raila had publicly announced that after "winning the presidential elections", he [Raila], would "invite John Githongo back to Kenya and ensure that those behind Anglo Leasing are apprehended and punished." Well, Githongo returned on his own in August 2008. What is Raila waiting for, or were those declarations just election rhetoric? Why should Kenyans trust anything else he says?

* * * * * * * * * * * * * *

Another incident where Raila really disappointed me concerned one of my mentors, a genial retired judge of the East African Court of Appeal called Bena Luta. Justice (Rtd) Luta was the late Tom Mboya's Permanent Secretary in the Ministry of Justice and a former advisor to Jaramogi. He is in his early 90s. For the entire period I worked as Raila's advisor, I discussed many issues with Justice Luta, trying to draw on his vast experience and knowledge. Justice Luta often visited my office with another quintessential gentleman, a retired physician called Dr Chabeda. Through me, they passed on countless well-reasoned briefs and pieces of advice to Raila, but not once did Raila seek a meeting with them.

I eventually took Justice Luta to see Raila and we had productive discussions on a number of issues including coalition management, power sharing, portfolio balance and corruption in government, none of which Raila pursued. Justice Luta was one of the staunch believers in the concept of co-presidency and he gave authoritative examples from ancient Rome. But the matter that would later engage me for two years revolved around his personal situation and an injustice that had been perpetrated against him.

More than 20 years ago, Justice Luta had had two large farms of approximately 2,800 acres in the Rift Valley in the Kitale area forcefully taken away from him by the Moi government. One farm consisted of about 1,800 acres where he did dairy farming and planted maize. He had another farm of more than 1,000 acres, which was also unlawfully expropriated. One day, under the despotic Moi regime, the provincial administration, police, GSU and Kenya wildlife goons attacked both farms, beat up workers, took away the animals and forcefully occupied them. The farms were divided up and given away. Portions of the farms were turned into "government institutions".

In the two decades since, Justice Luta has been seeking justice to no avail. He has been to virtually every government office in the land and been sent around in circles. After he had given me copies of the relevant materials and facts, I sent Raila an urgent memo and requested his prompt intervention. I also approached the Lands Minister James Orengo for his advice and intervention. Luta only sought compensation for one farm. Raila wrote to Orengo, directing that action be taken to compensate Justice Luta. Orengo sent a letter to Finance Minister Uhuru Kenyatta, seeking funds to compensate the old man. Then there was silence for four months.

Then followed more meetings between Justice Luta, Raila, Orengo and myself, followed by more letters. Eventually, Raila called in Isahakia and asked him to speak with PS Finance Joseph Kinyua. I found that bizarre and told Justice Luta so. It was incredible that Raila couldn't simply summon Uhuru, Orengo, Kinyua, Isahakia and PS Lands Dorothy Angote to a meeting at the end of which he could give specific directions on what was to be done.

After six months, Uhuru hadn't even acknowledged receipt of Justice Luta's letter. Subsequently, we went through more hoops of bureaucracy, more phone calls and more letters. But nothing happened. Isahakia never did anything. He often kept Justice Luta waiting at the reception for more than six hours, only for Luta to then be informed that Isahakia couldn't see the old man. Two years later, Justice Luta was still going through the revolving doors of bureaucracy at the Treasury and BP Shell Building, when he started receiving strange calls from people asking him to authorise them to pursue his compensation claim, on the proviso that he agreed to pay them 20 per cent of the total sum. He actually met with one of these conmen at the Safari Park Hotel. Even more strange was the fact that this man had a copy of his compensation file. Justice Luta sought my advice. After hours of discussion, Justice Luta declined to be party to what looked like a huge racket by people closely connected to State House and Treasury.

Around June 2011, I went back to Raila and asked him why it was taking so long for Justice Luta to be compensated. "I know, I know *Ja-Nyando*! But what can I do? Why don't you take him to Isahakia again, and ask him to call Kinyua?" Raila said, looking frightened and worried. It was puzzling why he seemed so agitated. What did he fear and why?

"But *Jakom*, why don't you just go and speak with the President or Muthaura about it? *Jakom*, the old man will die in filth while the state, which you partly head, is illegally holding his land, which is estimated to be worth about Sh1.5 billion!"

"You know these people…," he said in frustration as he walked away. He genuinely looked pained. But what I couldn't understand was why Raila refused either to summon Uhuru to a meeting or to approach Kibaki with this case. As you are reading this, Justice Luta is still walking the pavements between the Treasury and BP House. I bleed inside when I think of it.

There was also the case of an elderly man who arrived one late afternoon in my office holding tightly two three-month old issues of *the Star* newspaper in which my articles on Moi and the Uhuru/Ruto alliance had been published. When the secretary sought to know what the man's visit was about, he insisted that he couldn't say until he saw me. After five minutes, the man entered my office and embraced me like someone he had known all his life. "This is you? This is Miguna Miguna I'm holding?"

"Yes Mzee, this is him. And you, what's your name?"

"I'm an old man from Muhoroni. I've been reading your articles for a very long time. These two are masterpieces. I'm keeping them forever."

"Thank you, Mzee."

"Many years ago, Jaramogi helped me get a scholarship to East Germany where I studied political science...That was in the early 1960s. I'm now retired."

"That's fantastic. How was East Germany then?"

"Oh, it was great. Those were very good days. There were many people like you in those days. I can't say the same thing about many people nowadays. Everybody worships money, few stand up for the truth, for what is right and just."

He then explained to me how his daughter had been murdered by some police officers in 2004 in Msambweni, on the Kenyan South Coast. Apparently, she had gone to a bar, got involved in a small argument with a bouncer who had confiscated her mobile phone. She had then rushed to the local police station and reported the matter there, hoping that they would assist her retrieve her telephone from the bouncer. From there, the story became more bizarre and mysterious. The first her father knew of any of this, was a call from the police to say his daughter had died and the body was at the mortuary.

An autopsy was conducted. It was found that she had been raped and strangled to death. Subsequently, an inquest was held which, strangely recommended the prosecution of the bouncer, not any of the police officers at the station at the time of her death. The bouncer was arrested, but since he had had no contact with the young woman at the police station, the charges against him were dismissed. Thus began the father's relentless search for justice.

For seven years, the old man had on countless occasions visited the Msambweni Police Station, the Coast Provincial Police Officer, the Coast Provincial Criminal Investigations Officer, the Attorney General's office, the Police Commissioner – virtually every office he could think of – beseeching those in authority to arrest and prosecute the police officers who were at the station when his daughter was raped and strangled. At one time, a police officer was arrested and charged. Then predictably, the autopsy report went missing from the prosecution file, leading to his discharge. The old man told me that even though he had been shown the autopsy report before, many senior people at the State Law Office and the police headquarters were now pretending as if they had never seen the report.

After hearing his heart-wrenching story, I sent a memorandum to Raila, seeking his intervention. I advised the man that he needed to speak with the yet-to-retire Attorney General Amos Wako, the Police Commissioner Matthew Iteere and the CID director Ndegwa Muhoro. I dispatched the memo before the man left the office. And with him still sitting across my desk, I placed a telephone call to the Muhoroni MP Ayiecho Olweny, and to the Assistant Minister for Internal Security and Provincial Administration Orwa Ojodeh. I requested Ayiecho allocate time to meet the man with a view to having his case raised in Parliament. This was done within two weeks by Nyakach MP Ochieng' Daima. As for Ojodeh, I needed him to pile pressure on the police to deal with the matter once and for all. I'm sad to note that even though the matter was raised in Parliament and the government promised to "investigate" it and "report back to the House within two weeks", nothing much has happened. And Raila never responded to my memo addressed to him on this matter. The old man is still going through the revolving doors of bureaucracy.

Of course, when it came to Raila's business and financial interests, or government jobs for his relatives, things seemed to work out smoothly.

Kenyans know that when Raila joined the Moi government in 2002, he was a man of modest means. Yet in a period of ten years – between his short stint in Moi's government and Kibaki's Narc regime – he suddenly became a multi-billionaire. How did that happen? And why, as Prime Minister, did Raila continue to run most of his businesses from his office through Caroli, Isahakia and Opondo? In the technological 21st century wouldn't it have been wiser to place his business interests in a blind trust and have them managed from a distance so as to avoid perceptions of conflicts of interest, influence peddling, unjust enrichments or even corruption?

Why did Raila condone the appointment of his sisters to plum government positions soon after he became Prime Minister? Were his elder brother Oburu Oginga and his cousin Jakoyo Midiwo the most qualified members of ODM for Assistant Minister for Finance and Chief Whip positions?

How about the criminal and corruption allegations against his sister Beryl Achieng' Odinga who faced serious allegations of fraud, involving irregular disposal of public land and other assets? Raila simply ignored all those allegations against his sister. She wasn't even suspended following the allegations and criminal charges. Fortunately public pressure eventually forced her to resign from the position as chairperson of the Kenya Railways Retirement Benefits Board.

More recently, Raila stood up in Parliament and lobbied members to support the introduction of genetically modified foods (GMOs) in Kenya. The matter was hurriedly debated and a bill passed, despite the fact that scientific studies and expert opinions for or against the introduction of GMOs hadn't been tabled and discussed in Parliament. Raila believes that anything 'scientific' must be good for the country. He spent a considerable amount of time chastising members of Parliament who expressed skepticism over the matter.

I was astounded at the casual manner Raila and a horde of other ODM members gleefully supported GMOs. When I sent Raila a cautionary memorandum on the matter, citing Canada's decision not to support GMOs, he dismissed me even without a response. One of his assistant ministers, Ayiecho Olweny, even claimed, during telephone discussions with me over the issue, that I was one of those Kenyans that were "showing a phobia towards science". He had completely misapprehended and misrepresented the nature of our cautionary voices. To be sure, we weren't and couldn't oppose the advance of science. What we were, and still are, against is using Africa as a dumpsite for untested, unproven and potentially harmful experiments dubiously presented as being in 'the service of science'.

As usual, Raila has been casual with an important issue that would affect the lives of tens of millions of ordinary Kenyans. He and his wealthy friends can always afford to feed their families on expensive organic foods. Meanwhile, Monsanto and other GMO food exporters can be satisfied that the millions they spent lobbying MPs and political leaders has paid off. For Raila, it is never about the public or national interest, it's what is in his personal interest above everything else.

There are hundreds of stories I could tell about Raila's inability to perform his constitutional functions and his betrayals. But I hope that the ones I have told here help readers to form a picture of the dysfunction within the Grand Coalition Government in general, and within the operation of the OPM, specifically. I am not suggesting that the OPM was in charge of police investigations or activities at the State Law Office. What I am saying is that as the Prime Minister of the Republic of Kenya and the individual with the constitutional mandate to execute all government functions, Raila could and should have taken initiative to have these matters addressed. The Attorney General, the Police Commissioner, the Director of CID, and Minister in charge of Internal Security and Provincial Administration worked directly under him.

I, however, continued to challenge the merchants of impunity, again and again. I considered it part of my job to protect public interest. This made me a derided and feared figure in the corridors of power, but it was a price I was prepared to pay. I was becoming increasingly frustrated and angry that I had pinned my hopes on Raila and people like Orengo and Nyong'o. Unfortunately, all of them had gone to bed with the merchants of corruption and looked at me as an irritant. What we had fought for during the second liberation was forgotten; it was now "our time to eat". I got reliable reports that Raila, Orengo, Nyong'o and Kajwang' were jokingly comparing me to the *Mau Mau* who woke up one day in December 1963, to hear reports that Kenya had obtained formal independence, but refusing to believe it, chose instead to "return to the forest".

These are just but a few illustrative examples of Raila's betrayals. For me, leadership is not all about what many people refer to as "big ticket" items. Leadership for me, starts with the values, morals and integrity of the individual leader; how s/he treats members of his or her family, relatives, friends, colleagues and compatriots. A leader who would flagrantly betray people close to him is more likely to betray the country. In other words, if Raila has betrayed most of his friends, colleagues and comrades as I have demonstrated by these few examples (and they are nothing but the very tip of the iceberg), is he capable of keeping his promises to the nation?

CHAPTER FOURTEEN

THE FLIP-FLOPPER

Right from his appointment as the Prime Minister of the Republic of Kenya, the one dominant attribute of Raila's tenure was as a flip-flopper. Raila flip-flopped so often, and on virtually every issue and instance that many around him took this as one of his natural characteristics. Prof. Oyugi repeatedly reminded me that what I was seeing was the real Raila; the one he had known for a long time. He said it with both sadness and resignation. "*Mano e kaka wuod Jaduong' en nga*", he would say, meaning "that's the way the Old Man's son is," alluding to Jaramogi, Raila's venerable father. "He isn't like his father," Oyugi would add, in obvious exasperation. What concerned me was the emptiness, the confusion and the persistent lack of focus about and around Raila. I had had high hopes of the man. But once I had worked at close quarters with him, I felt underwhelmed. I was disappointed and tired of the constant dithering, inconsistencies, erratic reversals and goofs. From afar and to those who admired him, Raila looked impeccably incapable of mistakes. But close up, I soon realised that errors and omissions in judgement were an absolute given. I will give only a few examples for illustrative purposes.

Soon after Parliament started sitting – and in complete disregard for the Accord and the Constitution – Kibaki wrote to the Speaker of the National Assembly, Kenneth Marende, notifying him of his decision to nominate Stephen Kalonzo Musyoka as the Leader of Government Business (LGB) in the House. Kalonzo in turn, as "Leader of Government Business" submitted a list of nominees to the House Business Committee (HBC). The HBC is the nerve centre of government operations in Parliament. It is the HBC that discusses new business – notices of motion, motions, bills, amendments, et cetera. Without the HBC, nothing can be processed through the House; no legislation, money bills, budget, constitutional appointments, would see the light of day. So, it is by far the most important committee of the House.

Kibaki's attempt to get his man in place, which involved circumventing the Accord, the Constitution and all the principles of good governance, was an affront on democracy and the rule of law. Firstly, Kalonzo wasn't, strictly speaking, a coalition partner. Kibaki had surreptitiously appointed him Vice-President in January 2008 as the country burnt and the international community was scurrying to find a solution to the conflict, which was threatening the stability of the region. His ODM-K had entered government through – at least according to former Kalonzo confidante Joe Khamisi – a pre-election secret deal in which, Kibaki would rig the 2007 presidential election and then Kalonzo would be part of a coalition rescue deal. Kalonzo's party had no popular mandate. It was the country's third party (having gotten, even with the convenient vote-padding, 800 votes), but it was a distant third, after ODM and the PNU Alliance, as such it had no moral, political or legal authority to claim chairmanship of the HBC over ODM. And thirdly, Raila was co-principal with Kibaki.

Kibaki's Machiavellian manouevres clearly demonstrated that he hadn't accepted the political settlement he had signed on February 28, 2008. PNU had already won the battle on the control of the executive arm of government. The bureaucracy, the security agencies and the judiciary were still firmly under Kibaki's stranglehold, and now he was moving on the legislative side, which ODM should naturally have controlled by dint of its slight majority in Parliament. Kibaki had been emboldened largely by the incompetence of the Accord and Raila's cowardice; the blue party had smelt blood. All this was a bad portent for the future, not just of the Grand Coalition Government, but also of the country and the region as a whole. A constitutional crisis – which is what this amounted to – could cause instability in the country. Geopolitically, Kenya occupied a central place in the region; its instability would send major tremors, causing panic to investors, capital markets and the tourism industry. That wasn't and couldn't be good for the world.

I summoned the think tank, which met and quickly concluded that Raila had to countermand Kibaki by writing to Marende, and submitting his own nominee for the position of LGB. Orengo, Caroli and I subsequently prepared a detailed letter, citing the Accord, the Constitution, parliamentary precedence from many countries in the Commonwealth, and appealing to Kibaki to put the interests of Kenya above his own parochial interests or those of the PNU. Raila nominated himself as the LGB. This was a psychological coup for Raila in many respects.

He had taken the battle to Kibaki's doorstep. That was long overdue considering how shabbily Kibaki had been treating him. He had shown that he could be tough. By this act, Raila also reaffirmed his belief in and commitment to the rule of law.

Since Kibaki didn't sit through parliamentary proceedings – and had no intentions of doing so – Raila, his counterpart, had a legitimate demand – also as the coordinator and supervisor of the execution of all government functions, including that of ministries – to chair the committee responsible for government business and to be principally accountable for all government functions in the House. Although Raila already had his 30 minutes Prime Minister's Question Time during which he was quizzed on inter-ministerial issues, this new role would give him much needed clout. Strategically, it was a good place for an ODM leader to be; mobilising MPs, vetting notices of motion and bills and otherwise just being in charge. We made sure Raila pulled the trigger by delivering the letter to Marende. Parliament was sent spinning, but our actions reverberated beyond Parliament, through PNU, ODM, the government and media, all the way to Geneva, New York, Washington DC and 10 Downing Street. Parliament became the next battleground between the two coalition partners. Kibaki had fired the first shot. Raila and ODM had mobilised, but would they return fire?

Well, in a way Raila did. On April 26, 2009 he picked up the gauntlet Kibaki had thrown at him, cocked his gun and aimed it at Kibaki by threatening – publicly – that ODM would precipitate fresh elections so that Kenyans could elect a government of their choice capable of fulfilling their needs and aspirations. He reminded the PNU mandarins, for the umpteenth time, that he had won the 2007 presidential elections and that it was due to his 'generosity' that they were still squatting along the executive corridors of power on Harambee Avenue and at State House, Nairobi. Such rhetoric was Raila's natural terrain. Kibaki and his PNU hardliners knew that Raila was an unparalleled rabble rouser and mobiliser. Yes, he was lousy at the negotiating table. He was also a disaster in statecraft and administration. But what he lacked in governance skills, he made up for on the podium. Nobody, in the history of Kenya's multi-party democracy, could spur and incite a mob better than Raila. In another life, he would have made a stellar trade unionist.

The heated debate was fuelled further when Marende made a historic ruling sending back the matter to both Raila and Kibaki for 'resolution'. Most Kenyans hailed Marende's 'Solomonic' ruling. They also praised Raila for 'standing up to Kibaki' on a matter of principle. Many thought and expected Kibaki to concede that he was wrong and allow Raila, as the leader of the majority party in

Parliament, to chair the HBC. That was the decent thing to do. After all, he had hoarded all executive power. But Kibaki stood his ground and refused to budge.

Meanwhile, from April 30, 2009, Marende temporarily assumed the chairmanship of the HBC. The position of LGB was to remain vacant for more than a year. We had suggested that the control of the HBC was more significant than the LGB. The LGB, while visually important, meant very little if a party had no control over the HBC. It was the latter that deliberated over issues and made decisions. The LGB in the House only communicated decisions made by the HBC to the House. But we needed and deserved both.

Shortly after Marende's Solomonic ruling, the US, UK and German ambassadors to Kenya released coordinated statements welcoming the "wise and timely intervention by the Speaker". We knew that we had pushed the right buttons. All that remained was for Raila to fasten his seatbelt and enjoy the ride. The general feeling within ODM was that Kibaki would eventually relent. But we had to keep up the pressure.

Throughout our discussions as a party, Raila had agreed with this position. It was therefore our expectation that he would stick to it. And even assuming that he had changed his mind, he owed it to himself and the party to inform us if he was going to change tack in a timely fashion. That was just how good governance was practised in the modern world. One-man decisions wouldn't do anymore.

But Kibaki knew Raila very well. He knew how emotionally fragile, confused and inconsistent he was, especially in one-on-one meetings between the two of them. He knew that with Raila all he needed to do was to sit tight and wait until self-doubt started gnawing at Raila's resolve. That is what Kibaki did. And lo and behold, after eight months, in late March 2010, an announcement was released from the Presidential Press Service indicating that: "Following consultations between His Excellency the President and the Commander-in-Chief of Kenya's Defence Forces, Mwai Kibaki, and the Right Honourable Prime Minister, Raila Odinga, His Excellency the Vice-Presidency Stephen Kalonzo Musyoka has been appointed the Leader of Government Business in the House…" Suddenly, the crisis had exploded, but not with the expected bang, but a pathetic whimper. I was stunned. I protested to Raila that such a move would show him as a flip-flopper; that he had needed to wait Kibaki out; that after all, Marende was an ODM member and he chairing the HBC couldn't be bad for ODM. But the horse had bolted and was already galloping down the field.

Within days, Kalonzo officially took up his position, to the consternation of most ODM members. It completely deflated the party and demonstrated that Raila had no strategy, plan or programme; otherwise, why had we resisted Kibaki's move so hard and for so long only to crumble on our own? But even more shocking was the fact that Raila had got nothing in return. Instead, it was ODM which ended up making further concessions to the PNU – a lesser party.

PNU now dominated most key parliamentary committees. These reckless moves would later return to haunt the Orange party after Kibaki unilaterally sought to nominate five candidates to the constitutional key state positions of Chief Justice, Deputy Chief Justice, Director of Public Prosecutions, Attorney General and Director of Budget, in complete disregard of the provisions of the Accord and the Constitution.

The second major incident of flip-flopping occurred on Sunday, February 14, 2010 after Raila dramatically announced a three-month suspension of William Ruto as Minister for Agriculture and Sam Ongeri as Minister for Education for alleged corruption in their ministries. Raila had exercised the authority and power given to him under Section 15(a) of the old *Constitution of Kenya*, and Section 4(1) of the *National Accord and Reconciliation Act*. The suspension of the two cabinet ministers was necessitated by credible allegations of corruption by independent investigations and audit reports by PriceWaterhouseCoopers and the Internal Auditor General affecting not just both ministries, but also touching on the two ministers specifically. Recommendations were made that both the ministers and a number of senior officers working under them should be investigated with a view to establishing culpability and ensuring full accountability for billions of shillings of public funds that had been stolen and/or misappropriated.

One week earlier, the Prime Minister had publicly announced that he had consulted the President and recommended the suspension of both ministers with a view to having credible investigations conducted in both ministries. In taking action against errant public officials, the Prime Minister's sole intention was to demonstrate the government's commitment to the elimination of corruption and impunity in Kenya, issues which the President himself had made public pronouncements on but on which both he and the Prime Minister had done absolutely nothing to curb. By suspending the two ministers for three months, the PM indicated that his action was meant to provide a conducive environment for an independent, fair and professional investigation to occur. Failing to act was not an option for the PM.

Members of the think tank, most members of the Orange party, the media, civil society, the international community and many ordinary Kenyans greeted Raila's decisive action with jubilation. At long last, they said, "someone is cracking the whip on high level corruption". But the joy was to be short-lived. Kibaki swiftly issued a statement from State House, Nairobi, reversing Raila's decision and publicly rebuking his co-principal.

The media yelled "Kibaki countermands Raila" and forgot their short-lived jubilation. Raila instructed Salim, Orengo, Nyong'o and I to prepare a comprehensive statement on Kibaki's unprecedented decision to countermand and reverse Raila's suspension. We agreed that he needed to read the statement on arrival from Paris. Isahakia and Caroli were already supposedly serving their "suspension" over their involvements in the Maize scandal, yet on that Sunday, it was Isahakia who opened the Treasury Building offices for us, and even his own office, from where I edited and printed the statement

I provided what I considered a solid legal interpretation of the Accord and the Constitution on this matter. I was among a few close associates of Raila who encouraged him to ride the storm as both the public and the international community were on his side; he had clearly chosen to be on the side of the people and a field marshal in the fight against corruption, while Kibaki appeared, based on his pronouncements, to be sympathetic to the lords of corruption. It was a win-win situation for Raila. And for a few days he stayed the course.

However, soon – and predictably – Raila started wobbling, for absolutely no apparent reason. He sat on all subsequent statements Salim and I prepared for him on this issue. ODM issued lame protests about Kibaki's interference and threatened to boycott cabinet meetings until Kibaki withdrew his countermand and, for two weeks, most ODM ministers made good on their threats. Demands were made that the Permanent Committee should meet to deliberate on the issues, but those demands were all ignored by Kibaki. Raila made me write two letters to Kibwana, requesting a meeting so that we could jointly prepare an agenda and summon a meeting of the Committee, but Kibwana also ignored my letters. My advice to Raila was to take the initiative and summon the Committee; that he didn't need Kibaki's consent to do so just like Kibaki didn't need his consent to call a meeting. But Raila looked scared. He refused to summon a meeting. By the third week, ODM ministers, led by Raila, were attending cabinet meetings, which both Ruto and Ongeri also happily attended.

Raila had let us down again. He had failed to deliver. Although he had the gun cocked and was pointing it at Kibaki's head, he couldn't pull the trigger. If this was a real life confrontation, Kibaki would have emptied his magazine into the immobilised and trembling Raila. It was impossible to understand why Raila was apparently bent on self-destruction, but he would do this again and again, until his word to the country became meaningless; his numerous empty threats comical. Soon, the country realised that whenever Raila spoke of "consultations with Kibaki" over any issue, it was only a product of his fertile imagination. In reality, there were never, ever real, concrete *consultations* between the two.

Although Kibaki's Presidential Press Service would frequently correct and rebuff Raila (whenever he became too excited and revealed either that he had met Kibaki, "consulted" and/or that they had "agreed" over something) soon, even that became unnecessary: they simply ignored him, preferring to let him flutter uselessly like a moth drawn to a flame. Thus, in the public's view, Raila slowly degenerated into a pathetic, pitiful sight; somebody to be mocked and ridiculed, not to be taken seriously.

The third incident revolved around the constitutional review process. Both Mutakha and I considered this our baby in ODM; we lived, breathed, ate and drank the "process". We were both passionate about the pursuit of a new constitution. And we were always prepared. We had spent countless hours, weeks and months researching the issues. We had prepared succinct, coherent and ironclad briefs. We had explained all the contentious and non-contentious issues to the ODM's National Executive Committee (NEC), the Parliamentary Group (PG), the ordinary members, and ultimately to Raila, his cabinet, MPs, and especially members of the Parliamentary Select Committee. I kept the heat on PNU, relentlessly debating with them in the media.

There was consensus in the Orange party that we would do everything to bring a parliamentary federal system to Kenya. But we weren't naïve; we knew that one couldn't expect to get everything. So, we had set our "irreducible minimum"– at a parliamentary system of government. We knew that reactionary forces had spread false propaganda about *majimbo,* which is what the parliamentary system had become known as in popular and media parlance. Although we had gallantly tried to debunk the myths and the vile propaganda, we were prepared to concede full federalism for a well-structured and enhanced devolution. Unfortunately, the Committee of Experts (CoE) had departed significantly from the Bomas Draft Constitution and had already presented a "harmonised draft", which was more of a mongrel presidential system than a parliamentary one.

Devolution was better conceptualised, formulated and structured in the first Harmonised Draft Constitution (HDC); it had three tiers, with real, practical powers devolved to the grassroots where the majority of Kenyans live. The main problem was on the way chapters and provisions dealing with the executive and legislature were crafted. There were also rumblings on the Kadhi Courts. These are courts that were entrenched in the Constitution of Kenya, 1963, that reserved the role of resolving family (marriage, divorce and death/burial) and property disputes to Muslim courts headed by Kadhis and in accordance with Muslim law.

For more than 40 years, there hadn't been a major controversy over these arrangements. Even though there wasn't uniform support and consensus over their appropriateness and utility, Kenyans had long recognised the fact that virtually all its laws and the judicial system were based on Judeo-Christian precepts. Consequently, it was felt that granting Muslims the limited power to determine matters over their personal affairs touching on marriage, divorce, death/burial and property wasn't entirely unreasonable. However, some Christian fundamentalists, traditionalists and xenophobes still resented this limited space granted to Muslims at independence and were insisting that the Kadhi courts should be scrapped. They mischaracterized the courts as "introducing sharia law to Kenya". Of course nothing could be further from the truth.

The same forces that were fighting to keep the Kadhi courts from the new constitution were also hellbent on mischaracterising all provisions that sought to entrench and guarantee gender equality and reproductive rights as "legalising abortion". They vehemently opposed what they termed "attempts by liberals to introduce abortion, homosexuality, bestiality and other devious acts to Kenya through the back door." They castigated us as "agents of western imperialism." These ultra-conservative-anti-abortion-and-anti-Kadhi-court adherents were in the meantime advocating the retention of the death penalty. I often jibed at them on TV debates, asking why they were so concerned about the unborn, yet so unconcerned about the living. I asked: "why aren't you making the same level of noise about the ongoing extra-judicial killings; the atrocities committed by the military in the Mount Elgon area where thousands were slaughtered without justification; the thousands of Mungiki sect members who have been summarily executed in cold blood over the years; or those on death row?" There were no coherent responses.

However, we were confident that we could intellectually panel-beat the HDC into a form that the majority of Kenyans desired and would vote for overwhelmingly in a referendum.

Having attended and participated in all CoE workshops and seminars, I knew that the problem was the weak philosophical base of many of the CoE members. The committee was full of technicians without theoretical, ideological and practical content. They discussed "systems of government" without having first thoroughly understood what was on offer around the world, from ancient Greece to the modern South Africa. Mutakha and I were aware that the PNU negotiators had been instructed to push for a mongrel system, which they were calling hybrid. During our first retreat at Mombasa, the PNU team was thoroughly divided, with Gichiira Kebaara engaging Kivutha Kibwana in a shouting match, which degenerated into profanities and abuse, with Gichiira telling Kivutha that he [Kivutha] was an idiot.

At some point, Uhuru Kenyatta, who was leading the PNU team, had to call for a two-hour time off to cool frayed nerves. But unlike the dysfunctional ODM, the PNU team quickly gained its balance and began to push hard as a team. The three-day meeting ended in stalemate.

When we resumed in Nairobi, the PNU team started being mischievous and obstructionist. We held numerous meetings, all ending in deadlock. The country and the international community were becoming increasingly restless. I remember being invited for meetings by the ambassadors for the US, Germany, The Netherlands, the Head of the European Union Delegation, and representatives of the Panel of Eminent African Personalities based in Nairobi. All were eager to know what was holding up the process; whether ODM and PNU would ever agree in time for a new constitution before the next elections; whether the differences between the two parties were too deep to be resolved without further acrimony; and what, if anything, they could do to facilitate some agreement. They also met my counterpart, Prof. Kibwana. In fact, twice, Kibwana and I were meeting Ranneberger at his Muthaiga official residence, in different rooms. That was the intensity, anxiety and pressure of this period. The stakes were too high to be taken for granted.

One day, we had agreed that the two technical teams – ODM's and PNU's – comprising Mutakha Kangu and I for ODM;, and Kivutha Kibwana, Gichiira, Njee Muturi and Peter Kagwanja for PNU; with Kathurima M'Inoti representing the Kenya Law Reform Commission, were to conduct research and select not more than seven "best" hybrid, presidential and parliamentary systems of government. We had agreed that each team would prepare summaries and analysis of the various constitutions as well as table copies of the same for the teams' perusal. The purpose of these negotiations was for both parties to place their "best foot forward".

Mutakha and I submitted our summaries, analysis and copies of the South African, Ghanaian, Nigerian, Canadian, US, French and German constitutions. The South African, Nigerian, Canadian and German systems were both parliamentary and federal, the US and Ghanaian systems were presidential (with the US being a federal system while the Ghanaian one was unitary), and the French system was considered a hybrid, though it had a strong presidential bias. We cited the old Constitution of Kenya as a "mongrel" type, while the 1963 Constitution was parliamentary/federal.

However, when the PNU team started their presentation, they had neither an analysis nor copies of the constitutions they were relying on; all they had were summaries of constitutions of 52 African states – anything and everything from Cape Verde, Morocco, Tunisia, Egypt, Libya, DRC, Gabon, Ethiopia, Eritrea to Cameroon. This was before the reverberations of the Arab Spring.

As Kivutha spoke and spent considerable time on Gaddafi's and Mubarak's despotic constitutions, I put up my hand to seek clarification. "With all due respect Prof. Kibwana, you don't expect us to *sit here* and have you discuss some of *the most repressive, most despotic and retrogressive constitutions in the world*; do you? To begin with, we don't have that kind of time. Going through those constitutions will take us one whole year; time we don't have. Secondly, we had agreed that each team would present *not more than seven best constitutions* of the world representing *the three systems of government under discussion*. Asking us to look through military juntas and one-man dictatorships under the pretext of giving Africa priority when we know – unfortunately – that *most African countries don't have model constitutions or democratic systems*, is to me not just a waste of time; it is a gross injustice to the people of Kenya. We are spending tax payers' money in these meetings. And I for one will not sit through an examination of constitutions of *banana republics*..."

But Njee Muturi, Uhuru Kenyatta's personal assistant, interrupted before I could finish: "This is our presentation. We sat through yours quietly and we demand that you sit through ours quietly as well." He was supported by Kagwanja.

But I pushed forward. "Well, then we must decide what to do, because for me, I won't sit through that unnecessary pain. First, where are the copies of those constitutions you are summarising? We agreed that each team would bring copies for perusal by everyone. We tabled our copies before presenting; in fairness you must table yours, otherwise, how do we know that your summaries are accurate reflections of what are in the actual documents?" I posed.

"Miguna, we are going to make our presentation the way we choose. It is not up to you to tell us how to proceed," Kibwana retorted.

I briefly consulted with Mutakha before picking up my documents and saying, "In that case, I'm out of here. I think you guys are not serious. Mutakha, let's go."

I immediately departed and drove off. Barely 30 minutes later, while on Waiyaki Way, a reporter from the Nation Media Group called me "to find out if I have just stormed out of a meeting between PNU and ODM negotiators."

"Excuse me? Who gave you that information?" I sought to know.

"Never mind who gave it to me. Just confirm or deny the story."

"Well, if you must know, I did not actually 'storm' out of any meeting; but I left a meeting a few minutes ago."

"Is it true that you said Morocco is a banana republic?" He persisted.

I pulled over and stopped the car and gave him a rundown on what had happened before I left the meeting.

A few hours later, I couldn't believe my ears and eyes when I saw screaming headlines on TV, claiming that I had "disrupted the meeting before storming out" and that I had said all African countries were banana republics. Clearly, the Kenyan media wasn't just being manipulated and used to fight me as an individual, but it was also being used to fight all the progressive agendas on the table. I felt sad but fortified in my determination to forge ahead.

Mutakha and I briefed Raila the following day. Raila expressed his full confidence and support in our work. We subsequently briefed the entire ODM negotiating team, the parliamentary team and the party's joint National Executive Committee and Parliamentary Group. I prepared a detailed summary of events and analysed our options. We agreed that stalemates were inevitable during negotiations and that we might have achieved more during the Serena mediation process if we had strategically orchestrated stalemates, the way PNU did. Orengo and Sally confided in us that Martha Karua was very good in instigating stalemates and crises during the mediation talks, which, on careful analysis, perhaps got the PNU "more than they deserved."

Raila instructed us to prepare a simple outline of the three systems in bullet form, then he would request Kibaki to instruct his team to meet with Mutakha and I again to agree on those outlines. This assignment was firmed up within four days. Under the column dealing with the powers, functions and responsibilities of the President in a hybrid system, we stated that: The President would be elected directly through universal adult suffrage by secret ballot. S/he would be head of state, a symbol of national unity and commander-in-chief of the defence forces. The President chairs the National Defence Council; is responsible for external defence, external affairs and presides over state functions. S/he also appoints constitutional office holders, although this function may be perfunctory in certain instances. S/he appoints high commissioners and ambassadors as recommended by the Prime Minister. The President chairs special cabinet sessions on war and national emergencies. As well, s/he presides over the amnesty procedures. The President may be removed from office through impeachment.

Regarding the powers, functions and responsibilities of the Prime Minister, we indicated that s/he would assume his/her position by virtue of being the leader of the majority party or coalition in the National Assembly. S/he would head government. Under this system, as in the prime ministerial one, government is by cabinet. In other words, important executive decisions are made by Cabinet, not through the executive fiat of an individual as happens in a pure presidential system. However, most of these decisions still have to be ratified by parliament. The Prime Minister chairs cabinet meetings, appoints and dismisses public officers, including cabinet members. S/he is also the leader of the government business in the National Assembly; leads in public policy formulation and implementation; leads the process of initiating and implementing legislation; chairs the National Security Council; and heads inter-governmental relations. The Prime Minister may be removed through a vote of no-confidence in the National Assembly.

We also prepared a summary of both pure presidential and parliamentary systems.

Subsequently, our team tabled these comprehensive documents before a joint PNU and ODM meeting at Kibaki's Harambee House meeting co-chaired by Raila and Kibaki. They clearly outlined government and state functions. We did this in view of the Harmonised Draft Constitution that the CoE had prepared, which provided for a hybrid system where a President elected through universal adult suffrage would share power with a Prime Minister whose party commanded the majority seats in parliament.

It was in the course of the Harambee House negotiations where these documents were tabled that Raila dropped the ball. As people were debating and discussing, Raila suddenly said: "Your Excellency, I have a suggestion to make. I'm not sure if the suggestion will be accepted or rejected, but I get the feeling that we are not making progress. What would the PNU team's response be if we, the ODM side, suggested that we adopt a pure presidential system?"

Raila finished and fiddled with his pen. There was complete silence. Everyone was shocked. Uhuru was the first to recover and he said: "Your Excellency maybe our side need time to consult briefly before we can comment on the suggestion. But for the record, the PNU team appreciates the ODM's realisation that the presidential system is best for this country."

"OK, OK. We can break for a few minutes," the President said. The President and his PNU team left the room. The ODM team talked in hushed tones, mostly agreeing with Raila. I held my tongue briefly. I knew that Raila had betrayed us again.

When the PNU team returned, they stated that they were grateful for ODM's climb-down and would support the decision. Raila, Mudavadi, Ngilu, Mutakha and I then proceeded to his Treasury Building office for a prognosis. And it was there that Raila really shocked me. As soon as we sat down and started discussions, with Mutakha and I pointing out the "difficulties we will face trying to convince our people to support a presidential system that had all along been identified with the PNU team and which ODM had criticised before," Raila became agitated and growled: "Miguna, you can't win all the time; ok? Henry [Kosgey] complained to me that you were rude to him the other day. In your so-called classical examples, you had removed all power from the President and gave it over to the Prime Minister. This is *an elected President*, yet he has no power. Leave this to politicians…We will explain the decision to the people." Raila was clearly angry with me.

It didn't matter that Mutakha and I were saying the same thing; that what we were saying had been said more than a thousand times by virtually all ODM leaders; that it was what the country had identified as 'the ODM position' and one which opinion poll after opinion poll found most Kenyans preferred. Moreover, I didn't consider the position I was pushing was mine. I didn't have a personal interest or position divorced from that of the Orange party. Luckily, ODM's position was also that of the majority of Kenyans and one motivated by progressive and egalitarian philosophy. All we wanted was to expand the democratic space and institutionalise the rule of law and constitutionalism. We had discussed all these matters before and concluded that Kenyans needed to move away from the imperial presidency to a more accountable system of government. Kenyans were tired of a suffocating deity. Raila had supported that view until now. Why had he flip-flopped?

"And Sally was complaining the other day that he was rude to her too…" Musalia chipped in, seeing that I was caged. I couldn't believe it. The attack sounded choreographed. I recoiled back in my seat, waited for the meeting to end and then left. Later, when discussing this incident with Sally, she told me that, "that's the way our people behave. But why is Musalia trying to destroy our friendship? Why did he make that up?" Sally would subsequently set the record straight with Raila over Musalia's claims, but the damage had clearly been done.

As for Kosgey, he had taken offence at a presentation Mutakha and I had made over the systems of government; when I innocently stated that "we know that it would be difficult for people who served under Moi's one-party system to understand, come to terms with, and accept some of the changes being proposed. For instance, we appreciate the fact that the presidency has been a very powerful tool, symbol and instrument in this country and that over the years it has been used mainly to oppress Kenyans, but obviously those who benefited through the presidency might see it only in a good light. Change is painful; so we understand that."

Kosgey had retorted: "You people don't know what you are giving away; you don't know the power and benefits of the presidency." That was his argument. It didn't convince the more than 30 people in the room. Out of those many people in the room (as far as I am aware), only Henry Kosgey took offence at my presentation. Amazingly, Prof. Nyong'o, Orengo and Mutakha said almost the same thing without eliciting any grumbles. I thought Nyong'o was even more stinging. But that's life. Raila had freely chosen his friends and the system of government he preferred. He preferred raw power over good governance and constitutionalism. That's essentially what he had said.

All along, we had no idea that Raila was a closeted PNU who subscribed to the nonsensical argument that the leader of the majority party in parliament who becomes Prime Minister by virtue of his or her party emerging victorious after a general election hasn't been 'popularly elected by the people' merely because the people wouldn't have cast their ballots 'directly' for him. What a crock! How about the Speaker of the National Assembly who is elected by MPs? How about a Chief Justice who is appointed by the Judicial Service Commission? How about many, many other systems of appointment? Are they all illegitimate? Why would a President elected by about three million people in a country with an adult population of more than 20 million have legitimacy, but not a leader of a political party that receives either an equal amount of votes or even more? The argument was clearly faulty; it wasn't founded on firm logic, reason, law or constitutional interpretation. It was voodoo philosophy!

When the Parliamentary Select Committee on the constitutional review process met to deliberate over the "Revised Harmonised Draft", its ODM members were a disjointed group working at cross-purposes. By this time, William Ruto had peeled off with a large chunk of the Rift Valley MPs. He was practically in PNU by then and never attended ODM functions. He had long stopped submitting his monthly dues to the party. He never supported ODM agenda in Parliament. The same applied to more than 15 ODM MPs who supported him. Therefore, it was an act of recklessness for Raila and ODM as a party to have kept William Ruto, Isaac Rutto, Chacha Ganya, Aden Duale and Safia Abdi in the PSC. There was no way these five would back the party's agenda in Naivasha or at any fora where party issues were to be discussed, and where votes were required. During this period, Ababu Namwamba was straddling both sides. For an extended period of time, he had taken off with Ruto. In Naivasha, he couldn't be relied on 70%. He was brilliant, but unreliable.

Once you discounted the five "rebel" MPs and Namwamba, we were left with Musalia Mudavadi, James Orengo, Sally Kosgei, Millie Odhiambo and maybe one or two other people that never contributed to any discussions anyway. And having observed how the ODM team "negotiated", the only people we could count on were Orengo, Sally and Musalia. Both Musalia and Sally weren't lawyers, so there were technicalities that they might have found challenging, but they tried. Millie was another story. She wasn't reliable at all. Not only did she lack a good grasp of the issues, she was always taking off on tangents. Even as late as the two final days at Naivasha, she was still asking me to give her "notes on the important points" I wanted her to raise at the meeting. Mutakha and I had spoon-fed her (and many others) without much to show for it.

That left us with three genuine negotiators against more than 20 on PNU's side. Orengo, Sally and Mudavadi were intellectually solid but lacked grit. Orengo had become particularly unreliable, making strident arguments in ODM consultative meetings, but consistently unable to stand his ground once the PNU hardliners like Jeremiah Kioni, Martha Karua, Uhuru Kenyatta, Moses Wetangula and Kiraitu Murungi eyeballed him. To make matters worse, Orengo fell ill on the last days of the Naivasha meeting. After he fell ill, we were literally surrounded, outflanked and outgunned. But still things got even worse. Mutakha left Naivasha to travel to South Africa four days before the retreat ended. Caroli went AWOL, as usual. I felt stranded. The PNU side had a battalion of war-hardened generals and street fighters: Kivutha Kibwana, Kagwanja, Njiru, Njee Muturi, Justin Muturi, Mukhisa Kituyi, Sakaja and many others. I was so disappointed by our group that I seriously contemplated resigning right there in Naivasha. There we were negotiating the most important document in any country's life, yet ODM couldn't marshal even three technical people to help me. (Though ODM had airtight strategies and positions, it lost due to very weak negotiators.) Even more annoying, while Uhuru, Ruto, Kalonzo and others were around rallying their forces, Raila was nowhere to be found. He would emerge from the woods, after it was too late. In other words, we had lost the war before it had even begun. We had generals and soldiers with guns cocked, but they lacked strategy, tactics and stamina. Many were too scared or compromised to even pull a trigger.

So, when the PSC draft came off the press, I knew that it would be worse than the "Revised Harmonised Draft". And it was; far worse! And after combing through the PSC draft, my suspicions were confirmed. This new draft constitution, being hailed by various leaders as the salvation we had been waiting for, was in fact a giant leap backwards democratically.

The PSC claimed in its "report" to the CoE that its Proposed Draft Constitution "modified" the "Reviewed" Harmonised Draft. But no, in its wisdom, the PSC had usurped powers that didn't legally belong to it and rewritten the entire Draft Constitution. Without justification, the PSC had deleted large chunks of the preamble, values, cultural rights, bill of rights, devolution, the legislature and the entire system of government. The PSC proposal created an imperial President without adequate checks and balances. Not only was the President the head of state and government, s/he would appoint and dismiss all public officials including cabinet ministers, deputy ministers, ambassadors, high commissioners, permanent secretaries, heads of state, corporations and even judges, unilaterally and whimsically, at will. S/he was authorised to create and disband public offices, in addition to being the commander-in-chief of the defence forces; s/he could declare a state of emergency with approval of the cabinet. S/he was also permitted to propose legislation to the National Assembly. In the PSC draft, the President was also chairing both the National Security and Defence Councils.

Contrary to claims by the PSC that they had constructed proper checks and balances that would prevent abuse and misuse of power, the contents of the PSC draft said otherwise. For instance, the President was immune from both criminal and civil proceedings. The impeachment process was cumbersome and complicated. It was virtually impossible to remove a President once elected. That meant that if a rogue President refused to pay for food at a local restaurant or for the construction of his or her private residence, there would have been nowhere an innocent Kenyan could go to obtain justice.

In the PSC draft, the President created and disbanded all public offices. All public servants owed their positions to the President, who would appoint and and fire them at will. Moreover, the much touted "independent" judiciary was still very much a toy for the executive. The "independent" judiciary didn't have administrative, institutional, financial and political independence. The proposed "Judicial Service Commission" comprised mainly presidential appointees. It was to be chaired by the Chief Justice and composed of two judicial officers, the Attorney-General, the chair of the Public Service Commission and a secretary who was the Chief Registrar – all presidential appointees. The only "independent" members of the Judicial Service Commission would be two advocates and two lay members. A team of six senior public officers appointed by the President and four "outsiders" is what the PSC called an "independent" judicial service commission! It's not clear at all how the so-called "independent" judiciary would be a check on the executive.

In all likelihood, a President elected by 50 per cent plus one would have considerable sway in the National Assembly, which was categorised in the PSC draft, contrary to all historical precedents, as the "upper house". Yet, it was the same house that had been mandated with investigating, charging and passing judgment over a President facing impeachment. It amounted to the imperial President being the investigator, prosecutor and judge in his or her own case. That offended all principles of natural justice and well-established democratic tenets. Needless to say, the removal of a sitting President by impeachment would not work as s/he would directly or indirectly control the National Assembly. Nor was there a provision for removal through a vote of no-confidence.

The PSC had retained the provincial administration minus the provinces; they were floating in a vacuum cleverly created for the imperial President to continue dominating governance in the country. They had also proposed functionless "regional assemblies" without regions. And with 47 counties scattered all over the country, but largely concentrated in the Rift Valley and Eastern Provinces, it was difficult to see how the PSC draft improved the repealed system of government. In many ways it made it worse.

In other words, the PSC did not just retain the imperial presidency that had led to terrible abuse of power, repression, corruption; the entrenchment of the culture of impunity, tribalism and all manner of misrule; they had created a monster.

Both Prof. Yash Pal Ghai and I subsequently opined that the PSC draft was worse than the mongrel (old) constitution that Kenyans had overwhelmingly rejected and blamed for all their miseries for the past 50 years. Mutakha and I would later prepare briefs for Raila and the rest of the shambolic ODM team, trying to persuade them to oppose the so-called Naivasha draft. Yash Pal Ghai was equally infuriated. Anyang' saw our point and penned his reservations. Orengo was in denial, as usual. Raila was in hiding.

Had the CoE not intervened to salvage the situation, we would now be saddled with a more retrogressive constitution than the repealed one. Or maybe that was Raila's intention; to get undiluted executive powers if he managed to ascend to the presidency. They ignored my caution: that when drafting laws or constitutions we must try to come up with something that we would be contented to have our worst enemy rule or govern under or with, because no one knows what the future holds.

CHAPTER FIFTEEN

THE YO-YO MAN

On December 15, 2010, I was attending the annual conference organised by the Forum for Federations in Addis Ababa, Ethiopia, when the Prosecutor of the International Criminal Court, Luis Moreno-Ocampo came on live television at about 1.30pm and announced that he had issued summons against five prominent Kenyans and one radio journalist for crimes against humanity committed in Kenya during the cataclysmic violence that followed the contested 2007 presidential election. Every Kenyan at the conference was glued to the single flat screen TV in the hallway of the conference building at the UN facility in Addis. The announcement caused shockwaves throughout Kenya.

I had heard the names weeks before, when Moreno-Ocampo had made his most recent visit to Kenya. During his live TV address, Moreno-Ocampo clustered the names of his suspects into the two main political formations in Kenya: the Orange Democratic Movement (ODM) and the Party of National Unity (PNU). Case One comprised of William Kipchirchir Samoei arap Ruto, Henry Kosgey and Joshua Sang. These, the Prosecutor stated, were members of ODM who had allegedly perpetrated crimes against perceived PNU victims "in an attempt to get state power". Case Two comprised of Francis Karimi Muthaura, Uhuru Muigai Kenyatta and Mohammed Hessein Ali. These three allegedly committed the crimes against perceived ODM members "in order to retain state power".

Apart from radio journalist Joshua arap Sang, the five individuals Moreno-Ocampo had named weren't ordinary people in Kenya. They were men who wielded huge power and influence, thanks to their heritage, wealth and political position.

Born to peasant parents on December 21, 1966 in Kamagut, Uasin Gishu, Kenya, Ruto had risen from humble beginnings to reach almost the apex of political power at a relatively young age, thanks to the mentorship of Kenya's autocrat and former President Daniel Teroitich arap Moi. He was an ODM MP for Eldoret North and had served as Minister for Agriculture and Higher Education after the grand coalition government was formed in March 2008. On October 19, 2010, he had been suspended by the government on corruption charges involving alleged unlawful acquisition of public land. Although the case had been dismissed for lack of evidence, his discharge had been shrouded in mystery as evidence was later disclosed that the main witness who had failed to show up at the trial had been given a job in one of the parastatals of the Ministry of Agriculture when Ruto served as minister. He had been ODM's main pointman for Rift Valley Province and a Pentagon member during the 2007 elections. Under President Moi, Ruto had distinguished himself as an indefatigable mobiliser and Organising Secretary of the dreaded Youth For Kanu '92 (YK'92), a group formed to drum up support for Moi in the 1992 election and from where Ruto quickly rose to become an MP, then assistant minister, minister and Kanu's Secretary General. He had resigned from his post as KANU secretary general on October 6 2007 and joined the ODM.

Now, he was facing charges at the ICC for allegedly planning and organising crimes against supporters of President Kibaki's Party of National Unity. He is charged with three counts of crimes against humanity: murder, forcible transfer of population (mainly of Gikuyu ethnic group) and persecution. On January 23, 2012, the ICC confirmed the charges against Ruto and Joshua Sang, in a case that also involved Uhuru Kenyatta, Francis Muthaura, Henry Kosgey and Major General Mohammed Hussein Ali. One of the crimes Ruto is accused of being involved with is the Kiambaa Church Massacre of January 1, 2008. The Commission of Inquiry into the Post-Election Violence (CIPEV or what is popularly known as the Waki Commission) released its findings in 2009 and established among other things that "the incident which captured the attention of both Kenyans and the world was the deliberate burning alive of mostly Gikuyu women and children huddled together in a church in Kiambaa on 1 January 2008". The death toll was 17 burned alive in the church, 11 dying in or on the way to hospital, and 54 others injured who were treated and discharged.

Ruto was undeniably a controversial figure. He has been in and out of various Kenyan courts over allegations of fraud, land grabbing and corruption. In early 2009, Ruto narrowly survived a parliamentary censure motion over allegations that he orchestrated irregular allocations and sales of 2.6m bags of maize in June

2008 and had allegedly, as Agriculture Minister, improperly allocated maize to companies and individuals that were underserving, resulting in the loss of billions of taxpayer money. Even though he survived the censure motion, the scandal left a permanent stain on his image. Then, of course, there was his spirited campaign against the ratification of the reformist new Kenyan Constitution, which the public overwhelmingly approved in a referendum held on August 4, 2010.

Henry Kosgey was both an ODM national chairman and the Minister for Industrialisation. He had served in numerous cabinet portfolios under former President Moi. He also had significant wealth. Although he faced charges at the ICC, the pre-trial chamber declined to confirm them, together with charges against Hussein Ali.

Uhuru Muigai Kenyatta, born 26 October 1961, was the closest Kenya has had to an oligarch. Uhuru is the son of Jomo Kenyatta, Kenya's first President (1964-1978). His name, *Uhuru*, is Swahili for "freedom". Nominated to Parliament in 2001 by Moi, he became Minister for Local Government and despite his political inexperience, was handpicked by Moi as his successor. This caused major divisions and a dramatic fallout within the ruling party Kanu, precipitating Uhuru's loss in that election, which propelled Mwai Kibaki to power in December 2002. Uhuru subsequently became Leader of the Opposition in Parliament. However, during the 2007 elections, he backed Kibaki for re-election and was named Minister of Local Government by Kibaki in January 2008, before becoming Deputy Prime Minister and Minister of Trade in April 2008 as part of a coalition government. From 2009 to 2012, Uhuru served as both Deputy Prime Minister and Minister for Finance. Accused by the International Criminal Court (ICC) of committing crimes against humanity in relation to the violent aftermath of the 2007 election, he resigned as Minister of Finance on January 26, 2012 but remains Deputy Prime Minister. He is the Gatundu South MP.

On December 15, 2010, Uhuru was named as a suspect of crimes against humanity by the ICC prosecutor for planning and funding violence in Naivasha and Nakuru, mainly against the Luo and Luhya ethnic groups. He has been accused of funding and organising a Gikuyu militia group, the Mungiki, during the post-election violence. On March 8, 2011 he, together with the other five co-accused, was summoned to appear before the ICC pre-trial chamber.

On September 29, 2011, while seeking to exonerate himself, Uhuru Kenyatta put up a spirited fight as he was being cross-examined by ICC Chief prosecutor Luis Moreno-Ocampo in the Hague, denying any links with the outlawed Mungiki sect. He said Kenya's Prime Minister Raila Odinga should take political responsibility for the acts of violence and killings that followed the 2007 presidential elections in Kenya. He told the three judges that Raila "by telling his supporters election results were being rigged, fanned tensions and then failed to use his influence to quell the violence that followed the announcement of the 2007 presidential results."

Both Uhuru and Ruto have announced that they will vie for the presidency of Kenya in the upcoming elections despite the serious charges that the ICC pre-trial Chamber has confirmed against them.

Also facing serious charges at the ICC is the head of the Kenyan Civil Service, Secretary to the Cabinet and President Kibaki's Permanent Secretary, Francis Karimi Muthaura. The allegations against Muthaura cut close to the seat of power as they revolve around Muthaura's alleged facilitation of Mungiki's movement to and from Naivasha and Nakuru and their alleged meetings with President Kibaki at State House, Nairobi after the 2007 electoral debacle but before the commission of the crimes against humanity.

Hence, the ICC process hasn't just caused major political and legal tremors in Kenya; it has also caused significant political realignments, mainly arrayed against Raila. In both a dramatic and unprecedented move, Uhuru and Ruto have ganged up against Raila and have declared that they will do everything within their powers to stop Raila from becoming President. They have formed a loose alliance called the Group of 7 (or G7), whose primary intention is to galvanise seven major ethno-religious 'constituencies' – the Gikuyu, the Kalenjin, the Luhya, the Kamba, the Meru, the Muslims and other 'marginalised and smaller groups – against Raila's electoral quest.

Under these circumstances – and given his reform credentials – one would have thought and expected Raila to firmly stand up and strongly agitate for the ICC process as the most practical and desirable process of establishing the truth and seeking and obtaining justice for the victims of the crimes committed during the post-election violence. It wouldn't just have been good politics for Raila, it would also have been good statecraft. He needed to be steadfast and consistent. After all, opinion polls have consistently shown that more than 63 per cent of Kenyans trust the ICC process over the Kenyan judiciary. Even though the judiciary is undergoing major reforms, the culture of incompetence, corruption and impunity persist and will take time to eradicate.

Moreover, Raila was involved in instigating the ICC process. At the height of the post-election violence in January 2008, ODM instructed James Orengo, then an ODM-MP for Ugenya and an experienced lawyer of many decades, to send a petition to the International Criminal Court (ICC) and seek the Court's intervention in the past and ongoing crimes against humanity that the party believed had not just been committed, but were still being committed by Kenya's security forces and the pro-PNU Mungiki gangs, generally against innocent and unarmed civilians, and specifically, against ODM supporters. Thousands of innocent Kenyans – especially those perceived to be ODM supporters – had been murdered in cold blood; seriously injured; maimed; raped; displaced; and their properties either looted or destroyed, by the security forces and state funded militias like Mungiki. ODM didn't trust the police or the judiciary to dispense justice for the victims of these crimes. It was common knowledge that virtually all senior security agents had been single-handedly appointed by Kibaki and would therefore continue to serve his interests and those of the PNU. Similarly, the judiciary still lacked independence; it was still prone to influence and interference from the executive. Despite the formation of the coalition government, Kibaki still controlled the executive

Although newspaper reports claimed that Orengo had submitted the petition, he never made a copy available to members of the Pentagon Technical Team despite our many requests and reminders. This isn't to imply that Orengo didn't send a petition to the ICC, it's only to underline the fact that I have never seen a copy of the same.

Soon, Martha Karua (then the Minister for Justice, National Cohesion and Constitutional Affairs) and her colleagues in the PNU also announced that they had petitioned the ICC to investigate allegations of ODM's complicity in crimes against humanity; crimes that targeted members of PNU. In other words, as early as January 2008, both PNU and ODM had requested the ICC's involvement in Kenya. It must be assumed that both parties had full confidence in the ICC as an institution and the ICC statute as an instrument. Indeed, Kenya was already one of the states party to the ICC.

The second point is that by seeking the intervention of the ICC on crimes that had been committed within its territory, both parties had acknowledged the limitations of the domestic judicial system in dealing with the crimes in a timely and just manner. And since both parties represented the overwhelming majority of Kenyans, it is arguable that as far back as January 2008, most Kenyans supported the involvement of the ICC with respect to the post-election violence. This is an indisputable fact.

The ICC is an international criminal court, which is complimentary to national systems. This means that when there are *genuine* state actions or proceedings the court cannot intervene. And for the state actions or proceedings to be deemed genuine, the relevant state must be willing and able to act. In other words, there mustn't just be political will at the highest level of state and government; the institutions and actors at all levels must have the desire and capacity to deal with international crimes committed within the jurisdiction of that specific nation-state.

Since the ICC was established by states parties to the Rome Statute, the states have a right and primary responsibility to prevent, control and prosecute atrocities committed within their territorial boundaries. As the Court's first prosecutor, Luis Moreno-Ocampo, once stated: "Complementarity protects national sovereignty and at the same time protects state action." However, in the event that atrocities are committed inside the territory of a state party, and the state is either unwilling or unable (for a range of reasons) to bring the perpetrators to account, the relevant state or another state party have the option of referring the situation to the ICC; or the United Nations Security Council may pass a resolution to refer the situation to the ICC.

In addition, the prosecutor of the ICC has the right and option to make an application before the Court and seek an order permitting him or her to investigate the situation and seek an order or orders authorising him or her to prosecute those identified through the investigations, to bear the highest responsibilities over those atrocities. Atrocities such as genocide, war crimes, crimes against humanity, and other serious crimes targeting large groups of unarmed civilians fall under the ambit of the Rome Statute.

Essentially, the ICC has a common mission to ensure that the most serious crimes of concern to humanity are investigated and punished as a way of protecting millions of innocent people around the world. It is an independent and impartial court. However, it works in collaboration with state parties, non-parties, multilateral organisations, non-governmental organisations, universities, the business sector and the media in trying to prevent, curtail, expose and punish impunity in the world. In other words, it is both independent and interdependent at the same time. It cannot act alone. It can only achieve its mandate effectively and efficiently if it works closely and collaboratively with other members of the international community. This is particularly so in view of the fact that it isn't a state with an army, police, intelligence and other security agencies. Nevertheless, it has the capacity to conduct credible investigations. It also has the ability to conduct fair and impartial proceedings to determine whether or not the prosecutor has produced enough evidence upon which suspects and accused persons may be found guilty of the allegations or charges.

But to fulfill its mandate, the ICC requires the full cooperation of nation-states where atrocities have occurred. This is so because relevant evidence can only be obtained from crime scenes. This demands that ICC investigators must be allowed to comb those scenes, which are situated within the territory of nation-states. It might require that the state – whether a party or non-party – doesn't interfere with the work of the ICC; that it avails and protects witnesses and other evidence. The problem, however, arises where state actors are either responsible or complicit to the crimes alleged.

This is the case in Sudan and Kenya. In both cases, the ICC has alleged that senior members of the respective governments – going as high as the serving heads of state – were either directly (in the case of Sudan) or indirectly (in the case of Kenya), involved in the conception, planning, execution and concealment of the atrocities. In Kenya's case, Kibaki's own right hand man, Muthaura, faced serious charges, with allegations touching on the presidency. And someone many believe to be Kibaki's chosen successor, Uhuru Muigai Kenyatta, also faces similar charges. Not only was the heart of power accused of crimes against humanity, the ICC trials – if they proceed – would ultimately interfere with the succession arrangement. Defiance doesn't seem like a viable option in view of the fact that given Kenya's centrality in modern geopolitical calculations of the major powers (especially the ongoing fight against terrorism) having a pariah or fugitive presiding over the state doesn't look like something that would be permitted by the US or other major powers. Yet two of those accused – the wealthy Uhuru and Ruto -are still insistent on gunning for the presidency. Then of course, is that question: where would they hide from the reach of the international community? Kenya, after all, isn't the Democratic Republic of Congo.

Ultimately, the ICC's mandate is to protect victims of international crimes. Inasmuch as justice is the basic and primary mission of the court, it wasn't set up for the alleged perpetrators of international crimes. Those are guaranteed a fair, transparent and impartial process where their alleged involvements would be assessed and independent determinations made. But the focus and primary mission is the protection of victims. Whatever the prosecutor or the court does must serve the interests of justice.

On March 4, 2008, PNU members of the Serena Mediation Team – Martha Karua, Prof. Sam Ongeri, Mutula Kilonzo and Moses Wetangula – on the one hand, and their ODM counterparts – Musalia Mudavadi, William Ruto, Sally Kosgei and James Orengo – on the other, signed an agreement in which they provided for the establishment of a "Commission of Inquiry into the Post-Election Violence (CIPEV). Briefly, CIPEV's terms of reference were to "identify and agree on the modalities of implementation of immediate measures aimed at: ensuring the impartial, effective and expeditious investigation of gross and systematic violations of human rights and that those found guilty are brought to justice; identifying and prosecuting the perpetrators of violence, including state security agents; and, addressing issues of accountability and transparency".

The Parties to the National Dialogue and Reconciliation, together with the Panel of Eminent African Personalities (The Panel), agreed to the establishment of the CIPEV, which was supposed to undertake the following activities: to investigate the facts and circumstances related to the violence following the 2007 presidential election, between December 28, 2007 and February 28, 2008; to prepare and submit a final report containing its findings and recommendations for redress, any legal action that should be taken, and measures for future prevention; and to make recommendations as it deems appropriate to the Truth, Justice, and Reconciliation Commission. In effect, it was stated that Kenyan authorities, institutions, parties and others shall fully cooperate with the Commission of Inquiry in the accomplishment of its mandate in response to requests for information, security, assistance or access in pursuing investigations, including the following: adoption by the Government of Kenya of any measures needed for the Commission and its personnel to carry out their functions throughout the national territory with full freedom, independence and security; provision by the Government of Kenya and all Kenyan state institutions of all information in its possession which the commission requests or is otherwise needed to carry out its mandate, with free access provided for the Commission and its staff to any archives related to its mandate; freedom for the Commission to obtain any information it considers relevant and to use all sources of information which it considers useful and reliable; freedom for the Commission to interview, in private, any persons it judges necessary; freedom for the Commission to visit any establishment or place at any time; and a guarantee by the Government of Kenya of full respect for the integrity, security and freedom of witnesses, experts and any other persons who help in its work.

By Gazette Notice number 8661, dated September 11, 2008, President Mwai Kibaki gave an extension to CIPEV to "report on its findings and recommendations… not later than October 16, 2008." My considered view is that these terms of reference covered virtually everything: the integrity of the investigations, the credibility of the outcome of the investigations, and the undertaking by "the Kenyan authorities, institutions, parties and others" to respect and fully implement all the recommendations and findings of the CIPEV. All the parties were represented and they signed of their own free will. Having voluntarily established the CIPEV, funded and guaranteed its work as well as undertook to implement all its recommendations, any self-respecting government couldn't turn around and try to dissociate itself from the CIPEV.

In fact on December 16, 2008 Kibaki and Raila publicly signed a written undertaking that any public officer charged with offences related to the post-election violence would be immediately suspended from public office pending investigations. The officers would be fired if the investigations established that the accused had cases to answer. Yet in the case of the ICC suspects, both principals (Kibaki and Raila) didn't act when Moreno-Ocampo named the six suspects. They did nothing when the ICC pre-trial Chamber confirmed those charges against the four prominent Kenyans. And they have continued to do nothing even after the four accused have been sent to trial. Whereas I was getting suspended indefinitely without pay, my staff being fired summarily and my personal effects being detained over undisclosed and unparticularised manufactured allegations that didn't touch on my integrity; Raila kept mum over people charged with mass murder, mass forcible displacement of civilian populations, mass rape, commission of cruel, degrading and inhumane acts, among other serious criminal acts. Instead, Muthaura, Ali, Uhuru, Kosgey continued to earn their hefty salaries and perks; continued to be guarded and their homes protected by state security agents; and the costs of their legal defense and health care paid for by taxpayers, including myself. Not once did Raila publicly complain or register dissent against this outrageous abuse and desecration of public office.

After months of diligent investigations, the CIPEV published and launched their report, findings and recommendations in mid-December, 2008. The recommendations were:

1. A special tribunal, to be known as the Special Tribunal for Kenya be set up as a court that will sit within Kenya to investigate and try those persons bearing the greatest responsibility for crimes against humanity, relating to the 2007 General Elections.
2. The use of Kenyan law and also the International Crimes Act. The Special Tribunal will have both Kenyan and international judges, as well as Kenyan and international staff.
3. Both PNU and ODM shall, within 60 days of the presentation of the CIPEV Report to the Panel of Eminent African Personalities, sign an agreement establishing the Special Tribunal.Subsequently, an enabling law shall be enacted within 45 days..
4. *The date of commencement of the functioning of the Special Tribunal shall be determined by the President, in consultation with the Prime*

Minister, the Chief Justice, the Minister for Justice, National Cohesion and Constitutional Affairs and the Attorney-General, within 30 days after the giving of Presidential Assent to the Bill enacting the Statute. [Emphasis added]

5. If the Special Tribunal is not set up as stated above, a list containing names of and relevant information on those suspected to bear the greatest responsibility for crimes falling within the jurisdiction of the proposed Special Tribunal shall be forwarded to the Special Prosecutor of the International Criminal Court.
6. The Special Tribunal Bill shall be anchored in the Constitution of Kenya and shall not be subject to any legal challenges.
7. The Special Tribunal shall consist of four organs: the Chambers (including an Appeals Chamber) and the Prosecutor, which shall be independent of each other, the Registry, and the Defence Office.
8. The Tribunal Chambers shall be composed of 6 independent judges, three in the Trial Chamber, and three in the Appeals Chamber. The Presiding Judge of each Chamber shall be a Kenyan while the other two judges in each chamber shall be non-Kenyan but drawn from the Commonwealth..

(…)

13. The Special Tribunal shall have exclusive custody of all investigative material and witness statements and testimony collected and recorded by this Commission.

The Commission makes the following further recommendations:

1. The International Crimes Bill 2008 be fast-tracked for enactment by Parliament to facilitate investigation and prosecution of crimes against humanity.
2. The Witness Protection Act 2008 be fully utilised in the protection of all witnesses who will need such protection in the course of investigation, prosecution and adjudication of PEV cases.
3. The Freedom of Information Bill be enacted forthwith to enable state and non-state actors to have full access to information which may lead to arrest, detention and prosecution of persons responsible for gross violations.
4. *All persons holding public office and public servants charged with criminal offences related to post-election violence be suspended from*

duty until the matter is fully adjudicated upon. [Emphasis added]

5. Upon conviction of any person charged with post-election violence offences of any nature, such persons shall be barred from holding any public office or contesting any electoral position.

Quite clearly, the CIPEV provided a big window of opportunity for both President Kibaki and Prime Minister Raila Odinga to rally their troops together and have a "Special Tribunal for Kenya" established as a court within the territorial boundaries of the Republic of Kenya. The Special Tribunal was to conduct credible investigations and trials of persons bearing the greatest responsibility over crimes against humanity committed during the same period.

Both Kibaki and Raila received the CIPEV report and publicly committed themselves to its full and complete implementation. Indeed, they had two Special Tribunals drafted and taken to Parliament; both times the bills were rejected. In the first instance, the Special Tribunal Bill was rejected due to deficiencies, gaps and issues pertaining to attempts to shield some of the most responsible persons from accountability. The CIPEV didn't provide for immunity even of a sitting head of state. In the second instance, there was no political will. Both Raila and Kibaki gave confused and lacklustre support for the Bill, resulting in its rejection by Parliament. In fact the third attempt, which revolved around a qualitatively better bill, was rejected at the cabinet level; a level that neither the CIPEV report recommended nor the law required.

My view throughout was that both Raila and Kibaki, having undertaken to enforce all the recommendations, did not need to take the bill to the cabinet for approval; and even if they did (which was a deliberate attempt to scuttle the bills), this should have been a mere formality. It was inconceivable that a cabinet appointed by the two principals would reject anything they proposed and supported. In modern democratic practice, internal dissent is allowed (should even be encouraged); however, if a cabinet minister feels so strongly that their appointing authority is wrong, they have the option of resigning or being dismissed if they fail to resign.

In my view, no cabinet minister was going to oppose anything proposed by the President and the Prime Minister. The only logical explanation for Kibaki's and Raila's refusal to 'whip' the cabinet in support of the bills intended to establish the "Special Tribunal", was that either one of them or both of them were actually opposed to the establishment of a Special Tribunal. The question is: why? Why would one or both of them oppose a local process that would establish the truth and bring to account those who perpetrated the crimes during the PEV? More than 1,200 Kenyans had been murdered. More than 600,000 innocent civilians had been displaced, uprooted from places of their habitual residence. Billions of shillings worth of property had been destroyed. Tens of thousands had been maimed and seriously injured. Thousands had been raped. Tens of thousands had been subjected to inhumane, cruel and unjust punishment. Why wouldn't Kibaki and Raila want expeditious justice for the victims of these serious crimes? Could it be that either one or both of them feared that if credible investigations were conducted, it would disclose their direct or indirect involvement? If not, why didn't they comply strictly with the CIPEV recommendations?

Subsequently, The Special Rapporteur on Extrajudicial Summary or Arbitrary Executions, Prof. Philip Alston, visited Kenya from February 16-25, 2009. At the end of his visit he published his findings. The primary focus of his mission was on allegations of unlawful killings by the police in their day-to-day work, by the military (especially in relation to the conflict in Mt. Elgon), and by diverse actors in the PEV. Prof. Alston's main concern was "the impunity enjoyed by those responsible for the vast majority of these killings." He noted that "Kenya's international obligations also require it to effectively investigate, prosecute and punish all those responsible for the unlawful killings. The killings by the police are widespread. Some killings are opportunistic, reckless or personal. Many others are carefully planned. It is impossible to estimate reliably how many killings occur because the police do not keep a centralised database. But police shootings are reported every day of the week by the press and the total number is certainly unacceptably high…"

So widespread were the killings by the security forces that Raila once told me of a bizarre incident when the former Police Commissioner, Maj-Gen. Hussein Ali, and the Director General of the National Intelligence Service, Maj-Gen. Michael Gichangi, visited him at his Treasury Building offices, sat across from him and confessed to having been involved or having authorised the barbaric murder of about four Mungiki "negotiators" who were on their way to the Naivasha Maximum Prison to visit Maina Njenga who was then serving term at that prison. Some or all of the people killed had visited Raila and sought his assurance for their safety and security, which Raila had given, having spoken with both Gichangi and Ali. Both men had visited Raila's office on the heels of two other high profile cold-blooded assassinations on State House Road, near the halls of residence of the University of Nairobi. Oscar Kinga'ra and John Oulu were human rights defenders then running the Oscar Foundation. They had previously made allegations against some high profile public figures and top government officials, including John Michuki and Alfred Mutua.

Shortly after they had been killed in broad daylight, Raila publicly requested the assistance of the FBI through the American Embassy in Nairobi. The request was promptly accepted. However, the Minister for Internal Security and Provincial Administration, Prof. George Saitoti, rejected the offer from the Americans. The letter rejecting the offer wasn't even copied to Raila.

But rather than take steps to countermand Prof. Saitoti, Raila did nothing. The same way he did nothing after hearing "the confessions" from Ali and Gichangi. He didn't even raise those issues with Kibaki. Neither did he take them before the Permanent Committee on the Management of Grand Coalition Affairs. None of his lieutenants took the matter to Parliament either. All he did was lament to me and to others. That wasn't leadership and I reminded him of this.

In any event, after realising that the government had taken the country in circles for years the CIPEV Chairman, Justice Philip Waki, forwarded the envelope containing the names of people the inquiry believed should be investigated further (with a view to having some or all of them prosecuted) and bundles of evidence to Kofi Annan for onward transmission to the ICC.

However, before Annan delivered those documents to the ICC, he granted the Government of Kenya a brief extension and accorded them a further opportunity to set up the recommended Special Tribunal. When that also failed, Annan gave the Government a month to approach the ICC and seek an extension. I accompanied James Orengo, Mutula Kilonzo, Amos Wako and Amina Mohammed to both Geneva and The Hague in 2009 to seek a one-year extension. The ICC granted a 90-day extension, but with stringent conditions including detailed "reports" of the stage of the investigations, the crimes being investigated and the persons being investigated, by the end of September 2009.

When the Government failed to meet those conditions, the ICC Prosecutor, Luis Moreno-Occampo visited Kenya and was taken through the usual mumbo jumbo by Kibaki and Raila. On November 6, 2009, the ICC issued the "Decision assigning the situation in the Republic of Kenya to Pre-Trial Chamber II." On November 26, 2009, the Prosecutor filed the "Request for authorisation of an investigation pursuant to Article 15" of the Rome Statute. On March 31, 2010, the Pre-Trial Chamber II, by a majority decision, granted the Prosecutor's request for authorisation to conduct investigations into the PEV. Subsequently the Prosecutor conducted investigations in Kenya, resulting in his application for confirmation hearings, a petition that was granted with an order in 2010 sending the six for confirmation hearings.

Meanwhile Raila would breathe hot and cold. Privately he consistently told me how much he hoped and prayed that Uhuru Kenyatta and William Ruto were confirmed, tried and convicted at The Hague. In fact he expressed his hope that Ruto and Uhuru would have warrants of arrests against them and that on their first appearances at The Hague they would be detained until their confirmation hearings. He sounded desperate to remove both Uhuru and Ruto from the 2012 presidential race. But publicly (and predictably), he pretended to support a local tribunal. That wasn't genuine.

Deep down Raila had always prayed for the 'success' of the ICC process; not for justice to prevail, but as a means of sorting out his political opponents. Even within ODM Raila was always yo-yoing; stating his commitment to a local process, but privately quite happy at the speed and course the ICC process was taking. There were countless meetings between Raila, a senior European diplomat based in Nairobi and I, where we discussed the strategies of having ODM express support for the process. Salim would attend some of the meetings whenever he was in Nairobi. It was during one of those meetings that Raila made the decision to send Salim and I to The Hague during the first appearances of the Ocampo Six. The rationale was for the Ocampo Six and about 100 supporters, including more than 30 PNU and ODM-rebel affiliated MPs, not to dominate the airwaves with anti-ODM propaganda; we needed to bear witness to the proceedings and accurately relay what we observed back to Kenya.

Our trip was fully funded by the OPM. I subsequently published a detailed "journal" of the trip. It was therefore obnoxious for Jakoyo Midiwo to later claim that I had made that trip "alone, without permission from the Prime Minister". Not only was the aide-mémoire by ODM Secretary General, Prof. Anyang' Nyong'o, prepared and forwarded to the UN Security Council on direct authority and express instructions by Raila, the discussions took days and many, many hours to conclude.

While Anyang' feigned ignorance of the ICC process, Salim Lone, the European diplomat (whom I will not name because they are still serving and disclosing their name might jeopardise or compromise their position) and I argued strongly for ODM to publicly take a stand. Orengo waffled back and forth. One day he would be for the idea, then the following day he would oppose it. Rumours were swirling that he had been seen frequenting both Muthaura's and Permanent Secretary for Internal Security, Francis Kimemia's offices. In other words, Orengo created the impression that he might have been compromised. It reminded me of the incident in his office, when I unexpectedly dropped over to see him, only to meet one of President Kibaki's bodyguards. That tweaked my curiosity. Upon inquiry, Orengo told me that the young man had been with him "in the trenches during the Mageuzi days" (when he had been a political activist);

that he is the one who had helped the man join the GSU years before he became Kibaki's bodyguard. However, a few months after he had told me that hilarious story I accompanied Raila to the Aberdares where he was inaugurating "The Rhino Charge" with President Kibaki. After the event, as we went for lunch at a local hotel, I asked one of Raila's bodyguards if he knew the same Kibaki bodyguard Orengo had claimed was with him in Mageuzi. The man told me without hesitation: "That's one of Kibaki's worst guards. He is the one who blocked State House gate for Raila in December 2002. He has been with Kibaki since DP; how can Orengo say that?" Right there and then I realised that Orengo had become unreliable and that I could no longer trust him; not on the ICC and not on anything important. So when Orengo started stalling on the aide-mémoire, refusing to make time to review what I had drafted for Anyang's signature, as Raila had directed, I had the document delivered to the Security Council without his approval. Neither did we show the document to busybodies like Jakoyo or Oburu.

Throughout the ICC process, my focus has always been in the interest of justice; justice for the innocent victims of the atrocities that were committed in Kenya between 2005 and 2008. Tens of thousands of innocent and unarmed civilians were killed, maimed, displaced, traumatised and raped, many times with the direct involvement or complicity of state actors. These people have no ability to seek or obtain justice for themselves. Many are long dead. Some are too traumatised and damaged to be able to seek justice. Others are simply incapable due to limitations in their education, exposure, power equations (vis-à-vis the perpetrators) and socio-economic conditions.

Contrary to some vile propaganda, I have never pursued justice for the victims in the Kenyan situation because of any personal interests, vendetta or parochial political motive. I have no personal grudge against the six Kenyans that faced investigations by the ICC or the four who had their charges confirmed. Nor do I have any animus towards them or the four persons the Pre-Trial Chamber II confirmed charges against on January 23, 2012.

Moreno-Ocampo had no personal interest in Kenya or its politics when he sought permission from the Court to investigate the Kenyan situation. In fact his letter to the President of the International Criminal Court, Sang-Hyun Song, dated November 5, 2009, was a simple one-paragraph affair:

> In accordance with Regulation 45 of the Regulations of the Court, I have... determined, on the basis of information on crimes within the jurisdiction of the Court, that there is a reasonable basis to

> proceed with an investigation into the Situation in the Republic of Kenya in relation to the post-election violence of 2007-2008.

On November 6, 2009, President Song responded by constituting the Pre-Trial Chamber II to immediately take charge of the Kenyan situation, as requested by Moreno-Ocampo.

Eventually, the Pre-Trial Chamber II – composed completely of Europeans – made a determination to allow the prosecutor's application for investigation of the Situation. The Pre-Trial Chamber II subsequently issued summons against the six Kenyans. And on Tuesday, January 23, 2012, they confirmed the charges against four: Uhuru Muigai Kenyatta, Francis Kirimi Muthaura, William Samoei Ruto and Joshua arap Sang. As far as I am aware, neither the request to investigate or charge the group of prominent Kenyans nor the court orders authorising investigations and confirming the charges emanated from Washington, London, Rome, Paris or Berlin, as many Kenyan ICC detractors and critics have claimed without any basis or foundation.

I am, of course, alive to the (legitimate) charges that have been made by some eminent scholars, lawyers and states over the apparent dominance of the ICC process by Europe, especially Germany, UK, Italy, France and Spain, largely based on the perception that, because they have often contributed about 44% of the ICC's annual operation budget, they would, invariably, be able to pull some strings. The respected scholar Professor Mahmood Mamdani of Uganda has accused the ICC of dancing to the tune of Western states.

But the most recent, detailed and extremely caustic criticism of the ICC has been advanced by Dr David Hoile in his 2010 book *The International Criminal Court – Europe's Guantanamo Bay?* Apart from the budgetary-control argument, Dr Hoile thesis is premised on four other grounds. First, he argues that because the process that led to the establishment of the ICC was flawed, rushed, and NGO-driven (with Africa largely absent); and because the United Nations Diplomatic Conference of Plenipotentiaries on the Establishment of an International Criminal Court, which was held in Rome, Italy, from June 15 to July 17, 1998, "to finalise and adopt a convention on the establishment of an international criminal court," was adopted by a vote of 120 to 17, with 21 countries abstaining (with Iraq, Israel, Libya, China, Qatar, USA and Yemen voting against); the court doesn't have global legitimacy. Moreover, Dr Hoile continues, quoting another ICC critic, Prof. David Davenport: "The bar for approval of the Rome Statute was set remarkably low, with the court to be approved upon ratification of only 60 nations out of 189 in the United Nations...

For a court that purports to have worldwide jurisdiction, even over citizens of countries that do not sign the treaty, this is a narrow base of approval…Further, such a process takes no account of geographic representation, population base, or strategic considerations, but simply relies upon a one-nation-one-vote approach…"

But this is a slippery-slope argument. He posits that because seven of the ratifiers: San Marino, Nauru, Andorra, Liechtenstein, Dominica, Antigua and Barbuda, and the Marshall Islands had a population of about 347,000, "which is less than the population of New York's smallest borough of Staten Island," their votes shouldn't have counted equally with China (1.25 billion), USA (312 million), Indonesia (230 million), Russia (150 million) and Japan (125 million). "Thus, while the ICC may aspire to be a universal court exercising universal jurisdiction, the simple fact is that it does not qualify on either count," Dr Hoile concludes.

But Dr Hoile is aware that only countries or nation-states are members of the United Nations. States Parties to the ICC Statute voluntarily ratified it. Clearly, no States Party was coerced into ratifying the statute. Neither is any dissatisfied party prevented from withdrawing its membership. Similarly, only states are parties to the Rome Statute. Whether a country's population is 100 or 10 billion, its membership is one and it can only cast one vote. There is only one China as an entity. Despite the billions of inhabiters, China has only one government, headed by one head of state, with a single representative to global bodies such as the UN. Consequently, Antigua and Barbuda – despite their sparse population – have the same rights and privileges – as states under international law, conventions and treaties – with such well endowed states as China, India and the rest.

But once a state ratifies the Rome Statute and operationalises the ICC instruments, the Court becomes part and parcel of that country's judicial process. One cannot therefore legitimately argue that the Court is 'foreign' to African countries that freely ratify the ICC regime. The Court is complimentary to domestic courts. It's a court of last resort. It only kicks in when a States Party's authorities are unable or unwilling to deal with genocide, war crimes and crimes against humanity that have been committed within that state's territorial boundaries.

Dr Hoile strongly objects to what he characterises as serious flaws of the Rome Statute. He considers article 13(b) and 16 of the ICC Statute, which grants "special prosecutorial rights" (to refer or defer an ICC investigation) to the UN Security Council, a major defect. I agree with him. It is rather odd and unacceptable that of five founding, permanent members of the Security Council

– US, UK, France, China and Russia – three (US, China and Russia) have not ratified the Rome Statute – yet they sit and decide on which cases to refer to or defer from the ICC. If the Court is legitimate, upholds the highest international judicial standards and has universal jurisdiction over genocide, war crimes and crimes against humanity, why aren't the permanent members of the UN Security Council subjecting themselves to its mandate?

If the US has refused to join the ICC on the flimsy basis that there are "insufficient checks and balances on the authority of the ICC prosecutor and judges" and that "the Rome Statute creates a self-initiating prosecutor answerable to no state or institution other than the Court itself," doesn't it mean that the US is only interested on a judicial system it can "control?" How and why is it that Sudan, which isn't a States Party to the ICC, can have its head of state indicted and warrants for his arrest issued for serious violations of human rights and crimes against humanity in Darfur, yet the US, China or Russia cannot even have their soldiers, police officers or civilians indicted for the same or worse crimes?

Admittedly, the US legal system is more rigorous and accountable than that of Sudan. But the same cannot be said of Russia or China. Nor would that be sufficient justification for not permitting independent investigations of alleged violations by US authorities and security agents in other countries. In my view, if the US was serious about its concerns over alleged institutional weaknesses of the ICC system, the solution should be to ensure that those weaknesses are either eliminated or the system strengthened. The best option should have been to make the ICC a first-class judicial institution, not to oppose or fight it.

Thirdly, Dr Hoile states, quoting the Israeli researcher Seth Frantzman, that "the Court is primarily European-run. Yet those it judges are not from Europe; they are usually [taken] from their home countries and shipped to Europe to sit in a European prison…This is at best an unfair system and at worst a colonialist one." Dr Hoile charges that the Court's agenda is the "recolonisation of Africa."

That's a good point. However, I haven't seen any credible evidence to go that far in my assessment. Admittedly, the Court is 'dominated' by Europeans, and that situation needs to be redressed. Nonetheless, we need to openly acknowledge that poor training, corruption and political interference with the judiciary are afflictions Africa (for instance) has experienced more than North America or Western Europe. We need not quibble with obvious facts.

So the challenge is to both Africa and the world community as a whole to ensure that the ICC system should be fully representative of the entire world, with all its cultural, racial and religious differences. But we also need to acknowledge that the ICC critics have raised weighty matters that deserve to be addressed comprehensively. It's troubling that citizens of strong US allies like Israel are "immune" from investigation and prosecution while all African countries are supposed to be permanently within the ICC radar.

Back to the Kenyan situation: it is crystal clear that the ODM was not formally involved in the ICC proceedings at all, nor did any "outside forces" intervene on the party's behalf. Had that happened, no senior ODM member would or could have been investigated and indicted. In addition, those alleging "political interference" haven't credibly substantiated their claims.

Yes, I met with the ICC investigators on a number of occasions to give them my perspective and analysis on the "Kenyan Situation." Those meetings were held in public places in the Republic of Kenya. I met them both in my personal capacity as a Kenyan professional who has a stake and interest on seeing the culture of impunity exterminated from the country, and in my capacity as a senior advisor to the Prime Minister of the Republic of Kenya, who, like Kibaki, was a major stakeholder in the process.

I reasonably believe that many of President Kibaki's advisors, senior staff and ministers also held meetings with the same investigators. People like Francis Muthaura (the President's Permanent Secretary, Secretary to the Cabinet and Head of the Civil Service and one of those under investigation), Francis Kimemia (Internal Security Permanent Secretary), Thuita Mwangi (Foreign Affairs Permanent Secretary), Prof. Nick Wanjohi (the President's Private Secretary), Prof. Kivutha Kibwana (the President's advisor on constitutional review; my counterpart), Alfred Mutua (the so-called 'Government Spokesman' but clearly only that of the PNU-wing of government), Prof. George Saitoti (Minister for Internal Security), Mutula Kilonzo (then Minister for Justice), Moses Wetangula (then Minister for Foreign Affairs). They too, provided their perspectives, analysis and opinions on the matter.

We provided those perspectives as patriotic Kenyans interested in the cause of justice. I have stated elsewhere that for me it doesn't matter the racial or cultural identity of those helping us slay the dragon of impunity. As long as the ICC process results in justice being done, it shouldn't matter the colour, race or citizenship of the investigators, prosecutors and judges. After all, justice is supposed to be blind.

It's not legitimate to complain that the judges who presided over the confirmation hearings were all European when most of the suspects also hired European lawyers to act for them before the Court. In any event, those complaining about the racial identity of the judges should point out specific things that would demonstrate their "reasonable apprehension of bias" rather than simply throwing up unfounded allegations.

We have to recognise the fact that the appearance or trials of the 'prominent' Kenyans at the ICC sends an important message to everyone in Kenya – the rich, poor, powerful or powerless alike – that crime does not pay; that there is no shield against impunity; that no matter how long or difficult the search for justice might be, ultimately the long arm of the law catches up with everyone.

Nobody is above the law!

For me this is a vital and important lesson for the country. Whether those facing charges at The Hague are convicted or not becomes immaterial. Their appearance at The Hague has already served as a vital lesson to everyone.

This is why I have been unhappy, disappointed and impatient with the dithering and flip-flopping of the ODM and Raila on the ICC matter. Throughout the process, Raila and his ODM top brass have shown yo-yo leadership with this issue. It has been near impossible for Kenyans to know where Raila or the party stand. One day they breathe fire, threatening to boycott cabinet meetings or even to bring down the coalition and precipitate fresh elections because Kibaki has sent Kalonzo and other cabinet ministers for "shuttle diplomacy" gallivanting all over the globe in an attempt to scuttle the ICC process; yet the very following day Raila's sidekicks, including his own spouse, would be commiserating with the accused or the wives of the accused; asking the public to 'pray for them.' This is despite the fact that Raila and the ODM leadership has never openly and robustly called for justice and prayers for the hundreds of thousands of victims of the PEV.

The hypocrisy, cowardice and opportunism of the ODM top leadership was completely repulsive to me. It was also incongruent with the views and feelings of the overwhelming majority of Kenyans who continued to support the ICC process. I prepared a petition for the United Nations Security Council on behalf of ODM, in order to indicate that neither Raila nor the Orange party had been consulted nor agreed to what became known as the "Shuttle Diplomacy" by senior members of PNU led by the Vice-President, Kalonzo Musyoka, whose brief was to convince the UN Security Council that Kenya was both capable and ready to prosecute those the ICC had indicted. The intention was to have the cases deferred either for one year or for good so that upon being returned to Kenya, the "authorities" would take them over and launder the suspects by orchestrating their acquittals ahead of the next elections.

Up to this point, ODM had failed to clearly articulate its position vis-a-vis the ICC process. Privately Raila and the ODM leadership supported the ICC, but publicly their voices remained muffled. I had discussed this matter extensively with Raila, Mudavadi, Orengo, Nyong'o, Salim, our European diplomat and members of the think tank. They were unanimous that ODM urgently needed to transmit its position to the UN Security Council.

11 March 2011

Your Excellency,

RE: PETITION TO THE MEMBERS OF UN SECURITY COUNCIL REGARDING THE KENYAN CASES AT THE ICC

It is my pleasure and privilege to refer to the ongoing International Criminal Court proceedings relating to Kenya and the deferral request made by a section of the Government of Kenya to the United Nations Security Council.

Background:

The Permanent Mission of the Republic of Kenya presented to the United Nations and to all the Permanent and Observer Missions to the United Nations an Aide Memoire titled *"Kenya's Reform Agenda and Engagement with International Criminal Court (ICC)"*.

Kenya's Vice-President, H.E. Kalonzo Musyoka has led a delegation to the UN Secretary General to discuss the Aide Memoire, alongside the *Communiqué of the 17th Extra-Ordinary Session of the Intergovernmental Authority on Development (IGAD) Assembly of Heads of State and Government on Sudan, Somalia and Kenya*, and the *African Union Decision on the Implementation of the Decisions on the International Criminal Court* on the deferral/referral of the Kenyan Cases at the ICC.

It is important for the UN Members, the Security Council and Secretary-General to have a complete picture and understanding of the situation in Kenya before making any determination on the Aide Memoire from President Kibaki.

This petition presents a set of incontrovertible facts which will assist The Security Council and other interested parties to understand why the Kenyan Cases at the ICC should neither be deferred nor referred. These facts justify why the ongoing ICC process is the best and only means of securing justice to the innocent victims of Kenya's post election violence of 2007/8. It is imperative to underline the fact that the institutions, groups and individuals that were allegedly involved in the planning and execution of the crimes against humanity during the 2007/8 post-election violence in Kenya continue to operate unfettered and occupy important positions of power within and outside government.

Sixteen Reasons Why the Kenyan Cases at the ICC must neither be Deferred nor Referred to Kenya:

- The prosecution of the Kenyan Cases at the ICC does not pose any threat to international peace and security. To the contrary, failure to bring to justice the perpetrators of post-election violence poses grave danger to Kenya's internal peace and security.
- The ICC process was unanimously approved by the two parties under the Annan-brokered National Accord, and the instruments that paved the way for the process were signed by both the President and the Prime Minister for and on behalf of their respective political parties, which form a coalition.
- The great majority of Kenyans (more than eighty per cent) support the ICC process as the most credible method to fighting the culture of impunity in Kenya. Surveys by leading institutions in the country have repeatedly confirmed this position.
- Local (Kenyan) trials will be exposed to:
    1. political manipulation by leaders pleading the ethnic card;
    2. threats to witnesses, their families and friends. Indeed, many witnesses have been hunted down and killed by State security agents; and
    3. undue delays engineered by frivolous and vexatious applications.
- Local trials are not possible at the moment as there is no national judicial mechanism in place to handle the cases. There have been no investigations and prosecutions since the crimes were committed more than three years ago. Moreover, the criminal justice system has not been reformed to enable it to handle the cases. Although Kenya has enacted the International Crimes Act, it is in doubt as to whether Kenyan courts have jurisdiction over the international crimes committed before January 2009 when the Act became operational.
- The judicial reforms contemplated under the new Constitution have not been implemented. The judges and magistrates have not been vetted. There is no independent prosecutorial authority.
- The involvement of the ICC was necessitated by Kenya's rejection to establish a national judicial mechanism to deal with the crimes

committed. In fact, the Government of Kenya repeatedly made verbal and written commitments to cooperate with the ICC and indicated that if it was unable to prosecute the perpetrators of the 2007/08 post election violence by September 2009, the ICC should do so. Those written and public commitments were made by the Government to the ICC Prosecutor both at The Hague and during his official visits to Nairobi.

- Local trials will be used to shield the suspects from justice. This was recently demonstrated by the nominations of Mr Githu Muigai and Mr Kioko Kilukumi to the positions of Attorney-General and Director of Public Prosecutions, respectively, while they are on record as lawyers for two of the ICC suspects. In addition, an ICC suspect chaired the Panel that identified and nominated Justice Visram to the position of new Chief Justice. Although President Kibaki was forced to withdraw his nominations through public outcry, a court order and stinging resolutions of the National Assembly Speaker, the Judicial Service Commission, the Commission on the Implementation of the Constitution, the Law Society of Kenya, the Federation of Women Lawyers and nearly all Kenyan civil society groups; it demonstrated the extent to which President Kibaki's Party of National Unity and the six individuals summoned by the ICC would go to defeat the cause of justice.
- The request for a deferral of the Kenyan cases pending before the ICC has been made by one side of the Kenyan coalition government, namely the Party of National Unity headed by President Mwai Kibaki. The Orange Democratic Movement headed by the Prime Minister Raila Odinga, does not support that request.
- Because of the significant positions held in and influence the suspects wield within Government, they are the ones spearheading the deferral request as a means of defeating the cause of justice. Ultimately, the six suspects the ICC has summoned intend to use the deferral, if granted, as the basis of perpetuating the culture of impunity in Kenya.
- The deferral request should therefore be seen as evidence that the Party of National Unity and President Mwai Kibaki are both unwilling and unable to prosecute the six suspects for the crimes alleged by the ICC.

- Since 1992, each general election has been characterised by state sponsored violence and ethnic cleansings leading to mass deaths, evictions, rapes and arson. While there have been official judicial inquiries on these crimes, no prosecutions have ever been conducted, and no culprits have been punished.
- Extra-judicial killings have increased significantly since 2003. The United Nations Special Rapporteur on Human Rights, Prof. Philip Alston has investigated and made far-reaching findings and recommendations. However, the Government has not taken any action.
- Both the Cabinet and Kenyan Parliament have on more than two occasions rejected Bills for the establishment of a local tribunal for the cases and instead declared that the trials should be held at The Hague.
- The ICC process is the only opportunity that Kenyans have to break the culture of impunity and the circle of election-related violence.
- In view of the foregoing, the request for deferral does not qualify or merit consideration by the UN Security Council within the provisions of Article 16 of the Rome Statute, or through any other provisions. This is particularly the case because the Kenyan Situation at the ICC was not originated by a referral by the UN Security Council. Consequently, the request for a deferral is an unwarranted interference with the Court's mandate, its independence and impartiality.

We therefore submit that the request for a deferral by a section of the Kenyan Government be rejected as being incompetent and frivolous.

On behalf of the Orange Democratic Movement and the Prime Minister of the Republic of Kenya, The Rt. Hon. Raila Odinga, EGH, MP, I would like to request you to bring this letter to the attention of all Council Members of the Security Council and to have it issued as a document of the Council, as a matter of great urgency.

Please accept, Your Excellency, the assurances of my highest consideration.

Hon. Prof. Peter Anyang' Nyong'o
Secretary General

I am forever grateful to Anyang' for the aide-mémoire. Had we relied on Raila and Orengo, the document wouldn't have been delivered. I say that because Raila had become quite confused; changing his mind more frequently than the rest of us change underwear. But closely following on the heels of the aide-mémoire was another initiative that also took time to process. Initially, the idea was to try and seek a "friend of the court"(amicus curiae) status for ODM. We knew the rules were stringent and that we might not be granted the status, but the most important thing was for the country to see ODM defending the ICC process. As well, we felt that it was imperative to deliver a strong submission for the amicus application with the full knowledge that the contents of our application would be extensively covered by both local and international media. Unfortunately, Raila would say yes, before reneging on his word. Orengo and Salim also wavered on the affidavit. I was astonished when Salim raised objections on the two paragraphs that had been suggested by Paul Muite and Maina Kiai, both of whom Raila had asked me to consult before the affidavit was forwarded to The Hague. Salim argued that his objection was due to the fact that he believed Raila had specifically asked us not to include them; but that was only partly true.

The artificial and useless debate over PNU's deferral and Raila's 'referral' was getting under my skin. For months I had strongly advised Raila not to continue calling for the "referral" of the cases as no such term was known to law. Once, Raila even called an ODM parliamentary group meeting at his office boardroom and engaged me in the same debate, insisting that the word "referral" was there in the Rome Statute. I demanded that we examine the Rome Statute and see whether that was so. A copy of the Rome Statute was found and I went through it with a fine-toothed comb. After I was through, Raila started arguing that "referral" could mean "imputed" from Article 19 of the Statute. However, after I put up a spirited argument, as I loudly read through Article 19, Ababu and Orengo came to Raila's rescue, arguing that "we must find something on which we can argue for a referral".

At that point, I knew we were now engaged in an exercise in futility. To this day, I don't understand why Raila made arguments about a referral. Perhaps it was a political game to please Ruto and his ODM rebels that Raila was still trying to "help him". But Ruto isn't that stupid. He knew that that was a bare-faced lie bereft of intelligence or sophistication.

It's true that the initial draft I had taken to Raila was longer and more detailed; Raila had also asked me to seek Paul Muite's and Maina Kiai's input, which I did on the very following day. Needless to say, I felt that disregarding Muite's and Kiai's valuable contributions negated Raila's instructions and rendered our intellectual contributions somehow superfluous. However, due to considerable respect I had for Salim (and in order to avoid unnecessary misunderstanding) I excluded the highlighted portions. My suspicion was that when Salim saw reference to Justice Rawal, whom he was quietly lobbying for, and had mentioned as "a good candidate for chief justice," he developed cold feet.

Be that as it may, I am reproducing the two paragraphs containing the bolded/highlighted portions that Salim had (unreasonably) insisted should have been omitted. I'm doing so for both historical record and in order to avoid confusion.

> As a Cabinet Minister, I am aware that both the Cabinet and the National Assembly of the Republic of Kenya (hereinafter referred to as the "Parliament") have on more than two occasions rejected Bills for the establishment of an independent local tribunal intended to investigate and prosecute the serious crimes that were committed during the post-election violence of 2007/8, leaving the ICC process as the only opportunity that Kenyans have to break the culture of impunity and the circle of elections-related violence. I am aware of the fact that the judicial reforms contemplated under the new Constitution have not been implemented. I am further aware that the judges and magistrates have not been vetted as required by the Constitution. *It is pertinent to point out that when Chief Justice Gicheru appointed the Hon. Lady Justice Kalpana Rawal to take witness statements from Police Officers and Provincial Administration Officials, a Judge of equal jurisdiction, the Hon. Justice Musinga issued orders rejecting Lady Justice Rawal from taking the statements. (…)*
>
> As a member of the Government of Kenya, I truly believe that there are no credible investigations of the post-election violence cases that are ongoing. Moreover, I believe that because the Kenya Police was heavily implicated in the crimes that are subject to the ICC process – and the institution remains unreformed – it is difficult to expect it to investigate itself let alone those who are currently before the ICC. *Most important, the police investigative capacity and willingness is severely lacking in Kenya. There are too many cases of witnesses dying, not appearing, and cases dismissed for lack of sufficient evidence. I believe that trying the six cases or individuals in Kenya will seriously jeopardize the witnesses, some of whom will likely refuse to testify out of fear and intimidation. This will defeat the cause of justice.*

The affidavit was transmitted to The Hague by the law firm of *Rachier and Amollo Advocates*. Prof. Nyong'o had signed two sets of affidavits before travelling to Moscow that April. The first one was more detailed and included things that Salim had objected to. The second one had the two "offensive" paragraphs excised from it. The idea was to let Orengo review them before Salim, Orengo and I would decide on the correct version. But unknown to me, both Orengo and Salim were now of the idea that neither affidavit should be sent. They didn't give any reasons. Orengo was still "thinking" about the matter. The day Orengo was talking about "thinking" about the issue, the deadline was less than four hours away. A decision had to be made swiftly. So, when Rachier called me and asked what he should do with the documents, I told him to "file immediately". Rachier called me back to confirm that the documents were "gone". He also assured me that he hadn't given anybody a copy. Eventually, only Anyang', Rachier, Amollo, and I had copies.

Yet, inexplicably, the documents leaked to the media almost immediately. I considered it a major breach though I don't know up to today the source of the leak. And as soon as the newspapers carried the story, Jakoyo called me, yelling. I asked him why he was shouting. He replied that they were trying to help yet we were destroying. I didn't quite know what he was talking about until he disclosed that Raila had told him that I was the one behind the affidavit.

"Raila told me that it was your idea; that you are the one who took Nyong'o and Salim to his house in Karen when he had just arrived from abroad; that you ambushed him…"

"Wait a minute Jakoyo; are you listening to yourself? Have you just said that I ambushed the Prime Minister of the Republic of Kenya? Now, how do you imagine I could do such a thing? Did you also say that I am the one who took Nyong'o and Salim to Raila's home? Isn't Nyong'o my senior? Don't you think he would have been the one who took me to Karen?"

"You think I'm joking Miguna; I'll expose you in the media! I'm going to condemn you in the media."

"Well, do as you wish. I followed *Jakom's* instructions. You should have been happy that I was so efficient!"

Thus, Raila had flip-flopped again and again on grave matters with national and international implications. By then, I was convinced that Raila wasn't a leader. He couldn't manage even a group of squirrels. But the work had been done. Once more, my – in my opinion, noble – actions had put me in the firing line.

BOOK SEVEN

AGAINST THE CURRENTS

CHAPTER SIXTEEN

THE MAIZE SCANDAL

It was 6.30pm on Friday May 15, 2009, when I entered the presidential suite at the Nairobi Safari Club (popularly known as the "Lillian Towers"). The imposing white Crown Jewel of Kiambaa Member of Parliament Stanley Githunguri's vast estate attests not just to the man's deep pockets; it also says much about his murky Kanu roots.

Once upon a time, Githunguri was the Managing Director of the National Bank of Kenya. Growing up, we heard rumours – even in the far flung and remote villages of Kenya like Magina – that Githunguri was "a very smart man who made good use of an important state appointment and built himself a fortune that many have admired for decades; that he was a clever, frugal and tenacious businessman." Whether those rumours were true or false were immaterial to my visit that day. I could see from the discoloured carpet, the broken-down toilet and the neglected kitchenette inside the suite that the five-star hotel must have seen better days. But the elevators still chimed well; the waiters and other employees seemed well groomed and polite; they also smiled glowingly at arriving visitors. That lifted the heart after the hassle of finding a parking space. Another car had rammed me from behind just as I had squeezed my vehicle into a cramped space more than 50m from the main entrance. I had decided to ignore the damage – seeing it as part of the daily stresses of being a motorist in Nairobi.

At my request, Raila had set the secret meeting for 6.30pm. There were two items on the agenda. First, as Raila's senior advisor for coalition affairs, I had some thoughts on how to make Raila and his newly created office more effective; and second, I had conducted preliminary investigations on what became known as the "Maize Scandal" and unearthed what I believed were tentacles of the scandal at the OPM. I felt that if the latter issue was not addressed promptly and fully, it could derail both Raila and ODM's political fortunes.

Up to that point, I had only shared my findings with Orengo, who had drawn Nyong'o into our discussions. Both Orengo and Nyong'o had suggested to me that it would be better for them to raise those issues with Raila in my presence. I had chosen Orengo because of his liberation credentials, vast legal experience and the place he had assumed in ODM as the *de facto* Attorney General. He had also become my ideological and professional soulmate in ODM. Nyong'o had been picked due to his position as ODM's Secretary General. We knew that the ODM chairman Henry Kosgey was a certified Kanu Orphan who wouldn't understand my concerns over grand corruption that was threatening both Raila's and ODM's legacies in government. But even more importantly, I had assumed that because both Orengo and Nyong'o had progressive credentials, had participated in pro-democracy activism for many years, and were generally widely recognised as solid thinkers, they could and would be expected to be candid and open with Raila on such issues. I had approached them with the utmost good faith.

Coincidentally, one of the key pillars of the successful Raila visit to Toronto in October 2006, Waikwa Wanyoike, was visiting Nairobi in April 2009. He hadn't seen or spoken with Raila since a few days preceding the 2007 elections when he had visited Nairobi. Because he was flying back to Toronto that night – and given the terrible disorganisation at the Prime Minister's office – I had suggested that he should pass by Lillian Towers that evening and "greet Raila" before his departure. As was usual with Waikwa, he kept his word and time, arriving 30 minutes after I had made myself comfortable in the presidential suite. Orengo arrived soon after him. Waikwa and Orengo were well acquainted with one another from the old "street battles of the 1990s". We were reminiscing about the "bad" old days when Nyongo' arrived, breathless and late, as usual. Raila came 15 minutes behind Nyong'o.

We all greeted each other and chatted generally before Waikwa took his leave. There was then a two-minute awkward silence. Raila inquired about service. I went to the kitchen counter where a telephone handset was and called reception. As we were waiting for our orders to be brought up, Caroli strolled into the suite and took a seat slightly behind me. I was astonished. I hadn't invited Caroli to that meeting. Orengo and Nyong'o would confirm later that they hadn't mentioned the meeting to any other soul, which left Raila as the most likely "breacher" of our usual protocol.

This wasn't the first nor the last clandestine meeting we would hold with Raila. Invitations were selective depending on the issues or agenda up for discussion.

There were times Salim was present and there were times when either Orengo or Nyong'o were absent. I'm sure there were many meetings from which I was also absent (either because I hadn't been invited or because I wasn't in town). Quite appropriately, some things were done or discussed on a "need-to-know-basis".

But Caroli's presence wasn't just a small breach – as Raila, Orengo and Nyong'o knew very well – given the nature of my preliminary findings. Caroli's name featured significantly in the "Maize Scandal" allegations that we had come to discuss – as indeed it seemed to occur in various other corruption allegations. I had thought it appropriate for us to hold confidential and candid discussions without his presence before inviting him to clarify the issues that required his explanation. In fact, I had suggested – and all the other participants had agreed – that the meeting should take place outside the Prime Minister's Office precisely so that the alleged culprits wouldn't be privy to the discussions. But with him sitting there holding forth on something while apparently unaware why the meeting had been called, I knew that something was very wrong.

My law school training and extensive legal practice were invaluable in such situations. Properly trained and experienced courtroom lawyers know that vital information and pointers aren't just gleaned from dry facts and evidence. Whether it's during investigations, inquiries, fact-finding missions, examinations or trials; inklings, nuances and fleeting impressions are gauged when one observes another testify under oath or give an account of an event. Innocuous statements, expressions, gestures or other idiosyncratic things human beings engage in under pressure can suddenly gain currency. A nose twitch, dry lips, sweating or just uneasy glances often give away the guilty in the most uncanny manner. And when carefully analysed and pieced together, such statements or physical reactions can begin to congeal into something coherent, logical and revealing. Remarks made innocently or repeated by one or more people in describing an incident or event might expose some hidden conspiracy, which would otherwise have gone undetected. That's why trials have been in use since the Ancient world – they're effective.

As an experienced barrister, solicitor and mediator, I was keenly watching everyone's body language and facial expressions. I was also noting their temperaments, choice of words, or the quivers of their voices. My investigations had been preliminary and informal, but already I was getting the impression that I had rattled some nerves. "Captain, without any further delay, Miguna has prepared some things which he would like to present to you…" Prof. Nyong'o started, fumbling. Strangely, he deliberately omitted to inform Raila that one of the documents was the product of three weeks of intensive meetings and discussions among Raila's think tank, which I coordinated, that Anyang' sometimes chaired and of which Orengo was an integral member.

We had held several secret meetings at the Social Development Network (Sodnet) offices in Lavington, Prof. Nyong'o's private office at Mountain View estate, at the Nairobi Club and in a few other places within Nairobi. Members of the think tank who participated during those discussions, aside from the two ministers and I were: Prof. Oyugi, Oduor Ong'wen, Mugambi Imanyara, Mutakha Kangu, Adhu Awiti, Peter Wanyande, Salim Lone and Nabii Nabwera. Later, this group would be expanded to include Martin Oloo and Julius Kemboy. We had discussed a range of issues from the constitutional review process; ODM's position in government; and how to strengthen Raila's position in government.

The issue of the Maize, Triton Oil and other scandals had also been discussed during our meetings. We wanted to know more about them; how ODM figures might have been involved; and we devised damage control and other strategies in order to blunt their impact on our party and prepare ourselves early for elections, which we suspected could be held on any date, even before 2012.

So why, I wondered to myself, is he speaking as if he hasn't seen or been privy to the issues or documents yet when I had held extensive discussions with him and Orengo, they had reviewed my analysis and even made suggestions on some of the issues? And why is Caroli here, I asked myself further.

"Yes, Your Excellency, Miguna has prepared very good documents, which we thought he should share with you, too." Orengo added, making the bad situation even worse.

Why was Orengo calling Raila 'Your Excellency'? I was astonished by the depth of Orengo's lyrical sycophancy even at such informal, private meetings. At that point, I knew that whatever was to be discussed wouldn't go anywhere. I realised that I was alone; that the four people sitting there and pretending to be keen on "my presentation" had met before and discussed the same issues; it was possible that they had already resolved on what to do with "Miguna's findings". Although I felt very disappointed and angry I restrained myself.

I noted Caroli's sly smile and Raila's unease. "Ok, thank you for making it possible for us to discuss these important issues so as to seek their resolution. *Jakom*, the think tank has been meeting over a number of issues, but the two we wanted to discuss with you today are: The need to use Prime Minister's Circulars – one for coordination and the other for supervision – to assist you in discharging your constitutional duties. And second are our thoughts on the Maize Scandal," I began, trying very hard to stay on topic. I continued talking, as I distributed the documents to them, about how the 'Prime Minister's Circulars' might be a way for the PM's office to put Muthaura in his place. I then started reading various provisions of each circular for illustrative purposes.

"But *Ja-Nyando*, why do we need all that when I can call these people directly and give them instructions as I have been doing already?" Raila asked, appearing impatient.

"*Jakom*, these are our considered advice based on what we have observed especially Muthaura and other senior government officials, including the police and intelligence openly being insubordinate and defiant to you. We have thought of the best, most orderly and formal way through which you can stamp your constitutional authority within government. Sir, government bureaucracy works through formal instruments; verbal orders can be ignored without any record of the orders having been given..."

"Ok *Ja-Nyando*...I think this is unnecessary. Isahakia has already prepared another circular, which we can use..." He was dismissive.

"Ok *Jakom*, if you say so, though I have to let you know that the think tank was unanimous on this issue, having reviewed what Isahakia has done, which isn't just poorly conceived, drafted and doesn't seem properly targeted...But we can move on."

Orengo and Anyang' were as quiet as mice.

"Well, the other issue is over the Maize Scandal. Over the past few months, starting January this year, Kenyans from all walks of life have been making noise over the price of consumer goods, especially the skyrocketing price of maize and maize related products like *unga*. For the first time in a very long time you were booed in your own constituency of Lang'ata by women and youths chanting *"Unga! Unga! Unga!"* at you. We watched in shock last year as, while you met ODM delegates at the Bomas of Kenya, there was a background chant of "*Unga*! *Unga*!". The situation isn't getting better; it is, in fact, getting worse by the day. We have discussed this issue at length with the think tank and I have also made preliminary inquiries which suggest that our office might have been involved from the inception with this scandal..."

"Why do you call it a *scandal*...global commodity prices have gone up throughout the world; not just in Kenya...," Raila interjected.

"*Jakom*, I'm not the one calling it that; almost everyone is: the media, the civil society, the average *wananchi*..." I tried to explain.

"Go on but don't call it a scandal."

"OK, *Jakom*, our point is: *this* thing could take a life of its own and consume us all – the innocent and the guilty alike. In 2007, you campaigned on a zero tolerance to corruption platform. Kenyans believed and trusted you. Now is the time to show them that that wasn't just campaign rhetoric. For instance, take the issue of the shady importation of maize that many, including the Minister for Public Health, Beth Mugo, have claimed to be unfit for human consumption. I have disturbing information, which I believe to be credible – and some of it has been reported in the media already – that it was Caroli who issued verbal instructions to the Strategic Grain Reserve (SGR) to order the maize, even to enhance its price and then told the Managing Director of the National Cereals Board of Kenya (NCPB) to release the maize to the domestic market despite serious reports of its contamination. Sir, reliable reports indicate that Caroli telephoned Misoi, the NCPB Managing Director, *from our office line...*"

"Is that true Caroli? Did you call them from *our office line?"* Raila interjected again, looking at Caroli with anxiety written all over his face.

Right there, I knew that both Raila and Caroli were privy to those "interventions", otherwise, he wouldn't and shouldn't have cared where the calls emanated from. Whether Caroli used the office line or his mobile line or Caroli's grandmother's mobile phone didn't matter, really. What mattered was why Caroli should have been the one giving instructions to the NCPB over contaminated maize. The NCPB was under the Ministry of Agriculture. The SGR, which was legally responsible for such importations, wasn't solely controlled by the OPM. Permanent Secretaries for Agriculture, Special Programmes, Finance and Office of the Prime Minister were all signatories to the SGR's quota allocations. Caroli wasn't a member of the SGR. So, why was he calling the NCPB and not Isahakia, for instance? Caroli was Raila's private secretary; he wasn't a signatory to the SGR.

The scandal had actually started in late 2008. This was after the formation of the Grand Coalition Government. The Minister for Agriculture then was William Ruto, an ODM MP and an important member of the party's Pentagon. The primary allegation was that in late 2008, the government lifted a ban it had imposed on the importation of maize to allow "capable businessmen to import maize to supplement the local produce that was short of the minimum required to satisfy the local market or demands". Subsequently (through the connivance of senior government officials, including those that sat in Cabinet), crafty briefcase millers (paper speculators on the commodities markets) were awarded quotas by the SGR or awarded import permits by the NCPB. Schemes were devised to avoid price controls, leading to hefty profits on the maize imports by the crooks. But more poignantly were credible allegations that some of the maize imported by local businesses and briefcase millers was contaminated and unfit for human consumption. One such shipment from South Africa through the port of Maputo in Mozambique was claimed to have been imported by companies directly or indirectly connected with one Ahmed Kassam and Caroli Omondi, both of whom worked for or with Raila or were closely associated with him.

A close friend of mine and a member of ODM's national executive committee told me how she and other ODM members, including Raila's daughter Rosemary Akeyo, were issued with allotment letters by the then Agriculture Minister William Ruto. These letters would contain the number of bags allotted and an inflated (artificial) selling price. All they were required to do – and did – was to tender these allotment letters with Asian businessmen (mainly millers) in the Industrial Area in Nairobi and be paid the difference between the actual and the inflated price. The "businessmen" would then take the letters to the NCPB for their allocations. In other words senior ODM members, senior officers at the OPM and family members of the Prime Minister were alleged to have been deeply involved in the scandal. And I got this information from a person who was directly involved. Yet here I was with the PM who should have been concerned, showing absolutely no interest in the sources of my information and who the culprits were.

"*Jakom*, I didn't use the office line; I called him on my mobile phone. In fact, I think I only called him twice. The rest of the discussions occurred at the NCPB offices, where I went." Caroli answered, matter-of-factly. In law, that was a confession of involvement.

I glanced at Raila and saw him satisfied by that 'confession'. I was dumbfounded. Caroli had just admitted to having been involved in the dodgy importations, and Raila didn't look bothered at all. In fact, he sighed deeply when he heard Caroli asserting that the calls emanated from his mobile phone and not the office line. Did Raila think that Caroli's mobile line left no traces, that evidence from his calls couldn't be used to implicate not just Caroli, but also his boss? In any event, why did Raila take Caroli's word for it? Professional due diligence demanded that such assertions should have been backed up with corroborative proof, in the absence of which, we could and should have ordered for the mobile telephone records from Caroli's service provider(s).

Orengo and Nyong'o had suddenly gone mute. But I continued. "*Jakom,* there are other elements which need to be discussed. Firstly, Isahakia is a signatory to the SGR. How much did he know and when did he know it? If he knew about any irregularities regarding the orders, evasion of tax, the importation of contaminated maize, the irregular issuance of allotment letters (including to one of his business partners) or the existence of briefcase companies, did he inform you? If so, when and what did you do with that information? If he didn't inform you; why?The fact that this thing is being referred to as a 'scandal' by the media implies that you as the coordinator and supervisor of the execution of all government functions including that of ministries could be said to have been sleeping on the job; people like Naivasha MP, John Mututho have started demanding that you take political responsibility. What will our response be?

"Additionally, a company associated with Isahakia and his business associate Bare Shirr is mentioned as having bought or sold some of the maize; if true, we have to think of the implications. Stating that Isahakia wasn't directly involved might be technically correct (if at all) but optically it stinks to the high seas.

"Moreover, I have also received reports that it was our office that intervened to not have the contaminated maize returned to South Africa. The question many people are asking *Jakom* is why would you care? Why should it have been you authorising a private firm to inspect the maize that the Kenya Bureau of Standards (KEBS) has declared unfit for human consumption? If you don't have any pecuniary interests whatsoever in the shipment; why would you interfere with the work of the KEBS? "Finally, *Jakom*, and this is extremely delicate, someone came to my office and told me that Ruto allocated thousands of bags to Caroli, Rosemary, Fidel and other members of your family..."

Raila interrupted me then. "Stop right there Miguna," he shouted. "I think you are getting carried away by rumours. I was the person who created KEBS; I know its work and its institutional capacity. KEBS did a lousy job on that inspection. Yes, something leaked onto the maize in one of the containers; it was this thick, I believe about three metres deep into the container, the leakage...As soon as the limited contamination was discovered, the affected parts were scooped out. The rest of the maize is OK and good for human consumption..."

He suddenly stopped in mid-stream, which gave me an opportunity to conclude. As he spoke, he was demonstrating how thick the leakage had been on the container. It left a clear impression that Raila knew too much about that specific shipment for us to believe that he had no interest in it, not as Prime Minister, but as Raila Odinga the businessman. "I understand you *Jakom*. But I would like to propose a way forward. Firstly, I would like you to give me permission and sufficient funding and support to set up a specialised team to investigate this matter. I have explained to Jim and SG that in my experience, we would be better off knowing everything about this maize issue than knowing less. If I were retained as a lawyer in this matter I would investigate it thoroughly for me to competently offer advice. What am I suggesting? That I be allowed to send investigators to South Africa to trace who incorporated the two or three companies that imported the contaminated maize. I have heard rumours that those companies are associated with Caroli and Ahmed Kassam. This might be true or false. However, *Jakom*, you know that Ahmed has business cards which identify him as one of your *advisors* based in Johannesburg, South Africa. Yet nobody but yourself and perhaps Caroli knows what he is doing for you there... Caroli obviously holds a very senior position at our office. Some people will therefore try to connect all their business interests and activities to you. We need to deal with this thing once and for all."

My words hung in the air awkwardly. The meeting ended in an anti-climax. I never heard from Raila, Orengo or Nyong'o on this matter again. But I have no doubt that I had stumbled on a cover-up. My belief is that Ahmed Kassam was Raila's "sleeper agent." The amounts claimed to have been lost – money that should have gone into public coffers and the pockets of ordinary Kenyans – was a staggering $26m (equivalent, at a 2012 exchange rate, to Sh2.2 billion) – enough to feed millions of hungry Kenyans. But my enquiries were stalled in the fading glory of that down-at-heel presidential suite that evening. All my subsequent offers to investigate the OPM's role in the scandal were ignored.

For his part, Orengo constructed two palaces in his village in Ugenya for his two wives; he also went on to complete another one in the leafy Karen estate in Nairobi. The total cost of the three houses, all of which went up in one year, must be way above Sh1 billion. An interesting insight about Orengo is in order here: I have travelled with him on many official visits abroad. During two of those trips, he shocked both Mutula Kilonzo and I by such ostentatious spending that we wondered where the money was coming from. When we both accompanied the PM to Chicago in 2009, Orengo spent $6,000 on one suit and $500 on two belts. In Geneva, Switzerland Orengo bought a short sleeved shirt for $1,000. After that last purchase, Mutula said to me: "Miguna, what's the matter with Jim? How can he spend that kind of money on a shirt? Listen my friend, I'm not poor; in fact I'm probably richer than Jim, but I can't spend that kind of money on clothes. If you want to buy suits just tell me and I will give you someone to tailor them for you for less than $150, and he will come all the way from Hong Kong." He revealed to me that all his clothes were tailored by a man from Hong Kong.

My point is this: since becoming Prime Minister, Raila and some people very close to him have been 'eating' unthinkingly. To judge by the look of things, some of those close to him have either been doing this with his tacit or explicit knowledge, approval or even encouragement, or by exploiting his willful blindness. There certainly isn't any evidence that he has tried to reign-in the culprits. On the contrary, when confronted with credible allegations of graft around him, Raila openly and consistently defended and shielded the corrupt.

Much later, Ruto would face a censure motion in Parliament over the maize issue. Raila would waver and wobble, not knowing whether to stand by Ruto or to sacrifice him, especially in view of the swirling allegations that Ruto had drawn him into the scandal through his [Raila's] family members. Ruto also made spectacular allegations that he was just being 'scapegoated'; that "others were the architects of the scandal" thereby leaving open the possibility of embroiling Raila in the mess. In fact, I heard rumours that Raila and the ODM were instrumental in getting Ruto out of the parliamentary pickle. I heard, although it was not substantiated to me, that it was Raila who rallied ODM MPs, especially from Nyanza, to vote against the censure motion, and also that it was the OPM, which allegedly 'influenced' the appointment of Mary Ng'ethe – a key witness in the Ruto fraud case – to a government board in order to discourage her from testifying in that case, resulting in Ruto's acquittal for 'lack of evidence'. Apparently, that was Raila's alleged inducement to Ruto so that the latter wouldn't implicate him into the Maize Scandal.

Before the censure motion was debated in Parliament, I bumped into Ruto at Raila's Treasury Building office and inquired about the claim that he had ordered hundreds of thousands, if not millions, of gunny sacks through his company, Africa Merchant Assurance Company Limited (AMACO), through which many people were alleging that he had funneled hundreds of millions – or even billions – of illegally obtained cash. Of course, Ruto laughed off the allegations and went on to stage a spirited defence of himself on the floor of the House. By that time Ruto was already a close political buddy of Uhuru Kenyatta, whose supporters in Parliament rallied to Ruto's defence. Together with Raila's support, Ruto survived. But he had been badly bruised.

Later, as described earlier, Raila attempted to suspend Ruto in relation to the Maize Scandal (a move I supported, although Kibaki countermanded him) and pretended to have both Caroli and Isahakia "voluntarily step aside for two months until investigations were conducted". Kibaki later announced their suspension as well as that of the Permanent Secretary for Agriculture, Dr Romano Kiome and the Permanent Secretary for Special Programmes, Mohamed Ali Daud. During those "suspensions" I tried to impress upon Raila to let go of both Caroli and Isahakia. Not only were they soiling his reputation and associating both him and the OPM with corruption, but they were also undermining ODM's pledge on zero tolerance to corruption.

Of course, my attempts were futile. Both Caroli and Isahakia were in the office as if nothing had changed; Raila allowed them to continue coming in almost daily. They had keys to their offices. They were still in charge of their staff. In fact, in the case of Caroli, he was even allowed to unilaterally pick Dennis

Onyango to stand in for him during his brief and choreographed 'absence'. He chose Dennis because he believed that Dennis would have no interest or capacity to replace him. Both Caroli and Isahakia continued to attend official meetings at the PM's Office. They routinely used their offices; even Muthaura continued to deal with and through Isahakia. And they continued to draw full salaries and benefits at taxpayers' expense, even though they were only entitled to half salaries. Thus Caroli's and Isahakia's stepping aside was a charade; a PR exercise. But it exposed the PM as a fraud.

Meanwhile, rumours were rife that some of the illicit maize had been exported to South Sudan while the rest found its way into the domestic food chain, exposing millions of innocent consumers to serious health risks, including possible fatalities. I began to realise that for Raila and the ODM party the "war on corruption" had become just empty rhetoric. Raila had also latched onto a strategy learnt from Moi of "governance through taskforces and commissions", which essentially is whitewashing grand corruption. Needless to say, reports of the so-called investigations were never made public. Although I held a senior position at the OPM, I wasn't given a copy, even after I repeatedly requested them. There was clearly a well-calculated scheme to shield Caroli and Isahakia. But why? Well, because by and large, both Caroli and Isahakia actually did whatever they did first and foremost with Raila's tacit consent. Yes, they pilfered tens of millions here and there from a variety of "projects" but the trajectory remained the same. Like Kulei (Moi's personal assistant) before them they had become mere pawns in Raila's clever schemes to rip off the public. It was a very sad development.

Raila's management style (if it can be called that) was chaotic. As previously indicated, he never held regular and well structured meetings with his senior staff. The less than five (in about three years) I attended were unstructured and disorganised. Elementary and poorly drafted minutes were produced all right. But there were no follow-up meetings, or action taken on identified things that needed action. Resolutions were never implemented. Both Raila and his Permanent Secretary were constantly unfocused, undisciplined and ungovernable. (I would eventually rely on individual meetings with Raila alone or small meetings I would organise with Orengo, Salim, Prof. Edward Oyugi or Mutakha Kangu).

Raila might be very good (especially as a political comedian and conversationalist) at public rallies, roadside and funeral meetings, but he is disastrous in structured meetings. He is obviously a good listener. But he isn't a good and organised leader, manager or administrator. He rarely delegates, and when he does, it is often to the wrong people – people who are either incompetent or irredeemably corrupt, or both.

Now, many would argue that such ailments are widespread among world leaders throughout history and that Raila isn't an exception. That might be so, but any good leader that finds himself with Raila's many and serious failings ought to surround himself with well trained, knowledgeable, experienced, dedicated and loyal and had workers of integrity. The leader's work would then be to focus on his broad vision and legacy and leave the "operators" to implement decisions made. Unfortunately in Raila's case, most of the people he prefers don't have these qualities. In the office, for instance, only Sylvester Kasuku and I carried out our functions with diligence and national purpose; almost all the other senior officers were busy chasing deals. And Raila preferred the deal-makers to his ideologically clear and diligent work-horses.

The Efficiency Monitoring Unit (EMU), the Inspectorate of State Corporations and even the public service reform sector are based at the Prime Minister's Office. The first two are supposed to ensure efficiency, effectiveness and ethical conduct in the management of public affairs. But when was the last time Kenyans heard of what these important state institutions and organs have done to fight corruption, theft, waste and lethargy in government? The only time Kenyans hear of the EMU is when Raila and ODM needs it to cleanse one of their cabinet ministers who has found himself or herself entangled in a web of corruption. That has been the case with allegations of grand corruption at various ODM headed ministries such as Health, Water, Local Government and the Office of the Prime Minister itself. Do Kenyans even remember these organs and their mandates? Those who criticised Kibaki for his so-called "hands off" management style, like this author, have found Raila's style to be worse; it's an "I don't care attitude" couched in deception. It is greed, opportunism, selfishness and cynicism deceptively couched as "change". In my view, a flagrant fraud is being perpetrated on the Kenyan people. For years, I kept saying this to many Raila confidantes like Salim, Orengo, Oyugi, Sarah Elderkin, Nyong'o and others. Their response wasn't outright denial; they simply asked: "Who is better than him among the presidential candidates?" I have found that answer presented in the form of a question to be a cop-out.

Of course, there are many Kenyans far better than Raila in every respect. The fact that they might not have declared their candidatures, are less known, or have less media coverage or money, doesn't discount their qualities for leadership.

CHAPTER SEVENTEEN

INSTANT BILLIONAIRES

I walked into Raila's office with Caroli Omondi just before 8am one Wednesday morning in April 2011. There was something important I wanted the three of us to discuss. The previous day, I had visited Hon. (Dr) Sally Kosgei in her Ministry of Agriculture office at Kilimo House. What she had disclosed had shocked me. Dr Kosgei had informed me that she had heard that Caroli had purchased Heron (Court) Hotel, a three-star facility in Nairobi. Her information was that Caroli had purchased the hotel for between Sh800 million to Sh1 billion.

Many might ask why I found that shocking. Well, Caroli happened to be Raila's private secretary. Officially Caroli was the Principal Administration Secretary for the Office of the Prime Minister. His take home pay was less than Sh300,000. By April 2009, Caroli had worked for the OPM for exactly two years. Even if he was saving 90 per cent of his net income – an impossible feat in any society – he would still not have saved Sh800m within two years.

Caroli didn't come from a wealthy family, his father having retired as a high school headmaster a few years earlier. Before he started working at the OPM, he had had a short stint at the World Bank's Nairobi office as a legal officer earning a modest income. In December 2007, he had disclosed to me that he faced imminent loss of his prime properties in Nairobi, one in the Upper Hill area where a mortgage of Sh45m was outstanding and due, and another – the property where ODM operates its Orange House secretariat – in the Kilimani area of Nairobi where a further Sh25m mortgage was due. In December 2007, Caroli had driven what had looked like a beaten-up ten-year-old BMW saloon, with a market value (based on an intelligent guess) that couldn't have been more than

Sh450,000. That's less than $7,000. So by all accounts, Caroli hadn't been doing well financially then. In fact he had given every impression of being in a deep hole that he was struggling to crawl out of. How in the world had he suddenly become a billionaire, capable of purchasing a billion-shilling property one kilometre from the Central Business District (CBD)?

On top of that, he had shown me an apartment complex worth more than Sh600 m in the Diani area of Mombasa. The 48-unit apartment complex had been completed at the same time as he was said to have purchased the Heron (Court) Hotel. When he took me there in 2010, he had told me that his sister – a primary school teacher who rented a two-bedroom house in Mombasa – was the owner. Any reasonable person knows that on the salary of a primary school teacher in Kenya, even paying a monthly rent for that Sh5,000 house would be a major financial strain. In addition, Caroli had purchased three new top-of-the-range vehicles – one BMW X6, a BMW X5 and a Mercedes Benz ML class – all imported either directly from Germany or through South Africa. The estimated cost of these vehicles alone would have been close to Sh20m. The vehicles had been purchased barely one year after the formation of the coalition government. Also, he had constructed a massive ultra modern house in Gwasi, his rural home, the same year he completed the apartment complex in Mombasa and reportedly purchased Heron (Court) Hotel. Credible reports had it that within three years, Caroli had assembled assets worth more than Sh10 billion. The transformation of his lifestyle from that of a humble struggling young professional to that of a wealthy man seemed almost instantaneous.

How could he have acquired such massive wealth from a gross salary of about Sh250,000 per month? Where would Caroli have come across such sudden wealth?

Granted, Caroli had confided in me that he had "taken" £250,000 that Raila had given him to send to Atul Vadher in the UK. He claimed that Atul had disappeared with a similar amount from him, which he had given Atul to purchase a BMW X5 from the UK for him. The credibility of this story isn't material, except to note that within a short period of one year, Caroli was supposed to have "saved" or "landed" £250,000! As a result of this 'little misunderstanding' between Caroli and Atul, the friendship between Atul and Raila died a premature death. Nor is Raila currently on speaking terms with Lord David Steel who had "donated" Atul to Raila in 2007. Yet despite this irresponsible behaviour, Raila didn't reprimand or discipline Caroli, which suggests that Raila tacitly approved and encouraged Caroli's wrongdoing. Prior to this meeting, the veteran human rights defender, Maina Kiai had asked me:

"Miguna, regardless of how much he is 'eating', why does Caroli have to drive those expensive BMWs?"

It was with these facts and allegations in mind that I wanted to confront both Caroli and Raila with the information about the new purchase in order to highlight the incongruence between Caroli's meagre income and his opulent lifestyle. I had concerns that the incongruity between his lifestyle and his legitimate income as a public servant would lead people to cast aspersions about both Caroli and his role within the OPM. Such qualms would be normal in societies governed by the rule of law and where corruption, drug trafficking, money laundering and other financial improprieties aren't just frowned upon, but are criminalised and severely punished. But I was to receive the greatest shock of my life.

"*Jakom*, hear what Miguna is saying…that people are saying that I bought Heron Court," Caroli started as soon as we sat down around a small coffee table. He was laughing. He didn't wait for me to introduce the subject. I also noticed the casual and joking manner Caroli was approaching the issue, which I found unnerving.

"Hmmm…hmmm…hmmm, is that so? Miguna, what's wrong if Caroli bought Heron Court, hmm? What's wrong with that? What's wrong with Luos? Why are they talking too much, hmm? Who told them not to make money?" Raila dismissed me even before I could open my mouth.

Here was Raila, a purported agent of change, apparently lecturing me on why corruption was good and suggesting that the only problem was "Luos who were talking too much because they couldn't make money". I guessed he was alluding to me and Professor Edward Oyugi. He was saying: "Look at you. You are well-educated. You have extensive experience and now a big government job, yet all you can do is stand there and complain about Caroli making billions. Who prevented you from doing the same? What's wrong with you Miguna?"

I tried to explain that the issue wasn't one of making or not making money; nor was it about what was wrong with Luos; the real issue was that most people would immediately conclude that Caroli – and indirectly the PM – was involved in grand corruption. This, I said, would not just bring Raila's name into disrepute, but it would tarnish his reputation, that of his office and everyone who worked there with the permanent stain of graft, something that I found unacceptable, particularly because I didn't have my hand in the till. I added that it was worse for him because he would be running for President in 2012.

I continued: "*Jakom*, I didn't hear that story from a Luo, and even if I did, I find it completely reprehensible that you could dismiss it out of hand without even bothering to interrogate what it means; its legal and political implications…"

"Is that what you came here to report? I have no time to hear stories of people who can't make money..."

Raila carelessly spoke of Luos 'refusing to make money' yet each time he was approached by Luo professionals – businessmen and women as well as struggling entrepreneurs – trying to get legitimate loans or find legitimate business opportunities, which would only involve introducing them to many of his business contacts both locally and internationally, he refused to help them. Many of these Luo professionals and business people had spent their savings to support Raila's campaigns. Many had also fundraised for him. They were not interested in shady deals. They didn't want shortcuts. All they were looking for was a helping hand. Yet whenever Raila had an opportunity to speak to them, he always told them that they should go into business. Meanwhile, his consistent advice to those already in business was that they should work harder, ignoring the fact that that's what they have been doing, sometimes for decades.

Prominent Luo businessmen, like Awiti Hezron Bolo of Mombasa, who had spent tens of millions of his own hard-earned money promoting Raila's political ambitions, now couldn't access him. Neither was he able to get any business assistance from Raila.

Then there were others like Professor Larry Gumbe, a retired university teacher who had toiled as the Liberal Democratic Party's executive director for many years before Raila joined government through the National Alliance Rainbow Coalition (Narc) and who now ran his own engineering consulting company. Larry had applied for and won various competitive contracts only for these to be withdrawn or given to others who had given bribes or kickbacks without explanation. Whenever Larry brought those cases to me, I would write urgent memoranda to Raila with documents attached that proved the injustice Larry was facing, but I never heard back from Raila. All attempts I made to advocate on Larry's behalf were fruitless.

Many Luo businessmen like Eric Opon Nyamunga had similar if not worse experiences. Hanningtone Gaya, another Luo businessman in Nairobi, had donated his Toyota Land Cruiser and other personal goods – including giving his time, pro bono, to serve in Raila's 2007 think tank – only for Raila to return the vehicle in an un-roadworthy condition, with magical trinkets hidden in the dashboard.

Obel Nyanja was for many years a one-man Raila 'diplomat'. From his New Jersey base he spent millions on Raila's numerous US tours. Then, after more than 20 years in the US, he decided to relocate to Kenya. Obel came with a well-developed business plan to manufacture medicine. He wanted land and finance in order to construct a factory. He had lined up US companies he could collaborate with. Raila, who by then was Prime Minister, expressed interest and offered to assist him. But once Obel had arrived in the country, he couldn't secure an appointment with Raila. Thrice, I helped him meet Raila, who in turn handed him over to Caroli. Caroli met Obel once, but then never answered his calls again. After eight months of Obel struggling to track down Caroli and Raila, his savings had run out and he had to abandon his planned project and look for a job. He moved to Kisumu. Luckily, he eventually found gainful employment with a private company in Nairobi. He forgot about his dreams for a factory – at least for a while. It is alleged that in the meantime, however, Raila had his sisters registered as directors in Obel's company and as of the time of going to press, credible rumours which I have not yet been able to substantiate have it that he has approached some Italian investors and is proceeding with the plans of starting the factory without Obel's knowledge or involvement.

Or take the case of Raila's long-suffering photographer Dominick Otieno. Dominic worked for Raila for more than 15 years. On numerous occasions before Raila became Prime Minister, Dominick would go for months without pay. He relied on well-wishers to help him out whenever they could. I did so myself on many different occasions. After Raila became Prime Minister, it took Dominick nearly one year before he was given some little contract paying him peanuts. But as a focused and dedicated worker, Dominick saved some money and constructed for himself a small semi-permanent house in his village in Ugenya. When Raila and Ida were on a tour of Ugenya, someone in their entourage pointed out Dominick's small house to both of them, thinking that the two would be proud of their hard-working photographer. Later, as the entourage reached Ugunja market where Dominick had gone as part of an advance party to welcome the Prime Minister and take photographs from vantage positions, Ida approached him and within full view of the entourage, berated him, asking rudely: "Dominick, where did you get money to build a house?"

Dominick was both stunned and confused. He didn't know what Ida was talking about. He didn't consider his small semi-permanent structure in the village to be a "house" that might put Ida's nose out of joint. Why shouldn't Dominick, or any other person working with or for Raila, be able to save enough money and construct a decent house? Why was Ida concerned about Dominick's ability to construct a house when she seems apparently unconcerned about the billions of shillings that have gone down the drain at the OPM in the past three years alone? Why is there not more concern about the opulent lifestyle of Raila's children? Where did they get all the money to acquire flashy top-of-the-range vehicles and huge mansions in expensive neighbourhoods when we haven't seen what they do for a living?

Without fail – and for decades – Raila has sought and obtained tens of millions of shillings from Luos around the world, rich and poor. However, since becoming Prime Minister, most of those who contributed to Raila's political campaigns have found that the man forgot about them as soon as he got into power. Not that they had all been expecting anything in return. But it's human nature for those who have assisted someone to achieve something in life to expect even just a "thank you" in return.

In fact, many who have worked closely with Raila have often complained bitterly that he has never said "thank you," no matter what they did for him. He is the only person I have worked with who has never (for six years) asked – even out of curiosity: "how are your wife and children?" I have therefore concluded that Raila doesn't care about anybody else but Raila Odinga, his family and relatives. It took me six long years to realise this.

That Wednesday, as Raila dismissed my concerns about Caroli's alleged wheeler-dealing, I felt so disappointed. My attempts to address an obvious case of runaway corruption were being summarily dismissed by one many Kenyans held in high esteem as a paragon of moral rectitude. I shook my head and left.

I later shared this story with Salim and seriously contemplated resigning. In my view, Raila had chosen to either turn a blind eye to corruption or was involved himself, through Caroli. My impression, based on my keen observations of the goings-on within Raila's office, was that Caroli had lots of potential avenues of wealth to exploit. Apart from his alleged involvement in the Maize, Kazi Kwa Vijana (KKV), National Social Security Fund (NSSF), National Health Insurance Fund (NHIF) scandals and others, he has also been Raila's "business envoy" around the world. In addition, his varied titles as "Chief of Staff" and "Private Secretary" placed him in a position where peddling influence and offering access might have become a lucrative route for making millions.

The facts I disclose in this book about Caroli's operations are mainly derived directly from my conversations with him, or from my conversations with those who have direct or indirect information about his dealings. Take, for instance, when Caroli and Ahmed Kassam met sometime in 2011 in Caroli's office, to discuss how they could influence or manipulate Department of Defence (DoD) contracts. In my presence, Caroli had picked up his mobile telephone and called someone "senior in the military" who promised to meet Kassam in order to discuss the deal, which was claimed to be for military supplies from China worth billions of shillings. About three months later I read newspaper headlines about a deal gone sour and senior military officers suspended, retired or fired.

Caroli and Kassam never bothered with me because they knew I had no interest in their deals. They also knew that I was one of Raila's staunchest generals; hence, their expectation that I would keep my mouth shut. It is reasonable to assume that that occasion had not been a one-off; that Caroli and Kassam must have been involved in similar big deals before or after that. After all, on that occasion Caroli openly disclosed to me that Kassam had "purchased a fixed wing aeroplane". I can only assume the gravy train must have been thick with action.

On another occasion, Caroli talked to me – and I also heard him speaking on the telephone – about an oil deal involving Raila, Museveni and some "powerful men around Museveni". Some of my Kenyan readers might recall that Raila made a sudden trip to Uganda and met Museveni at State House, Entebbe, around mid-2009. The agenda of the visit wasn't publicly disclosed. During that visit Raila and Museveni purportedly agreed to work together in order to process and sell the oil currently being produced from Lake Albert in Uganda. Initially, Museveni was keen to construct a brand new refinery in Uganda to handle the production but Caroli informed me that Raila had managed to convince Museveni that it would be "cheaper and more profitable to do it in Mombasa".

Now obviously many people would say that Raila was only doing this for the economic good of Kenya. That's possible. However, it is also highly possible – and perhaps more probable or likely – that he was only doing it for his own personal, private interest, as Caroli told me. Why, for example, was the Ministry of Energy not involved in the discussions? Why was Caroli – Raila's Private Secretary – deeply involved in the discussions? Raila's dalliance with Museveni must therefore be seen, understood and interpreted from the context of the mutual self-interest of the two leaders rather than from any opportunistic political propaganda angle. In any event, Caroli was extremely excited about the oil deal with Museveni.

As I mentioned before, Caroli had dialled a number and spoke to someone he later said was "Museveni's right hand man". I'm not sure if the said person was Sam Kutesa or Eriya Kategaya, but my recollection is that he mentioned one of the two names.

Another area in which Caroli showed a keen interest was the National Social Security Fund (NSSF). So interested was he that he swore to ensure that "my man" becomes the Managing Trustee of the huge fund. He eventually managed to place his homeboy Kazongo in charge. Through his old classmate, roommate and friend from the University of Nairobi days, Ahmednasir Abdulahi, Caroli even managed to get a "friendly person" to chair the NSSF board. Luckily Caroli is also chummy with Francis Atwoli, the Secretary General of the Central Organisation of Trade Unions (COTU) of Kenya. With such connections, Caroli was said to hold frequent meetings with Kazongo and other important people at the NSSF. Those in the know say that the NSSF is a cash cow almost in the league of the Kenya Revenue Authority and that those "working closely with its top managers have suddenly become fabulously rich". Recently, however, Caroli and Kazongo seemed to have hit a rough patch at the NSSF, resulting in the latter's unceremonial ejection from his lucrative position and bitter accusations by the board against an unnamed 'influential official at the OPM' whom they accused of 'interference and unlawful attempts to manipulate the NSSF for his personal gain and greed.' The alleged NSSF scandal, which saw a reported loss of billions of taxpayers' money, bore the unmistakable imprimatur of Caroli.

Then of course, are Raila's (and through him, Caroli's) "connections" to Rupiah Banda, President of Zambia from 2008 to 2011. Caroli frequently boasted to me of their grandiose investments in the copper fields of Zambia. So thick were the connections that Raila sent Orengo and someone else to Zambia on the day Zambians voted in the September 2011 presidential elections.

In-between, Caroli was busy receiving money from a number of sources – old friends, colleagues, Raila's middle men and "venture capitalists" – keen on tapping into the well-oiled connections the new "Joshua Kulei" was building and cementing. One such case was filed at the High Court in Nairobi about one year ago in which Caroli was sued by two individuals, including one lawyer, for the refund of Sh5m he had been advanced for a "business deal" that never materialised. Before the plaintiffs had filed the case against Caroli, they had held a meeting attended by veteran lawyer Paul Muite and another lawyer Mugambi Imanyara, during which Caroli had undertaken to repay the debt. But he never had and so the case had culminated in the civil action. Caroli never defended the action. Subsequently, default judgment was entered and Caroli ordered to pay. As we went to press, I hadn't received any credible evidence that he had repaid the debt.

Mysteriously though, the court file recently "disappeared" from the High Court registry. Many believe that Caroli might have tried hiding evidence of this case. Unfortunately for him, all records of the court are public documents. I have perused the file from Mugambi Imanyara's office, one of the lawyers involved, and verified the facts in this case. As one of the two highest ranking public officials in Kenya, the onus is on Raila to prove that his hands are clean. As a highly placed and powerful public figure, Raila owes Kenyans a positive moral and constitutional duty to thoroughly explain the alleged dubious dealings linked to Caroli, Isahakia, Kassam and many others.

Finally, there is the case of the *Kazi Kwa Vijana* (KKV) programme, a youth employment initiative spearheaded by Raila and his office, though it also involved other state actors, departments and ministries. Contrary to newspaper reports, the KKV programme was coordinated by the OPM, where Caroli was the one placed in charge. Caroli chaired virtually all KKV meetings at the OPM; not Isahakia. Nevertheless, as the accounting officer in the Office of the Prime Minister, Isahakia remained responsible for the acquisition, sourcing and disbursement of funds.

There were other senior officers that worked closely with Caroli and Isahakia. These were: Prof. Hirohiko Hino, Ann Olubendi, Rachel Gesami and Patrick Chabeda. Publicly available information shows that the people of Kenya have spent about Sh10 billion on "youth employment" initiatives that have had little discernible impact. Where's the money gone? Well, I have reliable information about the crafty Caroli roping in two "key" people in the Ministry of Finance to ensure that we'll never know where those funds have gone.

The KKV scandal erupted after the leakage of a World Bank "in-depth audit review" of only Phase Two of the project, dated September 13, 2011. The PM and his ODM party didn't welcome the disclosure; they condemned the leakage. Why? How else was the public going to learn of the massive theft if the report hadn't been leaked? Why blame the heroic whistle blower(s) and not the thieves?

Having carefully reviewed the World Bank audit report, I found the evidence of theft compelling. Here are the hard facts from the World Bank audit report:

More than Sh33 million of our money was disbursed to senior civil servants and other ineligible third parties without following existing government and World Bank payment procedures. Millions were paid to unrelated project activities in breach of legal agreements and Bank policies and guidelines. In many cases, money was accrued in excess of the approved limits.

There were numerous payments made without proper supporting documents in clear breach of government and World Bank financial disbursement policies and guidelines. Other payments were made for contracts that contravened the Bank and government procurement procedures.

In the case of Mrs Gesami, she was illegally and concurrently placed on both the World Bank and government payroll. The PM's Office deliberately concealed the fact that she was a full-time public employee and misled the Bank into approving her hiring as a "consultant". She was consequently paid more than Sh5 million on top of her regular government earnings. That was fraud.

The PM's Permanent Secretary, Mohamed Isahakia, is cited – directly – five separate times. These are in addition to 16 other serious alleged irregularities touching on him. He paid Sh1.2 million in meal allowances to employees while they were at their work stations. He also irregularly paid Sh173,668 commuter allowance for employees at the PM's office. He hired 26 unauthorised interns and paid them. More than Sh1.5 million was paid out to unknown and unauthorised persons.

Private companies like Copy Cat Ltd, Parallel Media, ISIS Solutions, DT Dobie, Kenya Shell, Total Kenya Ltd, Morven and Kester were paid more than Sh23 million for unauthorised services rendered to employees at the PM's office. Retroactive payments were made on fraudulent invoices. Cash payments were made without supporting documents. The PM's personal secretary, administration secretary and other unauthorised persons were either paid, their personal vehicles serviced and illegal fuel cards irregularly issued. All these amounted to tens of millions of shillings of public money.

I subsequently published an article based on my analysis of the 'interim' World Bank report, which catalogued numerous cases of embezzlement and unlawful and irregular payments from the public till, and also lambasted the PM's subsequent response to the scandal. I hold the view that any public money embezzled – even Sh100 – by those entrusted with it for the public good ought to be severely punished. In the Maize Scandal the public lost, through open theft and looting, about Sh10 billion! Corruption is one of the worst cancers in our society. Together with tribalism and nepotism it illegally diverts billions of money that could go a long way to improving the standards of living for more than 40 million Kenyans.

In parliament Raila was forced to respond to questions about the World Bank's report from the MP for Saboti, Eugene Wamalwa (now Minister for Justice, National Cohesion and Constitutional Affairs), in which he sought to know how much money had been committed to the KKV project from inception; how much money had been lost through alleged corruption with respect to the KKV; who was responsible for the alleged loss of funds; and whether the PM would be prepared in the circumstances to take political responsibility for the losses.

At first, the PM, while admitting to the losses, tried to pour cold water on the amounts that had been misappropriated, arguing that the 'money lost was inconsequential'. But the amounts were not remotely 'inconsequential'. Raila admitted that more than Sh308m of public money had been lost – indeed squandered – by his office and related implementing ministries between 2008 and 2010 in what was only Phase One of the KKV. He also admitted that more than Sh20m had been misappropriated by his office in the year 2011 on Phase Two of the project. Raila disclosed that Phase One of the KKV project had been wholly funded by the public to the tune of Sh7 billion whereas the second phase of Sh4.3 billion had been funded by the World Bank. That is roughly Sh10.3 billion of public money. That money is capable of constructing, equipping and staffing more than 10,000 primary schools where millions of poor kids could have been given an education.

In my *Star* article, I pointed out that what that amount of money should have done should have been visible to all Kenyans, yet we clearly could not see any evidence of where it had all disappeared to. Instead, Raila was telling Kenyans that they had used a whopping Sh10.3 billion to purchase slashers and hoes and to pay a few thousand hungry youths in the countryside to dig trenches and clear roadsides. It was incredible, especially in view of the fact that the youths were being paid roughly Sh250 per day for a period of less than a year. We aren't even talking here of the hundreds of thousands of ghost workers that would have inevitably been paid hundreds of millions, which ultimately would have ended up in the pockets of those who had conceived of and perpetrated the fraud. If the funds had been properly utilised, I argued in my article, hundreds of thousands of the targeted youth could have been trained in various useful skills through which they could have obtained gainful employment and they would have had sustainable livelihoods.

In my article, I pointed out that the PM's admission in Parliament came grudgingly. It wasn't voluntary. Nor was he contrite. Curiously, he seemed to take back the admission of loss by later insisting, "no single cent has been lost". That's after reading out a litany of millions of irregular, unauthorised and clearly dodgy payments made out by his office in breach of the government's and the Bank's procedures and regulations.

A few days before, the PM had proclaimed himself "as white as cotton" over the allegations. He repeated that phrase in Parliament, but TV polls conducted that evening (following his statement in parliament) showed that more than 60% of viewers didn't believe him. A true statesman would have genuinely apologised and ordered a thorough investigations over the alleged fraud. He would have immediately relieved his officers named in the World Bank report: Rachel Gesami, Caroli Omondi, Mohamed Isahakia, Bernard Wandera and Patrick Chabeda. Kenyans expected their PM to show sensitivity on welfare matters, particularly on issues of good governance, accountability, transparency and corruption. They expected and deserved to see that their PM cared about them and would protect the public interests; not his own or his cronies' interests.

Yet, there he was – defending the indefensible. He essentially said: "yes, millions of taxpayers' money disappeared in my office under my watch…but that's not theft. Neither my officers nor I are responsible, either…" I found that perplexing and asked: "Well, who is then? Who authorised those millions to be paid out in breach of the law? Unauthorised payment is nothing but theft. Who will take responsibility for that?"

Instead of defending the public interests, the PM defended his senior staff. "Is he in tune with the values enshrined in the Constitution? Is he capable of upholding and implementing the Constitution?" my subsequent article asked.

Theft is a popular name for larceny. It is an act of stealing. It involves the intentional taking of someone's property without his or her consent. It includes illegal conversion or exerting unauthorised control over property. Embezzlement is theft. So is obtaining control over property by deception or false pretexts. Clearly, Kenyans never consented to the massive theft of the KKV project funds by senior officers at the PM's office and at other ministries

It shouldn't and doesn't matter the amounts involved. If a robber goes to a bank with a gun and forces the teller to give him Sh100 – by force, false pretext or through forgery – before attempting to flee with the money, it wouldn't and shouldn't matter if he is caught before he actually leaves the bank. It shouldn't matter that the teller might have been deceived or forced to give out the money. Theft would have been established. The thief acted on an intention. End of story!

Theft is what happened in the KKV scandal. (Oh yes, that's what it is!) Those who carried out the massive theft have been caught. They acted on their intentions. They stole public funds. Instead of firing the culprits and prosecuting them, the Prime Minister stated "all the misappropriated funds would be refunded to the World Bank". But that constitutes a double loss to the public, since the so-called refund had to come from the public coffers. Why should the PM let those who had stolen public funds go scot-free? I wondered. I concluded my piece by insisting that there should be zero tolerance of corruption.

"We must have full restitution, yes. But the thieves must also be severely punished. They should be prosecuted, convicted and sent away for a few years. They cannot continue to hold public office. They lost our trust. They must also be publicly shamed. The culture of impunity must not be allowed to persist.

"I am calling for both criminal and political responsibility for all implicated – starting with the PM, his PS, chief of staff, administration secretary, director of policy and all the senior staff mentioned in the World Bank audit report just like I did when William Ruto, Amos Kimunya and Moses Wetangula were in the dock over alleged embezzlement of public funds. Nobody is above the law!"

The article stung Raila so much that on the day it appeared, Patrick Quarcoo, the Radio Africa Group's Chief Executive Officer and *the Star*'s CEO, William Pike, confided in me that Raila called more than five separate times. That was in addition to Isahakia's numerous calls to *the Star*'s political editor, Paul Ilado. Pike said to me on the day my column appeared: "Raila is seething with rage over your KKV article…it stung them so much that they are demanding that we restrain you from attacking him any further…I personally found the article balanced. Even some of our directors who are not your fans called to say they liked it…".

By 2011, after three short years in the PM's office, Caroli had essentially become a billionaire. He told me that the Sh45 million mortgage for the Upper Hill property had been paid off and that he was assembling materials to construct a 17-storey ultra modern office/apartment block on that piece of prime property. The Sh25 million mortgage on the property where Orange House sits had also been cleared. He referred to the five brand new top-of-the-range European imported vehicles relaxing in his driveway, as being courtesy of "the Government of Raila *wuod* Odinga." Add to his property portfolio, the alleged piles of cash in various bank accounts here and abroad, the oil deals in Uganda, the mineral concessions in the DRC and Zambia, and we are speaking of billions of shillings – all accumulated since 2007!

These and many other dubious 'deals' have brought Caroli's reputation into so much disrepute that even some of Raila's close family members had openly celebrated when he had been temporarily "suspended" in February 2010. Ruth Adhiambo, Raila's younger sister called me on the day Caroli's suspension was announced, and cried: "Miguna, I'm on the sky right now…flying high into the sky…I'm tempted to strip naked and walk through Kisumu streets dancing stark naked because of joy! Caroli is gone; please tell me it is true that he is gone!"

Many others expressed similar sentiments. Secret cables from the US Embassy in Nairobi that were published in the WikiLeaks scandal, quoted the former US Ambassador to Nairobi, Michael Ranneberger as saying that "Mr Odinga is unable or unwilling to govern effectively, and to move the reform agenda forward…On February 14, 2010, Mr Odinga purportedly took action against William Ruto not only because he wanted to be seen as fighting corruption, but to divert attention from his family's involvement in the Maize Scandal…we have credible reports that members of the Odinga family, presumably with his knowledge and/or involvement, were involved in the Maize Scandal…" The secret cables also quoted both Lands Minister James Orengo and Agriculture Minister, Dr Sally Koskei, confiding in Ambassador Ranneberger about Raila's dismal administrative and leadership skills. Both ODM ministers allegedly called Raila 'incompetent, confused and disorganised' and squarely blamed him for the failure to streamline the operations of his office. According to the WikiLeaks, both Orengo and Sally stated that Raila's 'weak leadership had negatively impacted on the operations of his office, which had become ineffective…' The day the WikiLeaks' report was published in the Kenyan newspapers, Orengo called me in panic, seeking my advice on how he should respond to the disclosures.

"Jim," I said, "just ignore it. If the reports are true and accurate, you shouldn't worry. After all, they may just be what *Jakom* needs in order to wake up from his slumber…"

So some members of the Odinga family weren't celebrating his temporary downfall because they had any personal animus against Caroli; they just wanted Raila to clean up his office so that his 2012 prospects would look good. Some also suspected that Caroli was strategically inducing them into corrupt deals as an insurance policy for himself.

Yet when an opportunity had arisen with the KKV scandal for Raila to take immediate action to deal with the obvious embezzlement of public funds by senior officers in his office, he instead appeared in Parliament and presented a spirited defence of the culprits, arguing that "no money was lost". That was disgraceful for a man, a politician, and a leader who many of us had had great hopes for. Hundreds of millions of shillings of taxpayers' money had been embezzled. The evidence was there for everyone to see. Raila knew that. So why was he trying to mislead the country?

* * * * * * * * * * * * * *

Another name that has become synonymous with graft is that of Raila's Permanent Secretary, Mohamed Isahakia. At the time of writing, Isahakia, who is at least 63, has worked for the Government of Kenya for decades. Before that he worked as the Director of the National Museums of Kenya (NMK), where tens of millions of public money disappeared under his watch. He was arrested and charged with theft and misappropriation of public resources. The matter went to court and disappeared there, with claims that "he had repaid the money". Repaid or not, theft occurred, for which he was fired from the NMK.

But Isahakia is nothing but a mysterious survivor, for he resurfaced a few years after his troubled stint at the NMK as a Permanent Secretary in Daniel arap Moi's kleptomaniac and despotic regime, serving for years until he was fired, again, for alleged incompetence. Dr Sally Kosgei, who fired him while she was the

Permanent Secretary to the Office of the President, Secretary to the Cabinet and Head of the Civil Service, disclosed this information to me. So, why would Raila choose such a person as his Permanent Secretary when there were so many highly qualified and experienced young Kenyans with integrity around?

As I have already mentioned, Isahakia was mentioned in the Maize Scandal. But even more significantly, he was caught red-handed by the defunct Kenya Anti-Corruption Commission with stolen public assets worth more than 50 million shillings in the form of public houses in the Woodley Estate. On December 2, 2010, PLO Lumumba, the KACC Director, announced that he had repossessed 19 public assets – eight flats and 16 bungalows in Nairobi's Woodley estate – that had been illegally acquired and allocated to Mohammed Isahakia (PS, Prime Minister's Office); Musalia Mudavadi (Deputy Prime Minister and Minister for Local Government); the late Mulu Mutisya; lawyer Kennedy Ogeto; and two others. In a bizarre twist, PLO then announced that Isahakia and others had been "pardoned" for "voluntarily returning the houses to the public". Immediately this announcement was made, I wrote to Raila advising him that in view of that voluntary 'return' by Isahakia or repossession from him of the public assets, his position as Permanent Secretary to the Prime Minister had become untenable and he should therefore either resign or be fired. I subsequently discussed this matter with Raila several times. In late December 2010, I published an article in *the Star* in which I criticised Lumumba for not charging and prosecuting the culprits. I argued that Isahakia and others should only have been given amnesty after they had been charged. Amnesty, I argued, should only be in exchange for an admission and finding of guilt.

That wasn't the first or the last time I questioned Raila's judgment in employing Isahakia. Of course Raila did nothing about my advice nor about the public disclosures of massive rip-offs perpetrated by his PS. That was another significant sign that Raila not only condoned corruption; he encouraged it.

I also challenged the Kenya Anti-Corruption Commission (KACC), the National Cohesion and Integration Commission and the Truth, Justice and Reconciliation Commission (TJRC) to pursue these issues. But they did not. For his part, PLO Lumumba promised to unleash 'high voltage files' and 'fry both big and small fish' when he took over as director of the KACC. However, deadlines came and went without any arrests or prosecutions. Not only did he compromise his reputation by accepting an appointment by Moi as the inaugural Dean of Kabarak University's Faculty of Law, he also dubiously proposed unilateral "amnesties" as a mechanism of dealing with past cases of grand corruption. In my view, forgiveness without accountability was tantamount to the perpetuation of the culture of impunity. When he announced that he had "forgiven" the racketeers in the Woodley Estate case, because they had "voluntarily returned" the property they had illegally grabbed from the public more than 19 years previously, I was disgusted. No law gave PLO the power to forgive thieves and looters. The thieves hadn't been charged. The so-called amnesty hadn't been approved by a court of law as part of a plea bargain as required by law. There were no restitutions, no surcharges, no punishments; PLO simply appeared on TV and made a declaration. In my considered view, this was the height of impunity.

By all accounts, PLO was generally considered to be a good lawyer; why then did he speak about 'developing policies' to let thieves go scot-free when he had the *Anti-Corruption and Economic Crimes Act, Public Office and Ethics Act, The Public Procurement and Disposal Act, 2005, Public Procurement Regulations, 2006, Witness Protection Act, 2006* and the *Constitution of Kenya* with which to put them away for life? Whatever 'policy' PLO intended to develop couldn't supersede all those statutes and the Constitution?

I was equally astounded when I visited the KACC website and discovered that PLO had unashamedly posted 86 press releases and 79 speeches on the KACC website when his office had achieved so little. Under "Press Releases," there was an item called "Triton Case in Court" dated July 17, 2009 but the link was a dud. Curiously, the Press Release announced the "arrest" of Yagnesh Mohanlal Devani and some un-identified "senior management" of "Triton" and unnamed officials of "Kenya Pipeline Company". However, it is public knowledge that no such companies are registered in Kenya. Moreover, no specific charges were listed against Devani's name, nor were there any particulars of what charges Devani or the unidentified "officials" were facing, if any. The Press Release declared that the investigations were "complete". The overall impression was of shoddiness.

For more than one year when PLO Lumumba served as the KACC Director he never successfully investigated one single major case of corruption or economic crime. He didn't touch Goldenberg, Anglo Leasing, Ken-Ren, Triton, Grand Regency, Foreign Embassies, Maize, Free Primary Education, and the trillions that the Kroll Report disclosed had been stolen from us. And nor, perhaps unsurprisingly, did PLO ever touch Kabarak University and the Kiptagich Tea Factory and Farm, which I had publicly reminded him about as soon as he took over at the KACC.

And as PLO was embarrassing himself with the amnesty promise to thieves, sitting beside him was Tecla Namachanja, the acting chairperson of the wobbling TJRC. Apparently, they were both planning to have racketeers and looters forgiven through the TJRC. That was cynically creative. Forget about the fact that the law didn't allow them to do that.

The other well-paid comedian was Mzalendo Kibunjia of the National Cohesion and Integration Commission. The National Cohesion and Integration Commission's mandate is to ensure that all public entities employ their staff from all Kenyan communities, regions and gender; that not more than a third of their staff is from one tribe; and that there is no discrimination. However, if Kibunjia diligently examined the composition of the Office of the President, Ministry of Finance, Ministry of Internal Security and Provincial Administration, the State Law Office, Central Bank, Kenya Ports Authority, Kenya Revenue Authority, Consolidated Bank, Kenya Power, Kenya Industrial Research Development Institute (KIRDI) and Industrial and Commercial Development Corporation (ICDC), he would inevitably establish that one community – the Gikuyu – dominates all the senior positions – from head of department to minister.

Another financial scandal that demanded investigation came in the wake of the referendum into constitutional reform. In advance of the referendum, the state, through Francis Kimemia, the Permanent Secretary in the Office of the President in charge of Internal Security and Provincial Administration, released in excess of Sh1.25 billion to both ODM and PNU to use during the constitutional referendum campaigns. The money was surreptitiously sourced and released through Isahakia for ODM and Kimemia for PNU. (This was to avoid possible legal and accounting queries about why the state would be funding political parties to conduct what amounted to a political activity, albeit an important national one.) On the ODM side, Isahakia released (some of) the funds to the party through its Executive Director, Janet Ong'era, and Secretary General Prof. Anyang' Nyong'o. The Orange Party's chief accountant, Joshua Kawino, was peripherally involved, as was Prof. Peter Wanyande. On the OPM side, Isahakia 'worked with' Caroli, Ceasar Asiyo and Abdulrahman Iddris to funnel the money to different places. On the PNU side, Kiraitu Murungi, Peter Kagwanja and Stephen Njiiru took charge of the money.

The eventual misappropriation of this money affected me because I was a member of the Green Joint Secretariat, supposedly financed by these funds. The Secretariat, housed at the Kenyatta International Conference Centre, had been established by both ODM and PNU in or around May 2010. Its mandate was to spearhead the campaigns for the ratification of the new Constitution, scheduled for August 4. The agreement was that both the strategy and secretariat staff were to be paid fixed amounts for the three full months they would render services to the joint secretariat. However, after the teams had worked tirelessly for two months without any payment or reimbursements for their costs, a few individuals, namely: Prof. Anyang' Nyong'o (ODM), Kiraitu Murungi (PNU), Janet Ong'era (ODM) and Peter Kagwanja (PNU) decided to renege on the contract they had agreed on with all the secretariat staff and strategic team. This led to a ruckus resulting in a demonstration by the staff who were demanding their payment and ugly confrontations between the volunteers and the apparatchiks. Lawsuits were filed and Kagwanja was held hostage for a brief period of time. The matter eventually reached the media.

I wasn't present when the demonstrations occurred. However, at a private meeting held between members of the strategy team and Nyong'o, Murungi, Ong'era and Kagwanja, at the Nairobi Club, I had strongly argued for the contracts to be honoured. Soon thereafter, Anyang' and Caroli told Raila – who was at the time receiving treatment in hospital after brain surgery – that I was the ringleader of the group who were demanding payment. Of course I wasn't, though I fully supported the campaign for payment and the exposure of those who were misappropriating public funds. I later learnt that Raila knew and had been roped into the scam. As a result, Raila "instructed Isahakia" to withdraw me from the Green Joint Secretariat. The long and short of it was that, once more, Raila sided with those who were ripping off the public. Consequently, there was no reasonable prospect that anything he said or did would benefit the general public or society at large. For my part, I made noise and again demanded that Isahakia shouldn't just be fired without any delay; I also demanded that he be prosecuted to the full extent of the law. I penned an op-ed article on this matter after I realised that Raila wasn't going to do anything.

Thereafter, Raila and the rest of the office tried to avoid me like the plague. I didn't care. I hadn't taken the onerous public service position to please anyone. I was engaged to advice. To do that I needed to be professional, objective and competent. Raila hired me to provide him with unvarnished truth, which I would filter, using my professional mind, training and judgment. Had he wanted a court jester, they were in adequate supply in Kenya. Had he been looking for sycophancy – that too, was in good supply in Kenya, a country that tolerated Moi for twenty-four years!

At the end of it all, despite not paying their dedicated strategists and secretariat personnel what they had agreed on beforehand, more than Sh1 billion had still been "spent". Reports had it, that Ceasar purchased a brand new Mercedes Benz, Isahakia sped up the construction of a mansion in Karen, and others feathered their nests as well.

* * * * * * * * * * * * * * *

Those who raise or pursue corruption allegations around Raila are the ones who fall victim. People have all kinds of things to say about Raila's former chief of protocol, Tony Gachoka, but one thing no one can accuse him of is lack of candour. Despite reports to the contrary, Tony was actually very close to both Isahakia and Raila. In fact it was Isahakia and Raila who hired Tony ahead of everyone else at the OPM. In those days I didn't know Tony well. But later, I learnt that he actually tried to no avail to raise with Raila important issues about Isahakia's alleged involvement in embezzlement of public funds at the OPM. At the OPM it was Tony who first publicly linked Isahakia and the OPM to the Maize Scandal. And what happened to him? He was suspended, with pay, for "indiscipline". Tony was alleged to have "undermined his boss". In a letter dated March 13, 2009, Isahakia stated: "Your conduct continues to be disrespectful, malicious and amounts to complete insubordination intended to undermine the Office of the Prime Minister". A case of the pot calling the kettle black.

Tony has claimed numerous times that Raila betrayed him, in much the same way as he had previously betrayed Paul Muite, Gitobu Imanyara, Simeon Nyachae, Achieng' Oneko, Wamalwa Kijana, Anyang' Nyong'o, Joe Donde, Otieno Mak'Onyango, James Orengo, Dennis Akumu and many others. Tony claimed that he hadn't just campaigned vigorously for Raila in 2007; that he had "brought Charity Ngilu" to Raila's camp and that Raila's "thank you" was to kick him in the crotch. Many would quibble with Tony's argument without reflecting on what he was saying. But the more significant point is that it wasn't just Tony alone; others before and after him became victim to the same vindictiveness: Rateng' Oginga Ogegos, Herbert Ojwang's, Odeny Ngures, Dimba Jakobuyas, Dick Ogolas, Martin Shikukus and people like myself.

Salim had to 'resign' from a position of "spokesman" that he had never held 'officially' because he had never been given a contract. Salim himself told me that he hadn't been fully paid for his services; that he was leaving because of frustrations and disorganisation in Raila's office. Salim, too, had complained to Raila many times without end, about the alleged corruption and inefficiencies in his office. Sarah had similarly done so in the past. And so did Mugambi Imanyara, who lasted only five months at the OPM as Raila's "legal advisor", a position that was later "given" to Paul Mwangi, as a piece of Machiavellian political bait to the Agikuyu community.

Throughout my tenure I diligently and promptly reported all reports or suspicions of corruption to Raila. But not once did I receive any feedback from Raila or see any action taken. For instance, I sent numerous reports, memoranda and letters to Raila about Isahakia's alleged involvement in grand corruption, including the fraudulent acquisition of numerous public houses in the Woodley Estate in Nairobi. They did not elicit even one request for a meeting to discuss the accusations. Not even after I specifically requested such meetings. I also forwarded documents patriotic Kenyans provided to me on the goings-on at various ODM ministries like Immigration and Registration of Persons, Cooperative Development, Lands, Health Services, Industrialisation and Local Government. Without exception, Raila remained eerily silent.

Shortly after Raila was sworn in, members of the think tank, including myself, received a five-page document entitled, "Sabotage scheme against Raila" in which the author(s) detailed problems with how Raila's office was being (mis)managed. The report quoted a newspaper story in *The People on Sunday* of May 4, 2008 in which credible allegations were made of "a fierce war by officers at the Prime Minister's office" and stated that such news "barely scratched the bottom of what is really at stake for Raila Odinga and ODM" [Sic]. The story correctly relayed information about a turf war between Caroli and Isahakia before providing tantalising details about the latter's background and proclivities. These allegations would be repeated much later in a *Standard* newspaper report by Dennis Onyango before he joined the OPM. Onyango's report turned its guns on Caroli.

The five-page dossier blamed Isahakia for the "watering down of ODM's position during the negotiations over portfolio balance". It claimed that it was Isahakia who had persistently "changed ODM lists" on ministries and other government positions. The report claimed that Isahakia was working at the behest of the PNU on "a plot to fix Raila". It then went back to "other dirty deals" during the 2007 presidential campaign when "the Isahakia boys inflated transport, publicity and security procurements while major needs were left bleeding for want of money". It concluded by asking Raila to "sack this man".

Of course Raila did nothing about the report; he never even convened a meeting to discuss it. Isahakia later disclosed to me that he suspected that Caroli Omondi and Musalia Mudavadi's Private Secretary and Director of Communications, Kibisu Kabetesi were behind the preparation and circulation of the report. Omondi in turn blamed Isahakia for Onyango's newspaper article. The bad blood, turf wars and conflicts between these two became so heightened that at one point the newspapers reported that they had physically fought in the office. Many in ODM hated both Isahakia and Omondi, whom they blamed for every mis-step Raila made.

During my tenure at the OPM, I consistently registered my complaints about known and perceived corruption cases in and around the office; cases that involved senior officers, the Prime Minister's relatives and even ODM cabinet ministers. Many times ordinary members of the public approached me with leads, information and documents accusing various people close to the Prime Minister of engaging in corruption.

Some of this information would be relayed to me anonymously by people simply emailing or dropping documents at the office. Given the sad and long history of Kenya where whistle-blowers have been murdered, fired, stigmatised, shunned, neglected or victimised for sticking out their necks, no reasonable person could blame some of the informants for choosing to remain anonymous, or for fearing for their lives if they came out into the open. The whistle-blower in the notorious Goldenberg financial and political scandal that looted more than Sh200 billion from the public coffers, David Munyakei – a fearless Kenyan patriot – was summarily fired from his job at the Central Bank of Kenya in 1993, and deliberately relegated to the economic doldrums. He died a painful, dejected and isolated man. Raila was in the opposition when the Goldenberg scandal was dramatically revealed to the country. He – like many other anti-corruption pretenders – loudly, repeatedly and publicly promised the country that he would ensure that the truth about the biggest financial rip-off in Kenya would be fully investigated and the culprits severely punished. That was many years ago.

CHAPTER EIGHTEEN

CIRCLING WOLVES

At 6 feet 4 inches and 210 pounds, I am not a small man. In fact, many consider me humongous. I've not always been this big, though. I've certainly almost always been taller than my classmates and workmates, but until I started 'eating well' (or is it eating unhealthily?) following my admission to the Ontario Bar, I was always the lankiest fellow around. It's partly genetics and partly lifestyle; genetics because my paternal grandfather, Jomune, and my father, Miguna, were both about the same height, and my older brother Ondiek is exactly the same height as me. Growing up, I always marvelled at how tall he was. But in fact he was never the tallest man in Magina, my village. Magina is a village of tall men. There you will find James Ogada Onyango (nicknamed John Long), a man with a 7.2 feet frame. And he only just looms over the rest of the men in his family.

So growing up in Magina, my height never made me feel out of place. Nor was anyone ever intimidated by it. Actually, at Apondo primary school I wasn't even the tallest boy. Okore Wuod Oduma was, though I was one of the tallest. They jokingly called me *ongowang'* (the heron), a fond nickname that made clear that, though I was tall, my height didn't mean I was older, bigger, stronger or aggressive. There is a big difference between being articulate, firm or vocal and being combative. Throughout my life, I have never tried to take advantage of my height. Although bullying was common at both Onjiko and Njiiri's, I never picked on anyone. It's true that I don't suffer fools gladly, nor do I run away from fights. But truth be told, I am rarely the aggressor.

Let me admit that my voice – like that of my late mother and my siblings – tends to be loud and strong, especially when agitated. Like my mother and siblings, I not only have strong opinions, I'm also vocal. Many consider me articulate and well prepared. Even my most rabid enemies admit that I'm not an empty-headed bloke. Moreover, I have never been meek or fearful of power, wealth or position. I respect people, not based on their class, race, colour, position or wealth. I hold the view that respect is a two-way traffic; you must extend it to others for it to be granted to you. I believe that respect is *earned*. You earn it by your behaviour, integrity, contributions and achievements, not through pedigree, inheritance, station in life or dubiously acquired titles or positions. I abhor inequality and injustice. As this narrative demonstrates, I detested and fought for justice even as an 11-year-old teenager in Lambwe Valley. I continued the struggle at Onjiko, Njiiri's, Gilgil and virtually at every institution or organisation I have been affiliated with. My fierce defence of the ideals ODM stood for earned me tremendous support from Kenyans from all walks of life. This could have caused disquiet – even nervousness – from Raila and some members of the kitchen cabinet. Since my departure from the Office of the Prime Minister, I have read unfounded allegations that I was busy building a political base with which to take a stab at ODM's leadership. That's hogwash. It never even crossed my mind.

It may come as a surprise to many to know that I am also quite reserved and private. I hardly go out at night. I love listening to music and reading for hours on end. I am punctual and adhere to deadlines without fail. In fact, throughout my life, I've always completed school assignments ahead of my classmates. I work without supervision. Indeed, during the first year after my appointment as Raila's advisor, I rarely made public statements and never appeared in the media unless as part of a state or official event. That made some of my supporters refer to me in internet discussion platforms as "No Drama Miguna". I can, and often tend to be reticent, especially in the midst of important assignments. I consider myself both a strategist and tactician. Before I comment on or commit to anything, I subject the prevailing issue to thorough research, analysis and introspection. This could be frustrating to those used to shallowness, sycophancy or rushed decisions. Prior to the August 4, 2010 referendum, Carey Orege, the Permanent Secretary for Regional Development Authorities and Raila's first cousin, became so frustrated by my reservations concerning the involvement of public servants in what was purely a political process, he told me agitatedly, "Miguna, you think too much". I was startled. So was Israel Agina, until recently the longstanding Odinga family business manager, who agreed with my viewpoint. Orege said it as if there are limits beyond which thinking is bad. Folk like Orege – like many Kanu-era bureaucrats – believe in "following orders from above" without question, even if such orders are unlawful, irresponsible or unreasonable. They had faith in a system that, to paraphrase the late Sudan Peoples' Liberation Movement leader Dr John Garang, is "too deformed to be reformed". Beyond that, however, they also prefer a system where senior personalities are never challenged even if they do wrong. Unfortunately, that's the mentality that has allowed grand corruption and abuse of power to fester, take root and become "normal".

It would have been dishonest and a betrayal of everything I have stood for and represented if I abdicated responsibility in the pursuit of justice merely because of my employment. If anything, I felt it was imperative that I tried to instill higher standards in Kenya – as high as or even higher than in Canada. For a while, I joined those who had mistakenly embraced, supported – even followed – Raila Odinga, believing he would be an engine of change. What we should all have been doing – and which we must start doing – is being loyal to and serving the people of Kenya, irrespective of their cultural, ethnic, racial and gender differences. We need to put the country ahead of any and all parochial interests. In fact, for the short period of time I held the senior public position at the OPM, that's what I tried to do. I know many have and will continue to quibble with the thrust of the articles I wrote during that time, or indeed the fact that I returned to writing articles at all. That's all right with me. But people must be able to place my articles in their proper perspective and judge their contents, not whether they like or dislike my height, weight or other primordial characteristics. In the end, those who hurled abuse at me should understand that almost everything I did was not just with the express permission and encouragement from the Prime Minister, it was also intended to serve the public interest.

All the above is a preamble to my saying that after I returned from exile in 2007, I discovered – to my utter surprise and disappointment – that some people took offense not just at my opinions, but also at my physical appearance. The latter especially seemed odd. On careful thought, perhaps I shouldn't have been surprised: 24 years of Moi's totalitarianism must have caused permanent fundamental cultural, social, political and psychological deformities in our society, deformities we are forced to contend with for many years to come. Consistently – starting with the disgraced former chairman of the disbanded Electoral Commission of Kenya (ECK), Samuel Kivuitu – insecure people have gratuitously alleged that I have tried to intimidate them. Often, this accusation followed my contributions on topical issues, especially during the constitutional review process.

For centuries, *ad hominem* insults have been the weapon of choice of the lazy, the cowardly, the ignorant and the malicious. They distract and divert attention from the issues to the person. In my case, they intend to stifle, muzzle and defang me. The virulent attacks are aimed at transforming me into a conformist. Some people who have recently decried me as "arrogant" have never met me, but only acquainted themselves with me through my articles, media appearances or third party *ad hominem* slurs. But I suspect that some of the virulence directed at me has had nothing to do with either my physical appearance or the way I communicate. It's simply due to the fact that some people have chosen to be petty, mischievous, malicious and envious, or are trying to protect what they consider their turf. Many have taken umbrage at my persistent attack on corruption, tribalism and nepotism in Kenyan society, especially in the public service. Standing up against impunity has risks.

I'm not naïve. I know that the stakes have been high, for some, too high to be taken for granted. There are those in Kenya who have benefited immensely from the networks of corruption that permeate our country and society. There are those who feel genuinely threatened by what I – and others of my persuasion – represent. I believe in creating a society in which everyone has equal opportunities and access to mandatory basic quality education, health care and social amenities. I believe in giving everyone a fair chance in life, in a society grounded in social justice that entrenches, protects and guarantees fundamental rights to all citizens, without discrimination. Justice isn't a cliché for me. I strongly believe in it, in both form and substance.

I also believe in a transparent, accountable and democratic society where power and responsibility are only vested in people whose integrity and competence have been tested and weighed, in a society where dishonest and untrustworthy people can never hold public office. Yes, I unflinchingly believe in honour. I don't, and have never, subscribed to the view that politics is a dirty game. To do that would be to condone incorrigibility as a natural attribute of leadership.

So, during all my interactions, activities and involvements in government, I used these standards to vet and judge policy blueprints, draft legislations, the draft constitution prior to its ratification on August 4, 2010 and candidates for public service. I'm always guided by what is ethical, legal and constitutional. These were the core guidelines in all my advisory briefs and opinions to the Prime Minister, not ethnic, nepotistic or other considerations. I focused, throughout, on the "National Agenda," or what I believed it was. Whenever my understanding and belief in the "National Agenda" conflicted with the Prime Minister's, ODM's or the coalition government's agendas, I chose the "National Agenda". I have no apologies to make for this.

That explains why I consistently debated and argued with various ODM mandarins over the system of government, the devolution structure, and the content of the bill of rights. It was the reason why I supported a modern federal prime ministerial system rather than a suffocating presidential one. Whereas many senior ODM politicians and power barons single-mindedly focused on power; its acquisition and retention, I focused on how best to secure the "National Interest". For instance, whereas Raila and other ODM leaders waffled between a parliamentary system and a Presidential one; I never wavered. But my implacable adherence to my principles, even when they conflicted with what I was being told was the brand new party line – a line that hadn't been discussed and ratified by the party organs – inevitably led to conflict.

Take my war of words and ideas with Professor Makau Mutua. This man signs off his articles, published weekly by the Kenyan *Sunday Nation*, as "Dean and SUNY Distinguished Professor at the State University of New York at Buffalo Law School and Chair of the Kenya Human Rights Commission. This gives the impression that not only is he learned, wise and a champion of human rights, but that by virtue of the two positions he flaunts, that he is also responsible and fair. Makau and I have a bit of history. For four years running, between 2003 and 2007, I consistently challenged Makau's regular but biased, one-sided and gratuitous attacks on Raila Odinga, then one of the leading presidential candidates in Kenya. I felt that for a professor of law, Makau's articles – tacitly, and at times explicitly – encouraged ethnic intolerance and jingoism, particularly against the Luo. During those days, Makau was an obsessive apologist for President Kibaki. He never criticised the plunder, pillage, looting, gross human rights abuses (especially the extra-judicial killings by both the police and the Kenyan military) abdication of duty, refusal to obey court orders, abuse of public office and other excesses that Kenyans had witnessed in the first Kibaki administration.

Week after week, Makau would pillory Raila for both real and imagined sins. Despite being chair of what was then a leading human rights NGO, he never once attacked or criticised the Kibaki government for its worsening human rights record. But he went further and imputed that Raila was unelectable on the basis of being a Luo. In other words, Makau was providing fuel for the tribal and ethnic victimisation of an entire ethnic community, not because they had done anything wrong, but merely because they happened to have been born Luos. And so I responded in print and on the blogosphere to Makau. By the time I returned to Kenya in 2007, however, I had largely forgotten and forgiven Makau. Apart from my rebuttals to Makau's published articles, I had never myself attacked him.

Then very early one Sunday morning, on March 7, 2010, I received a telephone call from a colleague, Sylvester Kasuku, asking if I had seen that day's newspapers. "No, why are you asking?" I inquired. "Get the paper and read what Prof. Makau Mutua has written about you," he answered without elaboration. It was 7am and I was still in bed. Within ten minutes, I was reading Mutua's "An Open Letter to ODM's Miguna Miguna". I was stunned. Why had Makau deliberately chosen to address me as an ODM member (which I was), rather than as Prime Minister Raila Odinga's advisor?

Makau's article was mischievous in more ways than one. Firstly, although he purported to address me in my capacity as an ODM member, Makau stated at the outset that he was writing an open letter to me "because you are a senior public servant with the ear of Prime Minister Raila Odinga, one of the two most powerful men in Kenya". So, it wasn't because I was an ODM member after all. He got carried away and forgot the stated 'purpose' of his letter: "In that role", he claimed, "you must be held accountable for what you say and write publicly, and the decorum with which you comport yourself" he continued. That was fair enough. But then he plunged into uncharted territory. "The bottom line is that with responsibility comes accountability. Since you are the PM's advisor, it is impermissible for you to publicly express contrarian views that are independent of the PM's on matters of national importance. You are Mr Odinga's mouthpiece, and anything you say is deemed to be his official view. A cardinal rule is that servants in the king's court have no "public minds" of their own. Like ambassadors they only – and solely – represent the king... That's the reason Dr Alfred Mutua, once the ubiquitous but reviled voice of the Kibaki regime, is nevertheless a bellwether for what is cooking in State House. When Francis Muthaura speaks, everyone knows that he is speaking for President Kibaki. Both Dr Mutua and Ambassador Muthaura do not have minds of their own. Nor does Robert Gibbs, the White House press secretary, who is President Barack Obama's official megaphone (sic). Not even Secretary of State Hillary Clinton expresses views contrary to President Obama. She works for him to carry out his foreign policy agenda. She must march in lock step with him or step aside were she to publicly repudiate his official policies...

"I write this letter because of your vitriolic attacks on the Naivasha Consensus that has brought Kenya within an eyelash of a new constitution. The PSC – composed of equal parts ODM and PNU – rose to the occasion and hammered out a consensual draft constitution...Mr Odinga, like the statesman that he has become, publicly and fully embraced the PSC draft. He zealously declared at several rallies that ODM fully backed the PSC draft and that we would get a new constitution come hell or high water. In a word, Mr Odinga owned the Naivasha

Consensus and became its most prominent salesman. Prof Anyang' Nyong'o, ODM secretary-general, has publicly affirmed the party's support for the Naivasha draft. But I am shocked to read your screeds and diatribes against the Naivasha draft. You denounced it as a sellout for providing a presidential system and rejecting majimbo in its devolution scheme. Mr Miguna, were you speaking for yourself, or the PM? Or are you an aide gone rogue?

"...Do not compound my scepticism for people with a double name, like Boutros Boutros [Ghali]. I urge you to internalise my criticism as constructive advice if you want to avoid a disgraceful exit from the public stage".

That was a mouthful of gibberish. It wasn't logic. It wasn't law. Neither was that piece of balderdash based on rudimentary commonsense. Makau claimed at once that I was an ODM member, the Prime Minister's most trusted aide and mouth piece, yet went on to pontificate about my "contrarian" views and "open opposition to the PM". Where was he getting that from? Not once did he substantiate his claims. He didn't say where and when I had contradicted the Prime Minister. He couldn't really claim to be privy to the private and confidential discussions between the Prime Minister and me, unless one of us had told him about them, and I knew I hadn't. If he had been informed of our private discussions and been asked to attack me, he hadn't disclosed it in that article or at all. But I was curious about the last statement. Here was a professor teaching at an American university threatening me publicly with dismissal yet he wasn't working for the Kenyan government or the Prime Minister. Was there something I was missing? Had he been put up to this by the PM? Appallingly, why was Makau implying that an advisor should serve his principal – not the public interests or higher ideals – as a robot?

On March 8, 2010, I exercised my right of reply and published "Makau Mutua and his illusions deconstructed". I argued that "[I]n my current occupation as an advisor to the Prime Minister of Kenya on coalition affairs and joint secretary of the Permanent Committee on the Management of Grand Coalition Affairs, I learn daily. I have learnt that virtually everybody I meet is an expert on one aspect or the other of my job. Many want to influence what I think, say or do. Even more want to use me as a conduit for their influence over the PM. That's all right. Occasionally, I am disabused of the notion that there are true 'friends', especially in Kenya. Some of my most recent virulent attackers have been those I considered close 'friends', until I read their onslaught in the media. Prior to publishing their vitriol, some of them called and profusely expressed their agreement with and support for the articles they later attacked. I guess it comes with the territory. But of all attacks I have received, the one that has amused me most is that of a Kenyan professor working in a country reputed to be a bastion for freedom and democracy, the United States of America. I have been amused by Makau Mutua's diatribe against me, not because he was a friend, but due to the unreasonable, plainly false and illogical arguments he advanced under the pretext of 'constructive criticism'. Makau couched his flimsy attack in very peculiar terms; he warned that I could only retain my employment if I heeded and internalised his fatwa. So, Makau gives and Makau takes. That's fine with me, too.

"Makau compares what I do with spokespersons of Presidents Mwai Kibaki and Barack Obama, not with their respective advisors, Kivutha Kibwana and David Axelrod. Even those eating at the King's Palace know the fine distinction between an advisor and that of a press secretary/spokesperson. I guess Mutua either doesn't or has chosen to be willfully blind.

"Prof Makau alleges that as a 'servant of the King', I have neither the right to think for myself nor the freedom to express my thoughts publicly. He is not advising that I speak responsibly; he is issuing a fiat against any statement or thought that could contradict my Boss. He commands that whatever I say publicly cannot contradict the 'King'; and he doesn't care whether the King agrees with my statements or not, or whether the King is right or wrong. And that if Makau notices anything he perceives as 'contrarian' (his own word) to the King's views, either the King should fire me or publicly denounce my position to Makau's satisfaction. Otherwise, Makau would make sure I lose my job. Maybe Makau knows something I don't know.

"That, Makau says, is how 'civilised' societies conduct their affairs. In fact, he asserts that it is a cardinal rule that 'servants in the king's court have "no minds" of their own'. I don't know when that cardinal rule was manufactured, by whom or where, nor do I know why it only applies to me. Maybe it was concocted by Makau because of his strong dislike for my name. Should I change my name to Miguna Makau, as my friend Adongo Ogony sarcastically asked? Well, don't worry; *distinguished professors of law* don't bother with such minor details.

"What Mutua prescribes sounds to me like a Gestapo fiat or the one party dictatorship we had in Kenya, a dictatorship many Kenyans fought against, were exiled, jailed and died for.

"Makau also accuses me of having publicly opposed the PM on the PSC Draft. He forgets to say when, where or how, yet he proceeds to state, falsely, that I poured 'screeds and diatribe against the Naivasha draft', that I denounced it as a sellout for providing a presidential system and rejecting majimbo in its devolution scheme. I honestly don't know what all that verbiage means.

"Curiously, Makau signed his attack as 'the Dean and SUNY Distinguished Professor at the State University of New York at Buffalo Law School and Chair of the KHRC'. He omits to write, like I routinely do, that the 'views expressed are my own'. Does that mean the State University of New York and the Kenya Human Rights Commission authorised or endorsed his article? Are those Makau's personal views or the views of the organisations he is affiliated to?

"Makau published his attack on me two whole months after the Parliamentary Service Commission draft had been delivered to the Committee of Experts tasked with preparing the new constitution and my articles published by *the Star* on that PSC draft. As he wrote in support of the PSC draft, it is the final CoE 'Proposed Constitution' that is being debated around the country. Suspiciously, Makau has not commented on the CoE's final draft. For Mutua, I was the most important national issue last week. Despite what the pollsters have told us recently (that the majority of Kenyans prefer a parliamentary system of government), for Mutua, I ranked higher than corruption, the constitution, unemployment, extra-judicial killings, and the abortion debate.

"Among eminent progressive constitutional scholars who dismissed the retrogressive PSC Draft was none other than our own Yash Pal Ghai. Prof Ghai, like me, concluded that the PSC draft was worse than the current (old) Constitution. The PM, Prof Anyang' Nyong'o and ODM held the same view and made that known, publicly. Prof. Nyong'o published more than two articles in *The Standard* newspaper on the same. Did Makau miss all that? Does he want us to have any constitution, no matter how retrogressive?"

Before concluding, I posed the following eleven questions, which I sought Makau's responses to:

1. *What is my primary duty – the people of Kenya, the King or the State?*
2. *When you purported to represent Kibaki's former anti-corruption Permanent Secretary, John Githongo, during the Anglo Leasing scandal fallout, why didn't you raise issue that Githongo chose to expose the King's (Kibaki's) nakedness instead of blindly supporting the King?*
3. *Is there a difference between 'civil service' as understood in colonial and neo-colonial Kenya and PUBLIC SERVICE as understood in a free, independent and democratic country?*
4. *What kind of society do you want us to construct – one based on the cult of the personality or the one undergirded by accountability,*

transparency and the rule of law? If you believe in the latter, are those views consistent with the ones you extol in your attack of me?

5. *When and where did I disagree with the PM's and ODM's position on the Constitution? Can you give specific examples of the "vitriol," "diatribe," "megalomania" and "haughtiness" that you claim were in my articles?*
6. *Is there a difference between the retrogressive PSC-Naivasha Draft and the CoE's Proposed Constitution Draft?*
7. *Are you aware that PNU wants to mutilate the CoE Draft and revert to the retrogressive PSC-Naivasha Draft? If so, was that why you attacked me?*
8. *Is it your understanding that I am a slave/servant with no mind of my own and no freedom to express my opinions due to my employment?*
9. *Please educate me on the 'cardinal rule' of those who serve the public or state vis-a-vis their expression of personal opinions? How about those applicable at the King's Court? Where are those rules published?*
10. *Do you know the content of my letter of appointment and any documents I might have signed regarding what I can or cannot do?*
11. *Can you please point out anything – published or uttered by me publicly – that undermines the PM or ODM?*

Then came my parting shot: "Professor Mutua, we are trying to transform a country and construct a democratic system based on good governance, rule of law, constitutionalism and respect for human rights. We cannot afford sycophancy! You are beseeching me to sing for the King. Unfortunately, I must disappoint you, for I will keep singing for and with the Kenyan people."

My friend, colleague, Waikwa Wanyoike, also responded to Makau in an article titled "Makau Mutua's criticism of Miguna Miguna distorted facts," published in *the Star* on March 10, in which he argued, in part: "They say, great minds discuss ideas. Average minds discuss events and small minds discuss people. I will reserve the decision on whether this is discussion about ideas, events or people to the readers… There are many problems with Prof. Makau's opinion. The sum of them is that his arguments are hinged on fallacious premises. First, it is erroneous for Prof. Makau to equate Miguna's role to that of Dr Alfred Mutua or even that of Amb. Muthaura. The roles are neither equivalent nor comparable. In fact, Prof. Makau makes a big factual mistake in his argument when he states that Miguna is the PM's 'mouthpiece' or, if you like, the PM's spokesman. Miguna is not a spokesman. He is an advisor. In practical terms the two are like night and day. A spokesman is a person who parrots what his boss – or the person he seeks to speak for – says or believes. In a metaphorical sense a spokesman is the mouth of his boss, at least as far as his official duties are concerned. And maybe this is why Dr Alfred Mutua has been so good at what he does, although in strict terms his title is an anomaly since he is a spokesman for the President and PNU and not for the Kenyan government.

"Miguna's role is also not equivalent or comparable to that of Amb. Muthaura. Muthaura, as a chief government administrator is an executive whose role is to implement the government's directives. In doing so, he is largely guided, not by his own ideas, but the directions given by the Cabinet. Again, beyond the ability to understand the directives and develop mechanism of implementation, his work requires little, if any, of his own mind to perform. In contrast, the work of an advisor requires one to have and mostly use his own creative mind to complement the ideas of his boss or even offer criticism of his boss' views. The forum where such criticism should occur is but another issue, although at a time when the world is moving towards a more open political and legal accountability, gagging advisors may be the practice of the old political order.

"Ideally, a good advisor is one who is extremely independent in his or her thought process and who is not shy to offer those thoughts to his boss in an undiluted or undiplomatic version. The concept of having a political advisor is in fact for the purpose of making sure that the boss gets to hear honest, independent and possibly contrary views to his own when the situation requires. Personal independence, both in thought and expression therefore becomes an integral component of what makes a competent advisor…

"What is most disturbing of Prof. Mutua's criticism of Miguna is that it betrays the extent of the effects of the political socialisation we have had as a country on how we interact with our superiors. The subconscious behind Prof. Mutua's criticism seems to be inspired by the belief that it is wrong to question the ideas of our superiors, and if we dare to, we can only do so in whispers lest we offend their sensibilities.

"Maybe the country's perennial problems with leadership are because we have encouraged public servants to become sycophants of our leaders. May be it is time we started honouring those who tell it as it is instead of vilifying them. Maybe it is time we complimented leaders who are able to hire strong independent-minded advisors instead of cautioning them. May be it is time we trained our leadership to develop a stronger sense of political self esteem so that they are ready to hear and embrace new, honest and unadulterated views from those below them".

That was high-octane intellectualism from Waikwa. I believed that the two rebuttals would send Makau and whoever he was serving into the doldrums. But within a year, I was woken up from my naïvety when the Prime Minister informed me that he would be travelling to the US on the invitation of the same Makau Mutua. Granted, there is value to the saying that "in politics there are no permanent enemies; only interests". Nobody could begrudge Raila for trying to woo his erstwhile enemies. Makau might not even have been an enemy. Speaking with some longstanding 'friends' and colleagues of Makau – people who had gone to school and worked with him very closely; Makau's gratuitous public attacks on Raila might have been calculated to get him attention. And obviously they had achieved their purpose. Makau's friend also told me that "Miguna, the man is attacking you because deep down, Makau believes that he is more deserving of that position than you. It's green envy pure and simple." So, one can imagine how puzzled I was when Raila invited me to accompany him to Buffalo at the invitation of Makau. I went and Makau made comments to me about his belief that I was "the brain behind Raila's strategies". I treated it as a joke from an embarrassed host.

Otuma Ongalo, until recently working as an editor with the *The Standard* newspaper, was another media attack dog who formed a habit of regularly using me as his target practice. In the first six months of 2010, he must have attacked me at least once every month. Just between April 15 and April 30, 2010, he attacked me twice. It seemed to me that some people were intent on derailing the work I was doing. On one occasion, after I had published a rebuttal to his criticisms of Raila, he responded with an article that opined, "The more Miguna tries to brighten Raila's star the more he darkens it..." In that piece, he tried to justify his senseless attacks by implying that Raila stood a better chance of becoming President if we – his generals and soldiers – allowed Kenyans to misunderstand, misinterpret and otherwise support him blindly. Ongalo and others held the view that ideological and philosophical clarity and coherence weren't needed, that all a presidential candidate should be after was votes. They believed that a presidential candidate should be free to lie and mislead so long as s/he is able to get votes. In other words, Ongalo, Makau and others were stuck in the old order where victory was all that mattered, that it didn't matter how one acquired it. Presumably, one could lie, bribe, mislead, or even commit crimes to win.

I considered that approach dishonest and fundamentally flawed. I hold the view that what was – and is still needed – is open and honest politics; a kind of politics without rancour, hate, negative propaganda and dishonesty, a politics based solely on issues.

My other detractors – Kibaki's advisor and my permanent committee counterpart, Kivutha Kibwana, PNU's self-styled strategist Peter Kagwanja', PNU 'spokesman' Moses Kuria, Ongalo and Makau only represent a tiny portion of the buckets of vitriol that have been poured on me by self-appointed censurers. Over the past four years, I have been subjected to sporadic fireworks from all kind of intellectual arsonists. Muthui Kariuki, a man who has variously described himself as either Vice-President Kalonzo Musyoka's media or communications advisor, or his spokesman, was another stone-thrower who never lost an opportunity to try and derail me. His attacks increased in both intensity and volume during the constitutional review process from 2009 to 2010. The intention was to distract, bog down, sabotage and exhaust me so that I couldn't be effective in representing the interests of the Prime Minister, ODM and that of Kenyans. But no matter what they did, I refused to surrender. Eventually, it would appear, the conspirators – those in PNU and ODM – devised new, more creative strategies.

* * * * * * * * * * * * * *

On September 15, 2010, I received an internal memorandum from the Prime Minister (through his Private Secretary) instructing me to represent him at a 'Workshop for Permanent Secretaries/Accounting Officers on the Implementation of the New Constitution' scheduled for Friday September 17, 2010 from 8.30am at Serena Beach Hotel, Mombasa to Sunday September 19. I was requested to arrive in Mombasa on the evening of Thursday, September 16. The memorandum noted further that the Office of the Prime Minister would meet my travel costs to and from Mombasa while the Ministry of Public Service would be responsible for my accommodation and airport transfer costs. Shortly upon receipt of the PM's instructions, the OPM quickly issued me with a first class air ticket and the necessary per diem.

At the airport, en route to the workshop, I met Isahakia, who was also on his way there. As we waited for the flight, Isahakia, former trade minister, Mukhisha Kituyi, Njoki Ndung'u (now a Supreme Court judge) and I chatted cheerfully. Isahakia didn't disclose any discomfort or unease.

There were two minor hitches when I arrived in Mombasa. Firstly, I found that no arrangements had been made for my transport from the airport to the hotel. I ended up hitching a ride with Ken Mwige, then Secretary/CEO of the Public Complaints Standing Committee (popularly known as the Ombudsman's

Office). And once at the hotel, I discovered that I had no reservations. When I approached the Permanent Secretary for Public Service, Mr Ndambuki, he quickly assured me that he would find a room for me. Nonetheless, after waiting for two hours without a room, I had to find accommodation myself in an adjacent hotel. That was the first indication that something wasn't right.

The following morning when the workshop started, (as we sat there waiting for the proceedings to begin) it was the ODM Minister for Public Service, Dalmas Otieno, who started, in a very general manner, questioning the presence of "some people who are not accounting officers and were not invited to this meeting". He also cryptically referred to the fact that the workshop was a 'government function' and no journalists or 'people who write articles for pay' would be allowed in. "Nobody is going to be allowed to report on this function," he added, even though there was a battery of print and electronic media journalists present, on invitation, capturing his every utterance.Those were curious words. When I scanned the room, I noticed many people who weren't Permanent Secretaries, managing directors of state corporations or accounting officers. There was the so-called government spokesman, Alfred Mutua, Kennedy Kihara an officer from the Cabinet Office, Njoki Ndung'u (who was then a private consultant), Mukhisa Kituyi (also attending as a private consultant), and many other junior officers from the Office of the President. In fact, my friend and colleague, Mutakha Kangu, who wasn't a government employee, had been invited but couldn't attend because the invitation reached him too late, minus the necessary 'facilitations'. All these people looked unconcerned. I therefore decided to ignore Dalmas' utterances, which didn't seem to be directed at me specifically, though I suspected that he might have been alluding to me.

After the first tea break, Muthaura joined Dalmas' crusade. He insisted on going round the room for everyone to "introduce himself so that we can confirm whether everyone present was invited". This was baffling. Anyway, when he reached me, I indicated that I had a letter from the Prime Minister, instructing me to attend on his behalf. Neither Dalmas nor Muthaura seemed satisfied, though they moved on to others. When they returned to me, I took out the Prime Minister's letter and asked Isahakia to confirm what I was saying. Isahakia chose to cast his eyes on the table before him and feign ignorance. I then asked them to call the Prime Minister to confirm. But they were undeterred, insisting that I hadn't been invited to the meeting.

At that point I sought to know why my presence would be unwelcome in view of the fact that we were to deliberate over the implementation of the Constitution, which concerned all Kenyans, and that as the Prime Minister's advisor on coalition affairs, my presence was vital. I also pointed out that it was quite curious that some people would raise eyebrows at my presence yet the Office of the President had more than 20 people when only Isahakia and I were there for the OPM. Didn't they know that this was a coalition government?

Anyway, they again temporarily skipped me and went round, settling on another candidate for eviction: James Oswago, the Chief Executive Officer for the then Interim Independent Electoral Commission. Once I saw that, I collected my things and left the room, followed very closely by Oswago. No one else left the room.

Once outside, I notified Raila and Caroli of what had happened. Both of them glibly and independently blamed Isahakia for having failed to make appropriate arrangements. But I wasn't convinced that they were that bothered because they never asked to speak to him, to Dalmas or to Muthaura. Later, when I sent a four-page complaint to Muthaura and copied it to Raila, raising issue on the manner the OPM and ODM were being disregarded in important matters affecting not just the smooth running of the coalition government but also the governance of Kenya, Raila never responded.

It was then that I realised that I might have been sent to Mombasa as a set-up so that I could come into conflict with Muthaura and attract negative press attention. Indeed, that happened three months later – in October 2010 – when Caroli's friend and former university room-mate, Ahmednasir Abdulahi, published a sensational and defamatory piece about me in the November, 2010, issue of the *Nairobi Law Monthly* (NLM), titled "Miguna Miguna loses it again" purporting that I had "gatecrashed an invite-only event for Permanent Secretaries" at the Mombasa meeting and that I had had to be forcefully removed from the meeting by the police. The story was headlined "Grapevine" at the top and "Newsmaker" across my mug-shot picture. The article then claimed that "the incident came four months after Mr Miguna shamed the country at a conference reviewing operations of the International Criminal Court (ICC) in Kampala, Uganda".

Of course, none of that had happened, but I wondered how Ahmednasir had been privy to what had happened to me in Mombasa. He hadn't been present there. I also wondered why he was misrepresenting what had happened in Uganda. Logically, I could only see Caroli's and Raila's hands. Ahmednasir wasn't just Caroli's friend and former classmate at the University of Nairobi, he was considered a staunch PNU advocate and operative. He represented the National Security Intelligence Service and its Director, Michael Gichangi, at the Commission of Inquiry into the Post-Election Violence (CIPEV or the Waki Commission) and at the Independent Review Commission into the 2007 elections (also known as the Kriegler Commission). In other words, Ahmednasir was the blue-eyed boy of the traditional and old Kenyan power establishment. When I inquired from Caroli why Ahmednasir was attacking me he simply laughed it off.

I promptly issued a four-page letter demanding a retraction and a written apology from the *Nairobi Law Monthly* and its Editor-in-Chief, Ahmednasir Abdulahi; I also threatened to initiate legal action in the event of failure or refusal to accede to my demands. Ahmednasir responded, rudely, that there was nothing defamatory in the publication and that he would neither retract the story nor apologise for it. He went further to "warn" me that the NLM had fought and defeated mightier souls than I and that I was free to "try the Kenyan courts".

As a prominent member of the newly established Judicial Service Commission of Kenya, I honestly believed that Ahmednasir was trying to intimidate me and pull rank by invoking the judiciary's name, but I wasn't about to allow the culture of impunity to prevail. I, of course, reminded Ahmednasir that the NLM that had "triumphed" over the "mighty souls" wasn't the same one he was editing. On November 25, 2010 I filed a complaint against both Ahmednasir and the NLM with the Media Council of Kenya for having published the offending article, which I asserted was false, defamatory, misleading and malicious, and had caused serious injury to my name, character, reputation and profession.

Not only did Ahmednasir fail to respond to my claim within 14 days as stipulated by the *Media Council of Kenya Act*, but he completely ignored the complaint, only sending counsel on the day of the hearing and purporting to find rescue under the Constitution.

I successfully petitioned for an order barring him and the NLM from participating in the hearing and, after more than one year of waiting, the Media Council unanimously ruled in my favour, on March 15, 2012 that:

(a) The article was false, misleading, distorted, malicious and based on rumours;
(b) The article wasn't fair, accurate or unbiased;
(c) The headline in the story was provocative and alarming, and did not reflect and justify the material printed under it;
(d) The use of my picture and name harmed me;
(e) Ahmednasir as the Editor-in-Chief of the NLM, contravened the Code of Conduct for Journalism in Kenya;
(f) The article breached the *Media Act* and the Code of Conduct of the Practice of Journalism in Kenya; and
(g) I was entitled to all the relief sought.

The respondents were ordered to publish a prominent apology acceptable to me in the April 2012 issue of the NLM. Ahmednasir was further ordered to issue a written apology to me personally. Both respondents were fined a cumulative sum of Sh1.4 million.

This experience reinforced my belief that not every loudmouth shouting 'reform' is a reformer. Kenyans should critically examine those proclaiming themselves reformers or agents of change like Ahmednasir. They should ask: if he was a true reformer, how come some of his clients like the National Security Intelligence Agency have been – for decades – the embodiment of the culture of impunity in Kenya?

And, of course, there was nothing I had 'lost' at the ICC review conference Ahmednasir had referred to. I had been specifically instructed by Raila to attend the ICC review conference in Kampala, Uganda, from May 31 to June 11, 2010 with Mutakha Kangu, Lands minister James Orengo and then East African Cooperation minister Amason Kingi. The PNU side of government had sent the Permanent Secretary for Foreign Affairs Thuita Mwangi, Foreign Affairs minister Moses Wetangula and Attorney General Amos Wako. But only the latter attended.

Raila's instructions had reached me only days before the conference started. We hadn't received any invitation letters, no accreditations and no programmes. As part of a government delegation we were to be registered as participants through the Ministry of Foreign Affairs. Unfortunately, up to the day we travelled to Uganda we hadn't received any information from the ministry. All our telephone calls to Thuita Mwangi went unanswered. In fact, on the day we travelled Thuita had switched his mobile phone off. His secretary kept telling us that he was "out of the office" and that we should just leave messages and he would call us back, which he never did.

Orengo was trying to reach Thuita and Wetangula almost after every 15 minutes the day we departed, but he wasn't successful. Kingi was in Mombasa and hadn't been told about the conference or that the Prime Minister wanted him to attend for ODM. I was the first one to contact him. Mutakha was in Nairobi, but as someone who wasn't on the government's payroll, his per diem needed to be processed under a different stream and those usually took time.

It was by this point only three hours before we were due to travel and we still hadn't received any information. Luckily, my secretary had managed to secure an electronic air ticket; she had also booked a hotel room and collected my per diems. I had also managed to get Mutakha's. It was now 2.30pm. Orengo called to say Mutakha and I should go ahead and that he would travel the following day. For the first time, Orengo mentioned that Wako was also flying out that afternoon.

Mutakha and I met the attorney-general Amos Wako on the plane. I had obviously been publicly critical of him a few months earlier, in February, when he had weighed in – I had felt wholly inappropriately – in the stand-off between Raila and Kibaki over the latter's overturning of the former's suspension of Ruto and Education Minister Sam Ongeri over credible corruption allegations. I had lambasted Wako in print for his claim that the Constitution legitimised Kibaki's reversal of Raila's decision to suspend both ministers. Since then, however, we had worked cordially enough. Only that morning he had forwarded some documents to me regarding "the Government of Kenya position" on the ICC process. When I had discussed the matter with Raila and Orengo, they had told me that our job at the ICC review conference would be to make sure that Wako didn't deliver or read any documents at the conference without our (and ultimately ODM's) input. Their instruction to me had been that we were attending precisely to ensure that "ODM's voice was heard at the conference". Having been told that, we knew the drill.

Upon arrival at Entebbe International Airport, Wako was picked up by Ambassador Geoffrey Okanga in his official limousine. But Mutakha and I were left stranded. We hitched a ride with Orengo's personal assistant who thought Orengo had been on the same flight with us. On arrival in Kampala, we found out that we hadn't been registered for the conference. However, since Orengo's personal assistant had arrived two days ahead of us, she knew where registration was done. She took us there and, luckily, we were able to register. We subsequently checked into our hotel. Later that evening, we bumped into the Kenya's High Commissioner to Uganda, Major-General (Rtd) Okanga, who advised us to relocate to The Kampala Serena, where Wako was staying. He promised to pick up the tab. That evening Wako bought us dinner and we had a pleasant evening.

Early the following morning Mutakha and I discovered three things. First, accommodation at the Kampala Serena was charging double our per diem allocations and Ambassador Okanga would not be paying for the rooms or topping up the difference as he had promised the previous day. So we had to check out that day, otherwise we would only have been able to stay there for two nights. Second, the Embassy hadn't arranged for our inland or local transport, so we had to fend for ourselves. Despite having promised to pick us up, Okanga never showed up at the hotel that morning. And third, it would be much cheaper if we moved to a hotel on the conference grounds in Munyonyo. After breakfast that morning, Mutakha and I cleared our bills, checked out and took a taxi to Munyonyo where we booked in for the rest of the conference.

Contrary to unfounded allegations later peddled against me regarding this trip to Kampala, there was no conflict between me and Okanga.

Other than what I later recounted in the article published in *the Star*, titled *Scuttling the ICC investigations and prosecutions in Kenya is not an option: Lessons from Kampala – June 4, 2010,* there was nothing else that happened in Kampala. All I had done was to try and prevent Wako from sneaking in a document that had not been vetted by both sides of the coalition as "the Kenya Government position". Anything else being peddled against me regarding that incident is out of pure malice. Raila, Orengo and Kingi were impressed by the contributions that we made. I never heard about any "complaints" until October 2011 – 15 whole months after the conference. To date, nobody has produced a letter from any "complainant", and not from Wako, anyway. It was therefore grotesquely unfair for Ahmednasir and other malicious people to try and mislead the country with perfidious innuendo.

* * * * * * * * * * * * * *

Meanwhile, the PNU wolves were circling, baying for my blood. They began a well-choreographed onslaught that sought to demonise, isolate, alienate and stigmatise me.

There seemed to be a concerted effort to portray me as a bogey-man, but no one bothered to disclose what I had done or why whatever it was hadn't been appropriate. I could sense conspiracy everywhere. A few letters to the editor, mostly published under *noms de guerre* littered the daily newspapers. Cartoonists sporadically competed with op-ed writers for my scalp. PNU's "chief strategist," Peter Kagwanja, began to portray me as a tail-less stray dog of the British colonial-Mau-Mau period. It was obvious to keen observers that the articles attacking me were part of a carefully choreographed scheme intended to derail me. But the oddity was that I had actually stepped back from the limelight. I wasn't appearing on TV and radio programmes often. Although I occasionally debated with Kagwanja and Kibwana, I only participated when the issues under discussion concerned my core functions. Whenever I sought Raila's concurrence with my continued media engagement, especially after Kagwanja or Kibwana's sporadic broadsides, Raila would say, "You should have responded like yesterday". So I knew I had his permission, authority and blessing to return fire. However, I increasingly restricted even those responses to my weekly column that he himself had authorised. For the most part, I kept my contributions and advice to Raila and the ODM team to confidential memoranda, briefs, talking points and research. Yet PNU seemed aware of my confidential advice to Raila. On one occasion, Muthui Kariuki, Vice-President Kalonzo's self-styled spokesman and advisor, even alluded to them, threatening that "one day, those secret briefs you are writing to the PM will become public."

But who could have been leaking these? Clearly, other than meeting PNU people at structured and formal sessions, I had no direct link with the PNU formation. It meant, therefore, that some people within ODM who were fairly knowledgeable of my role and had unfettered access to Raila's actual office and documents, were leaking information or instigating the PNU hounds to attack me. There were a few possibilities: Caroli, Isahakia and Raila's two secretaries were the immediate suspects, but normally, secretaries wouldn't have the time for, nor the interest in, such briefs. That left only Caroli and Isahakia, with their subterranean adjutants, Dennis Onyango and Iddris, respectively, as the most probable suspects.

The Kenyan press is quite predictable. And since the attacks were being published in all three major dailies, I was sure that whoever was coordinating those attacks must have been fairly senior, well-funded and sophisticated. Kagwanja would later confirm these fears in the presence of Caroli and Mutakha.

On reflection and with the full benefit of time it is now clear to me that Makau's earlier attack on me where he had threatened me with a humiliating exit from "public office" could in all likelihood have been "sponsored" from within Raila's office. After two years, that puzzling visit to Buffalo now made sense.

It's true I didn't just have political enemies. I had also been trenchant in my criticisms of those holding public and constitutional offices but who had long abandoned or abdicated their mandate and responsibilities. Patrick Loch Otieno Lumumba, or simply PLO (then director of the Kenya Anti-Corruption Commission), Tecla Namachanja (then acting chairperson of the Truth, Justice and Reconciliation Commission) and Mzalendo Kibunjia (chairman of the National Cohesion and Integration Commission), were not only failing to discharge their legal mandates, they didn't seem to know what those mandates were. They addressed many press conferences, spoke at workshops and seminars, but beyond that they did absolutely nothing to discharge the onerous responsibilities the public had bestowed upon them. Corruption, tribalism, discrimination and violations of fundamental human rights – both historical and ongoing – which were their primary domain, remained unaddressed.

But even their lethargy couldn't, in my opinion, rival that of the newly installed Director of Public Prosecutions, Keriako Tobiko and the Commissioner of Police Matthew Iteere. These two weren't just failing in their duties; they were in many ways the very embodiments of the culture of impunity in Kenya. They rivalled, and in some ways even threatened to surpass former attorney general Wako's pathetic record. From the hundreds of rip-offs perpetrated against the innocent public, to the unsolved cases of extra-judicial killings and politically-orchestrated murders, to high-profile cases of drug trafficking, neither Iteere nor Tobiko had taken any proactive initiative to deal with them. The result of which was that the public abandoned any hope that the two of them would ever resolve anything.

For the more than five years that Tobiko was responsible for prosecutions at the State Law Office he never successfully prosecuted any major and known criminal. During his tenure there was a swathe of mega corruption cases and human rights abuses that were either not investigated or prosecuted to the end. Even in cases where the evidence was publicly available, Tobiko would either terminate the cases or have them thrown out on dubious technicalities. This is the period of Anglo Leasing, Triton, Ken-Ren, Grand Regency, the Free Primary Education scam, the Standard Group attack, the extra-judicial killings of suspected Mungiki members and the carnage that accompanied the post-election violence of 2007/8. To date, Tobiko hasn't successfully prosecuted any major perpetrator, not even those caught on live television committing heinous crimes! Arguably, for those five years Tobiko was operating under the 'embodiment of the culture of impunity,' Amos Wako. However, that structural impediment wasn't a real hindrance. There wasn't an instance where Tobiko tried to address impunity and Wako stood in his way, not that he has disclosed publicly to us anyway. From publicly available records, the two worked hand-in-hand.

And grand-scale corruption continued unabated. Apparently, even the alleged 'Chinese' company, Pan African Network Group Ltd, which was controversially awarded a lucrative digital distribution licence by the Communications Commission of Kenya (CCK), had nothing but convenient connections to China. Within the corridors of power, I was informed by the Karachuonyo MP and Chairman of the Parliamentary Select Committee on Energy, Transport, Information, Communication and Public Works, James Kwanya Rege, that the company that had been 'fraudulently' awarded the lucrative contract belonged to the 'High and Mighty in Kenya'. Just like the mysterious 'foreign' companies given hundreds of acres of fertile agricultural public land on the Coast and the dubious 'foreign' company given land and a multi-billion deal at Jomo Kenyatta International Airport.

No one could have perpetrated such brazen acts of theft and looting (which have been going on for eons) without the connivance of top government officials at the National Security Intelligence Service (NSIS), the Kenya Police, the State Law Office, the Ministries of Education, Foreign Affairs, Finance, Internal Security, Cabinet Office, the Treasury, the Central Bank, the CID, the Kenya Airports Authority, the Kenya Airways, Immigration and Customs and many other government departments. Above all, no one could have the nerve to pull off such audacious rip-offs if those sitting at State House weren't either complicit or compliant. Yet the criminal kingpins – some very well known – haven't been charged.

As I have repeatedly pointed out, Tobiko, PLO Lumumba, Iteere and even the CID Director Muhoro, have done absolutely nothing about these cases. That isn't surprising to many of us who know the pedigrees of the people holding top positions at the KACC, the directorate of public prosecutions and at Vigilante House. Tobiko hasn't been called the 'master of inertia' for nothing.

These and other transgressions motivated me to attack these individuals and their institutional, professional and personal failures in my weekly column in *the Star*. I called them to account week after week. I relentlessly exposed and attacked corruption in government. I condemned gross violations of human rights. I challenged the blatant abrogations of the Constitution. All this I did without fear or favour but I did it within the narrow strictures of the law. It didn't matter whether the perceived perpetrator was affiliated to ODM or PNU. It didn't matter whether the culprit was a professed supporter of Raila or Kibaki. My column generated so much heat from the 'merchants of impunity' and, in equal measure, overwhelming support from tens of thousands of readers, that I became a lightning rod. Those who supported me did so with exuberance, while those who opposed me became increasingly rabid.

Conceivably, it was principally my column that motivated people (especially those whom I had had in my sights) to conspire against me, by concocting stories, including the scurrilous allegation attributed to Kenya's High Commissioner to Uganda, Okanga, that I had been abusive to Wako when we had been attending that ICC review conference in Kampala more than a year previously. Mutakha, Kingi or Orengo never corroborated those made-up cow dung stories, nor could they.

I was aware of nefarious schemes and plots. I knew I hadn't done anything illegal or unethical for which they could conspire to have me charged and prosecuted. Undoubtedly, I had the right to express myself freely without hindrance. Raila was in a quandary; he liked many of my articles that strongly defended him against unfair attacks and he confessed this much to me numerous times, but he loathed my articles that criticised the corrupt, the drug pushers, the land grabbers, the money launderers and those who engaged in high level corruption but he couldn't come forward and say so. He had clearly authorised my regular weekly column in *the Star* – it was actually his original idea – but it was as if he had only intended that column to serve as his propaganda mouthpiece.

On careful reflection, I can now see that Raila also felt insecure as a result of the momentous support I was getting from the ordinary citizens, people who admired my courage, my honesty, my style and my ability to expose humongous transgressions against the ordinary citizen clearly and consistently. Raila was conflicted. Although he was the one who had requested me to take out a newspaper column so as to address, advance and articulate the party's position on important issues of the day, including his, now that my columns had become intoxicatingly popular among Kenyans, he had started resenting them – and in the process – their author. My columns reflected the ideals he had once defended or which he had purported to represent but his interests had changed. He had become powerful and rich and deeply compromised. He had crossed the class line and joined the aristocrats. Now I had become at times an embarrassment to him.

But he still sometimes needed me and my articles. There wasn't anybody in ODM, at his office or around him with the writing skills I had. Anyang' Nyong'o and Ababu Namwamba could write very well and they did, regularly. The problem was that they didn't have what my friend and Chief Executive Officer of *the Star* newspaper calls "the Miguna sting". Unlike many Kenyans, I am not good at sports or athletics and I can't sing. Nor am I an innovative scientific inventor. The gift God gave me was the ability to coin words and phrases in a manner that drives a point home. As some other friends have said "Miguna is a gifted wordsmith". I bow to them in humility and appreciation.

One of Raila's skills is his ability to scout for talent. He will then wow a person to co-opt that talent. But when you have served your purpose for Raila, he will move on without a backwards glance, leaving broken dreams, a sense of betrayal, desolation and, at least in the case of Paddy Onyango Sumba who would die unemployed, poor and lonely about a year after Raila became Prime Minister, a broken soul, too. But that's how I came to work with Raila.

Whenever Raila wanted a devastating knockout punch against his opponents, he never asked Ababu or Nyong'o to pen the pieces. He always asked me. And I delivered, not once, twice or thrice – but repeatedly over a number of years, until the media started unfairly caricaturing me as his sycophant and attack dog. I wasn't. Raila never told me what to write and I never actually wrote to please him. What I did and will do again for society at large was to conduct thorough research, summarise basic facts and then use simple plain English to enunciate points that had otherwise been concealed from the public. I shared information with the public that had traditionally been hidden from them. For instance, the Kenyan media had never explored and exposed the fact that William Ruto and Uhuru Kenyatta had never been gainfully employed in Kenya away from politics. Also, the media hadn't examined whether the sources of those two's fabulous wealth had been earned through hard work or entrepreneurship. One inherited almost virtually all his wealth while the sources of the other one's vast income remain a matter of conjecture on the streets of Nairobi. According to a scientific survey conducted by *the Star* newspaper in 2011, my column in *the Star* soon became the most popular piece in all Kenyan newspapers. It was *the* column to read. Politicians, diplomats, journalists and ordinary Kenyans literally waited for Tuesday to read my articles.

Unfortunately for Raila, I intended to use my column – and indeed used it – to serve a wider public good. Yes, I would articulate ODM issues, defend ODM and Raila whenever that was legitimately desirable or deserved; however, any time I found that Raila's interests – or those espoused by ODM – were in conflict with the law, the constitution, my ethics, or the general public good, I didn't spare him or the ODM, at least behind closed doors. I was polite but firm. Truth and justice were my guiding lights.

Looking back, I believe that my articles served many purposes. Firstly, they explained the Prime Minister's position on important national issues, particularly issues relating to the Accord, the whole question of power sharing, how decisions were made or ought to have been made within the context of the coalition government, and as a tool for creating space for both the Prime Minister and ODM within the Grand Coalition Government. There were many things I said which Raila might have loved to say but couldn't because of the nature of coalition politics, and also because he was a quintessential coward and opportunist; he wanted to look 'good' so let me look 'bad' for him.

That would have been tolerable if he had appreciated what I was trying to do for him. But even more importantly, the articles attempted to educate Kenyans on the instruments of coalition, the inner workings of government and their role in all that. Whenever there was controversy, I sought to explain it in its proper context and perspective. Often Orengo and Raila would mention, in passing, that this or that article played a vital role in explaining ODM's position. I was the only instrument ODM had and often used to vaccinate impunity. As a party, ODM had become a shell, only reactivated whenever controversy arose. In the end, I chose to use my head and pen instead of my fists and body. That couldn't be that threatening and intimidating, could it? All I sought was a good debate.

In a way, my column transformed me into some kind of a celebrity. Even the Internet based encyclopaedia, Wikipedia, wrote that I had become a "popular public intellectual" and conferred on me the honour of having "reduced Kibaki's and PNU's chief strategist, Peter Kagwanja, to an intellectual minnow in a television debate. That was in reference to a live debate I had with Kagwanja on Citizen TV's "Power Breakfast Show" on April 14, 2011. We discussed a wide range of issues from the ICC process to the prospects of each major Kenyan politician in 2012. And on each issue, the verdict from callers, viewers' texts and emails as well as subsequent YouTube posts was that I had slaughtered Kagwanja. However, rather than take it in his stride, Kagwanja published a pathetic broadside on me in *the Star* newspaper on April 22 in which he compared me to a tailless rabid dog, Rasputin, Robespierre and the (now expelled) ANC Youth League President Julius Malema. I had a full-page rebuttal printed four days later, on April 26.

But more touching was that Sarah Elderkin weighed in with a sterling defence of me on May 19, 2011. She wrote of me: "But first I need to say that I know Miguna and I have worked with him. I have found him intelligent, well-read, well-prepared, honest, stalwart, upright, hardworking and supremely committed to what is good, proper, right and just. I also know he is impatient and highly vocal about anything that contravenes these values, and that he does not suffer fools gladly. About his style of operation (never the substance), he and I have in the past had rather lively discussions. But I have learned to respect Miguna.

"He is one of the few people I know who actually reads complex legal and constitutional documents, when others are just too idle or too incompetent to put in the hard work required. Miguna patiently winkles out the loopholes otherwise overlooked, and bravely stands his ground against the inevitable attacks.

"It is a lonely position, and Miguna might not always be diplomatic. But diplomacy isn't everything. If things go well for us in this country, Kenyans will owe Miguna more than they know.

"Little wonder, then, that Miguna strikes back to defend himself when people deliberately try to downgrade his work with cheap shots vilifying him as a person."

That was Sarah, the doyenne of modern Kenyan liberation journalism! She had (and still has) style, flair. But more than anything else, Sarah was brutally honest. I shared this trait with her. We would argue for hours, sometimes days and weeks over all manner of things. We would do it by telephone, short text messages, emails and in person. Sarah was one of a very small group with whom I could discuss virtually any issue candidly, without any suspicion that our discussions would return to haunt me. Waikwa Wanyoike, Mutakha Kangu and Kathleen France were three others. They were true and genuine friends.

In the beginning, Raila seemed to resist my enemies' schemes to get rid of me. They would call and demand that I be fired whenever I published an article they didn't like. In fact, Raila once told me how Kibaki had called him fuming about an article, which *the Star* had mistitled, making it look like I had attacked him. According to Raila, Kibaki had demanded that he should prevail upon me to stop writing the column. On that occasion, Raila told me that he had informed Kibaki that having gone through the article, he found nothing wrong or objectionable in it, and that I had the right to free expression. That's what he told me. I was extremely proud of him then.

But as the 2012 elections beckoned and Raila's greed for power became more accentuated, he gave in, believing wrongly the fake assurances my enemies – and perhaps his enemies as well – gave him that they would work with him closely and even support his candidature for President, believing that would turn out to be one of the worst mistakes Raila would make in his entire political career. For unlike other people Raila had used and dumped people like Rateng' Oginga Ogego, Dimba Jakobuya, Herbert Ojwang' and Tony Gachoka, I wasn't prepared to go quietly.

I sometimes wonder if Raila's political enemies – the ones who goaded him into breaking with me – planned exactly the scenario now playing itself out. They wanted Raila to self-destruct. I can't even rule out that deep down, even hidden away in their subsconsciousness, Orengo and Nyong'o aren't loving what is happening. I am doing what they would have wanted to do, what they longed to do, but didn't have the guts, the discipline or the skills to do. Raila has in the past been extremely nasty to them, especially to Orengo. I was recently informed by one of Raila's closest confidantes still working with him in the government, that about ten years ago Raila used to publicly call Orengo "a dog", that he would say: "Orengo is a dog; what can a dog do?"

Well, ten years on, Orengo had actually become Raila's dog – metaphorically and practically speaking – wagging his tail whenever Raila approaches, barking at real or perceived enemies of Raila, or whenever Raila orders him to bark, and otherwise just being plain stupid around Raila. Nyong'o resolved a long time ago to go mute when before Raila, saying "Captain" in the kind of melodious voice I used to hear our village pastor use in reference to "Jesus *ja Paradiso*".

Raila never expected me to be any less biddable. He believed that he would simply snap his fingers and I would run back. That is how Orengo, Nyong'o, Kajwang' and the rest of them have made him think everybody behaves. Unfortunately, he met someone from the Great Lwanda Magere's lineage, someone who was prepared to remind him of the oath of office he took when he became Prime Minister. When Raila became PM he took an oath to "preserve, protect, and defend the Constitution". That means that he has to preserve, protect and defend the rights and freedoms of *all* Kenyans without exception, not just his own personal interests. By capriciously violating my rights, Raila has broken his oath of office and deserves to be exposed.

Almost one year after Makau's initial broadside against me, he would follow my suspension with another hollow rant. On August 20, 2011 – 6 days after the suspension – Makau gloated, "Why Miguna Miguna's sacking was long overdue". He cut to the chase, stating: "Today I want to reflect on Mr Miguna Miguna's disgraceful exit from the public stage. It was long overdue. But I have one piece of advice for Mr Miguna — don't attempt to go mano-a-mano with Prime Minister Raila Odinga. Accept your sacking with humility and move on. Remember the Chinese saying — the peacock that raises its head gets shot. A senior aide who loses his boss's confidence must go without making a fuss. It's unseemly to protest the sacking too loudly. It betrays a problem of entitlement. Servants in the 'king's court' don't have public minds of their own. Most advisors toil in darkness and don't compete with their bosses for attention. Here's why you got tossed."

This was egregious nonsense. Strictly speaking, I hadn't really been fired. And there wasn't anything disgraceful I had done. As someone purporting to be a human rights activist (after all he is the chairman of an NGO called Kenya Human Rights Commission), Makau should have been censuring Raila for violating my legal and constitutional rights, not urging him on. He also seemed to have forgotten my earlier eleven questions, which he hadn't responded to. But he continued.

"First, Mr Miguna forgot why he was useful to Mr Odinga. Presidential candidates — and Mr Odinga is one — must focus on winning elections. The candidate's men and women must do everything to make him electable. Any aide or advisor who doesn't understand this cardinal rule shouldn't be around. *The candidate's electability is at the centre of everything. Nothing else matters.* Aides must pour themselves body and soul into the candidate's fortunes. This is true the world over. President Barack Obama's advisors know this, or they'd be gone in a nanosecond. I believe that Mr Miguna forgot that his utility would end if his actions and words became counterproductive to Mr Odinga's election chances. That's why he had to go."

Not only had Makau not mentioned how and when my so-called utility ended, he also failed to explain how my suspension would contribute to Raila getting more votes. More significantly, Makau was suggesting that the end justifies the means. He wasn't standing up for the protection of fundamental human rights or for principles over expediency as Kenyans would have expected him to do. He was standing with a megaphone and a placard shouting: "Kill him in the most barbaric way if his righteous, truthful and honest voice will prevent you from getting power!" Power. That's all Makau cared about. Power at all costs. *Nothing else matters, he shouts!* But power for what?

"*A presidential campaign is like a choir, and the conductor is the candidate.* This is especially true in Kenya where the candidate is more important than the party. No one else in the party — or in the employ of the candidate — is allowed to compete with the candidate for attention. Some will counter that Mr Miguna was a State official, not a party hack. I say baloney," he continued. Makau was insisting that a professional lawyer hired by a powerful public figure like the Prime Minister, should be singing the praises of the leader, not using his professional training, knowledge and experience to guide, advise and advance the public good. He was condoning and encouraging the Big Man syndrome that had destroyed and desecrated one newly independent African country after another. And this was coming from a law professor based in the US! Makau wasn't seeking to help transform the backward and retrogressive culture of dictatorship and misrule in Africa; he wanted it enhanced.

Makau proceeded to accuse me of having "...spent his waking and sleeping hours — at taxpayer's expense — fighting ODM's wars against PNU. Mr Miguna made no secret that he'd take a bullet for Mr Odinga. Therein lay his fatal mistake. He confused himself with Mr Odinga. That's why he was accused of treating MPs like his subordinate underlings. Second, there can only be one lion king. If you doubt me, go see for yourself at the Maasai Mara. Parties must speak with one authoritative voice. That's why Eldoret North MP William Ruto must leave ODM. There can't be two rats in one hole, as an African proverb reminds us."

This was incredible. On the one hand, Makau had alleged that I was contradicting and disobeying my boss and that I shouldn't have. Instead, I should have been a sychophant singing Hosannah! Now, he was arguing that I had been too committed, too loyal, too dedicated and that I shouldn't have been.

Then he concluded using choice words reserved for distinguished university professors: "My view is that Mr Miguna grew too big for his breeches. He fancied himself ODM's "thinker" and key ideologue. To him, many of the MPs in ODM were reactionary. He regarded the PM's secretariat as anti-reform, lazy, and dim-witted. He would churn out many position briefs for the PM. *Whether he was right or not isn't the point.* But he reportedly never tired of reminding them of their incompetence. However, Mr Miguna thought he was "untouchable" because he had Mr Odinga's ear. That's naïve. The man made enemies everywhere — in ODM, among MPs, in the secretariat. That's why they all combined forces for a take-down. Mr Odinga had to choose between Mr Miguna and ODM. Third, Mr Odinga finally realised that Mr Miguna was a liability. The man reminds one of a child bully in a sandbox. He labours mightily to use 'big' words and phrases. This makes his writing look phony. What looks to some like intellectual arrogance is academic insecurity. Otherwise, there's no reason to hurl insults at everybody who disagrees with you. Add the uncouth language to his dress — especially the hats — and a rather comical image emerges. He actually reminds me of the former Zairian dictator Mobutu Sese Seko Nkuku Ngbendu wa Zabanga. That's a lot of pomp. Mr Odinga must have known that such a "comical image" conjures up bad African memories. That's no way to woo discerning voters. Finally, Mr Odinga may have suspected that Mr Miguna was simply using his "zealotry" to serve as pretext to advance himself. Mr Odinga is in robust health. But I am sure many Luo politicians are scheming to succeed him. Who will inherit the enviable Odinga mantle when Jaramogi's son retires from politics? Mr Miguna may have been positioning himself. But he's not alone, except perhaps he was too indiscreet. Mr Odinga may have been convinced by others of this clever plot. No politician enjoys talk of succeeding him."

In my rebuttal, which was published in the *Sunday Nation* and *the Star* one week later, I once more deflated Makau's intellectual ego: "It seems Makau doesn't believe in democracy or the rule of law. He believes that one should be condemned unheard. He doesn't care about rights and procedural fairness. And that coming from a 'university professor'? In the *Nyayo* tradition, Makau thinks an advisor is worthless and not entitled to any legal or constitutional protection. He asserts that I deserve anything the 'king' subjects me to no matter how inhumane or illegal. This is pitiful. He also states that an advisor must have no mind of his own; that the "king" is the choirmaster and the advisor just one of the singers. So how does one 'advice' the 'king' without having independent thoughts and ideas? Isn't Makau simply prescribing sycophancy? How is that useful for our nascent democracy?

"Makau asserts for the second time, that 'servants in the 'king's court' don't have public minds of their own…'. Hello? This is the twenty-first century Mr

Mutua! Transparency and accountability are values enshrined in the Constitution. More egregiously, Makau insists that I have disagreed with the PM and ODM publicly 'on a daily basis'. Can he give us dates, places and issues of the 'daily' diagreements?" Unbelievably, he stressed that it didn't matter whether I was right or wrong. Why shouldn't it matter? Would Makau support the demonisation and punishment of one who is innocent? So, all those wrongful convictions and miscarriages of justice are OK to Makau? I continued:

"When a presidential candidates sets out to woo voters, he must do so honestly and with integrity. The campaign platform and manifesto cannot be based on lies. 'Reform' and 'change' aren't words one should be allowed to use as subterfuges… And a candidate's character must be put under a microscope and judged on the basis of both his words and deeds; not on propaganda and rhetoric…It's not just about getting votes at any price. Integrity. Trust. Honesty. Discipline. Commitment. Care. These are the core values that determine electoral success. Unlike Makau, I don't believe that life is all about plots, schemes, conspiracies and tricks. There is no reason why Kenyan politics cannot be based on honesty, trust and integrity. If Makau thinks that I'm guilty for insisting on these cardinal principles, so be it."

BOOK EIGHT

PEELING BACK THE MASK

CHAPTER NINETEEN

THE FALLOUT

The summer of 2011 would turn out to be one of the most tumultuous periods of my life. But many of the events that came to a head then – and that almost certainly precipitated my savage public ejection from Raila's inner circle – had been set in train much earlier.

One of the issues that helped seal my fate that summer was the manner in which I unwittingly ended up being depicted as the architect of a bold manoeuvre to finally expel William Ruto from ODM. To recap slightly, from about March, 2011, ODM had been trying to find a process through which it could rid itself of the 'troublesome' Eldoret North MP, Ruto who had had running battles with both the ODM party leader, Raila, and the party itself and the 15 to 20 rebel MPs whom he led. By this time, the rebels were no longer voting with ODM in parliament, but were trying to take over another party, UDM (the United Democratic Movement), which had earlier been allied with ODM though it had actually been founded in 1999, during the dying days of Kanu's totalitarian rule by Kipruto arap Kirwa, William Ruto and Shakhalaga Khwa Jirongo, popularly known as Cyrus. In March, ODM had attempted to use the *Political Parties Act* to expel some of the perceived weakest of the rebel MPs on the logical grounds that since their constituents had elected them as ODM candidates they no longer had the right to represent those constituencies if allied with another party. This move, however, had become a legal quagmire because ODM had not followed the proper procedure.

Then, in late June 2011, I came up with the alternative idea (as explained in Chapter Eleven) to work with UDM leaders who were still loyal to Raila like Gen. Koech to disenfranchise the rebel MPs. My idea was that some UDM party members should use the *Political Parties Act* to file a constitutional petition at the High Court against the rebel MPs for claiming to be UDM when they had been elected as ODM members. It was unanimously agreed that, subject to the Prime Minister's concurrence, we should initiate this legal process that would hopefully then get rid of *all* the rebel MPs. Orengo was detailed to consult with Raila who was vacationing abroad and deliver his instructions to me.

Within two days I got Raila's instructions through Orengo, to find a lawyer who would go after Ruto, Aden Bare Duale, Joshua Serem Kutuny, Charles Cheruiyot Keter and Isaac Kiprono Rutto. There was a consensus that Ruto, as the king-pin, had to be included this time. Duale, Kutuny, Keter and Rutto were the best foot-soldiers Ruto had – articulate and indefatigable. Except for Keter, they were also deemed to be 'weak on the ground', hence the excitement to 'take them out', politically. If ODM won the resultant by-elections, that would be a major boost to its dwindling fortunes, especially in the Rift Valley. However, we reasoned that if ODM lost some or even all of the seats – which was highly unlikely then – it wouldn't make any significant difference because 'they were gone anyway'. The by-elections would compel the party to reactivate its networks in the region. The ensuing recruitments, mobilisations, campaigns and jostling might just be what the party needed to rejuvenate itself. The contests would be a morale boost for the Orange troops. In other words, we believed that it was a win-win situation for ODM.

I acted with alacrity and tracked down Senior Counsel Paul Muite, whom Orengo and I believed would have been the best lawyer for such a high profile and potentially politically volcanic case. Muite advised me that he couldn't handle it because he had declared his candidature for the presidency for Kenya in the forthcoming elections. But he arranged to meet me the following day, a Sunday, at the Muthaiga Country Club. I relayed this development to Orengo and Nyong'o who urged me to proceed. All I needed was Paul's guidance on the best lawyers around and as expected, he immediately recommended Cecil Miller. I called Miller instantly and he gave me an appointment for the next day, Monday July 4 at 8.30am. I arrived 30 minutes before our scheduled meeting and waited. At Miller's office, I used my mobile telephone to connect him with Nyong'o, James Orengo and Janet Ong'era so that they could be in the loop. Moreover, since the party – as the client – was paying, it was only wise to make sure that Miller got instructions directly from the party. Miller promptly agreed to act for the party even though he mentioned, as an aside, that he had represented one of the affected MPs in a matrimonial case many years previously. I advised Miller to draw up a retainer document setting out our understanding and his fees, which he did the same day. After a brief back and forth over the initial retainer deposit which Anyang' thought was too high, I was requested to persuade Miller to discount a significant chunk, which he promptly did. Anyang' and Janet issued him with an ODM retainer cheque by Tuesday, July 5. Miller requested copies of the MPs' membership and party nomination documents, which Anyang' and Janet quickly placed at my disposal. I had these delivered to Miller's office on July 5, and I breathed a sigh of relief.

Because I was scheduled to travel to Canada on July 10, I requested Cecil Miller to place everyone – Nyong'o, Orengo, Muite, Ong'era and myself – in any email correspondence with him over the case. I wanted us to agree on the contents of the application fairly quickly, preferably before I travelled. That wasn't possible. On July 13' Miller forwarded by email the draft application and supporting affidavit. By then, I was already in Toronto. I dutifully edited it, copying everyone in. Muite and Anyang' also forwarded their input, copied to everyone. I noticed, however, that they had changed the applicants from the two UDM members that UDM's chairman General John Koech had recommended to two ODM members – Raila's Meru-based sidekick, Mpuru Aburi, and Anyang's right-hand man, Kepher Odongo. Upon inquiry, I was informed that these changes had been made on the instructions of Ong'era and Anyang'. I felt it was a grave error. The reason why I had suggested UDM members was to distance ODM from the application. I knew that a significant portion of the ODM top leadership, including Orengo and the PM, were uneasy about projecting ODM as "pushing Ruto et al from the party". I didn't really understand the origins of their unease, but I respected it.

On July 20 at 7.07am, I received an email from Anyang', via his Ipad, stating simply: "Hope we can bang it today and let media know." The message was addressed to Muite and copied to Miller, Orengo, Ong'era and myself. Everyone understood that as ODM's instructions to have the petition filed, and Miller acted promptly. The media reaction was instantaneous and explosive. "Raila moves to expel Ruto!" most electronic and print media screamed. I fielded questions from the NTV (a television station owned by the Nation Media Group) and KTN (The Standard Group's television arm), explaining the basis of the action, and warning that from then on, ODM would take lightning action against those bent on rocking it from within.

When I had noticed that two ODM members were now the ones to sue Ruto and his brigade, I had assumed that the top leadership had now quashed any qualms about how pushing Ruto from the party might be perceived. Yet the day after the news broke that 'ODM had gone to court to force Ruto out', the leadership exploded in confusion. Jakoyo reacted furiously, claiming that 'Miguna and some reckless ODM radicals around the PM are destroying the party'. Raila called Ong'era and Nyong'o, yelling, claiming that he had no knowledge of the suit. Sensing 'danger', Orengo, Ong'era and Nyong'o panicked and implied that I had acted alone without instructions, conveniently forgetting that it was Nyong'o and Ong'era who had issued the retainer fee to Miller and that it was Nyong'o who had issued the final instructions through his 'bang it' email. Curiously, however, Raila didn't call me. Ong'era reported to me that the PM had called her shouting: "Who the hell is Miguna Miguna? Who the hell is Miguna Miguna? I've not seen him for six months!'" Why was Raila angry with me? And why was he lying about his knowledge of the legal action and when he had last seen me?

Raila had personally authorised the law suit. It was ODM that issued the retainer cheque to Miller to initiate action against the ODM rebels. The cheque had been signed by secretary general, Anyang' Nyong'o and the party's CEO, Janet Ong'era. Raila knew all these things. He also knew I held no official position in the party. Why was he blaming me. And how was the legal action politically inopportune when it was public knowledge that ODM had tried several times to rid itself of Ruto and his rebels?

Also, he had seen me less than a fortnight before. On July 9, 2011, at his invitation, I had accompanied Raila to Juba, South Sudan, for that country's independence inauguration. Something wasn't right, but I couldn't immediately put my finger on it.

I decided not to call the PM in the aftermath of the explosion. I also decided not to worry about what he had reportedly said to Ong'era and Nyong'o. I know Raila. I know how he plays his political games. I knew that a telephone discussion would only make the situation worse; he would shout and grumble about things he either hadn't thought through carefully or which he didn't even know. Often, he would shout just to look tough to those around him. It gave Raila a kick to diminish others. "Hmm..hmm…", was all he would say afterwards. It was the most juvenile way of dealing with difficult situations. It negated and eroded Raila's meagre leadership credentials. It exposed him as a degenerate; a leader lacking in probity. But I also didn't call Raila, because I knew that it was possible that he had simply overreacted in the heat of the moment, that time usually calms most of these human emotions. It was also possible that Ong'era and Nyong'o might have misunderstood and/or misreported Raila's reaction. I couldn't be sure. This wouldn't have been the first time he had behaved like this.

However, when I heard that Raila had summoned the party's National Executive Committee/Parliamentary Group meeting for the following day, July

22, I invited Orengo, Nyong'o and Prof. Oyugi for an urgent discussion. Nyong'o didn't turn up but Orengo and Oyugi did. We met at my Runda house until about 1.30am the following morning.

The strategy I presented was simple: ODM didn't own the law suit. It had been lodged by two ordinary party members in their own names. They didn't claim to be acting on behalf of the leadership. They stated that, as loyal members of the party, they wouldn't sit by and see others try to destroy what they had built. They had decided to defend the party. Why then should the PM or the party want to appear as if the two litigants were their agents? Wouldn't that achieve the exact opposite of what they had intended? Wouldn't that show their hands, hands they were desperate to hide, and all to crucify me for nothing? My view was that the party shouldn't even have called a meeting to discuss the matter.

Both Orengo and Oyugi bought the logic and the strategy. Oyugi and I asked Orengo to try and explain it to the PM early the following day, before the scheduled meeting. I thought that the PM shouldn't even attend the meeting. But actually, Orengo didn't seek out the PM next morning. He simply went to the meeting and sat there quietly until he noticed that the tide had turned against those like Jakoyo who wanted a resolution "condemning the action and Miguna Miguna". The Deputy Speaker of the National Assembly, Farah Maalim, and Magerer Langat led an onslaught supporting the legal action. And when the final tally was taken, only two lone voices – Olago Aluoch and Jakoyo Midiwo – opposed it. As usual, Raila had conveniently taken cover. Ong'era, Orengo and Magerer Langat called me almost immediately after the meeting backed the action; they were effusive and I exhaled. I was relieved. I mistakenly thought that the resolution marked the end of the brouhaha. Well, I was wrong.

It appears that Raila, Jakoyo and Oburu, in particular, didn't like what had happened. Or more accurately, they might have liked the end result but resented the fact that I would get credit for such a huge political breakthrough. They interpreted it as a clear indication that I had become too powerful. How could a joint NEC/PG of the party approve the legal action by more than two-thirds majority yet I hadn't even attended the meeting? How could the majority of the party executive and parliamentary wing overrule the party leader? From Magerer's excited call, I knew that Orengo had disclosed my strategic input to others. If Magerer knew my involvement even though I hadn't discussed it with him then others must also have known. Orengo had probably reported my position word-for-word to the meeting. That must have caused jitters and in Raila's kitchen cabinet. Something had to be done to cut me down to size. It had to be immediate and ruthless. 'Miguna is going to be an example to all!" would seem, from the events of the following weeks, to have been their well-concealed decision. It was a scheme full of animus.

* * * * * * * * * * * * * * *

In fact, the Ruto matter wasn't the only controversy dogging my every move in that third week of July when I should have been enjoying a peaceful family holiday. At about 8am on July 7, 2011, one day into what was supposed to be a month-long vacation, I had received a telephone call from one of Raila's secretaries, Rosemary Outa. She told me that Raila wanted me to accompany him to Juba, for South Sudan's independence inauguration in two days time, on July 9. These sudden summonses couldn't have come at a worse time. On July 10, I was scheduled to fly to Toronto to collect Atieno and Biko for our month-long holiday. To get to Juba on July 9, the Kenyan delegation was supposed to depart very early in the morning and return the same evening. We were going to use chartered flights.

I said yes grudgingly. I was conflicted. I had never been to Sudan – South or North. At any other time I would have really loved to go but I had preparations to make for Atieno and Biko. And, given the turbulent historical relationship between the two Sudans, I had qualms that a trip to Juba might imperil my cherished trip across the Atlantic. This time, we were going to spend our annual month's vacation in Kenya. My good friend and Lamu town clerk, Patrick Ouya, had offered to find accommodation for us on his picturesque and historical island. My family and I were eagerly looking forward to the impending trip. Anyango, and Achieng' were particularly excited; they had been packing their toys and clothes for weeks now. Technically, I had actually been on holiday since July 6. Yet I couldn't really say no. Raila was my boss. 'He must have a very good reason for inviting me.' And in any case, I reasoned, 'We are at work for the Nation, 24/7.'

The ODM delegation was at the airport by 6.15am on July 9. As we waited for our flight, the party mandarins discussed politics and other menial things. It was when we were still waiting that Janet brought up the issue of the chairman of the Interim Independent Electoral Commission, Isaack Hassan's refusal to comply with ODM's request for deregistration of its rebel MPs and 34 councillors, predominantly from the Rift Valley. A week before, I had prepared a petition for ODM's Secretary General, Nyong'o, to both Hassan and the political parties' registrar. They had both trashed ODM's petition. Instead of formally responding to ODM's request, Hassan had summoned a press conference and challenged ODM to "target the big fish in the party and stop harassing the small fish." Hassan's position was that before ODM could go after the councillors, it should deal with the errant MPs, starting with William Ruto. But that wasn't his mandate. Legally, he couldn't run ODM or tell it when or how to discipline its errant members.

"Miguna, why can't you expose this green snake called Hassan in your column? He has no mandate to tell ODM how to conduct its affairs," Janet asserted. The team subsequently discussed the idea for about 30 minutes before resolving that it would be a good idea if I wrote a column about Hassan as soon as possible. But because I knew how tight my schedule was going to be, I was coy about the idea. I promised to consider it. "No, you must find time to hit that man hard... He is being partisan. There is no legal reason why he is refusing to act. We have proven our case. The *Political Parties Act* is clear on this matter..." Nyong'o added. By the time we boarded, the ODM team was unanimous that I should expose Hassan's partisanship, hypocrisy, duplicity and incompetence. The onus was now on me to find time to do so.

Our flight to Juba departed from Jomo Kenyatta International Airport at around 9am. Raila was flying from Wilson Airport. Within two and a half hours, we were approaching Juba. It would take us another two hours to land due to the absence of a control tower and the influx of hundreds of charter planes flying in and out of the new South Sudan capital city. After landing, we walked across the runway, dodging taxiing and landing planes and VIP vehicles. It was miraculous that the day ended without accidents or fatalities. There were no customs or immigrations checks either.

At the John Garang Mausoleum where the ceremony was being held, there was complete disarray. (I was astounded that the South Sudanese government hadn't got its act together and built even a modest stadium – or even just rigged up some kind of canvas gazebo – in which to hold the celebrations). Even though we had been issued with VIP tags, with our names and countries prominently displayed, the South Sudanese officials at the Mausoleum pushed and shoved us aside, onto bare concrete pavements. Some cabinet ministers, diplomats, senior government officials and other dignitaries were pushed onto the grass. Raila and Ida managed to climb up to the dais reserved for invited delegations and heads of states and governments. But former President Moi, cabinet ministers Otieno Kajwang', Orengo and others weren't so lucky; they sat with us in the excruciating sun, on the concrete pavements. When South African President Jacob Zuma arrived, his security ended up jostling with South Sudanese security, and Zuma was almost hurled down the steps in the ensuing commotion. Yet it was Zuma who had actually provided the South Sudanese with the air defences and the ceremonial 24-four-gun salute for the occasion! Equally extraordinary, was that while the South Sudanese officials were being handed round refreshments, visiting dignitaries – even cabinet ministers – were being refused water, even when they begged for a glass!

By the end of the day, we were exhausted, thirsty and starving. I almost missed our flight back. The earlier confusion became worse after the event, with everyone running helter-skelter, looking for transport back to the airport. When I climbed into our plane on the way back, I found Raila and Ida already seated up front, close to the cabin. They avoided eye contact with me, and I wondered, fleetingly, why. I later learnt that Raila and Ida had abandoned their chartered plane due to rumours that some PNU politicians and his enemies in government were allegedly planning to shoot it down on its way back. If that was true, I wondered, why had he let others fly in that plane?

On Thursday, July 21, 2011, after much procrastination from me – I was somewhat distracted by the storm over the rebel MPs' eviction – and increased urging from Ong'era, I published an article in *the Star* titled 'IIEC chair Isaack does not deserve all the plaudits'. As in all the articles I have authored previously, I made factual and logical arguments based on publicly available information. I reiterated the arguments Anyang' had made in his petition to the IIEC chairman and the political parties' registrar. I questioned Isaack's grasp of the law and his independence and challenged his decision not to act positively on ODM's petition. To date, no one has refuted any of the factual assertions and issues in that article. The article was not about Isaack as such. It also addressed issues of good governance, discrimination, corruption and nepotism at the IIEC. Those are important issues that cannot be trivialised.

A few days after my article appeared another commentator, Boaz Gikonyo, whose byline identified him as an elections expert who had allegedly consulted with the IIEC, published an even more detailed article that contained specific allegations of corruption, mismanagement and nepotism within the electoral body headed by Isaack. Surprisingly, when Isaack and his fellow IIEC commissioners addressed a press conference a few days after Gikonyo's article and attempted to respond to Gikonyo's serious allegations, he glibly accused an un-named 'senior politician' of trying to 'rig the next (2012) elections in advance'. He also castigated what he termed 'attempts to interfere with and influence the IIEC'. Nothing concrete or specific was said, but I subsequently learnt that Isaack sought and obtained an appointment with the Prime Minister on or about August 1 – and twice more shortly after that – where he further complained about 'attempts to undermine him and the IIEC'. Again, nothing specific.

Curiously, I later learnt, Raila held two meetings with James Orengo, Francis Muthaura, Francis Kimemia, Alfred Mutua, Hassan Isaack, Caroli Omondi, Mohamed Isahakia, Jakoyo Midiwo and Oburu Odinga at his offices between August 1 and 2, at which I was the subject of discussion.

On or about August 2, Isaack announced through the media that 'the IIEC had conducted preliminary investigations and discovered some information on the laptop computer of the personal assistant to the IIEC's secretary and CEO, James Oswago'. The IIEC subsequently suspended Oswago's personal assistant and recalled Oswago from The Philippines, where he had travelled on official duty. Even though there were no allegations against me and I neither knew, nor had worked with Gikonyo or Oswago's personal assistant, the media suddenly latched onto my July 21 article, prominently quoting from it and drawing unsubstantiated claims that it might have been part of the 'wider scheme to influence and interfere with the IIEC' as a way of preparing 'groundwork for the rigging of the 2012 elections'. I was astounded. Nothing could have been further from the truth. Three weeks after my suspension Oswago would confide in me that, by August 4 when my suspension was announced, "the IIEC internal investigations had established that I wasn't involved at all in the so-called smear campaign and alleged attempt at rigging the next general elections." Even though Isaack had loudly declared that he had invited the Kenya Anti-Corruption Commission to investigate the allegations Gikonyo and I had made against him and the IIEC, almost one year later nothing has been heard from Isaack (who was soon hired as the chairman of the newly established Independent Electoral and Boundaries' Commission) or the defunct anti graft body or its successor.

Although virtually all the print and electronic media were discussing my article on the IIEC, none of them contacted me for comment or response to the unfounded allegations that they continued to repeat. Nor did anyone from the IIEC, the OPM, ODM, KACC or any other interested parties attempt to get my response. Consequently, I also didn't seek anyone out. I felt that I hadn't done anything wrong, had acted on ODM's instructions and therefore had no reason to worry. Besides I was supposed to be enjoying a holiday. Things, however, would quickly spiral out of my control.

Sometime in early July 2011, before my trip to Canada, I had received from the ODM secretariat an invitation for a two-day party strategy team retreat. I was a member of the team and the PM's think tank and as Raila's senior advisor for coalition, constitutional and legal affairs, it was routine that I represented him at all important party and government functions. The two-day retreat was initially scheduled for mid-July. However, I had indicated to Anyang' and Ong'era that I would be out of the country and unable to attend. Partly as a result of my request (or so I naïvely might have believed), the meeting was rescheduled to early August. On July 20, I prepared for Raila a strategic document titled, "A Confidential Assessment On 2012 and Beyond: The Need For A Major Transformation, The Campaign and Technical Teams." I argued, in part that: "The next (2012) elections could mark the beginning of the end of the significance of the so-called 'Regional Kingpins' play in consolidating and delivering votes of former provinces/regions for political parties and their 'national' leaders. This trend is consistent with a grassroots/popular/citizens movement that gained momentum in 2005. The Party Leader and the Party must go to the grassroots directly and engage in a dialogue for the development of a '2012 organic manifesto of change and hope'… the decision to support ODM in the last elections was made by the people at the grassroots. The so-called leaders then 'followed' the people."

The idea was to encourage Raila and the ODM leadership to focus on grassroots mobilisation and worry less about the rebellion of a few politicians. I continued, "Later, however, (and in order to allow the 'leaders' to save face), the party gave them prominent roles in the national campaigns. Unfortunately, most of the 'leaders' quickly and conveniently forgot that they were not responsible for the party's popular support around the country. But even more unfortunate has been the vast space created for those putative 'leaders', which they have occupied and tried to use to relegate the party and its national leadership to a subservient position, vis-à-vis theirs.

"This time around, the party is well advised to rely mostly on grassroots leaders, mobilisers and supporters at constituency and county levels as the pillars of the party in every part of the country. This does not mean that we should abandon the idea of identifying key regional leaders and working with them to galvanise support, firstly, for our presidential candidate, and secondly, for the party candidates. It only means that we should not hope to have or use any so-called regional leaders to 'herd' their respective communities to support our party and leader in the next and subsequent elections. With the pure presidential system firmly in place, focus will now shift to the strengths and weaknesses of each presidential candidate. In our view, this system will slowly downgrade, weaken and eventually render meaningless the 'middle man' phenomenon in politics in Kenya. Unfortunately, ethnicity might continue to play a significant role in both county and national elections in the foreseeable future. Eventually – as the country industrialises – and as has happened in mature democracies – people will begin focusing more on 'bread-and-butter' issues and less on ethnicity. But that time isn't here yet!"

Once I had outlined my thesis and justification, I presented the roadmap: "Given the situation outlined above, the party and its leadership have no option but to go to the masses/grassroots in a down-to-earth manner that identifies real issues and problems facing different communities. This is where our support – and real power – is. This is already happening with the Party Leader's repeated tours of Eastern, Coast, Central, North Eastern, Rift Valley and Western. But Nyanza and Nairobi must not be left behind. Ideally, because the Party Leader is more or less from these two 'regions', there might be an unfortunate tendency to overlook their importance in consolidating the support/votes for him and the party. We have studied the most recent opinion polls and note, with tremendous regret, the figures from Western and North Eastern, in particular. In and around 2007, the support for the PL and the party in North Eastern was consistently above 75%. In Western, the figure was consistently above 65%. At the moment, however, our support in North Eastern stands at 49%, while Western is about 59%. Similarly, our support in Nairobi has dwindled to 47.6%. We aren't happy about Nyanza, too. In our view, our overall support in Nyanza – for both the PL and party – should be in the ninety percentile. What this means is that we must go flat out to regain, consolidate and expand our support base. This will not be easy for several reasons. Firstly, unlike before, we are now part of the government. Our fortunes will rise or fall, partly, with that of the perceived successes or failures with the grand coalition government. And secondly, our overall performance in government has been mixed."

By July 24, having not heard back from Raila, I confidentially shared my strategic views with Orengo and Nyong'o. On the same day at 4.39am, Nyong'o forwarded to me "ODM's Final Strategic Plan (2) For 2012 General Elections," which he asked me to "please read…and pass on to the Cricket Team." The "Cricket Team" was the code name for the secret ODM campaign strategic team, which Oduor Ong'wen, Bartonjo Chesaini, Kibisu Kabatesi, Martin Oloo, Adams Oloo, Janet Ong'era, Rosa Buyu and I belonged to.

Meanwhile, the retreat for the Cricket Team was scheduled for August 4 and 5, 2011, at the Enashipai Resort and Spa in Naivasha. Those weren't good days for my family in more ways than one. Firstly, my wife, who was then completing her practicum at the United Nations Development Programme (UNDP) offices at Gigiri, Nairobi, was attending a three-day seminar at the Great Rift Valley Lodge, Naivasha, beginning August 3. I was therefore the one in charge of the children. And secondly, I had just arrived with Biko and Atieno in Kenya and all the five children were incessantly demanding – and were entitled to – outings, adventures and sightseeing. I had actually planned to travel with all of them to Naivasha so that the entire family could spend two days after both our respective retreats would have ended. With both of us gone to Naivasha, the children stayed with our housekeeper, Millicent. Looking back now, I thank God I didn't take them with me and I promise never to make the mistake of placing any party, political interests or person above that of my family again.

So, despite still being on leave, I arrived for the retreat about 11am on Thursday, August 4. I had driven myself there. I had earlier been pleasantly surprised at the unusual speed and efficiency at which the OPM had processed and released my per diem that morning. It had been done in two hours. Previously, it would take more than four days to process such a simple thing. At this point, I had no idea that the efficiency had nothing to do with a positive change in administrative prowess by those running the OPM; it was part and parcel of an intricate web of conspiracy against me being executed. The 'Retreat Programme" outlined arrival to be 11am, lunch from 12pm to 2pm, followed by a committee meeting at 2pm to 3pm. Our 'sponsor,' the National Democratic Institute's country director, Mary O'Hogan, was scheduled to present the NDI Survey for 2011 between 3 and 3.30pm, then there would be meetings on party development from 4.15 to 4.45pm, followed by a discussion of ODM's policy development framework at 4.45 and 5.30pm.

But something was definitely wrong. By 1pm, as Mary and I finished our lunch and headed to the meeting room, none of my Cricket Team colleagues had arrived. Moreover, apart from the ODM secretariat chief accountant, Joshua Kawino, none of the secretariat staff had arrived. And as Mary and I approached the seminar room, I received an unusual text message from Prof. Oyugi. "Ja-Loka, I understand that you are attending a meeting in Naivasha with Oduor Ong'wen; can you ask him to call me urgently?" I called Oyugi immediately. "Professor, he isn't here yet." Apparently, Oduor had told Oyugi that he was with me. I contacted Oduor and passed along Prof. Oyugi's message. When reached by Oyugi, Oduor allegedly claimed that he had been held up at the Office of the President's Harambee House building in a meeting of the 'Police Reform Committee' with the Minister for Internal Security, Prof. George Saitoti. However, simultaneously in a text message to me, he claimed that he had been "held up in a meeting with ODM MPs" at an undisclosed location in Nairobi. Why would Oduor be meeting ODM MPs when the strategic retreat had been planned way back in July? I wondered. A few minutes later, I spoke with Prof. Oyugi and we agreed that Oduor wasn't being truthful.

Something wasn't right. But at that point, neither Oyugi nor I knew what it was. That would soon become clearer.

At about 3.30pm, as the few of us who were there were discussing the NDI survey results and their implications for ODM, I started noticing numerous missed calls and texts from various senior ODM ministers – Lands Minister, James Orengo, Agriculture Minister Dr Sally Kosgei and Cooperative Development Minister, Joseph Nyagah. There were numerous missed calls from the media as well. My phone was on vibration. For 15 minutes, I ignored the calls and texts, thinking I would get back to Orengo, Kosgei and Nyagah during the tea break. But that was not to be. One text from Paul Ilado, *the Star's* political editor attracted my attention. It asked: "Can you confirm the suspension? What's your response?" Since I hadn't received any information (no letter, text, email or telephone call from anyone in government) about any suspension, I texted back: "Suspension of whom?" The answer came back: "You!" I further inquired from him who had told him about it and he responded that he was getting the 'suspension letter' in a few minutes and would get back to me.

Within minutes, I started receiving calls from all kinds of people – media and friends. I then texted the PM's spokesman Dennis Onyango and my close friends Sarah Elderkin, Prof Edward Oyugi and Sylvester Kasuku to find out if they knew or if they had heard anything. They promptly replied that they knew nothing. All my friends were in the dark. Dennis sent me a text indicating that he was with the PM in Kisumu and that I should treat the story as rumours.

Apparently not, for within minutes Joshua Kawino, who was sitting next to me, passed me his phone with the Nation Media Group's "breaking news". The top headline screamed, "Raila fires top aide." Even though the letter (when it was finally delivered to me 28 hours after it was reported verbatim in the media) said I was only suspended without pay, the media kept reporting that I had been "fired", which perhaps I had been, constructively, since the suspension was indefinite and without pay.

Quite clearly, something fundamental had happened. People seated across from me were beginning to stare. I was getting restless. I stepped outside and tried to call back Orengo. His line was busy. I tried Sally. Nobody answered. I then called Nyagah. There was no response. My heart was racing. I took a deep breath and went into the bathroom. Then I dialed Raila's line. No answer. I telephoned Ogeta, one of his bodyguards. Silence again. "Something is definitely wrong," I hissed. I then called Sarah. She answered. But she was also in total darkness. She wasn't getting through to anyone either. I returned to the room, sat there blankly for ten minutes before picking up my bags and fleeing. By then,

Adams Oloo, Bartonjo Chesaini and Kibisu had arrived. They all were avoiding eye contact with me. It was now 4.15pm. Later, one of my friends informed me that he had seen a similar 'news flash' on Facebook but had ignored it as rumour. By 4 pm, major TV, radio and electronic media were 'officially' announcing my "indefinite suspension without pay".

Once outside, I dialed Prof. Oyugi's line. He told me that he was watching the 'breaking news.' He didn't know anything more than what was now all over the major TV stations and radios. I was now packing my things. Prof. Oyugi's view, which I shared, was that I should head home. By 4.15pm, as I started the ignition on my vehicle, my secretary sent me a short text message to say that my personal assistant, messenger and she had received letters terminating their employment. No reasons had been given. At or about 5pm, as I pushed the accelerator to the floor, my personal assistant sent another text message saying they had received a letter from the permanent secretary in the PM's office, Dr Mohammed Isahakia, addressed to me. It was marked 'Top Secret' and the person who had delivered it had instructed them not to open it. A few minutes after that, as I flew down the Nakuru-Nairobi highway, my personal assistant called to say that some strangers had arrived at my office and were now changing the locks. My staff had been ordered to "leave now!" I had now been denied access to my possessions inside, even personal possessions such as my books.

It was now 6pm and I was trembling as I pushed the vehicle to its limits. Our housekeeper called to inform me that the Administration Police officer at my house had been "collected" and that there was now no security at the gate. "Is everybody OK? How are the children?" I asked, this time in complete rage at the abandonment of my family. "We are OK," the housekeeper responded. That gave me temporary solace.

Though I had never been in this position before, I realised a script was being followed. An announcement is made by a major media house that a prominent person has been fired. "Reasons" and "justifications" are quickly concocted. The story catches fire. The prominent person's career is in tatters. He goes into hiding and remains there, ashamed of the humiliation! Friends and relatives take cover. Enemies emerge, emboldened. Life goes on. It was obvious that the chain of events had been carefully choreographed.

As I drove back to Nairobi, another telephone call revealed that the "decision" to 'suspend' me had taken place that morning in Nairobi. Some people who were supposed to have been attending the Naivasha retreat – people I had considered my friends, people like Oduor Ong'wen – had been at that meeting. That explained why he had failed to show up but had given two conflicting stories of his whereabouts. It also explained why Adams Oloo and Chesaini had arrived in Naivasha about four hours late and hadn't been able to maintain eye contact with me. Kabatesi, too, had seemed unusually cagey. None of them had even greeted me.

I heard that at that Nairobi meeting ODM Chief Whip Jakoyo Midiwo had demanded that I be fired immediately. He had not apparently disclosed the reasons for this demand. A number of MPs present – I don't know how many – had supported him. But Budalangi MP Ababu Namwamba and another unnamed MP had defended me strongly, arguing that someone like me was needed by both the PM and the party, that if we wanted to triumph in the struggle ahead "we cannot get rid of Miguna". But Ababu had been arguing to the wind. The 'story' had already been carefully leaked and planted across the media and boy, were those journalists having a field day!

On my way to Nairobi, I gave the media my brief response to the hilarious hullabaloo. I told them that I had not received any information – letter, email, text or telephone call – about the suspension. I explained that I had been on vacation for nearly a month and that I had only that day gone to a party strategy retreat in Naivasha. I added that whatever might have been concocted as a 'reason' for the suspension was baseless and unfounded, and that I would neither be cowed nor would I waver. I then declined further comment until I received the letter.

I arrived home just before 7pm and found my children outside. Questions tumbled from them: "Daddy, why did the soldier leave? Daddy, are we going to have security? Daddy this, daddy that!"

"Shhhh...Quiet. Everything will be all right," was my response. I didn't have an explanation. I couldn't look at them. How could I explain to them that their father had been hung out to dry? Emotionally, I felt in pieces. I could see the confusion in the children's eyes. But I had no way of explaining anything. Nobody, had given me advance warning of all this and I was struggling to come to terms with it all by myself.

There was an endless torrent of calls and text messaages. Both well-wishers and doomsayers were competing with each other over me. My phone couldn't cope and 'died'. As I charged the phone, I responded to the most urgent ones, essentially repeating what I had told the media. Later, I watched the 9pm news and couldn't believe the disinformation, bias and propaganda. "Raila fires top aide over spat with IIEC," KTN, Citizen and NTV kept repeating. My image was everywhere. My article from July 21 was being displayed, misreported, and misquoted and 'dissected' by self-appointed cardinals of righteousness. "He had outlived his usefulness," some commentator sneered after the news.

I glanced over at Biko and Atieno, but my two older children who must have realised what was happening – even if they couldn't fully comprehend it or appreciate what might have caused it – were pretending not to notice anything. I wasn't ready to discuss anything. I couldn't, anyway, even if I had wanted to, because I was in total darkness myself. The following day, August 5, I made all the front pages. All the newspapers carried the same headline, more or less: "Raila kicks out key aide!" East Africa's leading newspaper, the *Daily Nation* screamed. "Raila fires top aide over spat with IIEC." *The Standard's* David Ochami began his lead story in a curious way: "The revolving door in Prime Minister Raila Odinga's office has taken yet another high-flying casualty after the PM suspended a key aide and withdrew his security…" Not left behind was *the Star*, the newspaper in which my weekly column appeared. "Raila Suspends Miguna; defiant advisor says move baseless." Paul Ilado reported that "Prime Minister Raila Odinga [had] yielded to pressure from ODM MPs and government officials and suspended his advisor on coalition affairs Miguna Miguna…" Nobody was disclosing who the complainants were or the particulars of their complaint. The allegations ran the full gamut: from the 'spat with IIEC' to 'complaints from ODM MPs and government officials.' I couldn't bring myself to read beyond the headlines. I tried hiding the newspapers from the children but my son, Biko, kept digging them out.

Amidst all that, I maintained my innocence and continued to dismiss what I knew of the claims made against me in the suspension letter – which I still hadn't received – as baseless. I stated that "The merchants of impunity will not win in Kenya and that I wouldn't be cowed…" I added that "the new constitution is very clear on the rights of citizens. You cannot arbitrarily dismiss anyone without due process." And as a pointer to what my stance on Raila would soon be, I added: "How are you sure that you are capable of embracing the new constitution? My staff did not do anything, so why victimise innocent Kenyans?" Curiously, on the same day, the newspapers quoted Raila's cousin and ODM chief whip as celebrating the suspension. He attempted to justify it too. "How do you sue the Attorney General of the government you serve in? [He was referring to an employment case I had brought, described below] How do you abuse fellow civil servants in the media? How do you criticise the Speaker of the National Assembly in the media yet you are junior to him in government structures? This is truly unacceptable. He lost it a long time ago and often wrote articles which gave the PM a bad name yet the PM was not even aware." That was Jakoyo, and most likely Raila speaking through him, attempting to justify the draconian action.

What was very clear to me is that whatever had happened had been carefully planned. The only drawback for them is that they couldn't conjure up coherent 'stories'. The ones they were peddling weren't persuasive. Even if they were, they were still required to provide me with notice, accord me due process and act in accordance with the law. Attempting to shame and defame me wasn't a legitimate way to go about ending my service.

A further reason being given for my suspension was a "failure to sign local agreement forms despite several appeals". It was more of a refusal than a failure. These are forms that had been forwarded to me by Isahakia more than a year after I was hired that sought to fundamentally alter the terms of my employment. They arbitrarily reduced my remuneration, allowances and benefits by half. The reader may recall that when I had been offered my position as advisor, Ambassador Muthaura had undertaken to issue me a letter of employment that offered an identical employment package to that of my counterpart, Kibwana. Indeed, Muthaura had even asked Kibwana to disclose to me his pay slip, which contained his salary, benefits and privileges, so that I knew what to expect from my letter of appointment. He had also asked me to write to Isahakia with those terms so that in turn Isahakia would write to him (Muthaura), confirming the same. He explained that that was the way the Kenyan bureaucracy worked. However, when I had received these subsequent "local agreement forms", which contained terms that were materially different and far lower than what I had been offered and accepted, I had written to Isahakia and Muthaura, stating that I would not sign the forms unless and until they were amended to reflect what I had been originally offered and had agreed to. They started paying me lower than we had agreed, prompting me to sue for breach of contract before the expiry of the limitation period of two years.

I never received a response to my letters asking for those amendments. The case had been set down for a hearing when Raila announced the suspension. There is no law preventing any government employee from suing the government for breach of contract. If this action was now being touted as a reason for my suspension it only showed the extraordinary hypocrisy of the Kenyan government, for, in the same period that I was suspended for no legitimate reason, the head of the civil service, Muthaura, the minister for finance and Deputy Prime Minister, Uhuru Kenyatta, the minister for higher education and ODM's deputy leader, William Ruto, the minister for industrialisation and ODM's chairman, Henry Kosgey, and the director general of Kenya Postal Corporation, Mag. Gen. (Rtd) Hussein Ali, were all facing charges at the International Criminal Court for having committed crimes against humanity in Kenya, against Kenyans. Yet, none of them had been suspended. Raila had even written – twice – to Muthaura, demanding that I be paid the same as Kibwana. He strongly argued for the adherence and applicability of the principal of "equal pay for equal work". On the contrary, the same government that was purportedly accusing me of "gross misconduct", because I had sued the Attorney General for breach of contract (which is how any case against the government in Kenya has to be worded), was helping those accused by hiring expensive British barristers to defend them, providing luxury vehicles, houses and paying for all the accused's expenses.

Laughably, Midiwo had also claimed that I had been suspended because I had attended the first appearances at The Hague of the six Kenyans charged with crimes against humanity. Yes, I had gone to The Hague – along with Salim Lone, Raila's former spokesman – but only at the express request of the Prime Minister. Our tickets and expenses had been paid for by the government – just as those of my counterpart, Kivutha Kibwana, President Kibaki's advisor, had been. Many others had travelled to the Hague at the government's expense too. To single me out for some kind of blame here was pure malice, and demonstrated the duplicity some people employ to hoodwink the public.

Other scandalous allegations about misrepresenting the PM's Office, harassment, intimidation and use of abusive language, were only added for colour. The letter, when it finally came, presented no particulars, just as with the other allegations. There is no indication who I subjected to abuse, where or when. Nothing. And of course, nobody has ever accorded me the opportunity to respond to these illegitimate and unfounded claims. I was completely disappointed that, under the new Constitution that I had played such a pivotal role in drafting and having ratified, I would be treated with such callous disregard for my legal and constitutional rights, including simple human decency, and by a man I had defended for many years with all my energy, a man I had loudly proclaimed to be a champion of democracy, the rule of law and constitutionalism.

On Friday, August 5, after breakfast, my son Biko went to the gatehouse at home and retrieved some papers from the roof, which I had no idea were there. There was an unsigned letter from Francis Kimemia, Permanent Secretary, Ministry of Internal Security and Provincial Administration, dated July 22, 2009, inviting me for dinner at State House on July 24, 2009, at 7pm, which I had never received. Then there was a copy of a nine-page document titled 'The assassination plot against Hon Raila Amollo Odinga and the prominent Gikuyus [sic] businessmen involved'. I had never seen that one, either. Then there were two copies each of unsigned confidential memoranda I had written to the PM on August 12 and 23, 2009, respectively. There were two copies of my article 'Reform the judiciary by transforming the law society and creating an independent judicial service council, not by removing tenure for judges', dated August 23, 2009, and one copy of my article 'Raila has power to release arrested youth under power sharing accord'. Clearly, the security that the state had stationed at my Nairobi home had been doing more than 'guarding' me and my family.

In the afternoon of August 5, I sent a short text message to Orengo and Nyong'o, expressing my disappointment at how I had been treated. Orengo didn't respond. Nyong'o claimed that he wasn't privy to the decision, but that he would contact me after returning to Nairobi from Mombasa where he was "attending a conference". I never heard back from him again. Not that I expected them to get back to me. I had just wanted them to know my feelings.

Early in the morning of Saturday, August 6, when one of my twin daughters, Suré, suddenly asked whether we could go and visit their uncle and aunts in Magina, I said yes before I had fully processed all the potential challenges that a "yes" answer implied. I was going to be the driver, bodyguard, baby sitter, mother and father rolled up in one, but I was ready for a different kind of challenge. The suspension, which had been intended to demoralise me, had only strengthened my resolve to not be defeated by it. And off we went, six happy campers, singing and joking in the vehicle as I drove, heading to Kisumu, as if nothing had happened.

I had the previous evening, sent Raila the following short text message: "Jakom, good evening! Those who are publicly abusing and undermining you and the party like Dualle, etc are sacred, Those looting and plundering public resources are cosy. But I who have sacrificed so much and defended you and fought for you and what I've believed to be higher ideals is sacrificed so inhumanely. For what? I who has gallantly stood up to the merchants of impunity is cut loose! Does anybody think this is the way to win elections? Does anybody believe that I have done anything? And so my staff is fired summarily without due process. I have not even received the letter or any other official communication about this. Is this Justice? Is this the change we've sacrificed our lives for? Awuoro! Awuoro! God bless you."

For three days, my five children and I swam in Lake Victoria, ate humongous and delicious tilapia fish and visited with the villagers in Magina.

On our return, we stopped for lunch at Nakuru where my good friend Prof. Tom Ojienda generously hosted us at the Nakuru Members' Club. Before hitting the road again, I made a couple of calls to Sarah Elderkin and *the Star*'s CEO, William Pike, about my article, "A Note for My Friends," which was scheduled to be published as my column of August 9. William was suggesting some minor changes that Sarah and I agreed would blunt the piece. As I drove, Sarah would call with an editorial comment here and there. I would pull over, note and mull over the comment, and keep driving. By the time I arrived in Kisumu later that afternoon, Sarah and I had reached a consensus that the article was ready.

I asked my friend Onyango Oloo, who founded and manages the leading Kenyan online political platform, *Jukwaa*, to post the piece for me there, the day before it was published in *the Star*. From the second it went up, Sarah keenly monitored the reactions on the blogosphere. Immediately, there was an incredible level of response. Within a few hours, there had been more than 20,000 hits and in excess of 400 comments, almost all expressing outrage at the way Raila had treated me. Subsequently, *The Daily Nation* also published my "A Note for my friends" a few days after it had appeared in *the Star*.

The support that Sarah gave me at that time was invaluable. Among my close friends, she had been the first to react in a manner that demonstrated genuine concern. She took personal umbrage over Raila's decision, the timing and the manner in which it had been done and expressed her disappointment to Raila too, in the following letter:

> *From Sarah Elderkin to Raila Odinga*
> Nairobi, August 6, 2011
> Dear Raila,
> Please find enclosed a number of documents related to Miguna's sacking which I'd advise you to read. I am sending them to you because I think they are otherwise things you will not read.
> They are:
> 1. Online responses to Miguna's sacking
> 2. A column by Otieno Otieno in the *Sunday Nation* (in case you missed it)
> 3. An article by Miguna that I understand will appear in *the Star* on Tuesday
> 4. Online responses to this article, which has already appeared on the internet.
>
> I am advising you to read particularly the online comments, because they largely speak of you, and of discontent with you and your office. I have not edited them and there was virtually no comment supporting the action of your office.
>
> I personally think that what has happened is appalling. When I heard of it, my first thought was Moi, and the trepidation with

which people awaited the one o'clock news and roadside declarations about their sacking. It is terrible that an action of your office should reduce me, of all people, to that kind of comparison.

Apart from being completely ill-advised that you rid yourself of one of the best brains you have around you (and you have got some nincompoops, that's for sure) this has been done in the most disgusting fashion. Public executions went out in the UK a couple of hundred years ago. They were mourned by some as a loss of a spectator sport.

That a man who has been so loyal to you and to the party and put so much of himself into defending it against destructive incursions from outside should be publicly lynched in this manner is something I cannot and will never be able to condone. It is primitive and uncivilised and inhumane. How is this person ever to retrieve his reputation and continue with his life? Was this necessary? It's a disgrace.

And that is not to go into the details. Suspended without pay? Apart from the fact that this is completely illegal, Miguna has five young children at home to take care of. Inhumane or what? What message does this give about you and your office?

You have people around you playing major roles who are irredeemably corrupt. Two of them were suspended earlier and then incomprehensibly reinstated. They were suspended on full pay and benefits. Now you have a man who is totally loyal and not involved in your office staff's blatant, well-known all over town, corruption, yet he is 'suspended' without pay and this is activated by one of those whose integrity I wouldn't trust beyond a yard away from me, someone the whole town talks about.

Miguna gets no chance to hear and answer allegations? This is against the most basic of labour laws and totally contrary to natural justice.

Hearing about it through the media, and in such a spectacular character-assassination way? Well, words fail me. I would never have thought any action by your office would come to this.

Issuing all Miguna's staff with sacking letters? What have they done? What depths of inhumanity can we sink to here? And then changing the locks on Miguna's office so he cannot even retrieve his own belongings. Is he a criminal now?

What a shabby, mean, indefensible and contemptible way to treat anyone. More important, what a demonstration of business as usual, new Constitution or not.

You know that I will defend you through thick and thin. However, I have my standards and integrity and I will not compromise those for anyone.

I consider it my duty and obligation to tell you privately exactly what I think of this utterly shameful episode. Only you can rectify the damage done, both to Miguna and, even more importantly, to yourself.

Please read the enclosed documents. Things in your office and in the party appear to have got drastically out of kilter with what we all thought we stood for.

Sarah

Sarah was livid. Unlike the timid, cowardly and hypocritical Anyang' Nyong'o and James Orengo who pussy-footed around the issues, communicating to me through third parties, imploring me to keep quiet as they tried to "talk with Raila" (which I'm sure they never did or if they did, only in the usual timid manner of "yes Sir"), Sarah candidly spoke her mind. Strangely, following the suspension, she advised me that she might have done me in by "recently praising you to Raila". She had observed over the years Raila becoming envious of people around him with talent. Apparently, Sarah felt that Raila was jealous of intelligent, disciplined and hard-working people with integrity.

A few weeks before I had been suspended, Sarah had told Raila and his wife Ida, how happy she was that I was working with him. According to Sarah, she had asked Raila to promote me: "Give Miguna a more meaningful job where he could make real decisions and help you deliver on your core mandate. Listen more to people like Miguna who take their time to do solid research then prepare detailed briefs on your core mandate". In one of my subsequent discussions with Raila's wife Ida, who had her government office opposite mine, she had mentioned that Sarah had praised me to them and urged Raila to give me a position with more substance. But it's now obvious that Raila resented the support I was getting from people like Sarah.

I'm not sure what Sarah had had in mind, but I knew the limitations of being an advisor. I had mentioned to her, in passing, that I wouldn't have minded serving either as attorney general or permanent secretary for justice. Both positions were vacant at the time. But I quickly reminded her of what Orengo and Caroli had said: "Miguna will jail everybody if is he is the attorney general or the director of public prosecutions or the director of the Kenya Anti-Corruption Commission."

I had been baffled. In ODM, Orengo was supposed to have been my ally: a progressive lawyer with solid reform credentials. Caroli, too, had pretended to be my friend. In any event, we had all worked under Raila in one party called ODM. That ought to have counted for something. But perhaps their fear was that I would have actually carried out my duties diligently in accordance with the law and without any fear or favour.

Two columnists – Otieno Otieno of the *Sunday Nation* and Godwin Murunga of *the Star* – boldly told Raila in successive articles immediately after the suspension, that he had made a fatal error by sacrificing his strongest and best fighter when he was going into war. In an article, "Why Miguna Miguna is irreplaceable on Raila team," Otieno argued that "...Kenyan politics is not a game of golf. Its brutish nature makes it almost suicidal not to rally enough Migunas to your side or hold tightly onto the one you have going into a tough presidential election battle. It doesn't look wise either to face up to a wounded opponent like Mr William Ruto or Mr. Uhuru Kenyatta with a battalion of safe-playing careerists and paper tigers. As political attack dogs go, they don't come any better than Mr Miguna. Fiercely loyal and passionate, he brings sharp intelligence to a job dominated by sycophants – which make him such a rare talent..." Murunga added that Raila needed not just intelligent defenders; he badly required those who could bravely tell him the truth.

The media continued to run stories and profiles of me. On Monday August 8, 2011, the *Daily Nation* had a special two-page pull-out titled "Love him, hate him, Miguna Miguna, the suspended aide to the Prime Minister, is no stranger to controversy. Are we seeing the last of him?" They retraced my background to the tumultuous University of Nairobi period and painted me as a man who "was destined to kick up controversy". What was – and has been missing – in all the stories written about me, is that I am a man who has fought against injustice and stood up for freedom and equality throughout my life; that I have always chosen to fight against oppression no matter how dire the consequences. When my children's worried faces were scrutinising mine for comfort and reassurance during the wall-to-wall coverage of my suspension, I showed them defiance, resistance and optimism. I needed them to know that even though we could no longer go to Lamu, I would provide them with protection, even with my bare hands

"A Note for my friends", was published in *the Star* on August 9. After seeing the trauma my family, relatives and friends were going through and their desperate attempts to come to terms with the reality that I had been cut loose and hung out to dry, this column was my attempt to calm nerves, if you will. I'm not sure if I succeeded. I didn't want to join the speculators; neither was I ready then to 'spill the beans'.

I explained in great detail what had transpired before the shocking news broke, and concluded by stating: "I know I am very passionate about Kenyan politics. I also know we have a tradition in this country of both allies and rivals massaging each other's egos, pretending everything is OK, and covering up each other's faults and transgressions. It is a tradition throughout Africa. We only have to look at the AU and at the way African leaders close ranks to defend some of the worst despots this continent has ever seen.

"So when I tell it like it is, and some people get stung, others might feel I go too far in my criticism. But that is because I want Kenya to become a better place, and I get angry when I see the reform process being undermined. I don't have any apologies to make about this.

"If anyone thinks that in my enthusiasm to champion what is right I have overstepped the mark, well, I apologise to their ingrained sensibilities. But I will not be silenced in my pursuit of what is right and good for this country, even if I pursue it alone".

In the weeks and months that followed my suspension, I would consult widely and discuss Raila's betrayal with many respected lawyers, scholars, human rights defenders, diplomats and media personalities. I also read reactions of readers and bloggers. Pleasantly, I discovered that tens of thousands of Kenyans and friends of Kenya strongly objected to the manner in which Raila had executed the suspension. They questioned why he hadn't met with me first and explained the "reasons", if there had been any. They criticised the fact that Raila had leaked the suspension letter to the media and defamed me while I was representing him at an ODM strategy meeting in Naivasha. They challenged why Raila hadn't suspended any of his senior officers who had been accused and continued to be accused of grand corruption. More still demanded to be told the specific charges against me, with facts, not innuendos and propaganda. They all felt that Raila had betrayed me before subjecting me to gratuitous abuse. Initially, many of these people called me, sent me text messages and emails. A few even visited me at home or took me out for breakfast, lunch or dinner. They expressed their sympathies and support. Many encouraged me to soldier on. A few lawyers like Muite advised me to take legal action in order to protect and defend my rights, which they believed had been flagrantly violated.

So, on August 11, having waited for Raila to respond to my text messages and unanswered calls in vain, and having received neither my outstanding dues or personal effects, Mugambi Imanyara sent a lawyer to me, whom he said he had retained for me as a way of supporting a "fallen friend". Through him, I subsequently filed an application for judicial review of the suspension at the High Court in Nairobi. I sought to nullify the suspension, not because I wanted the job back or would have resumed if the application had been granted; no, I commenced action as a way of telling Raila that he couldn't trample over my rights without resistance. I needed to demonstrate to the country my commitment to the rule of law. I felt that it was important for Kenyans to understand that power and wealth shouldn't place anyone above the law; that under and before the law, everyone is equal, or at least ought to be. I also wanted to demonstrate to everyone that my support and defense of Raila wasn't unconditional. My support was firmly pegged on Raila's consistent adherence to the principles of democracy, good governance and the rule of law.

On Thursday, August 11, Raila's daughter Rosemary called me. Although I had by now decided not to answer calls from Orengo, Caroli, Isahakia and Nyong'o, I took Rosemary's call. "I just called as a friend…" That's all she said. By then, I had openly challenged Raila's reform credentials and implied that he wasn't an agent of change. In the coming weeks and months, I would appear on countless TV shows, publish articles and write this book.

On August 12, I decided to revisit the issue of my suspension in *the Star* because some malicious people had continued to use the media to misrepresent what had happened. I explained that the offer of employment I had accepted from both the Prime Minister and Ambassador Francis Muthaura, had been for the position of senior advisor to the Prime Minister at Job Group "V", the same level as Muthaura, my counterpart Kivutha Kibwana and then Presidential advisor Raphael Tuju. I also explained that I hadn't sued to get my job back as such; I had commenced legal action in order to enforce my legal rights and to compel Raila to uphold the law and the constitution.

Revisiting the entire episode was painful but necessary. I needed to get certain things off my chest. I'm the kind of person who hates going to bed angry. My wife and children know this about me. I believe in having issues settled quickly so that they don't bog you down. So, I wasn't going to let Raila Odinga's transgressions weigh me down.

Whatever truly motivated Raila to suspend me is not known; at least by me. I believe the "reasons" – whatever they are – had nothing to do with the allegations advanced in the suspension letter. Nor are the "reasons" Raila's cousin, Jakoyo and Caroli broadcasted – that I was purportedly interfering in politics – legitimate. Furthermore, it was curious that they would be complaining about my role in politics when I was the most senior advisor to the Prime Minister on coalition affairs. Coalition affairs included political, constitutional, legal and parliamentary issues. The Prime Minister is first and foremost a politician. He got his position through politics. And as someone with ambitions of becoming President, everything Raila did or said had political import. Moreover, one cannot advise any politician without being involved in politics.

Whatever the reasons for the suspension, the manner in which it was done exposed Raila as a liar, a coward and an erratic, malicious and vindictive man. More than that, it demonstrated the terrible cold callousness of a man so cold-blooded that he did not care about my children and wife, nor about the contributions I had made, nor indeed the fact that his action had nothing to do with anything I had done. Raila and his family – Jakoyo Midiwo, Oburu Oginga and Ida Odinga – might have thought that they were eliminating a potential competitor to the Luo leadership mantle. They might have deluded themselves that by this single act of grand betrayal, they were preparing a smooth succession from Raila to Fidel or Jakoyo. However, by that act, Raila transformed a loyal, dedicated and disciplined general in the war for the third and final liberation of Kenya into a mortal enemy. He had knifed me in the back without warning, reason or justification. The act exposed a deeply buried psychological flaw that defies definition. It also exemplified the English saying: "no good deed goes unpunished."

To have suspended me through the media without notice or explanation, to have summarily fired my staff without any notice or reason within one hour of disseminating the suspension letter to the media, to have withdrawn my security and illegally withheld my salary and benefits defies logic and justification. But when he also had the locks on my office doors changed, with my personal effects inside, and then proceeded to deny me access to them, he went beyond what in common law is called malice aforethought. He breached all lines of human decency and crossed into the boundary of barbarism. That's why only the word evil defines how I feel about Raila's action. To those who are quibbling over my anger and apparent bitterness, I would like to say this: I am human and I have a right to feel angry and bitter. Nobody has the right to dictate to me how to feel, in view of what Raila has subjected me to. I will never sacrifice myself for Raila again, ever. I will never work with or for Raila ever again.

When, shortly afterwards, a friend of mine asked me what had happened, I could only say this: "Raila has made his bed. He must now sleep on it. If he made a bed of thorns; he must endure the pain. However, if he made a bed of roses; he is entitled to enjoy the aroma."

My wife is still now, slowly recovering from the shock. She was very angry at the manner in which Raila had treated me. She recalled her earlier misgivings about Raila. My daughter Suré was the only child who sought to know what had happened between Raila and me. We rambled on but couldn't conjure up a sensible answer. My wife said something about "Raila is not a good person…he betrayed your Dad" then stopped. I explained to the child that in the world, there were people who lie, who cheat, who hurt others for nothing and that Raila is one such person. My other children simply observed but didn't say anything. A day after I returned Biko and Atieno to Toronto, their mother, Tracey, called me to inquire about "what had happened". Biko had mentioned about the police officer's departure from the home and all the commotion in the media. "Well, whatever has a beginning has an end," I had said, and we had left it at that.

CHAPTER TWENTY

YOU'VE MADE YOUR BED, NOW YOU MUST SLEEP IN IT

"Why didn't you resign upon discovering that Raila Odinga was a political conman?" This is a question many people have asked in response to my decision to go public about Raila Odinga's fundamental and irreconcilable contradictions and betrayals. Some have argued that if I wasn't satisfied with the working environment at OPM, I should have left myself before I was pushed out. Others believe I should have gone public with the issues I am raising now as and when those concerns arose. For his part, Caroli Omondi, the Prime Minister's private secretary, went on national television to challenge me to file my complaints with the "authorities". 'Why write a book about allegations that should be reported to the Kenya Police?' others have asked.

Clearly, some of these questions and comments are fair and legitimate. Others, however, aren't expressed in good faith. Let's begin with the suggestion that I shouldn't have continued to work at OPM if I wasn't happy with Raila or the work environment. I consider this to be one of the most mischievous assertions. Firstly, if every time someone was unhappy with something at work they quit, any kind of corporate or institutional stability or positive change would be inconceivable. Our successes should be judged, not on our abilities to avoid conflicts or disputes which are inevitable in all human relations, interactions and civilisations, but on our abilities to manage and resolve them. Surrendering and/or fleeing might not always be the most prudent or desirable path. Challenging and overcoming adversity is more glorious than succumbing to difficulties. In my specific situation, the issues I encountered and often confronted were issues of governance, democracy, rule of law, constitutionalism or their absence and threats to them, thereof. These aren't issues one can or could resolve through quitting. Confronting and challenging the situations and persons that perpetuate the culture of impunity is, in my considered view, the best solution. Resignation in this case would only have entailed leaving government employment to the corrupt, the lethargic, the lazy and the incorrigible. My view is that the question is poorly conceived, constructed and asked. The proper question should be: why can't Raila and other latter day agents of change clean the skunks out of their offices? Yes, why can't they get rid of the merchants of impunity that are threatening to derail, sabotage and reverse all the reforms we fought for and are now trying to implement?

Secondly, the question of the timing of these criticisms is critical. It is a fair, proper and genuine question to ask but an even better question might be: did I or did I not disclose, challenge and oppose the ills I now rail against while I was working as a senior advisor to the Prime Minister of the Republic of Kenya? Have I really only spoken about these ills after I was suspended? Available public records disclose that I have been a thorn in the side of the establishment ever since I was a lanky teenager at the University of Nairobi. Those struggles, as the early chapters of this book bear out, resulted not just in my detention without trial and torture, they led to my exile. In exile, I had the option of taking the easy way out, making money and forgetting the past. But what did I do? I chose to continue the struggle against all forms of oppression, exclusion and exploitation. I fought against racism, discrimination and xenophobia in Canada and the political dictatorship in my homeland. I struggled for academic freedom as much as I did for racial equality. I demonstrated against cultural exclusivism and superiority as much as I have consistently done against tribalism. On my return to Kenya, I fought against the 2007 electoral fraud and civilian coup as doggedly as I am now fighting against Raila's emerging culture of intolerance, corruption and dictatorship. I did so before I was employed as Raila Odinga's advisor on coalition affairs. And I have continued to do so after my employment.

If anyone doubts the veracity of these claims then all they need do is log onto the internet or visit a public library. There they will find old newspaper cuttings, TV clips and radio recordings. They will encounter reels of my voice, my writings, my agitation. In the archives, there will be minutes upon minutes of ODM strategic meetings, ODM Pentagon records, minutes of government meetings as well as records of consultative meetings held by the Committee of Experts in Kenya. My name is writ large on the blogosphere. All of these records will prove that I have devoted years of my life to reading, researching, thinking, writing about and fighting for freedom, liberation, equality, equity, good governance, respect for human rights, adherence to the rule of law and constitutionalism.

I have done that out of choice and commitment, indeed for the more than 30 years I've been deeply and intricately involved in the struggle to make the world a better place than I found it. I wasn't doing it for Raila Odinga, or ODM or the grand coalition government. I was doing it for myself and for humanity. So, those claiming that I have only found my voice after the suspension are either trying to be too clever by half, or they suffer from a terrible bout of amnesia, either or both of which I decline to take responsibility for.

Caroli's ridiculous assertion that I shouldn't speak or write about the horrendous corruption and abuse of power I observed while working at the Office of the Prime Minister, that I should instead file a complaint with the so-called authorities, is comical. Caroli knows as well as anyone, that the record of the "Kenyan authorities" deserves another 600-page book or perhaps even a PhD dissertation – and I promise to attempt either of the two, in the near future. Since we obtained our flag of independence, the authorities have only excelled in the perpetration of runaway corruption, politically motivated (but unresolved) assassinations, extra-judicial killings, tribalism, nepotism, and the wanton plunder and pillage of public resources such as land and forests. The 'authorities' have never credibly, competently, effectively and successfully investigated the serious crimes that have bedevilled our country for the past 50 years: drug smuggling, human smuggling, gun running, money laundering, ethnic cleansings, murders, theft and the complete desecration of our national heritage. Instead of apprehending criminals – including organised ones – *the authorities* collude with them. Caroli knows that reporting these allegations to the authorities would at best result in the information herein being used to extort money from the culprits, and at worst, result in the victimisation and persecution of me, the whistle-blower. I don't engage in exercises in futility.

So, why did I choose to write a book? We cannot develop and prosper without our ability to think and challenge existing, dominant or prevailing ideas and concepts. And the most basic instrument of testing and synthesising ideas is through thinking. But thought cannot be captured other than by some form of immutable record, like a book. The written word is more or less permanent. Ideas never die; and ideas whose times have come cannot be completely sabotaged. It's as old as humanity itself, this idea of thought, disputation, discussion and debate. This book has been both inspired and an inspiration, written under the heavy yoke of artificially imposed privations, human cruelty and animus. I have written this book because I have experienced and observed things that I believe Kenyans and friends of Kenya deserve, and are entitled to know. I have an inherent and fundamental right over my own life's narrative, which really is the core theme of any memoirs.

Public figures – or those who have been in public life, even if, like myself, only fleetingly – owe it to the society that bestowed that privilege of service on them, to share their experiences, point out pitfalls, highlight successes and values, and to record those things for posterity. But this book is not just about me. It is also about Raila Odinga and his administration. Once a person – any person – opts to vie for the highest *elective* office in the land, they must accept – indeed they have no option but to accept – that their life, public and private, will and must be closely scrutinised to determine their suitability for service.

Watching my five children grow, I see and discern one who is so young yet so gifted at reading my mind that she can sit there watching her Dad and go upstairs to get a pen just at the exact moment that I need it. Another is so creative and resourceful that she comes up with answers so complex, so sophisticated and so obviously above her age, her learning and her experiences, things she would never have encountered before so that one wonders where she gets those ideas from. Yet another one is so driven, competitive and ambitious that, at her tender age, she is in a hurry to read and devour all books and written material she encounters, including this book. Then another is so patient and kind and generous that her spirit sometimes reminds me of my long departed mother and inspires me. And finally, one who is so interested, captivated and inspired by anything and everything automotive that at the age of three, he knew all makes and models of virtually all vehicles being produced around the world. So, here I am, surrounded by love, warmth and inspiration in my home and then, beyond its perimeter, by hate in equal measure, trying to wade my way through life just as earlier thinkers, writers and revolutionaries have.

Most have implied that in writing this book I might be reacting in anger and bitterness and not out of a principled position. Their scepticism is understandable. I can't deny that I have been angry. Neither can I deny that a tinge of bitterness is completely absent from my voice and perspective. I am a human being after all. What Raila did to me was inhumane. It was also unlawful and cruel. Even the most noble and forgiving person would have felt deeply betrayed and hurt. It was a blatant violation of my constitutional and legal rights. It also flagrantly violated the law of natural justice.

Yes, I didn't raise publicly most of the frustrations I felt for the two and a half years I worked at the PM's office. But I raised all these and other issues with Raila on various occasions privately, just between the two of us, and in the presence of a few trusted colleagues and confidantes. Most of these issues were raised with him both verbally and in writing. I had valid reasons for how I went about things and would do precisely the same if I ever found myself in similar circumstances. I couldn't, in good conscience, raise these issues publicly and still have continued to serve. If I had done that, many now criticising me would have called me irresponsible and uncouth and they would have had good reasons for saying those things. But more profoundly, I would have lost the trust and confidence of the person I was advising. Trust is a core component of the job of an advisor. Without it, one cannot be effective. On three separate occasions, I seriously contemplated resigning and consulted Sarah Elderkin, Salim Lone, James Orengo, Prof. Edward Oyugi and my wife. They all expressed support and understanding of what I was going through but they all advised me to stay put. Orengo, Sarah and Salim felt that ODM needed me at the OPM more than ever before. My wife was genuinely concerned about my future and our family's livelihood. They all urged me to persevere. It's therefore the height of dishonesty, hypocrisy or ignorance for some Raila sycophants to impute that I can't complain about what I experienced there merely because I didn't resign.

The decision to join the Raila Odinga presidential quest wasn't made whimsically. I carefully thought through the pertinent issues and weighed them up before taking the plunge. By 2006, I had been in Canada for about 19 years and most of the conditions that had previously prevented my return from exile no longer existed. Moi had retired in 2002. Multiparty politics had been reintroduced in 1992. The last time anyone had been detained without trial in Kenya was in 1988. So, quite clearly, the political environment had significantly improved. The only problem was that we were still in Kenya being governed under the old retrogressive constitution. So, when I was finally able to connect directly with Raila Odinga, I made the decision to work with him to change that. Other than what I had gathered from the media and third parties, I knew nothing about the man. I knew, of course, that he had spent eight years in detention without trial. I knew also that he was involved – at different stages of the struggle – in the constitutional review process. And I also knew that he was the son of Jaramogi Oginga Odinga, the doyen of liberation politics in Kenya.

By the time I was selling my house and relocating with my young family to Kenya, Raila had emerged as the ODM presidential candidate and I had declared that I would run for the Nyando Constituency seat. Together with Sarah Elderkin (with Adongo Ogony on the sidelines), we had prepared a searing statement for Raila's presidential campaign launch. It made fundamental undertakings and promises. It defined where the struggle for our national emancipation was. That struggle, we argued, needed clear vision, focus, courage, discipline and commitment. It demanded fearlessness. It wasn't about parochial personal interests. It wasn't about provincial considerations. The struggle for the third and final liberation of Kenya was and remained the struggle for democracy, equality, equity and respect for human rights. It was a struggle to create, entrench and perpetuate the culture of constitutionalism, the rule of law and respect for human rights. It was also the struggle not just for basic needs, but for creating a modern, technologically advanced and just society. At its core, it was the struggle for social justice.

How could I whimsically resign from such a grandiose scheme and vision? Raila and I were but two individuals in the struggle involving millions of Kenyans. How could I easily abandon the struggle, which wasn't about me, personally? Moreover, having left our secure existence in Canada far behind, there were pragmatic considerations. How would I support myself and my family? What would I tell my wife who was then completing her university studies, or my children who were attending school? They had taken a huge risk too, in coming from Canada to Kenya and trusting in my vision for our future.

Yes, I nursed the resignation option for more than one year. The idea and need for this book was largely conceived during that traumatic period. Barely six months after taking up my appointment, I had confided in Salim Lone, Professor Edward Oyugi, James Orengo, Sarah Elderkin, Joab Agar Okello, Banda Nyaware, Maurice Adongo Ogony and my wife the frustrations I was experiencing. I explained to them the contradictions I was observing in the PM. In fact, we had individually concluded that Raila Odinga was probably a political conman, a master manipulator, a man whose middle name was deception. That deep down he didn't seem to have the fire, the drive, the belief or the commitment for fundamental changes that we had for all those decades thought he had. But I was still at that point struggling to reconcile in my own mind the Raila I saw from day-to-day with the heroic vision I had once had of Raila the liberation hero. I couldn't quite believe that the chaotic carpetbagger before me bore no relation to the man who had once been prepared to sacrifice his own life for other Kenyans' freedoms. So I was disappointed, but my faith in Raila hadn't yet been entirely extinguished. In hindsight, I probably should have resigned but with the benefit of hindsight who wouldn't plot out their life differently?

Since my suspension, I have vented my criticisms of Raila and the OPM. For example, I published an article in October 2011 titled, "Raila, obey the Constitution or remain in the past", articulating some of the problems I had with

Raila's political direction. I know many people won't want to remember these pieces in their quest to portray me as something other than what I am. If I was desperate to get my job back, as some malicious people have falsely claimed, why was I writing and publishing these articles? If I was only interested in advancing my personal interests, why didn't I take on board the avalanche of opportunistic advice that I should keep my head down until the king remembered me? Why indeed was I continuing to make noise – the same noise I have been making since I was a teenager? And when eventually the king woke up from his slumber and attempted a half-hearted reinstatement, which I describe in detail in the last chapter of this book, why didn't I rush to resume my duties?

Raila Odinga has loudly and consistently claimed that he was a significant architect of the Constitution of Kenya, 2010, a constitution that enshrines, entrenches and guarantees everyone's fundamental rights and freedoms, including the right to the due process of law. Article 3 of the Constitution states that "every person has an obligation to respect, uphold and defend the Constitution". The Prime Minister – like the President – took an oath and swore that he would defend and uphold the Constitution. That's a positive duty on his part. He cannot choose which parts of the constitution to defend or uphold, and which parts or provisions to ignore or violate. Nor can he choose who those rights and freedoms apply to, where or when. Everyone is equal before and under the Constitution.

The Bill of Rights of the same constitution recognises, guarantees and entrenches every person's right to fundamental freedoms, dignity, social justice and the realisation of his or her potential. Significantly, the Bill of Rights applies to all law and binds all State organs and all persons. Power, wealth, class or position does not exempt anyone from the obligations under the Constitution. Indeed, Article 21 provides that it is a positive fundamental duty of the State and every State organ (and persons holding State power and responsibility) to "observe, respect, protect, promote and fulfil the rights and fundamental freedoms in the Bill of Rights".

Under the Bill of Rights, every person has the right to institute court proceedings if a right or fundamental freedom in the Bill of Rights has been denied, violated or infringed, or is threatened. Every person's freedom from torture and cruel, inhuman(e) or degrading treatment or punishment and the right to a fair trial, among others, is equally safeguarded. Freedom of conscience, religion, belief, opinion and expression are also guaranteed, as is the right to be free from all discrimination. Finally, article 35 states that every citizen has the right of access to information held by the State and by another person or other persons required for the exercise or protection of any right or fundamental freedom.

So, given that Raila claims to be an architect of that constitution and has been mandated by the Kenyan people to be one of its principal upholders, it is ironic that the manner in which Raila suspended me violated so many of my basic rights. And then, to add insult to injury, he tried to offer my talented colleague and good friend Mutakha Kangu, my staunch ally on the constitutional review process, *my* job. Wisely, Mutakha was alive to the fact that Raila's office was a nest of vipers and a den of confusion, disorganisation, envy, jealousy, sloth and corruption. He was sensible enough to realise that working with Isahakia and Caroli would be impossible for him. He knew they were lazy, malicious and very petty. He also knew that Raila wasn't interested in change and reforms, that he gave lip service to Agenda Four reforms. Deep down, Mutakha knew that Raila was now all about maintaining the status quo.

Raila has never come clean on why he turned against me. In the process, he has behaved like a rabid dog that bites itself and the owner. I am not suggesting I was Raila's owner. That would be obtuse. All I am doing is describing how rabid dogs behave. Because they are infected, they lose their senses and cannot distinguish themselves from other dogs. They cannot also distinguish a friend from a foe. A rabid dog bites anything and everything in its path. It's self-destructive. In my honest opinion, that's what Raila had degenerated into by August 4, 2011. He seemed incapable of separating his friends from his enemies. Nor was he capable of distinguishing petty from important issues. He spent too many hours bar-hopping like an adolescent. It was amazing to watch. He drank himself silly every day. He was rarely lucid or coherent. He also spent too much time with silly and cheap women – married and single, of all descriptions. He gave his personal security a hell of a time trying to keep him safe, secure and alive. He gave his strategists, minders and spin doctors like me hell trying to exercise damage control every time he opened his mouth. At times, two of his bodyguards – Ogeta and Lumumba – would plead with me to "please speak with *Jakom*. We know you are the only one who can do it…the rest are cowards…"

Raila was always seen in the company of women the Strategy Team jokingly referred to as 'the Pentagon groupies'. Many a time, we were appalled to find him eating food brought to him by women I felt to be wholly inappropriate such as Rachel Shebesh, Ann Kariuki and Esther Passaris. He seemed to have a strange weakness for women of all descriptions. If he wasn't drinking with such women, he was spending too much time with sycophantic nincompoops like Paul Gondi, Mike Njeru, Tony Chege (prior to December 30, 2007), Jakoyo Midiwo, Oburu Oginga, Caroli Omondi, Mohammed Isahakia, James Orengo and others I saw as simply lazy layabouts. Anyone with money, regardless of whether it was stolen or obtained by legal means, was given direct access to him: The Jimmy Wanjigis, Ahmed Kassams, the late Njenga Karumes, S.K. Macharias, Stanley Githunguris, Harun Mwaus, and Charles Njonjos – name them! The PM's office was host to a stream of characters holding briefcases and brown envelopes: drug dealers, money launderers, thieves, peddlers and pimps. Raila had become more of a political and a business dealer than a national leader. He was more comfortable with dubious wealthy men than with scholars, activists and intellectuals. In fact, Professor Oyugi kept reminding me, "*Ja-Loka*, Raila hates progressive intellectuals".

I now believe that, too. Raila, his family and relatives have become too greedy. They have also *all* become too wealthy too fast. They were in a mad rush to stash away billions of shillings they had not worked for. These are some of the most despicable things I witnessed working with Raila. His entire life is now driven by the worst kinds of human excesses: flesh, alcohol and money. He has become a walking contradiction. He pretends to be everything to everybody. To Moi, he wants to be seen as the worst and the greediest land grabber and wealth stasher. To Kibaki, he is a spineless coward who never stands up to any abuse, no matter how egregious. To Charles Njonjo and Company, he is a clueless man who never remembers his past. To the many women he spends his time with, he cares about nothing but sex. To those women he is also generous with money and jobs. Yet to his political male friends – those who shared detention camps, torture chambers, police cells and maximum-security prisons with him – he is cold, detached, unconcerned, insensitive, indecisive, envious and inhumane.

To please Moi, Francis Kimemia, Kinuthia Mbugua, Francis Muthaura, Moses Wetangula, Anyang' Nyong'o, Dalmas Otieno, Jakoyo Midiwo, Oburu Odinga and other newly minted oligarchs who were becoming very uncomfortable with my consistent exposure of corruption, Raila was prepared to 'assassinate' my character, reputation, career and future. And he did it, gleefully. He tried to besmirch my good name, reputation and character. I believe he personally authorised Isahakia to disseminate to the media concocted falsehoods about me in order to demonstrate to Moi and his orphans that he was tough and could deal with me. In exchange, he thought that Moi and Co would support him, throw him a political lifeline, if you will. But he miscalculated badly.

I'm not sure why Raila believes that he needs Moi and his relics of the last century. The majority of voters in Kenya are aged between 18 and 35. This constitutes about 65 per cent of the Kenyan electorate. This group is fairly educated, sophisticated and filthy poor. Most of them are also unemployed. They have no time for the Mois of this world. They want leaders who can and will improve their material conditions; those who have a vision and pragmatic plans to create employment and will build an environment conducive to development. They aren't interested in history, which is unfortunate. But happily, *they are specifically not interested in the history of rich oligarchs.*

So, Raila cosying up to Moi and Co gets him no political mileage whatsoever. If anything, it sinks him deeper into political muck. His traditional support base – the progressive element – has abandoned him, having discovered that he is a political conman. The youth have no time for him. They, too, have realised that his soccer commentaries, riddles and comedies don't put food on their tables. The Luos are deserting him in droves, too, having woken up to the hard reality that under Raila's premiership, the only Luos that are doing well are members of his immediate family. With my inhumane treatment, the Luo have finally said "enough!" They are voting with their feet at an alarming speed. Indeed, there isn't a single Kenyan in recent history who has attracted as much animus and as many complaints – both frivolous and genuine – as Raila Odinga. Those complaining about Raila aren't limited to any specific race, gender, class or ethnicity. Some are high-ranking politicians, civil servants, professionals, intellectuals, industry executives and junior officers, some even working at the OPM. Raila rides a storm of criticism every day, which makes his claim that my suspension was as a result of some undisclosed complaints all the more ridiculous.

Margit Helwig-Boettle, the German Ambassador to Kenya, took me to lunch at the Serena Hotel a few weeks after my ignominious trial by media. She had been with Raila in Kisumu when news of my suspension had broken. She had reportedly passed her mobile device to Raila and inquired if he knew about it. Raila had confirmed that he did. He had told her that I had had to go because he claimed I had "criticised the Speaker of the National Assembly Kenneth Marende and the Interim Independent Electoral Commission (IIEC) Chairman, Isaac Hassan." He was referring to two of my newspaper columns. The German Ambassador had tried to question the rationale, method and timing of the suspension, asking whether he had given me formal warnings, at which Raila had answered in the negative. She had then mentioned that in Germany, suspensions couldn't be done through the media and not without three formal warnings.

I learnt from my friend Onyango Oloo that Gitobu Imanyara, who had also then been present, had expressed his objections too. Oloo showed me a short text message Gitobu had sent him saying the same thing. Paul Muite telephoned me to say that he had actually spoken to Raila about the matter. In particular, Muite expressed shock at the manner in which the suspension had been announced (through the media), the illegality of withholding my salary and benefits, and the summary dismissal of my staff. He also mentioned that he couldn't understand why Raila had refused to release my personal effects to me. (All my dues, benefits and personal effects remain illegally detained by Raila to this day!) I guess it was the clearest sign that Raila had dictatorial tendencies, just like Moi.

Anyone who could do what Raila did to me is irredeemably unfeeling. He knew I had a wife and five children, all then students. My wife was completing her undergraduate studies at Daystar University. My older children were studying in Canada, while my younger three girls were at Makini School in Nairobi. All of them were returning to school at the beginning of September. The total cost of tuition and back-to-school purchases would be around Sh1.5m. In addition, I had spent more than $12,000 (about Sh1.4m) on return fares to Canada for the children and me. On top of it all, we needed money for daily sustenance. Raila knew all this and yet he ordered not just my suspension; he imposed additional punitive and unlawful conditions that I wasn't to receive any payment whatsoever.

Why would anybody do that except to inflict maximum suffering and pain? Why did Raila feel that my wife, children and I should be subjected to such hardship? Why did he order my security withdrawn when he knew that I had made enemies merely by being perceived as his strongest defender? Why did he change the locks to my office and refuse to release my personal effects? Why? My salary and benefits weren't coming from Raila's pocket. Nor was he paying for my security. So, why did he do what he did?

We had had our internal party and office disagreeements. I had vehemently opposed, on ideological grounds, ODM's desertion of its electoral commitment to pursue a parliamentary system in the constitutional review process. I had also objected to the inhumane manner in which peasants had been evicted from the Mau Forest, while a blind eye had been turned to oligarchs' business interests there. But these differences of opinion weren't just normal under the circumstances; they were also healthy and ought to have been encouraged.

Perhaps, also, the more I became popular, the more Raila became insecure. Raila knew that, unlike many people working with or for him, I had never relied on him for handouts. Nor had I relied on him to make me; I was already a successful barrister and solicitor when we met. Similarly, I had already made a name for myself as a commentator when we met. I had built my Runda house entirely from my savings before I moved to Kenya.

Why then would some pesky and malicious people question my intentions in writing this book? Like Raila, I have dreamed of higher political office. But while working at the OPM, I never said or did anything that anyone could remotely have construed as jockeying for power or leadership of ODM. Unlike my other colleagues, like Adhu Awiti who openly canvassed – even engaged in physical altercations with his political opponents – for leadership positions in the party and at the constituency level, I refrained completely from such activities. In any event, why is it right and proper for Raila to dream and not me? I have been a leader all my life. I wouldn't have been elected into leadership positions in secondary school, high school and university if I had no leadership skills. But I have also aspired to and been driven by high ideals.

I may have grown up dirt poor, but I can still dream as big as Raila Odinga. Where he might have felt a sense of entitlement because of his father's exalted position in society, I saw hills and valleys I had to climb and rivers and lakes I had to swim across if I was to reach my destination. Unlike Raila, my destination wasn't State House. I dreamt of it, of course. But as a pragmatist, I couldn't think that far.

CHAPTER TWENTY ONE

PEELING BACK THE MASK

I saw two missed calls from the Prime Minister of the Republic of Kenya, Raila Amolo Odinga. My Blackberry phone had just developed some strange mechanical problems and wasn't ringing. I had bought a replacement handset two weeks before, but because I hadn't imported all the 2,000-plus contacts into it, I was still using my old phone and hadn't heard or seen the incoming calls. It was Tuesday December 27, 2011, at 12.15pm. I had pulled up beside the road to take another call. The first missed call had been logged on my mobile at 11.49am; the second one at 11.50am. I had been expecting Raila's call.

That morning, I had had a breakfast date with my good friend and confidante, Patrick Quarcoo, the Chief Executive Officer of the Radio Africa Group, at The Sarit Centre. This was a follow-up to another breakfast Patrick and I had had at the Java Gigiri. Each breakfast date started at 8.30am, and lasted for more than three hours.

It wasn't unusual for Patrick and I (or his business partner and CEO of their newspaper, *the Star*, William Pike and I) to have an early breakfast meeting at this joint. Although I had pulled my column from *the Sta*r in November after what I had felt to be an inappropriate level of editorial interference. In my article about an attack on presidential candidate Raphael Tuju, references to Raila that were entirely germane to the piece had been excised without my permission – (this had come on the back of a request by the management 'to go easier on Raila', because he had been complaining…) I remained on excellent terms with both Patrick and William who had earlier stood by me at my darkest hour. Whenever we met, it was usually at Java, Gigiri. Indeed, if there is any meeting place in the republic I frequent more than any other, it is Java, Gigiri. I even have a specific corner table, which both my friends and the waiters at the Java call my "office." It is at this corner table that many important discussions on matters big and small have taken place over the years.

It was at this table, that I used to regularly meet Orengo, Prof. Oyugi, Mutakha Kangu, Nabii Nabwera, Waikwa Wanyoike, Mugambi Imanyara, Salim Lone, Mugambi Kiai, Laetitia van den Assum, Onyango Oloo, Dr Migot Adhola and plot, scheme, strategise, discuss, argue, debate, laugh, sentimentalise, agonise and resolve some of the most delicate, intractable and important national, even international, issues of our time. Of all my friends, it was Patrick, William and Laetitia who had spent more hours with me around that table than anybody else.

During the week of December 19, Patrick and I had had lunch like we had on many other occasions, and discussed my situation: first, some TV assignment he was working out for me with his media house; second, a media idea I had; and thirdly, we spoke of my unravelling, but unending situation with Raila. Patrick disclosed, very cagily, some details of his most recent discussions about me with Raila.

This wasn't the first time that Patrick had revealed that he had been talking about me to Raila. According to Patrick, Raila had promised to pay me all my dues even before the matter went back to court on November 4. And yet, for some strange and unexplained reason, Raila hadn't made good on his word. That was a sticking point for me. I told Patrick that I would now find it difficult to trust Raila on anything. But Patrick persisted, coming across as my honest, down-to-earth-friend who was just trying to do everything within his power to lift a fallen comrade out of the ditch that somebody had pushed him into. So, I heard Patrick out.

Raila had come up with what seemed like a genuine and *practical* solution to our *problem*. For the four months since August 4, I had consistently told any friends who had approached me with undefined and unauthorised 'offers' – such as Prof. Oyugi and Salim Lone – that *the issues* between Raila and I could only be discussed and resolved if Raila contacted me *directly.*

At least four times both Oyugi and Salim had spoken to me – separately – of plans to visit my house and discuss all the stumbling blocks to some kind of reconciliation between Raila and me, but each time, the meeting had never materialised. I waited for their confirmation telephone call to no avail. Then, they had suddenly stopped calling me. Oyugi had even stopped answering my telephone calls and texts. Salim was still responding, but more erratically, partly because of his book project and one or two deaths and ailments in his family. I concluded that someone somewhere (I wasn't sure who), was involved in some mind game with me. I'm not very good at political intrigues. I avoid them if I can. So, when Patrick had first mentioned that he had discussed me with Raila and suggested – to Raila and me – how we could resolve our issues amicably, I was quite sceptical, but out of my utmost respect for Patrick, I had told him that as long he could vouch for Raila, I was game.

Until the back-to-back breakfasts on December 26 and 27 I hadn't actually believed that Patrick was acting at the behest of Raila. However, when we met on December 26, Patrick had shown extraordinary passion and commitment, and given me undertakings that made me realise that something had changed. In fact, at the end of the December 27 meeting, Patrick had opened his wallet, taken out a $1 and torn it in two equal parts. He had looked at it pensively and said: "Here my brother; take one half, and I'll take the other half. Raila will call you today by midday. If he doesn't call, you keep that portion. However, if he calls, I get my dollar back." We had grabbed each other's hands tightly and had said together, as if on cue, "Deal!"

We had then parted, I, heading back home and Patrick scrambling to finish his day's meetings before heading back to his family in Kampala, Uganda. That's why I had been expecting Raila's call that day. It's also why I had called back after seeing his two missed calls. He hadn't answered and I had proceeded on my journey.

After 15 minutes, I saw another missed call from him, pulled onto the curb and called back. Once more, he didn't answer. However, barely two minutes later, as I was still sitting there in my vehicle, I looked at my Blackberry and saw "call from PM." I answered.

"Ja-Nyando, idhi nade?" he began, speaking in Dholuo, asking me how I was doing, but referring to me using the name of my birthplace's constituency. It's how Raila had greeted me since our meeting in Toronto in October 2006. He spoke just as he had done for all those long and difficult years when we had worked together strategising, scheming, planning, plotting and executing one tactical operation after another, laughing, arguing, and patting ourselves on the back for a job well done. I had promised Patrick that I would treat Raila with courtesy, respect and dignity. Every human being deserves that. That's the way I am; I believe in personal honour. I keep my side of the bargain. I deliver. I hold no petty, personal grudges, and I am absolutely free of vendetta and malice. Whatever I do, I do in good faith. My word is my bond. That's not just a cliché for me, it's the way I've lived my life.

"Adhi maber Jakom," I responded, assuring him that I was well, using the honorific *"Jakom,"* which is how I have always referred to him. (*Jakom* basically means "chairman" to the Luo community of Kenya.)

"I sent Patrick…Quarcoo to you. You spoke?"

"Yes *Jakom,* we spoke yesterday and today."

"Ok, where are you now?"

"I'm at home. Why?" That was a safe lie; I was in the neighbourhood.

"Well, because I wanted us to meet and chat."

"When and where would you like to do that?"

"You can come to the office, in 30 minutes? Hmm? Hmm?"

"Thirty minutes would be difficult *Jakom,* but I can make it in 45."

"Ok, 45 is ok."

"Oh, *Jakom,* I also would prefer not to come to the office, at least not today."

"Hmmm? Hmm? Hmm? Ok. Where would you like…because in another 30 minutes, I'll be going to the barber for a haircut, then I'm travelling out of the country later today…"

"We can do it at Serena, *Jakom.*"

"Hmmm? Hmm? Serena is ok; *kanyo ema adhiye kinyosi…*" He slipped back into Dholuo again, indicating that his barber was at Serena."

"Ok, *Ja-Nyando*; 45 minutes at Serena."

Immediately I hung up, I dialled my wife's telephone number. "Do you know who just called me?" I began.

"Who?"

"Raila."

"Hmmm! Really? *Janekono wacho ang'o?"* She wanted to know what 'that mad man' had to say for himself. My wife rarely expressed herself in colourful language, but ever since Raila had thrown me under a moving train she had become Raila's most vociferous critic. Since August 4, she couldn't even glimpse Raila on TV or see his picture in the newspapers without emitting some choice verbal projectile. She did it so frequently and with such venom that I at times had to remind her that no matter what the man had done, he was still a human being deserving of the same moral, legal and constitutional rights that I was demanding had to be observed. That's my wife; harmless, uncontroversial, polite, quiet and self-effacing, but when offended, betrayed, unfairly treated, or hurt, she will transform into the world's most lethal and unforgiving being. "He wants to meet with me. In fact, I'm heading out to meet him right now. He wants us to meet at his office but I've told him that I cannot go there now, not today. Anyway, what do you think?" I asked.

"Ok; *kiawa!"* Now, *kiawa* isn't a word that easily translates into English. It has no specific meaning. It's actually, all at once, for Luos, a sigh of uncertainty, cynicism, scepticism, doubt, wonder and polite disapproval. Having lived with

Jane now for more than ten years, I know when there isn't need for further discussion. This was one such moment. She had communicated her scepticism.

The next person I called was Patrick. I informed him that Raila had called and we were, in fact, to meet at the Serena, within minutes. I promised to keep him updated on the progress – if any – after the meeting.

I then turned my car around and headed straight towards town, reaching Serena within 25 minutes. It was as if the Nairobi traffic approved of our meeting; or perhaps very few people had obeyed the government order that all public servants were to resume work on December 27. Whatever, I literally "flew" to Serena. As I've indicated earlier, I'm a stickler for being on time for meetings or appointments. There was no way I would arrive late after having given my word to Raila. I was in my usual brown *safari* khaki pants and blue, long-sleeved shirt. There was no way in hell I was going to change into formal clothing.

By 12.40pm, I was seated at the Bambara lounge, typing away, trying to tidy up a chapter of this book that I had started writing earlier that morning. I had given my publisher a commitment that the entire book would be ready, in draft form, by early January 2012. They had in turn, given me their undertaking that the book would come off the press in the summer of 2012. And in view of Raila's (ongoing) interlocutions, I was even more determined to complete it and get it out of the way.

I knew that Raila and everyone around him must have been extremely nervous about the book. They knew me well enough to know that once I had promised the country, on live TV, that the book would be out before the next general elections, that I would do all it took to deliver on that vow. They were also scared of my way with words and what I might write about. My sixth sense, which I trust completely, was now sounding a red alert about the impending meeting. But I also knew that nothing short of death was going to stop me from delivering my book on time.

Then Patrick called. "Chief, I've been summoned."

"By whom?"

"By you know who! I'm on my way; will be with you in a few minutes."

I told Patrick where I was then sent Raila a text that I had arrived and was waiting in the Bambara lounge. However, by 1pm, he had neither arrived nor called. At around 1.15pm, I received a text message from Raila, saying he was on his way. He apologised for being late. That was nice and rare. Patrick arrived almost immediately after that and, like the business executive he is, quickly determined that we were better off having our conclave in a private room. Before I could say anything, he was at the reception desk. Two minutes later, he returned, declaring that he had secured us a private room.

Raila arrived at about 1.30pm. His bodyguard, Francis Oduor, came over to where Patrick and I were seated and gave me a hearty handshake. That was my first inkling that this was a huge political game, some cleverly crafted plot. Clearly, Oduor had been primed. Everyone had been given a role to play. I needed to carefully watch my step, everyone's movements and my surroundings. I was a pro; I knew which cards to play, and which to keep close to my chest. Raila is (in)famous for his 'political dexterity'. Nobody goes into a wrestling match with him unprepared. As he had once told me about Kalonzo, at the time they were competing to be the ODM's 2007 presidential candidate, "Miguna, when you are wrestling with someone, you try every trick in the book to fell him; you scratch, hold on and pull his scrotum, spit, gouge out his eyes, try to hit his knees and legs because, ultimately, the victor will be the person on top after the final bell is rung."

So, as I approached Raila, extending my hand, after our four-month orchestrated 'separation,' I was preparing myself emotionally and mentally.

"Ja-Nyando, how are you? How was your Christmas?" he asked, smiling as he grabbed my hand.

"It was OK. And yours?" I asked, reciprocating.

"Oh, I spent it in Bondo," he replied, as we walked towards the door to the private room.

In that brief exchange, I vividly saw not genuine friendship, good faith, or a reassuring signal that the man was ready to move on; I saw a poisoned chalice, being dangled precariously before me.

The conference-room was medium-sized and rectangular with an oval table in the middle, surrounded by chairs. Raila entered first and sat towards the middle of the table, with part of his back facing the door. Patrick followed closely and sat two chairs to his left. I quickly determined to sit one chair to the left of Patrick, but then noticed that it would place me at the head of the table, as if I was chairing the meeting. I stood there briefly, trying to make eye contact with both Raila and Patrick in order to assess whether that would be OK, but they didn't respond. So, I reluctantly sat at the head of the table. It was just the three of us.

Soon, a waiter walked in and asked for our orders. Raila ordered white coffee, Patrick ordered hot water with lemon, ginger and honey, what he and I called "dawa" at Java, Gigiri. I didn't feel like anything. The waiter returned with the drinks, plus a half-litre bottle of water for everyone, just as Raila was apologising, again, for coming late due to an endless stream of visitors at his office. He specifically mentioned a meeting with "the Chinese that took longer than expected". The small talk calmed some of the nerves in the room.

After he finished, there was a brief, awkward silence, which Patrick broke by clearing his voice and setting the ball rolling. "Thank you *Mzee* [a venerable Kiswahili word for an elderly person] for calling and attending the meeting. We all know why we are here. As you have already confirmed, you sent me to discuss the issues in contention with our brother, Miguna, and we are here to see if we can conclude those discussions and wrap that matter up before you leave today. What time is your flight, Sir?"

Patrick did the intro like a pro, which he surely was. I looked at him and smiled. Patrick was now some sort of mediator for both Raila and I, and he was executing his pro bono duties with the utmost professionalism. "I will perhaps now ask Miguna to state what his position is with respect to the issues and then we'll carry on from there," said Patrick, gesticulating to me to take up the conversation.

I tried to maintain eye-contact with Raila, but he kept looking downwards. That wasn't a good sign to someone who had lived in Canada for nearly two decades and placed significance in eye contact. I began by thanking Raila for, at long last, seeing the necessity and wisdom of getting in touch with me. I pointed out that immediately following the media announcement of the suspension I had tried to make contact, calling his mobile twice and sending him a text message, but without eliciting any response. I then mentioned that the manner in which my so-called suspension had been announced had been fundamentally unfair, inhumane, and in my view, completely unlawful and a demonstration of malice aforethought, which had all been compounded by the fact that I hadn't received any notice, nor had Raila met with me to explain why it had been done, or why it had been done in this way. In addition, I mentioned that it was illegal to suspend me indefinitely, without pay, to have locked up my personal effects and refused to give me access to them, and to have dismissed all my staff summarily for absolutely no reason. I dwelt at some great length on the callous and unwarranted manner my staff – two of whom had families that depended on their income – had been summarily fired, when everybody knew that the unfounded allegations against me had nothing to do with them. If the allegation was that I was discourteous to my colleagues and subordinates, my staff hadn't complained; instead, they were being victimised for refusing to be conscripted into other people's malicious and nefarious schemes.

I thanked Patrick for one of his companies' humanitarian offer of employment to my former messenger, although the decision had been William Pike's. Then I turned briefly to the allegations, stating that they were vague, general, bald and unparticularised. At all material times, I hadn't been provided with letters of complaint from anyone and my responses sought, as required by law; that my detailed demand for particulars had elicited absolutely no response, which could only be interpreted as further proof that the allegations were false. Nobody had provided dates, places, people and circumstances of the complaints that were specific and detailed to accord me a reasonable opportunity to respond, as required by law.

I indicated, as well, that since the announcement of the suspension, nobody had contacted me to seek my side of the story, nor had I been advised of any process instituted to investigate or to determine the veracity of the allegations on their merit. I said that I was astounded that "sources" around the PM had been quoted alleging that I had been suspended because I had gone to The Hague during the first appearance of the six Kenyans accused of crimes against humanity there, yet the PM himself had authorised the trip and directed Salim and me to go; that some had blamed me for insulting the former Attorney General, Amos Wako in Uganda when, again, the PM himself had authorised my trip and given me instructions on what to do while there. I asked Raila why he couldn't have simply asked Mutakha Kangu, Orengo or Amason Kingi who had accompanied me there for a report on what had happened instead of relying on rumours, innuendoes and misleading reports by the media. I told him that he knew why I had refused to sign the so-called "Local Agreement" which had been given to me more than one year after I had been appointed. The document had sought to fundamentally change the terms of my employment by reducing my remuneration to half of what I had been promised and upon which I had accepted the employment offer; and half of what my counterpart at the President's Office, Kivutha Kibwana, had been earning and continued to earn, thereby reducing me, my role, mandate and office to subservience in the coalition arrangement and operation vis-à-vis that of our coalition partner, PNU; a decision which even Raila had objected to in a letter to Muthaura, demanding that I be paid the same as Kibwana.

I emphasised to Raila that as a lawyer, I had fought long and hard to protect my clients' rights and interests throughout my professional life and that even as the Prime Minister's senior advisor on coalition affairs and Joint Secretary to the Permanent Committee on the Management of Grand Coalition Affairs my primary mandate had been to ensure that the coalition was managed, in all conceivable respects, as a coalition of equals. I questioned why he would not have wanted to ensure that I was not treated as a junior officer to my counterpart in all respects, and ventured that such treatment hadn't just been disgraceful, but illegal. I told him that I owed it to myself, to my profession and the dignity of the office, to either do as I have done for my clients, or even better. I pointedly told him that I would never sell myself short.

I then explained to Raila that every reasonable Kenyan, himself included, knew that the complaint that I had attempted to interfere with the Interim Independent Electoral Commission (IIEC) was completely unfounded, baseless and laughable. I didn't work for the Commission. Until my suspension, I hadn't heard of Major Oswago's personal assistant, on whose computer I understood some documents had allegedly been found. In any event, the young man had been Oswago's PA, not mine. Why someone of the PM's calibre should have thought that he needed to "sacrifice" me for Oswago beat logic, was unreasonable, unjust and very unfair. If Oswago and his PA had done something wrong – and I am not here suggesting that they did – why should I have been victimised? Was it because Oswago's position was more vital to the PM than mine? Why? Was it because the PM intended, or thought he could use Oswago – for whatever reasons – during the 2012 general elections? Mark you, it was I who had asked Oswago to apply for the IIEC job; he had been more interested in being the CEO of KACC.

The article I had written on incompetence, tribalism, nepotism and corruption at the commission had been requisitioned by ODM leaders. Raila knew that. Almost all my arguments had been contained in Prof. Nyong'o's letter to the IIEC – a letter I had actually drafted for Prof. Nyong'o, at his request. Why had I been sacrificed for carrying out the party's instructions? As well, the facts in my article were in the public domain and had never been credibly refuted by Hassan, or anybody else for that matter. Moreover, there was no evidence that I conspired with anyone at the IIEC to "attempt to rig the 2012 general elections" as had been scandalously alleged by Isaack Hassan.

Finally, I pointed out that Raila should never have discarded me like a piece of shit, throwing me to his political enemies, and mine (almost all of whom were my enemies because I had been Raila's strongest defender) without care, sensitivity, humanity or dignity.

When I finished, Raila began by acknowledging that I was a hard worker, intelligent and committed, that nobody doubted these things. He then stated that, by the same token, I was also alleged to be short tempered and some people claimed that I had hurt their feelings. He said that it was important that I knew and thought about that. Regarding the "reasons" for the suspension and the manner in which it had been executed, he said that he had authorised it after the brouhaha surrounding the allegations by Hassan that he, Raila, had been trying to interfere with the 2012 general elections by attempting to tinker with the formation of the Independent Electoral and Boundaries Commission (IEBC). He didn't assert that he was privy to any evidence linking me to any such attempts at alleged interference. He knew the allegations were hogwash, anyway.

He also mentioned that I had been very prolific in publishing articles in the media and that he had agreed with most of the opinions. He omitted to mention that he was the one who had asked me to start my weekly column in *the Star*. But he mentioned that the article I had published criticising the Speaker of the National Assembly, Kenneth Marende, for defending some MPs' refusal to pay taxes, had really aggrieved Marende. He didn't mention that he had disagreed with my article or that it was factually, logically or legally faulty; it was all about looking good.

Astonishingly, Raila mentioned that although he had authorised the suspension, his instructions hadn't been followed by my "enemies at the office". He sounded upset that those "enemies within" (whom he didn't mention) had purported to suspend me *sine die* and without pay which, in his own words, had been clearly illegal acts. He didn't say why he hadn't acted to right the wrongs committed by those "enemies." He tried to emphasise that he had intended the suspension to be temporary (very brief, he emphasised) "until the dust settled", after which I would have been reinstated, that he hadn't approved of releasing the suspension letter to the media, that he had wanted and would have preferred for it to have been a "hush, hush affair."

He omitted to explain why he hadn't simply instructed Isahakia to reverse what had been done if his instructions hadn't been followed correctly and, if Isahakia and those he referred to as my "enemies" had disobeyed his directives, what steps he had taken to deal with such serious acts of insubordination. Why had a loyal general been dehumanised for nothing yet those who had flagrantly disobeyed his orders been protected by him? He also didn't explain why he hadn't discussed the matter with me and explained his intentions beforehand, as he had done with Caroli and Isahakia when they had been "allowed" to "step aside" of their own volition before being "suspended" for three months because of credible allegations that they had both been deeply involved with the 'maize scandal'.

Earlier, when I had been outlining my case, I had asked the PM why Isahakia, who was more than 65 was still being kept on, even protected, when he would be the easiest person to remove by virtue of his age. "Why can't you just retire him?" I had asked. "Well, it's not that easy in an election year…" Raila had stated.

"But *Jakom*, can't you just do a sample, simple, unscientific survey by inquiring, starting from your drivers, bodyguards, secretaries, cleaners, cooks, et cetera, whom between Isahakia and me was most hated by his colleagues?"

"*Ja-Nyando*, I know Isahakia is hated more; in fact, I know that he has been frustrating many people, including Dr Adhu Awiti…"

"Thank you *Jakom*. It is good if you know."

So, quite clearly, Raila knew that I was innocent. He also knew that he had subjected me to barbaric treatment without any justification. But, in his mind, I could be sacrificed in the most beastly manner without fear that such treatment would generate enough of a political firestorm to jeopardise his ambitions. I was a Luo after all. Luos were supposed to be in Raila's back pocket; politically speaking. Isahakia, on the other hand, was a Somali who belonged to a tiny clan called "Isahakia". Even with numbers far below 5000, Raila was more assiduous in courting the tiny Isahakia clan than the numerically irrelevant Luo. My eyes were now wide open.

In order to save Raila's face (after all, he was still Prime Minister of the Republic and the leader of ODM), to avoid a back-and-forth discussion, which could belittle and undignify not just Raila but also myself and the occasion, I politely declined to respond once he was done. I wanted to avoid a situation where he left the place feeling ambushed and humiliated in front of Patrick. That's not my style, despite what my critics might think or believe. Contrary to popular myths (mainly peddled by vindictive and/or envious people) I conduct myself with absolute dignity.

I knew Raila knew the truth. At some point, Raila nonchalantly pulled out two documents from his coat pocket. The first one was an "opinion" by his office (I could see that from the letterhead, though he claimed it was from the Attorney General), recommending that I be terminated before December 30. Tactically appearing magnanimous, Raila stated that he had told his office that he would like to reinstate me instead. There was no mention of the "investigations", or any "reports" purporting to be recommendations arising therefrom. Nor did Raila mention why nobody had sought my side of the story. The second document was typed on a strip of plain copy paper. It contained my name and a new title of "Prime Minister's Advisor for strategic research, speech writing, new media, public policy and rapid response". I promptly told Raila that the "job" description falling under the new title looked like "clerical" duties, at which point he said that "we could still work on the appropriate job title, job description and agree on those details later". It sounded like 'talks about talks'.

I was very clear and categorical; I couldn't work with Isahakia, specifically, as he had stated that he didn't want to work with me, either. Also, through his actions, he had demonstrated malice aforethought. Raila said that was all right; that he was aware of Isahakia undermining other members of his staff like Dr

Adhu Awiti. He stated that nowadays, he approved Awiti's administrative requests himself, and that he would do the same for me. That elicited further comments from me, the gist of which was that if Isahakia continued to be his Permanent Secretary, there were bound to be unnecessary conflicts because, as the accounting officer, he would refuse to approve my office expenditure and would undermine me. What would happen if I needed my vehicle repaired or replaced, if I wanted to attend a conference or travel? Practically, were these things anybody would expect me to go to the PM with? Who would authorise payments or reimbursements? Administratively, who would assign staff, purchase equipment and do all the menial things, the nuts and bolts that move an office or institution? Was Raila prepared to hand me "authority to incur expenditure" so that my memos and requisitions could go directly to accounts? Further, given the fact that Raila had confirmed my innocence and my contract had not expired, why was there this attempt to change my job title and description?

It became abundantly clear to me that either Raila thought I was naïve, or he might have thought I didn't know or had paid little attention to the practical details of how ministries, offices, departments and institutions are managed and run on a daily basis; that I might be one of those sleep-walking, absent-minded intellectuals, or hot-headed political activists who are perpetually caught up with the big picture and forget, in a fanciful flight of idealistic naïveté, that ultimately resolutions and decisions must get implemented; that equally important, after policies have been conceived and drawn, and after decisions have been made, is execution; how things run, on a daily basis. What he might have conveniently forgotten, is that when I hosted him in Toronto in October 2006, I had been running a well-oiled law firm.

Raila believed, wrongly, that because he had unlawfully withheld all my pay for five months, I would be so desperate that any offer would be alluring. Suddenly, I realised that the draconian actions he had taken against me had been carefully executed; they were designed to reduce me to the level of a complete pauper so that whenever he snapped his fingers, I would run or crawl back, with my tail between my legs and say "yes sir!" to everything, no matter how ridiculous. Well, he was wrong and mistaken. I never cower, never bow and never beg.

Consequently, I firmly maintained that my preference was for a horizontal (or if possible, even a vertical) transfer to another government or state institution. I had in mind a position as a Permanent Secretary or the chief executive of a state corporation. I explained to Raila that due to the poisoned environment in the OPM, primarily caused by Isahakia and busybodies like Caroli and Jakoyo Midiwo, reinstating me would cause unnecessary conflicts (almost all of it artificially orchestrated by merchants of impunity), with the risk of ultimately undermining the core mandate of the office and that of the PM. I stated that a transfer would be in the best interests of the PM and myself. I mentioned that I didn't want to be handed a poisoned chalice. Further, I mentioned that I wasn't ready to hang myself with a rope someone was trying to force me to knot.

Unfortunately, Raila wasn't interested – or pretended that he wasn't interested – in seeing me go. He came up with another suggestion I declined, which was that as he was setting up his campaign secretariat, I could consider either heading or joining it, then I would continue to receive my remuneration from the exchequer. I thought that wasn't ethical and said I couldn't do it. I also didn't think it would have been wise. Moreover, I was aware that as of that date, his campaign secretariat had been up and running for at least three months already. How was I going to work with some of my former colleagues (many of whom I had coordinated before my suspension) who had been fed filth about me or even created false stories about me themselves? How would Raila or I rebuild the confidence and trust that he had, unjustifiably, crushed?

Raila desperately tried to (deceptively) make me believe that he was doing everything to get me back. Yet, it was also crystal clear – at least to me – that it was all about his self-preservation. "What is in it *for me*?" I kept asking. I tried to turn over the issues in my head quickly, but the conclusions weren't attractive. Politically, I didn't see much; not with Jakoyo, Oburu, Ida, Nyong'o, Orengo, Kajwang', Dalmas, Caroli and their mangled and frenzied cabal, trying to run the show; not on the basis of democracy, a clear progressive ideology, a transformative agenda or principles and nor, could I see a secure place for myself, given my self-styled enemies' paranoia about the 'Raila Succession'. Indeed, it seemed inconceivable that I had any future in the Orange party – not in its present formation, anyway. Even if I were to win any nominations fairly, would there be a realistic chance that I would be issued a certificate?

Are there fair-minded people out there who believe that Raila would consider me for any of the significant positions for which I am impeccably qualified? Why – when I had defended him like no other person – didn't he consider my candidature for the attorney general, director of public prosecutions, anti-corruption commission or any of the newly established constitutional implementation organs? Which of the people he supported for those positions matched my credentials, training, tested skills, integrity, passion and commitment to the permanent elimination of impunity in this country?

Yes, Raila was focused on his 2012 presidential bid and was desperate to deal with major "problems – real or imagined". And of all his current 'problems', post my suspension, I strongly believe that he had realised that I ranked higher than Ruto and Uhuru. Admittedly, Ruto was threatening to remove a huge chunk of the vote-block he needed to make it over the hump. Uhuru, too, was making it difficult, nay almost impossible, for him to break through in the Mount Kenya region. But what Raila feared more was the threat I posed to his carefully crafted, but phony edifice, to the façade that he was progressive, an agent of change, a reformer, even that he was a 'focused, indefatigable, good leader' who had what it would take to transform Kenya from its backward culture of impunity, runaway corruption, tribalism, nepotism and primitive cronyism to industrial splendour, where equity, equality, social justice, the rule of law and constitutionalism would prevail.

Raila knew that Ruto, Kalonzo – even Uhuru – could not effectively challenge him on these issues. Kenyans don't regard them as 'reformers'. In terms of 'liberation' credentials, they aren't at the same level as Raila; in fact, they don't register. More importantly, they are either regarded as people who openly opposed the new constitution, or 'watermelons' who would not want a quick, efficient and full implementation of the new charter that nearly 70 per cent of Kenyans supported in a referendum. He believes that he permanently crippled Raphael Tuju when he painted him with that culturally toxic tag of *andhoga* (betrayer), provoking Luos into frenzied, emotional, unfair attacks on Tuju, personally and politically.

Raila considers me his most potent enemy, the single most 'powerful' individual who could torpedo his ship. I might not have much money; in fact, I hardly have any. Ruto and Uhuru are regarded as billionaires as well as temporal custodians of two major ethnic vote blocks but they don't have credibility or legitimacy to effectively counter and neuter Raila's false claims to 'liberation' credentials. But I do. Not only have I worked for and with Raila very closely, I have been the only face in the entire ODM that Kenyans have, almost universally, acknowledged as incorruptible, focused, passionate and ideologically pure.

Fortunately for me – and as my friend Jared Okello dramatically confirmed to me recently – "everybody, even the oldest woman in the remotest part of the country, even cattle in the green slopes of the Rift Valley, knows that Miguna is and has been relentlessly pursuing the agenda for the common man; they know that Miguna has integrity, that he cannot be arm-twisted into doing anything wrong, that he cannot turn against the common man, be anti-people or evil; they know that almost everyone at the Office of the Prime Minister, at the senior positions, are there to eat..." Jared was trying to convince me to accept the reinstatement and return to the OPM.

Some of these thoughts were in my mind when I told Raila that joining him, his office or his campaign secretariat would be a tall order for reasons already stated or alluded to. Raila, who had a flight to India to catch at 5pm and who had been directed by the High Court to sort out my situation by December 30, cut to the chase. In order not to prolong the discussion, we agreed that a statement and reinstatement letter should be crafted, containing the following four items:

1. That the suspension of Mr Miguna Miguna, the Prime Minister's Advisor on Coalition Affairs, be rescinded, unconditionally, with immediate effect, since it was determined that all the allegations against him were unfounded
2. That Mr Miguna is hereby ordered reinstated, forthwith
3. That all arrears, emoluments and accrued interests owed to Mr Miguna, be paid to him, forthwith
4. That upon resumption of duty, Mr Miguna would be reporting *directly* to the Prime Minister.

There were no reinstatement conditions on me.

We further agreed that before Raila departed for his 10-day trip to India that evening, a press release from his office would be issued announcing the terms of our agreement, all of which would have been approved by me prior to its release. This would be easy as we had agreed on a draft containing the four items, a copy of which Raila left with. His office could thereon communicate with me by email. The same terms would be contained in a letter of reinstatement and addressed to me. Patrick, acting as our mediator and secretary, also retained a copy of the four items and the meeting ended, after we had all agreed that the statement and letter were to be issued by that evening at the latest. As usual, I also dutifully recorded the terms.

When the waiter came in with our bill and passed it over to Patrick, I suddenly realised that Raila had left us with an Sh11,000 debt, without even caring that I hadn't been paid since July 26, 2011. Nor did it seem fair that Patrick, who as a genuine friend was only trying to help us, should be saddled with such a huge bill. But that is how Raila is; it was not the first time he had walked from a restaurant, in my presence, without picking up the bill. He had once done that to me after asking that I arrange a small meeting with Prof. Oyugi, Oduor Ong'wen, Adhu Awiti and me at a restaurant Oduor Ong'wen and Prof. Oyugi owned in the Kilimani area of Nairobi. After we had eaten a sumptuous meal of fish, beef, chicken, a variety of vegetables, and the drinks had flowed freely, amidst strategy and discussions, Raila had simply walked away, leaving us with a bill of more than Sh35,000. Even his drivers, bodyguards and a few hangers on that rushed to the place after learning of his presence, had eaten. We had pooled our resources and found most of the sum, but the owners must have had tight margins that month.

A few months after that incident, I had accompanied Raila on a tour of Nyanza, with Orengo, Kajwang', Oburu, Jakoyo and some of his usual office entourage. We had flown on a Kenya Air force Force helicopter and landed in Kisumu around lunchtime. Upon arrival, Raila had asked us to join him for lunch at the Kisumu Yatch Club. Again, after a sumptuous meal with plenty of drinks on offer that the team, except yours truly, had partaken of the bill had been brought to me, and I had dutifully passed it over to Orengo. Seeing Orengo and I looking at the bill, Raila had asked us to pass it over to him. He had examined it closely and then asked for the manager. When the man had come, saying "yes sir, no sir," Raila had reprimanded him harshly, stating that the bill wouldn't be paid because we had been overcharged. The bill had been about Sh125,000.

It's true the charges had seemed excessive. But then again, I didn't know the price of the expensive looking bottles of champagne, wine and whisky that those around the table, except yours truly, had been drinking. I had also felt that we could and should simply have paid what we believed was a fair cost for the order. After all, the place was a going concern. The owners were there to make money, and they had offered us good hospitality in exchange for our money. In any event, I believe that it was callous, insensitive and an abuse of power for Raila to have taken advantage of his position and undermined another Kenyan's business.

But to get back to the Serena hotel on December 27, I also noticed something else, which I told Patrick about: Raila's body language. On arrival at the hotel, Raila had been cordial and chummy; now, he had just walked out without maintaining eye-contact with either Patrick or I, and he hadn't shaken our hands, as he customarily did when he was in a good mood. His mood had visibly deteriorated a few minutes before he left, as Patrick completed the draft agreement. Why? I told Patrick that it must have been because Raila expected me to be so excited about his "offer" for me to return to his office and his indication that all my arrears and emoluments would be paid, forthwith.

I had mentioned to Raila during the discussions on December 27, 2011, that even the half-pay the court had ordered for me for two months hadn't been paid to me in full (all my dues, arrears and gratuity still remain unpaid to this day); Isahakia had only released one third of the two-months pay, withholding the rest, for absolutely no reason. This was in contempt and violation of the court order.

Apparently, Isahakia had told someone I know very well that I wouldn't be paid a dime for as long as he was the Permanent Secretary at OPM.

Raila had said nothing about the continuing breach of the court order, but had lamented that I had enemies at the OPM who had resolved to use my suspension as a means of going to extremes to hurt me; that he hadn't approved my indefinite suspension without pay. At the meeting, it had been Raila who came up with the idea, which I welcomed, that I must be paid all the arrears forthwith. Both Patrick and I had been pleasantly surprised by that gesture, and had believed, naïvely, that it had been made in good faith.

Well, Patrick settled the bill. I then left for home as Raila went for his haircut. From his facial expressions and body language, I suspected that he wasn't up to any good. I warned Patrick not to hold his breath, despite Raila's promises. I warned that the old man was too old to change from being the quintessential political conman.

Patrick called me later to say that Raila had instructed Caroli to execute what we had agreed on. The following day, Caroli contacted me by phone and I relayed the gist of our agreement by email and requested him to confirm the same with Patrick. Patrick subsequently emailed Caroli, with a copy to me, confirming the terms. Yet, when I read the email draft press release Caroli had already – without my approval, as pre-arranged – sent out to the media, it mangled part of the terms and inserted something about court cases being terminated, "subject to notices" being served. Raila and I hadn't discussed that.

At about 5.30pm on December 28, I received a letter from Abdul Mwasera for the Permanent Secretary, OPM, purporting to be a "warning letter" and demanding:

(a) The investigations have revealed breach of discipline on my part.
(b) The letter equally serves as a warning to me "to desist from any breach of discipline as such a breach would attract further severe disciplinary action."
(c) I should note that before resumption of duty, I was "required to withdraw any pending court case(s) as regards to this matter."
(d) Upon reinstatement, I was "required to sign Local Agreement form G.P. 106 (Revised) before resumption of duty."
(e) I should "confirm in writing" that I "have read and understood the contents of this letter."

I was astounded. First, the letter was dated December 27, 2011, the same day as our discussions with Raila. That had two possible implications. The first possibility was that when I met Raila, he had already cooked up some plan with his underlings and cronies at the OPM and ODM, including possible outcomes of our meeting and approved the contents of the letter before he had come to meet me at Serena, thereby reducing the meeting to a Machiavellian ploy by him (in view of the letter from Mwasera, this seemed the most plausible reason). The other option, however, was that Isahakia and Co, ignoring Raila's instructions, had drafted what amounted to a warning letter and *not* a rescinding of the suspension. This would, of course, be in line with what Isahakia had been specialising in ever since his appointment as Raila's campaign manager for 2007 presidential election and subsequently as Raila's Permanent Secretary – rank insubordination.

Frankly, I saw Raila's Machiavellian fingerprints all over Mwasera's letter. His trip to India was part of the clever ploy; make it look like the 'rogue' elements at the OPM, Miguna's so-called enemies, were at it again. Look like a magnanimous, forgiving, kind, considerate, and good-hearted statesman, who had forgiven the Prodigal Son, opened his arms and embraced him, welcoming him back home. Meanwhile, keep the sharp, hot knife ready for the final kill. No Sir, I wasn't that naïve and stupid.

Raila and I had agreed that the reinstatement would be announced unequivocally, made unconditionally, and apply with immediate effect. Now, attempts were being made to impose unacceptable, illegal and unconstitutional conditions on me before resuming my duties. The letter Mwasera issued didn't state, categorically, as Raila and I had agreed, that *I had been completely vindicated, and that all the allegations that had been made against me were unfounded*. This was most important. I had emphasised, and Raila and Patrick had agreed without argument, that I needed my reputation restored. I needed my integrity, dignity and humanity respected and the damages that had been caused to them repaired, as much as was humanly and legally possible. I was morally and legally entitled to that. Based on my discussions with Raila, I knew that he understood that. In fact, he had expressed a view that he knew that he had subjected me to unlawful and inhumane treatment.

Mwasera's letter not only contradicted the press release that Caroli had issued, but it also didn't contain any of the four items Raila and I had agreed on less than 24 hours before. Mwasera's letter spoke of being a "warning letter" as well as being a "disciplinary action." Who was warning me? And what about? Who was purporting to be "disciplining" me? And what about? Was it Raila, with whom I had just had mutually respectful and cordial discussions, and with whom we had unanimously agreed on the four items? Was it Mwasera, three steps my junior?

Was it Isahakia, my equal in government, a party I had recently named in a court action for issuing an unlawful suspension letter, and a person the Prime Minister and I had agreed, I couldn't and wouldn't be working with, anyway? Or was it Caroli, my one step junior? Or could it be Jakoyo Midiwo and the larger Odinga clan? Who was throwing a wrench in this carefully crafted "deal?"

By authorising these junior colleagues to write me "warning letters" or issue statements on my "reinstatement," Raila was deliberately reducing me to the level of a complete lame duck, important in title and name only. I couldn't accept that. I had originally been appointed by the President of the Republic of Kenya, upon consultation with the Prime Minister of the Republic, through a letter written by Francis Muthaura, Permanent Secretary, Office of the President, Head of the Civil Service and Secretary to the Cabinet. My letter of appointment had been issued in the usual manner all senior government officers above the position of "secretary" are appointed. My reinstatement, therefore, should have been issued in the same manner. Mwasera's letter was therefore an outrage.

Within one hour of its receipt, I sent Caroli an electronic letter (or email), copied to Patrick, pointing out the errors and demanding that Mwasera's letter must be formally withdrawn and a fresh letter containing all the four terms we had agreed on be issued on or before December 30.

Later that evening, I also sent Raila a short text message, informing him that the letter from Mwasera wasn't acceptable and that I needed it replaced on or before December 30 2011. The text was also copied to Patrick and Caroli. However, December 30 came and went, without Mwasera's letter being withdrawn. Caroli's mobile line was now dead. Raila couldn't be reached. He hadn't responded to my text message. Patrick was now scrambling, panicking. The deal now stood in limbo but time was ticking away. Meanwhile, the media continued to report that "Miguna is back!" I knew the drill. So, at 7.32pm that day, being a decisive man and, like Raila, a keen student of Machiavelli I prepared my response to the so-called reinstatement letter and invited the media for a press conference at my Runda home on December 31, 2011, my adopted birthday. The notice read: "URGENT MEDIA NOTICE – ON Saturday, December 31, 2011, at 11am, Mr Miguna Miguna, will address a Press Conference at his Runda home…regarding his REINSTATEMENT as Prime Minister Raila Odinga's advisor on coalition affairs. Please keep time. Thank you. Miguna."

I found Raila's action contemptuous, disrespectful and in bad faith. It also exemplified poor leadership, confusion and cowardice. Raila had essentially reneged on the agreement we had entered into at the Serena Hotel on December 27, 2011. I knew that if I delayed too long, Raila's people would put it about that

I had returned to work, had received all my dues, and had accepted all the terms. Then, by the time Raila returned – ten days later – public opinion would have been firmly in his favour. And it would be too late for me to complain that I had been wrongfooted.

And so I planned that on the morning of New Year's Eve, the media would be the first to hear of my categorical rejection of my so-called reinstatement. I noticed something curious that morning. At about 7am, there were 15 missed calls from friends of mine – staunch Raila supporters – who would never normally call and certainly not earlier than noon. Raila was bent on preventing the press conference. I had mastered his tricks. So, I never answered or returned any of the calls. That steeled my determination, as I announced to the media:

> Ladies and Gentlemen,
> Fellow Kenyans,
> When I get involved in negotiations and conclude a deal – any deal – legal, personal, political or professional – I make sure that there are simple, clear and mutually understood ground rules, guidelines and principles, and that all parties involved, must undertake and solemnly promise, in good faith, before the commencement of such negotiations and after their completion, to be bound by all the terms and conditions of the final agreement, and to honour, respect and fully and honestly discharge all their undertakings, as prescribed in the agreement.
>
> On Wednesday, December 28, 2011, I promised the country that following the decision by the Rt. Hon. Raila Amolo Odinga, EGH, MP, Prime Minister of the Republic of Kenya, to unconditionally rescind my suspension he had announced on August 4 2011, and to order, with immediate effect, my reinstatement, as his Advisor on Coalition Affairs and Joint Secretary to the Permanent Committee on the Management of Grand Coalition Affairs [Caroli's statement had also referred to my old position]. I would take my time, *to analyse, digest and fully understand that decision* before I could comment further.
>
> I am not prone to intemperate, precipitous or exuberant decisions and declarations. Before making any decision – big, small, personal, legal, political or professional – I always spend a considerable amount of time consulting, analysing and carefully reflecting on all aspects of the decision, issues, circumstances and implications. I cross all the Ts and dot all the Is.

And once I have made my decisions, I stick with them, come hell or high water. That's because I am a strong believer and practitioner of the principles of honour, integrity, the rule of law and constitutionalism.

On Tuesday, December 27, 2011, from about 1.30pm to 3.30pm – a whole two hours – the Prime Minister and I met, in the presence of a mutual friend, at the Serena Hotel, in the City of Nairobi. It was the Prime Minister who called me, personally, and requested the meeting.

We had a courteous, respectful, dignified, cordial and professional meeting, which when it concluded, we – the two of us, alone – unanimously agreed, in good faith, that the Prime Minister would make the following announcement, that day, personally or through his office, before he travelled to India.

The agreement was in writing, and was witnessed by the mutual friend. It was to be unconditional and to be implemented immediately without any delay whatsoever. Both the Press Statement and letter of reinstatement were to contain the following terms:

1. That the suspension of Mr Miguna Miguna, the Prime Minister's Advisor on Coalition Affairs, be rescinded, unconditionally, with immediate effect, since it was determined that all the allegations against him were unfounded;
2. That Mr Miguna is hereby ordered reinstated, forthwith;
3. That all arrears, emoluments and accrued interests owed to Mr Miguna, be paid to him, forthwith; and,
4. Upon resumption of duty, Mr Miguna would be reporting *directly* to the Prime Minister.

We agreed that I would approve – as to form, nature and content – all statements and/or letters that would be issued with respect to this matter.

There were no other terms or conditions the Prime Minister and I agreed on, apart from the four items above.

Following the issuance, by the Prime Minister, of a Press Statement, that day, containing all the terms of the agreement, the Prime Minister was to immediately ensure that a letter containing the four terms agreed on, would be delivered to me, forthwith, and all the terms therein, and honoured fully, without any delay whatsoever.

Unfortunately, the statement that was released by one Caroli Omondi, on behalf of the Prime Minister, on December 28, 2011 – 24 hours after our agreement – did not, accurately, reflect and adhere to the terms of our agreement.

But even more egregiously, when I received a letter from the Office of the Prime Minister, signed by a junior officer on behalf of the Permanent Secretary, at 5.30pm on December 28 2011, but which was dated December 27 2011, the form, content and tone was totally at variance with the agreement the Prime Minister and I had entered into, in good faith. The letter was also inconsistent and contradicted the Press Statement released by Mr Omondi.

At about 5.30pm on December 28 2011, I formally communicated to Mr Omondi and the Prime Minister, in writing, electronically – twice – and indicated that both the Press Statement and the so-called letter of reinstatement, failed to communicate the terms of our agreement, as the Prime Minister had undertaken to do. I requested that the so-called reinstatement letter dated December 27 2011 be withdrawn, formally, and a fresh one containing all the terms the Prime Minister and I had agreed on, in good faith, be issued, on or before December 30 2011.

Unfortunately, as of the time of this Press Conference, my letters, and subsequent short text messages to both Mr Omondi and to the Prime Minister, have not been responded to, though they were clearly received, as Mr Omondi had confirmed receipt to the mutual friend of the Prime Minister and I.

In view of the foregoing, and conscious of my responsibilities as a Kenyan who believes in honour, good faith, the rule of law and principles of good governance and constitutionalism, I hereby announce that by a letter dated today's date and delivered to the Prime Minister already, I have declined to accept the decision to reinstate me, on terms and conditions contained in the letter by one Abdul Mwasera, dated December 27, 2011. A copy of my letter to the Prime Minister and that of Mr Mwasera, are attached, herewith.

We must develop and entrench both a culture and practice of honouring our words, respecting deals we make, and adhering to the principles of good governance, rule of law and constitutionalism.

I will not take questions.

I thank you.

Immediately afterwards, Caroli Omondi did some truly inept spin-doctoring, presumably in an attempt to divert attention from the hash he had made of my 'reinstatement'. He told the media that the reinstatement had only come about because Raila and the OPM pitied me now that I had "nothing to do and was complaining…". In fact, I was very happily occupied, writing this exposé of his office's corrupt ineptitude. He also claimed that my previous contract had expired which was, of course, egregious nonsense – it had been a three-year renewable contract, dated March 2009. But maybe those claims were actually his way of diverting the heat from more sinister goings-on. A friend later told me that immediately after Raila had purportedly reinstated me, Caroli had been overheard loudly stating to someone on the telephone, from his office at the OPM, "Don't worry, this is what will finish Miguna completely…he is finished!"

Based on a careful review of Mwasera's letter, it was clear that Raila wasn't acting in good faith. Yes, he had eaten humble pie and staged a climb-down, but surely that was because of his fatal fear of this book and what I had promised, in a K24 interview with host Jeff Koinange, would be "multiple volcanic eruptions". It was also crystal clear that he intended to stab me in the back. The fact that he hadn't fulfilled his part of the bargain as he had undertaken to do even though he was the one who had approached me, showed not just bad faith and deception, but also disclosed some concealed plot. If Raila was honest and genuine he would have fully honoured his word and undertakings. He would also have attempted to undo the damage he had inflicted upon me. After all, my dues weren't coming from his pocket. Instead, he never even bothered to respond to my letter. Nor has he made sure that I am paid my arrears, nor have my personal effects been released to me.

What if, my wife has asked me, Raila planned to destroy me – physically, politically and professionally – and was just using the reinstatement as a clever cover? What if, for instance, I died in a staged accident, shootout, robbery, random attack or deadly crossfire after the reinstatement? Wouldn't most people naturally suspect, if something happened to me, that since we had made up, it couldn't have been foul play? People would look elsewhere – to the PNU, non-existent ex-girlfriends, political and social enemies – for explanations of the tragedy.

What if the target was my book, its destruction and a plan to make sure it never got published? What if I became a victim of a staged sting operation, a staged crime of passion, a staged accident, a staged anything? How would I extricate myself from such a situation and regain my integrity and reputation again?

The plot reeked of Raila from pore to pore. I knew how he thought and operated. I had seen the way he had removed the so-called 'legal opinion from the AG' from his coat pocket, his eyes darting with guilt, when all I had seen was a memorandum from Mohamed Isahakia and Caroli Omondi, recommending my termination. I had also seen a small strip of typed paper containing my name, my new title and job description. But if the suspension was being lifted unconditionally – as Raila told both Patrick and I – why wasn't I being reinstated in the same position as before suspension? That had happened to Caroli Omondi, Mohamed Isahakia, Thuita Mwangi, Moses Wetangula and many others.

Payment of my arrears and emoluments wasn't a magnanimous act since I was, by law, fully entitled to them. The Government of Kenya owed me the money that Raila promised would be paid forthwith. I don't beg or apologise for seeking or getting my legal entitlements. Secondly, the issue of reporting directly to Raila wasn't new either; that's the way I had been reporting even before the unlawful suspension. The organogram of the OPM sets out clearly the chain of command; only Isahakia, Caroli and I reported directly to Raila. Again, this was put in writing to avoid anybody injecting himself into the equation. Thirdly, the issue of exoneration was the most important issue. It was imperative that Raila made it clear that the allegations made against me had been unfounded. People trying to quibble with these issues either don't understand the law or don't appreciate the rights involved. They might also be malicious or mischievous.

When one analyses this saga, one cannot help but wonder: does Raila have the requisite administrative, professional and leadership skills to run the OPM? The answer, based on the entire set of circumstances, is that he doesn't appear to. If he doesn't, as is now apparent, how can he possibly run a country? Is he competent to be a Commander-In-Chief of the Defense Forces? Does he have the knowledge, training, skills, experience, emotional intelligence, discipline and temperament to be the Chief Executive Officer of the Republic of Kenya? My answer is definitely not. Raila Odinga doesn't have the requisite skills to run even a kindergarten! He 'leads' and operates through confusion and chaos. That's not how anybody could possibly run a country in the 21st century, consulting magicians and traditional medicine men.

How come Raila approached me this time, when he had earlier, steadfastly refused to respond and agree to an out-of-court settlement? Why is it that nobody from Raila's office, from ODM or any of his sycophants had genuinely reached out to me or commented on my reinstatement, including some who had been very close to me before? Why the eerie silence? Could it be that they knew of the plot and were eagerly waiting to see if I would grab it before they moved in for the kill? Luckily, my gut had told me that Raila's move wasn't genuine or in my best interests.

If I had agreed to the outlandish terms Mwasera's letter demanded, I wouldn't and couldn't have written this book. I would have been gagged, forever. Furthermore, I wouldn't and couldn't have been able to pursue the legal action against Isahakia. No doubt the fine print in that 'local agreement' would have contained provisions purporting to bar me from using any information in the course of my duties and responsibilities, to write or publish articles, documents or books. That was targeted at this book. The intention was to vitiate and abrogate my constitutional right to free expression, to guarantee Raila a turbulence-free run-up to the 2012 general elections.

Aren't Raila and Kalonzo – two leading public servants – reportedly writing their memoirs? Wouldn't they be free to use, reflect on and partly rely on their experiences, including documents, relating to their current positions? What gives them the right and authority to do so but not me? In law, do people have rights based on their social class, positions, power, authority or wealth? Before a court of law, is there a distinction between parties: between the government and the state, those holding positions of power and an ordinary private individual? Isn't justice said to be blind?

But I also saw Isahakia's and Caroli's hands in all this. I had issued a libel notice against Isahakia following his defamatory publication and wide dissemination of the scandalous and libellous suspension letter. Caroli, as I have said before, has always feared any professional Luo who is viewed as competent and 'clean.' Now, they were trying to use the reinstatement to waive my rights to seek redress in court. That was partly the reason why their version of reinstatement was being made conditional on me agreeing to have "all court cases terminated or withdrawn" and signing the "revised" local agreement. No, Sir; I wouldn't take that bait.

I had been working for the people of Kenya, effectively, since I was a youth. One doesn't have to be formally employed in government to serve the people. In fact, often formal employment compromises and blunts one's commitment, dedication and passion. Many start focusing on feathering their nests. Look at Koigi Wamwere, Mukhisha Kituyi, Anyang' Nyong'o, James Orengo, Kiraitu Murungi – and of course, Raila Odinga. After their appointments into public office they changed, almost instantly, into something nobody could recognise. For my part, I have written extensively on issues of good governance, respect for human rights, the rule of law and constitutionalism. I have been involved in political activism for the betterment of our country for more than 30 years. I've been doing so without formal employment or remuneration and even after I relocated to Kenya, I worked, pro bono, for Raila Odinga for three years prior to being employed in government. And I continued writing and challenging the culture of impunity even when working as Raila's senior advisor. *The Constitution of Kenya 2010* is crystal clear; everyone who is employed in government or by a state agency works for the 'majestic people of Kenya.' I have consistently argued that other than matters of state security and intelligence, there isn't any secret that any democratic government can keep from its own people. *The people own the government.* They are the ones that elect it, give it a mandate, laws and the constitution with which to 'govern' – not rule – them. Government is only for expedient, practical reasons. All the information that is gathered or kept by the government – *ipso facto* – is deemed to belong to the people. It is the people who keep the government in check. Accountability, which is the cornerstone of any democratic system, is to the people, either directly through elections, recall or impeachment, or indirectly through parliament, the senate, county or municipal assemblies. Hence, for anyone to argue that there is a category of information that the people shouldn't have access to is not only wrong in law; such a position would also be wrong on the basis of both morality, public policy and the Constitution. Anybody who makes such an argument must be ignored and dismissed with the contempt s/he deserves. Being muzzled by censorship, extortion, intimidation or threats isn't something I would accept even with a million guns at my head. I didn't accept my position in March 2009 on the basis that certain rights would be waived or suspended. If that had been a condition of employment, I wouldn't have accepted the appointment.

Another fear from within the OPM that Mwasera's mischievous letter aimed to address was my appeal of Judge Mohamed Warsame's erroneous ruling of December 15 2011 on my judicial review application. It was crystal clear, as I had mentioned to the PM during our meeting, that Warsame's ruling that I was a 'political' appointee whose position could be terminated at any time and not a public servant with clearly laid out contractual rights, ignored commonsense, logic, legal principles, the rules of evidence and basic facts in the case. Since his ruling, many prominent lawyers I had spoken with, including Paul Muite, had advised me to appeal it as it committed so many errors it was impossible to enumerate all of them. Warsame's judgement was also replete with numerous grammatical, typographical, factual, logical and legal errors. The ruling was full of irrelevant bluster and bar-room gossip. It wasn't really written in English. It was a poorly constructed contraption of unrefined elementary comprehension. More than anything else, it was a demonstration of the mire our judiciary is deeply stuck in and a frightening sign of how far we still have to travel before we can say that our judiciary is fully reformed, well-trained, competent, ethical and capable of rendering justice.

How could Raila think that I would agree to the withdrawal of the appeal? How would that benefit me? Why would I want that faulty ruling to stay on record and become a defective precedent?

It is possible that the PM had for some time been looking for an opportunity to destroy me. Anything is possible. It is equally possible that the PM made the decision to destroy me after noticing my potential and how I could ruin his succession schemes. People like James Orengo, Anyang' Nyong'o, Otieno Kajwang', Dalmas Otieno, Jakoyo Midiwo and Caroli Omondi who have succession ambitions, might also have been driven by those ambitions. I say this because I can't otherwise explain why they seemed so excited about what they believed would be my total political destruction. But actually, I've never been in competition with any of them. Unlike most of them, I didn't hold elective office or operate from Parliament or Orange House. The ODM ministers and MPs had the bully pulpit from which they could reach local and international audiences. All I had was my column. They, too, could have written columns. In other words, there is no justifiable reason for their toxic jealousy.

Clearly, the manner of suspension was intended to cause maximum damage – financially, politically and professionally. Raila knew that without money, and no reasonable prospects of similar alternative employment given the unnecessary damage caused by the suspension, I wouldn't be able to execute a political entry within a year before the next general elections. Others have posited that Raila intended to force me back to Canada. I believe that. Unfortunately for him, I shall stay right here and continue with my good work.

Kenyans had hoped that the birth of a new Constitution would bury the old order. Unfortunately, the struggle to build a new order will take time and more effort; old despotic tendencies and practices are deeply entrenched in our psyches, system and institutions are refusing to give way. The corrosion hasn't just seeped deep into those we have always derisively referred to as "anti-reformers". Those who have suffered for the liberation cause, like Raila, have also been irretrievably contaminated by this social malaise. Instead of providing a beachhead for progressive forces within the retrogressive state, he has effectively converted. The corrosion of the old order has seeped through all the arteries of our society. The media, civil society, professions, institutions, unions and bodies are all infected.

An old man from Magina village, one who fought for our country's independence with Jaramogi, Okuto Bala and others – Dick Abuor Okumu –

recently called me and said: "*Ruath!* We value you. You are our light with which we see. You are a descendant of Lwanda Magere. I know you are our bull that scares others from our herd. I'm aware that you are sharp and know how to fight with your mind, pen and if need be, physically. But we are also aware that it is the brave rhinoceros whose hide is used to make shields. Please don't use cooking oil on a wild cat."

"Dick! I have heard you and I agree with you. You fought the colonialists, didn't you?"

"Yes I did – fiercely! Were Olonde and I fought with valour until we got freedom. Olonde spent five years in hard labour while I spent three. I've never regretted the sacrifices we made. So, yes, I understand where you are coming from."

"You did that while there are others, even in our village, who chose to work for the white man became clerks and 'prospered?'"

"That's true."

"And you did that knowing very well the dangers involved. You risked your life for the liberation of our people and country and through it all, you suffered indignity, long years of incarceration with hard labour, and when you were released (when independence was attained), you continued to suffer while those who collaborated with the colonialists were now chiefs, government clerks, district officers, district commissioners, and held other such lofty titles?"

"Yes my brother! I feel you."

"Dick! Do you regret having fought against colonialism, having fought for liberation? Do you feel that you might have been better off collaborating with the British?"

"Never! I would do it again and again if I were to relive my life over again!"

"Precisely my friend! We are fighting for the liberation, not just of the mentally, psychologically, socially and culturally captivated Luo. We are fighting so that we can complete the liberation struggle of Kenya you started, so that we can live in equality, social justice and freedom – everyone."

"I agree there. That's why Jaramogi wrote the book *Not Yet Uhuru*. We are yet to enjoy the fruits of *uhuru* we fought for."

"Now, you are concerned about the so-called fight between me and Raila Odinga. But who really started it? What are the root causes? Are we really fighting or is it just Raila fighting me? And why is Raila fighting me? Until Raila woke up one day and announced to the country through the media, that he had thrown me out and discarded me like a dog, had you ever heard that I had done anything to undermine, let alone fight Raila?"

"Of course not! You may not know *Thuon*, but Raila and his people are very dangerous. That's why we, the villagers are worried. Do you know that Raila, Adhu Awiti, Ayiecho Olweny, John Pesa, Dalmas Otieno and many so-called Luo leaders visit magicians at night to plot on who to sacrifice? Do you know that they used to visit a Tanzanian magician called Odemba? Do you know they visit *Kit Mikayi* in Seme in the middle of the night and sacrifice animals there. A black bull is not slaughtered in the normal way; it is strangled by hand before it is skinned and then they eat the meat as the magician performs his things? *Thuon*, Raila is dangerous!"

"Now Dick, you know how and where I grew up. You know my mother Suré nyar Njoga (may her soul rest in eternal peace!) You know that I am a person without envy. You know I don't steal and have never stolen. You know that I am incapable of being bought or bribed by anyone. You also know that my family and I don't believe in magic. Anybody who has never touched magic cannot be touched by magic. So, Raila and his Luo cabal can visit all the magicians in the world, from Odemba to the Chinese, but it will never work on me. So, relax! If I had stolen anybody's money, Raila wouldn't have sent Caroli to say to the press that I had nothing to do and was complaining that I was destitute! Didn't you hear what they said about me, as if the Government of Kenya belongs to their mothers? Is this Raila's government? Is it *Joka* Odinga's? You know I don't drink alcohol. You know I don't smoke. You know I don't go to bars, and am not susceptible to peer pressure. You know all these things about me but you also know that Raila has never said anything I did or have done to make him treat me in this way. You also know that there are people in Raila's office – Caroli Omondi, Mohamed Isahakia and other 'merchants of impunity' – who have been accused of massive theft of public resources – the Maize, Triton, Kazi Kwa Vijana, NSSF, NHIF and other scams – yet they remain permanent fixtures at Raila's office. Those are Raila's closest buddies. You know all of that? Why do you think that is so?"

"Yes my brother! We are also wondering why!"

"Dick, but you also know that Raila is a man just like Miguna, isn't it? He has two nuts like me, or does Raila have three?"

"Hahaha! My brother…He has only two."

"Well, Dick, did Raila's mother give birth differently from Suré nyar Njoga?"

"No *wuod ma*!"

"Let me tell you that Raila is evil – pure, undiluted evil! He has shot his best, most skilled, most courageous and loyal general in the back! Is that honourable? Do you support something like that?"

"No! I don't. In fact, we were discussing that today with other villagers and we resolved that you did well not to have accepted that job. We could see the hidden, concealed dangers and risks involved. Those people could murder you! The villagers saw through it; it was a ruse. Those people from Siaya have taken us, the people of Kano, for granted for a very long time. Look at Raila's office; where is anyone from Kano? Look at the entire government; where are our bright sons and daughters in there? Didn't we vote for Raila to a person?"

"Anyway Dick, this isn't about Siaya and Kano. It isn't about Raila's office and how many people from Kano are working there. This is about leadership, or to be more accurate, a grand failure of it in the person of Raila Amolo Odinga. Raila is not a leader. He is a vindictive, envious, jealous, confused, lecherous and evil man. I'm not the first, the only one, or the last he would do this to. If we allow him, we would be complicit in the perpetuation of the culture of impunity."

"They were saying that you were seen with Tuju?"

"Dick, *so what if I was seen with Tuju? Tuju is a Luo and a Kenyan, just like Raila and I, isn't he? Why shouldn't I be seen with him? What crime has he committed*? After all, I knew Tuju before I knew Raila!"

"Well, they are saying Tuju is working with Kibaki!"

"Dick, how about Raila? Isn't he a co-principal, the one who shares *mkate nusu* and sits next to Kibaki at all public functions, cabinet meetings, etc? Haven't you seen how satisfied Raila is while walking beside Kibaki, clasping his hand? Haven't you heard him say how good Kibaki is as a leader; that they are getting along perfectly, that Kibaki is not a dictator like Robert Mugabe?

"If Kibaki declared Raila *Tosha* today, would Luos stone Raila like they stoned Tuju or would they sing his praises, saying how he is a political genius? If Uhuru and Ruto endorsed Raila today, would Luos excommunicate him? *Why can't Tuju or anybody else have political ambitions just like Raila?* No public office, including the presidency was created for any one person or family. *The presidency of the Republic of Kenya is not hereditary.* Even if it was, from whom is Raila supposed to inherit it? Tuju is a Luo and a Kenyan, just like Raila. He has equal rights to Raila. The problem with most Luos right now, especially the poorest of the poor, is to mistakenly believe that Raila is their only chance to the topmost leadership of this country. Raila likes that line of delusional reasoning; he encourages and perpetuates it. That is the most unfortunate thinking and belief imaginable. Raila doesn't have to be President for Luos to do well economically, socially, politically, or otherwise.

"*The presidency isn't the beginning and the end of everything.* There are many communities in Kenya which have not produced any President and might not do so in a long time to come, but who are doing much better than the Luos. Let me tell you something; most Luos don't know and have never been told that Raila Odinga doesn't care about Luos. Raila Odinga cares about Raila Odinga and the larger Jaramogi family. He has been Prime Minister now for more than four years; what practical initiatives – economic, social, health, educational has he started, encouraged or facilitated in Luo Nyanza? *Where is the concrete evidence that if Raila were to become President, Luos, specifically and Kenyans, in general, would see any significant difference in the quality in their lives, that he would initiate genuine employment, investment, productive or infrastructural projects, not fake ones like the KKV, which was actually to divert public funds for 2012 campaign kitties*? If he couldn't do it in more than four years as Prime Minister, why should he be given another five years as President?"

"I see your point. We are with you all the way."

"That's good Dick. Now ask yourself these questions: *Raila has been Prime Minister now for close to five long years; what has he done for Kano? Kibaki and Uhuru have helped the coffee farmers, written off billions of shillings worth of bad debt. Why hasn't Raila done the same for sugar and cotton farmers?* Then our factories, instead of failing, could be offering much needed employment for our youth, more than sixty per cent of whom are loitering in the market places, with nothing productive or meaningful to do, while Agwambo is Prime Minister! What industries – other than the Odinga's Spectre International plant in Kisumu, which Moi essentially built for him as a bribe for helping him prop up the dying Kanu regime in 1997 – has Raila brought to Nyanza?

How about James Orengo; he is the Lands Minister; how come land demarcation in Nyanza has not been done? How many new hospitals, health centres and dispensaries has Anyang' Nyong'o constructed in Kano? How many unemployed Kano youth has Dalmas Otieno employed in the public service? I'm not suggesting that they do such things merely because they come from Nyanza; but Dick, look around you. You have travelled to Central Province. Do you think people in Magina, for example, live like those in Kiambu or Meru? Why? These are questions we can't run away from Dick, can we?"

"Yes *Thuon*, I see your point. Raila has failed us!"

"Dick, do you know someone called Reuben Ndolo?"

"Oh yes, the former MP for Makadara? That's a man as solid as steel, a real Raila defender!"

"And do you know someone called Rachel Shebbesh?"

"That nominated MP?"

"Yes, Dick. Now hear this; just yesterday, January 1, 2012, Ndolo told me that Rachel had told him that Raila had said he would kill Ndolo if he didn't stop 'seeing' Rachel. Now, do you know what that means?"

"What? That he would kill Ndolo for seeing that woman? Isn't she married?"

"Dick, precisely my point, my brother. But it says more about Raila; it isn't just shocking because Rachel is married. What is more shocking is that Raila could threaten to kill one of his bravest defenders and fighters because of a woman. One more thing; Raila met Rachel through Ndolo, not the other way round."

"We have always suspected that the man is both ungrateful and evil."

"Oh, one more thing Dick: do you know that it was Raila who conspired against Ndolo in the 2007 elections? That's betrayal. It is treachery. It is dishonesty. It is pure, unmitigated evil."

"Oh my God!"

"Yes, once Raila realised that Ndolo would win the Makadara seat after triumphing in the ODM nominations, he set out to undermine, to frustrate and ultimately to ensure Ndolo's defeat. In the presence of many people including yours truly, Raila picked up a phone and telephoned Charity Ngilu, asking her to put a Narc candidate in Makadara against Ndolo. Now you know how it goes in Makadara, don't you? Gikuyus are the majority, followed by Luos, Luhyas, Kambas, et cetera. By putting a Kamba/Narc candidate against a Luo/ODM candidate, Raila calculated that Ndolo wouldn't get solid ODM/Narc votes. That ensured the victory of a Gikuyu/PNU candidate. That's how Ndolo lost the election. And Raila did it again during the by-elections that were held recently in Makadara. *He hasn't just done it against Ndolo; he has been rooting out intelligent, focused, hardworking Luos with leadership potential since time immemorial. What do you think happened between him and Tuju?*"

"Tell me my brother, tell me."

"Well, before the 2002 general elections, Raila actually supported Tuju. Indeed, many complained then that he imposed Tuju on Rarieda. Raila's older brother Oburu had wanted to impose the late Moses Owiti a.k.a. *Malo Malo,* may his soul rest in peace. But Raila stood his ground. Tuju was a bright, hard working and rich young man. *Malo Malo* was like a *matatu* tout. Raila thought that Tuju would just be an asset for him, providing slick PR, good TV clips and tons of money for himself and his campaign. But Tuju proved to be more than that. He demonstrated to the country how an MP could make a difference at the constituency level. He also showed Raila and others how one could run public offices in a lean, efficient and professional manner. You have never heard Tuju cited in corruption; have you? You have never heard his name in tribalism and nepotistic indices. So, why do you think Raila fought and removed him from Rarieda? *Because Raila hates to see another Luo with money, influence and rising popularity.* He is insecure; he can't stand competition, even if not directed at him. That's the same reason Raila treated me worse than a dead wild beast."

"I'm listening my brother, I'm listening."

"Tuju isn't the first young, bright, hard working professional Luo that Raila has mistreated and abused. He did the same to his former personal assistant and think tank Rateng' Oginga Ogego and Odeny Ngure, whom Tuju replaced. Odeny was one of Raila's strongest defenders going into the 2002 general elections. And what was Odeny's crime? Raila claimed that Odeny was arrogant! Arrogant to whom? Arrogant because he openly, bravely and effectively took on Raila's detractors and enemies and demolished them? Instead of being grateful, Raila felt threatened and insecure. Raila is thankless and vicious. And how about Orengo and Nyong'o, his current sycophants these days? Weren't they chewed up and spat out for standing up to Raila on matters of principle? Dick, do you people prefer to see me weak, colourless and sycophantic like Orengo is now?"

"Oh no, *Thuon*; we would like you to remain strong, focused and strategic."

"Precisely! That's what I'm trying to do, in my little, modest way. I know I'm not wealthy. I can account for everything I own – and it's not much. Luckily, God has blessed me with a lovely and supportive family. God has also blessed me with a good brain and some very useful skills. I can think for myself. I can speak and write for myself – something I can't say about Raila Odinga. (The man is incoherent) I intend to use these gifts God gave me to feed my family, to protect myself and to pursue justice, truth and equality for everyone in this country, even if I do it alone. Though obviously, it would be more effective to fight this war together, in an organised fashion – not against Raila personally – but what he represents: the decaying, despotic old older.

"Luos call what Raila intended to do with me '*timo sango*'; the sacrifice of an innocent person to redeem another person, often a criminal, or one possessed with demons. He told me to my face that that's what he was doing, 'trying to save Major Oswago'. But Oswago also told me that he went to Raila and confronted him, asking him why he was using his name that way when everyone knew that he had done nothing from which he had to be saved. Oswago told me: 'Miguna, why is Raila saying he sacrificed you for me when both of us have done nothing wrong and Raila knows that?"

For me, it no longer matters why Raila does anything; he does it for Raila Odinga. Raila might be a deity to many people, but I have never elevated him to that position. I've been nothing but a loyal and dedicated general for Raila and ODM. But what did Raila do in recognition of my contributions? He hurt me, defamed me and tried to ruin me. *A king who does that to one of his most loyal servants, does not deserve the crown, and is not fit to rule or govern.* Raila has failed the most basic test of leadership.

"I don't believe – indeed I cannot believe – that Raila was always this despicable beast. There was a time when Raila was homeless, destitute, unemployed and couldn't even walk into a bar or restaurant and sit next to other Kenyans, not even his relatives. Restaurants and bars closed as soon as he appeared. Nobody would talk with him. He had no friends. That wasn't a very long time ago. He was then probably around my current age. He still rose to become Prime Minister, didn't he? So, what could possibly make people think that I can't become Prime Minister or President, for that matter? What is it God endowed Raila with that He denied me, eh? I intend to meet Raila and his friends at the 'liberation parade' after this country is fully free, or in Heaven, or in Hell!"

"Itieka Thuon! Itieka chuth!" (I'm satisfied, the Brave one! You've satisfied me completely!")

"I've made a decision, a final decision in relation to Raila Amolo Odinga: *I shall never, ever work with or for Raila Amolo Odinga again here on earth, in heaven or in hell.* My wife, children and relatives feel the same way. A man – any man – who can do what Raila did to me is capable of killing another person, an innocent person, for absolutely no reason at all, just so his ego and insecurities can be assuaged temporarily. If Raila was in possession of the only key to the door to heaven, I would ask to be directed to Hell, before running there with all my strength. I would demand to be shown the Castle of Fire where Obell Sibuor presides, and upon reaching there, I would request to be placed in the hottest furnace so that I could burn to ashes immediately. I would rather die than work with or for Raila Amolo Odinga. I mean it, with all my soul. It doesn't matter to me that he might be the next President. Kenya doesn't belong to him or to whoever becomes the next President. I have as much right to this beautiful land as Raila. That's how I feel about Raila Amolo Odinga."

"Got your point! *Joka* Wanga should return to their home!"

"Thank you Dick. Happy New Year!"

I recently received the following comments from my good friend Joab Okello Agar, an attorney and administrative judge in New York, US, following an interview with Jeff Koinange's *The Bench* on K24 that aired on Thursday, January 12, 2012.

> What struck me the most was your honesty. I was watching it with my wife who is not very political and when I asked for her opinion, she said that you are "honest" and it occurred to me right then that this is what sets you apart from the others. You are honest. *Raila has probably dealt with brave people but he has not dealt with brave and honest people.*
>
> The other impression I got was that you have opened up a new front in the struggle, that of individual rights. Most people do not understand that liberal ideology is based on individual rights. People like Raila probably understand freedom of speech, freedom of press, freedom to vote, democracy, etc., but [they] do not understand that *the cornerstone of all these progressive liberal concepts flows from the fact that human beings have fundamental individual rights that must be respected.* Most of us are ready to sacrifice the individual for societal rights not realising that there cannot be societal rights without individual rights.
>
> I believe your interviews have educated and emboldened Kenyans to start thinking and standing up for their rights in court and in other fora. Your experience with Raila…and hopefully a trial of the six prominent Kenyans at the ICC will help sensitise Kenyans to the rule of law and the understanding that *individual rights are the cornerstones of the liberal progressive tradition that we have been pursuing for years.*
>
> …This seems all very simple, however, we have a tradition where it is still very easy to convince people that the society is more important than the individual and therefore it is alright to sacrifice the individual for the society's 'good'. Politicians exploit this and it is the only argument against you that you should expect.

Integrity cannot be bought or sold, no matter how wealthy one might be, and integrity is the highest human attribute I believe I have and have been associated with. To my mind, it is the most precious human characteristic we all should seek. I would rather have my integrity intact and be a pauper than be a billionaire who is spat at whenever he has passed by. That is how people feel about Isahakia and Caroli; they are objects of pity and spite.

Truth telling, honesty and honour are three qualities I consider dear, so dear to me that I would sacrifice daily human comforts in exchange for them. I also hold dear to my heart my individual dignity, humanity and my right to think for myself, to express myself freely and to participate in all human endeavours guaranteed by law and our living Constitution.

I intend to protect my integrity with all my strength, intellect, soul and spirit. Truth never rots or decays so, I intend to dedicate my entire life to its propagation. Evil might triumph over good occasionally, but not forever. It's always better to be on the side of justice than to be on the side of injustice and evil. Good and righteousness ultimately prevail over evil. That's a guarantee.

There are two distinctive threads running through this book, and indeed, my life. The first one is the persistent and unrelenting quest for justice in every endeavour that I've been involved in. The second one is the desire, the courage and fearlessness to confront adversity and challenge impunity. I did it when I faced persecution as a young boy of not more than 11 in Nyatoto village in Lambwe Valley. I did it again at Onjiko secondary school, then at Njiiri's High School, then at the NYS in Gilgil, and then at the University of Nairobi. While in political exile in Canada, I did it again and again.

On March 6, 2009, when I was appointed a senior advisor to the Prime Minister of the Republic of Kenya and a Joint Secretary to the Permanent Committee for the Management of Grand Coalition Affairs, many thought I had 'arrived'. Many others expected me to sit on my hands, while my time away and join the gravy train. That's what Kenyans have been conditioned to expect and accept of senior public and state officers. "You go in, make yourself comfortable and keep your mouth, hands and pockets full." Therefore, my refusal to join the gravy train, my resistance to the culture of impunity, my consistent and persistent opposition to corruption, lethargy, laziness and incompetence, and my ability to rail against these vices loudly, aggressively, eloquently and both privately and publicly, naturally earned me mortal enemies, the kind of vicious powerful figures that don't brook dissent and don't accept defeat.

Many people have asked me: "Miguna, why did you do it? Why did you spend more than CAD 50,000 of your hard-earned money in 2007 to assist Raila's quest for the presidency? Didn't you do it for selfish reasons?" Some of these questions are being asked by people who have no interest in knowing the truth. Their primary intention is to expose me as someone who had vested interests but the truth is I didn't. Indeed, the truth, unfortunately for this group of people, is both stubborn and rather inconvenient. My answer has been consistent.

In 2002, I was among a very tiny minority among Luos who openly opposed the NDP/Kanu merger. I opposed it because I felt that Raila was dragging Luos into an alliance with Moi that had no national progressive agenda, that he had joined Kanu, not for the purpose of improving and expanding the democratic space but solely to advance his political ambitions. The first time I supported Raila was later in 2002, after he declared Kibaki fit for the presidency. I did so, not because I liked or supported Kibaki as a person (I have never done so for reasons I have stated in this book), but because I realised the strategic import of using Kibaki to stop Moi's cynical and retrogressive schemes of extending his despotic regime illegitimately through the hurriedly concocted candidacy of Uhuru Kenyatta. Many patriotic Kenyans, including myself, believed that it was better to have Kibaki assume the presidency under the Narc torch than allow Moi to succeed (himself) in perpetuating mediocrity, retrogression and impunity.

After the assassination of my friend Crispin Odhiambo Mbai in 2003, I was desperate to assist in the arrest, prosecution and severe punishment of those who killed him. I thought (wrongly, I have now painfully discovered), that Raila was an ally that could help me in that quest. As naïve as that might sound to some people, it was the primary impetus that drove me to seek him out. I've not given up the quest for justice for Odhiambo Mbai.

The third reason is what some people without a clear appreciation of my motivation, might characterise as selfish. I have harboured political ambition from my youth. Throughout my life, I have watched in horror as a tiny group of greedy people have attempted to defile, strangulate and – like feral beasts – maul the political process and turn it into nothing but a means for their personal enrichment and aggrandisement. This has gone on for far too long. Unfortunately, those with the requisite ideological understanding, commitment and discipline have rarely succeeded in organising themselves into a viable alternative political formation that could steer the country to a different, more equal, more liberal, more prosperous and hopeful future. Luckily, there was a confluence between my personal ambitions and the political panorama in Kenya in 2007.

Recently, an insightful cyber commentator, "*eberasi*," expressed a thought that many Kenyans tend to forget: "Kenya is larger than its warriors, rulers and even heroes. That is why they fight and die for her. Miguna may have issues with Raila Amolo Odinga and vice versa, but the way he was hounded out of office, exposed to insecurity, and left either [to] starve or crawl back is not any different from what Moi did. If it was wrong then, it remains wrong now…"

Five years after returning to Kenya, I regret to announce that I might have been wrong about Raila. He, like Kibaki and Kalonzo, isn't a genuine agent of change. He has proved to be as prone to corrupt, tribalistic and nepotistic tendencies as the worst of the merchants of impunity. He abuses power and doesn't uphold the law and the constitution. More importantly, he cannot be trusted. After the horrors of the post-election violence, the corrupt regrouped –

one under Kibaki's State House and Harambee House, and the other under Raila's Orange House and BP Shell House Building.

As my friend Agar says, there can never be societal rights without individual rights. Society is nothing but a conglomeration of individuals. Yet it is when individuals band together, in sufficient large numbers, in the quest for justice, that society liberates itself from bondage. The struggle for the total liberation of Kenya, of Africa and of all the repressed, oppressed and the exploited in the world is what I have been involved in, and it is what I shall continue to pursue. Therefore, if this book does nothing else, I hope it raises these issues and puts them in their proper perspective.

The book is also intended to unmask the duplicitous and deceptive life of Raila Amolo Odinga. I've done it for myself, for my family, for the country, for Africa and for humanity.

For that, I say TINDA!

EPILOGUE

PROJECT KENYA

I narrate these stories because it's important that readers understand what kind of historical events, incidents and circumstances have shaped and defined my life. For instance, they explain the probable reasons why I have rejected anything alcoholic throughout my life. But these stories also exemplify why I have lived a principled and focused life. The reason why I have held on to and will never compromise on my rights to free conscience, thought, expression and association are largely traceable to this early part of my life.

My deep commitment to respect fundamental human rights, the rule of law, justice and constitutionalism wasn't founded on flimsy rhetoric and empty theories; it is grounded on my life experiences. Had Nelson Mandela, Bantu Steve Biko, Joe Slovo, Ruth First, Walter Sisulu and other anti-apartheid warriors not resolved to defy the apartheid regime and join the struggle, how long would the black South Africans have spent in bondage? Wouldn't it have been easier, more 'pragmatic' from the personal survival perspective, for them to have taken a low profile and furthered their careers? How about the hazardous struggles of African slaves who risked everything for the ultimate freedom? Should we be proud or ashamed of Kunta Kinte for repeatedly attempting to escape from slavery but each time being caught and tortured and brutalised by the slave owners? Should we be ashamed or proud of Nat Turner and Frederick Douglass for championing the anti-slavery movement? Isn't the spirit and culture of struggle against injustice and oppression something honourable and inspiring?

Struggle demands sacrifices without which victory cannot be guaranteed. Whenever these sacrifices are made, nobody can tell with precision how it will all end. But end it always does, with victory on the side of justice. Evil might win a few bouts. Sometimes evil's temporary and fleeting 'triumphs' are so frequent and might last for decades until those without a firm grasp of history would mistake them for final victory. But good always, ultimately, wins. That's the tested verdict of history and it's not going to change. I have faced life-threatening experiences throughout my life. But each time I have closed an ugly chapter, I have opened a new one. Through it all, I have remained focused, firm, unbowed, unrepentant, unshaken and fearless. Surrender isn't an option.

My job description, as a senior adviser to the Prime Minister, didn't include lying or engaging in or condoning wrongdoing, neither did it include being deceptive. To advise entailed that I had to be thorough, objective, candid and balanced. Often, advising a senior public figure such as the Prime Minister of a country requires one to have the strength of character to express contrary opinions, to disagree not just with fellow advisers and colleagues, but also to have the fortitude to disagree with the public figure you are supposed to advise. Ultimately, even though I had been hired to advise the Prime Minister, I was required to do so strictly in line with the public interests and in accordance with the law. The national interests were more paramount than parochial ODM interests or those that only attached to Raila Odinga. I wasn't interested in power at any cost. To me, the end did not always justify the means. Both were important. I was, after all, a public officer. My remuneration came directly from public coffers.

I was lucky to have had a strong, generous and loving mother who taught me the values of honesty and loyalty when I was still very young. My mother also instilled in me the rebellious streak against injustice. The fearlessness I have exhibited throughout my life is part DNA and part conditioning. I was raised to reject oppression. My system is violently opposed to dishonest, deceptive and selfish people who would do everything to take advantage of others. I have also been lucky to have had a few genuine friends and comrades who have valued our friendship more than temporal things.

Undeniably, I have had my fair share of fair-weather friends too; here today (when things are good), gone tomorrow (when things are elephant). Fair-weather friends bombarded me with calls and text messages shortly after Raila announced the "reinstatement" that never was, until my mobile telephone died, literally, under their heavy attack. After I made it clear that I couldn't accept a cynical "warning letter" couched as a "reinstatement," the deluge of calls and texts from the fair-weather friends suddenly stopped raining. I knew the drill.

This is just an illustration of how painful this whole episode has been.

Having survived the hardship of being born and raised in Magina village, I never saw any hurdle too high to jump over. I have relied on my self-confidence, resourcefulness, discipline and love of hard work to triumph where others might have been deterred; these characteristics have enabled me to transform tragic incidents into salvations in disguise. This happened when as an 11-year-old boy I bolted out of that homestead in Lambwe Valley and charged into the pitch-dark night. It happened again after I had been detained incommunicado, then released from the infamous Nyayo Torture Chambers.

I know many do not know this, but I'm a highly introspective person. In fact, many times, Raila accused me of thinking too much. (Though he had no objection to the numerous 'think pieces' I penned in his defence.) This disquiet was only expressed about the copious notes I made during meetings. He felt exposed. (He shouldn't have if he believed that he was honest). I think about and analyse virtually everything I see. It can be frustrating to those around me but it has saved my life, repeatedly.

I plotted my escape from Kenya into exile in detention. Before my arrest, I had custody of all SONU stationery and equipment. I also had possession of the SONU files containing correspondence with global bodies such as Amnesty International, the International Students' Union, the Human Rights Watch and the United Nations High Commissioner for Refugees. As I endured torture and withering interrogation over concocted tales, I plotted how I was going to put that reservoir of information into good use, if only I was released.

I am an example of the immortal lesson that education is the universal equaliser. Through education, the poor cross class and cultural barriers; they breach artificial stratifications and aspire for a more equal and equitable society, which, with hard work and discipline, they often achieve. That ability to be decisive and pursue a different course with unflinching discipline and persistence has characterised my life throughout. Even my outspokenness is traceable to these earlier experiences; apart from the genetic imprint alluded to earlier. Over the years, I have learnt that cowardice, opportunism and greed ultimately kill the person afflicted by these human frailties.

Tom Joseph Mboya was an exceptionally gifted thinker, tactician and speaker. Historians say that Kenya has not known of such souring oratory since the assassination of TJ. Unfortunately, Mboya allowed his ravenous hunger for political power to undermine his ability to think and strategise. His mobilising abilities were legendary, but they ended up at the service of those who plotted his assassination. He betrayed one of the most fundamental rules of power: always conceal your intentions but never waver in your quest or ambition. A good strategist exhibits patience – at least outwardly – even as s/he bubbles within. Mboya was a tactical genius; he ensnared and hobbled Jaramogi with one innovative distraction after another. In the process, he mistook momentary and pyrrhic triumphs to be the ultimate victory. As he celebrated his extraordinary tactical manoeuvres over Jaramogi – with Kenyatta and his coteries cheering – he forgot to cover his exposed flank. He believed he was indispensable to Kenyatta. He trusted those he worked with too much.

In other words, Mboya was a contradiction: on the one hand, he had extraordinary talents and used that to rise rapidly to the pinnacle of power before he even turned 30. Yet on the other hand, he inadvertently forgot that his ascendancy placed him on the path of equally ambitious characters, some evil and others not so evil. He naïvely – and, one could argue, recklessly – believed that Jomo Kenyatta and his cronies would be so appreciative of his talents and performance in dismantling the Jaramogi Oginga Odinga juggernaut that they would reward him with the ultimate prize: the presidency. He was wrong. Mboya forgot that every human being is potentially evil and wicked and that if you discover such traits in anyone, you should, if for nothing else but your personal survival, place great distance between you and such a person. If you are able, you should avoid working with such a person permanently. Ultimately, any cautious and intelligent operative must not trust such a person again.

Dr. Robert Ouko couldn't learn that lesson because, like Mboya, the forces of retrogression didn't give him another chance. Diplomacy and cowardice don't provide security; outspokenness does.

That has remained my spirit, determination and focus. Many would argue that I committed the same error I blame Mboya and Ouko for. My response is that those saying so don't know the difference between lemon and lemonade; one is a fruit, the other a drink. The reason you are reading this book on Raila's pathological betrayal of his friends and cause – and neither Mboya nor Ouko were that lucky – is because of that difference. My sense of survival is so acute that if I were to die of human hands, I would die standing up; not on my knees or on my bed. That is a guarantee.

Although I might have looked like and might have stated that I trusted Raila completely, the truth is that I never actually did. My faith began to falter during the post-election crisis of 2007. When Raila addressed both local and international press in January 2008 and stated that as a general he wasn't supposed to go to the frontlines where his troops were, I was utterly astonished. Everyone I spoke with about it was equally dumbfounded – Salim Lone, Prof. Oyugi and Sarah Ederkin. Until then, I was giving excuses for his absence in the thick of it.

I felt that he was busy doing equally important and pressing things that were both necessary and essential to the success of our resistance against the electoral theft. After he made that statement, it suddenly dawned on me that we were dealing with a delusional character infused with a sense of divine entitlement.

Raila's careless statement about the role of a general made me ask: if a general doesn't go to the frontline to fight, who leads his troops? How does he motivate them? In what way does a general prove to his troops that he is willing and ready to sacrifice his life for them? Does a general hide in a bunker, a five-star hotel or a hole? To me Raila sounded like Saddam Hussein, pretending to be a brave warrior when in reality he was hiding in a hole. In my considered view, a true general must stand shoulder-to-shoulder with his troops. In fact, he must *lead* them in battle, and if necessary, fearlessly take a bullet for them. Clearly, Raila wasn't a good or a true general. It was at that point that I began to question his loyalty, trustworthiness, commitment and honesty.

During that interview, Raila also came across as both a cowardly and unconcerned leader who believed, wrongly, that the lives of his lieutenants and comrades weren't as valuable as his own. As he uttered these most unfortunate and irresponsible statements, tens of thousands of his supporters were being killed, maimed, raped and forcefully displayed in Central Province, Nairobi, Kisumu, Kakamega, Kericho, Eldoret, Nakuru, and Naivasha. Gory pictures of men, women and children dragged from commuter vehicles on the Nairobi-Kisumu highway and hacked and shot to death in the most brutal manner imaginable were being beamed on television and reported in the print and electronic media. Admittedly, Raila condemned the brutality being meted out to his supporters, primarily by the security forces and the Mungiki gang. A vicious and an unrepentant gang he is currently desperate to collaborate with in search of votes because of his insatiable greed for power and glory.

Raila's duplicitous, hypocritical and deceptive nature would be exposed again and again during and after the 2007 post-election crisis. I would sit in meetings where he would give his word and commitment to a person or group of people, then he would turn around in another session with a different person or group and assert the complete opposite. What I saw up close wasn't a leader capable of transforming Kenya into a modern, industrial, democratic and just society.

When Raila was released from his first stint in detention by Moi, he found his wife and children without a proper or stable home. Everywhere Raila went – even to Nairobi restaurants – people would avoid him like the plague. Friends, relatives and former colleagues would shy away from him for fear of being victimised by the state. He was treated like a leper. In fact, it was Dr. Ongong'a

Achieng' – Achieng' Oneko's eldest son – who took pity on Raila and assisted him in securing a mortgage (without collateral or down payment) at the Kenya Commercial Bank where Dr. Ongong'a was a senior manager, in order to purchase a house in Runda. Yet Raila the PM behaves as if he has forgotten that experience and background. He can no longer answer Ongong'a's telephone calls. He shows no empathy, sensitivity and concern about people in similar situations to the abject one he then found himself in.

More painfully, Raila has tried to put me in the same situation Moi unjustly placed him in. He finds the company of those who oppressed him more convenient than those engaged in the struggle against the culture of impunity. That's the kind of politics of yesteryear that we wanted to change. Yet it was the politics he embraced. What should I have done? Become a chameleon like him? No. I had long resolved to remain steadfast, truthful and honest. I am an unrepentant transformative radical. I have agitated for change since I was a small peasant boy.

I have never subscribed to the belief that all struggles need martyrs. Yes, sacrifices are inevitable in life, especially during protracted struggles, particularly of leaders of the struggle. But I have never believed that only cowards should enjoy the fruits of the struggles. Surviving struggles should be the most important duty of a revolutionary. Those who survive the struggle are heroes. They are the ones who evade capture and refuse to fall victim of their enemies. Only the dead are martyrs. I swore that I would resist being a martyr. I shall only be if the cause is just and I am on my feet.

As Jack Layton, the leader of the New Democratic Party of Canada and then leader of official opposition in the Canadian House of Commons stated in a letter to his friends just before he died on August 20, 2011: "My friends, love is better than anger. Hope is better than fear. Optimism is better than despair. So let us be loving, hopeful and optimistic. And we'll change the world."

It's hope that has kept me going, quite literally. Many times in my life, I've had nothing but hope; the dream that tomorrow will be different.

ACKNOWLEDGEMENTS

Many people have assisted me during the conception, planning and writing of this book. Some provided moral, emotional, financial and political support, while others encouraged me through their searing and consistent criticisms. It was actually the latter that made me complete writing this book in record speed if only to expose their duplicity and opportunism. Personal attacks have always solidified my commitment to social justice and equality.

I'm grateful for the support and encouragement I got from my brother Eric Ondiek Miguna, his wife Angeline (the petite lady we all call *Min Kari* or *Angelina*), and their children, Babu, Cary, Evance; Alex and the late Palvine; my surviving sisters Auma, Herina, Akinyi and Monica; my departed sisters Jane, Juma, Leah, Owino and Atieno; my father-in-law, Benson Omolo Awange, and my mother-in-law, Zipporah Auma. You kept the faith and spirit burning. I cannot forget my departed loving aunt Beldina Owuor (Nyar Ma), who kept me going – literally – during those difficult periods in Onjiko.

Kathy France: my friend of 20 years and the only book-keeper I have had throughout my professional career has proved to be a genuine friend, confidante, role model and solid rock. Kathy was introduced to me after I completed law school by a fellow artist and friend, Nqaba Msimang from South Africa. Kathy has been a solid rock in my life. She has served as my mother, guide, supporter, book-keeper, friend – name it. Of all my closest friends, Kathy has remained more steadfast than virtually everyone else: calling, emailing and checking on me days without number. She is still going strong at well over 70; a true African iron lady.

Another permanent feature in my life has been Denvon Nesbith. I met Denvon in Toronto after I joined Osgoode Hall Law School in 1990. Together with two of my best friends – Joma Nyakorema Nkombe and Livingston Wedderburn – we formed the Pan-African Law Society at York University through which we mobilised and agitated against racism and discrimination both at York and around

Toronto. Although Denvon, like many others, wasn't a law student, he joined our organization because we understood that the issues of systemic and institutional racism were not limited to Osgoode Hall Law School or York University. Denvon has remained a true friend throughout. Although he developed a severe kidney failure that forced him to prematurely leave his lucrative ICT consulting practice, he has remained brave and uncomplaining. Even though he attends dialysis thrice every week, Denvon developed my website in 2007 as a contribution to my political foray and has been managing it ever since. Without Denvon, even this book wouldn't have been published in record speed. He is the person who has been posting and updating the website, which in many ways hasn't just kept my readers, friends and supporters informed, but has also served as the security for everything I write. I pray that Denvon gets a donor soon so that he can continue to contribute towards the final liberation of Africa. I cannot thank Denvon enough.

Waikwa Wanyoike, whom I first met in 1997 and acted for as an asylum seeker in Toronto has been a good friend throughout.

My comrade Onyango Oloo has demonstrated, over and again, what true friendship means and that we must practice what we preach if we are serious about the commitments we proclaim. I thank him most sincerely for standing with me during this long quest for justice.

Tracey Wynter; Charles Roach, Esq.; Sarah Elderkin; Mutakha Kangu; Owen Ojuok; Dick Abuor Okumu; Tom Ogindo; Joab Agar Okello; Onyango Ogango; Prof. Edward Akong'o Oyugi; Mohamed Doli; Ambassador Rateng' Oginga Ogego; Paul Muite; Elly Ajwang'; Mary Ajwang'; Parselelo Ole Kantai; Salim Lone; Mugambi Kiai; Herbert Ojwang'; James Ogada Onyango; Marceline Odongo; Mrs. Jane Omolo; Mzee Omolo Tindi; *Japuonj* Enos Ochiewo Oyaya (*Rateng'*); Ambassadors David Collins (Canada) and Margit Helwig-Boette (Germany); Joanne Bund; Prof. Marilyn Pilkington; U-Sheak Koroma; Dr. Sally Kosgei; Prof. Eboe Hutchful; Prof. J. Esberey; Prof. Richard Sandbrook; Prof. Allan Hutchinson; Livingstone Wedderburn; Prof. Toni Williams; Prof. Ronald Manzer; Munyonzwe Hamalengwa, Esq.; Jeff Koinange; Dr. Willy Mutunga; Justice (Rtd.) Bena Luta; Prof. Larry Gumbe; Sylvester Kasuku; Prof. Tom Ojienda; Apollo Mboya; Anthony Munene; Jared Okello; Beth Gebroyohannes; Duncan Sandys Otieno Onguta; Anthony Ochieng' Owala; Duncan Osodo; Okulu Obadha (Mangy); the late irreplaceable Abaja Yambo; Millicent Agola; Erastus Omill Oloo; Peter Mutonyi Gakiri; Ogola JTO; Hussein Mohamed; Rosa Buyu; Joseph Nyagah; James Aggrey Orengo; Sheri Price; the late Yvonne Vera; John Hidaya Masuka; Regina Senjule; Julius Omware; the late Prof. Odera-Oruka; the late Prof. Owuor Anyumba; Prof.

Frederick Ochieng'; Dick Abuor Okumu; Benson Shiholo and Kiarie Kamau of the East African Educational Publishing; Jeremy Ng'ang'a; Peter Nyoro and Pamela Gitari of the Oxford University Press; Ruth Tesfemariam; Jacky Muka; the late Apollo Onyango Ong'or; *Japuonj* Joshua A. Owiti Osuri; Maurice Adongo Ogony; Richard Le Bars and Vincent Charron both of the Canadian High Commission in Nairobi; the Star newspaper CEO William Pike and the Radio Africa Group CEO Patrick Quarcoo, have been supportive, at one time or the other, in the course of this journey.

Ambassador Laetitia van den Assum (Netherlands) has proven through more than three years that cultural, racial, gender and religious differences are capable of being bridged and transformed into assets for development and prosperity. Amb. Van den Assum has demonstrated her patriotism to and love for Kenya more than most highly placed and privileged Kenyan politicians. Her deep friendship, care and generosity for me have been a source of encouragement and strength. Let me say thank you most sincerely.

My comrade Felix Mbutho, a South African diplomat in Nairobi, has been more solid than granite. He kept contact, calling and dropping at home, almost daily. Life is full of surprises. Felix and I call each other 'Comrade'. Indeed, he has lived up to that salutation.

Raphael Tuju and I call each other 'Brother'. That isn't a prefix I bestow on any head God had the mercy to create without good justification. For more than ten years that we have been friends, he has earned the adoration reserved for a true Brother.

To my *Comrade* and *Brother*, I wish to confirm that we kept the faith and delivered on time. I thank you both most sincerely for the friendship, generosity and human dignity you have shown.

Simon Buckby and Helen Wharton of Champollion of London, UK, came in handy at the last minute to salvage the project when many powerful and influential forces in Kenya seemed arrayed against me deserve a hearty thank you.

I am grateful for the support, commitment and exemplary work done by the team at Gilgamesh, led by the wonderful Max Scott. Charles Powell and Graham Edwards worked round the clock to ensure that I could fulfill my promise to Kenyans that this book would be available in July 2012. And they delivered, spectacularly! The speed at which they were able to release the book was unprecedented. Their experience in publishing and book design has produced a book I am very proud of.

Patricia Nicol, my inimitable editor, who served 12 years as a senior editor with the *Sunday Times* in both Scotland and London, worked tirelessly and demonstrated her great skills by transforming a 400,000-word manuscript into this beautifully crafted 588-page tome. She juggled her work while raising two young children, one who isn't even two years old. Without Patricia's dogged effort, skill and flexibility, this book couldn't have been released in time and on schedule. I am forever grateful to her.

There are many, many comrades, relatives, friends, colleagues and supporters who have kept calling and writing to me, sometimes almost on a daily basis, in order to express their solidarity with me and to keep up my spirits. I ask them to forgive me for not listing all of them. Even if I could remember everyone – an onerous task given the number of people involved – listing them would take half of this book. Let me just say: thank you to everyone.

I wouldn't live with myself if I left my departed mother, Suré *nyar* Njoga, out of this book, for without her care, suffering, sense of justice and sacrifices, I would never have made it past childhood, and this book would never have been written.

My family – both immediate and extended – has been outstanding throughout these difficult, trying and challenging times. This includes our dedicated housekeeper, Millicent Atieno Warindu.

My children Atieno (Atis nyar Apondo), Biko (Abuki) Thuon, Suré (Asuro), Anyango (Nyangi Juma) and Achieng' (Chichi my creative tutor) Roda – I cannot thank you enough. I know how you have suffered quietly, watching as your edifice, the confidence, security and stability that we all valued, suddenly appeared to crumble around us. You watched in silence as I successfully tried to shield you (perhaps unsuccessfully) from the ravages of corrosive selfishness, envy, jealousy and betrayal. I still remember Suré's persistent question: "Mommy, what happened between Daddy and Raila? I thought they were friends…" I couldn't answer that perceptive observation from a ten-year-old girl who had shouted "ODM…Raila!" louder than anybody else I knew in December 2007 when she was barely six. Time passes quickly. My love for you is unyielding.

Throughout this tedious and stressful experience, my wife, Jane, has been quietly but solidly loving and supportive. Without her consistent encouragement and emotional support, this work wouldn't have been completed on time and on schedule – nor would it have been of this superb quality.

Finally, the immortal caveat: none of my family members, comrades, friends, relatives, editors and supporters – other than me – is responsible for any errors or views expressed in *Peeling Back the Mask: A Quest for Justice in Kenya*.

APPENDIX 1

Guiding Principles and Institutional Framework for Managing the Affairs of the Grand Coalition Government (Coalition Agreement), prepared and tabled by the author at the Permanent Committee meeting in April 2009. Although the ODM members had unanimously adopted the document, they failed to push for its discussion and ratification at meetings held at the Harambee House in April 2009. The author attempted to reintroduce it at the Kilaguni retreat, but that, too, failed to materialise

GUIDING PRINCIPLES AND INSTITUTIONAL FRAMEWORK FOR MANAGING THE AFFAIRS OF THE GRAND COALITION GOVERNMENT

Between

ORANGE DEMOCRATIC MOVEMENT

-and-

PARTY OF NATIONAL UNITY

Dated at Nairobi on the ______ day of __________ 2009

THE GUIDING PRINCIPLES AND INSTITUTIONAL FRAMEWORK FOR MANAGING THE AFFAIRS OF THE GRAND COALITION AFFAIRS (hereinafter referred to as the "Guiding Principles And Institutional Framework") made this ______ day of April 2009

BETWEEN The ORANGE DEMOCRACTIC MOVEMENT Political Party registered under the Political Parties Act, 2008 (hereinafter referred to as "the ODM")

AND

The PARTY OF NATIONAL UNITY Political Party registered the Political Parties Act, 2008 (hereinafter referred to as "the PNU")

Background: Recalling the Agreement on the Principles of Partnership of the Coalition Government made on February 28, 2008 (hereinafter referred to as "the National Accord"), which Parliament approved by enacting the *National Accord and Reconciliation Act, 2008* (hereinafter referred to as "the *Act*");

Recognizing that the Grand Coalition Government has been formed to promote good governance, social justice, human rights, democracy, equity, the rule of law and constitutionalism; and

Pursuant to the formation of the Grand Coalition Government following the entrenchment of the National Accord in the Kenya Constitution by the enactment of the *Kenya Constitution Amendment Act Number 3 of 2008* (hereinafter referred to as "the *Amendment Act No. 3, 2008*)

NOW THE PARTIES HERETO AGREE AS FOLLOWS:

Article 1: Interpretation and Definitions

1.1 Definitions in the Guiding Principles and Institutional Framework, and any schedules or annexations/annextures to it shall, unless the context otherwise admits or requires, have (with or without the definite article) the following meanings:

1.2 In the Guiding Principles and Institutional Framework reference to the plural includes reference to the singular and vice versa.

1.3 Headings: Headings inserted in the Guiding Principles and Institutional Framework is for convenience of reference only and do not affect the interpretation of this agreement.

"**Commencement Date**" means the date when the Guiding Principles and Framework is signed.

"**Consensus**" refers to agreement without voting.

"**Discipline**" means the standard of conduct, accountability and transparency required of the Grand Coalition Government.

"**Dispute**" means disputes as defined in Article 6 herein.

Government" shall have the same meaning as provided in the Constitution of Kenya and as defined in the *Interpretation and General Provisions Act* and any other written law.

"**Grand Coalition Government**" means the Government of Kenya established under the Constitution of Kenya as amended by the *National Accord and Reconciliation Act, 2008* and *Constitution Amendment Act Number 3 of 2008.*

"**Joint Secretariat**" means the Secretariat headed by two Joint Secretaries of the Permanent Committee on the Management of the Grand Coalition Government.

"**Parties to the Grand Coalition Government**" means both ODM and PNU Coalition.

"**Permanent Committee on the Management of Grand Coalition Affairs**" (hereinafter referred to as "the Permanent Committee") means an organ of the Grand Coalition Government mandated with the responsibility of managing the affairs of the Grand Coalition.

"**Political Appointments**" refer to all appointments generally known as "Executive" and made by the President, the Prime Minister, the Vice-President, the Deputy Prime Ministers and Ministers. They include appointment of Permanent Secretaries; Heads of State Corporations; Provincial Commissioners; District Commissioners; Ambassadors, High Commissioners and Heads of Diplomatic Missions; Police Commissioner; Senior Military Officers; the Head of National Security Intelligence Service; Attorney General; Solicitor-General; members of the Judiciary; Members and Commissioners of the Public Service Commission; Chancellors and Vice-Chancellors of Public Universities.

"Portfolio Balance" means real power sharing which shall entail a mechanism and/or a scheme for sharing Executive authority and responsibility equitably and equally in Government by the two Grand Coalition Partners.

"Principal" means His Excellency President Mwai Kibaki and/or The Right Honourable Prime Minister Raila Amolo Odinga, or the persons occupying the offices of President and Prime Minister in the Republic of Kenya.

"State Protocol" refers to the official, formality, diplomatic and etiquette observed or required to be observed, including the rules and procedures observed on state or official occasions, treatment, remunerations, security and privileges accorded to the Principals.

"Quorum" means half of the members of both Party of National Unity (PNU) Coalition and Orange Democratic Movement (ODM) to the Permanent Committee on the Management of the Grand Coalition Affairs.

Article 2: Principles Governing the Operation of the Grand Coalition Government

2.1.1 That Kenya belongs to all Kenyans.

2.1.2 That the Grand Coalition Government is made up of the Two Principals and members of their respective Parties who have equal power, authority and responsibility with respect to the management of the Government of Kenya.

2.1.3 That the Grand Coalition Government's primary role is to serve all Kenyans and act in their best interests.

2.1.4 That good governance; respect for the rule of law and human rights; transparency and accountability shall guide the operation of the Grand Coalition Government.

2.1.5 That there must be real power sharing between the Grand Coalition Partners.

2.1.6 That there must be portfolio balance in the sharing of power, authority and responsibility in Government between the Grand Coalition Partners.

2.1.7 That decisions in Government and the public declaration of those decisions will be made jointly through constant consultations, concurrence, compromise and consensus.

2.1.8 That there shall be Collective Responsibility and One Government.

2.1.9 That there shall be Comparable State Protocol for both Principals.

Article 3: Aims and Objectives of the Grand Coalition Government

3.1 To stop violence and restore fundamental rights and liberties;

3.2 To address the humanitarian crisis, promote reconciliation, healing and restoration;

3.3 To address issues such as poverty, the inequitable distribution of resources and perceptions of historical injustices and exclusion through:

3.3.1 Undertaking constitutional, legal and institutional reform;

3.3.2 Tackling unemployment, particularly among the youth;

3.3.3 Undertaking Land Reform; and

3.3.4 Addressing transparency, accountability and impunity.

Article 4: Party Obligations

Each Party Shall

1.1 Commit itself to the realization of the values, aims, objectives and principles set out in this Agreement.

1.2 Support policies agreed upon and bills introduced in the National Assembly by the Grand Coalition Government.

1.3 Not do anything which directly or indirectly competes with or undermines the Grand Coalition Government or the advancement of its policies and programs or act in a manner that compromises the interests of the Grand Coalition Government as stipulated or contemplated by these Guidelines and Institutional Framework and the National Accord.

Article 5: Executive/Political Appointments

5.1 Executive/Political appointments, promotions, demotions, discipline, interdictions and dismissals affecting Government bodies, organs, agencies and boards, including Permanent Secretaries; Heads of State Corporations; Provincial Commissioners; District Commissioners; Ambassadors, High Commissioners and Heads of Diplomatic Missions; Police Commissioner; Senior Military Officers; the Head of National Security Intelligence Service; Attorney General; Solicitor-General; the Judiciary; Public Service Commission; Chancellors and Vice-Chancellors of Public Universities; and regulatory boards and agencies, shall be jointly made by both Principals pursuant to the "Mechanisms of Consultation" instrument.

5.1 All Executive/Political appointments must be made in accordance with the principle of portfolio balance between ODM and PNU Coalition.

Article 6: State Protocol

6.1 Both Principals shall have or be accorded equal treatment in terms of the official, formality, diplomatic and etiquette observed or required to be observed, including the rules and procedures observed on state or official occasions; identical terms of service including remunerations, security, housing and attendant privileges.

Article 7: Speaking for and within the Grand Coalition Government

1.4 The President and the Prime Minister shall jointly speak for the Government on major policy issues agreed to by the Grand Coalition Government.

1.5 No other public officer shall speak on behalf of the Grand Coalition Government except with express joint written authority of both Principals.

7.3 No Cabinet Minister or Assistant Minister shall contradict, oppose or act against a position or issue jointly taken or agreed on by the Grand Coalition Government or Grand Coalition Partners.

Article 8: Disputes

8.1 It shall be the responsibility of both Principals to endeavour to resolve any dispute that may arise relating to the interpretation of the National Accord and/or the Guiding Principles And Institutional Framework or the obligations under it, or any other matter which may prejudice the Grand Coalition Government.

8.2 Dispute Resolution: If a Dispute arises that has not been resolved by the Principals within twenty-four hours, it shall be referred to the Permanent Committee. The Permanent Committee shall negotiate in good faith to resolve the dispute.

8.3 Where a Dispute cannot be resolved by the Permanent Committee, either Party to the Grand Coalition may refer the matter for mediation or further resolution by the Panel of Eminent African Personalities, failing which, either Party to the Grand Coalition may give to the other Party to the Grand Coalition, written notice, that unless the matter is resolved within a period of seven (7) days the Grand Coalition will be terminated and fresh elections held within two (2) months of the Grand Coalition coming to an end. The Grand Coalition Government shall then hand over executive power and authority to the Party and/or Leader duly, legally and legitimately declared as winner after election conducted in accordance with the Constitution of Kenya.

Article 9: Validity of the Grand Coalition Agreement

9.1 These Guiding Principles And Institutional Framework for Managing the Affairs of the Grand Coalition Government are valid from the date they are ratified up to and including the date when the Grand Coalition Government ceases as provided for in the National Accord.

Article 10: Permanent Committee on the Management of the Grand Coalition Affairs

Article 10.1: Composition

10.1.1 The Permanent Committee shall be composed of the Two Principals and six nominees from each Grand Coalition Partner.

10.1.2 Each Grand Coalition Partner shall nominate and replace, in writing, any of its members to the Permanent Committee.

10.1.3 In order to maintain the integrity of the Permanent Committee's deliberations and decisions, non-members of the Permanent Committee can only attend the meetings of the Permanent Committee upon written invitation by both Principals through the Joint Secretaries.

11: Confidentiality

11.2 Confidential Information: All records, reports and other documents relating to the Grand Coalition Government are confidential whether oral, written or embodied in any other physical form except if:

11.1.1 The information was known to the receiving party on the date of its receipt; or

11.1.2 The information was in the public domain after the date of its receipt; or

11.1.3 The information had entered the public domain after the date of its receipt other than by unauthorized disclosure by a party or any other person.

11.1.4 Neither party shall disclose in whole or in part any confidential information received except as approved in writing by the Permanent Committee, or where necessary to carry out the terms of this agreement.

11.1.5 Before any confidential information is disclosed to a third party, the party about to so disclose shall inform the Permanent Committee of its intention to disclose and shall inform such third person of the confidential obligation under the agreement, and require such third person to be bound by the same confidential obligations.

12.2 Decisions

12.2.1 Decisions of the Permanent Committee shall be made by consensus.

12.2.2 No issue, policy platform or agenda shall be announced or implemented by the Grand Coalition Government without both Grand Coalition Partners consulting and agreeing beforehand.

12.2.3 Each Grand Coalition Partner has the right to present for deliberation, further refinement, redefinition and fine-tuning any issue relevant to the management of the Grand Coalition Government.

13.3 Frequency of Meetings

13.3.1 The Permanent Committee shall meet at least two times each month, specifically at 10:00 a.m. on the First Friday of each month or such other time or times as the Principals, jointly, deem fit.

14.4 Functions

In Partnership and Collaboration with Other Government Institutions, the Permanent Committee shall:

14.4.1 Define, refine, fine-tune and/or interpret any issue, term or provision in the Guiding **Principles and Institutional Framework and/or the National Accord instruments.**

14.4.2 Discuss and resolve disputes that arise in the Grand Coalition Government.

15.5 Quorum

15.5.1 For purposes of executing functions and mandate of the Permanent Committee, three (3) members from each Grand Coalition Partner and both the Principals shall constitute a quorum.

Article 11: Joint Secretariat

16.1 The Permanent Committee shall have a Joint Secretariat headed by two Joint Secretaries, one from each Grand Coalition Partner. The Joint Secretaries shall take minutes of all meetings and agree on the contents of the official minutes before its adoption and safe custody; keep all Permanent Committee's records in safe custody, prepare the Agenda for meetings and perform any and/or all functions as directed by the unanimous resolution of either the Permanent Committee or both Principals.

Article 12: Depository

17.1 The Registrar of Political Parties and the Panel of Eminent African Personalities shall be the Depositories of the Guiding Principles and Institutional Framework.

Dated and signed at Nairobi this _______ day of April 2009

______________________	______________________
H.E. Mwai Kibaki	Rt. Hon. Raila Amolo Odinga
President and Commander-in-Chief	Prime Minister
Party of National Unity Coalition	Orange Democratic Movement"

APPENDIX 2

Mechanisms of consultation and procedures of making executive/political decisions and appointments within the Grand Coalition Government and the Permanent Committee, tabled before the Permanent Committee by the author in April 2009. Although the ODM members had unanimously adopted the document, they failed to push for its discussion and ratification at meetings held at the Harambee House in April 2009. The author attempted to reintroduce it at the Kilaguni retreat, but that, too, failed to materialise.

During the life of the Grand Coalition Government (GCG) and that of the Permanent Committee on the Management of Grand Coalition Affairs (PCMGCA), both major and minor Executive decisions and appointments are made and will continue to be made.

Executive decisions on policy, governance, government structure and institutions as well as engagements of senior cadres in public, diplomatic and international service require real consultation and concurrence of the Two Principals in accordance with the principles of real power sharing and portfolio balance between two equal partners enunciated in the Agreement On The Principles of Partnership of The Coalition Government (National Accord).

The Black's Law Dictionary, 6th Edition

Defines **consultation** as an act of conferring; deliberation of persons on some subject; or conference between the counsel engaged in a case, to discuss its questions or arrange the method of conducting it.

Concur is defined as "express agreement."

Concurrence means "to agree"; "accord"; "act together"; "consent."

Consultative decision making requires parties to meet (directly or through representatives) in order to discuss, confer and then agree or consent, **in writing**, on an act to be performed.

Therefore, without agreement, concurrence or consent, **in writing**, by the Grand Coalition Partners, no Executive/Political Decision(s) and/or Appointment(s), demotions, dismissals or termination of contracts will occur. If either Principal has made or makes such a decision or decisions or appointment(s) without consulting and seeking the concurrence of the other Principal, the one who has not been consulted and has not concurred shall have a veto power, which shall be deemed exercised by virtue of non-consultation and non-concurrence.

EXECUTIVE DECISIONS AND APPOINTMENTS

Within the context of the existing Kenyan law, which the **National Accord** is an integral part of, the following mechanisms for consultations and procedures will apply when Executive/Political decisions are made to appoint, promote, demote, suspend, interdict, dismiss, contract, assign, engage or bestow on or withdraw from personnel in the public service powers, duties, responsibilities or privileges. Executive / Political appointments shall include but not be limited to all employment, engagements, assignments, contracts, benefits or privileges held or enjoyed through the proclamations, decisions or fiat of the Executive. In Kenya, these appointments, decisions or fiat exercised by the President, the Prime Minister, the Vice-President, the Deputy Prime Ministers and Ministers.

List of Executive/Political Appointments:

1 Permanent Secretaries
2 Head of the Civil Service
3 Secretary to the Cabinet
4 Secretaries in Ministries
5 Heads of State Corporations
6 Members of the Boards of State Corporations
7 Chair of Regulatory Boards and Agencies
8 Members of State Corporations other Boards and Agencies
9 Provincial Commissioners
10 District Commissioners
11 Ambassadors, High Commissioners and Heads of Diplomatic Missions
12 Police Commissioner
13 Office of the Government Spokesperson
14 Commandant of Administration Police
15 Commandant of the General Service Unit
16 Director, CID
17 Chief of General Staff of the Armed Forces
18 Controller and Auditor General
19 Internal Auditor General
20 Senior Military Officers
21 Director General of the National Security Intelligence Service

22	Attorney General
23	Solicitor-General
24	Judges of the Court of Appeal
25	High Court Judges
26	Registrar of the High Court
27	Registrar of Political Parties
28	The Ombudsman
29	The Central Bank Governor
30	Chair, Public Service Commission
31	Vice-Chair, Public Service Commission
32	Commissioners, Public Service Commission
33	Establishment and membership of Commissions of Inquiry
34	Management of Government Press
35	State Corporations Advisory Committee
36	Membership of the National Security Committee
37	Chancellors of Public Universities
38	Vice-Chancellors of Public Universities
39	Secondment to International Bodies, Agencies or Organs
40	Prerogative of Mercy
41	Participation and signing of all Bilateral and International Treaties and Agreements
42	Nominations to International Organizations

Mechanisms of Consultations and Procedures of Making Executive Decisions and Appointments

1. Full, Complete and Timely Disclosure

Any position that has been filled, Executive Decision(s) made, contract(s) or treaties signed, extended or terminated, and responsibilities, duties and privileges bestowed on any person or persons since the formation of the Grand Coalition Government with respect to the above list, must be declared forthwith, in writing, with or without request, by the relevant Government institution(s), agency or agencies or organ(s) to the Two Principals and the Joint Secretaries. This is to facilitate decision-making by consensus between the Two Principals.

2. Meeting of the Two Principals

The Two Principals shall meet, accompanied by the Joint Secretaries, monthly to discuss and identify ministries, departments, organs, agencies, diplomatic missions abroad and boards to be affected by Executive Decision(s) and/or Executive Appointments.

3. Directive to Identify Positions and Individuals to be Affected

The Two Principals shall direct two (2) representatives to identify institutions, organs, bodies, agencies, diplomatic missions abroad, positions and/or individuals to be affected by the Executive/Political Decision(s) and/or Executive Appointments mentioned herein.

4. Sharing of Positions

The identified positions shall then be shared out equally and Executive Decisions made jointly between President Kibaki/PNU Coalition and Prime Minister Raila Amolo Odinga/ODM based on their strategic, budgetary, public policy and national importance.

Neither Party has the power, authority or mandate to vet nominee(s) of his or its Grand Coalition Partner. Each Principal will scrupulously apply the principles of fairness, equity, inclusivity and transparency in filling his half share of the public service, diplomatic and international positions.

5. Announcement of Executive Decisions, Appointments, Promotions, Interdictions, Dismissals, Contracts and Treaties

Once the Two Principals and Grand Coalition Partners agree on the positions to be filled and individuals to be appointed, **signified in writing**, the President, Prime Minister, Vice-President, Deputy Prime Ministers and Ministers, as the case may be, shall issue out letters of appointment and ensure that the appointees are integrated in the Public, Diplomatic and/or International Service within one week of the agreement noted at item number 3 herein.

6. In Case Of Failure to Agree On Executive/Political Appointments

In case the Two Principals fail to agree on the appointment(s), engagements, contracts or decision(s) to be made, the matter shall be brought before the PCMGCA by either one Joint Secretary or both Joint Secretaries within two days of such disagreement occurring.

7. Positions Automatically Become Vacant

If the PCMGCA fails to resolve the matter within two days of the same being brought to it, the contested positions shall automatically become vacant. However, these positions must be filled through consultations and concurrence of the Two Principals, in writing, within two months of their vacancy occurring.

8. The Constitution of the Grand Coalition Government

The Constitution of the Grand Coalition Government must at all times reflect the principles of Real Power Sharing between two equal partners and Portfolio Balance pursuant to the provisions of the National Accord.

9. Evaluation of the Mechanisms and Procedures

The foregoing Mechanisms and Procedures for Executive/Political decision-making apply in regard to demotions, interdictions, suspensions, dismissals, contracts and treaties in all Public Service, Diplomatic and International engagements as well as in the cancellation of contracts, treaties, accords and protocols. They are designed to encourage discussion about the issues in contention and optimal ways of resolving them. Once resolved, the process requires that an evaluation procedure be engaged so that the results of the resolution process can be assessed and a determination made of the need for system enhancement, modification or entrenchment.

The PCMGCA should determine the agency or agencies or person(s) to carry out such evaluation. It is recommended that each Principal nominate two (2) independent professional evaluators to carry out this exercise quarterly.

APPENDIX 3

The Affidavit of Prof. Peter Anyang' Nyong'o dated 25 April, 2011, which was submitted to the International Criminal Court at The Hague by ODM.

AFFIDAVIT OF PROFESSOR PETER ANYAN'G NYONG'O
SWORN AT THE CITY OF NAIROBI, KENYA ON APRIL 25, 2011

I, PETER ANYANG' NYONG'O, of the City of Nairobi, Kenya, MAKE OATH AND STATE AS FOLLOWS:

1. I am the Secretary General of the Orange Democratic Movement (hereinafter referred to as the "ODM"). The ODM is a duly registered political party in accordance with the laws of Kenya. The leader of ODM is the Rt. Honourable Raila Amolo Odinga, who is also the Prime Minister of the Republic of Kenya.

2. I am also the Minister for Medical Services and a Member of Parliament for Kisumu Rural Constituency in the Republic of Kenya.

3. On or about February 28th, 2008, the National Accord and Reconciliation Agreement (hereinafter referred to as the "Accord") was signed between the ODM and the Party of National Unity Alliance led by the Honourable Mwai Kibaki, who is also the President of the Republic of Kenya. That agreement was later enacted in Parliament as the National Accord and Reconciliation Act, 2008 and entrenched in the Constitution. It was also preserved in the new Constitution, which was ratified through a referendum on August 4, 2010.

4. The Accord established the Grand Coalition Government in Kenya whose two partners are the ODM and the PNU Alliance, led by the Prime Minister, Raila Odinga, and the President, Mwai Kibaki, respectively. Under the Accord, the two sides share power and responsibilities in the Coalition equally.

5. As the Secretary General of the ODM, a cabinet minister in the Government of the Republic of Kenya and a Member of the Kenyan Parliament, I have personal knowledge of and reasonable beliefs on the matters I hereby depose. I have personal knowledge of how decisions are made by the Government of Kenya and how government processes work.

6. With respect to the current proceedings at the International Criminal Court (hereinafter referred to as the "ICC") against six Kenyan individuals, namely, William Samoie Ruto, Henry Kiprono Kosgey, Joshua Arap Sang, Francis Kirimi Muthaura, Uhuru Muigai Kenyatta and Mohammed Hussein Ali, I verily believe and the fact is that there have been no consultations between the Grand Coalition Government partners regarding the application(s) purportedly made by the Government of the Republic of Kenya pursuant to Article 19 of the ICC Statute. Specifically, I am aware that the President and the Prime Minister have not consulted and made any decision regarding this matter. Similarly, I am aware that the Cabinet has not met, discussed or made any resolution concerning this matter. Consequently, I verily state and the fact is that the purported application is not and cannot be that of the Government of the Republic of Kenya as claimed.

7. I verily believe and the fact is that the Admissibility Challenge purportedly filed by and/or on behalf of the Government of the Republic of Kenya, was actually only filed by and/or on behalf of one faction within the Government of the Republic of Kenya, namely, the Party of National Unity (PNU) headed by President Mwai Kibaki. The decision to file the Admissibility Challenge was not jointly arrived at by the President and the Prime Minister; nor was it a decision made by the Cabinet of the Government of the Republic of Kenya. Similarly, I am aware that there has been no decision in Cabinet or between the Prime Minister and the President regarding the request to the ICC to hand over a number of items, including but not limited to the evidence the Prosecutor has gathered, to the Kenyan authorities.

8. Further, I verily believe that the prosecution of the Kenyan Cases at the ICC does not pose any threat to international peace and security. To the contrary, failure to bring to justice the perpetrators of post-election violence poses grave danger to Kenya's internal peace and security.

9. The ICC process was unanimously approved by the two parties under the Kofi Annan-brokered National Accord, and the instruments that paved the way for the process were signed by both the President and the Prime Minister for and on behalf of their respective political parties, which form the grand coalition government.

10. I truly believe that the great majority of Kenyans (more than sixty one per cent) support the ICC process as the most credible method to start the fight against the culture of impunity in Kenya. I am aware of independent professional surveys by leading institutions in the country which have repeatedly confirmed this position.

11. Contrary to claims by lawyers that have been hired and instructed by the PNU faction within Government, I truly believe that local trials are not possible at the moment as there is no credible national judicial mechanism in place to handle the cases. I truly believe that there have been no investigations and prosecutions since the crimes were committed more than three years ago. Moreover, the criminal justice system has not been reformed to enable it to handle the cases. Although Kenya has enacted the International Crimes Act, it is in doubt as to whether Kenyan courts have jurisdiction over the international crimes committed before January 2009 when the Act became operational.

12. I am aware of the fact that the judicial reforms contemplated under the new Constitution have not been implemented. I am further aware that the judges and magistrates have not been vetted as required by the Constitution.

13. I truly believe that the Admissibility Challenge is evidence that the Party of National Unity and President Mwai Kibaki are both unwilling and unable to prosecute the six suspects for the crimes alleged by the ICC.

14. As a Cabinet Minister, I am aware that both the Cabinet and the National Assembly of the Republic of Kenya (hereinafter referred to as the "Parliament") have on more than two occasions rejected Bills for the establishment of an independent local tribunal intended to investigate and prosecute the serious crimes that were committed during the post-election violence of 2007/8.

15. I truly believe that at the moment the ICC process is the only opportunity that Kenyans have to break the culture of impunity and the circle of elections-related violence.

16. As a member of the Government of Kenya, I truly believe that there are no credible investigations of the post election violence cases that are ongoing. Moreover, I believe that because the Kenya Police was heavily implicated in the crimes that are subject to the ICC process – and the institution remains unreformed - none of the six individuals before the Court has been investigated, will be investigated or can be investigated by the Kenyan authorities. I am aware – and it is public knowledge - that none has been charged or is being prosecuted at the moment. Most important, the police investigative capacity and willingness is severely lacking in Kenya. There are too many cases of witnesses dying, not appearing, and cases dismissed for lack of sufficient evidence. I believe that trying the six cases or individuals in Kenya will seriously jeopardize the witnesses, some of whom will likely refuse to testify out of fear and intimidation.

17. Because of the foregoing, and on behalf of the ODM as a coalition partner in the Grand Coalition Government of the Republic of Kenya, I am humbly requesting the Court to reject the Application unilaterally and unprocedurally made by the PNU faction within government.

I make this affidavit truthfully in response to the purported Application by the Government of the Republic of Kenya pursuant to Article 19 of the ICC Statute and in support of the ODM's request for that application to be dismissed, and for no other or improper purpose.

SWORN BEFORE ME this 25th day of April 2011
at the City of Nairobi, Kenya

PETER ANYANG' NYONG'O

APPENDIX 4

Letter to Prof. Kivutha Kibwana dated 7 August 2009 regarding his attempts to interfere with the work of the Committee of Experts.

Dear Prof. Kibwana,

RE: A REBUTTAL OF PROF. KIBWANA'S "A CRITIQUE OF THE WORK OF THE COMMITTEE OF EXPERTS"

One of the "relevant actors" in the Constitutional Review process that you provided a copy of your "A Critique of the Work of the Committee of Experts (CoE)" dated 6th August 2009, has been kind enough to share it with me.

I wish that you had considered it prudent to have forwarded a copy of the Critique to me in view of our corresponding responsibilities in the national reform agenda, including the Constitutional Review process.

I also believe that the issues you have raised should have been brought to the attention of the CoE during the "Technical Consultations Forum" on the "contentious issues" that were held in Nairobi in June this year. Both of us were invited, attended and actively participated during those fruitful deliberations.

Because the Technical Consultations Forum were well structured, professionally moderated and proceedings were recorded verbatim, your comments and those of others would have been formally registered and considered thereby eliminating suspicions of ulterior motives while at the same time giving a reasonable opportunity for the CoE and other stakeholders to address them in an open, transparent and accountable manner.

The way your Critique was submitted to the CoE, in particular, creates unnecessary suspicions, poisons the environment within which the COE ought to do their job, and potentially contaminates the process. Given Kenya's history of institutional intolerance and state repression, some members of the CoE might consider or interpret your Critique as an attempt to intimidate, coerce, unduly influence or in some way control how they discharge their statutory mandates. This is particularly the case given your role as the President's Advisor on Constitutional Review and the fact that you chose to write as the "Presidential Advisor, Constitutional Review".

Section 16 of the *Act* stipulates that "[I]n the performance of its functions under this Act, the Committee of Experts shall not be subject to the control of any person or authority". Implicitly, one could infer that you have institutional power that if not exercised carefully may give the impression of an attempt to interfere with the functions of the CoE.

There is high possibility and potential that by the mere act of you submitting the Critique to the Chair of the CoE and copying it to the Minister for Justice – both of whom share ethnic affiliation with you - adverse inferences may be drawn. This is regrettable.

It is imperative that we exercise our discretions responsibly and in a productive manner, especially during these trying times. We cannot afford to politicize the work of the CoE!

However, since the issues you have raised and published are important, I have exercised my discretion and inherent jurisdiction to share my written observations with those you had copied your document to as well as other relevant actors.

I enclose a true copy of your Critique for ease of reference by all the recipients of this intervention.

My comments will closely follow the order of your ten-page presentation. They are made in good faith and as a means of engaging in the national conversation that will, hopefully, result in the promulgation of a people-focused constitution for Kenya.

Detailed Observations on Prof. Kibwana's "A Critique of the Work of the Committee of Experts"

Introduction

General Principles and Stages of the Process

The general principles and stages of the constitutional review process are articulated under the "Longer-Term Issues and Solutions: Constitutional Review" that was signed by representatives of both the Orange Democratic Movement and the Party of National Unity Coalition on 4th March 2008. They are as follows:

"The parties accept that the constitution belongs to the people of Kenya who must be consulted appropriately at all key stages of the process, including the formation of the process itself, the draft, the parliamentary process and any final enactment.

There will be five stages in the review of the Constitution and there will be consultation with stakeholders in each stage:

1. An inclusive process will be initiated and completed within 8 weeks to establish a statutory Review including a timetable. It is envisaged that the review process will be completed within 12 months from the initiation in Parliament.
2. Parliament will enact a special 'constitutional referendum law' which will establish the powers and enactment processes for approval by the people in a referendum.
3. The statutory process will provide for the preparation of a comprehensive draft by stakeholders and with the assistance of expert advisers.
4. Parliament will consider and approve the resulting proposals for a new constitution.
5. The new constitution will be put to the people for their consideration and enactment in a referendum."

In compliance with the stipulations above, a CoE was established by Parliament, as the representative and democratic organ of the Kenyan people.

The Statutory Mandate of the CoE

The Committee of Experts (CoE) is a statutory body created by an Act of Parliament, namely, *The Constitution of Kenya Review Act, 2008.*

Sections 23 and 24 of *The Constitution of Kenya Review Act, 2008* provides the mandate of the CoE.

Sec. 23 states that the Committee of Experts shall:

a) identify the issues already agreed upon in the existing draft constitutions;
b) identify the issues which are contentious or not agreed upon in the existing draft constitutions;
c) solicit and receive from the public written memorandum and presentations on the contentious issues;
d) undertake thematic consultations with caucuses, interest groups and other experts;
e) carry out or cause to be carried out such studies, researches and evaluations concerning the Constitution and other constitutions and constitutional systems;
f) articulate the respective merits and demerits of proposed options for resolving the contentious issues;

g) make recommendations to the Parliamentary Select Committee on the resolution of the contentious issues in the context of the greater good of the people of Kenya;
h) prepare a harmonized draft Constitution for presentation to the National Assembly;
i) facilitate civic education in order to stimulate public discussion and awareness of constitutional issues;
j) liaise with Electoral Commission of Kenya to hold a referendum on the Draft Constitution; and
k) do such other things as are incidental or conducive to the attainment of the objects and principles of the review process.

Sec. 25 of the *Act* authorizes the CoE to regulate its procedures. The CoE is mandated to hold such number of meetings in such places, at such times and in such manner as the CoE shall consider necessary for the discharge of its functions under the *Act*.

Accordingly, in my view, if you or anyone else had genuine interest in participating in setting up the terms of reference for the CoE, you ought to have done so before the *Act* was promulgated into law. On the other hand, if you either agrees with the terms set out in the *Act* or acquiesced to them through silence, *ipso facto*, you would be deemed to have forfeited the right of bring up issues that had already been settled at this late stage. Those issues could and should have been addressed before the *Act* was enacted by Parliament.

Alternatively – and as I have indicated above – you had the option of either raising the issues contained in your Critique in written Memorandum, upon request by the CoE pursuant to sec. 23(c) of the Act, or at the Consultations Forum that the CoE conducted in June 2009 pursuant to sec. 23(d) and 30(1) (b) and 30(2) of the Act. With the greatest of respect – and unless you would like to encourage the CoE to act irregularly and in contravention of the Act - I do not consider your Critique to be consistent with the CoE's statutory mandate.

In a publication titled: "Committee of Experts on Constitution Review: Invitation for proposals on contentious issues," the CoE explained and widely disseminated to all Kenyans – through print and electronic media – its statutory mandate, the mechanisms it had used in determining the "contentious issues," and invited submissions through memoranda on those issues. For a number of weeks subsequently, the CoE held consultations with stakeholders on ALL contentious issues. Since I met you at one of those meetings and listened keenly to your presentation, which contained many of the issues you have repeated in your Critique, I am sure the CoE has provided you with more than a reasonable opportunity to contribute during this important process.

I am puzzled by your assertions that you are unaware of the decision-making protocol used by the CoE. I am equally surprised by your accusation of the CoE of not letting Kenyans know who will make decisions and under what mandate, and with what consequences in the entire constitution-making process. Are you not a Kenyan? Haven't you actively participated in this process thus far? Who are the other Kenyans that you purport to advocate on behalf of? When did they appoint you their representative?

For sure, I am one of those Kenyans with whom you have never sought audience in order to ascertain whether or not I agree with your representations, which are presumably done for my benefit! Unless you have arrogated yourself the role of my representative or advocate – functions I have never relinquished for anyone - I strongly urge you to desist from appropriating my voice and advancing arguments that are inimical to my interests as a patriotic Kenyan.

You have not disclosed to us the identity of those Kenyans that have accused the CoE of "suppressing (or failing to identify) some contentious issues." I am sure you are aware that the CoE's mandate does not include the collection and collation of views of Kenyans on any of the issues in question. That work was competently done by the Constitution of Kenya Review Commission (CKRC). This is a CoE; not a Commission of Inquiry.

The CoE was not established in order to create more contentious issues than were identified during the *Bomas* Constitutional Review process. The artificial manufacture of controversies to derail the constitution-making process is not a useful exercise and I would advise you to be facilitative rather than recalcitrant. Kenyans have waited for far too long for a people-focused Constitution to entertain any shenanigans aimed at delaying, undermining or polluting the process.

Attempts at raising emotive issues as a way of ensuring that Kenyans never get the Constitution they yearn for cannot be tolerated. We should all restrain ourselves against temptations to engage in sophistry during this process.

1. *Non-articulation of broad principles around which to debate and make the new constitution*
Contrary to your demand that the CoE should develop and publicize "broad Principles Around which to Debate and Make the New Constitution," this is not the function and role of the CoE. But more significantly, the broad principles you are demanding already exist; they were developed by the "Kenya National Dialogue and Reconciliation" forum chaired by H.E. Kofi Annan. In point of fact, the specific instrument was signed on by the Serena Mediation Team on 4th March 2008. Its provisions are contained in the preceding paragraphs of this letter.

As a Professor of Law, I expected you to exercise due diligence in all relevant matters before making these unsupported, superfluous and clearly diversionary charges against the CoE.

2. *Lack of comprehensive CoE roadmap in the public domain*
The Act, which is a public document, provides a comprehensive and inclusive roadmap on the mechanisms the CoE must follow in order to discharge their mandate. It provides for the meetings, consultations, deliberations and record keeping of the CoE.

The CoE has not only widely disseminated the list of contentious issues, the method it used to arrive at them, held well publicized public meetings around the country and invited submissions on all issues; but it also provided to participants at the meetings, free of charge, copies of the Act.

Amazingly, you acknowledge then refute one such publicity in *The Standard* newspaper of 18th June 2009. Interestingly, you omit to mention that the same *roadmap* by the CoE appeared in various issues of the Saturday and Sunday *Standard*; the *Daily Nation*, the Saturday and Sunday *Nation*; *The Star*; *The People*; the *Kenya Times*; and the *East African*. Similarly, paid advertisement appeared during prime-time on KTN, NTV, Citizen and KBC television networks.

The consultative meetings, which were conducted with experts, stakeholders and the general public at large – what you refer to as "provincial public hearings" – were held in various locations; expensive and inexpensive alike. All the fora were accessible to the public.

These and other initiatives by the CoE are extremely expensive and time consuming. Given the limited resources and strict budget and timeline the CoE operate with, it deserves commendation; not condemnation.

The suggestion that because the CoE has not used flyers – a charge I am not in a position to confirm or deny – it has therefore failed to involve the Kenyan public who as a result "does not therefore have a holistic picture of the constitution-making journey" [sic] is, to say the least, reasoning of questionable logical pedigree. There is no scientific study or data you have adduced to support your sweeping assertions that only flyers reach the ordinary person while all the publicity so far conducted by the CoE have not reached an appreciable number.

Who did you commission to conduct such a poll, whom did they interview and when and where were their findings published?

During its consultative meetings, the CoE prepared and disseminated concise analysis of all the contentious issues. These were provided to all participants without discrimination. Are you implying those were not legible, coherent or enough?

3. *Absence of genuine involvement and broad consultation of stakeholders and Kenyans in general in the renewed constitution-making process*
I am not sure how you are privy to the number of submissions received to date by the CoE on the contentious issues, however, your assertion that the "CoE did not, through analysis, show how it isolated contentious issues," is further proof that you believe that the CoE must account to you on how it discharges its functions. How else was the CoE, which is comprised of 11 highly qualified professionals from diverse backgrounds, able to present us with 3 contentious issues if its members did not conduct an analysis of the submissions and available draft constitutions?

Are you imputing that the CoE is either incompetent or unethical? Why would you make such a strong and scandalous allegation without any evidentiary foundation? Is the charge advanced for colour only?

It is quite illuminating that you have not disclosed the source of your information that the stakeholders you have listed as not having been properly consulted by the CoE – the Parliamentary Select Committee, Leaders of Political Parties and Civil Society (both faith and secular) – have publicly complained of the same.

Wide consultations, public involvement and transparency are crucial for this process precisely because constitution-making is primarily a political process. Consensus-building is both essential and necessary for the process to succeed. However, context and balance are equally important.

As you are aware, the Constitutional Review process in Kenya did not start - and it will not end - with the work of the CoE. Kenyans have travelled this tortured terrain since 1966. As many have observed, Kenya's Constitutional Review process has been the most protracted, extensive, consultative and exhaustive of all processes around the world. No reasonable person can claim that the views of Kenyans on the new Constitution are unknown! Consequently, we cannot prolong the process forever. We must all play our part, patriotically, to move the process to a successful conclusion.

What might fatally imperil the work of the CoE are unfounded laundry-list of diversionary charges and artificial roadblocks like the ones contained in your Critique; not the absence of consultations by the CoE.

You ask the "CoE to be ready to open its sitting room and bedrooms for Kenyans to approach so that they know CoE is utterly transparent" [sic]. Are you sure transparency extends that far? Is this issue raised only to incite controversy? I hope not.

4. Delayed promotion of dialogue between stakeholders with opposing views

My understanding is that the CoE published the contentious issues, invited written submissions on them, held targeted consultations with both stakeholders and expert, and have travelled around the country where average Kenyans have made contributions to the process precisely in order to encourage dialogue and consensus building.

It is one thing to encourage dialogue; it is quite another to recklessly open old wounds that are beginning to heal and fresh ones that were not there before and then call it dialogue.

The Kadhi's Courts that you cite as an example of an issue that the CoE should encourage an amicable exchange of views on is NOT one of the contentious issues. The CKRC process never identified it as a contentious issue. For decades, Kadhi's Courts have been part and parcel of the Constitution of Kenya without causing controversy.

Why should people only interested in retaining the old retrogressive constitutional order be permitted to use the Kadhi's Court's as a subterfuge to undermine the entire process?

Needless to say, so far, the CoE has bent over backwards and allowed unnecessary public display of emotions by religious factions that should not have been condoned if the CoE was rigidly applying its mandate under the *Act*.

During the consultations over the three contentious issues, the CoE extended these and included extensive discussions on affirmative action and the Kadhi's Courts even though these two have never been contentious issues. Is that something to genuinely complain about?

Regarding political parties' involvement in discussions over what you have characterized as "the hybrid between parliamentary and presidential systems since it has been widely agreed that a hybrid of the two systems is required," I am flabbergasted by the manner you not only mischaracterize the gist of proceedings that have gone on, but also seem to discount what has already happened.

To begin with, you were present when representatives of all political parties and stakeholders discussed the system of government and the electoral system, including parliamentary, presidential and "mixed" systems. At no time did the majority of participants support the so-called "hybrid" system.

In point of fact, both the hybrid and presidential systems were the least popular. I invite you to consult the verbatim record of the CoE to satisfy yourself on this matter.

The new Constitution Kenyans yearn for will not be constructed through deceit, disinformation or subterfuge.

5. Undue delay in bringing reference group on board

You have to be careful not to over-reach. Trying to dictate how the CoE conducts its affairs is not just prohibited by law; your overt attempt to twist its work in one direction or the other offends every single tenet of independence and integrity, which are cornerstones of good governance, constitutionalism and the rule of law.

You have absolutely no legal, moral or political grounds to insist on when or how a Reference Group under section 31 of the *Act* is to be constituted. The *Act* does not dictate a timeline on when this has to be done. Sections 16, 23, 24 and 25 of the Act give exclusive jurisdiction over the functions of the CoE to the CoE itself.

Although you accuse the CoE of "uncautiously moving ahead in some of its work even before the new amendments to the review law are operationalised," [sic] the charge ought to be directed at you. Either you seem to have arrogated yourself the role of an advisor to the CoE or you have simply usurped the CoE's statutory role. I call for absolute caution on this matter.

6. What decisions can CoE make, what decisions must be made by representatives of Kenyans, what decisions fall on Kenyans themselves?

From the foregoing questions, it is apparent to me that you have not carefully read the *Act*. Sections 23, 24, 25, 28, 30, 31, 32, 33, 34, 35, 37, 38, 39, 40, 41 and 43 of the Act answer the questions you have posed.

7. Unclarity regarding the process used to resolve minor contentious Issues [sic]

I respectably submit that an issue is either contentious or it is not. Separating contentious issues into "minor" and "major" might be interesting for theoretical or intellectual debate at a University Seminar, however, for such an important undertaking like the constitutional-making process of a country such as Kenya, we need to deal with the practical reality of our situation as we find it; not as we would like it to be. Fortunately for Kenya, there are only three contentious issues.

Contentious issues identified by both the Bomas Constitutional Review process and the CoE settle this question.

Please, do not try to take us back. This process must move forward so that it can be concluded. That is what Kenyans deserve, want and must get.

8. Non-disclosure of non-contentious and minor contentious issues

This matter has been extensively dealt with in the "Introduction" and items 2 and 7 above.

9. Suppression or lack of identification of some contentious issues

Same answer as in the preceding item.

10. Non-flexibility as regards new contentious issues whenever they arise

Revert to item 8 above. Repeating the same question in different ways is not helpful in this debate.

11. Possible inclusion instead of exclusion in the Draft Constitution of issues for which Consensus is elusive

I concur with this sentiment except to add that it ought to have been presented during the consultative process. That way, it could have been subjected to interrogation by other participants thereby enriching the process.

12. Demonstration of clear partisanship and bias by CoE

To begin with, you were not at the first consultation meeting of the CoE held at the Intercontinental Hotel in Nairobi; I was. Your absence was noticed by all and sundry because you had been invited. In fact, when I sought an explanation from the CoE, I was informed that you had sent apologies.

For you to now claim that "the meeting was astounded when a leading member of CoE stated that the parliamentary system was preferable to the presidential system of government" is both misleading and scandalous.

I recall that you attended one subsequent meeting out of more than five. During the proceedings, everyone was given an opportunity to present their views. Members of the CoE participated both professionally and carefully like everyone else.

I do not recall the "meeting being astounded" by any view expressed by a "leading member of CoE" as you have claimed. It might be accurate had you stated that you were astounded. However, to ascribe your idiosyncratic feelings as those of "everyone" is pretentious, to say the least.

There was nothing astounding from presentations made by members of the CoE. If any indicated their preference regarding a system of government as opposed to one or others, such a view would have been supported by some facts, analysis and historical account.

You had the opportunity to challenge such a view openly and freely. If you chose not to do so, it is unfair to the member of CoE for you to attempt to intimidate, threaten or blackmail him for views s/he expressly in an open forum and in compliance with his or her statutory duty.

My observation is that you might not have been impressed by the fact that during the proceedings to which you were present, the majority of participants supported, with cogent reasons, the parliamentary system and opposed the presidential. But this could not have been news to you in view of the fact that the overwhelming majority of Kenyans supported the same system during the Bomas Constitutional Review process. However, to target an innocent member of the CoE is cowardly because you know very well that given your method of attack, s/he cannot respond to your allegations.

There is nothing more damaging to a professional's reputation than an unfounded allegation of bias. Normally, in a legal process, whoever makes such an allegation without facts and detailed particulars faces serious censure and costs consequences. Particulars must disclose the precise statement(s) made and the context in which they were made. You have advanced a very serious allegation that a "leading member of the CoE" astounded the meeting by stating that the parliamentary system was preferable to the presidential system, yet failed to support the allegation with clear facts and evidence.

Let us avoid frivolous attempts at impugning the integrity of members of the CoE. It does not help the process.

13. Personal views of CoE members should not colour the Draft Constitution

Theoretically, I share some of the views you have expressed under this item. However, I strongly disagree with the implication that any member of CoE is an empty vessel with no views and that if they do, that such views ought to play absolutely no role in the constitutional review process. If that were to be, then the CoE would not be called "experts", nor would Kenyans gain from expertise which is not supposed to exemplify itself. You have stated that the CoE are "advisors". How would they advise without expressing their opinions?

I would agree with you that members of the CoE must exercise extreme caution when expressing their views so as not to impose them on others. Also, I agree that members of the CoE are not to advance extraneous agenda and/or interests other than those supported by the majority of Kenyans, and that are in the best interests of Kenyans.

14. Does CoE promote the national as opposed to sectarian interest?

I wonder whether this was a serious or rhetorical question. If it was serious, who did you intend to provide an answer?

Clearly, the Act compels the CoE to promote the national as opposed to sectarian interest. Are you implying that this is not the case? If so, where is your evidence?

You assert that the membership of CoE was obtained through a partisan route; what exactly do you mean by that? Was the route the CoE was appointed any different from the ones that created the Commission of Inquiry on Post-Election Violence, the Independent Review Committee, the

Interim Independent Electoral Commission, the Interim Independent Boundaries' Commission and the Truth, Justice and Reconciliation Commission?

If it was different from the others; how different? If not, why have you picked on the CoE for ridicule?

15. Avoidance of official staff recruitment procedures

The more I read your catalogue of allegations against the CoE, the more I realize that your initial proclamation that "[T]his paper is written in good faith for purposes of enriching your national duty" is more hollow than it sounds.

What is more astounding than to be accused of bias, unethical conduct, incompetence and now something akin to tribalism and nepotism – all without facts and evidence?

Although I have no inside information about the operations of the CoE or any other Parliamentary Select Committee-driven body like you seem do have, I cannot help but wonder if you have shown the same level of keenness to the other outfits like you do to the CoE.

If you have not done so; why not?

For example, in the Monday, August 10, 2009 issue of *The Standard* newspaper, at page 20, there is a paid advertisement by the Interim Independent Electoral Commission (IIEC) on "Setting the Electoral Reform Agenda for Kenya".

On careful reading, one meets Mr. Kennedy Kihara, the acting Commission Secretary, who also just happens to be a serving Deputy Secretary and Director of State Functions in the Office of the President. A summary of his background in the advertisement goes further: "Mr. Kihara started his career in the Civil Service in 1984 as a District Officer and has risen through the ranks. He was Joint Secretary to the Task Force that managed the dissolution of the defunct Electoral Commission of Kenya and was secretary in several other Government task forces. He is also a board member in several parastatal boards."

The IIEC Secretary is the Chief Executive Officer of the Commission. He manages the IIEC on a day-to-day basis.

Before staff and Commissioners were hired, two vital conditions that one had to meet before submitting an application for consideration were: (a) One was not a former employee or Commissioner with the defunct ECK; and (b) One was not holding any public office in any capacity.

The first question, therefore, is: How did Mr. Kihara satisfy both conditions? Secondly, since the IIEC is supposed to be INDEPENDENT, how can Mr. Kihara, who is still substantively employed in the Office of the President, serving under a President who happens to be the Leader of the Party of National Unity (PNU), supposed to be INDEPENDENT so as to discharge his functions impartially, fairly, objectively and professionally without extraneous political party or other considerations.

In any event, can Mr. Kihara be effective at the IIEC given the fact that he holds two onerous substantive positions at the Office of the President while also serving on several boards of State Corporations?

Since Kenya went up in flames because of the manner the defunct ECK conducted the tallying and announced the Presidential election results on 30 December 2007, do we have confidence that Mr. Kihara can do better than Mr. Kivuitu? Let us remember that unlike Mr. Kihara, Mr. Kivuitu and all the former ECK Commissioners were not formally working at the Office of the President, yet they were still unable to withstand the pressure to tilt the presidential election results. Where is the guarantee that the IIEC will achieve what the ECK failed to do with a more sectarian person in charge of the Commission and the legal, administrative and financial foundations of the IIEC shakier than those of the ECK?

Professor, have you sent a letter of complaint over this matter to the IIEC? If not, why?

16. The risk of rushing the process

I am happy that you are the only person who has expressed concern that the long-stalled

Constitutional Review process might be "rushed" this time around. What worries me is that as an Advisor to the President on Constitutional Review, you are more concerned about the perceived "hurry" of the CoE to bring forth a new Constitution rather than the fact that according to the "Matrix of Implementation Agenda" prepared by the Serena Mediation Team, we are supposed to have a new Constitution by 22nd December 2009 – 12 months from the date of enactment of *The Constitution of Kenya Review Act, 2008*. The Act was enacted on 22nd December 2008.

That is my main worry on this issue Professor!

17. Inadequate information and transparency

Like a bogeyman, you keep throwing up all these issues as if your intention is to scare the COE into inaction through fright. I hope that you have not intimidated and frightened them to the extent that they will start going slow on the process to satisfy you and those who instruct you.

The standards you seem to be setting for the CoE has not been met by any of the statutory bodies formed post the National Accord.

Whereas I support a fully transparent, accountable and accessible system, let us avoid using the fact that we are still technological backward as a weapon to fight the CoE.

18. Delay of facilitation of non-partisan civic education

My impression is that the "Provincial meetings" you alluded to earlier are part of the civic education. Other aspects of that process will kick in once a draft has been prepared and approved by Parliament, pursuant to section 35 of the Act. As such, there is no need for panic. In my view, therefore, there is no basis for claiming that civic education has been delayed.

Conclusion

I have stated, and I will repeat, there is need for caution and restraint in these matters. The CoE require encouragement and support; not vilification, lectures and threats. Kenyans have waited patiently for far too long for a people-focused Constitution to permit any diversionary tactics aimed at undermining the quick completion of the process that will allow ratification by latest August 2010.

Secondarily, I trust that attention can be paid to the issues I have raised with regards to the perceived lack of independence of the IIEC Secretariat.

I look forward to hearing from you.
Yours very truly,

MIGUNA MIGUNA

Cc: The CoE, The Prime Minister, Minister for Justice, AG, and all stake holders.

APPENDIX 5

The Memorandum of Understanding between Raila Odinga and the National Muslim Leaders Forum (NAMLEF)

MEMORANDUM OF UNDERSTANDING

This Memorandum of Understanding (MOU) is made between Honourable Raila Amolo Odinga (Hon Raila Odinga) on one hand and the National Muslim Leaders Forum (NAMLEF) on the other.

At the time of execution of this MOU, on the one hand, Hon Raila Odinga has declared his intention to vie for the presidency of Kenya during the 2007 General Elections. He has sought the support of NAMLEF in getting the backing of the Muslim community in Kenya to back him for presidency.

In the MOU reference to Hon Raila Odinga is intended to include and bind all such persons working for him with authority during the campaign period, and thereafter will refer to his government.

On the other hand, NAMLEF a national umbrella platform of leaders of Muslim organizations desires to see our country Kenya as a just, harmonious, peaceful and prosperous nation based on good governance, constitutionalism and the rule of law, pro-poor policies, enhanced democratic space and where Kenyans effectively participate in shaping their destiny and the positive upliftment of the status and welfare of Muslims in Kenya and the correction of historical and structural injustices and marginalization meted on Muslims through deliberate policies and programmes.

In entering into this agreement, NAMLEF and the Muslim community in Kenya recognize the fact that President Mwai Kibaki's government has meted out calculated, deliberate, unprecedented discrimination, intimidation and harassment of sections of Kenyans, including

Muslims. NAMLEF and the Muslim community in Kenya desire to see an end to this. After due consultation, NAMLEF has arrived at a decision to support the candidature of Hon. Raila Odinga for presidency during 2007.

In this MOU reference to NAMLEF is intended to include and bind all such persons who have authority to commit NAMLEF or work under its authority.

This MOU therefore declares and commits Hon Raila Odinga and NAMLEF as follows:

That:

Hon Raila Odinga and NAMLEF agree to this MOU to take effect forthwith upon its signing. This MOU is made to secure and cement solidarity and partnership between Hon Raila Odinga and NAMLEF constituency based on values of mutual trust, honesty, integrity, transparency and good governance.

This MOU is made in utmost good faith and trust between Hon Raila Odinga and NAMLEF with the common objective of transforming our country Kenya into a proud, prosperous and just nation, where all Kenyans live in harmony realising their full potential without discrimination, subjugation or fear.

NAMLEF shall:

- Declare public support for Hon Raila Odinga's candidature for presidency.
- Support no other candidate for the Presidency for the 2007 General Elections.
- Mobilise the Muslim constituency countrywide to support Hon Raila Odinga's candidature for presidency.
- Provide Hon Raila Odinga's presidency with support and wise counsel.
- Maintain open links of communication during the presidency of Hon Raila Odinga.

Hon Raila Odinga shall:

- Embrace NAMLEF totally as his partner of choice in seeking the backing of the Muslim community, including access to and representation on all his presidential campaign organs. Upon successful election and serving as the president of Kenya: Continue to embrace NAMLEF as his partner of choice, providing support and sustain relations with it and the Muslim community. Accord NAMLEF both an advisory and partner role in his government on all Muslim affairs.
- Embark on the radical transformation of Kenya to be just, harmonious, peaceful and prosperous nation based on good governance, constitutionalism and the rule of law, pro-poor policies, enhanced democratic space and where Kenyans effectively participate in shaping their destiny through a genuinely devolved government.

- Initiate, within the first year, deliberate policies and programmes to redress historical, current and structural marginalization and injustices on Muslims in Kenya. This will include the entrenchment in the Kenyan constitution provisions that will outlaw the targeting and profiling of any Kenyan community (including Muslims) and subjecting them to human rights abuses, violations and discrimination under any guise whatsoever, as has specifically been witnessed by the Muslim community in the past. Specific action will include the setting up of a commission to inquire on deliberate schemes and actions of government, its agencies or officers, to target or interfere with welfare and social well being of Muslims in Kenya as citizens including renditioning of Kenyans to Somalia, Ethiopia ad Guantanamo Bay. Such schemes and actions will be put to an end and have public officers responsible for the same named and held to account. Accord immediately, within the first two years, North Kenya and the Coast Province and other neglected areas budgetary priority for infrastructural development in the sectors of road and telecommunications, water, housing, education and health, amongst others. Ensure equitable representation of Muslims in all public appointments.

NAMLEF as a credible national Muslim institution and Hon Raila Odinga as a credible national leader known for consistency, valour and statesmanship and vying for the highest position in Kenya commit themselves to this MOU.

Signed by Hon. Raila Odinga and

Sheikh Abdullahi Abdi

Witnessed by Farouk Adam, Said Mtwana and Hon. Najib Balala